Lecture Notes in Artificial Intelligence   9776

Subseries of Lecture Notes in Computer Science

LNAI Series Editors

Randy Goebel
  University of Alberta, Edmonton, Canada
Yuzuru Tanaka
  Hokkaido University, Sapporo, Japan
Wolfgang Wahlster
  DFKI and Saarland University, Saarbrücken, Germany

LNAI Founding Series Editor

Joerg Siekmann
  DFKI and Saarland University, Saarbrücken, Germany

More information about this series at http://www.springer.com/series/1244

Sven Behnke · Raymond Sheh
Sanem Sarıel · Daniel D. Lee (Eds.)

RoboCup 2016:
Robot World Cup XX

 Springer

Editors
Sven Behnke 🔟
University of Bonn
Bonn
Germany

Raymond Sheh
Department of Computing
Curtin University
Perth, WA
Australia

Sanem Sariel
Computer Engineering Department
Istanbul Technical University
Istanbul
Turkey

Daniel D. Lee
School of Engineering and Applied Science
University of Pennsylvania
Philadelphia, PA
USA

ISSN 0302-9743   ISSN 1611-3349 (electronic)
Lecture Notes in Artificial Intelligence
ISBN 978-3-319-68791-9   ISBN 978-3-319-68792-6 (eBook)
https://doi.org/10.1007/978-3-319-68792-6

Library of Congress Control Number: 2017956785

LNCS Sublibrary: SL7 – Artificial Intelligence

Printed on acid-free paper

This Springer imprint is published by Springer Nature
The registered company is Springer International Publishing AG
The registered company address is: Gewerbestrasse 11, 6330 Cham, Switzerland

Preface

RoboCup fosters robotics and AI research by setting formidable challenges, which bring researchers from around the world together through publicly appealing competitions and organized scientific meetings. RoboCup 2016 was held at Leipziger Messe, Germany, from June 30 to July 4. The competition inspired 31,500 visitors to watch 3,500 participants from 45 countries with over 1,200 robots compete in various disciplines. In the RoboCupJunior leagues the focus is on the technical education and development of middle and high school students through project-oriented robotic challenges. The research-oriented major leagues were held in the areas of: RoboCup Soccer, with eight leagues spanning simulated robots to full-size humanoid robots competing in soccer; RoboCup Rescue, with three leagues investigating how robots can support first-responders in emergency situations; RoboCup@Home, where the development of service robots in everyday environments is promoted; and RoboCup Industrial, with two leagues exploring future uses of robots in industrial applications.

Amazon Robotics held their annual Amazon Picking Challenge at RoboCup for the first time in 2016 co-located with RoboCup. The goal of the challenge is to strengthen ties between the industrial and academic robotic communities, and to promote shared and open solutions to unsolved problems in unstructured manipulation and automation. The contest focuses on vision, grasping, and motion planning to solve picking and stowing tasks, with prizes awarded based on how many items are successfully transferred in a fixed amount of time. In addition to the competitions, exhibitors from 60 companies displayed their latest results at the RoboCup venue.

This book highlights the approaches of champion teams from the competitions and documents the proceedings of the 20th annual RoboCup International Symposium that was held at the Leipzig Congress Center, adjacent to the competition venue, on July 4. Due to the complex research challenges set by the RoboCup initiative, the RoboCup International Symposium offers a unique perspective for exploring scientific and engineering principles underlying advanced robotic and AI systems. The highly experimental and interactive character of RoboCup, along with its unique opportunities to benchmark and validate research progress, provides a natural forum where novel ideas and promising technologies can be disseminated across a large and growing community.

For the RoboCup 2016 Symposium, a total of 63 submissions were received. The submissions were carefully reviewed by the 72 members of the international Program Committee who generously helped to read and evaluate each of the submissions. Each paper was scored and discussed by three reviewers. The committee ultimately decided to accept 34 regular papers and four papers for a special track on open source hard- and software for an overall acceptance rate of 60%. Among the accepted papers, 14 were selected for oral presentations and the remainder were presented as posters.

The RoboCup 2016 Symposium was fortunate to have three invited keynote speakers:

- Martin Riedmiller (Google DeepMind): "Intelligence Scores Goals: Machine Learning for Autonomous Robots"
- Davide Scaramuzza (University of Zurich): "Towards Agile Flight of Vision-Controlled Micro Flying Robots: From Active Perception to Event-Based Vision"
- Ruzena Bajcsy (University of California, Berkeley): "Framework for Individualized Dynamical Modeling of Human Motion"

Prof. Riedmiller described his group's history at RoboCup and how it has inspired their current work on deep reinforcement learning. Prof. Scaramuzza showed how novel vision sensors and algorithms can be used to guide quadrotors to navigate quickly through unstructured environments. Prof. Bajcsy presented her group's work on modeling human movement dynamics to better enable machine understanding for human–robot interfaces. Their three exciting presentations helped to attract over 600 participants to the symposium.

The Award Committee selected two best papers, printed first in the book:

- Best Paper Award for Scientific Contribution: Alexander Hagg, Frederik Hegger and Paul Gerhard Plöger, "On Recognizing Transparent Objects in Domestic Environments Using Fusion of Multiple Sensor Modalities"
- Best Paper Award for Engineering Contribution: Daniel Speck, Pablo Barros, Cornelius Weber and Stefan Wermter, "Ball Localization for Robocup Soccer Using Convolutional Neural Networks"

Additionally, three submissions were awarded HARTING Open Source Prizes for contributions that have made software and/or mechatronic design plans available to the general public on the basis of the open source principle. These papers are also featured in this book.

We want to first thank our program managers, Steve McGill and Marcell Missura, who were instrumental in overseeing the review process on EasyChair. We also want to thank the members of the Program Committee and our additional reviewers for their time and expertise to ensure the quality of the technical program, as well as the members of the Award Committee for their work during the symposium. Our thanks go to the Leipziger Messe team, who supported us in the preparation and running of the symposium, in particular Nora Furchner and Hanna Krajczy. We also thank all the authors and participants for their contributions and enthusiasm. Finally, we are grateful to the general chair of RoboCup 2016, Gerhard Kraetzschmar, who dedicated his complete time and energy, and the members of the Organizing Committee who helped make RoboCup 2016 one of the best RoboCup events ever. As symposium co-chairs, we had the great pleasure of working together and seeing each other in Leipzig. We sincerely thank the entire RoboCup community for their support and friendship!

December 2016

Sven Behnke
Raymond Sheh
Sanem Sarıel
Daniel D. Lee

Organization

Symposium Co-chairs

Sven Behnke   University of Bonn, Germany
Raymond Sheh   Curtin University, Australia
Sanem Sarıel   Istanbul Technical University, Turkey
Daniel D. Lee   University of Pennsylvania, USA

Program Committee

H. Levent Akin   Bogazici University, Turkey
Luis Almeida   University of Porto, Portugal
Minoru Asada   Osaka University, Japan
Jacky Baltes   University of Manitoba, Canada
Bikramjit Banerjee   University of Southern Mississippi, USA
Reinaldo A.C. Bianchi   University Center of FEI, Brazil
Joydeep Biswas   University of Massachusetts Amherst, USA
Ansgar Bredenfeld   Dr. Bredenfeld UG, Germany
Xiaoping Chen   University of Science and Technology of China
Eric Chown   Bowdoin College, USA
Esther Colombini   Technological Institute of Aeronautics, Brazil
Anna Helena   Universidade de São Paulo, Brazil
   Reali Costa
Bernardo Cunha   Universidade de Aveiro, Portugal
Klaus Dorer   Offenburg University of Applied Sciences, Germany
Christian Dornhege   University of Freiburg, Germany
Amy Eguchi   Bloomfield College, USA
Alexander Ferrein   Aachen University of Applied Sciences, Germany
Maria Gini   University of Minnesota, USA
Fredrik Heintz   Linköping University, Sweden
Koen Hindriks   Delft University of Technology, The Netherlands
Dirk Holz   Google Inc., USA
Luca Iocchi   University of Rome La Sapienza, Italy
Jianmin Ji   University of Science and Technology of China
Hiroaki Kitano   Systems Biology Institute, Japan
Gerhard Kraetzschmar   Bonn-Rhein-Sieg University of Applied Sciences, Germany
Gerhard Lakemeyer   RWTH Aachen University, Germany
Nuno Lau   University of Aveiro, Portugal
Daniel Lofaro   George Mason University, USA
Sean Luke   George Mason University, USA
Luis F. Lupian   La Salle University, Mexico
Olivier Ly   University of Bordeaux, France
Patrick MacAlpine   University of Texas at Austin, USA

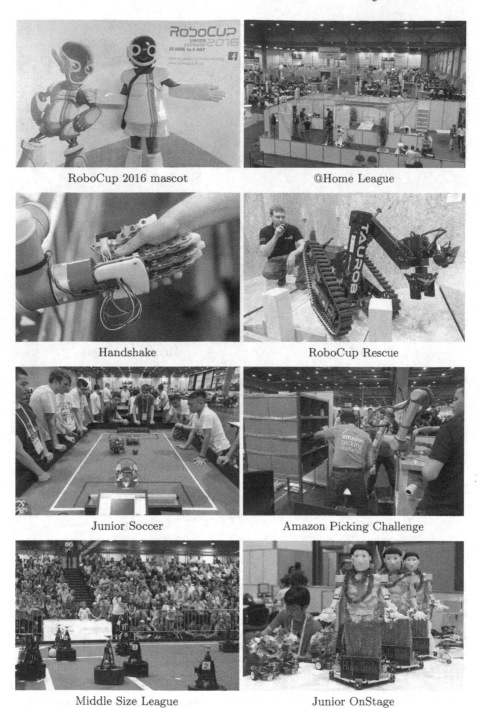

RoboCup 2016 mascot

@Home League

Handshake

RoboCup Rescue

Junior Soccer

Amazon Picking Challenge

Middle Size League

Junior OnStage

Fig. 1. Impressions from RoboCup 2016 (Image credit: Leipziger Messe).

@Home League

Standard Platform League

@Work League

Humanoid League

SmallSize League

Junior Rescue

Logistics League

Amazon Picking Challenge

Fig. 2. Impressions from RoboCup 2016 (Image credit: Leipziger Messe).

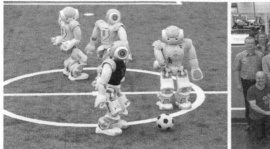

Standard Platform League

Board of Trustees

Social event party

Symposium lecture hall

Invited speaker: Martin Riedmiller

Invited speaker: Davide Scaramuzza

Invited speaker: Ruzena Bajcsy

Symposium poster session

Fig. 3. Impressions from RoboCup 2016 (Image credit: Leipziger Messe).

Contents

Best Paper Award for Scientific Contribution

On Recognizing Transparent Objects in Domestic Environments Using Fusion of Multiple Sensor Modalities

Alexander Hagg$^{(\boxtimes)}$, Frederik Hegger, and Paul G. Plöger

Department of Computer Science, Bonn-Rhein-Sieg University of Applied Sciences,
Grantham-Allee 20, 53757 Sankt Augustin, Germany
{alexander.hagg,frederik.hegger,paul.ploeger}@h-brs.de
http://www.h-brs.de

Abstract. Current object recognition methods fail on object sets that include both diffuse, reflective and transparent materials, although they are very common in domestic scenarios. We show that a combination of cues from multiple sensor modalities, including specular reflectance and unavailable depth information, allows us to capture a larger subset of household objects by extending a state of the art object recognition method. This leads to a significant increase in robustness of recognition over a larger set of commonly used objects.

Keywords: Object recognition · Transparency · Fusion · Modalities · Domestic robotics · Multimodal

1 Introduction

Object recognition is dominated by methods developed for color and depth cameras. Applications usually involve diffuse, textured materials. Environments in service robotics, as opposed to its industrial counterpart, tend to be much harder to control, increasing the need for high system robustness, whilst minimizing cost. The rise of low cost RGB-D sensors has begun to cut a path toward the latter goal but come with some old and new deficiencies. In this work we explore techniques to improve generalization and robustness with respect to realistic domestic environments and a wide set of objects, such as those that are transparent and cannot be described by the Lambertian reflectance model [12]. Such materials reflect large numbers of features from the environment and render common visual features unusable. Perception of transparent, reflective and refractive materials is one of the main problems that has not yet been solved in an affordable and generalizable way.

We combine a broader range of sensor modalities, which all have their benefits for certain material properties, similar to the categorization work by Marton et al. [17], for visual object recognition. Modalities are defined as a transformation, $\mathcal{M} : (I \rightarrow V) \rightarrow f(V)$, with I the image space, V the sensor's value

© Springer International Publishing AG 2017
S. Behnke et al. (Eds.): RoboCup 2016, LNAI 9776, pp. 3–15, 2017.
https://doi.org/10.1007/978-3-319-68792-6_1

range, and $f(V)$ the transformation onto an interpretation of the sensor's values. The transformation represents a hypothesis of a certain physical property in the scene based on evidence by certain sensor values.

We extend a state of the art approach that allows for multimodal inputs and use the sensor's weaknesses to our advantage. The depth sensor returns *nan* values for pixels for which no depth value is found, used to hypothesize a reflective or refractive material. We also provoke a saturated intensity response for specular materials by adding a light from a fixed position near the camera.

We evaluate the proposed approach on three main object categories: *diffuse textured, semi-transparent* and *composite*. The latter consists of a number of different materials from the first two categories. This set of materials covers most domestically used objects. Examples can be taken from Fig. 9. We compare our approach to the baseline system, LineMOD [9], and analyze the used modality spaces and sensor characteristics. Experiments are run in a standard tabletop scenario, assuming that most household objects are found on horizontal surfaces such as tables and cupboards.

In the next section, we will discuss modalities that specialize on transparent materials. Section 2 describes existing approaches and provide a more in depth insight into the approach we extended. In Sect. 3 we describe the modalities we used to increase the set of recognized objects, after which we evaluate our approach in the next section.

2   Related Work

Most object recognition methods assume object sets whose visual response can be described by the semi-Lambertian reflectance model. However, reflective and transparent materials are described based on the specular reflectance model [8]. Material-specific methods only serve a particular material or assume a controllable environment. Current approaches include measuring the polarization of light in highlights or using the refraction of a known background pattern to reconstruct a transparent surface. But these often require either full control of environmental lighting or a full model of the object and the environment behind it, which both do not apply to domestic environments.

A number of methods is based on the fact that specular reflection can cause light polarization changes. Koshikawa and Shirai [11] showed that these changes can be used to infer local surface normals. Saito et al. [20] applied this technique on specular reflectance highlights. Others used similar approaches, also based on the near infrared (NIR) spectrum, but were mostly hampered by tight illumination constraints [16,21]. Fritz et al. [7] formulate a Latent Dirichlet Allocation [5] in combination with SIFT [13], which describes patch appearance based on the local edge energy distribution of refraction (caused by the underlying material). Maeno and Nagahara [15] use a light field camera and model distortion by refraction. Both methods assume that the background has sufficient texture. Albrecht and Marsland [1] and Lysenkov and Rabaud [14] use the observation that NIR structured light cameras are not able to produce depth data for transparent and most reflective materials, as the light is scattered away. Their approaches require a prior full 3D model. Blake and Bulthoff [4] describe and use a principle that is based on a priori knowledge of the position of a dominant light-source and inferring features from specular highlights caused by object materials that adhere to the specular reflection model. Object recognition methods from this approach always assume either prior model knowledge or fully controllable illumination. Klank et al. [10] depend on large camera movements. Their method provides a slightly better than random guess on whether an object is transparent or not, not accounting for unexpected occlusion in one of the viewpoints. Albrecht and Marsland [1] use unavailable depth data from an RGB-D sensor to reconstruct transparent objects. Wang et al. [3] improve transparent object segmentation using unavailable depth data as well. Alt et al. [2] use unavailable depth data to enhance object borders from multiple view points. Both specular highlights and unavailable depth data from an RGB-D camera fulfil the requirements within an affordable robotics context.

Chiu et al. [6] focus on improving perception of geometrical data by fusing multiple modalities and thus possibly allowing for the better acquisition of non-transparent data. The approach does not focus on adding information on transparent objects but instead incorporates *missing information*, helping segmentation and localization of transparent objects.

Marton et al. [17] fuse sensor data from an RGB-D, a time of flight and a thermal sensor on a low level basis, although their categorization accuracy was only around 23% for glasses. Their framework focusses on probabilistic categorization and is not extensible to individual recognition tasks that enable localization and grasping. Another low level multimodal object recognition systems, LineMOD, was introduced by Hinterstoisser and Cagniart [9]. Their approach allows extension to other modalities and focusses on the recognition and localization task. We extend it and use it as a baseline system for evaluation.

3 Multimodal Approach

LineMOD, defined by Hinterstoisser and Cagniart [9], is used because of its low level multimodal model. The authors define a novel low level abstract template representation for cues from any modality. Their approach is based on locally dominant gradient orientation for features, requiring that a feature is representable as such. As we will show in Subsect. 3.1, the low level internal representation of LineMOD allows a wide range of modalities to be used. In common robotics scenarios, new objects are prone to appear often and household situations are subject to many user-introduced variations. By using quantization and spreading of bit-coded features, fast online learning whilst keeping generalization and robustness as high as possible makes the system fit for these scenarios.

The authors use complementary modalities, compensating for each other's weaknesses. We too want to add modalities in a complementary, decoupled way to enhance the recognition system towards other reflectance models without degrading the performance of the original modality set. The authors of LineMOD use two modalities: *maximum intensity gradients* to detect edges from desaturated RGB data and *maximum normal vectors* from depth data to detect surfaces from diffuse objects. As we seek to describe features as patches of pixels showing certain local behaviours in various modality spaces, we are able to describe edges of such patches using the same dominant gradient approach as is used in LineMOD.

3.1 Modalities

By introducing a larger set of modalities, we provide a richer multimodal input that takes into account both semi-Lambertian and specular reflectance models. Table 1 shows an overview of all used modalities. The modality $\mathcal{M}_1$ is based on *maximum intensity gradients*. It is used to describe an objects contour, as the original authors focus their recognition system on texture-less objects, where the foreground/background intensity difference is a good cue for the object's edge in the image. The gradients are calculated for each color channel to remove the influence of the object's and background's absolute color. This method is discriminant enough to describe texture as well, allowing the modality to describe both object edges as well as surface texture. The gradients are normalized in order to add robustness to contrast changes. The dot product between a template and the observed normalized vectors is used as a similarity measure.

Table 1. Modalities used in this approach

Modality	Physical property	$f(V)$	Range
$\mathcal{M}_1$	2D shape	Max. intensity gradients	$[0, \pi]$
$\mathcal{M}_2$	3D geometry	Max. normal vectors	$[0, \pi]^2$
$\mathcal{M}_3$	Transparency	Unavailable depth	$\{0, 1\}$
$\mathcal{M}_4$	Specular reflection	Max. intensity	$\{0, 1\}$

Dominant normal vectors from depth data, $\mathcal{M}_2$, based on NIR disparity images from the RGB-D camera, serve as a cue to the 3D shape of the visible surface. The features are defined as a least-square optimal gradient for a patch neighbourhood around the current pixel in the depth image. As a similarity measure, again the dot product between the template and perceived image serves as a similarity measure.

In addition to the modalities $\mathcal{M}_1$ and $\mathcal{M}_2$ we introduce two modalities $\mathcal{M}_3$ and $\mathcal{M}_4$. These modalities will allow the recognition of (semi-)transparent objects. As was already described by Albrecht and Marsland [1], the NIR pattern from the active RGB-D camera is reflected away from the camera or is irreversibly deformed by transparent objects. Large patches of unavailable depth data (observed as *nan* values in the depth image) are observed for transparent and reflective objects, which is shown in the bottom of Fig. 1. This can serve as a cue for the existence of a transparent material. It is not sufficient to accurately describe the material but does allow us to capture the 2D contour of the object, as can be seen in the lower part of Fig. 1. We can use the same dominant gradient feature as was used for M_1.

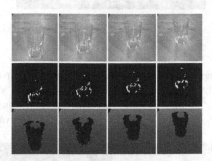

Fig. 1. Water glass in various positions (+7 cm each) from front to back. Top: raw RGB input, middle: thresholded intensity images showing specularity candidates, bottom: visible shape from unavailable depth data from NIR camera (black). (Color figure online)

As many household objects tend to be generally symmetric around the vertical axis and this approach assumes a tabletop scenario, we can interpolate parts of the objects 3D geometry by extruding the part of the contour where the object meets the table. We then use the interpolated 3D shape to find locally dominant normal orientations as was done for modality M_2.

The second modality M_4 we add to the pool is based on specular reflections, as in [21], which can be extracted by setting an absolute lower threshold to the intensity image. The specular reflections, caused by bundling of the environment light by the geometry of the object, were shown to be pose-invariant under the assumption of a dominant light by Netz and Osadchy [18]. Obviously, according to the laws of optical reflection, reflections of the environment by an objects surface are not invariant. We therefore introduce an off-the-shelf 20 lux LED light at a fixed position near the sensors to add an invariant lighting factor into the scene.

After reducing the RGB image to an intensity image by luminance based desaturation, pixels with intensity values beneath a certain threshold are discarded. The image now only contains highlight candidates as shown in the middle row of Fig. 1. The highlights caused by the active light are mostly constant, except for situations having direct sunlight, as can be seen in Fig. 2. The intensity histograms below show a clear bump in the high range. By removing all pixels except for the last five intensity bins, we find a conservative compromise between capturing many (overshot) specular reflections whilst preserving robustness. The histograms do show most candidate specular pixels are covered by using these five bins. Obviously, the environment lighting does change the amount and position of highlights and thus produces false positives.

Fig. 2. Thresholded intensity images in various lighting environments. Left to right: dark corner of a sparsely lighted room to a bright sunlight situation. Top: desaturated images, middle: thresholded images, bottom: partial intensity distributions, with intensity as an 8 bit integer value. Showing the last 30 single value bins.

Fig. 3. Left: original scene and right: specular highlight candidates. The white soap bottle cap produces a false positive.

Another source for false positive pixels are bright semi-Lambertian surfaces, as seen in Fig. 3. As an alternative to the model based recognition done in [19], we only consider specular candidates that also do not show available depth data. We achieve more consistent results by using this crossmodal feature. Specular highlights are now represented as patches of high values in intensity space, allowing us to use the intensity gradient feature that was defined in the baseline system for M_1.

As defined by Hinterstoisser and Cagniart [9], a template matrix with all 2D feature positions and their normalized cue values is constructed. Figure 4 shows features' relative positions that are maintained in our extension, as opposed to the baseline. The coke bottle is a good example to show that the surface coverage of the four-modal approach is much bigger compared to the original two-modal approach. This helps to get a much better result in position estimation. Another issue with the baseline approach is caused by it not being able to determine the relative position of the label on the object. It produces more false positives when other bottles are present, with labels positioned at different heights. On a final note, the new modalities tend to be complementary to the baseline features, promoting the idea of increased robustness by using complementary modalities from the baseline approach.

Figure 5 describes the pipelines that were used, whereby the *Specularity Cue* and the *Transparency Cue* belong to our extension.

Fig. 4. Comparison of two- and four-modal approach. Left: RGB image, middle: two-modal approach, right: extended approach with all four modalities. Intensity gradient features are represented in *red*, normal vector features in *green*, unavailable depth features in *purple* and specular highlight features in *blue*. (Color figure online)

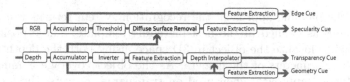

Fig. 5. Modality pipelines

Summarizing, we approach NIR pattern distortions by transparent objects and their specular reflections as binary patches, differing from the background, defined by its shape and position.

3.2 Feature Stability

RGB-D (and stereo) cameras produce unstable depth maps, caused by refraction of NIR patterns by an object's surface. Unstable patches of pixels, as shown on the right of Fig. 6, can invalidate a large subset of possible features, leading to a large amount of necessary templates per view.

Fig. 6. Left: maximum disparity fluctuation, represented as an intensity value. Right: the corresponding depth fluctuation.

On the other hand, our depth interpolation method, which is described in Subsect. 3.3 depends on the contour of the object being stable. Depth values tend to be very noisy on surface edges. We therefore use a per pixel running average to stabilize the depth data whilst minimizing the impact of preprocessing on the total processing time. By accumulating a number of frames and removing every pixel that reaches a *nan* value at least once over all frames, we are able to reduce the amount of unstable pixels from 4% to about 1%. An accumulator was also used for RGB values.

The specularity based modality is unstable in pose changes parallel to the camera plane. Figure 1 however shows, that for small pose changes, they are stable enough to be used under the assumption that the dominant light direction is known.

3.3 Localization

Similar to the baseline approach, the recognition system returns the positions of the features as defined in the best-matching template. These positions can then be used to localize the object in 3D space, using both the depth map and the extrinsic parameters of the camera. As the object coverage is much higher for the extended approach when used on transparent objects, the localization quality is also higher. Depth value assignment to *nan* valued pixels in the depth map is done using a scanline algorithm as depicted in Fig. 7, extruding depth values from the nearest horizontal surface beneath the object into the unknown depth values of the object. This approach is unique and stable enough to allow object recognition and enable the position estimation for transparent objects. In order to filter outlier pixels that occur especially around object edges (and jump between the objects location and the background), we remove these outliers using a statistical outlier filter, based on a Euclidean distance threshold.

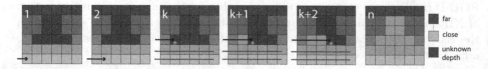

Fig. 7. Scanline depth interpolation. We traverse the depth map bottom-up and from left to right. Once we find a *nan* valued pixel, we traverse down the depth map and take the first valid depth value we find, pushing its value up into the unknown pixel. This algorithm depends on our pre-processing step, namely on removing most of the flickering noise that occurs especially on edges of objects.

4 Evaluation

In order to evaluate the impact of the new modalities on the object recognition performance, we compare the original LineMOD feature set with three different setups, described in Table 3. Tests are run on a Care-O-bot® 3 robot, equipped with a Kinect, using object poses found in common household scenarios, depicted in Fig. 8. We test nine objects from 3 different categories, three per category: *diffuse*, *transparent* and *composite* materials. With $\mathcal{M}_1$ and $\mathcal{M}_2$ allowing recognition of objects from the first category, $\mathcal{M}_3$ and $\mathcal{M}_4$ are expected to work mostly on the second category and all modalities to work together on the latter. A robustness test against object pose changes and a full test on all objects is performed. In all experiments, true positives are defined as a template response that contains the correct object name and a 3D centroid location that is within 5 cm. from the ground truth object centroid location. All other responses are false positives.

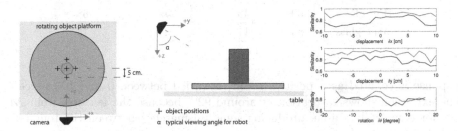

Fig. 8. Left: main experiment setup. Right: similarity response while displacing/rotating the object. The experiment is based on one templated object pose, with red representing the dual modal approach and blue the 4-modal approach. (Color figure online)

In a first experiment, templates of a soda bottle are built for both the baseline as well as the fully extended modality setups simultaneously, after which the template similarity values are extracted from the scene at varying object poses. Figure 8 (right) shows similarity responses whilst changing x, y and *theta* object coordinates. A single template shows similar behaviour for the extended approach, although a dip for x (parallel to the camera) movement can be seen, which can be explained by the bottle's label center not pointing towards the camera. Similarity values in general are lower for the 4-modal approach, which produces about twice as many features per object, whereby $\mathcal{M}_3$'s features are less stable, because of the instability of the interpolated depth values, and thus produces a lower similarity level.

In the second experiment, templates are created for 1000 different object poses (5 positions, depicted in Fig. 8, each from 200 rotated views). A template is only created when the database does not already contain a matching one, preventing duplicate templates. Table 2 shows the actual created number of templates per object, showing that the number of needed templates is greatly reduced when using a larger number of modalities.

The trained database is used in 250 recognition trials per object, which are performed with randomly generated object poses (on the rotating platform). Figure 10 shows the ROC curves on the entire object set for all four systems. The similarity threshold, which is used to decide whether a returned similarity

Table 2. Total number of templates per object for all four modality combinations

Set	$\mathcal{M}_1, \mathcal{M}_2$	$\mathcal{M}_1, \mathcal{M}_2, \mathcal{M}_3$	$\mathcal{M}_1, \mathcal{M}_2, \mathcal{M}_4$	All
Large noodles	309	60	256	79
Small noodles	358	87	286	108
Candle	345	67	273	85
Coke bottle	382	225	399	229
Sprite bottle	92	19	53	23
Soap bubbles	98	26	72	33
Water glass	262	33	169	48
Beer glass	300	48	249	68
Wine glass	83	11	44	13

response is counted as a positive result, is varied between 0 and 100 percent. The extension shows saturation at around 92% because the features from $\mathcal{M}_3$ are not completely stable, producing some mismatches between the templates and the scene.

Fig. 9. Object evaluation set with three categories of objects: *diffuse, composite* and *transparent.*

Adding any of the newly proposed modalities greatly improves the results, whereby the combination of all four produces the best results, although the system is never able to recognize all objects. Nevertheless, the modality combination seems a step into the right direction. The unknown depth modality introduces the largest improvement, which can be explained by the much higher object surface coverage that is reached with this modality. Recognition rates are shown in Table 3, showing a significant improvement. The right of Fig. 10 shows the results of a reduced experiment with all transparent objects removed from the object set, showing that even for *diffuse* objects, our extension improves sensitivity and thus robustness. Table 3 shows the resulting recognition rates, when picking the optimal similarity response decision boundary, which we found to be 75%, which is a bit lower than the boundary found by Hinterstoisser et al. The recognition rates on the diffuse-only object set are similar for all modality combinations,

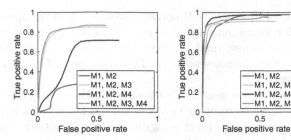

Fig. 10. Left: performance on the entire object set. Right: performance on the reduced set, not containing any transparent objects.

except using $\mathcal{M}_3$, which can be explained by the added edge noise, for the NIR light is deflected from those edges.

Table 3. Recognition rates

Set	$\mathcal{M}_1, \mathcal{M}_2$	$\mathcal{M}_1, \mathcal{M}_2, \mathcal{M}_3$	$\mathcal{M}_1, \mathcal{M}_2, \mathcal{M}_4$	All
All	28%	79%	71%	**81%**
Diffuse	**98%**	89%	97%	92%

Table 4 shows the average total time needed for a full database comparison, showing an approximate doubling of recognition time, caused by the processing of the added modalities.

Table 4. Average time needed for template comparison using all templates.

Set	$\mathcal{M}_1, \mathcal{M}_2$	$\mathcal{M}_1, \mathcal{M}_2, \mathcal{M}_3$	$\mathcal{M}_1, \mathcal{M}_2, \mathcal{M}_4$	All
Time [seconds]	0.031	0.058	0.064	0.065

5 Conclusion

We have shown that a combination of multiple modalities, designed for various physical aspects of materials, leads to an increase in robustness for object recognition. By reinterpreting color and depth data, we are able to distinguish objects from diffuse, transparent and composite categories. It improves recognition of these objects without significantly reducing the recognition rate and time of diffuse objects. The recognition rate is improved most significantly by use of an *unavailable depth* modality.

In future work, we will utilize NIR active lighting to find the specular reflection response in order to minimize false positives that are produced by unknown external light sources. A new modality will be added based on the fact that geometry, especially edges, causes noise in the depth map. This can serve as a cue for object borders.

Using a larger number of sensor modalities and making use of the weaknesses of low cost sensors allows to recognize objects from a large amount of material categories. For robotics, solving object recognition in an affordable, generalizable and robust way is of utmost importance, as it will increase the acceptance rate of users in the general public.

References

1. Albrecht, S., Marsland, S.: Seeing the unseen: simple reconstruction of transparent objects from point cloud data. In: Robotics: Science and Systems (2013)
2. Alt, N., Rives, P., Steinbach, E.: Reconstruction of transparent objects in unstructured scenes with a depth camera. In: IEEE International Conference on Image Processing, pp. 4131–4135. IEEE, September 2013
3. Wang, T., He, X., Barnes, T.: Glass object segmentation by label transfer on joint depth and appearance manifolds. In: IEEE Conference on Image Processing (ICIP), pp. 2944–2948 (2013)
4. Blake, A., Bulthoff, H.: Shape from specularities: computation and psychophysics. Philos. Trans. Roy. Soc. **331**(1260), 237–252 (1991)
5. Blei, D., Ng, A., Jordan, M.: Latent Dirichlet allocation. J. Mach. Learn. Res. **3**(3/1/2003), 993–1022 (2003)
6. Chiu, W., Blanke, U., Fritz, M.: Improving the kinect by cross-modal stereo. Br. Mach. Vis. Conf. **1**(2), 3 (2011)
7. Fritz, M., Bradski, G., Karayev, S.: An additive latent feature model for transparent object recognition. In: Advances in Neural Information Processing Systems, vol. 22, pp. 1–9 (2009)
8. Heath, T.L.: A History of Greek Mathematics: vol. 2. From Aristarchus to Diophantus. A History of Greek Mathematics. Dover Publications, New York (2000)
9. Hinterstoisser, S., Cagniart, C.: Gradient response maps for real-time detection of textureless objects. IEEE Trans. Pattern Anal. Mach. Intell. **34**, 876–888 (2012)
10. Klank, U., Carton, D., Beetz, M.: Transparent object detection and reconstruction on a mobile platform. In: IEEE Conference on Robotics and Automation (ICRA), pp. 5971–5978 (2011)
11. Koshikawa, K., Shirai, Y.: A model-based recognition of glossy objects using their polarimetrical properties. Adv. Robot. **2**(2), 137–147 (1987)
12. Lambert, J.: Photometria. Eberhard Klett Verlag, Augsburg (1760)
13. Lowe, D.G.: Distinctive image features from scale-invariant keypoints. Int. J. Comput. Vis. **60**(2), 91–110 (2004)
14. Lysenkov, I., Rabaud, V.: Pose estimation of rigid transparent objects in transparent clutter. In: IEEE Conference on Robotics and Automation (ICRA), pp. 162–169 (2013)
15. Maeno, K., Nagahara, H.: Light field distortion feature for transparent object recognition. In: IEEE Conference on Computer Vision and Pattern Recognition, pp. 2786–2793, June 2013

16. Mahendru, A., Sarkar, M.: Bio-inspired object classification using polarization imaging. In: International Conference on Sensing Technology, pp. 207–212. IEEE, December 2012
17. Marton, Z.C., Rusu, R.B., Jain, D., Klank, U., Beetz, M.: Probabilistic categorization of kitchen objects in table settings with a composite sensor. In: 2009 IEEE/RSJ International Conference on Intelligent Robots and Systems, pp. 4777–4784. IEEE, October 2009
18. Netz, A., Osadchy, M.: Using specular highlights as pose invariant features for 2D–3D pose estimation. In: IEEE Conference on Computer Vision and Pattern Recognition, pp. 721–728 (2011)
19. Osadchy, M.: Using specularities for recognition. In: IEEE International Conference on Computer Vision, vol. 2, pp. 1512–1519. IEEE (2003)
20. Saito, M., Sato, Y., Ikeuchi, K., Kashiwagi, H.: Measurement of surface orientations of transparent objects by use of polarization in highlight. Syst. Comput. Jpn. **32**(5), 64–71 (2001)
21. Zhang, L., Hancock, E.: A comprehensive polarisation model for surface orientation recovery. In: IEEE Conference on Pattern Recognition, pp. 3791–3794 (2012)

Best Paper Award for Engineering Contribution

Ball Localization for Robocup Soccer Using Convolutional Neural Networks

Daniel Speck$^{(\boxtimes)}$, Pablo Barros, Cornelius Weber, and Stefan Wermter

Department of Informatics, Knowledge Technology, WTM Hamburg Bit-Bots,
University of Hamburg, Vogt-Koelln-Strasse 30, 22527 Hamburg, Germany
2speck@informatik.uni-hamburg.de

Abstract. In RoboCup soccer, ball localization is an important and challenging task, especially since the last change of the rule which allows 50% of the ball's surface to be of any color or pattern while the rest must remain white. Multi-color balls have changing color histograms and patterns in dependence of the current orientation and movement. This paper presents a neural approach using a convolutional neural network (CNN) to localize the ball in various scenes. CNNs were used in several image recognition tasks, particularly because of their capability to learn invariances in images. In this work we use CNNs to locate a ball by training two output layers, representing the x- and y-coordinates, with normal distributions fitted around the ball. Therefore the network not only locates the ball's position but also provides an estimation of the noise. The architecture processes the whole image in full size, no sliding-window approach is used.

Keywords: RoboCup · Convolutional neural network · Deep learning · Tensorflow · Ball detection · Ball localization · Noise · Filtering

1 Introduction

In RoboCup humanoid soccer standard computer vision algorithms frequently utilize color and edge information for ball tracking [2,6,8,17], because such algorithms are rather easy to implement and do not require lots of test data. For example, one of the common solutions is to search for round shapes in the picture and try to find the center of this shape [2]. Most of the standard algorithms are computationally cheap and deliver usable results. However, since there is no intelligent decision whether an object is a ball or not, they detect false positives quite often. Furthermore, since the complexity of the tasks of RoboCup has increased [20], the motivation for new solutions is growing. For instance, until 2014 the ball's color was all orange, but from 2015 onwards the specifications have changed to a ball with at least 50% white color leaving the rest of the ball open for any color combinations [20]. These changes in complexity adversely affected the results of many algorithms which were used up to now, because the color distribution now significantly changes in dependency of the camera's

S. Behnke et al. (Eds.): RoboCup 2016, LNAI 9776, pp. 19–30, 2017.
https://doi.org/10.1007/978-3-319-68792-6_2

Fig. 1. One of the balls currently used in Robocup. The white color of the ball is almost identical compared to the color of the goal posts and the endlines. In the center image one can see the overemphasized red channel; this happens occasionally with our robot's camera and the lighting in our laboratory. The left and center images show non-moving balls with a distance of 0.5 m to the robot. The right image shows a moving ball with a distance of 1.0 m to the robot. (Color figure online)

direction (plus lighting) and the orientation of the ball itself. Figure 1 shows the contrasting appearance of the ball for different orientations and movement.

The new ball specifications motivate intelligent approaches that are less dependent on assumptions like a homogeneous color of the ball. Moreover, technical advances make neural approaches possible in terms of computational power [1]. In sum the hypothesis of this paper is that a neural architecture should outperform standard algorithms which were used so far and especially be able to learn invariants for getting a much better rate of true positives and reduce misclassification. In general we think that without preprocessing and with a sufficiently large dataset a deep neural architecture should be able to learn the mentioned invariants, because the raw information covers not only more variation but also a more distinctive feature set. LeCun et al. have already shown that deep networks are able to learn visual features for comparable tasks in robotics [15]. Here, we present a CNN which localizes the ball and outputs a distribution that can be utilized for determining the noise in the input signal.

CNNs have often and successfully been used for object classification tasks [7,12,14,22] while in the last years also several CNNs for object localization have been proposed and showed good results [3,4,16,19,21]. However, e.g. sliding-window approaches are not optimal for ball localization in RoboCup soccer. Due to the large change in size of the features representing the ball when it is moving away or towards a robot the ball would cover several segments of a sliding-window solution quite often. Therefore we decided to let our architecture always classify the full image and manipulate the output, not the input, by feeding a probability distribution over the width and height of the image as the teaching signal. Apart from that, deep learning architectures like convolutional neural networks seem to be novel in the RoboCup humanoid league for object localization tasks.

For evaluating our architectures we randomly chose single frames of a non-moving ball or a few frames out of sequences as test images and measured the accuracy. In the sequences the ball is moving in various directions. We started with clean scenes with just a few objects and the ball, but our current dataset contains more images with robots, goal posts and miscellaneous objects (tables, chairs, windows, doors, humans, heaters) in the background.

In the Sect. 2 we go into detail about our proposed architecture. In Sect. 3, we describe the methodology of our approach: the used data set, the experiments in detail, our evaluation method and results. Finally, in Sect. 4, we present our conclusion and possible future work.

2   Proposed Architecture

2.1   Convolutional Neural Networks

Fully-connected neural networks (e.g. MLPs) use lots of memory when they are designed for complex computer vision tasks. The vast amount of weights increases rapidly with the network's size. In contrast, CNNs filter the input information in the first layers [12]. The 2D data of an image is convolved by different kernel filters which extract characterizing features in the convolution layer. In subsequent layers this information is pooled and subsampled [12]. At the end different filters extracted the features by being applied over an image. These can be color distributions, shapes, specific patterns and so on. Properly designed and trained deep architectures can supply robust, state-of-the-art results [24]. In our approach we utilize the strengths of CNNs in classification tasks and combine this with altering the output layer to predict the ball's location with a distribution instead of absolute coordinates or bounding boxes.

2.2   Teaching Signal

Our teaching signal is a normal distribution fitted around the center of the ball's real coordinates. Hence, one 800-dimensional vector for the x output layer (width of image) and one 600-dimensional vector for the y output layer (height of image). The normal distributions parameter μ is the center of the ball, while σ was set to 20. An example of one teaching signal is shown in Fig. 2. Using a normal distribution as the teaching signal ("labels") lets the network converge faster since a pixel-precise prediction would be harder to learn and has no substantial advantage in ball localization or tracking. Furthermore, the shape of the network's output data can be interpreted for approximating the current process's noise: in clean images the distributions (output) mostly had maxima of similar width, height, and shape. Reflections, blurring, and other visual distortions frequently caused wider maxima and noised shapes. For that reason the use of probability distributions as the teaching signal was a huge benefit, enabling a faster convergence and supplying additional information about the noise in the input data. Moreover Larochelle et al. stated that a high number of solutions that deliver a small training error increase the chance of the network converging into local minima [13]. In consequence, there is a decreased chance for the network to learn invariants and represent a generalization of the problem, ensuring the test error to be low, too. By using a probability distribution it is far less likely for the network to find a solution that only results in a decreased training error, because a maximum in the distribution consists of many classes

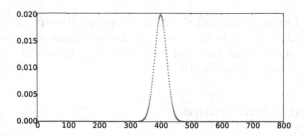

Fig. 2. A sample normal distribution that is taken as the teaching signal for the x output layer of the network. In this hypothetical sample image the ball is located at $x = 400$, therefore the normal distribution has a μ of 400. The width σ is 20.

being activated, therefore there are far less possible solutions with a low training error rate. Figure 2 shows an example for a probability distribution fed to the network for training.

2.3 Activation Functions

We used three different activation functions: the "traditional" rectified linear units (ReLU) [18], rectified linear units with an upper bound of 6 (ReLU6) [11], and soft-sign activation [5]. A ReLU activation is defined by:

$$h(x) = max(0, x). \tag{1}$$

where x represents a feature vector (the input for one complete layer) and h is the activation transformed by the activation function, calculating the output of one layer. The networks using ReLU6 converged faster regularly. ReLU6 activation is defined by:

$$h(x) = min(max(0, x), 6). \tag{2}$$

The upper bound of 6 in ReLU6 activation preserves the network of having too high activations since every activation runs into a hard limit and saturation. Additionally the precision of floating point numbers is higher around 0 and gets lower with values much higher than 0. As a consequence, our network learned features faster with ReLU6. A faster convergence and slightly better test results were provided by using soft-sign activation:

$$h(x) = \frac{x}{|x| + 1}. \tag{3}$$

The soft-sign activation function's shape is comparable to $tanh(x)$ but it saturates slower. This makes the soft-sign activation less dependent on weight initialization, which improves the forward activation as well as the backward learning [5].

2.4   Weight Initialization

One of the most challenging parts for deep neural networks is the initialization of weights [5]. If the weights are initialized to high the signal diverges while being propagated through the network; if the weights are too small it converges to zero or falls into a local minimum. The first scenario results in an activation of the output layer which does *not* deliver usable results. Instead of a proper distribution with an activity bump, the activation is large for all neurons while the second scenario results in an output that is very similar for nearly every input signal – the delta between different outputs for different inputs is very small. Many networks showed a convergence when their weights were initialized with a normal distribution $\mathcal{N}(\mu, \sigma^2)$, where $\mu = 0$ and $0.01 \leq \sigma^2 \leq 0.2$. This was the case throughout many different parameter settings in the majority (about 60%) of experiments. However, the results of the first experiments depended on heavy empirical testing which was very time-consuming. Better results were delivered by *normalized initialization* [5] (sometimes also referred to as *Xavier initialization*) which gives a good approximation for initializing the weights. This is especially useful because this approach showed good results in combination with soft-sign activation. Basically, the weights W between layer j and layer $j+1$ are initialized with a uniform distribution (U) with upper and lower bounds defined by:

$$W \sim U \left[-\frac{\sqrt{6}}{\sqrt{n_j + n_{j+1}}}, \frac{\sqrt{6}}{\sqrt{n_j + n_{j+1}}} \right]. \tag{4}$$

where n_j is the amount of neurons in layer j and n_{j+1} the amount of neurons in layer $j + 1$. Besides the distribution shown in Eq. 4 it is also possible to approximate the variance of a normal distribution with normalized initialization by taking Eq. 4 as the variance for a normal distribution and set $\mu = 0$. For ReLU activation this initialization also works but has to be scaled up a bit because of the ReLU activation's lower bound of 0.

2.5   Optimization Algorithms

The experiments started with "traditional" gradient descent optimization for the learning algorithm but big data sets need a huge amount of training steps for the networks to converge. This problem was solved by using a stochastic gradient descent algorithm: Adam. Adam was developed by Kingma et al. and successfully proposed especially for deep networks with a high amount of parameters [10].

2.6   Models

For demonstrating that networks with less neurons actually can achieve at least comparable results in ball localization we decided to develop two architectures. Model 1 delivered the best results for our experiments so far and after achieving this accuracy we abstracted from model 1 to create a network with less neurons to lower the computational costs of running the architectures.

24   D. Speck et al.

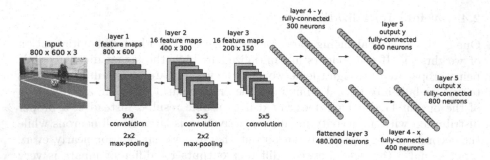

Fig. 3. Graphical illustration of the architecture of model 1.

Model 1 is illustrated in Fig. 3. It has only three convolutional layers, pooling is applied on the first two layers. The aim was to find out if less convolution and especially less pooling leaves more "raw" information that could be interpreted by the fully-connected classifiers in the last layers. The model was evaluated with and without dropout. If dropout was used, it was applied on every layer except the output layer with a dropout rate of 0.5 for training and no dropout for testing. Instead of dropping single connections, always whole neurons have been dropped out. The initial bias for the fully-connected layers was zero and 0.01 for the convolutional layers, which showed a marginally faster convergence for this architecture.

Model 2, illustrated in Fig. 4, has a decreased number of fully-connected neurons. The training time for 10,000 training steps was reduced by 20% in comparison to model 1. Further decreasing the training time needs a more aggressive use of pooling to reduce the dimensionality, but in our case this procedure lowered the test error rates drastically. Again, dropout is applied on every layer but the output layer with the same rates for training and testing as model 1.

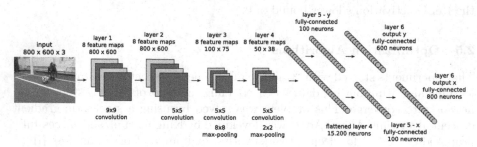

Fig. 4. Graphical illustration of architecture model 2.

3   Experimental Results

3.1   Dataset

CNNs need a large training data set [15]. All images of our data set have been recorded in our laboratory, which has a play field set up according to the

RoboCup humanoid league rules but scaled down in size. The dataset contains 1,160 images; 80 are used as test images while 1,080 are used for training the network. The images portray various scenes, some are very clean with just the ball on the field, others cover a goalkeeper robot, the goal posts, a striker robot, and several arbitrary objects in the background (like tables, chairs, a heater, windows, a door). See Fig. 5 for examples. Mostly the distance to the ball is between 0.5 and 5.0 m. 400 images show a non-moving ball at various locations, while the rest are sequences of a moving ball. Roughly 20% of the training and test images contain a robot, a goal post or something similar right next to the ball and in almost 50 images the ball is partly covered, e.g. by the legs of a robot. The images are of dimension $800 \times 600 \times 3$ (width $\times$ height $\times$ RGB-channels) without *any* preprocessing. Hence, the dataset contains images with reflections, blurry images, images with overemphasized color channels, and so forth. Especially the red channel is intensified in some images, letting white walls appear pink.

Fig. 5. Illustration of some test images used for evaluation, taken from the robot's camera. (Color figure online)

3.2 Experimental Methodology

For evaluation we use a *top-11 error rate*, it describes if the top-11 activations (activity bump of the network) in one feed-forward step matches with the top-11 values of the teaching signal. Due to the symmetric shape of a normal distribution this guarantees the top-11 activations of the network to be 5 pixels around the real center of the ball. Hence, we basically count how many of the top-11 activations of the network are found in the teaching signal and build the mean over this. Only if the ball and therefore the normal distribution is exactly at a corner, this has a worst case of 10 pixels around the ball's center.

3.3 Results

Overall all networks showed a convergence after about 15,000 to 30,000 training steps. For the easier, cleaner images they started to converge after approximately 8,000 training steps, while about 15,000 training steps were needed for the more complicated ones. Table 1 shows the full results of our networks classifying the test images. Model 1 (soft-sign) offered the best results. It outperformed model 2 and the other activation functions. Regardless of which model was used, soft-sign

Table 1. Results for full training (40,000 training steps).

Network	top11 x peak	top11 y peak
Model 1 soft-sign	**81%**	**75%**
Model 1 ReLU6	74%	71%
Model 1 ReLU	72%	69%
Model 2 soft-sign	71%	70%
Model 2 ReLU6	66%	68%
Model 2 ReLU	65%	63%

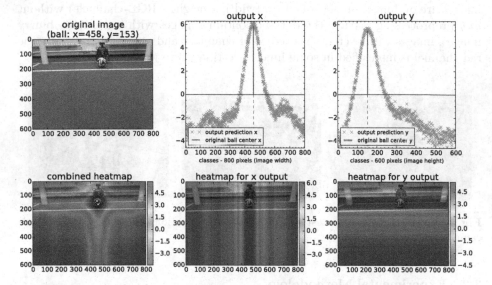

Fig. 6. In the first row the original test image is displayed. The real coordinates (x, y) for the ball are $(458, 153)$. The x- and y-output, generated by the network for this specific test image, is also shown in row 1. The second row shows the heatmaps for the combined output (left), the x-output (center), and the y-output (right). The top11-activation is plotted into the left image in the second row with red dots. (Color figure online)

activation delivered the best results, ReLU6 was always off by some percent and ReLU even lower. Hyperbolic tangent and sigmoid activation were only tested in the very first experiments and were dropped due to unsatisfactory results.

The network's output is visualized by plotting the top-11 prediction as well as a heatmap on top of the test images. The heatmaps and the distribution plots, illustrated in Fig. 6, show that the network is classifying accurately.

3.4 Architecture Benchmarks

For an evaluation of our architecture's running time we used the full network (model 1) on a modern laptop (Intel Skylake i7 U-Series; mobile processor for low power consumption: 15 W TDP). Running the complete test data set took this processor 74.43 s, with a mean of 0.91 s per image. Even on our new Hambot robots the full architecture is too big for the RAM (2 GB). Hence, we scaled down model 1 and retrained it. The architecture (layers, configuration, ...) is the same, but the input size is 200 × 150 and the output vectors for the x- and y-axis are 200- and 150-dimensional vectors. With this configuration our robots were able to load and work with the network. A processing of the full test data set took our robot 24.05 s (laptop: 2.079 s), with a mean of 0.304 s (laptop: 0.026 s) per image. The performance of model 1's downscaled version dropped: to roughly correspond to the top-11 error we evaluated a top-3 error which was 58% (top3 x) and 52% (top3 y) in total. Especially images with a ball-robot distance of over 2 m dropped drastically in performance (some of these images were below 30%). Near distances up to 1 m mostly showed error rates of roughly 70%. Thus, either faster processors for robots are necessary (to run the bigger nets) or low classification rates at medium to high distances have to be accepted.

4   Discussion

In most experiments the soft-sign activation networks dominated in performance, hence it is the best choice for this particular network design and the task of ball localization. Additionally the normalized initialization led to better results and faster convergence. Overall, model 1 as well as model 2 delivered usable results, while model 1 was the better choice, guaranteeing a very precise prediction in about 80% of the test images. For more complex images the discrepancy to the real coordinates often was less than ±10 pixels. Even results with a higher discrepancy may be useful in a game since the approximated location of the ball is much more important than a pixel-precise knowledge of it's position. Additionally, when catching the ball as a goal keeper or kicking the ball as a striker, pixel-precise information is unnecessary, since the hardware is not able to kick or catch balls with such a precision. As a consequence, distributions that point in the right direction are an efficient way for ball localization, especially when the discrepancy to the real coordinates is low enough. Furthermore this gives an approximated idea about the uncertainty in the input signal: clean shaped distributions cover low noise and high accuracy, while noisy input data distorts the distribution's shape. Despite this, less than 5% of the test images were classified incorrectly, leading to unusable results. In 90% of the test images the ball was found reliably and the rest showed noisy activity bumps. However, even these noisy activations were stable enough to filter the output, e.g. with a DBSCAN algorithm. Nonetheless, our architecture relies on a big training data set and the prediction results worsen a lot, if the input signal differs much from the training data. Thus, there is still work to be done. For example, our training data set is too small: in some situations the endlines or goal posts (because of their white color and in some angles round-shaped appearance) shift the network's attention, moving the activity bumps in between the ball and these objects. This most likely happens because many images cover no goal posts or only small parts of it. Also, scenes showing a partly covered ball led to mis-localizations, and scenes with no ball falsely led the network to output some location. Slightly less than half of such scenes were classified correctly. As a consequence, for such cases, there are clearly not enough training samples and therefore invariances learned by the network to produce reasonable output.

5 Conclusion and Future Work

We proposed a deep neural architecture, which is able to reliably locate the ball, although no pre-training was used. If supplied with enough training data (showing different ball orientations, speeds/trajectories, color distributions, distances, and other characteristics), it should outperform standard algorithms. The low computational power of robots compared to a computer limits the size of the network. For that reason we concentrate on developing an architecture for achieving satisfactory accuracy while keeping in mind the limited computational power of the robots. Hence, the current setup achieves the results with just a few layers and not *too* many neurons. The current architectures take no longer than 10 to 20 h to train and can be run on modern robots with small changes. Our networks are able to deliver a reasonable performance in locating *multi-color* balls with arbitrary color patterns. Additionally, our architecture not only predicts the ball's location but does this with producing a distribution over the full width and height of the image. Therefore it delivers information about the noise, also. Figure 6 shows that for an accurate prediction the distributions on the output layer have a single bump with a spiky maximum. Additionally the x- and y-output bumps are of a similar shape (width, height). This can be seen in the majority of the test images when fed to the network, which proves the idea of the distribution output.

One aspect for developing a better architecture, to learn a better representation of invariances, will be to create a larger, more complex data set. Therefore more images are needed where the ball is partly covered, as well as images with no ball at all. Even mirroring the training data set's images improved our results: the top-11 accuracy of the test images went up to **83%** (top-11 x) and **76%** (top-11 y) for model 1. Thus, a bigger training data set with more varying images should stabilize the results. Up to now our data set only has few images that hide the ball e.g. between the legs of a robot. Learning inhibitory feedback should further improve the performance so images with no ball at all and a zero learning signal as well as more images with robots or other objects partially covering the ball should be the next milestone.

Another goal is to filter the noise and to predict the ball's movement over several frames with a recurrent neural network. As already mentioned, the cluster points even for test images with a low accuracy are close enough to each other to approximate the right direction to the ball. One possible and interesting solution is a neural Kalman filter [9]. It predicts a new/subsequent value for some observed feature based on previous input and observation noise as well as process noise. A neural implementation renders this task more complicated but also more dynamical, which should increase the filter's precision in the dynamical environment of RoboCup humanoid soccer. Standard implementations are used often but their success heavily relies on the knowledge of process and measurement errors. Szirtes et al. have shown that a neural architecture can learn predictable features along with the noise on specific features of the input information [23]. This information can be filtered by specific local neurons rendering the solution highly dynamical for feature rich, noisy environments. A way to keep the filter and prediction part computationally cheap and neurally reasonable is to use an Elman network. Potentially future work could connect both parts of the architecture even more: when the recurrent neural network outputs the next prediction of the ball's location, this information could be used to direct the attention of the convolutional neural network to the corresponding area in the image. Deep architectures can supply very good, robust results for those tasks [24].

Acknowledgement. We would like to thank Stefan Heinrich for reviewing this paper, the Hamburg Bit-Bots (http://robocup.informatik.uni-hamburg.de/) (esp. Nils Rokita, Fabian Fiedler), for assistance in working with the robots and giving feedback, and Nathan Lintz for constructive discussions about TensorFlow (https://www.tensorflow.org/), which was used to build our architecture. The work was made in collaboration with the TRR 169 "Crossmodal Learning", funded by the DFG, and partially supported by CAPES Brazilian Federal Agency for the Support and Evaluation of Graduate Education (p.n.5951135).

References

1. Bestmann, M., Reichardt, B., Wasserfall, F.: Hambot: an open source robot for RoboCup Soccer. In: Almeida, L., Ji, J., Steinbauer, G., Luke, S. (eds.) RoboCup 2015. LNCS, vol. 9513, pp. 339–346. Springer, Cham (2015). doi:10.1007/978-3-319-29339-4_28
2. Coath, G., Musumeci, P.: Adaptive arc fitting for ball detection in Robocup. In: Proceedings of APRS Workshop on Digital Image Analysing, Brisbane, Australia, pp. 63–68 (2003)
3. Erhan, D., Szegedy, C., Toshev, A., Anguelov, D.: Deep neural networks for object detection. In: Advances in Neural Information Processing Systems, pp. 2553–2561 (2013)
4. Erhan, D., Szegedy, C., Toshev, A., Anguelov, D.: Scalable object detection using deep neural networks. In: 2014 IEEE Conference on Computer Vision and Pattern Recognition, pp. 2147–2154 (2014)
5. Glorot, X., Bengio, Y.: Understanding the difficulty of training deep feedforward neural networks. In: AISTATS, vol. 9, pp. 249–256 (2010)
6. Hanek, R., Schmitt, T., Buck, S., Beetz, M.: Towards RoboCup without color labeling. In: Kaminka, G.A., Lima, P.U., Rojas, R. (eds.) RoboCup 2002. LNCS, vol. 2752, pp. 179–194. Springer, Heidelberg (2003). doi:10.1007/978-3-540-45135-8_14
7. Hinton, G.E., Srivastava, N., Krizhevsky, A., Sutskever, I., Salakhutdinov, R.R.: Improving neural networks by preventing co-adaptation of feature detectors. arXiv:1207.0580, pp. 1–18 (2012)

 8. Jamzad, M., Sadjad, B.S., Mirrokni, V.S., Kazemi, M., Chitsaz, H., Heydarnoori, A., Hajiaghai, M.T., Chiniforooshan, E.: A fast vision system for middle size robots in RoboCup. In: Birk, A., Coradeschi, S., Tadokoro, S. (eds.) RoboCup 2001. LNCS, vol. 2377, pp. 71–80. Springer, Heidelberg (2002). doi:10.1007/3-540-45603-1_8
 9. Kalman, R.E.: A New Approach to Linear Filtering and Prediction Problems (1960)
10. Kingma, D.P., Ba, J.L.: Adam: a method for stochastic optimization. In: International Conference on Learning Representations, pp. 1–13 (2015)
11. Krizhevsky, A., Hinton, G.: Convolutional Deep Belief Networks on CIFAR-10 (2010, unpublished manuscript)
12. Krizhevsky, A., Sutskever, I., Hinton, G.E.: ImageNet classification with deep convolutional neural networks. In: Advances in Neural Information Processing Systems, pp. 1–9 (2012)
13. Larochelle, H., Bengio, Y., Louradour, J., Lamblin, P.: Exploring strategies for training deep neural networks. J. Mach. Learn. Res. **10**, 1–40 (2009)
14. LeCun, Y., Bottou, L., Bengio, Y., Haffner, P.: Gradient based learning applied to document recognition. Proc. IEEE **86**(11), 2278–2324 (1998)
15. LeCun, Y., Kavukcuoglu, K., Farabet, C.: Convolutional networks and applications in vision. In: ISCAS 2010–2010 IEEE International Symposium on Circuits and Systems: Nano-Bio Circuit Fabrics and Systems, pp. 253–256 (2010)
16. Malik, J., Girshick, R., Donahue, J., Darrell, T.: Rich feature hierarchies for accurate object detection and semantic segmentation. In: 2014 IEEE Conference on Computer Vision and Pattern Recognition (CVPR), pp. 580–587 (2014)
17. Murch, C., Chalup, S.: Combining edge detection and colour segmentation in the four-legged league. In: Australasian Conference on Robotics and Automation (ACRA 2004) (2004)
18. Nair, V., Hinton, G.: Rectified linear units improve restricted Boltzmann machines. In: Proceedings of the 27th International Conference on Machine Learning (ICML 2010), pp. 807–814 (2010)
19. Oquab, M.: Is object localization for free? Weakly-supervised learning with convolutional neural networks. In: Proceedings of the IEEE Conference on Computer Vision and Pattern Recognition, pp. 685–694 (2015)
20. RoboCup-Team: RoboCup Soccer Humanoid League Rules and Setup (2015)
21. Sermanet, P., Eigen, D., Zhang, X.: OverFeat: integrated recognition, localization and detection using convolutional networks. arXiv preprint arXiv:1312.6229 (2013)
22. Szegedy, C., Reed, S., Sermanet, P., Vanhoucke, V., Rabinovich, A.: Going deeper with convolutions, pp. 1–12 (2014)
23. Szirtes, G., Póczos, B., Lrincz, A.: Neural Kalman filter. Neurocomputing **65–66**, 349–355 (2005)
24. Zhang, K., Liu, Q., Wu, Y., Yang, M.H.: Robust visual tracking via convolutional networks. CoRR abs/1501.0, pp. 1–18 (2015)

Oral Presentations

Kick Motions for the NAO Robot Using Dynamic Movement Primitives

Arne Böckmann[✉] and Tim Laue

Fachbereich 3 – Mathematik und Informatik,
Universität Bremen, Postfach 330 440, 28334 Bremen, Germany
{arneboe,tlaue}@informatik.uni-bremen.de

Abstract. In this paper, we present the probably first application of the popular *Dynamic Movement Primitives (DMP)* approach to the domain of soccer-playing humanoid robots. DMPs are known for their ability to imitate previously demonstrated motions as well as to flexibly adapt to unforeseen changes to the desired trajectory with respect to speed and direction. As demonstrated in this paper, this makes them a useful approach for describing kick motions. Furthermore, we present a mathematical motor model that compensates for the NAO robot's motor control delay as well as a novel minor extension to the DMP formulation. The motor model is used in the calculation of the Zero Moment Point (ZMP), which is needed to keep the robot in balance while kicking. All approaches have been evaluated on real NAO robots.

1 Introduction

Kick motions are an essential part of robot soccer. In recent years, the speed of the game has increased a lot with most teams now being able to stably walk at high speeds. Thus, fights for the ball are more common. A flexible kick motion that is able to adapt to different and changing ball locations as well as to different kick speeds on the fly while keeping the robot in balance during pushes from other robots is a huge advantage in such situations.

Several methods to design and execute flexible kick motions have already been developed. For instance, Müller et al. [8] model the kick foot trajectory using hand-crafted piecewise Bézier curves, which are modified on the fly to adapt to different ball positions. However, handcrafting Bézier curves is a complex and time consuming task. Wenk and Röfer [18] tackle this problem by automatically inferring trajectories based on the ball position, kick velocity, and kick direction. While this method works, it does not allow the user to influence the resulting trajectory, i. e. creating special purpose kicks like backward kicks is not possible.

In this paper, we present a middle ground between the two above-mentioned approaches: A kick motion that can be hand-crafted easily by using kinematic teach-in or be created by a multitude of optimization algorithms while retaining the ability to adapt to different ball positions and kick velocities. This is done by using a modified version of Dynamic Movement Primitives (DMPs) [4]

© Springer International Publishing AG 2017
S. Behnke et al. (Eds.): RoboCup 2016, LNAI 9776, pp. 33–44, 2017.
https://doi.org/10.1007/978-3-319-68792-6_3

to describe the kick trajectory. During the kick, the robot is dynamically balanced using a Linear Quadratic Regulator (LQR) with previews to keep the Zero Moment Point (ZMP) inside the support polygon. This involves a new way of estimating the ZMP based on a model of the motor behavior of the NAO.

The remainder of the paper is organized as follows: Sect. 2 introduces the motor model that is the basis of the ZMP calculation, Sect. 3 explains the ZMP estimation and introduces the balancing algorithm while Sect. 4 introduces DMPs and explains how we use them to model a kick trajectory. Sections 5 and 6 wrap up the paper with an evaluation of the kick motion and a conclusion.

2   Model-Based Motor Position Prediction

As described below, the NAO's motor response delay is usually 30 ms. Thus, the ZMP balancer needs to take into account that the motor will not be at the currently measured position when the current command reaches the motor. Our solution to this problem is to predict the current motor position using a mathematical model and to use this prediction in our control algorithms.

2.1   Determining the NAO's Motor Response Delay

The NAO's motors are position-controlled using the proprietary NaoQi software. It processes the commands and relays them to an ARM-7 micro controller at 100 Hz. The controller distributes the commands over RS-485 to several dsPIC micro controllers which are responsible for controlling the actual motors. Measured motor positions travel back the same chain [3]. This chain together with the slow control rate of 100 Hz induces a delay between sending a command and being able to measure a reaction of the motor.

To determine the actual delay, a motor is moved from a resting position into a random direction and the time between sending the command and measuring a movement is recorded. A movement is registered as soon as the measured motor position deviates from the position that the motor was in when the command was issued. No threshold is used. For measuring, the internal sensor is used. This is done 100 times for each leg motor of four different NAOs, thus, we get 4400 measurements in total. As shown in Fig. 1, the vast majority of motor reactions occurs at 30 ms. The measured average distance of the reactions at 10 and 20 ms is $0.087°$. This is below the maximum accuracy of the motors, which is $0.1°$. Therefore, we can assume that the measurements at 10 and 20 ms are due to sensor noise. However, the measurements at 40 ms cannot be discarded as noise. Taking a closer look, it seems that some joints in some robots are more prone to responding after 40 ms than others, suggesting that hardware wear or defects might cause a delayed measurement.

Thus, for a fully repaired robot it is safe to assume that the motor response delay is 30 ms. Actually, the delay might be anywhere between 20 and 30 ms, but due to the 100 Hz duty cycle, more precise measurements are not possible.

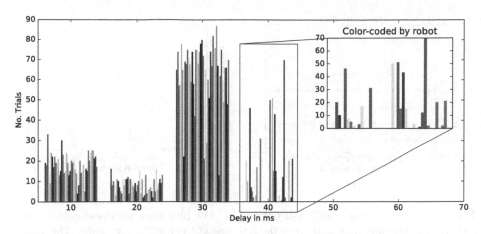

Fig. 1. Histograms of motor response delay. Each bar is one motor of one robot. The zoomed part shows the motors that responded after 40 ms, color-coded by robot. The experiment was conducted using the leg motors of four robots and repeating each trial 100 times. Thus, 4400 responses were measured in total.

2.2   A Model to Estimate the Motor Position

We propose to model the behavior of a motor as second order dynamical system based on a mass spring damper:

$$T^2\ddot{y}(t) + 2DT min(\dot{y}(t), V_{max}) + y(t) = u(t), \quad T, D, y, u \in \mathbb{R} \quad (1)$$

T is the time constant, $y(t)$ is the motor position at time t, D is a dampening constant, V_{max} is the maximum motor velocity that is used to limit $\dot{y}(t)$, and $u(t)$ is the requested motor position at time t.

The parameters (T, D, V_{max}) need to be set in a way that the model optimally mimics a motor. This can be achieved by minimizing the error function J:

$$J = \sum_{s \in S} \sum_{i=0}^{|s|} d(i)(m(i) - s(i))^2 \quad (2)$$

S is a set of step responses for a given motor, $|s|$ the number of measurements in step response s, $m(i)$ the position of the model at the i-th step, $s(i)$ the actual motor position at the i-th step and $d(i) = 0.85^i$ a decay function.

The decay function d emphasizes the short term model quality over the long term, i. e. we prefer parameters that provide a better short term prediction over parameters that provide an overall good prediction. This is done because in our use case the model is only used to predict a short amount of time.

Sets of step responses can be generated by applying step functions, which jump from zero to their respective values instantly, with different step heights to the motor. Figure 2(a) shows a set of step responses that has been recorded and the respective optimal model response. For fitting, the first three samples of the step response should be ignored to make up for the motor response delay.

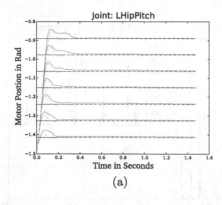
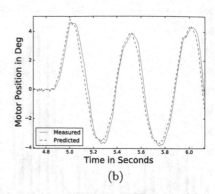

(a)   (b)

Fig. 2. (a) Step responses and their optimal fit. The blue lines are the step functions, red are the step responses, and green the response of the best fitting model. The model of the depicted LHipPitch joint has an error that is slightly above average (see Table 1). (b) Prediction and actual motor response of a motor while walking (Color figure online)

Table 1. Error in leg motor predictions

Joint	Avg. error	Variance
LAnklePitch	0.196°	0.04
LAnkleRoll	0.153°	0.02
LHipPitch	0.216°	0.053
LHipRoll	0.111°	0.009
LHipYawPitch	0.048°	0.003
LKneePitch	0.363°	0.145
RAnklePitch	0.216°	0.054
RAnkleRoll	0.170°	0.025
RHipPitch	0.307°	0.092
RHipRoll	0.097°	0.007
RKneePitch	0.297°	0.118

Table 2. Errors when applying model parameters that have been optimized for one NAO to five different NAOs

Robot	Avg. error over all leg joints	Variance
Original	0.185°	0.057
NAO 1	0.159°	0.055
NAO 2	0.183°	0.065
NAO 3	0.179°	0.056
NAO 4	0.181°	0.071
NAO 5	0.197°	0.061

2.3   Model Evaluation

To show that the model can be used to predict the real world motor positions of the NAO, we compared the model response and the actual motor position while executing a five second walking motion. For the comparison, the real motor values have been shifted in time to remove the measurement delay. Figure 2(b) shows an excerpt of the experiment of the LHipRoll motor. The average absolute error over all leg joints is 0.185° with a variance of 0.0573. Thus, the model seems to be able to predict the motor behavior with sufficient accuracy. Detailed results for each motor can be seen in Table 1.

We were also interested in the portability of the model parameters. As documented in Table 2, a repetition of the experiment on different robots (always using the same model again) was successful.

3   ZMP-Based Balancing

The robot needs to be kept in balance while kicking. A good measure for the balance of a robot is the Zero Moment Point (ZMP). A robot is said to be dynamically stable if the ZMP is inside the support polygon [17].

The center of pressure of the support polygon and the Zero Moment Point are coincident [12]. Therefore, it is possible to use the pressure sensors under the NAO's feet to measure the ZMP, if it exists. However, the sensors are quite inaccurate and often faulty. To avoid using these sensors, we estimate the ZMP $(z_x, z_y)^T$ based on the cart-table model proposed by Kajita et al. [5]:

$$\begin{pmatrix} z_x \\ z_y \end{pmatrix} = \begin{pmatrix} c_x \\ c_y \end{pmatrix} - \frac{c_z}{g} \begin{pmatrix} \ddot{c}_x \\ \ddot{c}_y \end{pmatrix} \tag{3}$$

$(c_x, c_y, c_z)^T$ is the center of mass (COM) and $g \approx 9.81$ the gravitational force. Due to the measurement delay and the high sensor noise, we estimate the COM using the motor model and forward kinematics $(c_x^m, c_y^m, c_z^m)^T$. The motor model is initialized using sensor readings at the beginning of the motion. While the kick motion is being executed, the model is not updated from sensor readings.

Tilting the robot over the edges of the supporting foot does not influence the estimated ZMP. To detect such situations, we calculate the scaled difference $P\Delta\Theta = P(\gamma - \phi)$ between the expected torso orientation γ as provided by the motor model and the measured torso orientation ϕ as provided by the IMU and scale the COM accordingly [1]. The unitless constant factor P needs to be adjusted manually. We chose $P = (30, -30)^T$. Figure 3(a) shows how the ZMP behaves with and without tilt detection.

To be able to measure outside influences, e. g. someone pushing the robot, we replaced the COM acceleration by the acceleration of the torso $\ddot{o}$ as measured by the NAO's IMU. This can be done because the COM is usually inside the torso and thus both accelerations are similar.

Thus, the final ZMP is calculated by:

$$\begin{pmatrix} z_x \\ z_y \end{pmatrix} = P\Delta\Theta \begin{pmatrix} c_x^m \\ c_y^m \end{pmatrix} - \frac{c_z^m}{g} \begin{pmatrix} \ddot{o}_x \\ \ddot{o}_y \end{pmatrix} \tag{4}$$

To finally balance the robot, an LQR preview controller as described in [2, 16, 18] has been implemented. The inputs of the controller are the current ZMP and current COM as well as the next 50 desired ZMP positions. Figure 3(b) shows an overview of the balancing sub-system.

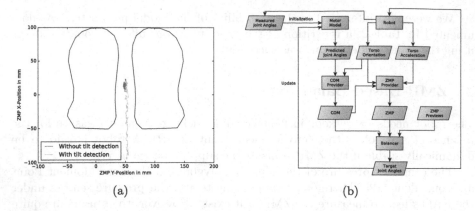

Fig. 3. (a) The red and blue lines show the estimated ZMP position with and without tilt detection while the robot is being tilted backwards. (b) The balancing process. (Color figure online)

4   Describing Kicks Using Dynamic Movement Primitives

The kick trajectory is described by using Dynamic Movement Primitives (DMPs) [4,13]. For the sake of simplicity, this chapter only considers one-dimensional DMPs but they can be easily scaled to n dimensions as long as the dimensions are independent of each other, i. e. for translational movements. For rotational movements, a special DMP formulation has been introduced by Ude et al. [15]. However, for kick motions it is sufficient to simply keep the foot level to the ground, thus no rotational DMP was used in this paper.

DMPs model goal-directed movements as weakly non-linear dynamical systems. They consist of the canonical system and the transformation system.

The *canonical system* s describes the phase of the movement:

$$\tau \dot{s} = -\alpha_s s \tag{5}$$

The phase s replaces the time in the transformation system. Intuitively, it drives the transformation system similar to a clock [9]. s conventionally starts at 1 and monotonically converges to zero. τ is the execution time of the movement. As long as τ remains constant, a closed solution for the canonical system exists [9]:

$$s(t) = exp(\frac{-\alpha_s}{\tau} t) \tag{6}$$

α_s determines how fast s converges. The value of α_s has to be chosen in a way that s is sufficiently close to zero at the end of the execution. We chose α_s by setting $s(\tau) = 0.01$ and solving (6) for α_s.

The *transformation system* is defined by two first order differential equations:

$$\tau \dot{z} = \alpha_z(\beta_z(g - y) - z) + sf(s) \tag{7}$$
$$\tau \dot{y} = z \tag{8}$$

τ is the execution time of the movement, α_z and β_z are damping constants, g is the goal position of the movement, y is the current position of the movement, s is the current phase as defined by Eq. 5 and $f(s)$ is called the forcing term.

The dampening constants are set for critical dampening, i. e. $\beta_z = \alpha_z/4$. We chose $\beta_z = 25$ and $\alpha_z = 6.25$, but the exact values do not matter as long as the system is critically dampened.

The forcing term defines the movement's shape. With $f(s) = 0$, the system is just a PD controller converging to g and reaching it at time τ. One could say that f superimposes its shape onto the PD controller. To ensure that f does not keep the system from reaching the desired goal position, f is scaled by the phase, thus diminishing the influence of f towards the end of the movement. To be able to express arbitrary movements, f is typically chosen to be a radial basis function approximator:

$$f(s) = \frac{\sum_{i=1}^{N} \psi_i(s)w_i}{\sum_{i=1}^{N} \psi_i(s)}, w_i \in \mathbb{R} \qquad (9)$$

ψ_i is the i-th Gaussian radial basis function with mean c_i and variance σ_i^2:

$$\psi_i(s) = exp(-\frac{1}{2\sigma_i^2}(s - c_i)^2) \qquad (10)$$

The weights w_i can be chosen to create any desired function and thus define the shape of the whole movement. Different learning and optimization approaches can be used to find the weights for a certain movement, e. g. Schaal et al. [14] describe how to imitate a given trajectory.

Since the goal position g is part of Eq. 7, the shape also depends on g. This means that the weights can only force the system into a certain shape for one specific value of g. When g changes, the shape "bends" to reach the new goal position. In general, this is undesired behavior and is solved by scaling f if g changes. However, we found that kick motions "bend" in a natural way (Fig. 4), i. e. if the goal position is moved closer to the start position, the robot will swing

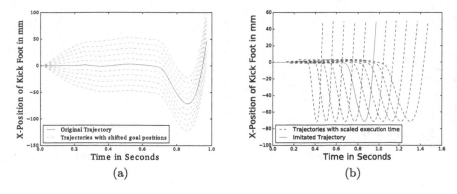

Fig. 4. (a) Behavior of the kick motion when the goal position is adapted. (b) Temporal scaling capability of the DMP.

further back and vice versa. This is exactly the behavior that one would expect from a kicking motion because it ensures that the distance between the inflection point and the goal position remains the same. This is important because the kicking velocity depends on this distance.

Thus, the DMP formulation allows us to define an arbitrary movement in task space and later scale its execution time as well as to move the goal position while retaining a sane shape.

A major downside of the formulation is that the final velocity is always zero making it unsuitable for kick motions because kick motions need to reach the target with a specific velocity. Solutions to this problem were proposed by Kober et al. [6] and Mülling et al. [9]. They replaced the goal g in Eq. 7 with the position, velocity and acceleration of a moving target g_p.

$$\tau\dot{z} = \alpha_z(\beta_z(g_p - y) + \tau\dot{g}_p - z) + \tau^2\ddot{g}_p + sf(s) \tag{11}$$

While Kober et al. used a target that is moving on a straight line, Mülling et al. used a fifth order polynomial.

$$g_p(t) = \sum_{i=0}^{5} b_i t, \quad \dot{g}_p(t) = \sum_{i=i}^{5} ib_i t^{i-1}, \quad \ddot{g}_p(t) = \sum_{i=2}^{5}(i^2 - i)b_i t^{i-2} \tag{12}$$

The coefficients b_i are calculated by applying the bounding conditions:

$$g_p(t_0) = y_0, \quad \dot{g}_p(t_0) = \dot{y}_0, \quad \ddot{g}_p(t_0) = \ddot{y}_0 \tag{13}$$

$$g_p(\tau) = g, \quad \dot{g}_p(\tau) = \dot{g}, \quad \ddot{g}_p(\tau) = 0 \tag{14}$$

Due to the time dependency, the coefficients need to be recalculated if τ changes.

In this way, a new parameter $\dot{g}$ is introduced. It represents the velocity at the end of the movement. However, the weights now depend on $\dot{g}$ as well. This means that if the goal velocity is changed, the shape of the movement will change. As shown in Fig. 5(a), the trajectory reacts to changes in the goal velocity with

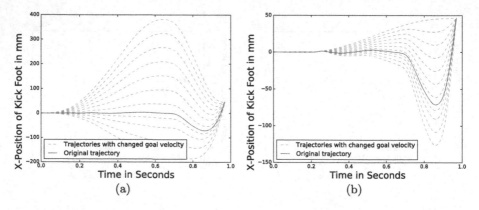

Fig. 5. Reaction of the DMP to changes in the final velocity. (a) Shows the reaction of the original DMP while (b) shows how the DMP reacts with our new scaling term A.

huge changes and becomes inexecutable. We propose to fix this by scaling the forcing term with the novel factor $A = (\dot{g}_{new} - \dot{y}_0)/(\dot{g} - \dot{y}_0)$, where $\dot{y}_0$ is the starting velocity of the trajectory and $\dot{g}_{new}$ is the new goal velocity. Figure 5(b) shows that this produces much better results. If the velocity is increased, the wind up phase gets longer, if it is reduced, the wind up phase gets shorter until it completely disappears if the requested goal velocity is zero. This is exactly the behavior that one would expect from a kick motion.

Thus, the final form of the DMP used in our experiments is:

$$\tau \dot{z} = \alpha_z(\beta_z(g_p - y) + \tau \dot{g}_p - z) + \tau^2 \ddot{g}_p + sf(s)A \tag{15}$$

$$\tau \dot{y} = z \tag{16}$$

$$\tau \dot{s} = -\alpha_s s \tag{17}$$

This DMP responds well to changes in goal position and goal velocity. It is noteworthy that both parameters can be changed mid-execution without causing discontinuities. The implementation used in our experiments has been released as part of the B-Human Code Release 2015 [11] and is available online[1].

5   Evaluation

Several experiments have been done to evaluate the kick motion. The setup is identical for all experiments: The robot is standing at the side line of the field and kicks the ball into the field, as depicted in Fig. 7. All experiments have been done with the official RoboCup SPL ball of 2015, a Mylec street hockey ball that is 65 mm in diameter and weighs 55 g. Each experiment consists of 30 kicks.

We used the Royston H-Test [10] with a significance level of 0.05 to determine that the measured kick distances are normally distributed. Normally distributed kick results indicate that the results have only been influenced by natural noise, i. e. there is probably no systematic error in the test setup or the implementation.

To compare the performance of the kick motion to an existing one, we used imitation learning [14] to learn weights that imitate the kick motion of team B-Human of 2015 [8, 11] and executed 30 kicks with each leg and each kick motion. The results can be seen in Table 3 and Fig. 6.

To test the generalization qualities of the kick motion, we conducted four experiments with different ball positions and velocities. In the first experiment, the ball is positioned 65 mm to the left. In the second experiment it is moved 80 mm forward, the third and fourth experiment reduced the kick velocity by 1/4 and 1/2 of the original kick velocity respectively. The results can be seen in Table 4. To reach the position of the left ball, the robot had to fully stretch the leg. Therefore, the knee motor could not be used to generate a forward force, thereby significantly reducing the reached kick distance. The other experiments show a reasonable scaling towards the desired kick distance. Videos showing the kick generalization can be found at https://youtu.be/g73pPCWcQvw and https://youtu.be/eANtiAiMmTg.

---

[1] https://github.com/bhuman/BHumanCodeRelease/tree/master/Src/Tools/ Motion.

Table 3. Kick distance comparision between the B-Human kick motion of 2015 and an imitation of that motion. The data for the imitated kick with the right leg contained two outliers. If those outliers are removed the result is normally distributed as well.

	B-Human left	Imitated left	B-Human right	Imitated right
Avg. distance	5.3 m	4.3 m	4.61 m	3.6 m
Avg. angular deviation	5.62°	8.06°	9.69°	7.48°
Avg. ball location (cm)	$(-2.53, 496.93)$	$(-1.63, 430.03)$	$(7.52, 453.53)$	$(4.41, 361.56)$
Royston H-value	4.48	0.407	1.62	3.08
Royston p-value	0.106	0.812	0.43	0.000062
Is normal distributed	Yes	Yes	Yes	No

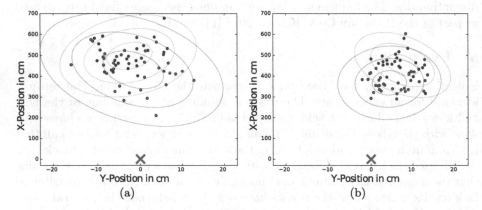

(a)   (b)

Fig. 6. Kick positions of the B-Human and imitated kick motions: The red cross is the kick origin. The dots are the positions where the balls came to a halt. The blue dots originate from the B-Human kick, the red dots from the imitated kick. (a) Shows the results of kicks with the left foot while (b) shows the right foot. (Color figure online)

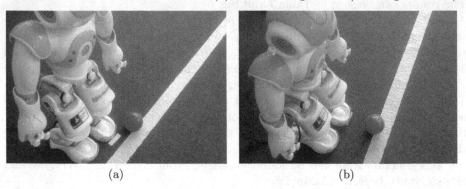

(a)   (b)

Fig. 7. Ball position generalization experiments: In (a) the ball was moved 65 mm to the left, in (b) it was moved 80 mm to the front.

Table 4. Kick distance results for generalized kicks. The data of the left generalization contained one outlier. If it is removed, the result is normally distributed.

	Left ball	Forward ball	3/4 speed	1/2 speed
Avg. distance	1.31 m	3.29 m	2.4 m	1.83 m
Avg. angular deviation	5.91°	4.98°	5.83°	4.73°
Avg. ball location (cm)	(12.63, 130.93)	(22.87, 328.0)	(5.44, 239.16)	(2.96, 182.90)
Royston H-value	6.17	1.15	3.65	3.43
Royston p-value	0.04	0.56	0.144	0.142
Is normal distributed	No	Yes	Yes	Yes

6 Conclusion

We presented a kick motion for the NAO robot that can imitate arbitrary kick trajectories and adapt them to different ball positions as well as different kick velocities. The kick motion is modeled using a slightly modified variant of DMPs. While executing the kick, the robot is kept dynamically stable using a ZMP preview controller. Additionally, we proposed a model of the NAO's motors and used it to improve the calculation of the ZMP.

We have shown that this method of generating kick motions works but cannot kick the ball as far as a manually tuned motions. However, they are more versatile. The ball does not need to be placed perfectly to be kicked and the kick speed can be adjusted. Additionally, the underlying DMPs are easy to extend and lend themselves well to a multitude of optimization algorithms [7].

The kick motion presented in this paper has been successfully used in the corner kick challenge competition at RoboCup 2015.

Acknowledgement. We would like to thank the members of the team B-Human for providing the software framework for this work.

References

1. Alcaraz-Jiménez, J.J., Herrero-Pérez, D., Martínez-Barberá, H.: Robust feedback control of ZMP-based gait for the humanoid robot Nao. Int. J. Robot. Res. **32**(9–10), 1074–1088 (2013)
2. Czarnetzki, S., Kerner, S., Urbann, O.: Applying dynamic walking control for biped robots. In: Baltes, J., Lagoudakis, M.G., Naruse, T., Ghidary, S.S. (eds.) RoboCup 2009. LNCS, vol. 5949, pp. 69–80. Springer, Heidelberg (2010). doi:10.1007/978-3-642-11876-0_7
3. Gouaillier, D., Hugel, V., Blazevic, P., Kilner, C., Monceaux, J., Lafourcade, P., Marnier, B., Serre, J., Maisonnier, B.: Mechatronic design of NAO humanoid. In: Proceedings of the 2009 IEEE International Conference on Robotics and Automation (ICRA 2009), Kobe, Japan, pp. 2124–2129 (2009)

4. Ijspeert, A.J., Nakanishi, J., Hoffmann, H., Pastor, P., Schaal, S.: Dynamical movement primitives: learning attractor models for motor behaviors. Neural Comput. 25(2), 328–373 (2013)
5. Kajita, S., Kanehiro, F., Kaneko, K., Fujiwara, K., Harada, K., Yokoi, K., Hirukawa, H.: Biped walking pattern generation by using preview control of zero-moment point. In: Proceedings of the 2003 IEEE International Conference on Robotics and Automation (ICRA 2003), Taipei, Taiwan, vol. 2, pp. 1620–1626 (2003)
6. Kober, J., Mülling, K., Krömer, O., Lampert, C.H., Scholkopf, B., Peters, J.: Movement templates for learning of hitting and batting. In: Proceedings of the 2010 IEEE International Conference on Robotics and Automation (ICRA 2010), Anchorage, Alaska, USA, pp. 853–858 (2010)
7. Kober, J., Bagnell, J.A., Peters, J.: Reinforcement learning in robotics: a survey. Int. J. Robot. Res. 32(11), 1238–1274 (2013)
8. Müller, J., Laue, T., Röfer, T.: Kicking a ball – modeling complex dynamic motions for humanoid robots. In: Ruiz-del-Solar, J., Chown, E., Plöger, P.G. (eds.) RoboCup 2010. LNCS, vol. 6556, pp. 109–120. Springer, Heidelberg (2011). doi:10.1007/978-3-642-20217-9_10
9. Mülling, K., Kober, J., Krömer, O., Peters, J.: Learning to select and generalize striking movements in robot table tennis. Int. J. Robot. Res. 32(3), 263–279 (2013)
10. Royston, J.: Some techniques for assessing multivarate normality based on the Shapiro-Wilk W. J. Roy. Stat. Soc.: Ser. C (Appl. Stat.) 32(2), 121–133 (1983)
11. Röfer, T., Laue, T., Richter-Klug, J., Schünemann, M., Stiensmeier, J., Stolpmann, A., Stöwing, A., Thielke, F.: B-Human Team Report and Code Release 2015 (2015). http://www.b-human.de/downloads/publications/2015/CodeRelease2015.pdf
12. Sardain, P., Bessonnet, G.: Forces acting on a biped robot. Center of pressure - zero moment point. IEEE Trans. Syst. Man Cybern. Part A Syst. Hum. 34(5), 630–637 (2004)
13. Schaal, S.: Dynamic movement primitives - a framework for motor control in humans and humanoid robotics. In: Kimura, H., Tsuchiya, K., Ishiguro, A., Witte, H. (eds.) Adaptive Motion of Animals and Machines, pp. 261–280. Springer, Tokyo (2006). doi:10.1007/4-431-31381-8_23
14. Schaal, S., Peters, J., Nakanishi, J., Ijspeert, A.: Control, planning, learning, and imitation with dynamic movement primitives. In: Proceedings of the Workshop on Bilateral Paradigms on Humans and Humanoids, IEEE International Conference on Intelligent Robots and Systems (IROS 2003), Las Vegas, Nevada, USA, pp. 1–21 (2003)
15. Ude, A., Nemec, B., Petric, T., Morimoto, J.: Orientation in cartesian space dynamic movement primitives. In: Proceedings of the 2014 IEEE International Conference on Robotics and Automation (ICRA 2014), Hong Kong, China, pp. 2997–3004 (2014)
16. Urbann, O., Tasse, S.: Observer based biped walking control, a sensor fusion approach. Auton. Robots 35(1), 37–49 (2013)
17. Vukobratović, M., Borovac, B.: Zero-moment point—thirty five years of its life. Int. J. Humanoid Rob. 1(1), 157–173 (2004)
18. Wenk, F., Röfer, T.: Online generated kick motions for the NAO balanced using inverse dynamics. In: Behnke, S., Veloso, M., Visser, A., Xiong, R. (eds.) RoboCup 2013. LNCS, vol. 8371, pp. 25–36. Springer, Heidelberg (2014). doi:10.1007/978-3-662-44468-9_3

Learning a Humanoid Kick with Controlled Distance

Abbas Abdolmaleki[1,2,3(✉)], David Simões[1], Nuno Lau[1], Luis Paulo Reis[2,3], and Gerhard Neumann[4]

[1] IEETA, DETI, University of Aveiro, Aveiro, Portugal
{abbas.a,david.simoes,nunolau}@ua.pt
[2] DSI, University of Minho, Braga, Portugal
lpreis@dsi.uminho.pt
[3] LIACC, University of Porto, Porto, Portugal
[4] CLAS, TU Darmstadt, Darmstadt, Germany
neumann@ias.tu-darmstadt.de

Abstract. We investigate the learning of a flexible humanoid robot kick controller, i.e., the controller should be applicable for multiple contexts, such as different kick distances, initial robot position with respect to the ball or both. Current approaches typically tune or optimise the parameters of the biped kick controller for a single context, such as a kick with longest distance or a kick with a specific distance. Hence our research question is that, how can we obtain a flexible kick controller that controls the robot (near) optimally for a continuous range of kick distances? The goal is to find a parametric function that given a desired kick distance, outputs the (near) optimal controller parameters. We achieve the desired flexibility of the controller by applying a contextual policy search method. With such a contextual policy search algorithm, we can generalize the robot kick controller for different distances, where the desired distance is described by a real-valued vector. We will also show that the optimal parameters of the kick controller is a non-linear function of the desired distances and a linear function will fail to properly generalize the kick controller over desired kick distances.

Keywords: Contextual policy search · Motor learning · Humanoid robot · Non-linear policies

1 Introduction

Designing optimal controllers for robotic systems is one of the major tasks in the robotics research field. Hence, it is desirable to have a controller that can control the robot for different tasks or contexts in real time, for example a soccer robot should be able to kick the ball for any desired kick distance which can be chosen from a continuous range of kick distances. We define a task as a context. Context is a vector of variables that do not change during a task's execution, but might change from task to task. In this paper for example, the context is

© Springer International Publishing AG 2017
S. Behnke et al. (Eds.): RoboCup 2016, LNAI 9776, pp. 45–57, 2017.
https://doi.org/10.1007/978-3-319-68792-6_4

the distance the ball travels after being kicked and can be chosen by the agent. The kick task is one of the most important skills in the context of robotic soccer [1]. Typically the kick controllers are only applicable for a discretized number of desired distances. For example three sets of parameters for the kick controller is obtained which are applicable for long, mid and short distance kicks. Such a controller limits the robot to properly pass the ball to its teammates. Controlling the robot to kick the ball (near)optimally for different distances, allows the agents have a lot more control and options regarding their next decision, which could affects the game's outcome. Our goal is to find a parametric function that given a desired kick distance, outputs the (near) optimal controller parameters. In the other word we would like to obtain a policy $\pi(\theta|s)$ that sets the parameters θ of a robot kick controller given a context s which is the desired kick distance. In order to optimize the robot controller parameters given an objective function, there are many algorithms proposed by the scientific community [2–9]. However, many of these algorithms usually optimize a parameter set for a single context, such as optimizing a kick for the longest distance or the highest accuracy [10]. In other words, these algorithms fail to generalize the optimized movement for a context to different contexts. In order to generalize the kick motion to, for example, different kicking distances, typically the parameters are optimized for several target contexts independently. Afterwards, to generalize movements to new unseen contexts and to obtain a continuous policy $\pi(\theta|s)$, regression methods are commonly used [11,12]. Although such approaches have been successfully used, they are time consuming and inefficient regarding the number of needed training samples. In such a method, data-points obtained from optimizing the kick controller for context s cannot be re-used to improve and accelerate the optimisation for context s'. This is due to the fact that optimizing the controller parameters and generalizing them are two independent processes and the correlation between different contexts is ignored during the optimisation. Therefore in this paper we propose to use contextual relative entropy policy search (CREPS) algorithm which searches for the optimal parameters of the policy $\pi(\theta|s)$ in one run optimisation process a. In the other word in CREPS, optimizing the controller parameters and generalizing them happens simultaneously and therefore the correlation between different contexts can be exploited in order to accelerate the optimisation. CREPS, however, has a major drawback related to its search distribution update. The distribution might collapse prematurely to a point-estimate, resulting in premature convergence. On the other hand, the CMA-ES algorithm [2] which is not a contextual algorithm has shown to be able to avoid premature convergence. Therefore we combine the update rules of CREPS and CMA-ES resulting to the contextual relative entropy policy search with covariance matrix adaptation (CREPS-CMA). We will show that CREPS-CMA avoids premature convergence. Hence we will use CREPS-CMA for optimising the kick controller. We will also show that a non-linear function of desired kick distance clearly outperforms a linear one. This effect has been also observed for the humanoid walking task [13]. Now our robot is able to kick the ball for a continuous range of desire kick distances. This is in contrast with our previous approach where we had 3 sets of parameters for short, mid and long distance kicks.

2   The Approach

We used a simulated Nao robot shown in Fig. 1 for our experiments. Our movement pipeline is composed of two main parts: a kick controller, which receives parameters θ and converts them into joint commands for the robot's servos; and a policy function, which maps a given context s for a specific kick distance into the corresponding parameter vector θ. The pipeline for the kick task, whose context is the kick distance s with a straight kick direction with respect to the torso, is shown in Fig. 2.

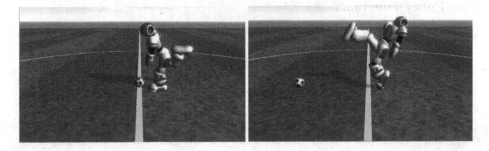

Fig. 1. The initial (left) and final (right) positions of an exemplary kick movement.

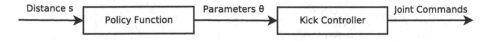

Fig. 2. The pipeline of our contextual kick movement.

2.1   Kick Controller

We have a kick controller which is a simple keyframe-based [10] linear model and we also have stability module as in [1] that stabilize the robot during performing the kick movement. A keyframe, as defined in [10], is a complete description of joint angles, either absolute or relative to the previous keyframe. Our keyframe based controller is defined by the following parameters:

- The initial keyframe, represented as a vector α of joint angles with dimension l,
- The final keyframe, also represented as a vector β of joint angles with dimension l.

- The action time t that is the amount of time the robot takes to move from the initial to the final keyframe. The joint angles are linearly interpolated across t to create the corresponding movement.

During performing kick only the legs joints move and remaining joints (arms and head joints) are kept constant. As each leg has 6 joints, α and β are 12-dimensional vectors. Therefore considering the action time t, our kick controller has 25 parameters to set. The controller receives a 25-dimensional parameter vector $\boldsymbol{\theta}$, which is then interpolated and coded into motor commands. Figure 1 shows the initial and final positions of an exemplary kick. The stability module has its constant parameters which doesn't change from task to task, please see [1] for more details of our stability module. Now we need to find a policy function of kick distance s that sets our controller parameters with the proper parameters $\boldsymbol{\theta}$ for any given desired kick distance.

2.2 Policy Function

Our goal is to find a function in form of

$$\mu(s) = \boldsymbol{A}^T \varphi(s),$$

that given a context vector s with dimension d_s, outputs a optimal parameter vector $\boldsymbol{\theta}$ with dimension d_θ such that it maximise our objective function $R(\boldsymbol{\theta}, s)$: $\{\mathbb{R}^{d_s}, \mathbb{R}^{d_\theta}\} \rightarrow \mathbb{R}$. Where $\varphi(s)$ is an arbitrary feature function of context s that outputs a feature vector with dimension d_φ and the gain matrix A_π is a $d_\theta \times d_\varphi$ matrix. Typically $\varphi(\boldsymbol{s}^{[i]}) = [1 \quad \boldsymbol{s}^{[i]}]$, which results in linear generalization over contexts. In order to achieve non-linear generalization over contexts, we can use normalized radial basis features (RBF) as a feature function:

$$\varphi(\boldsymbol{s}^{[i]}) = \frac{\psi_j(\boldsymbol{s}^{[i]})}{\sum_{j=1}^{K} \psi_j(\boldsymbol{s}^{[i]})}, \quad \psi_j(\boldsymbol{s}^{[i]}) = \exp(-\frac{(\boldsymbol{s}^{[i]} - c_j)^2}{2\sigma^2}),$$

where K is the number of RBFs and centres $\{c_j\}_{j=1...K}$ are equally spaced in the range of s, based on the desired number of RBFs K, and σ^2 is the bandwidth of the RBF. The bandwidth represents how related contexts are. A large bandwidth means that contexts are very similar and therefore the relationship is (near)linear. A bandwidth of 0 is an extreme case where movements are not generalizable at all, and each context has its independent optimal parameters. Both K and σ^2 are hand-tuned parameters. RBF features have been shown to enable algorithms to learn non-linear policies which greatly outperform their linear counterparts on non-linear tasks, such as walking [13], so we expected a performance increase. Now the task is to learn the optimal gain matrix A. As we don't have the labelled data to fit A, we need to use a reinforcement learning method.

2.3   Learning Policy Function

In order to learn the policy function $\mu(s)$ we use a contextual policy search algorithm called CREPS-CMA. CREPS-CMA is an extension of contextual REPS [8,14] which is capable of multi-task learning. The goal of CREPS-CMA is to find a function $\mu(s)$ that given a context s, it outputs a parameter vector θ such that $\{s, \theta\}$ maximises the objective function $R(s, \theta)$. The only accessible information on the objective function $R(s, \theta)$ are evaluations $\{R_k\}_{k=1...k}$ of samples $\{s_k, \theta_k\}_{k=1...k}$, where k is the index of the sample, ranging from 1 to the number of samples N. CREPS-CMA maintains a stochastic search distribution $\pi(\theta|s)$ over the parameter space θ of the objective function which is used to generate samples θ given s. The search distribution $\pi(\theta|s)$ is modelled as a linear Gaussian policy, i.e.,

$$\pi(\theta|s) = \mathcal{N}\left(\theta | A^T \varphi(s), \Sigma_\pi \right),$$

where the mean of the distribution is our policy function $\mu(s)$ we are searching for and covariance matrix Σ_π controls the exploration of the algorithm. CREPS-CMA is an iterative algorithm. First it initializes the search distribution $\pi(\theta|s)$ by defining A matrix and covariance matrix Σ_π with arbitrary values[1]. Afterwards in each iteration, given context samples[2] $\{s_k\}_{k=1...k}$, the current search distribution $q(\theta|s)$ is used to create samples $\{\theta_k\}_{k=1...k}$ of the parameter vector θ. Subsequently, the evaluation $\{R_k\}_{k=1...k}$ of samples $\{s_k, \theta_k\}_{k=1...k}$ is obtained by querying the objective function $R(s, \theta)$. And

---

Algorithm 1. Contextual stochastic search algorithm

Initialize $\pi(\theta|s)$
Repeat
    Set $q(\theta|s)$ **to** $\pi(\theta|s)$
    Use a uniform distribution to generate context samples $\{s_k\}_{k=1...N}$
    Sample parameters $\{\theta_k\}_{k=1...N}$ **from current search distribution** $q(\theta|s)$ **given context samples** $\{s_k\}_{k=1...N}$
    Evaluate the reward R_k **of each sample in the sample set** $\{s_k, \theta_k\}_{k=1...N}$
    Use the data set $\{\theta_k, s_k, R_k\}_{k=1...N}$ **to compute a weight** d_k **for each sample**
    Use the data set $\{s_k, \theta_k, d_k\}_{k=1...N}$ **to update the new search distribution** $\pi(\theta|s)$
Until search distribution $\pi(\theta|s)$ **converges.**

---

[1] With initializing we can define the region of the space that we would like the algorithm starts searching.

[2] Please note that the way we sample contexts s_k depends on the task. Throughout this paper we use a uniform distribution to sample contexts s_k which is desired kick distance. The intuition behind it is that all the kick distances have same importance for us.

dataset $\{s_k, \theta_k, R_k\}_{k=1\ldots k}$ is used to compute a weight $\{d_k\}_{k=1\ldots k}$ for all samples. Each weight is a pseudo-probability for the corresponding sample. Subsequently, using $\{s_k, \theta_k, d_k\}_{k=1\ldots k}$, a new Gaussian search distribution $\pi(\theta|s)$ is estimated by estimating a new A matrix and covariance matrix Σ_π. The new search distribution will give more probabilities to the samples $\{s_k, \theta_k\}_{k=1\ldots k}$ with better returns $\{R_k\}_{k=1\ldots k}$. This process runs iteratively until the algorithm converges to a solution. After all we are interested in the matrix A to construct our policy function $\mu(s)$. Algorithm 1 shows a compact representation of contextual stochastic search methods. Now we briefly explain how CREPS-CMA computes weights and what are the update rules of the search policy.

2.4 CREPS-CMA

The key idea behind contextual REPS [8] is to ensure a smooth and stable learning process by bounding the relative entropy between the old search distribution $q(\theta|s)$ and the newly estimated policy $\pi(\theta|s)$ while maximising the expected return. This results in a weight

$$d_k = \exp\left((\mathcal{R}_{s\theta} - V(s))/\eta\right)$$

for each sample $[s_k, \theta_k]$, which we can use to estimate a new search distribution $\pi(\theta|s)$. $\mathcal{R}_{s\theta}$ denotes the expected performance when evaluating parameter vector θ in context s and $V(s) = \varphi(s)^T w$ is a context dependent baseline which is subtracted from the return $\mathcal{R}_{s\theta}$. The parameters w and η are Lagrangian multipliers that can be obtained by minimising the dual function, given as

$$\min_{\eta, w} g(\eta, w) = \eta\epsilon + \hat{\varphi}^T w + \eta \log\left(\sum_{K=1}^{N} \frac{1}{N} \exp\left(\frac{R^{[k]} - \varphi(s^{[k]})^T w}{\eta}\right)\right).$$

where $\hat{\varphi} = \sum_{K=1}^{N} \varphi(s^{[k]})$ is the expected feature vector for the given context samples. We optimize this convex dual function by gradient decent. Now given dataset $\{s_k, \theta_k, d_k\}_{k=1\ldots N}$ and the old Gaussian search distribution

$$q(\theta|s) = \mathcal{N}\left(\theta | A_q^T \varphi(s), \Sigma_q\right),$$

we want to find the new search distribution $\pi(\theta|s)$ by finding A_π and Σ_π. Therefore we need two update rules, one for updating the context-dependent policy function $\mu_\pi(s)$ of the search distribution and another one for updating the covariance matrix Σ_π of the distribution.

Context-Dependent Mean-Function Update Rule. The matrix A can be obtained by the weighted maximum likelihood, i.e.,

$$A = \left(\Phi^T D \Phi + \lambda I\right)^{-1} \Phi^T D U, \tag{1}$$

where $\Phi^T = [\varphi^{[1]}, \ldots, \varphi^{[N]}]$ contains the feature vector for all context samples $\{s_k\}_{k=1\ldots N}, U = [\theta^{[1]}, \ldots, \theta^{[N]}]$ contains all the sample parameters, D is the diagonal weighting matrix containing the weightings $\{k\}_{k=1...N}$ and $\lambda \boldsymbol{I}$ is a regularization term. λ is a very small number such as $1e{-}8$.

Covariance Matrix Update Rule. Standard contextual REPS directly uses the weighted sample covariance matrix as $\boldsymbol{\Sigma}_\pi$ which is obtained by

$$\boldsymbol{S} = \frac{\sum_{k=1}^{N} d_k \big(\boldsymbol{\theta}_k - \boldsymbol{A}^T \varphi(\boldsymbol{s}_k)\big)\big(\boldsymbol{\theta}_k - \boldsymbol{A}_\pi^T \varphi(\boldsymbol{s}_k)\big)^T}{Z}, \tag{2}$$

$$Z = \frac{\big(\sum_{k=1}^{N} d_k\big)^2 - \sum_{k=1}^{N}(d_k)^2}{\sum_{k=1}^{N}(d_k)}.$$

It has been shown that the sample covariance matrix from Eq. 2 is not a good estimate of the true covariance matrix [15], since it biases the search distribution towards a specific region of the search space. In other words, the search distribution loses its exploration entropy along many dimensions of the parameter space, which causes premature convergence. This is a highly unwanted effect in policy search. To alleviate this problem, inspired by rank-μ update rule of CMA-ES [2], which is not a contextual algorithm, we combine the old covariance matrix and the sample covariance matrix from Eq. 2, i.e.,

$$\boldsymbol{\Sigma}_\pi = (1-\lambda)\boldsymbol{\Sigma}_q + \lambda \boldsymbol{S}.$$

There are different ways to determine the interpolation factor $\lambda \in [0,1]$ between the sample covariance matrix $\boldsymbol{S}$ and the old covariance matrix $\boldsymbol{\Sigma}_q$. For example, in [15], the factor $\lambda \in [0,1]$ is chosen in such a way that the entropy of the new search distribution is reduced by a certain amount, while also being scaled with the number of effective samples. We will extended REPS by using the rank-μ covariance matrix adaptation method of CMA-ES algorithm [2] which has been shown to be effective for avoiding premature convergence, i.e.,

$$\lambda = min\left(1, \frac{\phi_{\text{eff}}}{d_{\boldsymbol{\theta}}^2}\right), \phi_{\text{eff}} = \frac{1}{\sum_{k=1}^{N}(d^{[k]})^2}$$

where ϕ_{eff} is the number of effective samples and $d_{\boldsymbol{\theta}}$ is the dimension of the parameter space $\boldsymbol{\theta}$.

3   Experiments

[3]In this section, first we evaluate CREPS-CMA algorithm. Hence we use standard optimization test functions [16], such as the Sphere, the Rosenbrock and the Rastrigin (multi-modal) functions. We extend these functions to be applicable for the contextual setting. The task is to find the optimum 15 dimensional parameter vector $\boldsymbol{\theta}$ for a given 1 dimensional context $\boldsymbol{s}$. We will show that CREPS-CMA

---

[3] Matlab source-code of CREPS-CMA algorithm is available on-line at https://dl.dropboxusercontent.com/u/16387578/ContextualREPSCMA.zip.

performs favourably. Afterwards, We use CREPS-CMA to optimize our kick controller for different desired kick distances for a simulated Nao robot[4] and will show our accuracy results, with both linear and non-linear policies. According to the results non-linear policy outperforms the linear one.

3.1   Standard Optimization Test Functions

We chose three standard optimization functions, which are the Sphere function

$$f(\boldsymbol{s}, \theta) = \sum_{i=1}^{p} \boldsymbol{x}_i^2,$$

the Rosenbrock function

$$f(\boldsymbol{s}, \theta) = \sum_{i=1}^{p-1} [100(\boldsymbol{x}_{i+1} - \boldsymbol{x}_i^2)^2 + (1 - \boldsymbol{x}_i)^2],$$

and also a multi-modal function, known as the Rastgirin function

$$f(\boldsymbol{s}, \theta) = 10p + \sum_{i=1}^{p} [\boldsymbol{x}_i^2 - 10\cos(2\pi\boldsymbol{x}_i)],$$

where p is the number of dimensions of θ and $\boldsymbol{x} = \theta + \boldsymbol{A}\boldsymbol{s}$. The matrix A is a constant matrix that was chosen randomly. In our case, because the context $\boldsymbol{s}$ is 1 dimensional, A is a $p \times 1$ dimensional vector. Our definition for $\boldsymbol{x}$ means the optimum θ for these functions is linearly dependent on the given context $\boldsymbol{s}$. The initial search area of θ for all experiments is restricted to the hypercube $-5 \leq \theta_i \leq 5, i = 1, \ldots, p$ and contexts are uniformly sampled from the interval $0 \leq \boldsymbol{s}_i \leq 3, i = 1, \ldots, z$ where z is the dimension of the context space $\boldsymbol{s}$. In our experiments, the mean of the initial distributions has been chosen randomly in the defined search area. We compared CREPS-CMA with the standard Contextual REPS. In each iteration, we generated 50 new samples. The results in Fig. 3 show that CREPS-CMA could successfully learn the contextual tasks while standard Contextual REPS suffers from premature convergence.

3.2   Kick Task Results

We use a Nao humanoid robot simulated in RoboCup 3D simulation environment which is based on SimSpark[5]: a generic physical multiagent system simulator. The robot has 22 degrees of freedom, six in each leg, four in each arm, and two in the neck. We use CREPS-CMA to train a simulated NAO robot by optimising the kick controller explained in Sect. 2 using both linear policies, i.e., $\varphi(\boldsymbol{s}^{[i]}) = [1 \quad \boldsymbol{s}^{[i]}]$ and a RBF based non-linear policy. The desired kick distance s varies from 2.5 m to

---

[4] https://www.ald.softbankrobotics.com/en.
[5] http://simspark.sourceforge.net/.

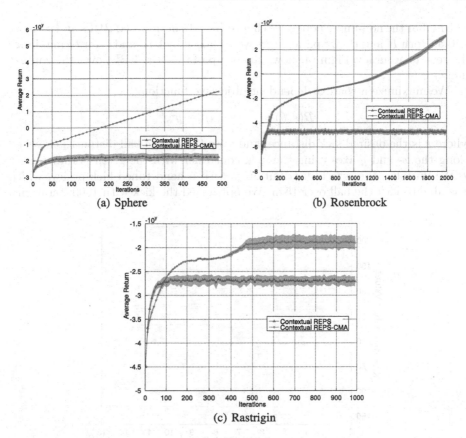

Fig. 3. The performance comparison of CREPS and CREPS-CMA for optimising contextual versions of standard functions (a) Sphere, (b) Rosenbrock and (c) Rastrigin. The results show that CREPS-CMA clearly outperforms CREPS in all three benchmarks while CREPS suffers from premature convergence.

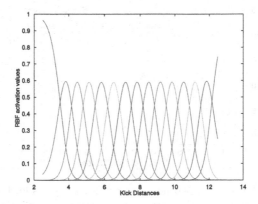

Fig. 4. The 15 RBFs setup used for generating features.

12.5 m. For the non-linear policy, we choose $K = 15$ normalized RBFs and σ^2 is set to 0.5. Both K and the σ^2 parameters were chosen by trial and error to maximize the results accuracy. Figure 4 shows the setup of the used RBFs over the context range.

We maximize a context dependent objective function

$$R(s, \theta) = -(x - s)^2 - y^2,$$

where s is the desired kick distance, and x and y are the ball distances travelled along the x- and y-axes using the kick controller with the given parameter set θ. We initialize the search distribution π with a hand tuned kick policy, which was able to kick the ball over 15 m. We optimized the kick with 1000 iterations.

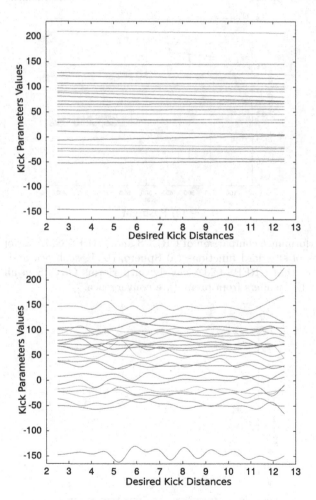

Fig. 5. The learned linear (left) and non-linear (right) policies for kick distances of 2.5 to 12.5 m. The y-axis represents the controller parameter values for a given desired kick distance, and the x-axis represents the desired kick distance.

Each iteration generates 20 new samples where the contexts were sampled uniformly. Each sample was evaluated 5 times, and was averaged to smooth out the noisy returns. In order to simulate competition conditions, for evaluating each sample, we placed the robot in 5 different positions around the ball and it had to perceive the ball, move towards it, position itself in place and then kick it towards the target goal using the kick controller. We compared the performance of the linear policy with non-linear one. Figure 6 shows that the non-linear policy clearly outperforms the linear one and the accuracy of the non-linear policy is considerable.[6] The average error of the linear policy was 0.82 ± 0.10 m while we achieved an average error of 0.34 ± 0.11 m using the non-linear policy. As expected, using a non-linear policy improves the accuracy of the results with order of magnitude. In fact, the average error is more than halved. This also demonstrates the non-linearity nature of robotic tasks such as kick task and the usefulness of using RBF functions to capture this non-linearity. Figure 5 shows the learned linear and non-linear policies for generalizing the 25 parameter kick controller for different kick distances. We can see that the learned linear policy is a linear approximation of its corresponding non-linear policy.

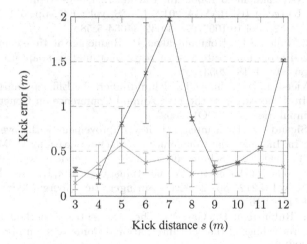

Fig. 6. The performance of the learned linear (blue) and non-linear (red) policies. The x-axis represents the desired kick distance, in meters, while the y-axis represents the error with respect to desired kick distance, also in meters. (Color figure online)

4 Conclusion

We used a recently proposed contextual policy search algorithm to generalize a robot kick controller for different desired kick distances, where a context is described by a real-valued vector of distances. We have modified the algorithm,

---

[6] Demonstration video of the non-linear kick controller using the magma challenge tool [17] is available on-line at https://www.dropbox.com/sh/0iimyykf6xejj6g/AADg9iCNJZAbu3Voe2UKsmQza?dl=0.

naming it CREPS-CMA. Using CREPS-CMA, we have successfully learned linear and non-linear policies over the context of kick distances. The non-linear policy outperforms its linear counterpart, and allows a humanoid robot to kick a ball with flexible distances and with satisfactory accuracy results, which could leads to a better control and coordination in a robotic soccer match. In this research, we also demonstrated the non-linearity of a kick task. In future we will use more complex kick controllers such as dynamic motor primitives.

Acknowledgment. The first author was supported by FCT under grant SFRH/BD/81155/2011. The work was also partially funded by the Operational Programme for Competitiveness and Internationalisation - COMPETE 2020 and by FCT Portuguese Foundation for Science and Technology under projects PEst-OE/EEI/UI0027/2013 and UID/CEC/00127/2013 (IEETA and LIACC). The work was also funded by project EuRoC, reference 608849 from call FP7-2013-NMP-ICT-FOF.

References

1. Ferreira, R., Reis, L.P., Moreira, A.P., Lau, N.: Development of an omnidirectional kick for a NAO humanoid robot. In: Pavón, J., Duque-Méndez, N.D., Fuentes-Fernández, R. (eds.) IBERAMIA 2012. LNCS, vol. 7637, pp. 571–580. Springer, Heidelberg (2012). doi:10.1007/978-3-642-34654-5_58
2. Hansen, N., Muller, S.D., Koumoutsakos, P.: Reducing the time complexity of the derandomized evolution strategy with covariance matrix adaptation (CMA-ES). Evol. Comput. **11**, 1–18 (2003)
3. Sun, Y., Wierstra, D., Schaul, T., Schmidhuber, J.: Efficient natural evolution strategies. In: Proceedings of the 11th Annual Conference on Genetic and Evolutionary Computation (GECCO) (2009)
4. Stulp, F., Sigaud, O.: Path integral policy improvement with covariance matrix adaptation. In: International Conference on Machine Learning (ICML) (2012)
5. Rückstieß, T., Felder, M., Schmidhuber, J.: State-dependent exploration for policy gradient methods. In: Daelemans, W., Goethals, B., Morik, K. (eds.) ECML PKDD 2008. LNCS, vol. 5212, pp. 234–249. Springer, Heidelberg (2008). doi:10.1007/978-3-540-87481-2_16
6. Mannor, S., Rubinstein, R., Gat, Y.: The cross entropy method for fast policy search. In: Proceedings of the 20th International Conference on Machine Learning (ICML) (2003)
7. Theodorou, E., Buchli, J., Schaal, S.: A generalized path integral control approach to reinforcement learning. J. Mach. Learn. Res. **11**, 3137–3181 (2010)
8. Kupcsik, A., Deisenroth, M.P., Peters, J., Neumann, G.: Data-efficient contextual policy search for robot movement skills. In: Proceedings of the National Conference on Artificial Intelligence (AAAI) (2013)
9. Abdolmaleki, A., Lioutikov, R., Peters, J., Lua, N., Reis, L.P., Neumann, G.: Regularized covariance estimation for weighted maximum likelihood policy search methods. In: Advances in Neural Information Processing Systems (NIPS), MIT Press (2015)
10. Depinet, M., MacAlpine, P., Stone, P.: Keyframe sampling, optimization, and behavior integration: towards long-distance kicking in the RoboCup 3D simulation league. In: Bianchi, R.A.C., Akin, H.L., Ramamoorthy, S., Sugiura, K. (eds.) RoboCup 2014. LNCS, vol. 8992, pp. 571–582. Springer, Cham (2015). doi:10.1007/978-3-319-18615-3_47

11. Wang, J.M., Fleet, D.J., Hertzmann, A.: Optimizing walking controllers. ACM Trans. Graph. (TOG) **28**(5), 168 (2009)
12. Niehaus, C., Röfer, T., Laue, T.: Gait optimization on a humanoid robot using particle swarm optimization. In: Proceedings of the Second Workshop on Humanoid Soccer Robots in conjunction with the, pp. 1–7 (2007)
13. Abdolmaleki, A., Lua, N., Reis, L.P., Peters, J., Neumann, G.: Contextual policy search for generalizing a parameterized biped walking controller. In: IEEE International Conference on Autonomous Robot Systems and Competitions (ICARSC) (2015)
14. Daniel, C., Neumann, G., Peters, J.: Hierarchical relative entropy policy search. In: International Conference on Artificial Intelligence and Statistics (AISTATS) (2012)
15. Abdolmaleki, A., Lua, N., Reis, L.P., Neumann, G.: Regularized covariance estimation for weighted maximum likelihood policy search methods. In: Proceedings of the International Conference on Humanoid Robots (HUMANOIDS) (2015)
16. Molga, M., Smutnicki, C.: Test functions for optimization needs (2005). http://www.zsd.ict.pwr.wroc.pl/files/docs/functions.pdf
17. The MagmaOffenburg RoboCup 3D Simulation Team. Magma challenge tool [computer software]. http://robocup.hs-offenburg.de/en/nc/downloads

Boundedness Approach to Gait Planning for the Flexible Linear Inverted Pendulum Model

Leonardo Lanari[1], Oliver Urbann[2($\boxtimes$)], Seth Hutchinson[3],
and Ingmar Schwarz[2]

[1] Dipartimento di Ingegneria Informatica, Automatica e Gestionale,
Sapienza Università di Roma, Rome, Italy
[2] Robotics Research Institute, TU Dortmund University, Dortmund, Germany
[3] Electrical and Computer Engineering, University of Illinois, Champaign, IL, USA
oliver.urbann@tu-dortmund.de

Abstract. In this paper, we solve the gait planning problem by using the Flexible LIP model, which has been shown to be more realistic w.r.t. the LIP for cost-effective or compliant biped robots for gait generation. We extend a stable inversion approach to obtain bounded Center of Mass (CoM) reference trajectories and show several advantages compared to preview control: avoidance of numerical integration, lower computation time, exact tracking of reference Zero Moment Point (ZMP) trajectories, and the ability to come to an immediate stop.

Keywords: Boundedness · Stable inversion · Preview control · LIPM

1 Introduction

In this paper, we apply the trajectory planning and control methods derived in [12,13] to the Flexible Linear Inverted Pendulum (FLIP) model for bipedal locomotion introduced in [19]. The result is a computationally efficient method for planning bounded trajectories using a model that is more realistic than the Linear Inverted Pendulum (LIP) model used by many researchers (e.g., [10]) in the past.

Several models of bipedal locomotion have been introduced that are intended to capture dynamic aspects that are not present in the LIP model. Pratt et al. [16] include a flywheel to model the dynamics of a rotating body. In [1,15], the dynamics of the swinging leg are taken into account by including extra masses in the model. Dau et al. [4] propose a specific extension to the LIP model by a function that can be utilized to model various dynamical issues.

While multiple-mass models are an indisputable improvement, another important dynamical aspect in robotics is compliance, elasticity and flexibility. These can arise as a desired compliance, as in the COMAN [19] and TORO [7] humanoids. But elasticity can also be an undesired property of cost-effective robots like Nao by Aldebaran Robotics. While compliance is a reasonable attribute for a humanoid robot expected to operate in an environment with humans, the necessity of light-weight and cost-effective robots is evident.

© Springer International Publishing AG 2017
S. Behnke et al. (Eds.): RoboCup 2016, LNAI 9776, pp. 58–70, 2017.
https://doi.org/10.1007/978-3-319-68792-6_5

Thus, in our previous paper [19] we presented a novel model called the Flexible Linear Inverted Pendulum model (FLIPM) that includes elasticity and has a proven positive impact on walking stability. In this paper we further investigate this model and give a new interpretation as an interconnected system of a flexible system and the cart-table model of Kajita et al. [9].

Along with improvements in the modeling, different enhancements or alternative approaches to the preview control of [9] have also been proposed. For example, the combination of an observer with the preview control showed a stabilizing effect in simulation [3] and on a physical robot [2]. It is also possible to include multiple sensor sources [21] and reactive stepping [20] ideas. Model Predictive Control as proposed by Diedam et al. [5] allows also reactive stepping without defining an a-priori reference ZMP.

The novel concept of Capture Point (CP), defined as the point on the floor where the robot has to step in order to come to a full stop, was initially introduced in Pratt et al. [16]. Englsberger et al. [6] applied this concept to a walking algorithm which is the base for Missura and Behnke [14] to include a state estimation.

In this paper we want to exploit the novel FLIP model and generate a stable gait by using the boundedness approach introduced in [12,13] which provides a certain number of possible advantages. First an analytical solution can be derived, given a desired ZMP trajectory, for the CoM trajectory thus allowing efficient real-time implementations. Moreover this approach can also be seen as an extension of the Capture Point concept with its benefits as the determination of stopping strategies or sudden change of plans.

In Sect. 2 we illustrate the FLIPM and its interpretation as the series interconnection of two sub-systems. This separation allows, in Sect. 3.2, the development of a novel controller. To show a direct application of both the FLIPM and the boundedness approach, we explicitly illustrate the derivation of the state reference trajectories when a piecewise constant desired ZMP is chosen. The necessity of an impulsive control input is also highlighted together with an alternative approach. Experiments finally show the performance of the obtained controller in Sect. 5. Conclusions and future work are then addressed.

2 FLIP Dynamical Model

In this section we first describe the idea behind the Flexible Linear Inverted Pendulum Model (FLIPM), and write it as two systems in series. As explained in the introduction, it is intended to model elasticity in various parts of the robot: motors, gears, light-weight links and possible PD controllers, which can be imagined as a spring and a damper. Comparably to LIPM, it is a linear model and thus can still be efficiently applied. Note that it does not model vertical flexibility as height changes would lead to a nonlinear model.

We begin with the cart-table model proposed by Kajita et al. [9], here extended as in Fig. 1. A massless table stands on the ground with a cart on top at height z_h, with mass m_1 at position c_1. The cart can accelerate itself such

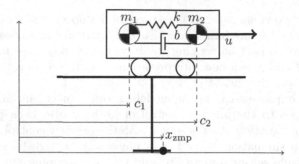

Fig. 1. The cart-table representation of the FLIPM

that the table stands stably even if the cart is not located above the stand of the table, in which case the Zero Moment Point (ZMP) x_{zmp} is located in the support polygon of the table.

To model the elasticity, we add a second mass $m_2 \ll m_1$ with position c_2, located within the cart. The second mass is connected to mass 1 by a spring-damper mechanism, with spring constant k and damper constant b, modeling elastic parts of the robot like motors, gears etc. Thus mass 2 models everything that is located *before* all elastic parts of the robot, and mass 1 everything *after* the elasticity. In this model, the control input is a force applied to mass 2. In Fig. 1 the acceleration of mass 1 due to the spring and damper is the acceleration achieved by the wheels on the table. While both masses are used in the dynamic model, to simplify calculations the second mass is not included in the ZMP.

The corresponding equations of motion are

$$m_1\ddot{c}_1 = -b(\dot{c}_1 - \dot{c}_2) - k(c_1 - c_2) \tag{1}$$
$$m_2\ddot{c}_2 = b(\dot{c}_1 - \dot{c}_2) + k(c_1 - c_2) + u \tag{2}$$

and the ZMP (neglecting the contribution of mass 2) is given by

$$x_{zmp} = c_1 - \frac{z_h}{g}\ddot{c}_1 = c_1 - \frac{1}{\omega_o^2}\ddot{c}_1 \tag{3}$$

where $\omega_o^2 = g/z_h$ (which is the pendulum frequency for the LIP). Computing the overall transfer function from u to x_{zmp} which, after some manipulations, takes on the form

$$F(s) = \frac{x_{zmp}(s)}{u(s)} = \left(\frac{1 - \frac{1}{\omega_o^2}s^2}{s^2}\right)\left(\frac{bs + k}{m_1 m_2 s^2 + (m_1 + m_2)(bs + k)}\right) \tag{4}$$

it is interesting to recognize the typical cart-table transfer function $F_{ct}(s)$ from the acceleration $\ddot{c}_1$ and the ZMP

$$F_{ct}(s) = \frac{x_{zmp}(s)}{\ddot{c}_1(s)} = \frac{1 - \frac{1}{\omega_o^2}s^2}{s^2} \tag{5}$$

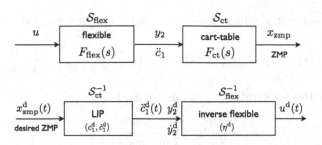

Fig. 2. FLIPM as a series interconnected system (up) and its inverse (down)

and a second transfer function

$$F_{\text{flex}}(s) = \frac{\ddot{c}_1(s)}{u(s)} = \frac{bs + k}{m_1 m_2 s^2 + (m_1 + m_2)(bs + k)} \tag{6}$$

from the input force u to $\ddot{c}_1$ which can be thought as the contribution of a *flexible system* S_{flex}. In the sequel it is important to notice that S_{flex} is both stable and minimum-phase due to the presence of a stable zero at $-k/b$. The overall system $F(s) = F_{\text{ct}}(s) F_{\text{flex}}(s)$ can be interpreted as the conceptual series interconnection of the cart-table S_{ct} and the flexible system S_{flex} as shown in Fig. 2.

If $m_2 = 0$ the transfer function (4) reduces to $F_{\text{ct}}(s)/m_1$ which is consistent with u being a force while in the classic cart-table the input is an acceleration.

In order to find the same explicit series interconnection in the state space, we make a change of coordinates. We choose the first two components as $x_1 = c_1$ and $x_2 = \dot{c}_1$ with

$$\dot{x}_1 = x_2, \qquad \dot{x}_2 = u_1, \qquad y_1 = x_1 - \frac{1}{\omega_o^2} u_1$$

and $u_1 = \ddot{c}_1$, which leads to the cart-table model S_{ct} with transfer function $F_{\text{ct}}(s)$. The original version of the cart-table [9] had also the acceleration $\ddot{c}_1$ as a state variable in order to obtain a strictly proper transfer function.

We choose as the two final state components the relative position and velocity

$$\begin{pmatrix} x_3 \\ x_4 \end{pmatrix} = \begin{pmatrix} c_2 - c_1 \\ \dot{c}_2 - \dot{c}_1 \end{pmatrix} \tag{7}$$

so that we obtain, by setting

$$\bar{M} = \frac{1}{m_1} + \frac{1}{m_2} = \frac{m_1 + m_2}{m_1 m_2} \tag{8}$$

the following state space representation (A_2, B_2) of S_{flex}

$$\begin{pmatrix} \dot{x}_3 \\ \dot{x}_4 \end{pmatrix} = \begin{pmatrix} 0 & 1 \\ -k\bar{M} & -b\bar{M} \end{pmatrix} \begin{pmatrix} x_3 \\ x_4 \end{pmatrix} + \begin{pmatrix} 0 \\ 1/m_2 \end{pmatrix} u \tag{9}$$

The output matrix C_2, which gives the transfer function $F_{\text{flex}}(s)$

$$F_{\text{flex}}(s) = C_2(sI - A_2)^{-1}B_2 = C_2 \begin{pmatrix} s & -1 \\ k\bar{M} & s + b\bar{M} \end{pmatrix}^{-1} \begin{pmatrix} 0 \\ 1/m_2 \end{pmatrix} \qquad (10)$$

and therefore the acceleration $\ddot{c}_1$ as output y_2, is

$$C_2 = \begin{pmatrix} \dfrac{k}{m_1} & \dfrac{b}{m_1} \end{pmatrix} \qquad (11)$$

The previous series separation allows the direct use of the framework and results of [12,13] for the $\mathcal{S}_{\text{ct}}$ subsystem. The basic idea is illustrated next.

3 Stable Inversion Approach

After briefly recalling the basic idea of [13] for the LIP, we take advantage of the series interconnection previously identified for the FLIPM.

3.1 Stable Inversion for the LIP

For the LIP, the problem consists in finding, for a given desired output ZMP denoted as $x_{\text{zmp}}^{\text{d}}(t)$, the corresponding bounded CoM reference trajectory and feedforward input $u^{\text{d}}(t)$ which guarantee exact tracking: if the state is initialized on the bounded state reference trajectory, the cart-table driven by $u^{\text{d}}(t)$ will ensure zero output tracking error. This reference state trajectory (CoM state) can then be translated, through inverse kinematics, into a joint reference trajectory to be tracked by the local joint controllers.

Using the framework of [12] we transform an *exact tracking* problem for the cart-table into a *stable inversion* one for the LIP, i.e. the inverse of the cart-table system. The LIP is then forced by $x_{\text{zmp}}^{\text{d}}$ and has its generic state trajectories exponentially diverging unless a specific initial state for the unstable part is chosen (the LIP has an unstable pole in $s = \omega_o$). These initial conditions which guarantee a bounded state evolution for a given $x_{\text{zmp}}^{\text{d}}$, should verify the so-called *boundedness condition* (see [13] for further details) which involves only the unstable dynamics of the LIP as in [6,8,18].

For the LIP system

$$F_{\text{ct}}^{-1}(s) = \frac{s^2}{1 - \frac{1}{\omega_o^2}s^2} \qquad (12)$$

the boundedness condition extend the concept of capture point of [16] and, for any given analytical expression of the desired ZMP $x_{\text{zmp}}^{\text{d}}(t)$, we are able to obtain a bounded CoM position trajectory in an analytical closed form (so also the velocity and acceleration have closed form analytical expressions) thus providing a useful tool for real-time implementation.

3.2   Stable Inversion for the FLIPM

For the FLIP model, we seek the bounded reference trajectory for c_1, analogous to finding the CoM trajectory for the LIP. To do so, we extend the approach recalled in Sect. 3.1 to the FLIPM by using the particular series interconnection highlighted in (4): the inverse of a series interconnection is the series (in reverse order) of the single inverse systems and thus we can use all our previous results for the LIP part. In Fig. 2 the overall inverse system is expressed in terms of $\mathcal{S}_{ct}^{-1}$, i.e. the LIP, and $\mathcal{S}_{flex}^{-1}$ which denote the inverse system of respectively $\mathcal{S}_{ct}$ and $\mathcal{S}_{flex}$.

Moreover, being $\mathcal{S}_{flex}$ minimum phase, its inverse $\mathcal{S}_{flex}^{-1}$ is stable. Therefore since the boundedness constraint involves only the unstable dynamics, obtaining a stable inverse for the FLIPM reduces to using the boundedness constraint for the unstable part of the LIP and just inverting $\mathcal{S}_{flex}$. All previous results obtained for the LIP can therefore be extended.

To explicitly derive $\mathcal{S}_{flex}^{-1}$ we rewrite the dynamics of $\mathcal{S}_{flex}$ using a change of coordinates which also highlights the dynamics of the zeros (the zero-dynamics) and thus enables the direct derivation of a *reduced order inverse system* [17]. Since $\mathcal{S}_{flex}$ has relative degree one - we need to differentiate the output once to make the input appear explicitly - we choose as new coordinates the output $z = y_2$ and $\eta = x_3 = c_2 - c_1$

$$\begin{pmatrix} z \\ \eta \end{pmatrix} = \begin{pmatrix} k/m_1 & b/m_1 \\ 1 & 0 \end{pmatrix} \begin{pmatrix} x_3 \\ x_4 \end{pmatrix} \tag{13}$$

so that, in these new coordinates, system $\mathcal{S}_{flex}$ becomes

$$\dot{z} = \left(\frac{k}{b} - b\bar{M} \right) z - \frac{k^2}{m_1 b} \eta + \frac{b}{m_1 m_2} u \tag{14}$$

$$\dot{\eta} = \frac{m_1}{b} z - \frac{k}{b} \eta \tag{15}$$

$$y_2 = z \tag{16}$$

By definition, the dynamics of η, when the output is restricted to be identically zero ($z = 0$), gives the dynamics of the zeros (one zero at $-k/b$ for the flexible system as clearly confirmed by the transfer function $F_{flex}(s)$). The reduced order first order flexible system inverse $\mathcal{S}_{flex}^{-1}$ is then directly obtained as

$$\dot{\eta} = -\frac{k}{b} \eta + \frac{m_1}{b} y_2(t) \tag{17}$$

$$u = \left(\frac{b}{m_1 m_2} \right)^{-1} \left[\frac{k^2}{m_1 b} \eta + \dot{y}_2(t) - \left(\frac{k}{b} - b\bar{M} \right) y_2(t) \right] \tag{18}$$

where u is solved from (14) and z is taken from (16). Being $\mathcal{S}_{flex}^{-1}$ stable, if we apply the bounded $y_2^d(t) = \ddot{c}_1^d(t)$ obtained from the LIP (see Sect. 3.1 and Fig. 2) as input, the resulting state evolution $\eta^d(t)$ and output $u^d(t)$ will be bounded for any initial state[1]. Note that the output $u(t)$ in (18) depends also on its input derivative $\dot{y}_2 = \dddot{c}_1$.

Going back to the original system with the new coordinates (13), we can summarize the overall procedure by noting that if the FLIPM is driven by $u^d(t)$ and has a state evolving as $(c_1^d, \dot{c}_1^d, \eta^d, \ddot{c}_1^d)$, then the output will exactly track the desired ZMP $x_{zmp}^d(t)$. The analytical closed form expression of $c_1^d(t)$, for a given x_{zmp}^d, is readily obtained using the boundedness condition of [13]. An example is discussed in the following section.

4 A Carried Out Example: Piecewise Constant ZMP

In order to illustrate the overall approach and its potential, we choose the most demanding reference ZMP trajectory: an instantaneous variation at time T, i.e. $x_{zmp}^d(t) = u_{step}(t - T)$ where $u_{step}(\cdot)$ denotes the Heaviside step function. The boundedness condition applied to the chosen $x_{zmp}^d(t)$ leads to

$$c_1(0) + \frac{\dot{c}_1(0)}{\omega_o} = e^{-\omega_o T} \tag{19}$$

which coincides with the Capture Point condition of [16]. A possible corresponding reference trajectory c_1^d of the LIP is given by[2]

$$c_1^d(t) = \frac{1}{2} e^{\omega_o(t-T)} \cdot (1 - u_{step}(t - T)) + \frac{1}{2}(2 - e^{-\omega_o(t-T)}) \cdot u_{step}(t - T) \tag{20}$$

where the first term shows the anticipatory behavior emphasized in [9]. Note that the resulting desired velocity $\dot{c}_1^d$

$$\dot{c}_1^d(t) = \frac{\omega_o}{2} \left(e^{\omega_o(t-T)} - 2\sinh(\omega_o(t - T)) \cdot u_{step}(t - T) \right) \tag{21}$$

is still continuous[3] while the acceleration $\ddot{c}_1^d(t)$ is not. We still need to also compute η^d, but since it is the solution of (17) driven by $y_2^d = \ddot{c}_1^d$,

$$\eta^d(t) = e^{-k/bt} \eta^d(0) + \frac{m_1}{b} \int_0^t e^{-k/b(t-\tau)} \ddot{c}_1^d(\tau) \, d\tau \tag{22}$$

it can be obtained analytically by substituting $\ddot{c}_1^d$ and evaluating the integral.

Finally, in order to compute the feedforward term u^d using (18) for the particular chosen desired ZMP, we note that the third derivative of c_1^d

$$\dddot{c}_1^d(t) = \frac{\omega_o^3}{2} \left(e^{\omega_o(t-T)} - 2\sinh(\omega_o(t - T))u_{step}(t - T) \right) - \omega_o^2 \, \text{Imp}(T) \tag{23}$$

---

[1] Note that the stable dynamics of the inverse should be consistently initialized, for example $\eta^d(0) = x_3(0)$, in order to obtain identically null tracking error.

[2] This choice corresponds to the stable dynamics initialized to 0 (see [13] for details).

[3] Note that, due to the special structure of $c_1^d(t)$, the impulses that appear from the derivation of the step functions in (20) cancel out. Similarly for the acceleration.

is needed and therefore an impulse $\mathrm{Imp}(T)$ appears in the desired feedforward

$$u^{\mathrm{d}}(t) = \frac{m_2 k^2}{b^2}\eta^{\mathrm{d}}(t) - \frac{m_1 m_2}{b}\left(\frac{k}{b} - b\bar{M}\right)\ddot{c}_1^{\mathrm{d}}(t) + \frac{m_1 m_2}{b}\dddot{c}_1^{\mathrm{d}}(t) \qquad (24)$$

which makes the implementation difficult. From a theoretical point of view, this result is consistent with the FLIPM model: in order to make the ZMP change instantaneously we need an impulsive input. Note that if $x_{\mathrm{zmp}}^{\mathrm{d}}$ were continuous, at this point we would have obtained an analytical result that could be directly implemented, which would be extremely beneficial for real-time applications.

4.1   Approximate Inverse

The presence of the impulse in (24) emanates from the chosen challenging $x_{\mathrm{zmp}}^{\mathrm{d}}$ and from the system $\mathcal{S}_{\mathrm{flex}}$ having relative degree one and therefore the need of $\dot{y}_2$ in (18). A possible way to avoid this derivation is to make a relative degree zero approximation of $\mathcal{S}_{\mathrm{flex}}$ by adding a high frequency zero in $F_{\mathrm{flex}}(s)$, i.e.

$$F_{\mathrm{flex}}^{\mathrm{a}}(s) = (1 + \tau s)F_{\mathrm{flex}}(s) = \frac{(1+\tau s)(bs+k)}{m_1 m_2 s^2 + (m_1 + m_2)(bs+k)} \qquad (25)$$

which can be rewritten, after some manipulations, as

$$F_{\mathrm{flex}}^{\mathrm{a}}(s) = \frac{b\tau}{m_1 m_2} + \frac{\alpha s + \beta}{m_1 m_2 s^2 + (m_1 + m_2)(bs+k)} \qquad (26)$$

with

$$\alpha = \frac{1}{m_1 m_2}\left[\tau(k - \bar{M}b^2) + b\right], \quad \beta = \frac{k}{m_1 m_2}(1 - \bar{M}b\tau) \qquad (27)$$

Since only the numerator of the transfer function has changed, we can use the same state Eq. (9) as for $\mathcal{S}_{\mathrm{flex}}$, while the output is now given by

$$\ddot{c}_1 = \begin{pmatrix} \beta m_2 & \alpha m_2 \end{pmatrix}\begin{pmatrix} x_3 \\ x_4 \end{pmatrix} + \frac{b\tau}{m_1 m_2}u = C_a\begin{pmatrix} x_3 \\ x_4 \end{pmatrix} + D_a u \qquad (28)$$

Being the relative degree 0, the inverse system is readily found as

$$\dot{x}_i = (A_2 - B_2 D_a^{-1}C_a)x_i + B_2 D_a^{-1} \qquad (29)$$

$$u = -D_a^{-1}C_a x_i + D_a^{-1}\ddot{c}_1 \qquad (30)$$

with $x_i = (x_3, x_4)^T$ and A_2, B_2 defined in (9). When the ZMP trajectory is given by a step function, we have avoided the triple derivative of c_1^{d} which introduced the impulse. The choice of the high frequency zero needs to be done consistently with the sampling time and the system parameters.

4.2   Some Interesting Applications

The previous analysis shows that we can obtain closed form expressions for the FLIPM reference state corresponding to a given x_{zmp}^{d}. The same boundedness framework, however, allows to solve a simultaneous CoM/ZMP problem which allows to solve for both a desired ZMP which satisfies some additional constraints and the corresponding CoM (which for the FLIP refers to c_1). For example, in the same spirit of the Capture Point, a change of plan or a sudden obstacle could require the humanoid to stop as soon as possible, if possible in one step. This is equivalent to requiring a step recovery from a generic initial state $(c_1(0), \dot{c}_1(0))$. Considering a generic instantaneous step at time T of length α, since the boundedness constraint

$$c_1(0) + \frac{\dot{c}_1(0)}{\omega_o} = \alpha e^{-\omega_o T} \tag{31}$$

applied to the FLIPM involves only the unstable dynamics of the LIP, we can solve (31) either in the step length α - as shown next in Sect. 5 - or in the step duration T. While this solution guarantees that, after the step is taken, c_1 converges asymptotically to 0, other interesting choices can also be studied by considering both parameters α and T to be still determined. We can, for example, add the additional requirement that the humanoid should immediately stop when the step is taken without the asymptotic convergence to the rest upright position. This can be achieved by solving simultaneously

$$c_1(0) + \frac{\dot{c}_1(0)}{\omega_o} = \alpha e^{-\omega_o T} \qquad c_1(0) - \frac{\dot{c}_1(0)}{\omega_o} = \alpha e^{\omega_o T} \tag{32}$$

where the second condition ensures a deadbeat behavior. Solving in α and T

$$\alpha = \frac{1}{\omega_o} \sqrt{\omega_o^2 c_1^2(0) - \dot{c}_1^2(0)} \qquad T = \frac{1}{2\omega_o} \ln \left(\frac{\omega_o c_1(0) - \dot{c}_1(0)}{\omega_o c_1(0) + \dot{c}_1(0)} \right) \tag{33}$$

Analyzing the existence of T leads to interesting considerations.

   We envisage to explore and implement, for the FLIPM, this and several other possibilities illustrated in [11] together with a smoother choice of the ZMP desired trajectory as the typical Constant/Cubic/Constant profile used for representing single/double/single support patterns.

5   Experiments

As in [19] we show the superiority of the FLIPM compared to the LIP, we give a comprehensive comparison between the boundedness approach and the preview control w.r.t. the tracking error and execution time. Additionally, we show how the approximate inverse system performs on a system that is hard to control due to the spring-damper-system even in the case of a stopping capture step.

5.1 Dynamic Simulation

To verify that the system is capable of generating a stable gait, we apply it in the rigid body dynamics simulation environment SimRobot that is based on the Open Dynamics Engine. In [19] the Nao is utilized as an example for a robot with elasticities, thus we also utilize a model of it here. As this robot is position controlled, we directly apply $c_2^d = c_1^d + \eta^d$ without numerically problematic integration steps that would be required using preview control [21]. We thus have a reference c_1 that exactly matches the reference, while preview control uses an optimization function which allows tracking errors.

Figure 3 depicts the results of a walk forward at 10 cm/s that is interrupted by an unforeseen instant stop at 14.7 s executed utilizing a capture step. In this simulation we use high values for k and b (1000, 200) as the simulated robot reveals a low elasticity. The frequency of control and simulation is 100 Hz. As it is implemented in C++[4], it can also be applied on a physical robot in real-time at this frequency.

To show stability we consider directly the body orientation as shown in Fig. 3, rather than the measured ZMP. As can be seen, a low oscillation occurs during the walk that does not affect stability. It is a consequence of the simulation of the collisions between the feet and the ground, which are not fully rigid. At the stopping step the oscillation stops immediately indicating a correct determined final position.

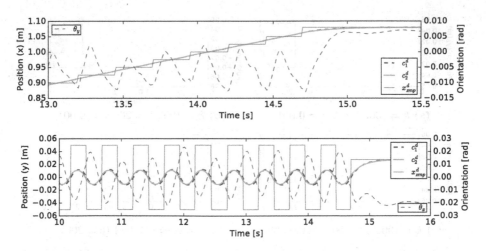

Fig. 3. Results of the dynamic simulation with control and simulation frequency of 100 Hz applying the exact system (Sect. 3) implemented in C++

---

[4] https://github.com/OliverUrbann/FLIPM.

5.2   Comparison

Figure 4 shows the application of the approximate system to the state space equation $x_{t+1} = Ax_t + Bu_t^d$ that represents the FLIPM as presented in [19]. The control output u_t^d is obtained and applied to the state space by integration enabling a comparison with a preview controller.

The walk initially consists of 10 steps with a sudden stopping (capture) step at 1.8 s. With low values for b the tracking error of the reference ZMP is low, even in case of an interrupting and unforeseen stop by a capture step. Rising values of b require an adaption of τ to compensate the arising tracking error.

In contrast to Sect. 5.1, Fig. 4 is obtained using a high control frequency of 2 kHz. While this leads to satisfying results applying the boundedness approach, the preview controller in Fig. 4(d) performs partially better. However, in fact preview control is not applicable at these frequencies as the time for calculating the depicted 3 s is 204.9 s using a Python script on a Core i5 PC. This is a consequence of the preview that must be approx. 1 s, thus requiring to calculate 2000 future frames in each time step. In contrast, calculation time is approx. 1 s for the simulation of 3 s using the boundedness approach. Thus, it needs 1/3 of the available time for calculation and is therefore even at 2 kHz real-time capable using Python. At lower frequencies, where preview control is also real-time capable, e.g. at 100 Hz where computation time is 0.5 s, it reveals higher tracking errors (see [19]) and a jitter in the resulting ZMP. Therefore, at frequencies where the controller is real-time capable, Boundedness Control performs better.

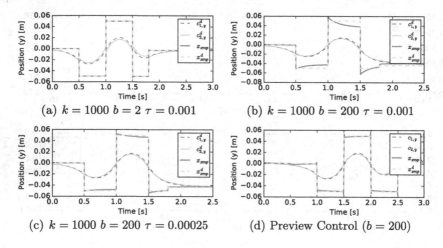

(a) $k = 1000$ $b = 2$ $\tau = 0.001$

(b) $k = 1000$ $b = 200$ $\tau = 0.001$

(c) $k = 1000$ $b = 200$ $\tau = 0.00025$

(d) Preview Control ($b = 200$)

Fig. 4. Comparison of different choices of k, b and τ for the approximate iterative system and preview control (without capture step).

6   Conclusion

In this paper, we presented a boundedness approach for gait planning based on the Flexible Linear Inverted Pendulum Model (FLIPM). Applying a stable inversion to a series connection of LIP and the flexible system we are able to obtain a reference trajectory for the CoM and a control output. We show several advantages compared to preview control like Capture Point determination, computation time etc.

As future work we will investigate an advantage of preview control: closed-loop control. While the experiments show stable results, a system applying a control output may drift due to integration steps. Additionally, sensor feedback will be investigated due to its importance for physical robots.

Acknowledgements. This work is partially supported by the EU H2020 RIA project COMANOID.

References

1. Buschmann, T., Lohmeier, S., Bachmayer, M., Ulbrich, H., Pfeiffer, F.: A collocation method for real-time walking pattern generation. In: 2007 7th IEEE-RAS International Conference on Humanoid Robots, pp. 1–6, November 2007
2. Czarnetzki, S., Kerner, S., Urbann, O.: Applying dynamic walking control for biped robots. In: Baltes, J., Lagoudakis, M.G., Naruse, T., Ghidary, S.S. (eds.) RoboCup 2009. LNCS, vol. 5949, pp. 69–80. Springer, Heidelberg (2010). doi:10.1007/978-3-642-11876-0_7
3. Czarnetzki, S., Kerner, S., Urbann, O.: Observer-based dynamic walking control for biped robots. Robot. Auton. Syst. **57**(8), 839–845 (2009)
4. Dau, H., Chew, C.M., Poo, A.N.: Proposal of augmented linear inverted pendulum model for bipedal gait planning. In: 2010 IEEE/RSJ International Conference on Intelligent Robots and Systems (IROS), pp. 172–177 (2010)
5. Diedam, H., Dimitrov, D., Wieber, P.B., Mombaur, K., Diehl, M.: Online walking gait generation with adaptive foot positioning through linear Model Predictive control, vol. 24, pp. 1121–1126. IEEE (2008)
6. Englsberger, J., Ott, C., Roa, M., Albu-Schaffer, A., Hirzinger, G.: Bipedal walking control based on capture point dynamics. In: 2011 IEEE/RSJ International Conference on Intelligent Robots and Systems (IROS), pp. 4420–4427, September 2011
7. Englsberger, J., Werner, A., Ott, C., Henze, B., Roa, M.A., Garofalo, G., Burger, R., Beyer, A., Eiberger, O., Schmid, K., Albu-Schäffer, A.: Overview of the torque-controlled humanoid robot TORO. In: 2014 14th IEEE-RAS International Conference on Humanoid Robots (Humanoids), pp. 916–923, November 2014
8. Hopkins, M.A., Hong, D.W., Leonessa, A.: Humanoid locomotion on uneven terrain using the time-varying divergent component of motion. In: 14th IEEE-RAS International Conference on Humanoid Robots (Humanoids), pp. 266–272, November 2014
9. Kajita, S., Kanehiro, F., Kaneko, K., Fujiwara, K., Harada, K., Yokoi, K., Hirukawa, H.: Biped walking pattern generation by using preview control of zero-moment point. In: IEEE International Conference on Robotics and Automation (ICRA), pp. 1620–1626 (2003)
10. Kajita, S., Kanehiro, F., Kaneko, K., Fujiwara, K., Yokoi, K., Hirukawa, H.: A realtime pattern generator for biped walking. In: ICRA, pp. 31–37. IEEE (2002)

11. Lanari, L., Hutchinson, S.: Planning desired center of mass and zero moment point trajectories for bipedal locomotion. In: 2015 IEEE-RAS 15th International Conference on Humanoid Robots (Humanoids), pp. 637–642, November 2015
12. Lanari, L., Hutchinson, S.: Inversion-based gait generation for humanoid robots. In: IEEE/RSJ International Conference on Intelligent Robots and Systems (IROS), pp. 1592–1598 (2015)
13. Lanari, L., Hutchinson, S., Marchionni, L.: Boundedness issues in planning of locomotion trajectories for biped robots. In: 2014 14th IEEE-RAS International Conference on Humanoid Robots (Humanoids), pp. 951–958, November 2014
14. Missura, M., Behnke, S.: Balanced walking with capture steps. In: Bianchi, R.A.C., Akin, H.L., Ramamoorthy, S., Sugiura, K. (eds.) RoboCup 2014. LNCS, vol. 8992, pp. 3–15. Springer, Cham (2015). doi:10.1007/978-3-319-18615-3_1
15. Park, J.H., Kim, K.D.: Biped robot walking using gravity-compensated inverted pendulum mode and computed torque control. In: Proceedings of the 1998 IEEE International Conference on Robotics and Automation, vol. 4, pp. 3528–3533 (1998)
16. Pratt, J.E., Carff, J., Drakunov, S.V., Goswami, A.: Capture point: a step toward humanoid push recovery. In: 2006 IEEE-RAS 6th International Conference on Humanoid Robots (Humanoids), pp. 200–207 (2006)
17. Silverman, L.M.: Inversion of multivariable linear systems. IEEE Trans. Autom. Control 14(3), 270–276 (1969)
18. Takenaka, T., Matsumoto, T., Yoshiike, T.: Real time motion generation and control for biped robot -1st report: walking gait pattern generation. In: IEEE/RSJ International Conference on Intelligent Robots and Systems (IROS), pp. 1084–1091 (2009)
19. Urbann, O., Schwarz, I., Hofmann, M.: Flexible linear inverted pendulum model for cost-effective biped robots. In: 2015 IEEE-RAS 15th International Conference on Humanoid Robots (Humanoids), pp. 128–131, November 2015
20. Urbann, O., Hofmann, M.: Modification of foot placement for balancing using a preview controller based humanoid walking algorithm. In: Behnke, S., Veloso, M., Visser, A., Xiong, R. (eds.) RoboCup 2013. LNCS, vol. 8371, pp. 420–431. Springer, Heidelberg (2014). doi:10.1007/978-3-662-44468-9_37
21. Urbann, O., Tasse, S.: Observer based biped walking control, a sensor fusion approach. Auton. Robots 35(1), 37–49 (2013)

A Closed-Loop Gait for Humanoid Robots Combining LIPM with Parameter Optimization

Andreas Seekircher[✉] and Ubbo Visser

Department of Computer Science, University of Miami,
1365 Memorial Drive, Coral Gables, FL 33146, USA
{aseek,visser}@cs.miami.edu

Abstract. Even with the recent advances in the area of dynamic walking on humanoid robots there is still a significant amount of manual calibration required in practice due to the variances in the hardware. That is in order to achieve the performance needed in environments such as RoboCup. We present a LIPM-based closed-loop walk, that adapts to differences in the physical behavior of the robot by optimizing parameters of the model directly on the NAO while walking and executing other tasks. A significant amount of errors in the model predictions can be reduced without using a more complex model simply by adjusting the LIPM to fit the observed behavior. Our experiments show that the optimized model yields a more controlled, faster and even more energy-efficient walk on different NAO robots and on various surfaces without additional manual parameter tuning.

1 Introduction

A stable walk is one of the most important skills of a humanoid robot for most tasks. In an environment such as RoboCup, being able to walk to the ball and position for a kick is an essential skill that decides whether a team is successful. The walk has to be fast, but also stable and accurate. On physical robots, this often requires manual calibration and parameter tuning.

In this paper, we present a new walking engine for creating a balancing, dynamic walk for the NAO with the focus on optimizing parameters of the used model from observations gathered while the robot is walking. The goal is a walk that does not require manual fine-tuning, exact calibration or a long training to be stable in different simulators or on different NAOs or surfaces (Fig. 1).

The paper is organized as follows: we discuss relevant work in the next section and describe the generation of the walk motion in Sect. 3. Section 4 describes the optimization of the walk model. Our experiments and results are explained in Section 5, followed by the conclusion in Sect. 6.

2 Related Work

Many approaches for dynamic walking are based on simplified physical models, such as the inverted pendulum [11] or extensions of it, e.g. [14]. These models

© Springer International Publishing AG 2017
S. Behnke et al. (Eds.): RoboCup 2016, LNAI 9776, pp. 71–83, 2017.
https://doi.org/10.1007/978-3-319-68792-6_6

Fig. 1. The NAO walking on artificial grass and outside with shoes without extra calibration.

can also be used to define constraints on CoM/ZMP trajectories for a stable walk [10] or for preview control or model predictive control for walking [23,26]. In [9] a ZMP-based approach is use for walking on slopes or stairs. Additionally, there are many approaches for balance controllers, e.g. for lateral disturbance rejection [16], balancing through foot placement adjustment [25], ankle-, hip- and step-strategies [1,28] or balancing based on contact forces [20]. These approaches can produce very stable, dynamic walking motions and balancing when there are external disturbances. However, the models are never perfect and variances in physical robots could add a bias that reduces the stability of the walk. Therefore, in practice a lot of time might be needed to calibrate individual robots.

Other approaches for walking use methods such as evolutionary strategies, genetic algorithms or parameter optimization to generate or improve walking motions. These approaches can fine-tune a motion to a specific robot and do not depend on an accurate calibration. A common approach is to create a para-meterized walk motion (e.g. feet trajectories) and use parameter optimization or evolutionary strategies to find good parameters [3,21,27]. Approaches for walking based on optimization are often evaluated using only simulations. For example, [12] optimize parameters for walking in Webots using Gaussian PSO, policy gradient RL and evolutionary hill climbing and compare the performance of the different methods. [15] use CMA-ES [7] to optimize walk parameters for the RoboCup 3D Simulation League. Nevertheless, there are promising result for similar approaches on physical robots [2,8]. In [4], the forward walking speed of a physical humanoid robot is improved significantly by optimizing parame-ters of an open-loop walk (e.g. step frequency, swing amplitude) and parameters for a feedback controller using Policy Gradient Reinforcement Learning (PGRL) and Particle Swarm Optimization (PSO). [19] optimize a gait on a physical humanoid robot using PSO. Other approaches optimize the parameters of cen-tral pattern generators that generate the walk motion [5,13,22,24,29]. Many approaches for gait generation using optimization show promising results, but they usually require a long training and can be tedious to execute on physical robots. Also, a human operator might be needed to prevent damages from eval-uating parameters that create an unstable motions. A method that needs 1000 fitness functions evaluations [4] or a 3 h training [19] is too time-consuming if it has to be done for 6 robots within a limited time.

Ideally, the robot should not require an explicit walk training, but improve the walk while it is performing other tasks and it should not evaluate parameters directly that might cause it to fall. Therefore, we use a model-based approach (using LIPM, a linear inverted pendulum) to generate a walk that we combine with an offline optimization that can constantly run in the background and provide improved parameters based on current measurements.

3   LIPM-Based Gait Generation

This section describes the implementation of a walking engine for a dynamically generated walk on the NAO. It uses a linear inverted pendulum as a model for the motion of the center of mass of the robot. A center of mass reference trajectory is generated for a requested walk speed and the steps are created according to the model. We estimate the robots state using sensor measurements to react to errors and disturbances.

3.1   The Inverted Pendulum Model and Walk State Representation

We use the linear inverted pendulum model as in [11]. It assumes that the center of mass stays at a constant height h. The position and velocity of the center of mass in the plane at height h can be calculated by

$$x(t) = x_0 * cosh(k * t) + \dot{x}_0 * \frac{1}{k} * sinh(k * t) \tag{1}$$

$$\dot{x}(t) = x_0 * k * sinh(k * t) + \dot{x}_0 * cosh(k * t) \tag{2}$$

with $k = \sqrt{\frac{g}{h}}$, where g is the gravitation and $x_0, \dot{x}_0 \in \mathbb{R}^2$ are the position and velocity of the mass at $t = 0$ (see [6]).

The state of the robot is reduced to the foot positions relative to the center of mass and the mass velocity. Given the position of the supporting foot and assuming a center of pressure in the center of the support polygon, we can use the model to predict the position and velocity of the mass. The swing leg is independently controlled and moved along an interpolated trajectory towards a step target position. However, the movement of the swing leg changes the mass position which has to be taken into account in the movement of the support foot. Using this representation, we can predict the outcome of full steps given the step duration and step targets (assuming the swing leg reaches the target position). We try to keep the ZMP always very close to the center of the support polygon. Thus, the mass trajectory for the current step can not be changed much. Most errors are compensated by adjusting the step duration and the target of the swing leg, which affects how the mass continues to move after the support exchange.

In contrast to some other implementations, we did not derive equations for step positioning or balancing directly from the equations of the pendulum model. Instead, the model is used as a black box, which is used to predict the successor state for a given walk state and selected a step values. We use the model in several components to approximate the correct values for walk actions numerically using the model predictions. This is not the most efficient implementation, but it allows us to experiment with the model without having to update other modules.

3.2   Step Planning

The behavior of the robot can request different walk directions and velocities. The walking engine has to make sure that this velocity is reached as fast as possible without falling. The previous walking engines used by the RoboCanes agent did not always generate stable motions. Sudden changes in the requested walk speed could make the robot fall. This could be avoided by adding additional limits on the acceleration, but choosing limits manually often reduced the responsiveness of the walk too much.

In this approach we let the walking engine control the acceleration. The maximum acceleration depends on the physical behavior of the robot, which is modeled by the pendulum model. The walk should be generated based on the physical behavior of the model and guarantee a feasible mass acceleration. Generating steps is done in two steps. First, we calculate the reference trajectory for the requested walk speed. The states defining this trajectory are then used as desired states for the step planning.

The center of mass reference trajectory describes the required mass movement for a given walk velocity and step frequency. It can be described completely by the two states (foot positions and mass velocity) during the support exchange. These states and the step values have to be chosen such that the velocity is maintained and the same steps can be repeated to walk with the requested speed. Since the duration of the steps is given by the step frequency and the average velocity is given, we can calculate the distance that has to be covered by the two steps. Thus, the step length and the target positions for the swing legs can directly be calculated. The only unknown value is the mass velocity at the support exchange that yields the same velocity after executing the two steps. If the velocity is too high, the velocity will increase over the two steps. If the velocity is too small, it will decrease further. Using these predictions and an approximated gradient we can approximate the velocity in a few iterations (error less than $1\,mm/s$ after 5 iterations). Therefore, the optimal values at the support exchange states for a requested speed are known and can be used as desired values in the step planning.

The task of the step planning is to choose the current step, such that the robot can reach the reference trajectory. The duration and the swing target of the current step are chosen such that the predicted state after the next action is as close as possible to the corresponding support exchange state defined by the reference trajectory (similar to the capture step foot placement strategies used e.g. in [16–18]). We approximate the best step values similar to the calculation of the velocities in the reference trajectory iteratively using the pendulum model. Due to errors in the joint control or external disturbances, it can be necessary to adjust the step time and step target position for the current step. The step planning updates these values in every control cycle. First, the remaining step

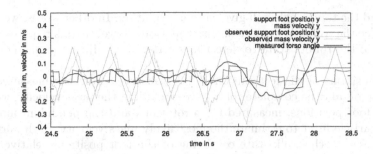

Fig. 2. Generated walk motion without using sensor feedback on a physical NAO (lateral direction). The robot is pushed a little and can not recover from it.

time is calculated such that the lateral velocity at the end of the step is close to the velocity defined in the reference trajectory. Using this time and the current position of the support foot, the mass position at the end of the step can be predicted using the model. The support position and mass movement during the next step depend on the step target for the current step. Therefore, the step target position is chosen, such that the state after the next step is close to the ideal support exchange state from the reference trajectory (again using model predictions). If the requested walking speed changes, the reference trajectory will immediately change to the new trajectory. However, the step planning will choose feasible steps that will not make the robot fall and reach the requested speed after a few steps.

If there were no errors in the model, the predictions would be accurate and the steps optimal. However, the variances and disturbances on a physical robot add too many errors that add up and make the robot fall quickly (see Fig. 2). Sensor feedback has to be used to react to errors. Nevertheless, the better the model fits to the actual physical behavior of the robot, the smaller are the errors and only smaller adjustments in the steps are needed.

3.3   State Estimation and Closed-Loop Walk

The walk can only be robust if it reacts to unexpected errors in the motion. These can be caused by external disturbances, inaccurate joint control or also by the errors in the model. Many walk motions control the joints using a high hardness and try to move the joints exactly along the planned trajectories. If the joints move this way with high force, errors in the model would only move the ZMP inside the support polygon. Neither the joint angles, nor the torso angle would give information about the error unless the error is already too large, the ZMP reaches the edge of the support polygon and the robots starts to fall. Force sensors could be used to detect the error, but they can be unreliable on the NAO. Therefore, we use a lower hardness in the ankles and hip. This allow the joints to not move exactly to the set angles. If the generated motion is not correct for the current state (e.g. accelerating too fast), the differences in the reached joint angles and the torso angle will give more information. In other words, we do not try to force the robot to execute an exact motion. However, this requires a good tracking of the robots state to detect any errors and adjust the planned steps quickly.

The positions of the feet can directly be observed from the measured joint angles. To obtain the complete robot state including the mass velocity, we combine the foot positions, measured torso rotations and the pendulum model by using a particle filter to estimate the most likely mass velocity. Each particle is a hypothesis for the walk state consisting of the foot positions relative to the mass, the mass velocity and the torso angle. This filter is based on the idea to estimate the mass velocity not only from IMU values, but to combine those values with the knowledge of the model and the observed joint angles. Even though the model is expected to have errors and the point of estimating the state is to react to unexpected errors and differences to the model, the robot will not move completely different. Therefore, we update the particles state using the model, but add high noise values to not loose track of the state in the case of disturbances. Additionally, the directly measured To update a particle state using the model we have to decide which foot is the supporting foot which is used as pendulum origin. We use the support foot of the internal state used for generating the motion, but we have to take the control delay into account. Every time the step planning changes the supporting foot, it will take several control cycles until the effect can be observed in the measurements. Instead of setting the delay manually, we added a delay parameter to the estimated state in the filter which represents the number of cycles control delay. This way the filter finds the delay that fits best to the model and observations (and is adjusted automatically, e.g. for the simulator or a physical robot).

We use the estimated velocity, measured foot positions and torso angles as observed walk state. From the observed walk state we predict the current walk state using the estimated delay. This state reacts very quickly to disturbances, but is also noisy. Therefore, it is merged into the internal walk state of the motion generation using small factors ($f * \text{observation} + (1 - f) * \text{internalState}$). These

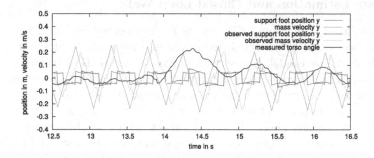

Fig. 3. The support foot positions and velocities in y direction (lateral) using the closed loop walk. The support foot position and velocity set by the walk are now adjusted slightly, if the observed state differs from the expected values.

factors are set manually such that the robot reacts fast enough to disturbances without reacting to much to noise in the sensor values. We use values around 0.01 for the foot positions and mass velocity (which seems low, but this update is done 100 times per second on the NAO) and 0.5 for the torso angle.

The plot in Fig. 3 shows an example of the walk on a physical NAO. The error is not increasing and the walk is stable. Towards the end of the plot the robot was pushed from the side and is able to recover from that.

Even though the walk is stable, there are errors in every step even without external disturbances. The robots does not behave exactly as predicted using the model, which prevents it from following the reference trajectory. Therefore, it will not walk with the requested walk speed.

4 Model Optimization

Without external disturbances the errors in the model should be as small as possible for a controlled, stable walk. There will always be a high variance in the motion on a physical NAO, but repeating errors might be caused by a bias in the model which can be corrected. Using sequences of observed walk states, we optimize parameters of the model using CMA-ES to improve the predictions. This improves several components such as the state estimation or the step planning. The movement of the inverted pendulum only depends on its length. The height of the center of mass of the NAO could be measured, but there are errors. A shorter or longer pendulum might model the motion of the robot better, since the exact center of mass position is not known. Similarly, an error in the CoM in lateral or sagittal direction might cause errors in the predictions. The model predictions will never match the observed movement, but a bias should be avoided. The pendulum model itself will not be modified by the optimization, but we add parameters to the mapping from the estimated state of the robot to the model. We add offsets for the CoM position in x, y and z direction, offsets for the estimated velocity, factors to adjust the measured foot positions in x direction and a factor for the cycle time. Some of these parameters might not be physically reasonable. However, the point of using a parameter optimization to fit the predictions to the observations is to improve the model without knowing exactly what is causing the errors and which parameters need to be changed. We let the optimization explore which parameters can help with improving the predictions (e.g. as expected the time factor is always very close to 1).

We collect data for the optimization by observing several steps with different mass velocities. The initial state in each recorded state can be used to predict the complete step using the model. The difference between this prediction and the observed positions and velocities are the error that is minimized. The evaluation of parameters does not require to walk using potentially bad parameter values. The optimization is done on the gathered data by calculating several positions on the trajectories using the model and comparing the result positions and velocities to the observed values to calculate an overall mean squared error for the used parameters. This can run on a physical robot in the background with low priority.

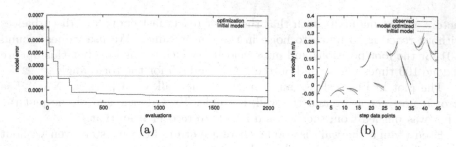

(a)   (b)

Fig. 4. (a) An example run for the model optimization on a physical NAO. (b) The velocities of the observed steps from the physical NAO used for the optimization.

After a constant amount of iterations it stops and the robot can immediately use the new parameters.

Figure 4a shows an example run of this optimization using data from a NAO robot. The 10 model parameters were optimized using CMA-ES with a population size of 20. Figure 4b shows the velocities of the step observations and the values predicted by the model before and after the optimization. The parameters are only adjusted slightly, but the predictions are improved. This would be very tedious/impossible to do manually for multiple robots.

5   Experiments and Results

We conducted several experiments using different physical and simulated robots to evaluate the effect of the optimization on the walk. The experiments were executed using two different simulators and different physical NAOs. The simulator Webots contains a NAO H21 model, which is very similar to the physical NAOs. The simulator SimSpark uses a robot model similar to the NAO, but with slightly different dimensions and masses. Additionally, it is possible to modify some parameters of the robot model (e.g. longer legs, wider hips). In our experiments, we use the robot types used by the RoboCup 3D Soccer Simulation League. The optimization of the model parameters runs for 20 s, then gathers new step data and restarts the optimization. In the experiments using physical robots, it was executed directly on the robot.

We compare some results to the previously used walking engine based on the walk of the RoboCup team B-Human [6], which is a very stable closed-loop walk based on the inverted pendulum model. However, integrated in the RoboCanes agent, it depends highly on an accurate calibration of the NAO and on several parameters that can be set manually. We found a configuration that is very stable, but the acceleration is limited and the robots can not react quick enough in many situations. Sometimes the balancing ignored the requested walk speed completely to walk stable. The results used for comparison are created using the best configuration we found which was used by the team RoboCanes in several competitions.

In the first experiment, the robot walks on a spot (the requested speed is 0) for several minutes. The lateral movement is most important in this experiment, which depends on the step timing and selection of step target positions. The robot should make steps such that it maintains a stable oscillation from left to right without much variance. The model parameters are optimized using information from only a few steps. If better parameters are found, the walking engine directly starts using these parameters, which decreases the average prediction error of the model. The better the predictions for the movement of the mass are, the better are the step target positions that are chosen in the beginning of each step and the step target position does not have to be updated much during the step.

If the robot model would be perfect, the robot would be able to choose each step such that the robot's state at the end of each step is the state defined by the reference trajectory. Figure 5 shows the variance in the support foot positions at the end of the steps made by a physical NAO. Without the optimization the robot walked slowly forward (the feet move toward negative x) and the feet are further apart than the position from the reference trajectory (which is based on the 50 mm hip offset of the NAO's legs). Using the optimized model, there is still a similar variance in the step targets but the bias is reduced and the robot does not walk forward anymore.

For the next experiments the robots receive walk requests that change from 150 mm/s forward to 150 mm/s backward every 3 s. The walking engine is expected to accelerate towards the requested walk speed as fast as possible, but without falling. The resulting values are averaged over 5 min.

Table 1 shows that the optimization reduces the overall prediction error. In this experiment, we use odometry information from the motion of the torso (position and angle) relative to the feet to calculate the approximate current walk speed. If errors in the predictions prevent the robot from walking with

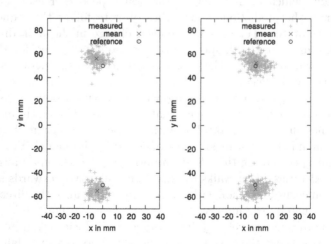

Fig. 5. Variance in the positions of the support foot at the end of each step on a physical NAO without (left) and with the optimization (right).

Table 1. Observed values for the forward/backward walk with 150 mm/s with different robots. The second row for each robot contains the results using the optimization.

		Mean prediction error				Mean step change		Walk speed err. in mm/s	
		x	$\dot{x}$	y	$\dot{y}$	x	y	Mean	Std. dev.
Webots	NAO	−0.2	1.5	2.0	−12.0	0.25	0.81	−37.0	23.8
		−0.4	3.2	1.1	−3.7	−0.4	0.25	−28.5	18.2
SimSpark	type0	−0.2	1.4	0.8	−4.8	−0.1	0.4	−24.4	16.5
		0.4	−2	0.6	−5.6	0.08	0.5	−3.8	20.8
	type3	−0.1	0.4	0.9	−5.3	−0.08	0.51	−12.9	15.7
		0.2	−0.4	0.4	−1.1	0.04	−0.01	−8.6	19.1
Physical	Nao1	2.7	−16.8	4.6	−29.8	1.05	2.48	61.0	106.3
		1.3	−4.7	1.4	−0.8	0.32	−0.16	38.0	45.7
	Nao2	1.6	−10.3	4.9	−32.0	1.26	2.94	64.8	102.9
		0.3	−1.2	0.5	8.8	0.32	−0.15	24.8	77.5
Physical	Old walk	-	-	-	-	-	-	−51.8	88.6

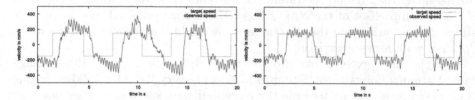

Fig. 6. Forward/backward walk with 150 mm/s on a physical robot using the new walk without optimization (left) and with optimization (right).

the desired speed, the robot measures that but consistently chooses wrong step target positions which do not change the walk speed correctly. Therefore, a smaller error in the predictions allows the robot to follow the requested walk speeds more accurately. For 0.5 s before each change in the walk direction, we comparing the measured walk speed with the requested speed for the average speed error shown in Table 1. The optimization reduces the error and standard deviation of the walk speed.

Without changing any parameters and without optimization, the new walking engine walks too fast backwards, such that it can not slow down and falls. For the experiments on the physical robot without the optimization, it was already necessary to manually set a mass offset of 5 mm in the model. Figure 6 shows measured walk speeds using this offset and no optimization on a physical robot. The walk speed varies and it walks too fast. The velocity backwards is too high, such that it sometimes takes longer to slow down and change the direction. With optimized parameters, the improved prediction yields a more stable walk that maintains a more constant velocity. The backwards velocity is still too high, but not as much as without the optimization and the robot does not fall.

Since the observed walk speed does not depend on information from the walking engine, we can compare these results with the speeds of the previously

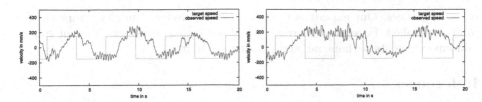

Fig. 7. Results for the forward/backward walk using the old walking engine. With our current parameters this walk accelerates slowly to be stable (left). The old walk with a higher acceleration limit (right).

used walking engine. This walk is very stable, but Fig. 7 shows that it accelerates much slower and the forward velocity is faster than backwards. One of the parameters of this walk controls the maximum velocity change. However, increasing this parameter does not necessarily improve the walk. With a higher allowed acceleration the walk is less controlled and the torso starts oscillating more. When the walk is too unstable, the old walk even ignores the walk request completely to only balance as shown in Fig. 7.

We conducted several more experiments, all showing that the optimization yields a more controlled, more stable walk. On hard surfaces (e.g. thin carpet in RoboCup competitions) the walk can be very fast, but it can also walk in different environments without manual parameter tuning. By automatically adjusting the model it is able to walk stable on soft artificial grass or outside on pavements with shoes that add extra weight.[1] As a byproduct, the lower hardness in the joint control reduces the sum of the currents in the hip and knee joints by approximately 10% compared to walking with full hardness.

6   Conclusion

We have implemented a closed-loop LIPM-based dynamic gait for the NAO. Components such as the reference trajectory generation and step planning use a LIPM to generate the motion. We added several parameters to the model that can be modified to improve the model predictions. These parameters are simple offsets and scaling factors that can compensate systematic errors caused by variances in the hardware of physical robots.

We optimize the model parameters using CMA-ES to fit the model to observations of the robot's movement. The experiments show, that the optimization reduces bias in the predictions by approximately 50% to 90% (varies depending on walk requests, robot, environment). It is able to improve the walk, even if it uses only a few observed steps to adjust the parameters and runs with limited computational resources, e.g. on the 1.6 GHz Atom CPU of a physical NAO. The optimization does not require an explicit training and takes less than a minute on a NAO such that the parameters can be updated while the robot is executing

---

[1] Video material: http://www.cs.miami.edu/home/visser/tmp/walking/.

other behaviors. Our experiments show that the reduced model errors yield a more controlled, faster and energy-efficient walk that works on different robots and environments without manual parameter tuning.

References

1. Aftab, Z., Robert, T., Wieber, P.B.: Ankle, hip and stepping strategies for humanoid balance recovery with a single model predictive control scheme. In: Proceedings of the IEEE-RAS International Conference on Humanoid Robots (2012)
2. Chernova, S., Veloso, M.: An evolutionary approach to gait learning for four-legged robots. In: Proceedings of the IEEE/RSJ International Conference on Intelligent Robots and Systems (IROS), vol. 3, pp. 2562–2567. IEEE (2004)
3. Dallali, H., Kormushev, P., Li, Z., Caldwell, D.: On global optimization of walking gaits for the compliant humanoid robot, COMAN using reinforcement learning. J. Cybern. IT **12**(3), 39–52 (2012)
4. Faber, F., Behnke, S.: Stochastic optimization of bipedal walking using gyro feedback and phase resetting. In: 7th IEEE-RAS International Conference on Humanoid Robots, pp. 203–209. IEEE (2007)
5. Gökçe, B., Akin, H.L.: Parameter optimization of a signal-based omni-directional biped locomotion using evolutionary strategies. In: Ruiz-del-Solar, J., Chown, E., Plöger, P.G. (eds.) RoboCup 2010. LNCS, vol. 6556, pp. 362–373. Springer, Heidelberg (2011). doi:10.1007/978-3-642-20217-9_31
6. Graf, C., Röfer, T.: A center of mass observing 3D-LIPM gait for the RoboCup standard platform league humanoid. In: Röfer, T., Mayer, N.M., Savage, J., Saranlı, U. (eds.) RoboCup 2011. LNCS (LNAI), vol. 7416, pp. 102–113. Springer, Heidelberg (2012). doi:10.1007/978-3-642-32060-6_9
7. Hansen, N., Müller, S.D., Koumoutsakos, P.: Reducing the time complexity of the derandomized evolution strategy with covariance matrix adaptation (CMA-ES). Evol. Comput. **11**(1), 1–18 (2003)
8. Hebbel, M., Kosse, R., Nistico, W.: Modeling and learning walking gaits of biped robots. In: Proceedings of the Workshop on Humanoid Soccer Robots of the IEEE-RAS International Conference on Humanoid Robots, pp. 40–48 (2006)
9. Huang, W., Chew, C.M., Zheng, Y., Hong, G.S.: Pattern generation for bipedal walking on slopes and stairs. In: 8th IEEE-RAS International Conference on Humanoid Robots, pp. 205–210. IEEE (2008)
10. Kajita, S., Kanehiro, F., Kaneko, K., Fujiwara, K., Harada, K., Yokoi, K., Hirukawa, H.: Biped walking pattern generation by using preview control of zero-moment point. In: Proceedings of IEEE International Conference on Robotics and Automation (ICRA), vol. 2, pp. 1620–1626 (2003)
11. Kajita, S., Kanehiro, F., Kaneko, K., Yokoi, K., Hirukawa, H.: The 3D linear inverted pendulum mode: a simple modeling for a biped walking pattern generation. In: Proceedings of IEEE/RSJ International Conference on Intelligent Robots and Systems (IROS), vol. 1, pp. 239–246 (2001)
12. Kulk, J., Welsh, J.S.: Evaluation of walk optimisation techniques for the NAO robot. In: 11th IEEE-RAS International Conference on Humanoid Robots, pp. 306–311. IEEE (2011)
13. Liu, C., Chen, Q.: Methods synthesis of central pattern generator inspired biped walking control. In: Deng, Z., Li, H. (eds.) Proceedings of the 2015 Chinese Intelligent Automation Conference. LNEE, vol. 338, pp. 371–379. Springer, Heidelberg (2015). doi:10.1007/978-3-662-46466-3_37

14. Liu, J., Urbann, O.: Bipedal walking with dynamic balance that involves three-dimensional upper body motion. Robot. Auton. Syst. **77**, 39–54 (2016)
15. MacAlpine, P., Barrett, S., Urieli, D., Vu, V., Stone, P.: Design and optimization of an omnidirectional humanoid walk: a winning approach at the RoboCup. In: 2011 3D Simulation Competition. In: AAAI (2012)
16. Missura, M., Behnke, S.: Lateral capture steps for bipedal walking. In: 11th IEEE-RAS International Conference on Humanoid Robots, pp. 401–408. IEEE (2011)
17. Missura, M., Behnke, S.: Omnidirectional capture steps for bipedal walking. In: Proceedings of IEEE International Conference on Humanoid Robots (Humanoids) (2013)
18. Missura, M., Behnke, S.: Balanced walking with capture steps. In: Bianchi, R.A.C., Akin, H.L., Ramamoorthy, S., Sugiura, K. (eds.) RoboCup 2014. LNCS (LNAI), vol. 8992, pp. 3–15. Springer, Cham (2015). doi:10.1007/978-3-319-18615-3_1
19. Niehaus, C., Röfer, T., Laue, T.: Gait optimization on a humanoid robot using particle swarm optimization. In: Zhou, P., Menegatti, B. (eds.) Proceedings of the Second WS on Humanoid Soccer Robots in Conjunction with the 2007 IEEE-RAS International Conference on Humanoid Robots (2007)
20. Ott, C., Roa, M., Hirzinger, G.: Posture and balance control for biped robots based on contact force optimization. In: 11th IEEE-RAS International Conference on Humanoid Robots, pp. 26–33 (2011)
21. Rokbani, N., Benbousaada, E., Ammar, B., Alimi, A.M.: Biped robot control using particle swarm optimization. In: IEEE International Conference on Systems Man and Cybernetics (SMC), pp. 506–512. IEEE (2010)
22. Shafii, N., Lau, N., Reis, L.P.: Learning to walk fast: optimized hip height movement for simulated and real humanoid robots. J. Intell. Robot. Syst. **80**, 1–17 (2015). doi:10.1007/s10846-015-0191-5
23. Strom, J., Slavov, G., Chown, E.: Omnidirectional walking using ZMP and preview control for the NAO humanoid robot. In: Baltes, J., Lagoudakis, M.G., Naruse, T., Ghidary, S.S. (eds.) RoboCup 2009. LNCS (LNAI), vol. 5949, pp. 378–389. Springer, Heidelberg (2010). doi:10.1007/978-3-642-11876-0_33
24. Torres, E., Garrido, L.: Automated generation of CPG-based locomotion for robot nao. In: Röfer, T., Mayer, N.M., Savage, J., Saranlı, U. (eds.) RoboCup 2011. LNCS (LNAI), vol. 7416, pp. 461–471. Springer, Heidelberg (2012). doi:10.1007/978-3-642-32060-6_39
25. Urbann, O., Hofmann, M.: Modification of foot placement for balancing using a preview controller based humanoid walking algorithm. In: Behnke, S., Veloso, M., Visser, A., Xiong, R. (eds.) RoboCup 2013. LNCS (LNAI), vol. 8371, pp. 420–431. Springer, Heidelberg (2014). doi:10.1007/978-3-662-44468-9_37
26. Wieber, P.B.: Trajectory free linear model predictive control for stable walking in the presence of strong perturbations. In: 6th IEEE-RAS International Conference on Humanoid Robots, pp. 137–142 (2006)
27. Wu, S., Pan, G., Yu, L.: Dynamic walking gait designing for biped robot based on particle swarm optimization. In: International Conference on Control Engineering and Communication Technology (ICCECT), pp. 372–377 (2012)
28. Yi, S.J., Zhang, B.T., Hong, D., Lee, D.: Active stabilization of a humanoid robot for impact motions with unknown reaction forces. In: IEEE/RSJ International Conference on Intelligent Robots and Systems (IROS), pp. 4034–4039 (2012)
29. Zhang, Q., Tang, T., Zhang, D., Yang, S., Shao, Y.: Optimized central pattern generator network for NAO humanoid walking control. In: IEEE International Conference on Robotics and Biomimetics (ROBIO), pp. 1486–1490. IEEE (2013)

Opponent-Aware Ball-Manipulation Skills
for an Autonomous Soccer Robot

Philip Cooksey$^{(\boxtimes)}$, Juan Pablo Mendoza, and Manuela Veloso

Carnegie Mellon University, Pittsburgh, PA, USA
pcooksey@andrew.cmu.edu

Abstract. Autonomous robot soccer requires effective multi-agent planning and execution, which ultimately relies on successful skill execution of individual team members. This paper addresses the problem of ball-manipulation for an individual robot already in possession of the ball. Given a planned pass or shoot objective, the robot must intelligently move the ball to its target destination, while keeping it away from opponents. We present and compare complementary ball-manipulation skills that are part of our CMDragons team, champion of the 2015 RoboCup Small Size League. We also present an approach for selecting the appropriate skill given the state of the world. To support the efficacy of the approach, we first show its impact in real games through statistics from the RoboCup tournament. For further evaluation, we experimentally demonstrate the advantages of each introduced skill in different sub-domains of robot soccer.

1 Introduction

The RoboCup Small-Size League (SSL) is a multi-robot domain consisting of teams of six robots that play soccer in a highly dynamic and adversarial domain. Overhead cameras track the positions of the ball and each robot, which are fed into a centralized computer shared by both teams [8]. Each team must autonomously coordinate their robots and manipulate the ball to score more goals than the opponent and win. Both team coordination and individual skills are important aspects of this problem. This paper addresses the latter, focusing on planning and execution for opponent-aware ball manipulation.

To plan tractably in a domain as complex and time-sensitive as robot soccer, one can separate the team planning aspect of the problem –e.g., to whom and where the robot controlling the ball should pass– from the execution of the plan –e.g., how to pass/move the ball to the chosen teammate– [3]. This paper focuses on the individual's plan and the execution of it: we address the problem of a robot that is tasked with moving the ball to a specific target location under opponent pressures. This location is assumed to be given by a separate team planner, but the robot can evaluate different methods of achieving its task, given its ball-manipulation skills.

To manipulate the ball, most teams in SSL have converged to similar mechanisms: a kicker to impart momentum on the ball, and a dribbler bar to dribble

S. Behnke et al. (Eds.): RoboCup 2016, LNAI 9776, pp. 84–96, 2017.
https://doi.org/10.1007/978-3-319-68792-6_7

Fig. 1. CMDragon's robot, with a ball touching its dribbler bar (horizontal black cylinder). The dribbling bar can be spun to put backspin on the ball for semi-control.

the ball (see Fig. 1). Their ball-manipulation skills thus depend on these mechanisms, and the optimal skill depends on the state of the opponents: kicking the ball to its target is a highly accurate method of moving the ball, provided no opponents are nearby to steal the ball before the kick, or to intercept it before it reaches its destination. Alternatively, the robot can dribble the ball to a better location before kicking, which is less reliable in the absence of opponents, due to the risk of losing the ball while dribbling, but may be better than directly kicking it if there are opponents nearby.

This paper illustrates the effect of different skills, by using the mechanisms above in different complementary ways to create opponent-aware ball-manipulation plans. First, we specify four macro-skills that the robot can take: align to shoot the ball, align to shoot using the dribbler, move the ball to a more beneficial location using the dribbler, and kick the ball. We define in detail the algorithms and physical limitations of these skills. Then, we use a skill decision algorithm to select among these skills depending on the state of the opponents.

We provide evidence of the efficacy of our approach using two methods: statistics gathered from the RoboCup 2015 competition, and in-lab experiments. The RoboCup statistics provide evidence of the effectiveness of the approach in real competitive games. To collect experimental data in a more controlled setup, we ran repeated experiments of various soccer scenarios that illustrate the advantages of each of the defined skills. These experiments show that the various skills are successful in different scenarios, which supports the need for an opponent-aware decision process among the skills, as well as within each skill.

Research into accurate dribbling has been previously studied as a way of maintaining control over the ball while navigating. Researchers have used modified potential fields to avoid non-moving obstacles along with constraints on motion to dribble in the RoboCup Middle-Size League [4]. Similar to our omnidirectional soccer robots, researchers have analyzed the kinematics and control needed for dribbling a ball along a path [6]. The only research that models the dynamics of a multi-body environment uses a physics-based robot motion planner [9]. The downfall of this approach is the enormous computational cost of modeling and predicting every robot in the environment. Our work is unique in that it focuses on developing a method of ball-manipulation with opponent awareness while still being computationally feasible in real-time.

2   Problem

In the robot soccer problem, each robot in the team must be able to effectively perform the individual skills selected by the team. In this paper, we assume that a robot ρ at location $\boldsymbol{p}_\rho$, currently in possession of the ball, must move the ball from its current location $\boldsymbol{p}_b$ to a target location $\boldsymbol{p}_t$, chosen by a separate team planner [7]. Thus, the robot needs to decide how to best move the ball to $\boldsymbol{p}_t$.

Our robots can manipulate the ball via two mechanisms: (i) a *kicker* enables the robots to impart momentum on the ball and thus perform shots or passes, and (ii) a *dribbler bar* enables the robots to impart backspin on the ball, and thus drive while maintaining contact with the ball. Kicking the ball enables the robots to move the ball quickly, but without protecting it. Dribbling the ball enables them to move the ball while guarding it; however, this method of moving the ball is slower, and it sometimes fails due to the robot losing control of the ball.

Due to the hardware design of the robots, the robot must have the ball immediately in front of it to be able to dribble it or kick it –i.e., the robot must face in direction $\phi = (\boldsymbol{p}_b - \boldsymbol{p}_\rho)$, and be at a distance of approximately $r_\rho + r_b$ from the ball, where r_ρ and r_b are the radius of the robot and ball, respectively. Furthermore, the robots are only capable of kicking in the forward direction ϕ. Thus, to execute a pass or a shot, the robot must be facing both the ball and the target location $\boldsymbol{p}_t$.

To intelligently decide how to move the ball to $\boldsymbol{p}_t$, the robot must know (i) how to use its dribbler and kicker effectively, and (ii) how to evaluate the probability of success of different ways of using them. The use of the kicker and evaluating how likely it is for a pass or a shot to be successful has been researched previously [2], and we use similar techniques here. The following sections focus on our approach to using the dribbling bar effectively, and how to best choose among different dribbling and kicking skills.

3   Individual Skills

This section covers the opponent-aware ball manipulation skills. First, possession and alignment are defined, which formulate the robot's requirement to remain in control of the ball and to align to the target. Next, we describe the Skill Decision Algorithm, which is an opponent-aware algorithm that implements the skills in an intelligent way. Lastly, we detail the two new dribbling skills used in the Skill Decision Algorithm.

3.1   Possession and Alignment

Robot, ρ, has two conflicting objectives when in possession of the ball: aligning with the ball towards its target (*alignment*), and maintaining possession of the ball from the opponents (*possession*). In the previous CMDragon team, the focus was purely on *alignment* which we define as

$$\mathbb{A} = \frac{\phi}{|\phi|} \cdot \frac{(\boldsymbol{p}_t - \boldsymbol{p}_\rho)}{|\boldsymbol{p}_t - \boldsymbol{p}_\rho|} < \epsilon_a \wedge |\boldsymbol{p}_b - \boldsymbol{p}_\rho| < \epsilon_d \tag{1}$$

such that it is aligned with the target angle by less than $\cos^{-1}(\epsilon_a)$ and close enough to the ball within some ϵ_d [1].

However, opponents introduce a threat that removes any guarantee on *possession*, and, by only considering *alignment*, the ball is often stolen. This can be contributed to two factors: the arc travel time of ρ and the opponent's proximity to the ball. Figure 2 demonstrates where the arc distance to *alignment* can take longer than the opponent's distance. In our simplified example, the opponent is very close in proximity to ρ and has an easy opportunity to gain *possession* of the ball by heading directly to it.

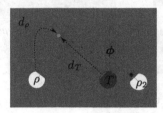
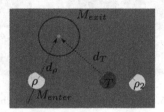

Fig. 2. ρ drives to a position near the ball that aligns to pass to ρ_2 while T drives directly to take the ball.

Fig. 3. Variables used to determine if ρ should drive directly to the ball since T is threatening to take possession.

We define the objective of *possession* by describing d_ρ and d_T as our robot's and the closest opponent robot's distance to the ball respectively, M_{enter} as a proportional gain added to d_ρ, and M_{exit} as a constant distance from the ball. Shown in Fig. 3, a *possession threat* ($\mathbb{P}$) is then defined to be true if

$$\mathbb{P} = d_\rho + (d_\rho * M_{enter}) > d_T \vee d_T < M_{exit} \qquad (2)$$

Our approach always maintains *possession* before considering *alignment*. If there is a *possession threat* then ρ drives directly to the ball and dribbles the ball. ρ is free to just align itself if there is no threat.

3.2 Skill Decision Algorithm for Individual Skills

Based on the robot's manipulation mechanisms, we have created four skills that can be used to move the ball to its target:

Kick (K): Kicks the ball to p_t. The quickest method of moving the ball to the target.

Align-non-dribbling ($A_{\neg D}$): aligns behind the ball by moving to the location $p_b + \frac{(p_b - p_t)r_\rho}{|p_b - p_t|}$, where r_ρ is the radius of the robot. Shown in Fig. 4.

Dribbling-rotate (D_R): Dribbles the ball by approaching the closest location $p_b + \frac{(p_\rho - p_b)r_\rho}{|p_\rho - p_b|}$ while facing the ball. It then quickly rotates to align to p_t. Shown in Fig. 5.

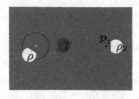 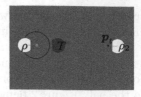

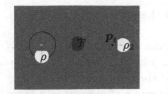

Fig. 4. Align-non-dribbling: drives around the ball to align to pass to target, p_t, defined by the circle.

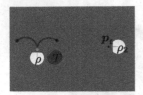 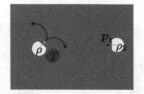 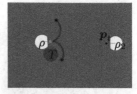

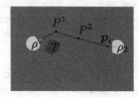 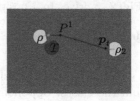

Fig. 5. Dribbling-rotate: dribbles the ball and then turns to align to pass target, p_t

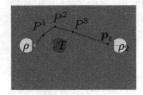

Fig. 6. Dribbling-move: dribbles the ball and pushes it along the path to p_t while avoiding obstacles.

Dribbling-move (D_M): Dribbles the ball by approaching it directly, and then moves the ball by pushing it toward p_t, while avoiding obstacles. Shown in Fig. 6.

The Skill Decision Algorithm (SDA), used by ρ at each time step, is shown in Algorithm 1. The team-goal's evaluation, $E(p_t)$, is determined by multiple factors including: open angle, opponent interception time, and pass/shoot distance, which combines to create a probability of succeeding [2]. If $E(p_t)$ is less than or equal to a threshold δ then the skill D_M is chosen to improve the current state, i.e., to improve the $E(p_t)$. If greater than δ then SDA checks alignment, $\mathbb{A}$, with p_t. If $\mathbb{A}$ then SDA kicks the ball to p_t. Otherwise, SDA checks if there is a *possession threat*, $\mathbb{P}$, since aligning might lose the ball. If $\mathbb{P}$ then SDA uses the skill D_R to grab the ball, protecting it, while still quickly aligning itself to kick to p_t. Otherwise, SDA uses the more robust $A_{\neg D}$ skill to align itself around the ball.

Algorithm 1. Skill Decision Algorithm. **Input:** Team goal success probability, aligned with ball and target, and possession threat. **Output:** Skill.

---

    function $SDA(E(\boldsymbol{p}_t), \mathbb{A}, \mathbb{P})$
        if $E(\boldsymbol{p}_t) <= \delta$ **then**   ▷ Low success probability
             $s = D_M$ ▷ Move the ball to target location
        else   ▷ Higher success probability
            if $\mathbb{A}$ **then**   ▷ Checking alignment
                 $s = K$ ▷ Kick if aligned
            else
                if $\mathbb{P}$ **then**   ▷ Check if an opponent is near
                     $s = D_R$ ▷ Dribble the ball before an opponent steals it
                else
                     $s = A_{\neg D}$ ▷ We have time to align nicely
                end if
            end if
        end if
        return s ▷ Skill to execute
    end function

3.3 Dribbling-Rotate

D_R's priority is to align to $\boldsymbol{p}_t$ as quickly as possible. D_R dribbles the ball while maintaining an inward force to compensate for the centrifugal forces of the ball in order to maintain control as shown in Fig. 7. It faces in the direction ϕ that provides the necessary centripetal force to maintain the ball on the dribbler of the robot: facing slightly inwards while turning provides a component of the normal force from the robot that always points towards the center of the circumference. Given the robot drives forward with speed s while gradually changing its orientation with speed ω, forming a circle of radius R, the constraint $s = \omega R$ holds in this case. The necessary angle offset ϕ can be obtained analytically by noticing that all the forces in Fig. 7 need to cancel out in the rotating reference frame. Therefore, we obtain the pair of equations:

$$|\boldsymbol{f}_N| \sin \phi = |\boldsymbol{f}_C|$$
$$|\boldsymbol{f}_N| \cos \phi = |\boldsymbol{f}_F| \tag{3}$$

Then, given the acceleration of gravity g, the coefficient of friction of the carpet μ, and the mass of the ball m (which cancels out in the end), we obtain:

$$|\boldsymbol{f}_N| \cos \phi = m\omega^2 R$$
$$|\boldsymbol{f}_N| \sin \phi = \mu m g \tag{4}$$

Solving these equations for ϕ gives the result for the desired heading:

$$\phi = \tan^{-1}\left(\frac{\omega^2 R}{\mu g}\right) \tag{5}$$

We estimated μ by starting from measurements of when the robot kicks the ball. Then we locally optimized to the value that gives the best dribbling performance.

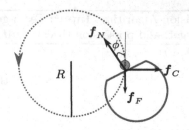

Fig. 7. Robot dribbling ball while facing slightly inwards. There exists an angle ϕ for which the forces are balanced.

3.4 Dribbling-Move

D_M's priority is to keep *possession* while driving towards p_t and avoiding all opponents and teammates. The priority of *alignment* naturally occurs as ρ drives toward p_t as shown in Fig. 6. In Algorithm 2, D_M determines if ρ has the ball by checking: (i) if it is in front of ρ, B_{front}, (ii) close to ρ, B_{close}, and (iii) located somewhere on ρ's dribbler, $B_{ondribbler}$. If ρ loses the ball then D_M drives directly to the ball to regain possession. The path used to drive to p_t is generated by a Rapidly-exploring Random Tree (RRT) where the opponents and teammates are obstacles, as defined in [5]. The path is made of multiple intermediate locations, $(P^1, P^2, \ldots, P^{n-1}, p_t)$. After any point P^n, D_M is always slightly turning ρ's forward direction towards the next point P^{n+1} by some empirically tuned γ.

Algorithm 2. Dribbling-Move. **Input:** State of the world, robot, ball, and target. **Output:** Location and angle.

---

function $Dribbling - Move(W, R\ B, p_t)$
$R_b = B_{loc} - R_{loc}$
$B_{front} = R_b.x > 0$
$B_{close} = R_b.x < MaxRobotRadius + (2 * BallRadius)$
$B_{ondribbler} = |R_b.y| \leq DribberWidth$
$B_{lost} = \neg(B_{front} \vee B_{close} \vee B_{ondribbler})$
$\{P^1, P^2, ..., p_t\} = RRT(p_t, W)$
$T = TurningThreat(W)$
    if B_{lost} **then**
        $\{P^1, P^2, \ldots, p_t\} = RRT(B, W)$
        else if $|R_{angle} - P^1_{angle}| > \alpha \vee |R_{loc} - P^1| < D_{min}$ **then**
            $\theta = P^1_{angle}$
            if T **then**
                $\theta = P^1_{angle} + 180°$
            end if
            return $\{R_{loc}, \theta\}$
        end if
    $\theta = R_{angle} + (R_{angle} - P^1_{angle}) * \gamma$
    return $\{P^1, \theta\}$
end function

This maintains control of the ball while dribbling and moving. If the turning angle goes beyond a threshold, α, then D_M stops and rotates in place with the ball. α was empirically tuned by testing the limits of turning before the dribbler lost the ball ($\alpha = 40°$ for our experiments). If there is a *turning threat* such that an opponent, in close proximity, is in the direction ρ is turning, then it turns in the opposite direction to protect the ball from being stolen [7]. D_M is complete once it arrives at p_t.

4 Results

4.1 RoboCup

In this section, we analyze the semi-final and the final game of the 2015 RoboCup Small-Size league, shown in the Table 1. We used the new skills (D_R, D_M) and SDA during these games in the tournament. The data was collected by analyzing the log files of the games. For our purposes, we defined a successful pass if it got to its intended target, and a $\mathbb{P}$ as described earlier in this paper. In the tables, the second column is the number of times a skill succeeded in passing the ball while the third column is the success of those passes actually reaching the teammate. This distinction is important since the skill might pass around the $\mathbb{P}$ but the teammate fails or the ball is intercepted.

The semi-final game is divided into two parts since for roughly half the game only $A_{\neg D}$ was used. In the first part, there were 14 passes with $\mathbb{P}$ and only 3 were successful using only $A_{\neg D}$. In the second part, we used SDA with the rule that dribbling was only allowed on the offensive side of the field. Therefore, on the defensive side, $A_{\neg D} + \mathbb{P}$ was used 6 times, succeeding 1 time. On the offensive side, D_R passed 11 times and succeeded 4 times with no clear improvement. D_M did improve with 7 successful passes out of 10 times. Interestingly, D_M was never used when not under pressure by an opponent, which was the major cause of the low value of $E(p_t)$ (< 0.1). Therefore, D_M started in a situation with a vastly low probability of success and under $\mathbb{P}$, but still it succeeded 7 times in getting away from the opponents and finding a better pass.

Table 1. Semi-final and final game in 2015 RoboCup small-size league. Statistics for the three maneuvering skills.

Semi-Final game against STOx's		
Skill	**(Success/Total)**	**(Success/Total)**
First Part	**Total # of Uses**	$\mathbb{P}$ + **Pass**
$A_{\neg D}$	17/32	3/14
Second Part		
$A_{\neg D}$	9/28	1/6
D_R	11/15 ($\forall\mathbb{P}$)	4/11
D_M	10/17 ($\forall\mathbb{P}$)	7/10

Final game against MRL		
Skill	**(Success/Total)**	**(Success/Total)**
	Total # of Uses	$\mathbb{P}$ + **Pass**
$A_{\neg D}$	10/29	3/13
D_R	23/36($\forall\mathbb{P}$)	11/18
D_M	10/23 ($\forall\mathbb{P}$)	6/10

In the final game, we used SDA for the entire game with the same offensive restriction to dribbling. Again, we see poor performance for $A_{\neg D} + \mathbb{P}$ with 3 successful passes out of 13. D_R performed much better in this game with 11 successful passes out of 18, and D_M performed well again with 6 successful passes out of 10.

Real games only provide sparse amounts of information on the benefit of the added skills because they are short and unreproducible. Still, they provide evidence on the algorithm's performance in real-world conditions against unknown opponents for which they were designed to handle. The results show that $A_{\neg D}$ is very unsuccessful when there is a *possession threat*, and by implementing more intelligent ball-manipulation skills we could improve the success rate against unknown opponents. Based on our review of the competition games there were clear times when D_R was better than D_M and vice versa. To better understand our analysis of the game, we introduce *passing with marking* to challenge our robot with situations often found in soccer, specifically those with *possession threats*.

4.2 Passing with Marking

Passing with marking is a sub-domain of soccer that uses marking to induce a state where the probability of successfully passing is lowered due to the proximity of the opponent(s), i.e., a *possession threat*. The domain starts with one robot ρ being marked by a close opponent Taker, T, at some distance d_T. ρ is placed closest to the ball while T blocks the initial pass. As T's distance to the ball, d_T, decreases, it is more likely to gain possession or block the pass. The objective is for ρ to pass to ρ_2 before T steals the ball or kicks it out of bounds. We define stealing the ball as when T has the ball within a robot radius plus a ball radius for at least 1 second. This constraint ends stalemates where both robots are driving into the ball and not moving. The domain is defined by a bounded area, and the teammate ρ_2 moves within this area to get open for the pass defined by its own team objective [7].

We devised two scenarios of the *passing with marking*: EXP1 where ρ is facing the ball and T, shown in Fig. 8, and EXP2 where ρ faces away from T with the ball near its dribbler, shown in Fig. 9. We ran both EXP1 and EXP2 in

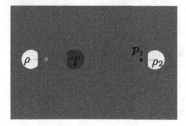

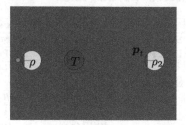

Fig. 8. (EXP1) Used in the simulation evaluation, it is a passing with marking domain where T is facing off against ρ, who must kick to ρ_2.

Fig. 9. (EXP2) Used in the simulation evaluation, it is a passing with marking domain where ρ must get around the ball to align itself to kick to ρ_2.

a physics-based simulation. For each test, we used only one of the approaches to see if the skill could pass the ball to ρ_2 using only that approach. We also devised two opponents that change the performance of the approaches. The *Drive to ball* opponent heads for the ball and tries to grab a hold of it. The *Clear ball* opponent attempts to kick the ball out of bounds, which usually involves it heading towards either the right or left side of ρ to kick it away.

EXP1 induces a state where T is blocking the initial pass and as d_T decreases it has a higher chance of stealing the ball away from ρ. This is clearly demonstrated in Table 2 where for both opponents the non-dribble approach $A_{\neg D}$ often fails to pass to its teammate. However, $A_{\neg D}$ does surprisingly better than D_R against the *Drive to ball* for two reasons. First, D_R fails at this task because as ρ approaches the ball so does T, and they often get stuck in a stalemate as D_R's forward velocity pushes against T. Second, $A_{\neg D}$'s success is due to luck as it kicks the ball immediately off of T and on occasion can get the rebound and pass to ρ_2. As d_T increases, the ball bounces less and $A_{\neg D}$ does not get as lucky as shown in Table 2. D_M performs the best against *Drive to ball* since when it gets into the stalemate position it can sometimes rotate in place with the ball and move to a better passing position. The rotation in place allows D_M to succeed where D_R failed. Both D_R and D_M did very well against clear ball because the same stalemate position did not arise as often since T is trying to get to the side of the ball in order to kick it out of bounds. This gave our approaches the opportunity to dribble without getting stuck.

Table 2. Passing with marking for 100 episodes on each approach where the experiment EXP1 is shown in Fig. 8.

Physics-based simulation EXP1 (success/100)					
	Opponents				
Approach	Drive to ball				Clear ball
	$d_T = \{260, 360, 460, 860\}$ mm				$d_T = 260$ mm
$A_{\neg D}$	15	11	2	1	3
D_R	4	2	0	14	89
D_M	35	48	53	97	84

EXP2 induces a state where ρ has to get around the ball in order to align itself to pass to ρ_2, while T puts pressure from the back as it tries to steal the ball. In Table 3, $A_{\neg D}$ did the worst out of the three approaches, and its small success against *Drive to ball* is because T would sometimes get stuck behind ρ and remain behind it. D_R and D_M both did well against *Drive to ball*. D_M was the best because it simply rotated in place first to align itself and it did so in the opposite direction of T. This meant that T was often circling around on the backside of ρ, giving it a clear pass. However, the rotating in place was D_M's downfall against *Clear ball* since T would stay on facing direction until ρ rotated to a side and then T would kick it away. The reason D_R did the best against

Table 3. Passing with marking for 100 episodes on each approach where the experiment EXP2 is shown in Fig. 9. Total is success plus failed.

Physics-based simulation EXP2 (success/100)			
	Opponents		
Approach	Drive to ball	Clear ball	
	$d_T = 590$ mm	$d_T = \{590, 690\}$ mm	
$A_{\neg D}$	21	4	8
D_R	84	48	85
D_M	96	22	18

Table 4. Passing with marking using real-robots with 10 episodes each.

Real-robot experiment (success/10))	
	Opponents
Approach	Clear ball
	$d_T = 355$ mm
$A_{\neg D}$	0
D_R	2
D_M	5

Fig. 10. ($A_{\neg D}$): ρ rotates around the ball to pass but loses it as the opponent kicks it away. (D_M): ρ, using Algorithm 2, goes directly to the ball, slides past the opponent to the right, and passes to the teammate. ρ was 75 mm and T was 355 mm away from the ball in their initial positions. T was running *Clear ball*.

Clear ball was because, as it circled around, it created more distance between itself and T. For the same reason, it performed better as d_T increased where D_M remained relatively the same.

We do not have a way of automating experiments on real-robots, and robots wear with use so it is not cost effective to run hundreds of experiments on the real-robots. We did run the EXP1 with the *Clear ball* opponent on our real-robots. Each approach was tested 10 times, and the results in Table 4 are slightly different than our simulated experiment. $A_{\neg D}$ did very poorly as predicted by simulation but the performances of D_R and D_M were not as expected. This difference can be attributed to factors on the complexity of executing skills in a stochastic environment with noisy actuators and perception. D_M still performs well on passing to the teammate. D_R would often continuously circle while T blocked the pass and the ball was eventually stolen. An example run of $A_{\neg D}$ and D_M is shown in Fig. 10.

5 Conclusion

We set our goal of improving the CMDragon team by better understanding the failing points of the previous team's approach to ball-manipulation. *Possession threats*, or lack of opponent awareness, stood out as a major downfall as purely aligning to the target led to opportunities for opponents to steal. The second major issue was passing even when the probability of success given to the robot, from the planner, was low. Since the previous team only had one option, the best they could do was to kick the ball and hope for luck.

Our solution to *possession threats* was to drive directly to the ball and dribble it. If the probability of success was high enough then we used D_R to quickly turn to the $\boldsymbol{p}_t$ and pass. For the low probability, our solution was to use D_M to move the ball to the target location to get a better evaluation for a pass. We then combined these skills into the Skill Decision Algorithm that defined when each skill should be chosen in order to best serve the individual and the team.

The results show an improvement in pass success using our method in both the real games and simulation experiments. Future work includes learning the possession threat parameters for individual teams during the game. There might also be more sophisticated parameters for choosing which skill to execute in the Skill Decision Algorithm. This can be seen in our simulated experiments, which showed that there exists certain scenarios where one approach outperforms the other. Further, our results indicate that one skill is not enough to solve the complexity of outmaneuvering an opponent, and that a combination is best suited to solve the problem.

The problem with having the planner plan every skill for each robot is not feasible for many real-time domains. The planner gives its best goal with what it can feasibly plan, but the robot itself must execute the skill to accomplish the goal. We demonstrate in this paper that increasing the sophistication of the individual robot skills improves the performance of the team. The robot can choose to execute the team goal differently based on the current state of the world. And by changing its skill, the robot can improve its probability of success. For multi-robot teams in adversarial environments, the individual robot must have sophisticated skills that can handle different scenarios with complex opponents. A team is therefore successful when the individual robot can choose skills that improve the team goal and/or improve itself in the environment.

References

1. Biswas, J., Cooksey, P., Klee, S., Mendoza, J.P., Wang, R., Zhu, D., Veloso, M.: CMDragons 2015 extended team description paper. In: Robocup 2015 (2015)
2. Biswas, J., Mendoza, J.P., Zhu, D., Choi, B., Klee, S., Veloso, M.: Opponent-driven planning and execution for pass, attack, and defense in a multi-robot soccer team. In: Proceedings of AAMAS 2014, the Thirteenth International Joint Conference on Autonomous Agents and Multi-agent Systems, Paris, France, May 2014
3. Browning, B., Bruce, J., Bowling, M., Veloso, M.: STP: skills, tactics and plays for multi-robot control in adversarial environments. J. Syst. Control Eng. **219**, 33–52 (2005). The 2005 Professional Engineering Publishing Award
4. Damas, B.D., Lima, P.U., Custódio, L.M.: A modified potential fields method for robot navigation applied to dribbling in robotic soccer. In: Kaminka, G.A., Lima, P.U., Rojas, R. (eds.) RoboCup 2002. LNCS, vol. 2752, pp. 65–77. Springer, Heidelberg (2003). doi:10.1007/978-3-540-45135-8_6
5. Lavalle, S.M., Kuffner Jr., J.J.: Rapidly-exploring random trees: progress and prospects. In: Algorithmic and Computational Robotics: New Directions, pp. 293–308 (2000)
6. Li, X., Wang, M., Zell, A.: Dribbling control of omnidirectional soccer robots. In: 2007 IEEE International Conference on Robotics and Automation, pp. 2623–2628. IEEE (2007)
7. Mendoza, J.P., Biswas, J., Zhu, D., Cooksey, P., Wang, R., Klee, S., Veloso, M.: Selectively reactive coordination for a team of robot soccer champions. In: Proceedings of AAAI 2016, the Thirtieth AAAI Conference on Artificial Intelligence, Phoenix, AZ, February 2016
8. Zickler, S., Laue, T., Birbach, O., Wongphati, M., Veloso, M.: SSL-vision: the shared vision system for the RoboCup small size league. In: Baltes, J., Lagoudakis, M.G., Naruse, T., Ghidary, S.S. (eds.) RoboCup 2009. LNCS (LNAI), vol. 5949, pp. 425–436. Springer, Heidelberg (2010). doi:10.1007/978-3-642-11876-0_37
9. Zickler, S., Veloso, M.: Efficient physics-based planning: sampling search via non-deterministic tactics and skills. In: Proceedings of the Eighth International Joint Conference on Autonomous Agents and Multi-Agent Systems (AAMAS), Budapest, Hungary, pp. 27–33, May 2009

Distributed Averages of Gradients (DAG): A Fast Alternative for Histogram of Oriented Gradients

M. Hossein Mirabdollah, Mahmoud A. Mohamed$^{(\boxtimes)}$, and Bärbel Mertsching

GET Lab, University of Paderborn, 33098 Paderborn, Germany
{mirabdollah,mahmoud,mertsching}@get.upb.de
http://getwww.upb.de

Abstract. We propose a compact descriptor for the purpose of dense image matching and object recognition. The descriptor is calculated based on local gradients about each point in an image. It contains the averages of gradients at four different windows surrounding a center point. The descriptor is calculated much faster than histogram of oriented gradients (HOG). Additionally, it will be shown that it is more discriminative than HOG. We used the new descriptor for two applications needed in RoboCup competitions very often. First, computation of dense optical flows and 3D scene reconstruction from two views. Second, human face detection.

1 Introduction

Finding local descriptors for image points is an active and challenging field of research in image processing and computer vision communities. In this regard, several works can be named, suggesting different types of local descriptors for sparse feature matching or dense matching purposes. For the sparse feature matching, the following methods can be remarked: SIFT [11], SURF [2], BRIEF [4], ORB [17], BRISK [10], LIOP [19] and MRRID [7]. An evaluation of these methods can be found in [1,12]. According to these works, although SIFT and SURF are relatively old methods, they still outperform many of the new methods by delivering higher rates of correct matches. Nevertheless, the SURF method is known to perform poorly in case of in plane rotations. We found out that this is due to a simple neglect in the calculation of the SURF descriptor, where the averaged vectors are not projected on the axis of oriented coordinate frames.

SIFT descriptors are generated based on the histogram of oriented gradients (for 8 bins) at 16 windows surrounding a point. In case of the SURF method, the sum of gradient components and the sum of absolute values of gradient components in 16 windows about a point are used to form a descriptor vector with the length of 64. Unfortunately SIFT and SURF are slow methods and are not appropriate for real time applications. Hence, later, methods based on binary descriptors such as BRIEF and ORB were proposed to meet real time requirements. The BRIEF descriptor is generated based on pairs of test points

© Springer International Publishing AG 2017
S. Behnke et al. (Eds.): RoboCup 2016, LNAI 9776, pp. 97–108, 2017.
https://doi.org/10.1007/978-3-319-68792-6_8

in a neighborhood of a point. As BRIEF is not rotation invariant, later ORB was proposed to achieve the rotation invariant version of BRIEF. In the BRISK method, binary patterns are extracted based on a regular radial symmetric pattern about a point. In this method the intensities of the neighborhood of the point are smoothed with Gaussian kernels of different sizes. These considerations make the precision of BRISK slightly better than BRIEF and ORB. Binary descriptors are fast to create, and also in the matching process, the Hamming distance (XOR operation) and bit counting can be used to speed up the matching process dramatically.

The aforementioned methods work well for sparse matching purposes; nevertheless, the good performances are due to the long descriptors created based on large neighborhoods of features. However, as we may need to use feature descriptors for other purposes such as dense image matching, object and action recognition, using such long descriptors demands high computational loads. In literature, compact descriptors such as census [20], MLDP [14] and HOG [5] were used for the computation of dense optical flows. HOG is also used in object and human action recognition. Among the mentioned descriptors, HOG showed a promising performance because it considers both the magnitudes and the directions of gradients in a local window [16]. Nevertheless, the computation of HOG is expensive as it necessitates the calculation of gradient angles. On the other hand, in HOG the spacial distribution of gradients is neglected, which degrades its discrimination. In this paper, we propose a new compact descriptor with the length of 8 bins, inspired from the SURF descriptor. We name the descriptor distributed averages of gradients (DAG), which outperforms HOG both in the sense of computation time and also discrimination.

The paper is structured as follows: In Sect. 2, the gradient based descriptors are reviewed. Section 3 describes how DAG is constructed. In Sect. 4, the application of DAG for the computation of dense optical flow and face detection is presented. DAG is evaluated in Sect. 5. Section 6 concludes this paper.

2   Gradient-Based Descriptors

In this section SIFT and SURF descriptors are reviewed as they are tightly related to HOG and DAG. In the SIFT method, HOG descriptors at 16 different windows surrounding a feature point are calculated. Then descriptors are formed by ordering the values of bins in vectors with the lengths of 128. Calculation of HOG is based on local gradients of an image about a point in a window. Given an image $I(x,y) : \Omega \rightarrow \mathcal{R}$, gradient vectors for a pixel (x,y) are computed as follows:

$$\mathbf{v}(x,y) = [v_x \; v_y]^T = [I_x(x,y) \; I_y(x,y)]^T \tag{1}$$

where $I_x = \frac{\partial I}{\partial x}$ and $I_y = \frac{\partial I}{\partial y}$. To form HOG, the magnitudes m and angles α of gradients should be calculated:

$$\alpha = atan2(v_y, v_x)$$
$$m = \sqrt{v_x^2 + v_y^2} \tag{2}$$

For the calculation of HOG for a point such as (x, y), the gradients in a rectangular neighborhood of the point is taken into account. In this regard, n bins $(b_1 \ldots b_n)$ spanning $0° \ldots 360°$ should be created. The value of each bin is formed as follows:

$$b_i = \sum_{\beta_i < \alpha_j < \beta_{i+1}} m_j \tag{3}$$

where $\beta_i = \frac{360}{n}(i - 1)$. A popular number for bins is eight, which has been used in SIFT. HOG has two main shortcomings: first it needs relatively high computation loads for the calculation of gradient angles. Second it discards the geometry of the occurrence of gradients. Obviously, in SIFT, HOG descriptors are calculated at different sub-windows about a feature, which means that the geometry of gradients will also be taken into account in another way.

Unlike SIFT, SURF descriptors are generated by averaging gradient components and also their absolute values to form a vector containing of 4 elements $[\sum v_x, \sum v_y, \sum |v_x|, \sum |v_y|]^T$. By calculating such a vector for 16 surrounding windows about a point, a descriptor vector with the size of 64 is obtained.

3   Distributed Averages of Gradients

As mentioned in the introduction section, long descriptors of the feature matching methods are keys to achieve high correct matching rates. However, in case of dense matching based on differential techniques, using such long descriptors gives rise to very high computation loads. On the other hand, compact versions of the descriptors mostly with the lengths of eight have been used for dense optical flow calculations. In this regard, we propose a compact descriptor inspired by the SURF descriptor, in which the averages of gradients in only four surrounding windows about each pixel are utilized (Fig. 1).

Additionally, unlike SURF which utilizes only small sub windows, in our proposed descriptor, window sizes can be changed but the number of windows remains always four. Additionally, these four windows are overlapping which make them robust against abrupt changes of the gradients at the borders. Furthermore, to keep the descriptor compact, we did not utilize the average of absolutes of gradient components. Instead the average of gradients for each sub window $w_i : i = 1, 2, 3, 4$ is simply calculated as follows:

$$\mathbf{v}_i = [v_{i,x}\ v_{i,y}]^T = \frac{1}{N} \sum_{(x,y) \in w_i} \mathbf{v}(x, y) \tag{4}$$

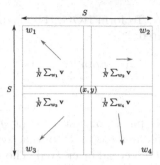

Fig. 1. DAG construction. Each arrow indicates the average of gradients in a window.

where $N = (S/2 + 1)^2$. By concatenation of the four vectors, a descriptor vector as following is formed:

$$\mathbf{d} = [v_{1,x} \; v_{1,y} \; v_{2,x}, v_{2,y}, v_{3,x}, v_{3,y}, v_{4,x}, v_{4,y}]^T \tag{5}$$

The descriptor vector can also be normalized to achieve robustness against illumination changes. We abbreviate the normalized version as NDAG.

3.1 Rotation Invariant DAG

To make DAG rotation invariant, a normal vector in the direction of the average of gradients in a neighborhood of each point is taken into account: $\mathbf{g} = [g_x \; g_y]^T$. We also use the orthogonal vector to $\mathbf{g}$, namely $\mathbf{k}$, to form a local coordinate system based on $\mathbf{g}$ and $\mathbf{k}$. The four windows about the keypoint is scanned using four sets of vectors:

$$\{\mathbf{g}_1 = -\mathbf{g}, \; \mathbf{k}_1 = \mathbf{k}\}, \{\mathbf{g}_2 = \mathbf{g}, \; \mathbf{k}_2 = \mathbf{g}\}, \{\mathbf{g}_3 = -\mathbf{g}, \; \mathbf{k}_3 = -\mathbf{g}\}, \mathbf{g}_4 = \mathbf{g}, \; \mathbf{k}_4 = -\mathbf{g}\} \tag{6}$$

To address pixels in surrounding windows, we simply use the following equation:

$$\mathbf{x} = [x \; y]^T = h\mathbf{g}_i + w\mathbf{k}_i \tag{7}$$

where i is the index of a window, $h = 0, \ldots, \frac{S}{2} + 1$ and $w = 0, \ldots, \frac{S}{2} + 1$. After the calculation of the averages of gradients in four windows, it is important to project the averages on the axis of the rotated coordinate system ($\mathbf{g}$ and $\mathbf{k}$). This step is not done in the SURF method which gave rise to its poor performance in case of in plane rotations.

4   Applications of DAG

In this section two applications of DAG are proposed: first for the computation of dense optical flow, and second for face detection.

4.1 Dense Optical Flow Using DAG

We apply DAG for the computation of the optical flow. To this end, we use combined local global methods proposed in [16]. Given two images I and I', DAG descriptors are extracted for all pixels in both images. As a result, for each image, one image with 8 channels is created to store the eight components of DAG descriptor. We name the 8-channel images S and S' associated to the images I and I' respectively. Consequently, we define a cost function consisting of data and regularization terms as explained in [16]:

$$\min_{u,v} E(u,v) = \sum_{\Omega} (\lambda E_{data} + \gamma E_{smooth} + E_{dual}),\qquad(8)$$

where

$$E_{data} = \rho(x,y,u,v)\qquad(9)$$

$$E_{smooth} = \|\nabla u\| + \|\nabla v\|\qquad(10)$$

$$E_{dual} = \frac{1}{2\theta}(u - \hat{u})^2\qquad(11)$$

where λ, γ and θ are the importance weights for each term. $\rho(.)$ is a similarity function as follows:

$$\rho(x,y,u,v) = \sum_{i=1}^{8} (S_i'(x+u,y+v) - S_i(x,y))^2\qquad(12)$$

where i is the channel index. To calculate optical flows, the cost function in Eq. 8 can be minimized based on the dual variable technique explained in [16].

4.2 DAG for Face Detection

One of the main task of a rescue robot is exploring a disaster environment to find living survivors. In this regard, the robot should be able to distinguish between the victims and other objects. Obviously, human face is an important feature by which victims can be determined more reliably comparing to other features. We have implemented a face detection framework which can work based on different types of descriptors. In this framework, a descriptor for a region of interest is extracted. Then a SVM (support vector machine) classifier for two classes, face and non-face, is trained. To achieve better detection rates, in the framework a multi-camera system is used, which consists of thermal and video cameras. The thermal images are segmented based on a temperature threshold to provide a list of regions which may contain faces. We align the thermal images with the video camera images using a simple calibration process. Thus, for each region in the thermal image, a corresponding region in the video image can be found (see Fig. 2). For each region in an image from the video camera, a descriptor based on DAG is generated. In this regard, each region is divided into regular blocks of the size $N \times N$. Then for each block a DAG descriptor (or other descriptors) is generated. Afterwards, the descriptors are concatenated to form a global descriptor for each region. The extracted feature vector contains fine detailed information of an image such as edges, spots, corners and other local texture features.

Fig. 2. Face detection using thermal and video images.

5   Evaluation and Experimental Results

5.1   Sparse Matching

To evaluate the discriminating ability of DAG, we used the KITTI training dataset [8] for optical flows. This dataset includes 194 pairs of images and provide the ground truth of flows between each two images. We compared DAG, normalized DAG (N-DAG), HOG, normalized HOG (NHOG) and ORB as a baseline method. The reason that we selected ORB was that we wanted to evaluate the performance of different methods given the same inputs. In this regard, we extracted Shi-Thomasi features [18] at eight levels of pyramids with the scale factor 0.8 and computed descriptors for the features based on different methods. The total average of extracted features was 3953. We used two measures for the evaluation:

$$\text{precision} = \frac{\text{number of correct matches}}{\text{number of matches}}$$
$$\text{recall} = \frac{\text{number of correct matches}}{\text{number of all features to be matched}}$$

To have a uniform matching strategy, we used 2 nearest neighbor (2-nn) matching method. In this method, for each feature in the first image, namely $\mathbf{f}_1$ with the descriptor $\mathbf{d}_1$, two matched features in the second image, namely $\mathbf{f}_{2,1}$ and $\mathbf{f}_{2,2}$, with the descriptors $\mathbf{d}_{2,1}$ and $\mathbf{d}_{2,2}$ are found. If the Euclidean distances of the descriptors are $d_1 = ||\mathbf{d}_1 - \mathbf{d}_{2,1}||$ and $d_2 = ||\mathbf{d}_1 - \mathbf{d}_{2,2}||$, a matching is assumed to be correct if $d_1/d_2 < 0.8$; otherwise, no matching is considered for $\mathbf{f}_1$.

We conducted two experiments to evaluate the performance of upright and rotated descriptors. In the first experiment, we evaluated the upright versions

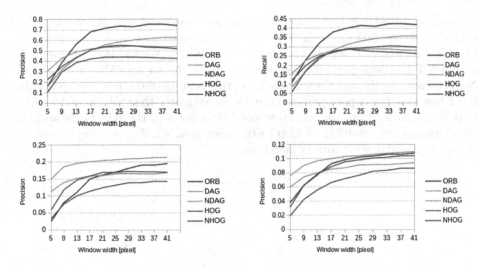

Fig. 3. Precision and recall curves for high quality features (top) and low quality features (bottom).

of all of the methods for two different groups of features: first, features with the qualities more than 0.005 and second features with the qualities between 0.001 and 0.005. We would like to see how the methods work for features with good and bad qualities. It is an important issue for dense matching purposes as typically most of the points have low gradient responses. In Fig. 3, the precision and recall curves for different methods with respect to the window widths can be seen. We can see that for small window sizes NDAG performs much better than the other methods but for larger windows ORB has better performance. Comparison of DAG and HOG shows that the precision and recall of DAG increase more and more as the window size increases; whereas the performance of HOG after the window size 21 degrades. It signifies that DAG is more capable to capture local informations in comparison to HOG at bigger window sizes. The reason that NDAG works better than DAG is that in small windows illumination changes affect the average of gradients adversely. Therefore, as normalization of DAG makes it robust against illumination changes, better performance of NDAG is reasonable. On the other hand, HOG is already robust against illumination changes thanks to its binning process. Therefore, its normalization only leads to losses of information.

Concerning the performances of the methods for low quality features, we see that DAG outperforms all other methods. The poor performance of ORB lies in the fact that most of the low quality features are located on almost homogeneous regions such as roads and in this case the binary descriptors are more vulnerable against the measurement noise rather than the gradient based methods.

In the second experiment, we rotated the second images of each image pairs to evaluate rotation invariance of DAG. In this experiment, we also ran the SIFT method, which might be interesting to readers how it works for these sequences.

Unfortunately, SURF had a very poor performance and was not comparable with any of the other methods. Therefore, we did not take it into account in this experiment. Figure 4 depicts the comparison results. We see that all methods except SIFT experiences relatively large drops at the angles $45°k$ ($k = 1, \ldots 7$). Nevertheless, ORB and then DAG have the best performances. Surprisingly, SIFT has a relatively poor performance. We investigated the problem and noticed that it originates from the nature of outdoor images in the KITTI dataset. In these images, repeatability of blob features are low, which gives rise to missing many of candidates for correct matching.

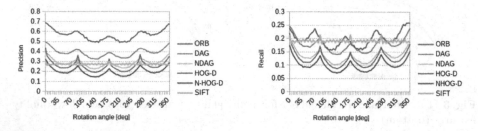

Fig. 4. Precision and recall curves in case of in plane rotations.

5.2 Computation of Dense Optical Flow and 3D Scene Reconstruction

We applied the DAG descriptor to compute dense optical flows for the KITTI [8] dataset as explained in Sect. 4.1. The KITTI dataset provides a very challenging testbed for the evaluation of optical flow algorithms. Pixel displacements in the data set are generally large, the images exhibit less texture regions, strongly varying lighting conditions, and many non-Lambertian surfaces, especially translucent windows and specular glass, and metal surfaces. Moreover, the high speed of the forward motion creates large regions on the image boundaries that move out of the field of view between frames, such that no correspondence can be established.

For evaluating the estimated optical flow, we calculated the average end-point error AEE, the average angular error AAE, and the percentage of pixels with an AEE of more than 3 pixels, which also known as bad pixels [8]. In all experiments, we used the fixed point iteration algorithm to optimize the objective function in Eq. 8. In order to deal with large displacement optical flows, we used the coarse to fine technique [3]. Furthermore, we used the normalized version of HOG and the normalized version of DAG. Because the normalized descriptors are robust against illumination changes, and also thanks to the normalization, a constant smoothness parameter can be applied regardless of the magnitudes of gradients. We used the following parameters setup for all descriptors, pyramids scale factor 0.9, the smoothness parameter $\lambda = 10$, outer fixed point iteration was 4 image warp, and inner fixed point iteration was 10 times. For DAG and HOG, we used the window size 7 and 5 respectively, which yielded the best results.

For KITTI training dataset, Table 1 shows the average AEE and the average of the percentage of bad pixels for 194 sequences. As shown in Table 1 DAG outperforms HOG in the AEE but the percentage of bad pixels for HOG is slightly better than DAG. Furthermore, Table 2 shows a comparison among DAG, HOG, and MLDP for some sequence of KITTI training dataset. As shown in this table DAG outperforms other descriptors. In Fig. 5, the computed flows for the sequence 0 using different methods are visualized. We can see that DAG works very well in the estimation of flows in low texture regions. It supports the previous results for sparse feature matching.

One of the main application of dense optical flow is 3D scene reconstruction based on the structure from motion techniques. These techniques are especially important for outdoor environments, where RGB-D cameras cannot be used due to their limitations an also 3D range sensors cannot be an option due to their high prices. In Fig. 5, the reconstruction of the scene for sequence 0 of KITTI is visualized. We used the techniques proposed in [13] for the camera motion estimation and the 3D scene reconstruction. We observe that the structure of the scene at many places is reconstructed well. Especially, the ground plane is rebuilt very well, showing the ability of the combined techniques in providing fine information for terrain analysis purposes.

We have also computed the optical flows based on the DAG descriptor for the KITTI test dataset and submitted to KITTI website under the name of DAG-Flow. Table 3 shows a comparison among algorithms used local descriptors for optical flow estimation.

Table 1. Average of the AEE and the average of the percentage of outliers for the KITTI training dataset.

	Average AEE	Average percentage of outliers
DAG	2.16	8.16
HOG	2.19	8.12
MLDP	2.85	8.89

Table 2. The AEE and the percentage of bad pixels for some sequences of KITTI training dataset.

Sequence no	0		14		25		101		115		131		139		141	
	AEE	%AEE	AEE	%AEE	AEE	%AEE	AEE	% AAE	AEE	%AEE	AEE	%AEE	AEE	%AEE	AEE	%AEE
DAG	1.69	9.01	8.80	17.67	7.12	23.00	8.74	21.97	0.75	3.88	1.40	8.43	1.10	5.50	4.63	14.85
HOG [16]	3.07	13.16	8.98	22.10	7.63	26.99	8.56	26.91	2.05	8.27	2.10	13.29	3.21	10.27	6.53	19.64
MLDP [14]	4.39	19.67	9.54	22.16	9.48	35.76	17.84	39.45	1.30	7.72	2.08	14.42	1.42	8.26	9.09	23.17

The average elapsed time for the computation of the optical flow for each pair of images were obtained. The optimization algorithm model ran on an Intel

Table 3. KITTI test dataset. The average of the AEE and the average of the percentage of outliers for some methods using local descriptors for the optical flow estimation.

	Average AEE	Average percentage of outliers
TVL1-HOG [16]	2.0	7.91
MLDP-OF [14]	2.4	8.67
CRTflow [6]	2.7	9.43
TGV2CENSUS [15]	2.9	11.03
DAGflow	2.3	8.41

Fig. 5. KITTI training data set. Row 1: sequence 000000_10 and frame 000000_11. Row 2: color coding of the estimated optical flow and the error map using DAG. Row 3: estimated optical flow and error map using HOG [16] descriptor. Row 4: reconstructed scene from two views. (Color figure online)

Core2Duo with a 2.5 GHz processor executing C++ codes. The computation time for DAG was 12.10 s, while for HOG and MLDP was 22.70 s and 16.26 s respectively.

5.3   Face Detection

For evaluating the performance of DAG descriptor for the face detection, we have used the Frontal Face Dataset from the Caltech 101 categories [9]. Caltech data set contains images for 101 objects. The face dataset contains 450 images with the resolution of 896 × 592 pixels. The images were captured from 27 people in different lighting conditions, various face expressions and different backgrounds. In our setup, every image is partitioned into 15 × 15 block. For training and testing the detection algorithm, we used positive images from the Frontal face dataset, while images from other objects as negative images. For training the SVM classifier, we used 100 positive images and 100 negative images. We tested the algorithm using 450 positive image and 450 negative images. We evaluated the accuracy of the algorithm by calculating the false positive and false negative ratios. Interestingly, the face detection algorithm based on DAG detected all the 450 faces correctly and the number of false detection was always zero; whereas, the algorithm based on HOG failed to detect some faces (false negative). In Fig. 6 some samples of faces are presented, which the SVM classifier based on HOG failed to detect.

Fig. 6. Samples of false detection of SVM classifier based on HOG feature vector. Left frame 88, middle frame 193, and right frame 338.

6 Conclusion

In this paper a new compact descriptor for the purpose of dense image matching and object recognition is proposed. The descriptor is calculated based on local gradients of each pixel in an image by calculating the average gradients at four different regions surrounding a center point. The descriptor can be calculated much faster than histogram of oriented gradients as there is no need for calculation of the angle of each gradient and also the binning step is skipped. Additionally, it was shown that the proposed descriptor is more discriminative than HOG based on two different types of experiments conducted in this paper.

References

1. Opencv feature descriptor comparison report (2015). http://computer-vision-talks. com/articles/2011-08-19-feature-descriptor-comparison-report/. Accessed 23 Mar 2016
2. Bay, H., Ess, A., Tuytelaars, T., Van Gool, L.: Speeded-up robust features (SURF). CVIU **110**(3), 346–359 (2008)
3. Brox, T., Bruhn, A., Papenberg, N., Weickert, J.: High accuracy optical flow estimation based on a theory for warping. In: Pajdla, T., Matas, J. (eds.) ECCV 2004. LNCS, vol. 3024, pp. 25–36. Springer, Heidelberg (2004). doi:10.1007/ 978-3-540-24673-2_3

 4. Calonder, M., Lepetit, V., Strecha, C., Fua, P.: BRIEF: binary robust independent elementary features. In: Daniilidis, K., Maragos, P., Paragios, N. (eds.) ECCV 2010. LNCS, vol. 6314, pp. 778–792. Springer, Heidelberg (2010). doi:10.1007/978-3-642-15561-1_56
 5. Dalal, N., Triggs, B.: Histograms of oriented gradients for human detection. In: Proceedings of CVPR, pp. 886–893 (2005)
 6. Demetz, O., Hafner, D., Weickert, J.: The complete rank transform: a tool for accurate and morphologically invariant matching of structure. In: Proceedings of BMVC (2013)
 7. Fan, B., Wu, F., Hu, Z.: Rotationally invariant descriptors using intensity order pooling. TPAMI **34**(10), 2031–2045 (2012)
 8. Geiger, A., Lenz, P., Stiller, C., Urtasun, R.: Vision meets robotics: the KITTI dataset. IJRR 1231–1237 (2013)
 9. Fei-Fei, L., Fergus, R., Perona, P.: Learning generative visual models from few training examples: an incremental Bayesian approach tested on 101 object categories. In: Workshop on Generative-Model Based Vision CVPR (2004)
10. Leutenegger, S., Chli, M., Siegwart, R.Y.: BRISK: binary robust invariant scalable keypoints. In: Proceedings of ICCV, pp. 2548–2555 (2011)
11. Lowe, D.G.: Distinctive image features from scale-invariant keypoints. IJCV **60**(2), 91–110 (2004)
12. Miksik, O., Mikolajczyk, K.: Evaluation of local detectors and descriptors for fast feature matching. In: Proceedings of ICPR, pp. 2681–2684 (2012)
13. Mirabdollah, M.H., Mertsching, B.: Fast techniques for monocular visual odometry. In: Gall, J., Gehler, P., Leibe, B. (eds.) GCPR 2015. LNCS, vol. 9358, pp. 297–307. Springer, Cham (2015). doi:10.1007/978-3-319-24947-6_24
14. Mohamed, M.A., Rashwan, H.A., Mertsching, B., Garcia, M.A., Puig, D.: Illumination-robust optical flow using local directional pattern. IEEE Trans. Circ. Syst. Video Technol. **24**, 1–9 (2014)
15. Ranftl, R., Gehrig, S., Pock, T., Bischof, H.: Pushing the limits of stereo using variational stereo estimation. In: Proceedings of IV, pp. 401–407 (2012)
16. Rashwan, H.A., Mohamed, M.A., García, M.A., Mertsching, B., Puig, D.: Illumination robust optical flow model based on histogram of oriented gradients. In: Weickert, J., Hein, M., Schiele, B. (eds.) GCPR 2013. LNCS, vol. 8142, pp. 354–363. Springer, Heidelberg (2013). doi:10.1007/978-3-642-40602-7_38
17. Rublee, E., Rabaud, V., Konolige, K., Bradski, G.: ORB: an efficient alternative to SIFT or SURF. In: Proceedings of ICCV, pp. 2564–2571 (2011)
18. Shi, J., Tomasi, C.: Good features to track. In: Proceedings of CVPR, pp. 593–600 (1994)
19. Wang, Z., Fan, B., Wu, F.: Local intensity order pattern for feature description. In: Proceedings of ICCV, pp. 603–610 (2011)
20. Zabih, R., Woodfill, J.: Non-parametric local transforms for computing visual correspondence. In: Eklundh, J.-O. (ed.) ECCV 1994. LNCS, vol. 801, pp. 151–158. Springer, Heidelberg (1994). doi:10.1007/BFb0028345

Classifying the Strategies of an Opponent Team Based on a Sequence of Actions in the RoboCup SSL

Yusuke Adachi, Masahide Ito, and Tadashi Naruse[✉]

Graduate School of Information Science and Technology,
Aichi Prefectural University, Nagakute, Japan
im161001@cis.aichi-pu.ac.jp, {masa-ito,naruse}@ist.aichi-pu.ac.jp

Abstract. In this paper, we propose a new method for classifying the strategies of an opponent in the RoboCup Soccer Small-Size League. Each strategy generates a sequence of basic actions selected from a kick action, a mark action, or other similar actions. Here, we identify strategies by classifying an observed sequences of basic actions selected by an opponent during a game. This method greatly improves our previous method [9] in the following two ways: the previous method was applicable mainly to set plays, whereas this restriction is lifted in our new method. Additionally, our new method requires a lower computational time than the previous method. Assuming that our team was the opponent team, our team's strategies were evaluated using the Rand Index, yielding a value exceeding 0.877 in 3 out of 4 games. A Rand index value exceeding 0.840 was obtained from an analysis of the 4 opponent teams (1 game for each opponent team). These Rand indices represent a high level of classification algorithm performance.

1 Introduction

The strategies used in the RoboCup Soccer Small Size League (SSL) have been extensively developed in recent years so that each team's robots take action in response to an opponent's predicted behavior. It has become increasingly important for teams to learn about their opponent's behavior. Some studies have developed approaches to learning an opponent's strategies in the SSL [2, 9]; however, because these methods use robot trajectory data and require long computational times, they are mainly applied to set plays.

To overcome these problems, we propose a new method for classifying an opponent's strategies. We focus on a sequence of basic actions, or simply a sequence of actions, wherein the basic action is a 4-tuple defined as the <action name, start position, end position, duration>. A typical action is a kick action, a pass action, a shoot action, or other similar actions. Sequences of actions are clustered into several groups such that each group includes a sequences of actions derived from a strategy. The advantage of this method derives from the ease with which this method predicts a future subsequent action, making it possible to take preemptive counter actions.

© Springer International Publishing AG 2017
S. Behnke et al. (Eds.): RoboCup 2016, LNAI 9776, pp. 109–120, 2017.
https://doi.org/10.1007/978-3-319-68792-6_9

In the following sections, we describe a method of extracting robot actions and applying a clustering method by defining a dissimilarity measure of a sequence of actions. Finally, we provide experimental results and discuss the availability of the method.

2   Related Work

Erdogan and Veloso [2] proposed a method for classifying an opponent's behaviors in the SSL, and they applied their classification method to the attacking behaviors in set plays during real SSL games. The opponent's behaviors were expressed as trajectories of offensive robots to which they applied a cluster analysis by computing the similarity of the behaviors. Yasui et al. [9] also proposed a method of classifying an opponent's behaviors using an approach similar to that of Erdogan. Yasui et al. applied their method to learn their opponent's behaviors during set plays as they occurred online and in real time. They demonstrated experimentally that an opponent's behaviors could be classified about 2 s before ball actuation. These studies demonstrated the effectiveness of learning an opponent's behaviors; however, because these methods use robot trajectory data and require significant computational times, they are mainly applied to set plays.

Trevizan and Veloso [6] proposed a method for comparing the strategies of two teams in the SSL. They divided a time series representing a game into non-overlapping intervals that they labeled episodes. They used 23 variables, including the distance between a robot and the ball and the distance between a robot and the defense goal, to characterize the episode. They used the mean and standard deviation of each variable over an episode to reduce the data size. Therefore, n episodes with f variables could be represented using a matrix of size $2f \times n$. They computed the matrix norms of two episode matrices for teams A and B and evaluated the similarities between the strategies of teams A and B. Their method then compared the similarities between the two teams' strategies. Their study's objective differed from the objective addressed in this paper.

Visser and Weland [7] proposed a method of classifying an opponent's behaviors based on a decision tree constructed for use in the RoboCup soccer simulation league. Time series data, consisting of the ball-keeper distance, ball speed, number of defenders in the penalty area, and other game parameters, were used to construct a decision tree that predicted the goalkeeper's (GK's) movements, including GK stays in goal, GK leaves goal, GK returns to goal, over several games. Learning based on a decision tree is a type of supervised learning. We propose an unsupervised learning algorithm for use in on-line real-time learning.

3   Robot Action Detection

In this paper, we use data logged during RoboCup 2015 competition. The logged data comprise a time series of robot positions and orientations, ball positions, referee commands, and other game parameters, logged every 1/60 s.

The strategies were classified by defining the following 8 actions: passer robot mark, shooter robot mark, ball-keeping robot mark, pass wait, kick ball, kick shoot, kick pass, and kick clear. A time series of logged data was converted to a sequence of these actions for use as an input to our classification process. (The not available (NA) action was suitably inserted if a part of the time series could not be converted to any of the 8 available actions.)

In this section, we describe how the robots' actions were detected using the logged data. The basic method is one that we have proposed in [1]. We extend that method in this section.

3.1 Mark Actions

In [1], mark actions consist of three actions: "passer mark", "shooter mark", and "ball-keeping robot mark". We improved the detection algorithms described in [1] and describe some of these improvements in the following subsections.

Passer Mark. In his passer mark algorithm, Asano did not consider whether a passing robot surely existed. In his algorithm, the passer mark was detected, even if a robot simply ran after the ball. We corrected this fault as follows.

Definition of symbols

$\overrightarrow{T_{i,f}}$: the position of the teammate robot T_i at time f.

$\overrightarrow{O_{j,f}}$: the position of the opponent robot O_j at time f.

$\overrightarrow{B_f}$: the position of the ball at time f.

$\overrightarrow{T_{S,f}}$: the position of the teammate robot with the shortest distance to the line connecting the ball $\overrightarrow{B_f}$ and the robot $\overrightarrow{T_{i,f}}$. We considered $T_{S,f}$ to be the receiver robot.

We computed the distance $D_{j,i,f}$ between $O_{j,f}$ and the line connecting $T_{i,f}$ and $T_{S,f}$, as shown in Fig. 1. If either or both of the inner products $\overrightarrow{V_1} \cdot \overrightarrow{V_2}$ and $\overrightarrow{V_4} \cdot \overrightarrow{V_5}$ were negative, γ_p was added to $D_{j,i,f}$, where γ_p is a constant, because it was desirable to exclude non-mark cases (See Eq. (1)). Averaging the $D_{j,i,f}$'s over the interval $[f, f + n - 1]$ gave the following equation, and with it we judged

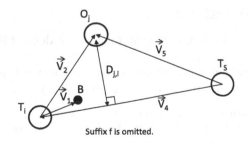

Fig. 1. Passer mark.

whether or not O_j marked a passer robot. (O_j marked the passer T_i at time f if the $MarkPass_{j,i,f}$ variable were equal to 1,)

$$MarkPass_{j,i,f} = \begin{cases} 1 & if\ \frac{1}{n} \sum_{k=f}^{f+n-1} D_{j,i,k} \leq TH_p \\ 0 & otherwise \end{cases} \qquad (1)$$

where TH_p is a given threshold and n is a given constant[1].

The detection algorithm is given below.

```
/*Passer mark*/
1    for(f = 0; f < f_end; f + +)
2     for(j = 0; j < 6; j + +)
3      for(i = 0; i < 6; i + +) {
4        compute D_{j,i,f} and MarkPass_{j,i,f}
5        memorize MarkPass_{j,i,f} }
```

Shooter Mark and Ball-Keeping Robot Mark

A shooter mark is often carried out near the goal area, and a mark robot usually stands some distance from a shooter. As an evaluation metric, we defined the distance between a (mark) robot and a line connecting the shooter and the center of the goal mouth. We then computed the $MarkShoot_{j,i,f}$ variable using an equation[2] similar to Eq. (1). (For a $MarkShoot_{j,i,f}$ variable of 1, O_j marks the shooter T_i at time f.)

A ball-keeping robot mark is a mark other than the passer mark and the shooter mark. We used, as an evaluation metric, the weighted sum of two distances, that is, the distance $D1_{j,i,f}$ between the ball-keeping robot T_i and the (mark) robot O_j and the distance $D2_{j,i,f}$ between the (mark) robot O_j and a line connecting the ball-keeping robot T_i and the ball.

$$D_{j,i,f} = \alpha D1_{j,i,f} + \beta D2_{j,i,f} \qquad (2)$$

We then computed the $MarkBall_{j,i,f}$ variable using the similarity equation[3], Eq. (1). (For a $MarkBall_{j,i,f}$ variable equal to 1, O_j marked the ball-keeping robot T_i at time f.)

3.2   Pass Waiting Action

The pass waiting action was not discussed in [1]. We defined it here for the first time.

Let O_b be the opponent robot nearest to the ball. It was reasonable to assume that a candidate robot waiting to receive a pass was the one on the left side of

---

[1] We used $TH_p = 400\,mm$ and $n = 3$ in our experiments.

[2] In the equation, the threshold is denoted by TH_s, and we used $TH_s = 400\,mm$ in our experiments.

[3] In the equation, the threshold is denoted by TH_b, and we used $TH_b = 800\,mm$ in our experiments. Both α and β in Eq. (2) were set to the value 0.5.

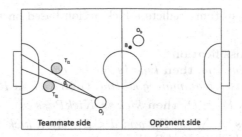

Fig. 2. Pass waiting action.

O_b, as shown in Fig. 2. O_j in Fig. 2 is one such candidate. The shootable angle θ_j could then be computed. If an opponent robot with a shootable angle exceeding a given threshold were present, the opponent was defined as being in a pass waiting action. To reduce the influence of noise, the shootable angle was averaged over some interval in time. The variable $WaitPass_{j,f}$ is given by

$$WaitPass_{j,f} = \begin{cases} 1 & if\ \frac{1}{n} \sum_{k=f}^{f+n-1} \theta_{j,k} \geq TH_w \\ 0 & Otherwise, \end{cases} \tag{3}$$

where $\theta_{j,k}$ is the shootable angle of robot O_j at time k. As the threshold value of TH_w, we used a threshold of $8°$ $(= 0.14\,\text{rad})$, and the length of the interval n was 3 in our experiments.

3.3   Kick Actions

In RoboCup Soccer, the kick actions as well as the mark actions are important. We proposed a kick action detection algorithm using the logged data reported in [1] and its modification in [8]. For the purposes of this paper, we classified kick actions according to the kick purpose: kick for shoot, kick for pass, or kick for clear. A kick action that did not belong to any of these three purposes was also considered. This section describes the kick action detection algorithm.

Definition of symbols

Kick actions = {KickShoot, KickPass, KickClear, KickBall}. KickBall is a kick action other than one of the first three actions.
L_b: a line segment that begins at the kick point P_s and ends at the last point P_e, along which the ball's trajectory is straight. Let $\overrightarrow{P_b}$ be its vector form.
$\overrightarrow{P_{oi}}$: a vector beginning at the kick point and ending at the opponent's robot O_i.
P_{gl}, P_{gr}, P_{gc}: edge points and center point of the teammate goal mouth.
d, D_G: a distance between P_e and P_{gc} and a given threshold.

The following algorithm predicts a kick action based on the location of the end point L_b.

/*Kick action classification*/

1   **if** L_b *crosses side line* **then** *kick is KickClear*
2   **else if** L_b *crosses teammate goal line* **then** *kick is KickShoot*
3   **else if** $\left| \overrightarrow{P_{oi}} \times \overrightarrow{P_b} \right| < D_1$ **then** *kick is KickPass*
4   **else if** P_e *is in* $\triangle P_s P_{gl} P_{gr}$ *and* $d < D_G$ **then** *kick is KickShoot*
5   **otherwise** *kick is KickBall*

In line 3 of the above algorithm, $\left| \overrightarrow{P_{oi}} \times \overrightarrow{P_b} \right| < D_1$ computes how close P_{oi} is to the line segment L_b.

Finally, an action other than any of the above 8 actions was expediently classified as a NA action.

4   Action Decision Algorithm

The previous section described the action detection algorithm. Next, a sequence of actions was calculated for each opponent robot. Multiple actions could be predicted simultaneously for a robot. In this case, we selected an action according to the priority of the action, where the priority of a kick action was the highest, followed by a pass waiting action, and finally by a mark action. The time series of logged data was then converted to a time series of actions[4] and was finally converted into a sequence of actions:

$$A_P[n] = \left[\begin{pmatrix} action_{n1} \\ \overrightarrow{p_{sn1}} \\ \overrightarrow{p_{en1}} \\ frame_{n1} \end{pmatrix}, \cdots, \begin{pmatrix} action_{ni} \\ \overrightarrow{p_{sni}} \\ \overrightarrow{p_{eni}} \\ frame_{ni} \end{pmatrix}, \cdots, \begin{pmatrix} action_{nt} \\ \overrightarrow{p_{snt}} \\ \overrightarrow{p_{ent}} \\ frame_{nt} \end{pmatrix} \right], \quad (4)$$

where $A_P[n]$ is a sequence of actions for robot n, $\overrightarrow{p_{sni}}$ and $\overrightarrow{p_{eni}}$ are the start and end times of the $action_{ni}$, respectively, and $frame_{ni}$ is the duration of $action_{ni}$. The ith element of a sequence of actions is denoted by

$$A_P[n][i] = \begin{pmatrix} action_{ni} \\ \overrightarrow{p_{sni}} \\ \overrightarrow{p_{eni}} \\ frame_{ni} \end{pmatrix} \quad (5)$$

A Note on the Time Series of Actions. Any time series of actions usually contains false actions. Preprocessing is needed to remove such actions.

- An action that only continues over a couple of frames should be classified as a false action and, as a result, is replaced by the succeeding action. The kick actions are an exception because short kick actions can occur at the edge of the field.

---

[4] This series of actions is defined over each time frame.

- If an action is broken into two actions by a false action, the two actions should be unified into a single action.
- If a false action cannot be replaced by any of the 8 actions, the time series is padded with an NA action.

5   Dissimilarities Between the Action Sequences

We defined a dissimilarity metric of two sequences of actions using Eq. (4). To do so, we first defined a dissimilarity measure d_0 of two actions $A_{P_1}[n_1][t_1]$ and $A_{P_2}[n_2][t_2]$ as follows,

$$
d_0(A_{P_1}[n_1][t_1], A_{P_2}[n_2][t_2]) =
$$
$$
\begin{cases}
\alpha \cdot \text{frame\_diff} + \beta \cdot \text{p\_dist} + \gamma \cdot \text{diff\_size\_cost} \\
\quad \text{if } action_{n_1 t_1} = action_{n_2 t_2} \\
\alpha \cdot 2.0 + \beta \cdot \text{p\_dist} + \gamma \cdot \text{diff\_size\_cost} \\
\quad \text{if } (action_{n_1 t_1} \in \text{Kick}, action_{n_2 t_2} \notin \text{Kick}) \text{ or} \\
\quad (action_{n_1 t_1} \notin \text{Kick}, action_{n_2 t_2} \in \text{Kick}) \\
\alpha \cdot 1.0 + \beta \cdot \text{p\_dist} + \gamma \cdot \text{diff\_size\_cost} \\
\quad otherwise
\end{cases}
\tag{6}
$$

where α, β, γ are the weights, and frame_diff, p_dist, and diff_size_cost are explained in the following paragraph.

The value of frame_diff is given by the following equation,

$$
\text{frame\_diff} = \left| \frac{frame_{n_1 t_1}}{frame\_play_{n_1 t_1}} - \frac{frame_{n_2 t_2}}{frame\_play_{n_2 t_2}} \right|,
\tag{7}
$$

where $frame\_play$ is the duration of the sequence of play $A_P[n]$. Frame_diff takes a value between 0 and 1.

The value of p_dist is given by the following equation,

$$
\text{p\_dist} = \min \left\{ \frac{|(\overrightarrow{p_{sn_1 t_1}} - \overrightarrow{p_{sn_2 t_2}})|}{FieldLength}, 1.0 \right\} + \min \left\{ \frac{|(\overrightarrow{p_{en_1 t_1}} - \overrightarrow{p_{en_2 t_2}})|}{FieldLength}, 1.0 \right\},
\tag{8}
$$

where $FieldLength$ is the length of the side line of the field. P_dist takes a value between 0 and 2.

The diff_size_cost is given by the following equation,

$$
\text{diff\_size\_cost} = \min \left\{ \frac{1}{3} \left(\frac{\text{long\_size}}{\text{short\_size}} - 1.0 \right), 2.0 \right\},
\tag{9}
$$

where $\text{long\_size} = \max(frame_{n_1 t_1}, frame_{n_2 t_2})$ and $\text{short\_size} = \min(frame_{n_1 t_1}, frame_{n_2 t_2})$. Diff_size_cost takes a value between 0 and 2.

Next, we defined a dissimilarity $d_1(A_{p1}[n_1], A_{p2}[n_2])$ between two sequences of actions $A_{P_1}[n_1]$ and $A_{P_2}[n_2]$ of robots n_1 and n_2.

Action sequences do not always have the same length; therefore, we defined the dissimilarity as the degree of overlap between the shorter sequence of actions and the longer sequence of actions. The computational algorithm is given below.

Step 1. Let *short* be the shorter sequence, and *long* be the longer sequence. Let the length of *short* and *long* be *short_size* and *long_size*, respectively. Let *kick_num* be the number of kick actions in *long*. Let i and j be counter variables with an initial value of 1. Let *start_j* and *limit_j* be the start of the search pointer and the end of the search pointer, with an initial value of 1. Initialize d_1 to 0.

Step 2. For the ith action in *short* sequence, decide the search range in the *long* sequence as follows,

$$
\begin{aligned}
ls &= \text{long\_size}/\text{short\_size} \\
limit\_j_1 &= i + ls \\
limit\_j_2 &= \min(start\_j + ls, \text{long\_size}) \\
limit\_j &= \max(limit\_j_1, limit\_j_2).
\end{aligned}
\tag{10}
$$

For the ith action in the *short* sequence, search coincident actions over the range *start_j* and *limit_j* within the *long* sequence.

Step 3. If a coincident action is found, compute

$$
d_1 = d_1 + d_0(A_{P_1}[n_1][i], A_{P_2}[n_2][j]),
$$

and *start_j* $= j + 1$. If such an action is not found, compute

$$
d_1 = d_1 + d_0(A_{P_1}[n_1][i], A_{P_2}[n_2][i]).
$$

If $i <$ short_size, then $i = i + 1$, and go to Step 2; otherwise, go to Step 4.

Step 4. Out of *kick_num* kick actions in *long* sequence, remove actions that match the kick action in *short* sequence. Let the number of remaining kick actions be *kick_unused*. Add *kick_unused* to d_1 as an additional cost,

$$
d_1 = d_1 + kick\_unused.
$$

Finally, we defined a dissimilarity d_2 between plays. A play includes six robot action sequences, so we considered the correspondence between any 2 sequences. The dissimilarity d_2 was defined by

$$
d_2(A_{P_1}, A_{P_2}) = \min_{\sigma \in S_6} \{\text{Tr}(FP_\sigma)\}
\tag{11}
$$

$$
F = [f_{ij}]
\tag{12}
$$

$$
f_{ij} = \{d_1(A_{P_1}[i], A_{P_2}[j])\},
\tag{13}
$$

where P_σ is a permutation matrix and $\text{Tr}(A)$ is the trace of matrix A.

The team's behavior was classified using the group average method [3] to cluster the sequences of actions under the dissimilarity metric d_2.

6   Deciding on the Number of Clusters

Determining the number of clusters was important. If the range of the number of clusters was given in advance, we could use the Davies–Bouldin index [4]. By contrast, Yasui et al. proposed a method for deciding the number of clusters independently of the range [10]. Their method is given by the following procedure. First, compute

$$W(K) = \sum_{i=1}^{K} \sum_{X_k \in C_i} \sum_{X_l \in C_i} d_2(A_{P_k}, A_{P_l}). \tag{14}$$

This equation computes the sum of the distances for any two elements in a cluster, summated over all clusters, assuming that the number of clusters is K. Then, using $W(K)$, compute

$$W'(K) = W(K)/W(1), \tag{15}$$

and

$$\arg\max_{1 \leq K \leq N}(W'(K) \leq h), \tag{16}$$

where h is a threshold value determined in advance. The number of clusters is decided by Eq. (16).

7   Experiment: Our Team's Strategy Classification

In RoboCup 2015, we competed in 4 official games and recorded logged data from each game. These data were then used in a classification experiment, assuming that our team was the opponent. In the experiment, we used $\alpha = \beta = \gamma = 1/3$ in Eq. (6) and $h = 0.06$ in Eq. (16)[5].

In this section, we classified our team's strategies experimentally. The set play data were used in the experiment. A set play began at ball re-placement and ended at ball interception or ball-out-of-field. The clustering results obtained from the 4 games[6] are shown in Figs. 3, 4, 5 and 6.

The Rand index [5] was used to evaluate the classification results. We determined the correct classification for each game, as determined in comparison with the clustering results obtained by inspection (the human clustering method). The Rand index for each game is given in Table 1. The Rand index values were high for each game except for the No. 2 game. In the No. 2 game, the opponent team

---

[5] For the parameter h, we ran the program over the range $0.03 - 0.07$ and found that $h = 0.06$ gave the best results.

[6] The number of clusters was not known in advance in this experiment, so the k-means method could not be used. Ward's method and the group average clustering apply under circumstances of an unknown number of clusters. In our experiment, these approaches gave similar clustering results. The computational cost of the group average clustering was lower than the cost associated with Ward's method; therefore, we used the group average clustering.

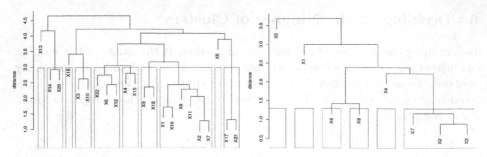

Fig. 3. Dendrogram for game No. 1.   **Fig. 4.** Dendrogram for game No. 2.

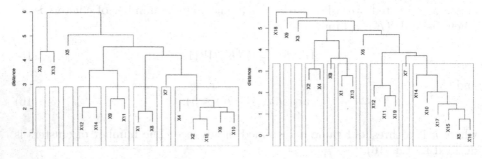

Fig. 5. Dendrogram for game No. 3.   **Fig. 6.** Dendrogram for game No. 4.

Table 1. Rand index (RoboDragons)   **Table 2.** Rand index (opponents).

Game	No. 1	No. 2	No. 3	No. 4
Rand index	0.892	0.750	0.924	0.877

Game	No. 1	No. 2	No. 3	No. 4
Rand index	0.901	0.889	0.874	0.840

malfunctioned so that the detection of mark actions did not work well, resulting in a lower Rand index. In other games, a cluster identified by human clustering was found to be divided into two clusters by the computer clustering method. This lowered the Rand index slightly; however, from a practical perspective, this was not a serious problem.

8   Experiment: Opponent Team Classification

The strategies of each opponent team in the RoboDragons' official games were classified. Figures 7, 8, 9 and 10 provide the classification results, and Table 2 lists the Rand indices. Table 2 reveals that the Rand indices assumed values between 0.840 and 0.901. For comparison, Erdogan et al. obtained values between 0.87 and 0.96 by using the trajectory data. Our experimental results revealed that high Rand index values similar to Erdogan's results were obtained from the action sequence data. This experiment revealed the cluster division problem discussed in previous sections. Future work to improve this problem is necessary.

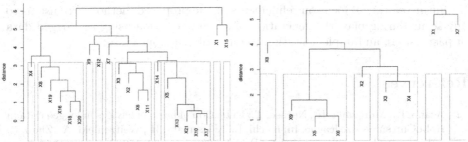

Fig. 7. Dendrogram for game No. 1 (opponent).

Fig. 8. Dendrogram for game No. 2 (opponent).

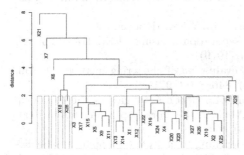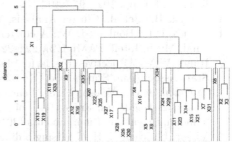

Fig. 9. Dendrogram for game No. 3 (opponent).

Fig. 10. Dendrogram for game No. 4 (opponent).

9   Computational Time

The total clustering analysis computational time was measured for game No. 4, in which 35 set plays were executed. This calculation included the computational time associated with the preprocessing of a time series of actions, the creation of a distance matrix, and the clustering using the group average method. We got an average computational time of 0.67 ms and a maximal computational time of 1.82 ms, which show that the real-time computation of clustering is possible.

10   Concluding Remarks

We have proposed a classification method based on an opponent's actions in this paper. A sequence of actions was derived from a time series of data logged from an SSL game. A sequence of actions includes less data than the logged data, permitting faster computation. An evaluation of this method using the Rand index revealed that clustering using the proposed method provided a good classification of an opponent team's behaviors (strategies, in most cases). The computational time was so small that real-time computation was possible using this method.

Future work will focus on refinements of the proposed method, extensions to any scene during play, the generation of a counter action using the logged data of past games, and implementation to our RoboDragons system.

References

1. Asano, K., Murakami, K., Naruse, T.: Detection of basic behaviors in logged data in RoboCup small size league. In: Iocchi, L., Matsubara, H., Weitzenfeld, A., Zhou, C. (eds.) RoboCup 2008. LNCS (LNAI), vol. 5399, pp. 439–450. Springer, Heidelberg (2009). doi:10.1007/978-3-642-02921-9_38
2. Erdogan, C., Veloso, M.: Action selection via learning behavior patterns in multi-robot domains. In: Proceedings of International Joint Conference on Artificial Intelligence 2011, pp. 192–197 (2011)
3. Everitt, B.S., et al.: Cluster Analysis, 5th edn. Wiley, Hoboken (2011)
4. Davies, D.L., Bouldin, D.W.: A cluster separation measure. IEEE Trans. Pattern Anal. Mach. Intell. PAMI **1**(2), 224–227 (1979)
5. Rand, W.M.: Objective criteria for the evaluation of clustering methods. J. Am. Stat. Assoc. (Am. Stat. Assoc.) **66**(336), 846–850 (1971)
6. Trevizan, F.W., Veloso, M.M.: Learning opponent's strategies in the RoboCup small size league. In: Proceedings of AAMAS 2010 Workshop on Agents in Real-Time and Dynamic Environments (2010)
7. Visser, U., Weland, H.-G.: Using online learning to analyze the opponent's behavior. In: Kaminka, G.A., Lima, P.U., Rojas, R. (eds.) RoboCup 2002. LNCS, vol. 2752, pp. 78–93. Springer, Heidelberg (2003). doi:10.1007/978-3-540-45135-8_7
8. Yasui, K., et al.: A new detection method of kick actions from logged data of SSL games. JSAI Technical report SIG-Challenge-B201-6 (2012). (in Japanese)
9. Yasui, K., Kobayashi, K., Murakami, K., Naruse, T.: Analyzing and learning an opponent's strategies in the RoboCup small size league. In: Behnke, S., Veloso, M., Visser, A., Xiong, R. (eds.) RoboCup 2013. LNCS, vol. 8371, pp. 159–170. Springer, Heidelberg (2014). doi:10.1007/978-3-662-44468-9_15
10. Yasui, K., Ito, M., Naruse, T.: Classifying an opponent's behaviors for real-time learning in the RoboCup small size league. IEICE Trans. Info. Syst. **J97–D**(8), 1297–1306 (2014). (in Japanese)

A 3D Face Modelling Approach for Pose-Invariant Face Recognition in a Human-Robot Environment

Michael Grupp[1]($\boxtimes$), Philipp Kopp[2], Patrik Huber[3], and Matthias Rätsch[2]

[1] Technische Universität München, Munich, Germany
michael.grupp@tum.de
[2] Reutlingen University, Reutlingen, Germany
philipp.kopp@student.reutlingen-university.de,
matthias.raetsch@reutlingen-university.de
[3] University of Surrey, Guildford, UK
p.huber@surrey.ac.uk

Abstract. Face analysis techniques have become a crucial component of human-machine interaction in the fields of assistive and humanoid robotics. However, the variations in head-pose that arise naturally in these environments are still a great challenge.

In this paper, we present a real-time capable 3D face modelling framework for 2D in-the-wild images that is applicable for robotics. The fitting of the 3D Morphable Model is based exclusively on automatically detected landmarks. After fitting, the face can be corrected in pose and transformed back to a frontal 2D representation that is more suitable for face recognition. We conduct face recognition experiments with non-frontal images from the MUCT database and uncontrolled, in the wild images from the PaSC database, the most challenging face recognition database to date, showing an improved performance.

Finally, we present our SCITOS G5 robot system, which incorporates our framework as a means of image pre-processing for face analysis.

1 Introduction

Among the technologies for biometric identification and verification, face recognition has become a widely-used method, as it is a non-intrusive and reliable method.

However, the robustness of a facial recognition system is constrained by the degree of head pose that is involved and the recognition rates of state of the art systems drop significantly for large pose angles. Especially for tasks where a great variation in head pose has to be expected, like in human-robot interaction, pose-invariant face recognition is crucial. The rise of collaborative and assistive robots in industrial and home environments will increase the demand for algorithms that can adapt to changing settings and uncontrolled conditions. A humanoid robot's cognitive ability to interpret non-verbal communication during conversations relies also heavily on the face of the human counterpart.

© Springer International Publishing AG 2017
S. Behnke et al. (Eds.): RoboCup 2016, LNAI 9776, pp. 121–134, 2017.
https://doi.org/10.1007/978-3-319-68792-6_10

The impact of head pose on the face analysis performance can be minimised by using normalisation techniques that transform non-frontal faces into frontal representations. This type of image pre-processing can loosely be classified into two categories:

- 2D methods (cylindrical warping, AAM (active appearance models) [7], 2D warping [2])
- 3D methods (3DMM, GEM (generic elastic models) [22], mean face shape [3])

As the 2D methods are trained on 2D data, the warping will only be an approximation of the underlying 3D rotation. They also do not model imaging parameters like the pose of the face and illumination, and face parameters like expressions, explicitly. Instead, these parameters are inherent and implicitly encoded in the model parameters. When dealing with larger pose ranges than around ±40° in yaw angle, a single 2D model is often no longer sufficient and a multi-model approach must be used (e.g. [8,13]).

The use of a 3D face model has several advantages, especially when further analysis involving the shape of the face is required, like in emotion detection. To correct the pose for face recognition, a 3D representation of the face can be rotated easily into a frontal view. At close ranges, the use of a 3D or RGB-D sensor can provide the additional depth information for the model. However, since the error of depth measurements increases quadratically with increasing distance when using RGB-D sensors like Microsoft Kinect [17], they are not suitable for acquiring image data from a distance. On the other hand, 2D cameras are more widely-used in existing platforms and cost-efficient, so that a method combining the advantages of 2D image acquisition and the analysis with a 3D model is needed.

The 3D Morphable Model (3DMM) [6] satifies this need by providing a para-meterised Principal Component Analysis (PCA) model for shape and albedo, which can be used for the synthesis of 3D faces from 2D images. A Morphable Model can be used to reconstruct a 3D representation from a 2D image through fitting. Fitting is the process of adapting the 3D Morphable Model in such a way that the difference to a 2D input image is as small as possible. Depending on the implementation, the fitter's cost function uses different model parameters to iteratively minimise the difference between the modeled image and the original input image.

Existing fitting algorithms solve a complex cost function, using the image information to perform shape from shading, edge detection, and solve for both shape and texture coefficients [11,15,24–26]. Due to the complexity of the cost functions, these algorithms require several minutes to fit a single image. While the execution time may not be crucial for offline applications, real-time robotics applications require faster solutions. More recently, new methods were intro-duced that use local features [16] or geometric features (landmarks, edges) with a fitting algorithm similar to the iterative closest point algorithm [4].

In this paper, we present and evaluate a complete, fully automatic face mod-elling framework consisting of landmark detection, landmark-based 3D Mor-phable Model fitting, and pose-normalisation for face recognition purposes. The whole process is designed to be lightweight enough to run in real-time on a standard PC, but is also especially intended to be used for human-robot interaction in uncontrolled, in the wild environments. The theory is explained in Sect. 2. In Sect. 3, we show how the approach improves the recognition rates of a regular COTS (commercial off-the-shelf) face recognition system when it is used as a pre-processing method for pose-normalisation on non-frontal and uncontrolled images from two image databases. Finally, we show how our approach is suitable for real-time robotics applications by presenting its integration into the HMI framework of our SCITOS robot platform in Sect. 4. Section 5 concludes the paper and gives an outlook to future work.

All parts of the framework are publicly available to support other researchers: the C++ implementations of the landmark detection[1] and the fitting algorithm and the face model[2], as well as a demo app that combines both[3].

2 Landmark-Based 3D Morphable Model Fitting

In this section, we will give a brief introduction to the 3D Morphable Model and then introduce our algorithm to recover pose and shape from a given 2D image. We will then present our pose-invariant texture representation in form of a so-called isomap.

2.1 The 3D Morphable Model

A 3D Morphable Model consists of a shape and albedo (colour) PCA model constructed from 169 3D scans of real faces. These meshes first have to be brought in dense correspondence, that is, vertices with the same index in the mesh correspond to the same semantic point on each face. The model used for this implementation consists of 3448 vertices. A 3D shape is expressed in the form of $\mathbf{v} = [x_1, y_1, z_1, \ldots, x_V, y_V, z_V]^{\mathrm{T}}$, where $[x_v, y_v, z_v]^{\mathrm{T}}$ are the coordinates of the vth vertex and V is the number of mesh vertices. The RGB colour values are stacked in a similar manner. PCA is then applied to both the vertex- and colour data matrices separately, each consisting of m stacked 3D face meshes, resulting in $m - 1$ shape eigenvectors $\mathbf{S}_i$, their variances $\sigma_{S,i}^2$, and a mean shape $\bar{\mathbf{s}}$, and similarly for the colour model ($\mathbf{T}_i$, $\sigma_{T,i}^2$ and $\bar{\mathbf{t}}$). A face can then be approximated as a linear combination of the respective basis vectors:

$$\mathbf{s} = \bar{\mathbf{s}} + \sum_{i=1}^{m-1} \alpha_i \mathbf{S}_i, \quad \mathbf{t} = \bar{\mathbf{t}} + \sum_{i=1}^{m-1} \beta_i \mathbf{T}_i, \tag{1}$$

where $\boldsymbol{\alpha} = [\alpha_1, \ldots, \alpha_{m-1}]^{\mathrm{T}}$ and $\boldsymbol{\beta} = [\beta_1, \ldots, \beta_{m-1}]^{\mathrm{T}}$ are vectors of shape and colour coefficients respectively.

---

[1] https://github.com/patrikhuber/superviseddescent.
[2] https://github.com/patrikhuber/eos.
[3] http://www.4dface.org.

2.2 Shape and Pose Reconstruction

Given an image with a face, we would like fit the 3D Morphable Model to that face and obtain a pose invariant representation of the subject. At the core of our fitting algorithm is an affine camera model, shape reconstruction from landmarks, and a pose invariant textural representation of the face. We thus only use the shape PCA model from the 3DMM and not the colour PCA model, and instead use the original texture from the image to obtain the best possible image quality for subsequent face analysis steps.

Similar to Aldrian and Smith [1], we obtain a linear solution by decomposing the problem into two steps which can be alternated. The first step in our framework is to estimate the pose of the face. Given a set of 2D landmark locations and their known correspondences in the 3D Morphable Model, we compute an affine camera matrix. The detected 2D landmarks $x_i \in \mathbb{R}^3$ and the corresponding 3D model points $X_i \in \mathbb{R}^4$ (both represented as homogeneous coordinates) are normalised by similarity transforms that translate the centroid of the image and model points to the origin and scale them so that the Root-Mean-Square distance from their origin is $\sqrt{2}$ for the landmark and $\sqrt{3}$ for the model points respectively: $\tilde{x}_i = Ux_i$ with $U \in \mathbb{R}^{3 \times 4}$, and $\tilde{X}_i = WX_i$ with $W \in \mathbb{R}^{4 \times 4}$. Using ≥ 4 landmark points, we then compute a normalised camera matrix $\tilde{C}$ using the *Gold Standard Algorithm* [14] and obtain the final camera matrix after denormalising: $C = U^{-1}\tilde{C}W$.

The second step in our framework consists of reconstructing the 3D shape using the estimated camera matrix. We estimate the vector of PCA shape coefficients α_s:

$$\arg\min_{\alpha_s} \sum_{i=1}^{3N} (x_{m,i} - x_i)^2 + \lambda \|\alpha_s\|^2, \tag{2}$$

where N is the number of landmarks and λ is a weighting parameter for the regularisation that is needed to only allow plausible shapes. x_i are the detected landmark locations and $x_{m,i}$ is the projection of the 3D Morphable Model shape to 2D using the estimated camera matrix. Subsequently, the camera matrix can then be re-estimated using the now obtained identity specific face shape, instead of only the mean face. Both steps are iterated for a few times - each of them only involves solving a small linear system of equations.

In the experiments with automatically detected landmarks, we use a cascaded regression based approach similar to Feng et al. [12]. After an initial estimate, i.e. placing the landmarks in the region found by a face detector, we extract local features (HOG [9]) to update the landmark locations until convergence towards their actual position. The detected 2D landmarks have known corresponding points in the 3D Morphable Model, and these points are then used to fit the model. The combination of the regression based landmark detection and the landmark-based 3D Morphable Model fitting results in a lightweight framework that is feasible to run on videos (all components run in the order of milliseconds on a standard CPU).

2.3 Pose-Independent Face Representation

After fitting the pose and shape, a correspondence between the 3D mesh and the face in the 2D image is known for each point in the image. We use this correspondence to remap the original face texture from the image onto a pose-invariant 2D surface that covers the face from all angles. We create such a generic representation with the isomap algorithm [27]: it finds a projection from the 3D vertices to a 2D plane that preserves the geodesic distance between the mesh vertices. Our mapping is computed with the algorithm from Tena [23].

The isomap of different persons are in dense correspondence with each other, meaning each location in the map corresponds to the same physical point in the face of every subject (for example, a hypothetical point $x = [100, 120]$ is always the center of the right eye). It can consequently show the accuracy of the fitting and is therefore a plausible representation of the result.

Figure 1 shows an isomap and a frontal rendering side by side. The isomap captures the whole face, while the rendering only shows the frontal parts of the face. As the face in the input image is frontal, with most parts of the face visible, there is little self occlusion. In case of large poses, a major part of the isomap can not be filled with face texture, and these regions will be marked black (for example, a small black spot next to the nose can be observed in the figure).

Fig. 1. Example picture from PaSC (left), frontal rendering (middle) and pose invariant isomap representation (right).

3   Face Recognition Experiments

To analyse the performance of our approach, we have run experiments on two different image databases (MUCT and Point and Shoot Challenge (PaSC)). Our experiments are face verification experiments, which means that the system has to verify the identity of probe images compared to a set of gallery images via matching. The results are then statistically analysed regarding the ratio of the two possible error types, the false acceptance rate (FAR) and false rejection rate (FRR) and plotted into detection error tradeoff (DET) curves [19], using the ground-truth subject-ID information provided in the metadata of the image databases. In the experiments on the PaSC database (Sect. 3.2), we filter the probe and gallery images according to different head poses.

We used a market-leading, commercial face recognition engine for the process of enrolment and matching[4]. As a reference measure, all experiments were also conducted using the original, unprocessed images from the databases (denoted as *org*). With this reference, we are able to analyse the impact of using our approach compared to a conventional face recognition framework without 3D modelling.

3.1   Experiments on the MUCT Image Database

The MUCT Database consists of 3755 faces of 276 subjects and is published by the University Of Cape Town [20]. For our experiments only persons without glasses and their mouths closed were used. After this filtering, 1221 pictures were left. The pictures are taken from 5 different cameras that cause different pose angles and there are in total 10 different lighting schemes applied to the pictures. Moreover, the size of the faces within the images is quite large and the subjects are placed in a controlled lab environment. MUCT comes with 76 manually labeled landmarks given for every image, from which we used 16 for the initialisation of our landmark-based 3DMM fitting (*LM*).

In total, we used the unprocessed images (*org*) and the pose normalised renderings coming from our fitting method (*LM*). We ran a verification experiment on these images, leading to similarity matrices with 1 490 841 scores for both methods. Using these scores, a DET curve was plotted, of which a relevant part is depicted in Fig. 2.

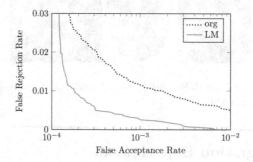

Fig. 2. DET curve showing the fewer recognition errors when using our landmark-based fitting method (*LM*) on the MUCT image database. The dotted line shows the result for the experiment with the original images without pose normalisation (*org*).

It is clear to see that the verification errors of the face recognition drop significantly when our landmark-based modelling approach is used to correct the head pose. This experiment shows that when pose is the major uncontrolled factor, like on MUCT, the usage of our *LM* approach leads to a clearly improved face recognition performance.

---

[4] Our results obtained with commercial systems should not be construed as the vendors' full-capability results.

3.2 Experiments on the Point and Shoot (PaSC) Image Database

For our proposed use case in assistive or humanoid robotics, MUCT is not representative of typical in the wild images we encounter. To verify the performance in heavily uncontrolled settings, we decided to do further investigations on a larger, more challenging database. The Point and Shoot Challenge (PaSC) is a performance evaluation challenge for developers of face recognition systems initiated by the Colorado State University [5].

As the name depicts, the images and videos used in the challenge are taken with consumer point and shoot cameras and not with the help of professional equipment. The database offers 9376 still images of varying resolution up to 4000×3000 pixels and labeled metadata. The arrangement of the image sceneries raises some major challenges for the automated recognition of faces. The pictures were taken in various locations, indoors and outdoors, with complex backgrounds and harsh lighting conditions, accompanied by a low image quality due to blur, noise or incorrect white balance. Additionally, the regions of interest for face recognition are also relatively small and of low resolution because the photographed people are not the main subject of the scenery.

In a direct comparison, the verification rate on PaSC equals only 0.22 at 0.001 FAR, in contrast to the more controlled databases MBE (0.997), GBU (0.8) and LFW (0.54) [5].

Because of these harsh, uncontrolled conditions, which are similar to a real life scenario, we chose this image database for our experiments and applied our fitting algorithm (LM) to the images. Like the previous experiment on MUCT (Sect. 3.1), it was a verification experiment using the same COTS face recognition algorithm.

Influence of the Number of Landmarks. Our experiments on PaSC are intended to be as near to a realistic scenario as possible. Therefore, we used the automatic landmark detection of [12] instead of using manually annotated facial landmarks. The detector and our fitting algorithm (LM) allow the use of different landmark schemes, which can vary in their amount. We tested three different sets of 7, 13 and 49 landmarks, which are visualised on the 3D Morphable Model in Fig. 3(a). To compare the different amounts of landmarks, their corresponding results for the face recognition experiment on PaSC are shown in Fig. 3(b). It can be observed that a higher number of facial landmarks leads to a higher quality 3DMM fitting, which then leads to a better verification performance.

Performance Evaluation Across Head Pose. One of the key questions of this work is whether our approach can improve the performance of face recognition under uncontrolled conditions, especially when dealing with head pose.

To allow a more detailed interpretation of the results, we generated head pose annotations for the PaSC database. We used OpenCV's implementation of the POSIT algorithm [10] to calculate the yaw angles for each image in the database. POSIT estimates the pose of an object from an image using a 3D reference model and corresponding feature points of the object in the image. In

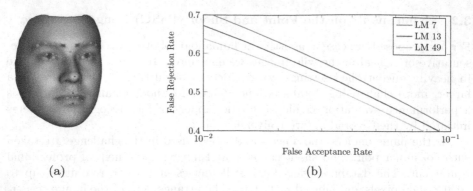

(a)   (b)

Fig. 3. Evaluation of different sets of facial landmarks. (a) Visualises the landmark sets on the mean face of the 3D Morphable Model. red: 7; red + blue: 13; red + blue + green: 49. (b) Shows a DET curve for face recognition on PaSC when using the different sets of landmarks (7, 13 and 49) for our *LM* fitting algorithm. (Color figure online)

our case, the 3D model was the 3D Morphable Model and the feature points were facial landmarks.

We used this yaw angle annotation to filter the scores into different groups of yaw angles. The results obtained with our method were then compared to the results without any face modelling. For comparison, we also tested the performance of a commercial face modelling system (*CFM*) using the same workflow. The *CFM* uses additional modelling capabilities like mirroring (to reconstruct occluded areas of the face) and deillumination. Figure 4 depicts frontalised renderings of the commercial system and our fitter. In total, we compared all images of PaSC against each other and the yaw angle filter separated the scores into 10° bins that span from −70° to +70°.

Fig. 4. From left to right: example images from PaSC (cropped to area of face for this figure) and their frontalised renderings from the commercial face modelling solution and our landmark-based fitter.

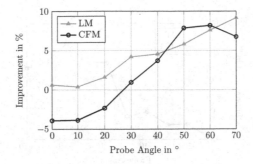

Fig. 5. Face recognition improvement over the baseline COTS system of two face modelling approaches. Different probe angles are compared against a frontal gallery. *(blue):* our 3DMM landmark fitting *(LM)*, *(black):* commercial face modelling system *(CFM)*. (Color figure online)

To better see how the pose normalisation methods improve the performance, the resulting curves show the absolute difference of the false rejection rate to the baseline without face modelling *(org)* at a specific operating point. This type of diagram allows a more simple and clearly arranged representation of the results at different head poses.

In Fig. 5, such a curve from the experiment is shown. A set of gallery images of 0° yaw is compared to sets of probe images from 0° to 70°. As gallery databases in face recognition applications often contain frontal images, this experiment reflects a common use case. At the operating point 0.01 FAR, we then plot the improvement for each group of yaw angles. The commercial face modelling solution shows its first improvements over the conventional face recognition starting at 30° yaw. Surprisingly, our 3D Morphable Model based method is even able to slightly improve the matching performance for frontal images. Although the COTS face recognition system was used outside of the specification for the large yaw angles, we are able to improve the performance for the whole pose range. By using the original image's texture, our fitter *(LM)* does not alter the face characteristics and corrects only rotations in the pitch or roll angles.

In the next two experiments, we take a look at how well the system operates when the gallery is also not frontal. In Fig. 6, the results for the experiment with a 20° and a 40° gallery can be seen. In this case, matching the faces is a much more difficult task, especially when the subjects look in different directions and large areas of the faces are not visible due to self-occlusion. While we are still able to improve the face recognition capabilities in the experiment with a 20° gallery, our method *LM* struggles to keep up with the commercial solution for a 40° gallery. The ability to reconstruct parts of the non-visible texture is a key component of the commercial modelling system *(CFM)* in such a use case which our system currently doesn't offer. Although, for the robotics application, which we present in Sect. 4 of this paper, it is likely that frontal images are used for the gallery enrolment.

130   M. Grupp et al.

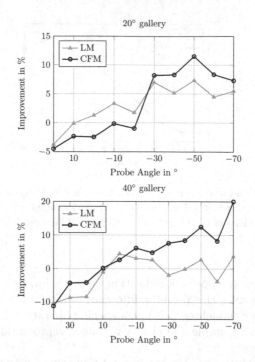

Fig. 6. Face recognition improvement over the baseline COTS system of two face modelling approaches. Different probe angles are compared against a 20° and 40° gallery. *(blue):* our 3DMM landmark fitting (*LM*), *(black):* commercial face modelling system (*CFM*). (Color figure online)

4   Application on a Robot System

Our fast and accurate 3D face modelling method is particularly suitable for face analysis tasks in assistive or humanoid robotics. In the following, we demonstrate our efforts in this field by illustrating how we integrate our approach into a mobile robot's software framework (Fig. 7).

A mobile robot platform combined with an HMI system is the basis for our research on human-robot interaction. The robot is based on a SCITOS G5 drive system with onboard industrial PC which is able to navigate autonomously in indoor buildings. For mapping and localisation ability, as well as collision avoidance, two laser scanners are attached to the base (SICK S300 and Hokuyo URG-04LX). Using this base platform, the robot is able to approach humans safely. The HMI part of the robot consists of a touch-based display and a head with moveable, human-like eyes. On top of the robot, we mounted a pan-tilt-unit (PTU; Directed Perception D46-17), where additional sensors and cameras can be installed. The PTU adds an additional degree of freedom which is used for camera positioning to enhance the tracking process.

To align the cameras to the region of interest, we track people by applying an adaptive approach which uses a particle filter to track the position and size

Fig. 7. Schematic overview of the framework for human-robot interaction on our SCI-TOS G5 platform. Our proposed landmark based 3D Morphable Model fitter acts as a pre-processing method for various face analysis tasks.

Fig. 8. Frames from a video of a subject turning from left profile to right profile view. The bottom row shows the pose-invariant isomap representations after fitting. Black regions depict self-occlusion/invisible parts of the face and thus cannot be drawn. On the two most extreme pose images, the initialisation with the face detector fails.

of the target and estimates the target motion using an optical flow based prediction model. Furthermore, an SVM-based learning strategy is implemented to calculate the particle weights and to prevent bad updates while staying adaptive to changes in object pose [18,21]. At this point, the 3DMM pose normalisation of our approach can be used for the image of the tracked face. It can be either applied continuously or if the pose of the subject is greater than a certain threshold (using the knowledge obtained in the experiments of Sect. 3.2).

Key frames of an example video taken from our robot system are presented in the upper row of Fig. 8. The OpenCV object detection with a face cascade [28] was used to initialise the regression based landmark detector, which then automatically found 15 facial landmarks. The fitting results, represented in isomaps, are shown in the second row of Fig. 8. On the robot, we use the frontal renderings as an input for the same face recognition engine that was also used for the experiments. To distinguish the person's identity properly, the system should generate a rather high score for this positive match. The pose normalised renderings allow the face recognition algorithm to achieve a clearly higher score compared to the original, unprocessed images. Possible use cases for a robot of this kind are industrial mobile robotics, shop or museum tour guides or a surveillance system (e.g. in a supermarket). In all these cases, the robot has to interact naturally with technically unskilled people. It is therefore convenient to be able to analyse people independent of their pose, without requiring them to look at the robot directly. Identification, age and gender estimation on pose normalised renderings offer the possibility to personalise the robots behaviour.

5   Conclusion and Further Work

We proposed a powerful method for head pose correction using a fully automatic landmark-based approach for fitting a 3D Morphable Model. By using an efficient fitting algorithm, our approach can be used for tasks which require a fast real-time solution that can be also used on live video streams. In contrast to existing work, we focus on an evaluation of our approach with automatically found landmarks and in-the-wild images and publish the whole 3DMM fitting pipeline as open source software (see Sect. 1).

An experimental evaluation on the two commonly-used image databases MUCT and PaSC showed the significance of our approach as a means of image processing for facial recognition in both controlled and heavily unconstrained settings. For recognition algorithms that are mostly trained for frontal faces, a rotation of the head means a loss of information that results in a lower matching score. We showed that our methodology is capable of improving the recognition rates for larger variations in head pose. Compared to a commercial face modelling solution, our approach keeps up well and even outperforms it in certain scenarios. The addition of 3DMM pose normalisation certainly brings advantages compared to a conventional face recognition framework when the setting is uncontrolled - like in robotics, surveillance or consumer electronics.

Furthermore, we presented our software framework on a mobile robot platform which uses our pose normalisation approach to allow a more reliable face analysis. We are currently doing further research on age- and emotion-estimation systems to expand the abilities of our robot. In the future, we also plan to statistically evaluate the effect on their performance when using our landmark-based pose normalisation, like we did for face recognition in this paper.

Acknowledgements. The authors would like to thank Huan Fui Lee and the RT-LIONS robocup team of Reutlingen University. We would also like to thank CyberExtruder, Inc. for supporting our research.

References

1. Aldrian, O., Smith, W.A.: Inverse rendering of faces with a 3D morphable model. IEEE Trans. Pattern Anal. Mach. Intell. **35**(5), 1080–1093 (2013)
2. Asthana, A., Jones, M.J., Marks, T.K., Tieu, K.H., Goecke, R.: Pose normalization via learned 2D warping for fully automatic face recognition. In: BMVC, pp. 1–11 (2011)
3. Asthana, A., Marks, T.K., Jones, M.J., Tieu, K.H., Rohith, M.: Fully automatic pose-invariant face recognition via 3D pose normalization. In: IEEE International Conference on Computer Vision (ICCV), pp. 937–944 (2011)

4. Bas, A., Smith, W.A., Bolkart, T., Wuhrer, S.: Fitting a 3D morphable model to edges: a comparison between hard and soft correspondences. arXiv preprint (2016). arXiv:1602.01125
5. Beveridge, J.R., Phillips, P.J., Bolme, D.S., Draper, B.A., Givens, G.H., Lui, Y.M., Teli, M.N., Zhang, H., Scruggs, W.T., Bowyer, K.W., et al.: The challenge of face recognition from digital point-and-shoot cameras. In: IEEE Sixth International Conference on Biometrics: Theory, Applications and Systems (BTAS), pp. 1–8 (2013)
6. Blanz, V., Vetter, T.: A morphable model for the synthesis of 3D faces. In: Proceedings of the 26th Annual Conference on Computer Graphics and Interactive Techniques, pp. 187–194. ACM Press/Addison-Wesley Publishing Co. (1999)
7. Cootes, T.F., Edwards, G.J., Taylor, C.J.: Active appearance models. IEEE Trans. Pattern Anal. Mach. Intell. **23**(6), 681–685 (2001)
8. Cootes, T.F., Taylor, C.J.: Statistical models of appearance for computer vision. Technical report, University of Manchester (2004)
9. Dalal, N., Triggs, B.: Histograms of oriented gradients for human detection. In: IEEE Computer Society Conference on Computer Vision and Pattern Recognition (CVPR), vol. 1, pp. 886–893. IEEE (2005)
10. Dementhon, D.F., Davis, L.S.: Model-based object pose in 25 lines of code. Int. J. Comput. Vis. **15**(1–2), 123–141 (1995)
11. Egger, B., Schönborn, S., Forster, A., Vetter, T.: Pose normalization for eye gaze estimation and facial attribute description from still images. In: Jiang, X., Hornegger, J., Koch, R. (eds.) GCPR 2014. LNCS, vol. 8753, pp. 317–327. Springer, Cham (2014). doi:10.1007/978-3-319-11752-2_25
12. Feng, Z.H., Huber, P., Kittler, J., Christmas, W., Wu, X.J.: Random cascaded-regression copse for robust facial landmark detection. Signal Process. Lett. **22**(1), 76–80 (2015)
13. Feng, Z.-H., Kittler, J., Christmas, W., Wu, X.-J.: Feature level multiple model fusion using multilinear subspace analysis with incomplete training set and its application to face image analysis. In: Zhou, Z.-H., Roli, F., Kittler, J. (eds.) MCS 2013. LNCS, vol. 7872, pp. 73–84. Springer, Heidelberg (2013). doi:10.1007/978-3-642-38067-9_7
14. Hartley, R.I., Zisserman, A.: Multiple View Geometry in Computer Vision, 2nd edn. Cambridge University Press, New York (2004). ISBN 0521540518
15. Hu, G., Chan, C.H., Kittler, J., Christmas, B.: Resolution-aware 3D morphable model. In: BMVC, pp. 1–10 (2012)
16. Huber, P., Feng, Z.H., Christmas, W., Kittler, J., Rätsch, M.: Fitting 3D morphable models using local features. In: ICIP (2015)
17. Khoshelham, K.: Accuracy analysis of kinect depth data. In: ISPRS Workshop Laser Scanning, vol. 38, pp. 133–138 (2011)
18. Kopp, P., Grupp, M., Poschmann, P., Böhme, H.J., Rätsch, M.: Tracking system with pose-invariant face analysis for human-robot interaction. In: Informatics Inside (2015)
19. Martin, A., Doddington, G., Kamm, T., Ordowski, M., Przybocki, M.: The DET curve in assessment of detection task performance. Technical report (1997)
20. Milborrow, S., Morkel, J., Nicolls, F.: The MUCT landmarked face database. Pattern Recogn. Assoc. S. Afr. (2010). http://www.milbo.org/muct/
21. Poschmann, P., Huber, P., Rätsch, M., Kittler, J., Böhme, H.J.: Fusion of tracking techniques to enhance adaptive real-time tracking of arbitrary objects. In: Conference on Intelligent Human Computer Interaction (IHCI) (2014)

22. Prabhu, U., Heo, J., Savvides, M.: Unconstrained pose-invariant face recognition using 3D generic elastic models. IEEE Trans. Pattern Anal. Mach. Intell. **33**(10), 1952–1961 (2011)
23. Rodríguez, J.R.T.: 3D face modelling for 2D+3D face recognition. Ph.D. thesis, University of Surrey (2007)
24. Romdhani, S., Vetter, T.: Estimating 3D shape and texture using pixel intensity, edges, specular highlights, texture constraints and a prior. In: IEEE Computer Society Conference on Computer Vision and Pattern Recognition, vol. 2, pp. 986–993 (2005)
25. van Rootseler, R., Spreeuwers, L., Veldhuis, R.: Using 3D morphable models for face recognition in video. In: Proceedings of the 33rd WIC Symposium on Information Theory in the Benelux (2012)
26. Tena, J.R., Smith, R.S., Hamouz, M., Kittler, J., Hilton, A., Illingworth, J.: 2D face pose normalisation using a 3D morphable model. In: IEEE Conference on Advanced Video and Signal Based Surveillance, pp. 51–56 (2007)
27. Tenenbaum, J.B., de Silva, V., Langford, J.C.: A global geometric framework for nonlinear dimensionality reduction. Science **290**, 2319–2323 (2000)
28. Viola, P., Jones, M.: Rapid object detection using a boosted cascade of simple features. In: IEEE Computer Society Conference on Computer Vision and Pattern Recognition, vol. 1, pp. I-511–I-518 (2001)

UT Austin Villa RoboCup 3D Simulation Base Code Release

Patrick MacAlpine[✉] and Peter Stone

Department of Computer Science, The University of Texas at Austin, Austin, USA
{patmac,pstone}@cs.utexas.edu

Abstract. This paper presents a base code release by the UT Austin Villa RoboCup 3D simulation team from the University of Texas at Austin. The code release, based off the 2015 UT Austin Villa RoboCup champion agent, but with some features such as high level strategy removed, provides a fully functioning agent and good starting point for new teams to the RoboCup 3D simulation league. Additionally the code release offers a foundational platform for conducting research in multiple areas including robotics, multiagent systems, and machine learning.

1 Introduction

The RoboCup 3D simulation environment is a 3-dimensional world that models realistic physical forces such as friction and gravity, in which teams of autonomous soccer playing humanoid robot agents compete with each other. Programming humanoid agents in simulation, rather than in reality, brings with it several advantages, such as making simplifying assumptions about the world, low installation and operating costs, and the ability to automate experimental procedures. All these factors make the RoboCup 3D simulation environment an ideal domain for conducting research in robotics, multiagent systems, and machine learning.

The UT Austin Villa team, from the University of Texas at Austin, first began competing in the RoboCup 3D simulation league in 2007. Over the course of nearly a decade the team has built up a strong state of the art code base enabling the team to win the RoboCup 3D simulation league four out of the past five years (2011 [14], 2012 [8], 2014 [9], and 2015 [11]) while finishing second in 2013. It is difficult for new RoboCup 3D simulation teams to be competitive with veteran teams as the complexity of the RoboCup 3D simulation environment results in an often higher than expected barrier of entry for new teams wishing to join the league. With the desire of providing new teams to the league a good starting point, as well as offering a foundational platform for conducting research in the RoboCup 3D simulation domain, UT Austin Villa has released the base code for its agent team. This paper presents the code release. Due to space constraints some details of the agent code release are left out, but are covered in other documents including a team technical report [13].

The remainder of the paper is organized as follows. In Sect. 2 a description of the 3D simulation domain is given. Section 3 gives an overview of the code

S. Behnke et al. (Eds.): RoboCup 2016, LNAI 9776, pp. 135–143, 2017.
https://doi.org/10.1007/978-3-319-68792-6_11

release and what it includes. A high level view of the agent's architecture is provided in Sect. 4 with several of the agent's features (walk engine, skill description language, and optimization task infrastructure) highlighted in Sect. 5. Section 6 references other code releases, and Sect. 7 concludes.

2   RoboCup 3D Simulation Domain Description

The RoboCup 3D simulation environment is based on SimSpark [17], a generic physical multiagent system simulator. SimSpark uses the Open Dynamics Engine[1] (ODE) library for its realistic simulation of rigid body dynamics with collision detection and friction. ODE also provides support for the modeling of advanced motorized hinge joints used in the humanoid agents.

Games consist of 11 versus 11 agents playing on a 30 m in length by 20 m in width field. The robot agents in the simulation are approximately modeled after the Aldebaran Nao robot,[2] which has a height of about 57 cm, and a mass of 4.5 kg. Each robot has 22° of freedom: six in each leg, four in each arm, and two in the neck. In order to monitor and control its hinge joints, an agent is equipped with joint perceptors and effectors. Joint perceptors provide the agent with noise-free angular measurements every simulation cycle (20 ms), while joint effectors allow the agent to specify the speed and direction in which to move a joint.

Visual information about the environment is given to an agent every third simulation cycle (60 ms) through noisy measurements of the distance and angle to objects within a restricted vision cone (120°). Agents are also outfitted with noisy accelerometer and gyroscope perceptors, as well as force resistance perceptors on the sole of each foot. Additionally, agents can communicate with each other every other simulation cycle (40 ms) by sending 20 byte messages.

In addition to the standard Nao robot model, four additional variations of the standard model, known as heterogeneous types, are available for use. These

Fig. 1. A screenshot of the Nao robot (left), and a view of the soccer field during a game (right).

---

[1] http://www.ode.org/.

[2] http://www.aldebaran-robotics.com/eng/.

variations from the standard model include changes in leg and arm length, hip width, and also the addition of toes to the robot's foot. Teams must use at least three different robot types, no more than seven agents of any one robot type, and no more than nine agents of any two robot types.

Figure 1 shows a visualization of the Nao robot and the soccer field.

3   Code Release Overview

The UT Austin Villa base code release, written in C++ and hosted on GitHub,[3] is based off of the 2015 UT Austin Villa agent. A key consideration when releasing the team's code is what components should and should not be released. A complete full release of the team's code could be detrimental to the RoboCup 3D simulation community if it performs too strongly. In the RoboCup 2D soccer simulation domain the former champion Helios team released the Agent2D code base [1] that allowed for teams to be competitive by just typing make and running the code as is. Close to 90% of the teams in the 2D league now use Agent2D as their base effectively killing off their original code bases and resulting in many similar teams. In order to avoid a similar scenario in the 3D league certain parts of the team's code have been stripped out. Specifically all high level strategy, some optimized long kicks [2], and optimized fast walk parameters for the walk engine [7] have been removed from the code release. Despite the removal of these items, which are described in detail in research publications [2,6,7,10,12–14], we believe it should not be too difficult for someone to still use the code release as a base, and develop their own optimized skills (we provide an example of how to do this with the release) and strategy, to produce a competitive team.

The following features are included in the release:

- Omnidirectional walk engine based on a double inverted pendulum model [7]
- A skill description language for specifying parameterized skills/behaviors
- Getup (recovering after having fallen over) behaviors for all agent types
- A couple basic skills for kicking one of which uses inverse kinematics [14]
- Sample demo dribble and kick behaviors for scoring a goal
- World model and particle filter for localization
- Kalman filter for tracking objects
- All necessary parsing code for sending/receiving messages from/to the server
- Code for drawing objects in the RoboViz [15] monitor
- Communication system previously provided for drop-in player challenges[4]
- An example behavior/task for optimizing a kick.

What is not included in the release:

- The team's complete set of skills such as long kicks [2] and goalie dives
- Optimized parameters for behaviors such as the team's fastest walks (slow and stable walk engine parameters are included, as well as optimized parameters for positioning/dribbling [7] and approaching the ball to kick [9])
- High level strategy including formations and role assignment [6,12].

---

[3] UT Austin Villa code release: https://github.com/LARG/utaustinvilla3d.
[4] http://www.cs.utexas.edu/~AustinVilla/sim/3dsimulation/2015_dropin_challenge/.

4 Agent Architecture

At intervals of 0.02 s, the agent receives sensory information from the environment. Every third cycle a visual sensor provides distances and angles to different objects on the field from the agent's camera, which is located in its head. It is relatively straightforward to build a world model by converting this information about the objects into Cartesian coordinates. This of course requires the robot to be able to localize itself for which we use a particle filter incorporating both landmark and field line observations [4,9]. In addition to the vision perceptor, the agent also uses its accelerometer readings to determine if it has fallen and employs its auditory channels for communication.

Once a world model is built, the agent's control module is invoked. Figure 2 provides a schematic view of the UT Austin Villa agent's control architecture.

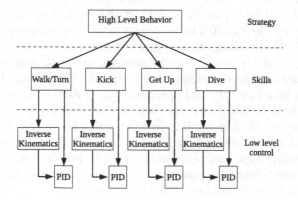

Fig. 2. Schematic view of UT Austin Villa agent control architecture.

At the lowest level, the humanoid is controlled by specifying torques to each of its joints. This is implemented through PID controllers for each joint, which take as input the desired angle of the joint and compute the appropriate torque. Further, the agent uses routines describing inverse kinematics for the arms and legs. Given a target position and pose for the hand or the foot, the inverse kinematics routine uses trigonometry to calculate the angles for the different joints along the arm or the leg to achieve the specified target, if at all possible.

The PID control and inverse kinematics routines are used as primitives to describe the agent's skills. In order to determine the appropriate joint angle sequences for walking and turning, the agent utilizes an omnidirectional walk engine which is described in Sect. 5.1. Other provided useful skills for the robot are kicking and getting up from a fallen position. These skills are accomplished through a programmed sequence of poses and specified joint angles as discussed in Sect. 5.2. One of the kicking skills provided in the code release uses inverse kinematics to control the kicking foot such that it follows an appropriate trajectory through the ball as described in [14].

High level strategy has been removed from the code release, however some sample behaviors such as dribbling and kicking the ball into the goal are included.

5   Feature Highlights

The following subsections highlight several features of the UT Austin Villa code release. These features include an omnidirectional walk engine (Sect. 5.1), skill description language (Section 5.2), and optimization task infrastructure (Section 5.3). When combined together these features provide a nice platform for machine learning and optimization research.

5.1   Omnidirectional Walk Engine

Agents use a double inverted pendulum omnidirectional walk engine [7] to move. The omnidirectional walk is crucial for allowing the robot to request continuous velocities in the forward, side, and turn directions, permitting it to approach continually changing destinations (often the ball).

The walk engine has parameterized values that control such things as step height, length, and frequency. Walk engine parameters are loaded at runtime from parameter files and can be switched on the fly for different walking tasks (e.g. approaching the ball, sprinting, and dribbling). A slow and stable set of walk engine parameters is included with the release, and these parameters can be optimized to produce a faster walk [7].

5.2   Skill Description Language

The UT Austin Villa agent includes skills for getting up and kicking, each of which is implemented as a periodic state machine with multiple *key frames*, where a key frame is a static pose of fixed joint positions. Key frames are separated by a waiting time that lets the joints reach their target angles. To provide flexibility in designing and parameterizing skills, we designed an intuitive skill description language that facilitates the specification of key frames and the waiting times between them. Below is an illustrative example describing a kick skill.

```
SKILL KICK_LEFT_LEG

KEYFRAME 1
setTarget JOINT1 $jointvalue1 JOINT2 $jointvalue2 ...
setTarget JOINT3 4.3 JOINT4 52.5
wait 0.08

KEYFRAME 2
increaseTarget JOINT1 -2 JOINT2 7 ...
setTarget JOINT3 $jointvalue3 JOINT4 (2 * $jointvalue3)
wait 0.08
.
.
.
```

As seen above, joint angle values can either be numbers or be parameterized as $<varname>, where <varname> is a variable value that can be loaded after being learned. Values for skills and other configurable variables are read in and loaded at runtime from parameter files.

5.3   Optimization Task Infrastructure

A considerable amount of the UT Austin Villa team's efforts in preparing for RoboCup competitions has been in the area of skill optimization and optimizing parameters for walks and kicks. An example agent for optimizing a kick is provided with the code release. Optimization agents perform some task (such as kicking a ball) and then determine how well they did at the task (such as how far they kicked the ball) which is known as the agent's *fitness* for the task. Optimization agents are able to adjust the values of parameterized skills at runtime by loading in different parameter files as mentioned in Sect. 5.2, thus allowing the agents to easily try out and evaluate different sets of parameter values for a skill. After evaluating itself on how well it did at a task, an optimization agent writes its *fitness* for the task to an output file.

Optimization agents can be combined with machine learning algorithms to optimize and tune skill parameters for maximum *fitness* on a task. The UT Austin Villa team uses the CMA-ES [3] policy search algorithm for this purpose. During optimization, agents try out different parameter values from loaded parameter files written by CMA-ES, and then the agents write out their *fitness* values indicating how well they performed with those parameters so that CMA-ES can attempt to adjust the parameters to produce higher *fitness* values. UT Austin Villa utilizes overlapping layered learning [10] paradigms with CMA-ES to optimize skills that work well together.

When performing an optimization task, agents are able to change the world as needed (such as move themselves and the ball around) by sending special training command parser commands[5] to the server.

6   Other Code Releases

There have been several previous agent code releases by members of the RoboCup 3D simulation community. These include releases by magmaOffenburg[6] (Java 2014), libbats[7] (C++ 2013), Nexus[8] (C++ 2011), and TinMan[9] (.NET 2010). The UT Austin Villa code release (C++ 2016) expands on these previous code releases in a number of ways. First the UT Austin Villa code release offers a

---

[5] http://simspark.sourceforge.net/wiki/index.php/Network_Protocol#Command_Messages_from_Coach.2FTrainer.

[6] http://robocup.hsoffenburg.de/uploads/media/magmaOffenburg3D-2014Release.tar.gz.

[7] https://github.com/sgvandijk/libbats.

[8] http://nexus.um.ac.ir/index.php/downloads/base-code.

[9] https://github.com/drewnoakes/tin-man.

proven base having won the RoboCup 3D simulation competition four out of the past five years. Second the release provides an infrastructure for carrying out optimization and machine learning tasks, and third the code is up to date to work with the most recent version of the RoboCup 3D simulator(rcssserver3d 0.6.10).

7   Conclusion

The UT Austin Villa RoboCup 3D simulation team base code release provides a fully functioning agent and good starting point for new teams to the RoboCup 3D simulation league. Additionally the code release offers a foundational platform for conducting research in multiple areas including robotics, multiagent systems, and machine learning. We hope that the code base may both inspire other researchers to join the RoboCup community, as well as facilitate non-RoboCup competition research activities akin to the reinforcement learning benchmark keepaway task in the RoboCup 2D simulation domain [16].

Recent and ongoing work within the RoboCup community is the development of a plugin[10] for the Gazebo[11] [5] robotics simulator to support agents created for the current RoboCup 3D simulation league simulator (SimSpark). The UT Austin Villa code release has been tested with this plugin and provides an agent that can walk in the Gazebo environment. As the development of the plugin continues further support of the Gazebo plugin by the UT Austin Villa code release, such as providing getup behaviors that work in Gazebo, is planned.

A link to the UT Austin Villa 3D simulation code release, as well as additional information about the UT Austin Villa agent, can be found on the UT Austin Villa 3D simulation team's homepage.[12]

Acknowledgments. This code release is based upon the work of all past UT Austin Villa RoboCup 3D simulation team members. We thank all the previous team members for their important contributions. This work has taken place in the Learning Agents Research Group (LARG) at UT Austin. LARG research is supported in part by NSF (CNS-1330072, CNS-1305287), ONR (21C184-01), and AFOSR (FA9550-14-1-0087). Peter Stone serves on the Board of Directors of, Cogitai, Inc. The terms of this arrangement have been reviewed and approved by UT Austin in accordance with its policy on objectivity in research.

References

1. Akiyama, H., Nakashima, T.: HELIOS base: an open source package for the RoboCup soccer 2D simulation. In: Behnke, S., Veloso, M., Visser, A., Xiong, R. (eds.) RoboCup 2013. LNCS (LNAI), vol. 8371, pp. 528–535. Springer, Heidelberg (2014). doi:10.1007/978-3-662-44468-9_46

---

[10] https://bitbucket.org/osrf/robocup3ds.
[11] http://gazebosim.org/.
[12] http://www.cs.utexas.edu/~AustinVilla/sim/3dsimulation/.

2. Depinet, M., MacAlpine, P., Stone, P.: Keyframe sampling, optimization, and behavior integration: towards long-distance kicking in the RoboCup 3D simulation league. In: Bianchi, R.A.C., Akin, H.L., Ramamoorthy, S., Sugiura, K. (eds.) RoboCup 2014. LNCS, vol. 8992, pp. 571–582. Springer, Cham (2015). doi:10.1007/978-3-319-18615-3_47

3. Hansen, N.: The CMA evolution strategy: a tutorial, January 2009. http://www.lri.fr/~hansen/cmatutorial.pdf

4. Hester, T., Stone, P.: Negative information and line observations for Monte Carlo localization. In: IEEE International Conference on Robotics and Automation, May 2008

5. Koenig, N., Howard, A.: Design and use paradigms for gazebo, an open-source multi-robot simulator. In: Intelligent Robots and Systems 2004, (IROS 2004). In: 2004 IEEE/RSJ International Conference on Proceedings, vol. 3, pp. 2149–2154, September 2004

6. MacAlpine, P., Barrera, F., Stone, P.: Positioning to win: a dynamic role assignment and formation positioning system. In: Chen, X., Stone, P., Sucar, L.E., Zant, T. (eds.) RoboCup 2012. LNCS (LNAI), vol. 7500, pp. 190–201. Springer, Heidelberg (2013). doi:10.1007/978-3-642-39250-4_18

7. MacAlpine, P., Barrett, S., Urieli, D., Vu, V., Stone, P.: Design and optimization of an omnidirectional humanoid walk: a winning approach at the RoboCup 2011 3D simulation competition. In: Proceedings of the Twenty-Sixth AAAI Conference on Artificial Intelligence (AAAI-12), July 2012

8. MacAlpine, P., Collins, N., Lopez-Mobilia, A., Stone, P.: UT Austin Villa: RoboCup 2012 3D simulation league champion. In: Chen, X., Stone, P., Sucar, L.E., van der Zant, T. (eds.) RoboCup 2012. LNCS, vol. 7500, pp. 77–88. Springer, Heidelberg (2013). doi:10.1007/978-3-642-39250-4_8

9. MacAlpine, P., Depinet, M., Liang, J., Stone, P.: UT Austin Villa: RoboCup 2014 3D simulation league competition and technical challenge champions. In: Bianchi, R.A.C., Akin, H.L., Ramamoorthy, S., Sugiura, K. (eds.) RoboCup 2014. LNCS, vol. 8992, pp. 33–46. Springer, Cham (2015). doi:10.1007/978-3-319-18615-3_3

10. MacAlpine, P., Depinet, M., Stone, P.: UT Austin Villa 2014: RoboCup. 3D simulation league champion via overlapping layered learning. In: Proceedings of the Twenty-Ninth AAAI Conference on Artificial Intelligence (AAAI-15), January 2015

11. MacAlpine, P., Hanna, J., Liang, J., Stone, P.: UT Austin Villa: RoboCup 2015 3D simulation league competition and technical challenges champions. In: Almeida, L., Ji, J., Steinbauer, G., Luke, S. (eds.) RoboCup 2015. LNCS, vol. 9513, pp. 118–131. Springer, Cham (2015). doi:10.1007/978-3-319-29339-4_10

12. MacAlpine, P., Price, E., Stone, P.: SCRAM: Scalable collision-avoiding role assignment with minimal-makespan for formational positioning. In: Proceedings of the Twenty-Ninth AAAI Conference on Artificial Intelligence (AAAI-15), January 2015

13. MacAlpine, P., Urieli, D., Barrett, S., Kalyanakrishnan, S., Barrera, F., Lopez-Mobilia, A., Ştiurcă, N., Vu, V., Stone, P.: UT Austin Villa 2011 3D simulation team report. Technical Report AI11-10, The University of Texas at Austin, Department of Computer Science, AI Laboratory, December 2011

14. MacAlpine, P., Urieli, D., Barrett, S., Kalyanakrishnan, S., Barrera, F., Lopez-Mobilia, A., Ştiurcă, N., Vu, V., Stone, P.: UT Austin Villa 2011: a champion agent in the RoboCup 3D soccer simulation competition. In: Proceedings of 11th International Conference on Autonomous Agents and Multiagent Systems (AAMAS 2012), June 2012

15. Stoecker, J., Visser, U.: RoboViz: programmable visualization for simulated soccer. In: Röfer, T., Mayer, N.M., Savage, J., Saranlı, U. (eds.) RoboCup 2011. LNCS, vol. 7416, pp. 282–293. Springer, Heidelberg (2012). doi:10.1007/978-3-642-32060-6_24
16. Stone, P., Sutton, R.S., Kuhlmann, G.: Reinforcement learning for RoboCup-soccer keepaway. Adapt. Behav. **13**(3), 165–188 (2005)
17. Xu, Y., Vatankhah, H.: SimSpark: an open source robot simulator developed by the RoboCup community. In: Behnke, S., Veloso, M., Visser, A., Xiong, R. (eds.) RoboCup 2013. LNCS (LNAI), vol. 8371, pp. 632–639. Springer, Heidelberg (2014). doi:10.1007/978-3-662-44468-9_59

Progress in RoboCup Revisited: The State of Soccer Simulation 2D

Thomas Gabel$^{(\boxtimes)}$, Egbert Falkenberg, and Eicke Godehardt

Faculty of Computer Science and Engineering,
Frankfurt University of Applied Sciences, 60318 Frankfurt am Main, Germany
{tgabel,falken,godehardt}@fb2.fra-uas.de

Abstract. A remarkable feature of RoboCup's soccer simulation leagues is their ability to quantify and prove the exact progress made over years. In this paper, we present and discuss the results of an extensive empirical study of the progress and the currently reached state of 2D soccer simulation. Our main finding is that the current decade has witnessed a continuous and statistically significant improvement of the overall level of play, but that the magnitude of the progress made has dropped clearly when compared to the previous decade. In accordance to this, we envision possible future prospects for the 2D league that might respond to our empirical findings.

1 Introduction

At RoboCup 2015, two-dimensional simulated soccer players competed with one another at a world championship tournament for the 20th time. The long history of this competition as well as the continued interest of the community in the 2D soccer simulation league made us ask the question what progress has been made in this league throughout the years. We answered this question quantitatively at the RoboCup Symposium 2010 [3] by presenting the results of an extensive empirical evaluation with which we measured the progress of playing performance within the time window from 2003 to 2007.

With eight years having passed since the end time of the interval considered in the study mentioned, we think it is time to revisit the 2D simulation league and to pose the same as well as further questions. For those questions to be answerable, however, we need a stable soccer simulation platform. In [3], we had addressed the time period from 2003 to 2007 during which there was such a stable platform since the 2D league's simulation software, the Soccer Server [6], underwent no changes. In the paper at hand, our focus is on analyzing and assessing the developments during the more recent time interval (2010 to 2015) where also no modifications were made to the platform. Beyond this, we intend to compare our current findings to the results of the first stable period (2003–2007), identify similarities and differences and draw corresponding conclusions. Finally, we are going to address the question what are the recommendations, avenues, and prospects for the further development of the soccer simulator and the 2D league as a whole given the experience and the results reported.

© Springer International Publishing AG 2017
S. Behnke et al. (Eds.): RoboCup 2016, LNAI 9776, pp. 144–156, 2017.
https://doi.org/10.1007/978-3-319-68792-6_12

In Sect. 2, we provide necessary background information on soccer simulation and its course of development during the two recent decades. We also raise a number of questions that shall be addressed with our studies and outline our experimental setup. Section 3 presents in depth the results of our evaluations and in Sect. 4 we aim at drawing conclusions from our findings.

2   Background

Researchers and students who have been active in the RoboCup domain for more than a single year, will easily come to the conclusion that the overall level of play at RoboCup tournaments is increasing gradually. While this observation will certainly be shared by both, participants as well as spectators, it is diffi- cult to quantitatively prove its correctness. To this end, the soccer simulation leagues adopt a special role because no hardware development and maintenance are necessary, but instead soccer-playing agents as well as belonging coaches are merely some pieces of software [1]. This allows for repetitive and detailed evalu- ations as well as for forming quantitative statements of a team's strengths and weaknesses [2]. But it also allows for analyses of simulated soccer teams across various years. Given these circumstances, we are in the lucky position to derive empirically grounded statements regarding the quantitative playing strength of teams from different years and, in so doing, come up with evidence for or against a significant progress of RoboCup's soccer simulation branch.

2.1   Periods of Stability

In the 2D Soccer Simulation League all competitions are based on the Soccer Server software [6] which implements soccer playing as a completely distributed multi-agent system in a two-dimensional plane while adhering to the official soccer rules to the largest degree possible. During the 20 years of its existence this simulator has gone through various extensions and changes (see [1,3] for an overview), but it has also experienced periods of stability, i.e. a number of successive years where the technical and maintenance committees in agreement with the soccer simulation community decided to introduce no changes (apart from bug fixes) and, hence, to keep the simulation platform stable.

These periods of stability are of special interest in the scope of this paper, since a stable platform is a fundamental prerequisite for doing analyses, experi- ments, and evaluations with published soccer team binaries from different years. Stated differently, a non-stable platform (e.g. due to the introduction of a new feature into the simulation) prevents us from performing a meaningful and fair comparison of teams that were developed for different versions of the simulator.

Figure 1 shows the alternating periods of stability and further-development of the Soccer Server starting from the Pre-RoboCup event at IROS 1996 in Osaka. After seven years of intensive development, in 2003 the Soccer Server went into its *first stable period* (FSP) covering five years. This happened in parallel to the establishment of the 3D Soccer Simulation League. When, however, the 3D

1996		2002	2003	5 Years	2007	2008	2009	2010	6 Years	2015
			First Stable Period (FSP)					Second Stable Period (SSP)		

Fig. 1. Alternating periods of Frozen and continued soccer server development

league moved to modeling humanoid robots instead of simple spheres in 2007, the 2D committees decided to end the stable period and introduce new features and significant changes to the 2D simulation, which resulted in new simulator versions with a changed feature set for the 2008, 2009, and 2010 competitions. Since 2010, however, the simulation has been kept stable once again such that we can now speak of a *second stable period* (SSP, six years so far, 2010–2015 and lasting) with full compatibility of all team binaries released with these years.

2.2 Experimental Goals and Setup

Goals. Given the fact that the 2D Soccer Simulation League has seen two stable periods, within which a meaningful and fair evaluation across years is possible, we are going to answer the following questions in the remainder of this paper:

1. We address the question whether further progress has been made in soccer simulation 2D throughout the years of the SSP. This is similar to our analyses for the FSP (2003–2007) published in [3].
2. We are going to compare the progress indicators of both stable periods and draw corresponding conclusions.
3. We want to analyze the current state of the 2D Soccer Simulation League more thoroughly by focusing on individual teams' further development during the recent years.

Platform. Within the SSP, Soccer Server versions from 14.0.3 to 15.2.2 were used. As already said, any changes introduced in this period were targeted solely at bug fixing and installation support. In total, there have been only two minor modifications that might interfere with older teams and hence might have an impact on our experiments. First, the drop ball time (e.g. maximal time to execute a corner kick) was cut to half in 2011 in order to push back time wasting. Second, a defect in the coach language implementation has been corrected which could be exploited by older teams to their advantage. In order to compensate these corrections and to enforce maximal compatibility with all teams from 2010 to 2015 we conducted all our experiments using server version 15.0.0.

Team Selection. As in our 2010 study for the FSP [3], we proceed on the assumption that a year's joint level of play can be read from the quality of its top representatives. In Sect. 3.3 we will empirically underpin the validity of this assumption. In order to enforce comparability with the results of the mentioned study for the FSP, we again let any year from 2010 to 2015 be represented by its top four teams, i.e. those teams that made it to the semi-finals in the respective year's RoboCup world championships. Thus, in total we utilized 24 officially released team binaries from the six years of the SSP. When addressing the first two of the three questions posed above, we refrain from naming teams by their actual names, but use "year_place" identifiers for better readability. The matching from identifiers to verbose team names can be found in Tables 1 and 2 in the Appendix.

Experiments. We retrieved all considered historic team binaries from the web archive[1], made them work in our evaluation setting, and let them play multiple matches against one another using Soccer Server version 15.0.0. All matches were performed on a cluster of identical machines. Since we allowed any team to face any other team at least fifty times, we had in total more than 17.000 matches which corresponds to approximately 120 days of simulated soccer.

3   Empirical Results

In accordance to the research questions posed above we divided our experiments into three parts. We start by presenting the results of our general progress analysis that focuses on soccer simulation's further development within the SSP. We then compare these findings to the progress that the 2D league had made within its FSP and, finally, we more critically question how to characterize its currently reached state and by which driving factors it has emerged.

3.1   General Progress Analysis

In this part of our study we allowed each of the 24 representatives of the SSP to face each other team 50 times under regular settings. We determined for each team the average score (number of goals shot vs. number of goals received) from these $23 \times 50 = 1150$ matches and plotted this information in the left chart of Fig. 2 (standard deviations are omitted for readability). Apparently, teams from later years score on average more goals while they receive less. Furthermore, polygons formed by interconnecting data points of the same year seem to shift slightly to the bottom right of the diagram. While this observation is less obvious than in the similar chart for the FSP from 2003–2007 [3], it nevertheless represents a first indication of the fact that there has been some progress in soccer simulation 2D during the last six years.

The accompanying bar chart in the right of Fig. 2 shows the share of points each team obtained within this set of experiments, where as in human soccer a victory is awarded with three points, a draw with one and a defeat with zero points. Thus, winning all of the 1150 matches would yield 100% (3450) while drawing all matches would yield 33.3%. With 82.1% of the maximal number of points the 2015 champion turned out to be the strongest team. Interestingly, teams originating from later years (bars with lighter shades of gray) place predominantly in the top half of the ranking whereas older binaries (darker shades of gray) are to be found mainly on the rear ranks.

---

[1] http://archive.robocup.info.

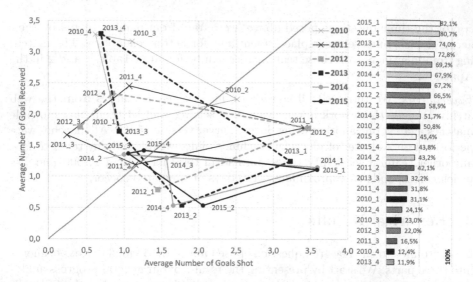

Fig. 2. Left: average scores for each of the 24 representatives from the second stable period when playing repeatedly against all other teams. Right: corresponding share of points achieved by each team within this empirical study.

While we have concentrated on individual teams so far, we now focus on a comparison of entire years where, as stressed in Sect. 2, we let the joint strength of a year be represented by its four top teams. In Fig. 3, we visualize the results of this year-vs-year comparison in a matrix-like representation. Each cell of this matrix shows the results of a large-scale tournament (of 800 matches each) where all representatives from the year indicated by the row played against all teams from the year indicated by the column. The bars within each cell show both, the distribution of points among both years as well as the average scores. For all matrix elements (y_1, y_2) with data it holds that $y_1 < y_2$, i.e. we have the "newer" teams in the columns and we visualize it with a darker color. Therefore, we can easily read from the chart, that in any constellation y_2 performed superior to y_1. The larger the difference $y_2 - y_1$, the clearer the dominance of the newer team. For $y_1 = 2014$ and $y_2 = 2015$, however, we find that both years are nearly equally strong (points are distributed as 49.7:50.3). So, the first general conclusion from the mentioned evaluations are that (a) there has been substantial progress within soccer simulation 2D during the six years of the SSP and (b) that this kind of progress has slowed down recently.

3.2   Comparative Progress Analysis

The decision to freeze the Soccer Server development in 2003 and, thus, to enter a stable period had not been taken recklessly back in 2002 (see [3] for background information). The empirical study [3] on what happened within this period of stability has emphasized to what extent the 2D community has drawn benefits in

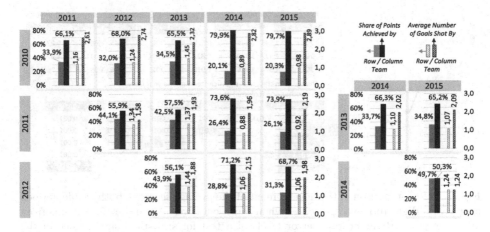

Fig. 3. Representatives from one year (row index) played multiple times against all teams from any other years (column index) of the SSP. Distribution of points (3/1/0) as well as average scores (over 800 matches) are plotted for each combination.

terms of increasing overall playing performance. Given the observations reported in Sect. 3.1, a highly interesting question to ask is whether the impact of the SSP has been as substantial as the impact of the first one.

To answer this question we now no longer target individual top teams or year-vs-year comparisons, but instead let the joint set of representatives of any year play repeatedly against *all* teams from all other years. For example, we made each of the four 2010 representatives play 50 times against all top teams from 2011 through 2015, which made a total of 4000 matches for each year considered. In the right part of Fig. 4 we present the averaged scores over these 4000 matches for the six years from 2010 to 2015 including the score quotient (average number of goals scored divided by the average number of goals received). The belonging chart in the left of this figure contrasts these results with the results of the FSP. Apparently, the progress made in that time period has been much clearer because the steps from year to year were larger in terms of scoring more goals while receiving less on average. Furthermore, when comparing the starting point of the FSP (2003) with the average results achieved four years later (2007), we have to acknowledge that in this stable period the average number of goals shot has been increased by a factor of 3.27 and the goals received has been reduced by factor 8.56. By contrast, from 2010 to 2014 (also after four years of time) these increment/reduction factors are only 1.78 and 2.59, respectively. These facts are indicative of a clear decline in the progress being made in soccer simulation 2D even under stable conditions.

With 4000 samples per year group, we can quite reliably state whether a change (measured by the average score) from one year y_1 to a second one y_2 is statistically significant or not, assuming a nearly normally distributed number of goals scored and received. To this end, we interpreted each average score as a two-dimensional data point and applied a multivariate analysis of variance,

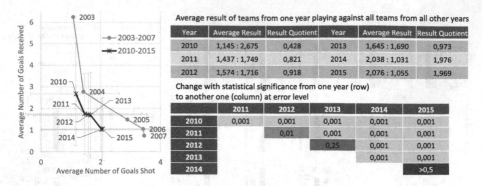

Fig. 4. Left: comparison of the development of the average scores in both stable periods over years. Right top: average scores when representatives of one year face teams from all other years. Right bottom: error levels of a test for statistical significance in the change of the average score from the row-indicated year to the column-indicated one.

given the empirically measured match results and group means (average scores). In so doing, we employed Wilks' Λ test statistic, which for large n (as in our case) is nearly χ^2-distributed [4], and determined the significance levels at which the null hypothesis has to be rejected (null hypothesis: mean vector (goals shot, goals received) is in every year the same). The results are listed in the matrix in the bottom right part of Fig. 4. The most important finding is that there has been a change at significance level of 0.1% from any year to any other one, if $y_2 - y_1 \geq 2$ (all non-diagonal entries). As far as changes from a year to its immediate successor year are considered, we do also find significance at a level of 0.1%, however, with three exceptions. From 2011 to 2012 the test statistic allows us to infer a change of the average score at a significance level of 1%, only. By contrast, for the transition from 2012 to 2013 and from 2014 to 2015, no statistically significant changes can be attested (error levels of 25% and >50%, respectively).

While our analyses so far has concentrated on average scores in conjunction with the law of large numbers, we now compare both stable periods from the win-draw-lose point of view. Part (a) of Fig. 5 visualizes the dominance of a year's (y_2) representatives over the teams from the predecessor year (y_1) by showing the share of points ($\frac{pts(y_2)}{pts(y_1)+pts(y_2)}$) achieved when all representatives face one another multiple times (number of matches: 800 for the SSP, 240 for the FSP). The interesting point to observe here is that for the SSP we arrive at much smaller levels of dominance over preceding year. Since a value of 50% means equality (i.e. no progress made) the low numbers between 50 and 56% for 2011/13/14, respectively, do also correspond to the statistically not significant levels of progress in terms of average scores reported above.

Here, a considerable difference to the FSP is distinctive which even becomes clearer in part (b) of Fig. 5 where the shares of matches won/drawn/lost are visualized, when teams play against representatives from all other years (data

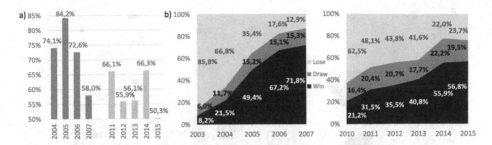

Fig. 5. (a) Representatives from the year (y) shown in the abscissa played repeatedly against teams from the immediate predecessor year $(y-1)$. Share of points achieved by teams from y are shown. (b) Distribution of matches won/drawn/lost by teams from one year when repeatedly facing all representatives from all other years of the same stable period.

from 4000 matches for each year). Although the FSP lasted shorter than the SSP, a more distinguished slope in the performance over the years can be observed which also hints to the fact that the SSP started out from a significantly more saturated starting state which, in turn, allowed for much smaller improvements over the years.

3.3 Team-Focussed Progress Analysis

The goal of this section is to characterize and circumscribe certain special aspects of the current state of the 2D Soccer Simulation League as they have emerged during the SSP.

Dominance of Top Teams. All our experimental investigations presented so far are based on the assumption that the strength of one year can be read validly from the level of play of its best representatives. We validated this claim by having a separate set of tournaments where we made ranks 1–4 from the RoboCup world cup play against ranks 5–8 repeatedly in any combination. This way we found that in such a setting the top four teams carve out 89.1% of the points whereas the ranks 5–8 yield 10.9%, only. The corresponding average score is 2.38:0.34 from the point of view of the top four. While such a kind of dominance may hold even for real soccer (perhaps less pronounced), we also have to acknowledge that the top places have been achieved more and more often by the same teams throughout the years. This fact is visualized in part (a) of Fig. 6 (see the Appendix for plain team names) where the sums of the points of those teams are compared that (1) have/had the same affiliation (institution) and (2) made it to the top four for at least one year within a stable period (again: all teams played vs. all others, awarding 3/1/0 points as usual).

It is interesting to observe that the best team of the FSP (Team A) yielded 26.7% of all points, whereas the dominating team of the SSP (Team B) carves out 37.6%. The same holds, if we consider the best two/best four teams of each stable period: In the FSP they jointly obtained 49.8% (top 2) or 76.4% (top 4),

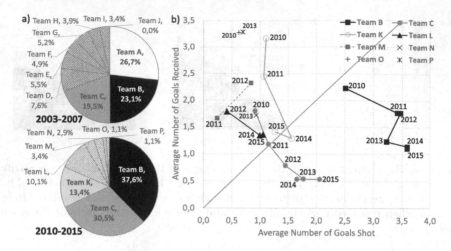

Fig. 6. Dominance of Established Teams in the 2D League: (a) point distribution over successive years partitioned by teams from identical institutions. (b) Evolution of these teams throughout the second stable period in terms of average scores.

in the SSP, by contrast, even 68.1% (top 2) or 91.6% (top 4). Moreover, the overall number of teams from different affiliations that made it to the semi-finals has decreased from 10 within the 5 years of the FSP to only 8 within the 6 years of the SSP. A conclusion to be drawn from these facts is that the performance gap between leading teams and the rest is more and more increasing.

Part (b) of Fig. 6 shows the same data points as the scatter plot in Fig. 2 (identical set of matches as raw data), however, this time teams from the same institution, i.e. with the same group of human developers, are now connected. This way, the dominance of the current top teams becomes even more transparent, since only teams B and C happen to position themselves below the identity function, hence scoring on average more goals than they receive. Moreover, this visualizations highlights to which extent teams improved over time.

(Un)Worthy Champions. One of the still appealing and exciting features of 2D soccer simulation is the randomness in the simulation introduced by the Soccer Server. As in human soccer, this may result in that a team can (with a low probability) beat a stronger one and, hence, kick the stronger one out of the tournament unexpectedly. From the point of view of the actually stronger team this situation is probably very "annoying", specifically if it occurs during a final match. Figure 7 stresses the fact that the 2D Soccer Simulation League indeed had this situation once within the SSP (in 2010). In all years following, however, the provably stronger team became world champion indeed. This issue has also been addressed by Budden et al. [2] who proposed a tournament format which is aimed at minimizing fluctuations from true team performance.

Aging Binaries. A dangerous development that might arise in a situation where a group is dominated by a small fraction of its members (as delineated at the beginning of this section) is that some kind of over-specialization is generated.

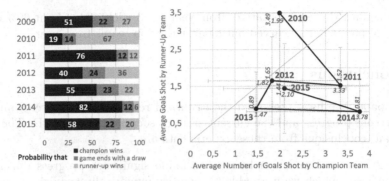

Fig. 7. Average results of 100 replays of the final matches throughout the second stable period: share of matches won/drawn/lost (left) and average scores from the champion's perspective (right).

Translated to the soccer simulation domain this means that most, if not all, participants start optimizing their teams' strategies specifically against the most recent versions of last year's winner or runner-up teams. If this kind of incestuous overfitting takes place, then we should expect to see that (much) older team binaries start to come off better the older their date of publishing. In order to investigate this issue, we determined for all team binaries considered in this study (a) how well they played when they made it to the top four (and thus became a representative for its year) by playing against all other representatives from its year and (b) how much better or worse (relative to (a)) they performed when playing against the representatives of the following year. We continued this analysis for all remaining years of the SSP denoting the time elapsed as the "age" of the respective team binary.

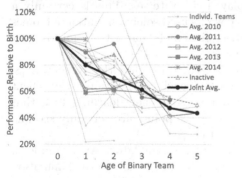

Fig. 8. No sign of over-specialization: team binaries do, in general, perform worse the older they get.

Although there are minor exceptions, Fig. 8 shows clearly that there is no indication that – with a team binary's increasing age – its performance starts increasing again due to reasons of over-specialization of the other teams against the most recent top teams. This finding is also confirmed by looking at the top team (Team A, binary version originating from 2010) of the FSP which has been inactive throughout the SSP (data series "Inactive"). This team's performance, though slightly above the average, decreases a little from year to year, and there is no sign of a turn-around in terms of improving performance with increased age. To sum up, on average a team binary published and used in year y loses about 10–20% of its strength per year and will, for example when playing against the representatives from year $y + 3$, yield only about 60% of the number of points it had carved out against the top teams from year y.

4 Conclusions

In this paper, we have presented the empirical results of a large-scale analysis of the recent progress and the current state of soccer simulation 2D. The most important conclusions from these experiments are:

- The 2D soccer simulation league has made significant progress during the recent years which we were able to quantify numerically thanks to fact that the software platform has been kept stable from 2010 to 2015.
- When compared to an earlier stable period (2003–2007) the magnitude of the progress made has been much smaller.
- The league is currently strongly dominated by a very small set of teams making it rather difficult for new teams to catch up. However, so far we do not find evidence for incestuous overfitting team strategies.

Having a stable period is extremely useful for the league and the community as a whole since it allows for studies and analyses as the one at hand. So, the policy of fixing the simulator for a couple of years should definitely be continued. With respect to the changes between the first and the second stable period this paper has shown that the league entered the SSP at a relatively mature and saturated level which did not allow for as large jumps in performance as in the FSP. Speaking about the future and a possible 2D soccer simulation agenda, we, therefore, envision three possible target directions.

- Enforce and implement finer-grained analyses of the progress of simulated soccer in terms of analyzing team play and strategies. This is certainly a shortcoming of the study at hand, since we focused solely on match outcomes without validating the actual team strategies, their maturity in multi-agent cooperation, or their level of adaptiveness.
- Enforce more focus on 2D soccer-related research benchmarks. Keepaway [8] and half-field offense [5] as well as the former coach competition are excellent examples. They might be complemented by some new learning task that becomes part of the official competitions. These points are certainly striking with regard to RoboCup's ambitious 2050 vision.
- Have a really bold, yet useful extension of the simulator. An example of such a move would be to add parts of the third dimension to the simulation (e.g. flying balls leaving the ground) and, hence, extend it from 2D to (more or less) $2\frac{1}{2}$D. This idea is not new, it had been under discussion in the technical committee already a few years ago. Among its advantages are the fact that it would *not* interfere with the 3D league which has moved to modelling humanoid robots. Furthermore, it would still allow for focusing primarily on issues of multi-agent cooperation and team play, also in conjunction with learning approaches. Also, it might at least partially level the ground making

it more attractive to new teams to enter the competition, as every team will have to adapt to the changes. Moreover, it might allow for bridging the gap to research in (human) soccer analysis where the 2D league's missing third dimension for the ball is a key obstacle [7]. Finally, it might address several of the findings brought up in this paper by allowing for a future third stable period starting out from a less saturated starting point.

Acknowledgements. The authors would like to thank Bernd Dankert for his support in conducting the empirical experiments.

Appendix

Table 1. RoboCup world championships' top teams in the 2nd stable period

	1	2	3	4
2010	HELIOS (JPN)	WrightEagle (CHN)	Oxsy (ROM)	ESKILAS (IRN)
2011	WrightEagle (CHN)	HELIOS (JPN)	Marlik (IRN)	Oxsy (ROM)
2012	HELIOS (JPN)	WrightEagle (CHN)	Marlik (IRN)	Gliders (AUS)
2013	WrightEagle (CHN)	HELIOS (JPN)	YuShan (CHN)	Axiom (IRN)
2014	WrightEagle (CHN)	Gliders (AUS)	Oxsy (ROM)	HELIOS (JPN)
2015	WrightEagle (CHN)	HELIOS (JPN)	Gliders (AUS)	Oxsy (ROM)

Table 2. List of all teams among top four from 2003–07 and 2010–15

Id	Plain Team Name	Id	Plain Team Name	Id	Plain Team Name	Id	Plain Team Name
A	Brainstormers (GER)	E	OPU-Hana (JPN)	I	Mersad (IRN)	M	Marlik (IRN)
B	WrightEagle (CHN)	F	TsinghuAeolus (CHN)	J	Everest (CHN)	N	YuShan (CHN)
C	HELIOS (JPN)	G	AmoyNQ (CHN)	K	Oxsy (ROM)	O	ESKILAS (IRN)
D	STEP (RUS)	H	UvATriLearn (NED)	L	Gliders (AUS)	P	Axiom (IRN)

References

1. Akiyama, H., Dorer, K., Lau, N.: On the progress of soccer simulation leagues. In: Bianchi, R.A.C., Akin, H.L., Ramamoorthy, S., Sugiura, K. (eds.) RoboCup 2014. LNCS (LNAI), vol. 8992, pp. 599–610. Springer, Cham (2015). doi:10.1007/978-3-319-18615-3_49
2. Budden, D., Wang, P., Obst, O., Prokopenko, M.: RoboCup simulation leagues: enabling replicable and robus investigation of complex robotic systems. IEEE Robot. Autom. Mag. **3**(22), 140–146 (2015)
3. Gabel, T., Riedmiller, M.: On progress in RoboCup: the simulation league showcase. In: Ruiz-del-Solar, J., Chown, E., Plöger, P.G. (eds.) RoboCup 2010. LNCS (LNAI), vol. 6556, pp. 36–47. Springer, Heidelberg (2011). doi:10.1007/978-3-642-20217-9_4

4. Johnson, R., Wichern, D.: Applied Multivariate Statistical Analysis. Prentice Hall, Upper Saddle River (1998)
5. Kalyanakrishnan, S., Liu, Y., Stone, P.: Half field offense in RoboCup soccer: a multiagent reinforcement learning case study. In: Lakemeyer, G., Sklar, E., Sorrenti, D.G., Takahashi, T. (eds.) RoboCup 2006. LNCS (LNAI), vol. 4434, pp. 72–85. Springer, Heidelberg (2007). doi:10.1007/978-3-540-74024-7_7
6. Noda, I.: Soccer server: a simulator of RoboCup. In: Proceedings of the AI Symposium 1995, pp. 29–34. Japanese Society for Artificial Intelligence (1995)
7. Perl, J., Grunz, A., Memmert, D.: Tactics analysis in soccer - an advanced approach. Int. J. Comput. Sci. Sport 12, 33–44 (2013)
8. Stone, P., Sutton, R., Kuhlmann, G.: Reinforcement learning for RoboCup-soccer keepaway. Adapt. Behav. 3(13), 165–188 (2005)

An Integration Challenge to Bridge the Gap Among Industry-Inspired RoboCup Leagues

Sebastian Zug[1]([✉]), Tim Niemueller[2]([✉]), Nico Hochgeschwender[3],
Kai Seidensticker[1], Martin Seidel[1], Tim Friedrich[4], Tobias Neumann[5],
Ulrich Karras[6], Gerhard K. Kraetzschmar[3], and Alexander Ferrein[5]

[1] Otto-von-Guericke University, Magdeburg, Germany
{zug,seidenst,maseidel}@ovgu.de
[2] Knowledge-Based Systems Group, RWTH Aachen University, Aachen, Germany
niemueller@kbsg.rwth-aachen.de
[3] Bonn-Rhein-Sieg University of Applied Science, St. Augustin, Germany
{nico.hochgeschwender,gerhard.kraetzschmar}@h-brs.de
[4] KUKA Roboter GmbH, Augsburg, Germany
tim.friedrich@kuka.com
[5] MASKOR Institute, FH Aachen University of Applied Sciences, Aachen, Germany
{t.neumann,ferrein}@fh-aachen.de
[6] RoboCup Executive Committee, Essen, Germany
ulrich-karras@t-online.de

Abstract. Manufacturing industries are changing rapidly towards more flexibility and autonomy. The RoboCup Logistics League (RCLL) and RoboCup@Work tackle research questions in this domain focusing on automated reasoning and planning, and mobile manipulation respectively. However, future scenarios will require both aspects (and more) and will most likely operate with more heterogeneous systems.

In this paper, we propose a cross-over challenge to foster closer cooperation among the two leagues to address these challenges. We outline four integration milestones and propose a specific scenario and task for the first milestone. The effort is driven by stakeholders of both leagues.

1 Motivation

In industry, cyber-physical systems (CPS) in the context of Industry 4.0 [1] have received a lot of attention recently. They strive to combine computation with sensing and actuation. The canonical meaning in industry are embedded computers and networks which monitor and control the physical processes and have a wide range of applications in assisted living, advanced automotive systems, energy conservation, environmental and critical infrastructure control, or manufacturing. Robots are one, if not the, most complex form of CPS.

Competitions, on the other hand, represent an important keystone in engineering education and research [2]. The combination of challenging tasks and motivating team work attracts students to work hard for a good performance and ranking. In order to reach this goal the students have to coordinate their

© Springer International Publishing AG 2017
S. Behnke et al. (Eds.): RoboCup 2016, LNAI 9776, pp. 157–168, 2017.
https://doi.org/10.1007/978-3-319-68792-6_13

interdisciplinary team similar to a "realistic" development process. This involves topics such as software engineering, methods research, project management and interface definition among others.

RoboCup [3] is the best-known international initiative to foster research in the field of robotics and artificial intelligence through such competitions. It is particularly well-known for its soccer leagues, but application-driven leagues such as RoboCup Rescue or RoboCup@Home [4] become more prominent every year. In this context, RoboCup@Work (@Work) [5] and the RoboCup Logistics League (RCLL) [6] are industry-inspired leagues based on scenarios known as Factory of the Future (FoF) or Smart Factory. These are context-aware production facilities that consider, for instance, object positions or machine status to assist in the execution of manufacturing tasks [7]. It can draw information from the physical environment or from a virtual model, for example, from a process simulation, an order, or a product specification. It is designed to cope with the challenges that arise from the desire to produce highly customized goods which result in the proliferation of variants [7] and therefore smaller lot sizes.

While both leagues share the same basic problems such as navigation, object handling, or device interaction, there are also significant differences. @Work tasks are focused on grasping and mobile manipulation operations, while the RCLL concentrates on research questions about task-level planning and scheduling, automation in an industrial production workflow, and multi-robot system integration process. However, in an industrial scenario implementing a realistic production process both aspects – complex manipulation *and* optimized resource planning have to be considered.

In this paper, we propose a *cross-over challenge* that requires involvement of teams of both leagues to cooperate on a common task. As we will outline, the aim is to foster cooperation of the two leagues; it is not intended that one leagues will be subsumed by the other. Since both individual leagues' tasks are already complex by themselves, we intend to start with simple cooperation of the robots that essentially involves cross-league communication through their respective refboxes in 2016. We will also outline, how we intend to increase and strengthen cooperation and allow for more integration in future competitions.

In the remainder of the paper we briefly introduce the two leagues in Sect. 2 and review a proposal for an industrial umbrella league (Sect. 3). We then outline how the cooperation and integration may be developed in Sect. 4. We then describe the proposed cross-over challenge in Sect. 5 before we conclude in Sect. 6.

2   League Descriptions

In this section, we describe the RoboCup Logistics League and RoboCup@Work, and give a brief overview of similarities and differences.

2.1   RoboCup Logistics League (RCLL)

The industry-oriented RoboCup Logistics League[1] (RCLL) tackles the problem of production logistics in a smart factory. Groups of three robots have to

---

[1] RoboCup Logistics website: http://www.robocup-logistics.org.

plan, execute, and optimize the material flow and deliver products according to dynamic orders in a simplified factory (Fig. 1). The challenge consists of creating and adjusting a production plan and coordinate the group [6].

A game is split into two major phases. In the *exploration phase*, the robots must determine the positions of machines assigned to their team and recognize and report a combination of marker and light signal state. During the *production phase*, the robots must transport workpieces to create final products according to dynamic order schedules which are announced to the robots only at run-time.

Fig. 1.   Teams   carologistics (robots with additional laptop) and Solidus (pink parts) during the RCLL finals at RoboCup 2015. (Color figure online)

The RCLL focuses on the topics of automated planning and scheduling, reasoning under uncertainty, and multi-robot cooperation. Other robotics aspects are intentionally kept simpler, e.g., handling of the machines or perception. The planning is open to a variety of approaches, from local-scope (single robot) to global-scope (overall fleet) planning, to distributed and centralized approaches [8]. A capable simulation of the environment is available as open source software to further corroborate this focus [9]. The RCLL task and its simulation also form the foundation for a Robot Planning Competition Tutorial at ICAPS 2016[2] [10].

2.2   RoboCup@Work League

The RoboCup@Work league[3] (short @Work) is the latest within the family of RoboCup challenges. It is inspired by industrial mobile manipulation scenarios and accordingly covers a large spectrum of current research topics related to the Factory of the Future (FoF) (Fig. 2).

The competition combines a number of separate runs addressing navigation, grasping and handling tasks of different complexity. The manipulation objects are motivated by industrial scenarios (profiles, nuts, screws).

Fig. 2.   @Work robot of the robOTTO team in front of a rack grasping an object.

In one of the tasks during a competition the robot has to recognize the correct objects, transport them from one shelf to another and place them into object-specific cavities, thus benchmarking object perception, navigation and precision placement capabilities of the robot. For all the tasks different instances allow for different levels of complexity and therefore

---

new teams as well as experienced teams are provided with a challenging environment setting. The referees evaluate the correct execution of tasks, collisions with the environment and score the fastest run according to specifications set in the rulebook.

2.3 Comparison of the Main Objectives

Table 1 compares some of the similarities and differences between the two leagues. The focus lies in organizational, environmental and hardware topics. The most prominent difference is the common robot platform. The RCLL requires the Festo Robotino as base platform, while @Work is open to different robots. However, since the beginning of the @Work competition, the KUKA youBot emerged as de-facto standard platform for this league. Both, the Robotino as well as the KUKA

Table 1. Comparison RoboCup Logistics League and RoboCup@Work

	Criteria	RoboCup Logistics League	RoboCup@Work
League	Established	2010 (Demo) 2012 (Competition)	2012 (Demo) 2014 (Competition)
	Teams (RC 2016)	10+	10+
	Competition Mode	Parallel runs in shared arena	Individual runs
	Disciplines	1 + 3 challenges	9 + 2 challenges
Referee box	Communication	Broadcast/Multicast with Protocol Buffer encoding	Broadcast/Multicast with Protocol Buffer encoding
	Task generation	Randomized order combination and machine placement	Distribution of the objects and their destination
	Visualization	Arena/Map w/robots, Task, Time, Score	Arena, Current task, Time
	Scoring	Production steps, Delivery, Exploration Reports	-
Common Platform	Robot	Festo Robotino	KUKA youBot
	Locomotion	holonomic (3 Wheel)	holonomic (4 Wheel)
	Manipulator	Typically Gripper	5 DoF Arm w/ gripper
	Connectivity	Wifi and LAN	LAN
	Embedded PC	Intel i5, 2.4 GHz, 8 GB RAM, 64 GB SSD	Intel Atom 510, 1.66 GHz, 2 GB RAM, 32 GB SSD Flash
	Circuit Boards	Motor, Power, I/O	Motor, Gripper, Power
	Power Supply	2x lead acid batteries	lead acid battery
Adaptations	Common Hardware Modifications	Gripper, Extra Computer, Sensor Mounts	Gripper, Kill switch, Elevated sensor platform, Wifi, CPU
	Common Sensors	Laser Range Finder, Odometry, Bumper, Cameras, IR-sensors, RGB-D camera	Laser Range Finder, Odometry, Cameras, RGB-D camera
Arena	Maximum size	14 m × 8 m	10 m × 12 m
	Operating Level	90 cm	0–15 cm
	Devices	Festo Modular Production Systems (MPS)	Round table, Conveyor belt
	Obstacles	Opposing robots, MPS stations	Barrier tape, Variable obstacles
Obj.	Number	1 (∼250 variants)	13
	Motivation	Industrial workpieces	Industrial components
	Heterogeneity	Single shape, various colors	different shapes and colors

youBot can be extended and modified with different sensor configurations. This gives teams flexibility in designing their robot to suit their research needs. The arenas of both leagues are of comparable size and includes networked devices to be used for various league specific tasks. For example, a conveyor belt is employed in @Work for the conveyor belt test whereas the Festo Modular Production System (MPS) is employed for the whole competition. A key difference of the leagues is the mode of competition, whereas RCLL performs parallel runs in a shared environment whereas in @Work the environment is not (yet) shared. This can be explained with the different scientific objectives of the leagues. In RCLL the focus is on multi-agent planning and scheduling whereas in @Work the focus is on mobile manipulation including the required capabilities such as perception, control and motion planning. The different objectives yields also in a heterogenous design of the competition objects – @Work includes a breadth of different object instances (variants in shapes and colors) whereas RCLL covers the depth of the variants of one object.

2.4 Other Industry Motivated Robotic Leagues

Outside of RoboCup there are further competitions with an industrial background. The Amazon Picking Challenge addresses the manipulation process of daily objects. The scenario reflects the commissioning process in a warehouse. Different goods have to be localized, grasped and placed to a box [11]. The second version of the challenge is held in Leipzig during the RoboCup 2016.

In contrast, the Airbus Shopfloor Challenge is focused on the simulation of the production process [12]. During the first performance at the ICRA 2016 the teams had to present a robot that could drill holes in a metal plate. The number of holes and their quality define the evaluation criterion.

Another competition targeting the industrial domain is the RoCKIn@Work competition [13] which is part of the recently finished EU-funded project RoCKIn. In RoCKIn@Work several task and functionality benchmarks related to mobile manipulation scenarios in small and medium sized factories are performed. A focus of RoCKIn@Work and RoCKIn in general was on developing experimental methodologies, benchmarking procedures and competition infrastructure and testbeds. The RoCKIn project significantly contributed to RoboCup@Work and vice versa as several elements from RoCKIn (e.g. testbed [14]) are in the meanwhile employed in RoboCup@Work.

3 RoboCup Industrial Umbrella League

Movements like *Industry 4.0* document an increased interest in industry towards more autonomy in manufacturing processes. These are based on cyber-physical systems that combine computing processes and physical interaction in heavily networked systems. In our context, we assume *autonomous mobile robots* as one of the most complex classes of such systems [15]. As such, testbeds are required for benchmarking methods and systems for smart factories. In 2016, the

RoboCup Industrial umbrella league [16] has been established with the mission to combine the efforts in the context of RoboCup towards this goal. Given the key differences (single- vs. multi-robot, scenario vs. solution design, multiple short-term tests vs. single long-term test, focus on manipulation vs. planning and scheduling) that we have outlined in Sect. 2, we strongly believe that merging the leagues is in neither league's best interest in the near future. However, we do see a high potential for cooperation on the technical level. *Long-term alignment of the research agenda* could keep diversity and cooperation alive through the common cross-over tasks. This would, at the same time, allow for the individual development and focus of the leagues. This would be akin to the organization of RoboCup soccer leagues. While the leagues have an overall common scheme of multi-robot systems playing soccer, the organization stays decentralized to a certain degree. The benefit is that ideas, methods, and sometimes software or even hardware components are shared across the different sub-leagues without forcing them to merge or otherwise one being subsumed by the other.

As a first endeavor in this context, several major stakeholders of both leagues are cooperating towards the creation of a single common autonomous referee box (refbox)[4]. This project is based on the RCLL refbox efforts started in 2013. It had been adopted for the RoCKIn@Work competition [14] and from there adopted in RoboCup@Work. With the recent effort, the idea is to create one common infrastructure (reasoning engine, communication, code base) and then model the specific scenarios. This would also greatly simplify the crossover challenge presented in this paper, as both sides would use the same executing machinery for the refbox.

4 RCLL/@Work Cross-over Challenge Development

Besides the will and effort of stakeholders of both leagues to drive the overall integration as described above, also needed is a technical integration effort to pave the way for cooperating robots. Based on our observation of the RCLL and @Work, we expect there to be four major milestones on the way to full integration as depicted in Fig. 3: the transition from different to commonly used object to handle (A), the operation in a common arena or space (B), the operation of each other's on-field devices (C), and finally direct robot interaction (D). These levels of integration configure four component classes (manipulation objects, arena, devices and robot interaction) in different ways.

Each of these levels requires considerable effort. For (A), the gap in the operational height of the robots must be overcome. For (B), a certain level of acceptance is required in both leagues as some "field-time" will have to be devoted to the testing of a common task. For (C), the operational height becomes an even more pressing issue, since now the interaction must be two-way. In (A), it is sufficient to move objects from the higher to the lower level. And for (D), an extensive communication infrastructure and robot-to-robot handling must be implemented. In the following, we analyze the levels and evaluate challenges.

---

[4] Code available at https://github.com/robocup-industrial/rci-refbox.

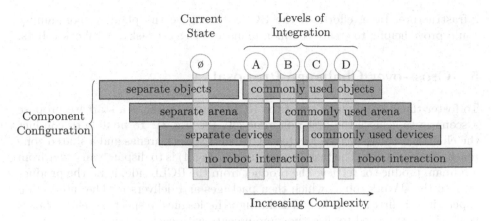

Fig. 3. Levels of interactions between both leagues

The separate objects configuration ø reflects the current situation with different types of objects (as listed in Table 1) where both leagues operate completely separated.

The use of common objects (A) can be achieved in multiple ways, ranging from using the superset of both leagues and expecting robots of either league to be able to handle all of them – a goal that probably @Work teams can accomplish more easily. More likely, however, is to use a subset with only some objects from both leagues.

Using separate workspaces (B) is possible via manipulation objects transferred from one area to another. Objects have then to be transferred by external means like a conveyor belt. Intersecting arenas with commonly used parts increase the complexity of the scenario significantly where collision-free operation and an effective trajectory planning for a heterogeneous multi-robot application has to be performed – a task that is currently performed only in the RCLL.

Shared devices (C) would exist only in commonly used areas. This component class involves all electrical elements of the arena beside the robots such as production units, transport systems, or storage elements. Common use of the same resources requires communication among the robot and teams to avoid conflicts – something that RCLL at the moment implements only at the team-level and @Work not at all. As outlined in Table 1 this is not yet the case.

Intermediate robot interaction (D) can require direct hand-overs among robots, or operating a machine at the same time (e.g., one robot feeds a work item that another operates the machine or needs to collect the object on the other side). Members of the @Work league will be able to adapt more easily due to their focus on manipulation and handling. A balance could be achieved by an @Work robot handing an object to an RCLL robot, combining both handling capabilities, which is nonetheless a challenging problem [17]. Additionally, this also requires combined or cooperative task-level planning – which is a focus area in the RCLL. This would require an even extended common communication infrastructure. Here, efforts of the RCLL to engage the planning community could prove helpful to create common plans and suggest tasks to @Work robots.

5   Cross-over Challenge Proposal

To foster the close cooperation of the RCLL and @Work, as a start we propose a scenario to achieve the first milestone (A) (cf. Fig. 3). To be able to conduct the challenge, we assume co-located RCLL and @Work arenas and a shared zone reachable from both. The task (represented in Fig. 4) is to dispatch an order from a human, produce or retrieve the product from the RCLL side, hand the product over to the @Work robot, which then packages and delivers it. The integration aspect in this first step is handled through the leagues' respective referee boxes that will be extended to directly communicate with each other.

In the following, we outline the task in more detail, before stating requirements and challenges.

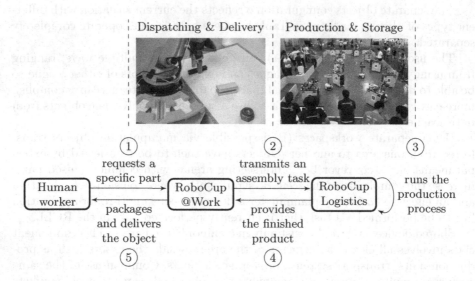

Fig. 4. Workflow of the scenario and the interaction between @Work and the RCLL.

5.1   Scenario and Task

We emulate an industrial process in a multi-stage production and packaging scenario with human-robot interaction and cross-vendor robot cooperation depicted in Fig. 4. It clearly distinguishes the task to be performed by the robots of the respective leagues and roughly follows the following steps. A human worker initiates production by requesting a specific product ①. The request is processed by the @Work referee box (refbox) and immediately communicated to the RCLL refbox ②. It generates an order and sends it to an RCLL robot for completion ③.

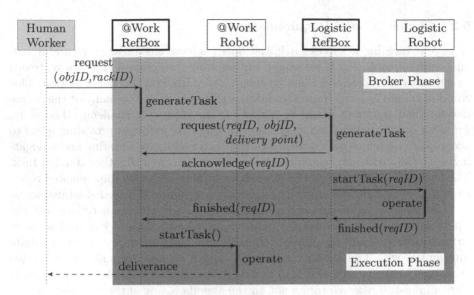

Fig. 5. The sequence diagram depicts the interaction between the @Work and RCLL referee boxes related to an object request. The green part illustrates the generation of the two separate tasks, the blue one their execution. (Color figure online)

Once production is completed, the product is supplied to a shelf or similar in the shared zone and informs the RCLL refbox, which in turn informs the @Work refbox of the availability of the product ④. This informs an @Work robot which picks up the object and puts it into a box, that is then delivered to the human worker ⑤.

A basic requirement for multi-robot cooperation is the capability to communicate with each other. In this scenario, this is handled through the respective refboxes. Robots communicate with their respective refbox and the refboxes with each other. We chose this approach to minimize the teams' efforts. They can keep using the same communication channels as in their respective leagues. While we encourage a common communication infrastructure in the future, enforcing this in the very first cross-over challenge would most likely be a roadblock for some teams. A number of speech acts are required between robots and the refboxes, which are depicted in Fig. 5.

After generating the corresponding task related to the workers request, the @Work refbox transmits the requiered information – Request ID, Object ID and the expected delivery point – to the RCLL refbox. In case of a successful task generation the RCLL refbox acknowledges the request and starts the run. The RCLL refbox will announce the completion if the object is available at the delivery point. At the end, the @Work task is executed, the robot grasps the object and delivers it.

5.2 Challenges and Requirements

A key feature for a successful initiation of a new challenge is a careful balance of its complexity. If we would aim for more integration right away, teams would be overstrained and could be demotivated from further participation. This could also influence the respective leagues themselves, as too many of the scarce development resources would be bound for the cross-over challenge. Therefore, we focus on communication integration through the refboxes providing goals to accomplish for teams within their own respective scenario. Entering and navigating in the shared zone – outside of their arenas – poses a slightly extended task. The execution of the requests by the robots combines already implemented robot capabilities with slight adaptations in order to minimize the needed adjustments.

The scenario addresses several challenges which are characteristic for the smart factory of the future: (a) connect mobile robots and external sensors, (b) integrate different specialized robot systems, and (c) apply an intermediate interaction with human workers. Hence, based on this scenario the intended cross-over challenge is a first step to bridge the gap between the two leagues. It also emphasizes research topics not on the agenda of any of the two leagues, like handling heterogeneity of systems.

The object that can be handled is constrained by the handling capabilities of the RCLL robots and MPS stations. Therefore, the common object used will be of cylindrical shape similar or even the same as in the RCLL. This is intentional in the RCLL to keep the focus on planning and scheduling, rather than mobile manipulation, since this is the very focus of @Work.

The transfer of the object from the RCLL to the @Work robot is a major challenge as the gap in the operational height must be bridged. While RCLL robot operate roughly at table height, the robots in @Work handle objects roughly at the ground level and small shelves. Several options were discussed from active elevators to passive slides. An alternative considered is to use a robot arm to bridge the distance.

An additional node for human input has to be added to the @Work arena. It is required to recognize and interpret the incoming request.

6 Conclusion

Future manufacturing industries that strive to offer production for more individualized goods and generally smaller lot sizes will require more flexibility and a number of new technologies. Such systems will most likely be heterogenous (either due to incremental upgrades to existing production facilities or to avoid vendor lock-in) and at least partially autonomous. Both, the RoboCup Logistics League (RCLL) and RoboCup@Work operate under the premise that autonomous mobile robots will play a role to achieve this goal. They each focus on distinct areas, in particular mobile manipulation in RoboCup@Work and automated multi-robot reasoning, planning, and scheduling in the RCLL.

As a *first step* towards a more heterogenous scenario we propose a *cross-over challenge* that involves robots from both, @Work and the RCLL, each bringing in their particular strengths. The cross-over task has to balance required effort and challenges posed to motivate teams to participate. We propose to base the *first challenge* on the already available referee box used in the two leagues and *focus on communication* to coordinate the robots and devices in both arenas. The interaction is then done through the refbox, such that the teams from the respective leagues do not need to adjust to a new infrastructure initially.

At the moment the *complexity level* of the scenario is *limited intentionally*. We have outlined *four milestones for future development* and closer cooperation and argued that we need to start with a simple motivating scenario. Eventually, the cross-over challenge will cover a larger variety of topics relevant to smart factories than the individual leagues alone. Yet, keeping the two leagues separate allows to foster development on their respective focus areas, automated task planning and mobile manipulation, respectively. The highest level of integration would benefit from the common referee box that is currently being worked on.

The cross-over task does not only pose challenges to participating teams. It requires a major effort by organizing teams and event organizers to create the necessary infrastructure, from aligning the competition arenas, over a handover device, to the refbox communication. This effort is one of the first cooperative projects within the recently established *RoboCup Industrial* umbrella league.

As to the best of our knowledge, such a common challenge and the explicit structure overarching several (comparable) leagues is a novelty in RoboCup. For example, we are not aware of any cross-over game or common organizational structure in robot soccer. Therefore, this project explores new ways of inter-league cooperation, and research and development alignment.

Acknowledgments. T. Niemueller was supported by the German National Science Foundation (DFG) research unit *FOR 1513* on Hybrid Reasoning for Intelligent Systems (https://www.hybrid-reasoning.org).

References

1. Kagermann, H., Wahlster, W., Helbig, J.: Recommendations for implementing the strategic initiative INDUSTRIE 4.0. Final Report, Platform Industrie 4.0 (2013)
2. Beer, R.D., Chiel, H.J., Drushel, R.F.: Using autonomous robotics to teach science and engineering. Commun. ACM **42**(6), 85–92 (1999)
3. Kitano, H., Asada, M., Kuniyoshi, Y., Noda, I., Osawa, E.: RoboCup: the robot world cup initiative (1995)
4. Wisspeintner, T., Van Der Zant, T., Iocchi, L., Schiffer, S.: RoboCup@Home: scientific competition and benchmarking for domestic service robots. J. Interact. Stud. **10**(3), 392–426 (2009)
5. Kraetzschmar, G.K., Hochgeschwender, N., Nowak, W., Hegger, F., Schneider, S., Dwiputra, R., Berghofer, J., Bischoff, R.: RoboCup@Work: competing for the factory of the future. In: Bianchi, R.A.C., Akin, H.L., Ramamoorthy, S., Sugiura, K. (eds.) RoboCup 2014. LNCS (LNAI), vol. 8992, pp. 171–182. Springer, Cham (2015). doi:10.1007/978-3-319-18615-3_14

6. Niemueller, T., Ewert, D., Reuter, S., Ferrein, A., Jeschke, S., Lakemeyer, G.: RoboCup logistics league sponsored by festo: a competitive factory automation testbed. In: Behnke, S., Veloso, M., Visser, A., Xiong, R. (eds.) RoboCup 2013. LNCS (LNAI), vol. 8371, pp. 336–347. Springer, Heidelberg (2014). doi:10.1007/978-3-662-44468-9_30

7. Lucke, D., Constantinescu, C., Westkämper, E.: Smart factory - a step towards the next generation of manufacturing. In: Mitsuishi, M., Ueda, K., Kimura, F. (eds.) Manufacturing Systems and Technologies for the New Frontier. Springer, London (2008). doi:10.1007/978-1-84800-267-8_23

8. Niemueller, T., Lakemeyer, G., Ferrein, A.: The RoboCup logistics league as a benchmark for planning in robotics. In: WS on Planning and Robotics (PlanRob) at International Conference on Automated Planning and Scheduling (ICAPS) (2015)

9. Zwilling, F., Niemueller, T., Lakemeyer, G.: Simulation for the RoboCup logistics league with real-world environment agency and multi-level abstraction. In: Bianchi, R.A.C., Akin, H.L., Ramamoorthy, S., Sugiura, K. (eds.) RoboCup 2014. LNCS (LNAI), vol. 8992, pp. 220–232. Springer, Cham (2015). doi:10.1007/978-3-319-18615-3_18

10. Niemueller, T., Karpas, E., Vaquero, T., Timmons, E.: Planning competition for logistics robots in simulation. In: WS on Planning and Robotics (PlanRob) at International Conference on Automated Planning and Scheduling (ICAPS), London, UK, June 2016

11. Correll, N., Bekris, K.E., Berenson, D., Brock, O., Causo, A., Hauser, K., Okada, K., Rodriguez, A., Romano, J.M., Wurman, P.R.: Lessons from the amazon picking challenge. arXiv preprint arXiv:1601.05484 (2016)

12. Airbus Group: Airbus shopfloor challenge - competition website. http://www.airbusgroup.com/int/en/people-careers/Working-for-Airbus-Group/Airbus-Shopfloor-Challenge-2016.html. Accessed 27 May 2016

13. Amigoni, F., Bastianelli, E., Berghofer, J., Bonarini, A., Fontana, G., Hochgeschwender, N., Iocchi, L., Kraetzschmar, G., Lima, P., Matteucci, M., Miraldo, P., Nardi, D., Schiaffonati, V.: Competitions for benchmarking: task and functionality scoring complete performance assessment. IEEE Robot. Autom. Mag. 22(3), 53–61 (2015)

14. Schneider, S., Hegger, F., Hochgeschwender, N., Dwiputra, R., Moriarty, A., Berghofer, J., Kraetzschmar, G.K.: Design and development of a benchmarking testbed for the factory of the future. In: 20th IEEE Conference on Emerging Technologies Factory Automation (ETFA), September 2015

15. Niemueller, T., Lakemeyer, G., Reuter, S., Jeschke, S., Ferrein, A.: Benchmarking of cyber-physical systems in industrial robotics - the RoboCup logistics league as a CPS benchmark blueprint. In: Cyber-Physical Systems - Foundations, Principles, and Applications. Elsevier (2017, to appear)

16. Niemueller, T., Lakemeyer, G., Ferrein, A., Reuter, S., Ewert, D., Jeschke, S., Pensky, D., Karras, U.: Proposal for advancements to the LLSF in 2014 and beyond. In: ICAR - 1st Workshop on Developments in RoboCup Leagues (2013)

17. Yamashita, A., Arai, T., Ota, J., Asama, H.: Motion planning of multiple mobile robots for cooperative manipulation and transportation. IEEE Trans. Robot. Autom. 19(2), 223–237 (2003)

Dynaban, an Open-Source Alternative Firmware for Dynamixel Servo-Motors

Rémi Fabre, Quentin Rouxel[✉], Grégoire Passault, Steve N'Guyen,
and Olivier Ly

Rhoban Football Club Team, LaBRI, University of Bordeaux, Bordeaux, France
{remi.fabre,quentin.rouxel}@labri.fr

Abstract. In this paper, we present an alternative open-source firmware for the Dynamixel MX-64 servo-motor. We discuss software features to fully exploit the hardware capabilities of the device. In order to enhance the default controller, a friction model and an electric model of the motor are embedded into the firmware. The parameters of the model are found using a black-box optimization algorithm. A feed-forward method is proposed to follow position, speed and torque trajectories. The approach is tested with a highly dynamic kick movement on our humanoid soccer robot *Sigmaban* whose torque trajectories are computed using a classic rigid body inverse dynamics. The comparison between the default control strategy and the proposed one shows significant improvements in terms of accuracy, delay and repeatability.

Keywords: Open-source · Model-based control · RoboCup · Humanoid robot

1 Introduction

Servo-motors offer a full turnkey solution for controlling electric motors and are heavily used in the field of robotics. Commercial servo-motors are the most common, but their proprietary firmware can't be enriched by the community and limits the realm of possible. The default control approach typically relies on angular feed-back and a Proportional-Integral-Derivative (PID) controller. This method is easy to use and offers good results when static positions are needed but is unsatisfactory when following complex trajectories which tend to be delayed and distorted. In particular, humanoid robots often call for precise, highly dynamic and torque-heavy movements. Achieving these with the out-of-the-box controller has proven to be difficult.

Instead of waiting for an angular error to appear, a feed-forward (FF) approach preemptively sends a command that produces the predicted torque to follow a given trajectory. To achieve that, the internal behavior of the motor must be modeled and the external torques and moments must be accounted for. The PID controller is only used to compensate unforeseen perturbations and model's inaccuracies.

© Springer International Publishing AG 2017
S. Behnke et al. (Eds.): RoboCup 2016, LNAI 9776, pp. 169–177, 2017.
https://doi.org/10.1007/978-3-319-68792-6_14

In this paper we present an open-source firmware[1] for the Dynamixel MX-64 servo-motor that is fully compatible[2] with the default one. Advanced features and possible enhancements are discussed but the main focus is given to the embedded implementation of a feed-forward control strategy. A friction model and an electric model of the motor are chosen. A wide set of detailed measures is taken and the CMA-ES evolutionary algorithm is used to identify the model's parameters. As application, a mechanical model of the humanoid robot *Sigmaban* [1] is used and the inverse dynamics of a football kick are computed[3]. Finally, the kick is played on the robot and the impact of the method is quantified.

1.1   Related Works

Open projects related to servo-motors have been around for years. OpenServo[4] is a mature project that offers low cost electronic boards but uses an 8-bit micro-controller that lacks the computational power of the ARM cortex M3 found in the Dynamixel. The DDServo project[5] [7] provides open hardware and firmware for the RX-28 and RX-64 motors, advanced control techniques are discussed and simulated but are not implemented. The Morpheus firmware[6] is an alternative firmware for the AX12 servomotor. A detailed friction characterization was carried by [6] and was used to choose a friction model. A model of the AX12 servo-motor was detailed in [4]. Schwarz and Behnke [3] use an ideal DC motor model and friction model covering the Stribeck effect.

The presented adds the inertia of the motor and its gear-box which, given the high ratio of the gear-box, appears to be meaningful. The main novelty of the proposed approach is the integration of a model-based feed-forward control into the original micro-controller instead of using the servo-motor as a black-box. Moreover, an offline evolutionary algorithm[7] is used in order to fit the model to an arbitrary rich set of measures. The quality of the results is of an order of magnitude better than what was achieved by hand-tuning the parameters.

2   An Open Source Firmware

Current Sensing: An interesting announced feature of the MX-64 series is the current sensing. Since the current is proportional to the torque, one would think that the servo-motor can be torque controlled. Unfortunately, testing the servo-motor with its default firmware proved otherwise. A high precision resistor of $5\,m\Omega$ called *rSense* is connected in series with the motor. The resistor's voltage is amplified and read through an Analog to Digital Conversion (ADC) pin.

---

[1] Dynaban: https://github.com/RhobanProject/Dynaban.

[2] http://support.robotis.com/en/product/dynamixel/mx_series/mx-64.htm.

[3] Rigid Body Dynamics Library: http://rbdl.bitbucket.org/.

[4] OpenServo project: http://www.openservo.com/.

[5] DDServo project: https://github.com/wojtusch/DDServo.

[6] Morpheus firmware: https://actuated.wordpress.com/ax12firmware/.

[7] CMA-ES Library: https://www.lri.fr/~hansen/html-pythoncma/.

The current appears to be very noisy and asymmetrical with the sign of the rotational speed. External measures showed that the current sensing issues are hardware related. Much better results were recorded when the *rSense* was held a few centimeters away from the motor and connected with copper cables. In the presented work, the current measure is considered unreliable as a feed-back information with the default electronics and thus not used.

High Precision and High Frequency Measures: When recording a physical value from a servo-motor with the default firmware, the delay between the actual measure and the moment the read is performed through the serial bus is poorly known. Moreover, the frequency of the measure is dependent on the communication bus. An open firmware allows for very specific, hardware time-stamped, high frequency measures. For instance, it is possible to read the current position at a frequency of 10 kHz, store the values in RAM for the duration of the experiment and send the values to the user through the serial port.

Model Based Estimation of the Torque Produced by the Motor: While the current measure proved to be unreliable, it is still possible to estimate the produced torque with a model-based approach. Knowing the voltage applied by the Pulse Width Modulation (PWM) signal and knowing the current speed, the model can estimate the electrical torque created by the motor and the friction torque. These values are updated at 1 kHz and are available to the user through the communication protocol.

The average speed is used where the instantaneous speed is needed, therefore a strong trade-off between precision and delay is present. Taylor expansion based algorithms, and Kalman filter based algorithms [2] are a few options that may enhance the speed estimation in a future work.

Feed-Forward Trajectory Control Mode: The embedded electrical and friction models can be used to follow position, speed and torque trajectories simultaneously. Knowing $\omega(t)$, $\omega(t + dt)$ and $\tau_o(t + dt)$ the needed command voltage can be calculated:

$$u(t + dt) = k_e \times \omega(t) + \frac{R}{k_e} \times (\tau_o(t) + \tau_a(t) + \tau_f(t)) \qquad (1)$$

$$\tau_a(t) = \frac{\omega(t + dt) - \omega(t)}{dt} \times I_0 \qquad (2)$$

where ω is the rotational speed, τ_o is the output goal torque set by the user, τ_a is the torque needed to accelerate the rotating parts of the motor which moment of inertia I_0 is a model parameter (empty shaft, gear box) and τ_f is the friction torque given by the friction model. R and k_e are constants of the DC motor.

The user is responsible for providing ahead of time a position and a torque trajectory to the firmware. The torque trajectory provided is the torque needed to accelerate the objects attached to the motor and also needed to oppose the torques applied on the motor's shaft (weight, inertia, contacts). The firmware is responsible for deducing the voltage command needed to accelerate the motor rotating parts (shaft, gear box).

The chosen trajectory representation is polynomial. The trajectories are communicated to the firmware as a 4th order polynomial for the trajectory position and a 4th order polynomial (5 float values) for the torque trajectory. The speed trajectory is internally deduced by derivation of the first polynomial. Trajectories are typically 150 ms long although the duration is user-configurable for each trajectory. A second set of polynomials can be buffered into the firmware to allow for continuous transitions between several trajectories.

In this mode, the speed is never deduced from the encoder, making the model's contribution to the voltage command a full open-loop feed-forward approach. The loop is closed in 2 ways:

A PID controller whose goal is solely to follow the position trajectory is used in parallel. The actual voltage command is the sum of the two contributions. (PID + FF) If the PID command is strongly opposite to the model-based command, the second will be ignored until their contributions are compatible. To avoid instability injections with this method, an hysteresis is used to decide the switching ON or OFF of the model contribution.

The user can take corrective actions in the next trajectory (150 ms later) and even choose to stop the current trajectory playing at any time.

3   Models

3.1   DC Motor

The chosen model for the Direct Current (DC) motor has only 2 parameters and expresses the classical linear trade-off between speed and torque at a given voltage U. R is the terminal resistance and k_e is the back-EMF constant

$$U = \tau \times \frac{R}{k_e} + k_e \times w \tag{3}$$

3.2   Friction

In [6] it was shown that the model (Fig. 1) was a good fit for geared transmissions at low speeds but failed at high speeds. The non-linearity between friction torque and speed that is responsible for the mismatch was not observed in the speed range of the motor, probably because the maximum speed of the motor (410 deg/s) is low enough to avoid it. Therefore, the classical Stribeck effect based friction model was chosen. In order to simplify the model and reduce its computational impact on the micro-controller, the parameter δ was fixed to 1 in Eq. 4. The same simplification was done by [3] (Fig. 2).

$$\tau_f = k_{vis} \times \omega \ - \ sign(\omega) \times (\beta \times \tau_s + (1 - \beta) \times \tau_{cc}) \qquad \beta = e^{-|\frac{\omega}{\omega_{lin}}|^{\delta}} \tag{4}$$

where ω_{lin} is the parameter defining the area of influence of the Stribeck effect, k_{vis} is the viscous friction constant and τ_{cc} satisfies: $\tau_f(\omega_{lin}) = \tau_c$.

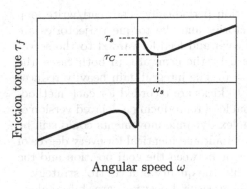

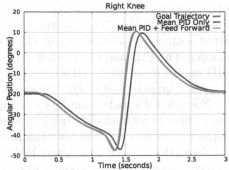

Fig. 1. Classic friction model   **Fig. 2.** Average right knee trajectory

4 Model Fitting

In order to quantify the validity of the actuator models and determine its parameters the following steps are followed:

A set of 113 measures of 1 s each are performed on a MX-64 servo-motor with nothing attached to its shaft. Predefined voltage command trajectories are implanted in the firmware and are followed and recorded with a 0.1 ms precision hardware timer. Three types of command trajectories are used, flat step commands (in order to have constant speeds), saw-tooth patterns and brutal step changes (in order to create important accelerations).

The exact same measures are recorded again on the same MX-64 with a load of approximately 0.28 kg at 12 cm.

A simple motor simulator is implemented using the electrical model and the friction model. The simulator is used to replay the voltage commands and estimate the motor position. A Root Mean Square (RMS) error is then computed for each one of the 226 measures. Therefore, a fitness function is computed. The function takes 7 model parameters (k_e, r, k_{vis}, τ_s, τ_{cc}, w_{lin}, I_0) and returns a score quantifying the quality of the model relative to a set of measures.

The CMA-ES python implementation is then used in order to maximize the fitness function. A previously hand-tuned set of model parameters is used as the starting point. Activating the restart strategy, specifying a standard deviation for each parameter and having a good starting set of model parameters are the three most important options to get the algorithm to perform well. The best match has a score 56 times better than the hand tuned solution.

5 Experimenting a Highly Dynamic Kick on Sigmaban

A dynamic kick motion is generated off-line. Standard inverse dynamics are used on a robot model to compute a torque trajectory for all degrees of freedom. The robot begins and ends the movement in single support on the left leg in a statically stable posture. The positions are sent to the motors with the classic

PID approach by updating the goal position periodically. The read/write loop frequency is 100 Hz. The position trajectories and the torque trajectories are fitted with cubic polynomials of 150 ms each and feed-forwarded to the servo-motors. The PID and the models are used by the firmware. In both cases, the PID gains are set to $P = 16$, $I = 1$, $D = 0$. The integral gain heavily reduces the static error on the starting position. 10 kicks are recorded for each method.

Note that if a control method was capable of reproducing a delayed version of the command without deforming it, complex dynamic movements could still be performed as long as the delay remains constant and identical for every degree of freedom (DoF). Therefore, a raw RMS error between the goal position and the measured position is not enough to quantify the quality of a control strategy.

For each measure and for each DoF, the measured positions are shifted along the time axis until their correlation with the goal trajectory is maximum. The shift value expresses the time delay, while the RMS error of the shifted measures expresses the deformation relatively to the ideal trajectory. The delay and the deformation are averaged over the 10 measures (Fig. 3).

The Cartesian trajectories of the right foot and the trunk are considered in a similar way.

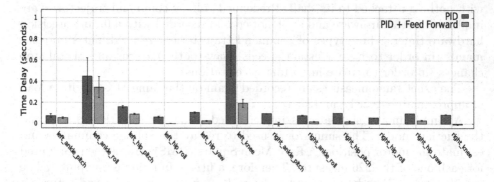

Fig. 3. Delays (and standard deviation) for each DoF and control strategy

The delay appears to be significantly reduced when the feed-forward control is used. The right_knee, which is the DoF performing the most dynamic trajectory, has an average delay of 86 ms with the PID only approach whereas its average delay is −8 ms with the feed-forward approach. The average delay for all DoFs with the PID only approach is 91 ms against 23 ms with the feed-forward control.

Note that the DoFs left_ankle_roll and left_knee have almost flat position trajectories during the kick, therefore their calculated delay is very noise depen-dent and will be ignored in the results interpretation. This is consistent with the fact that the delay's standard deviation is several times higher with these two DoFs. Also, note that a negative delay can be measured when the feed-forward overcompensates the command (Figs. 4 and 5).

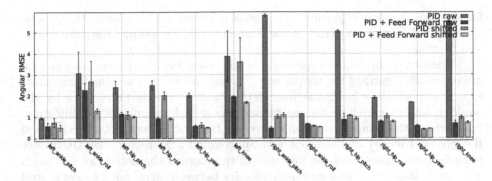

Fig. 4. RMS error (in degrees) (and standard deviations) for each DoF and control strategy, with and without time shifting

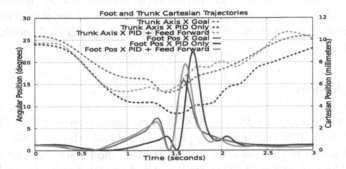

Fig. 5. Average trajectories in Cartesian space of the trunk orientation and kicking foot position for each control strategy

Once the measures are time shifted, the RMS error gap between the two approaches reduces. The first strategy (PI) has an average deformation error value of 0.95 against 0.74 for the second (PI + FF). Moreover, while the standard deviation of the deformation is comparable between the 2 approaches for low torque DoFs (kicking right leg servos), it is 3 times higher with the PID approach for high torque DoFs (supporting left leg servos). Therefore, the model-based control offers a better repeatability, especially when the applied torques are high.

When considering the Cartesian trajectory of the right foot and of the trunk, the average delay found for the PID approach is 80 ms against 0 ms with the feedforward (here, the delay was found by minimizing the RMS while time-shifting the curve with a step of 5 ms). The RMS error of the shifted PID trajectory is 46% higher than the RMS error of the second method (0.57 against 0.39). This value represents the deformation of the overall kick motion.

The enhancements in terms of deformation were expected. A PI controller creates a non-constant delay, which increases when high speed variations and high torques are applied, thus deforming the output trajectory. In contrast, the feed-forward approach preemptively sends a command to achieve the needed speed to follow the trajectory while compensating for output torques, inertia and friction.

Notice that the whole experiment could have benefited from an external ground-truth regarding the torque and position measures. The remaining errors can be explained as being the sum of the models imperfections, both by the model itself not matching the reality and the model parameters identification. Specifically, the temperature's influence on the system was not included and the physical model of the robot was approximate. Moreover, the DC motor manufacturer states[8] that the tolerance of the motor's characteristics can reach $+/-10\%$, important hardware discrepancies between servo-motors were indeed measured. Therefore, an improvement of the presented method would be to find a set of model parameters for each servo-motor. Finally, the backlash was not accounted for. While most of the backlash comes from the gearbox and is detected by the encoder, the short and brutal modifications of friction created by the backlash are not handled. A backlash hysteresis model [5] could be tried in future work.

6   Conclusion

The open source firmware for the MX-64 servo-motor presented in this paper is meant to be a tool offering a complete control over the actuator. A simple electric DC motor model and a traditional friction model are embedded into the firmware. The parameter identification method, which uses a black box optimization algorithm and a wide set of generic measures, proved to be much more accurate than what was achieved through specific measures and hand tuning. A combined feed-forward and feed-back implementation is tested on the humanoid robot Sigmaban with a highly dynamic football kick whose inverse dynamics is calculated. When compared to a PI controller, the proposed approach absorbs almost all the delay, significantly reduces the deformation and enhances the repeatability of heavy torque movements.

Acknowledgment. The authors would like to thank Stéphane Ygorra for his help and guidance in the project.

References

1. Fabre, R., Gimbert, H., Gondry, L., Hofer, L., Ly, O., N'Guyen, S., Passault, G., Rouxel, Q.: Rhoban football club team - description paper (2016)
2. Pan, M.-C., Lin, Y.F.: Further exploration of Vold-Kalman-filtering order tracking with shaft-speed information-ii: engineering applications. Mech. Syst. Sig. Process. **20**(6), 1410–1428 (2006)

---

[8] Motor data and operating ranges of maxon DC motors: http://www.maxonmotor.com/academy.

3. Schwarz, M., Behnke, S.: Compliant robot behavior using servo actuator models identified by iterative learning control. In: Behnke, S., Veloso, M., Visser, A., Xiong, R. (eds.) RoboCup 2013. LNCS, vol. 8371, pp. 207–218. Springer, Heidelberg (2014). doi:10.1007/978-3-662-44468-9_19
4. Mensink, A.: Characterization and modeling of a dynamixel servo. In: Technical report, University of Twente (2008)
5. Ahmad, N.J., Khorrami, F.: Adaptive control of systems with backlash hysteresis at the input. In: American Control Conference (1999)
6. Waiboer, R., Aarts, R., Jonker, B.: Velocity dependence of joint friction in robotic manipulators with gear transmissions. In: ECCOMAS Thematic Conference Multibody Dynamics (2005)
7. Wojtusch, J.: Development of electronics and control for servo actuators in robotic applications. In: Diploma Thesis (2011)

Poster Presentations

RoCKIn and the European Robotics League: Building on RoboCup Best Practices to Promote Robot Competitions in Europe

Pedro U. Lima[1]([✉]), Daniele Nardi[2], Gerhard K. Kraetzschmar[3], Rainer Bischoff[4], and Matteo Matteucci[5]

[1] Instituto Superior Técnico, Universidade de Lisboa, Lisbon, Portugal
pedro.lima@tecnico.ulisboa.pt
[2] Università di Roma La Sapienza, Rome, Italy
nardi@dis.uniroma1.it
[3] Bonn-Rhein-Sieg University, Sankt Augustin, Germany
gerhard.kraetzschmar@h-brs.de
[4] KUKA Roboter GmbH, Augsburg, Germany
Rainer.Bischoff@kuka.com
[5] Politecnico di Milano, Milano, Italy
matteo.matteucci@polimi.it

Abstract. This paper describes activities that promote robot competitions in Europe, using and expanding RoboCup concepts and best practices, through two projects funded by the European Commission under its FP7 and Horizon2020 programmes. The RoCKIn project ended in December 2015 and its goal was to speed up the progress towards smarter robots through scientific competitions. Two challenges have been selected for the competitions due to their high relevance and impact on Europes societal and industrial needs: domestic service robots (RoCKIn@Home) and innovative robot applications in industry (RoCKIn@Work). RoCKIn extended the corresponding RoboCup leagues by introducing new and prevailing research topics, such as networking mobile robots with sensors and actuators spread over the environment, in addition to specifying objective scoring and benchmark criteria and methods to assess progress. The European Robotics League (ERL) started recently and includes indoor competitions related to domestic and industrial robots, extending RoCKIn's rulebooks. Teams participating in the ERL must compete in at least two tournaments per year, which can take place either in a certified test bed (i.e., based on the rulebooks) located in a European laboratory, or as part of a major robot competition event. The scores accumulated by the teams in their best two participations are used to rank them over an year.

Keywords: Robot competitions · Benchmarking · Domestic robots · Industrial robots

© Springer International Publishing AG 2017
S. Behnke et al. (Eds.): RoboCup 2016, LNAI 9776, pp. 181–192, 2017.
https://doi.org/10.1007/978-3-319-68792-6_15

1 Introduction

In 2012, under its 7th Framework Programme (FP7), the European Commission (EC) launched a first Call for Coordination Actions to foster research in robotics and benchmarking through robot competitions. A consortium composed of six partners (five of which represented by the authors of this abstract) applied and got funding for a three-year project that ended successfully in December 2015.

The goal of RoCKIn[1] (Robot Competitions Kick Innovation in Cognitive Systems and Robotics) was to speed up the progress towards smarter robots through scientific competitions. Two challenges have been selected for the competitions due to their high relevance and impact on Europes societal and industrial needs: domestic service robots (RoCKIn@Home) and innovative robot applications in industry (RoCKIn@Work). As it is clear from the designations, both challenges were inspired by activities in the RoboCup community, but RoCKIn extended them by introducing new and prevailing research topics, such as networking mobile robots with sensors and actuators spread over the environment, in addition to specifying objective scoring and benchmark criteria and methods to assess progress. RoCKIn goal was to bring back to RoboCup some of these newly introduced aspects, and this is currently happening through negotiations with the RoboCup@Home and RoboCup@Work technical committees. Moreover, at least three new RoCKIn teams that had not participated in RoboCup@Work and RoboCup@Home before applied and qualified to RoboCup 2016.

The RoCKIn project has taken the lead in boosting scientific robot competitions in Europe by (i) specifying and designing open domain test beds for competitions targeting the two challenges and usable by researchers worldwide; (ii) developing methods for scoring and benchmarking through competitions that allow to assess both particular subsystems as well as the integrated system; and (iii) organizing camps whose main objective was to build up a community of new teams interested to participate in robot competitions.

Within the project lifetime, two competition events took place, each of them based on the two challenges and their respective test beds: RoCKIn Competition 2014 (in Toulouse, France) and RoCKIn Competition 2015 (in Lisbon, Portugal), with the participation of 12 teams and more than 100 participants. Three camps were also organized, in 2013 (Eindhoven, together with RoboCup 2013), 2014 (Rome) and 2015 (Peccioli, Italy, at the ECHORD++ Robotics Innovation Facility).

A significant number of dissemination activities on the relevance of robot competitions were carried out to promote research and education in the field, targeting the research community, in industry and academia, as well as the general public. The potential future impact of the benchmarking methods developed on robotics research was recognized by many researchers worldwide, and an article on the topic was published in the Special Issue on Replicable and Measurable Robotics Research of the IEEE Robotics and Automation Magazine in 2015 [1].

---

[1] http://rockinrobotchallenge.eu.

RoCKIn's success was a consequence of the experience accumulated over the years in RoboCup by the consortium members as organizers and participants of the respective RoboCup competitions. The lessons learned during RoCKIn paved the way for a step forward in the organization and research impact of robot competitions. The authors expect many of these to be brought back to RoboCup, improving the quality and impact of the @Home and @Work leagues.

A continuation of RoCKIn is already under way, based on the European Robotics League (ERL) concept, again funded by the EC under the new Horizon2020 (H2020) programme. Teams participating in the ERL must compete in at least two tournaments per year, which can take place either in a certified test bed (i.e. based on ERL/RoCKIn's rulebooks) located in a European research laboratory, or as part of a major robot competition event. The scores accumulated by the teams in the best two participations are used to rank them, leading to the awarding of prizes during the annual European Robotics Forum event. This brings extra visibility to robot competitions and to RoboCup in Europe, since we plan to hold some of the major tournaments as part of RoboCup world or regional events.

This paper highlights the main contributions of RoCKIn to benchmarking robotics research through robot competitions: task and functionality benchmarks, as well as the corresponding benchmarking methods, are introduced in Sect. 2. Scoring methods and metrics are described in Sect. 3, rulebooks, test beds and datasets in Sect. 4. Camps and competition events major outcomes are referred in Sect. 5. Section 6 concludes the paper with an outlook to the new concept for robot competitions currently underway in Europe: the European Robotics League.

2 Task and Functionality Benchmarks

RoCKIn's approach to benchmarking experiments is based on the definition of two separate, but interconnected, types of benchmarks [2]:

- Functionality Benchmarks, which evaluate the performance of hardware and software modules dedicated to single, specific functionalities in the context of experiments focused on such functionalities.
- Task Benchmarks, which assess the performance of integrated robot systems facing complex tasks that usually require the interaction of different functionalities.

Functionality Benchmarks are certainly the closest to a scientific experiment from among the two. This is due to their much more controlled setting and execution. On the other side, these specific aspects of Functionality Benchmarks limit their capability to capture all the important aspects of the overall robot performance in a systemic way. More specifically, emerging system-level properties, such as the quality of integration between modules, cannot be assessed with Functionality Benchmarks alone. For this reason, the RoCKIn Competitions integrate them with Task Benchmarks.

In particular, evaluating only the performance of integrated system is interesting for the application, but it does not allow to evaluate the single modules that are contributing to the global performance, nor to put in evidence the aspects needed to push their development forward. On the other side, the good performance of a module does not necessarily mean that it will perform well in the integrated system. For this reason, the RoCKIn benchmarking competitions target both aspects, and enable a deeper analysis of a robot system by combining system-level and module-level benchmarking.

System-level and module-level tests do not investigate the same properties of a robot. Module-level testing has the benefit of focusing only on the specific functionality that a module is devoted to, removing interferences due to the performance of other modules which are intrinsically connected at the system level. For instance, if the grasping performance of a mobile manipulator is tested by having it autonomously navigate to the grasping position, visually identify the item to be picked up, and finally grasp it, the effectiveness of the grasping functionality is affected by the actual position where the navigation module stopped the robot, and by the precision of the vision module in retrieving the pose and shape of the item. On the other side, if the grasping benchmark is executed by placing the robot in a predefined known position and by feeding it with precise information about the item to be picked up, the final result will be almost exclusively due to the performance of the grasping module itself. The first benchmark can be considered as a system-level benchmark, because it involves more than one functionality of the robot, and thus has limited worth as a benchmark of the grasping functionality. On the contrary, the latter test can assess the performance of the grasping module with minimal interference from other modules and a high repeatability: it can be classified as module-level benchmark.

Let us consider an imaginary, simplified RoCKIn Competition including five tasks $(T_1, T_2, \ldots, T_5)$. Figure 1 describes such imaginary competition as a matrix, showing the tasks as columns while the rows correspond to the functionalities required to successfully execute the tasks. For the execution of the whole set of tasks of this imaginary RoCKIn Competition, four different functionalities $(F_1, \ldots, F_4)$ are required; however, a single task usually requires only a subset of these functionalities. In Fig. 1, task T_X requires functionality F_Y if a black dot is present at the crossing between column x and row y. For instance, task T_2 does not require functionalities F_2 and F_4, while task T_4 does not require functionality F_1.

The availability of both task and functionality rankings opens the way for the quantitative analysis of the importance of single functionalities in performing complex tasks. This is an innovative aspect triggered by the RoCKIn approach to competitions. To state the importance of a functionality in performing a given task, RoCKIn borrows the concept of Shapley value from Game theory [5]. Let us assume that a coalition of players (functionalities in the RoCKIn context) cooperates, and obtains a certain overall gain from that cooperation (the Task Benchmark scoring in the RoCKIn context). Since some players may contribute

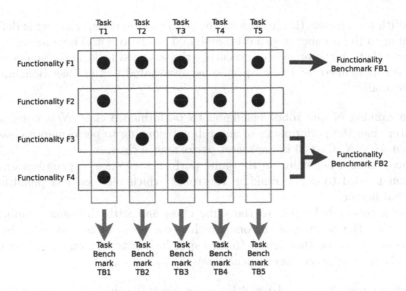

Fig. 1. Functionalities vs Tasks Matrix.

more to the coalition than others or may possess different bargaining power (for example threatening to destroy the whole surplus), what final distribution of generated surplus among the players should arise in any particular game? Or phrased differently: how important is each player to the overall cooperation, and what payoff can (s)he reasonably expect? Or in the RoCKIn jargon: how important is each functionality to the reach a given performance in a Task Benchmark?

Assuming that all scores are expressed according to the same scale, the Shapley values of the single functionalities can be calculated as:

$$\Phi_i = \frac{1}{n!} \sum_\pi [\nu(C_\pi(i) \cup i) - \nu(C_\pi(i))] \tag{1}$$

where i is a functionality, n is the total number of functionalities, π is a permutation of the n Functionality Benchmark scores, $C_\pi(i)$ is the set of functionalities that precede i in the permutation π, and $\nu()$ is the score of the set of functionalities specified as argument. Examples of the application of Shapley values to task benchmarking can be found in RoCKIn deliverable D1.2 [2].

3   Scoring Methods and Metrics

The scoring framework for the evaluation of the task performance in RoCKIn competitions is the same for all tasks of RoCKIn@Home and RoCKIn@Work, and it is based on the concept of performance classes used for the ranking of robot performance in a specific task.

The performance class that a robot is assigned to is determined by the number of achievements (or goals) that the robot reaches during its execution of the task. Within each class (i.e., a performance equivalence class), ranking is defined according to the number of penalties assigned to the robot. These are assigned to robots that, in the process of executing the assigned task, make one or more of the errors defined by a task–specific list associated to the Task Benchmark. More formally:

- The ranking of any robot belonging to performance class N is considered better than the performance of any robot belonging to performance class M when $M < N$. Class 0 is the lowest performance class.
- Among robots belonging to the same performance class, a penalization criterion is used to define ranking: the robot which received less penalties is ranked higher.
- Among robots belonging to the same class and with the same number of penalties, the ranking of the one which accomplished the task in a shorter time is considered the highest (unless specific constraints on execution time are given as achievements or penalties).

Performance classes and penalties for a Task Benchmark are indeed task-specific, but they are grouped according to the following three sets (of which here we define the semantics; the actual content is specific to each Benchmark):

- set DB = disqualifying behaviors, i.e. things that the robot must not do;
- set A = achievements (also called goals), i.e., things that the robot should do;
- set PB = penalizing behaviors, i.e., things that the robot should not do.

Once the content of each of the previous sets is provided as part of the specifications of the relevant Task Benchmark, the following 3-step sorting algorithm is used to apply the RoCKIn scoring framework:

1. if one or more of the disqualifying behaviors of set DB occur during task execution, the robot gets disqualified (i.e., assigned to class 0, the lowest possible performance class), and no further scoring procedures are performed for it;
2. the robot is assigned to performance class X, where X corresponds to the number of achievements of set A which have been accomplished by the robot;
3. a penalization is assigned to the robot for each behavior of the robot belonging to set PB that occurs during the execution of the task.

One key property of this scoring system is that a robot that executes the required task completely will always be placed into a higher performance class than a robot that executes the task partially. In fact, penalties do not change the performance class assigned to a robot and only influence intra-class ranking.

It is not possible to define a single scoring framework for all Functionality Benchmarks as it has been done for Task Benchmarks in the previous chapter. These, in fact, are specialized benchmarks, tightly focused on a single functionality, assessing how it operates and not (or not only) the final result of its operation. As a consequence, scoring mechanisms for Functionality Benchmarks cannot ignore how the functionality operates, and metrics are strictly connected to the features of the functionality. For this reason, differently from what has been done for Task Benchmarks scoring methodologies and metrics are defined separately for each Functionality Benchmark of a Competition. In RoCKIn, Functionality Benchmarks are defined by four elements:

- Description: a high level, general, description of the functionality.
- Input/Output: the information available to the module implementing the functionality when executed, and the expected outcome.
- Benchmarking data: the data needed to perform the evaluation of the performance of the functional module.
- Metrics: algorithms to process benchmarking data in an objective way.

RoCKIn Deliverable D1.2 [2] provides more details and examples on scoring and ranking team performance in task and functionalities, as well as methods to combine task rankings to determine the competition winner.

4   Rulebooks, Test Beds and Datasets

The RoCKIn@Home test bed (see Fig. 2) consists of the environment in which the competitions took place, including all the objects and artefacts in the environment, and the equipment brought into the environment for benchmarking purposes. An aspect that is comparatively new in robot competitions is that RoCKIn@Home is, to the best of our knowledge, the first open competition targeting an environment with ambient intelligence, i.e. the environment is equipped with networked electronic devices (lamps, motorised blinds, IP cams) the robot can communicate and interact with, and which allow the robot to exert control on certain environment artefacts.

Fig. 2. RoCKIn@Home test bed: left - 3D layout; right - real setup

The RoCKIn@Home rulebook [3] specifies in detail:

- The environment structure and properties (e.g., spatial arrangement, dimensions, walls).

- Task-relevant objects in the environment, split in three classes:
    - Navigation-relevant objects: objects which have extent in physical space and do (or may) intersect (in 3D) with the robots navigation space, and which must be avoided by the robots.
    - Manipulation-relevant objects: objects that the robot may have manipulative interactions (e.g., touching, grasping, lifting, holding, pushing, pulling) with.
    - Perception-relevant objects: objects that the robot must only be able to perceive (in the sense of detecting the object by classifying it into a class, e.g., a can; recognizing the object as a particular instance of that class, e.g., a 7UP can; and localizing the object pose in a pre-determined environment reference frame.)

During the benchmark runs executed in the test bed, a human referee enforces the rules. This referee must have a way to transmit his decisions to the robot, and receive some progress information. To achieve this in a practical way, an assistant referee is seated at a computer and communicates verbally with the main referee. The assistant referee uses the main Referee Scoring and Benchmarking Box (RSBB). Besides basic starting and stopping functionality, the RSBB is also designed to receive scoring input and provide fine grained benchmark control for functionality benchmarks that require so.

The RoCKIn@Work test bed (Fig. 3) consists of the environment in which the competitions took place (the RoCKIn'N'RoLLIn medium-sized factory, specialized in production of small- to medium-sized lots of mechanical parts and assembled mechatronic products, integrating incoming shipments of damaged or unwanted products and raw material in its production line), including all the objects and artefacts in the environment, and the equipment brought into the environment for benchmarking purposes. An aspect that is comparatively new in robot competitions is that RoCKIn@Work is, to the best of our knowledge, the first industry-oriented robot competition targeting an environment with ambient intelligence, i.e. the environment is equipped with networked electronic devices (e.g., a drilling machine, a conveyor belt, a force-fitting machine, a quality control camera) the robot can communicate and interact with, and which allow the robot to exert control on certain environment artefacts like conveyor belts or machines.

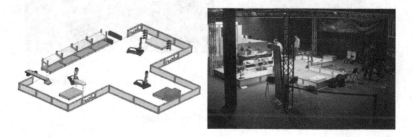

Fig. 3. RoCKIn@Work test bed: left - 3D layout; right - real setup.

The RoCKIn@Work rulebook [4] specifies in detail:

- The environment structure and properties (e.g., spatial arrangement, dimensions, walls).
- Typical factory objects in the environment to manipulate and to recognize.

The main idea of the RoCKIn@Work test bed software infrastructure is to have a central server-like hub (the RoCKIn@Work Central Factory Hub or CFH) that serves all the services that are needed for executing and scoring tasks and successfully realize the competition. This hub is derived from software systems well known in industrial business (e.g., SAP). It provides the robots with information regarding the specific tasks and tracks the production process as well as stock and logistics information of the RoCKIn'N'RoLLIn factory. It is a plug-in driven software system. Each plug-in is responsible for a specific task, functionality or other benchmarking module.

Both RoCKIn test beds include benchmarking equipment. RoCKIn benchmarking is based on the processing of data collected in two ways:

- internal benchmarking data, collected by the robot system under test;
- external benchmarking data, collected by the equipment embedded into the test bed.

External benchmarking data is generated by the RoCKIn test bed with a multitude of methods, depending on their nature. One of the types of external benchmarking data used by RoCKIn are pose data about robots and/or their constituent parts. To acquire these, RoCKIn uses a camera-based commercial motion capture system (MCS), composed of dedicated hardware and software. Benchmarking data has the form of a time series of poses of rigid elements of the robot (such as the base or the wrist). Once generated by the MCS system, pose data are acquired and logged by a customized external software system based on ROS (Robot Operating System): more precisely, logged data is saved as bagfiles created with the rosbag utility provided by ROS. Pose data is especially significant because it is used for multiple benchmarks. There are other types of external benchmarking data that RoCKIn acquires; however, these are usually collected using devices that are specific to the benchmark. Finally, equipment to collect external benchmarking data includes any server which is part of the test bed and that the robot subjected to a benchmark has to access as part of the benchmark. Communication between servers and robot is performed via the test bed's own wireless network.

During RoCKIn competitions and events, several datasets have been collected to be redistributed to the Robotics community for further analysis and understanding about the Task level and Functional level performance of robotics systems. In particular, data from the Object Perception (@Home and @Work) and Speech Understanding Functional Benchmarks was collected during RoCKIn Competition 2014 and RoCKIn Field Exercise 2015. The datasets are available and will continue to be updated in the RoCKIn wiki[2].

---

[2] http://thewiki.rockinrobotchallenge.eu/index.php?title=Datasets.

RoCKIn Deliverables D2.1.3 [3] and D2.1.6 [4] provide the full rulebooks for the two Challenges, including details of the RSBB and CFH referee boxes and pointers to the deliverables where details of the MCS and benchmarking system are available.

5   RoCKIn Camps and Competitions

Within the project lifetime, two competition events took place, each of them based on the two challenges and their respective test beds:

- RoCKIn 2014, in La Cité de L'Espace, Toulouse, 24–30 November 2014: 10 teams (7 @Home, 3 @Work) and 79 participants from 6 countries.
- RoCKIn 2015, in the Portugal Pavilion, Lisbon, Portugal, 17–23 November 2015: 12 teams (9 @Home, 3 @Work) and 93 participants from 10 countries.

Organizing each of the competition events followed and improved established RoboCup best practices for the organization of scientific competitions:

1. issuing the Call for Participation, requiring teams to submit an application consisting of a 4-pages paper describing the team research approach to the challenge, as well as the hardware and software architectures of its robot system, and any evidence of performance (e.g., videos);
2. selecting the qualified teams from among the applicants;
3. preparing/updating and delivering the final version of the rulebooks, scoring criteria, modules and metrics for benchmarking about 4–5 months before the actual competition dates, after an open discussion period with past participants and the robotics community in general;
4. building and setting up the competition infrastructure;
5. setting up the MCS for ground-truth data collection during benchmarking experiments, listing all data to be logged by the teams during the competitions for later benchmarking processing, and preparing USB pens to store that data during the actual runs of the teams robot system;
6. preparing several devices and software modules required by the competition rules (e.g., referee boxes, home automation devices—remotely-controlled lamps, IP camera, motorised blinds—and device network, factory-mockup devices—drilling machine, conveyor belt—objects for perception and manipulation, visitors uniforms and mail packages, audio files and lexicon);
7. establishing a schedule for the competitions and their different components;
8. establishing the adequate number of teams awarded per competition category and preparing trophies for the competition awards;
9. realizing the event, including the organization of visits from schools, and the availability of communicators who explain to the audience what is happening, using a simplified version of technically correct descriptions.

Three camps were also organized:

- RoCKIn Kick-off Camp, in Eindhoven, the Netherlands, 28 June till 1 July 2013, during RoboCup2013: 12 participants. The camp consisted of several lectures by the partners, on RoCKIn challenges and activities, covering sub-jects such as: principles for benchmarking robotics; raising awareness and disseminating robotics research; as well as discussion on developing robot-ics through scientific competitions like RoboCup. In addition to the lectures, attendees got first-hand experience of demo challenges, tests, and hardware and software solutions during the RoboCup@Home and RoboCup@Work practical sessions.

- RoCKIn Camp 2014, in Rome, Italy, 26–30 January 2014: 19 teams (11 @Home, 8 @Work), corresponding to a total of 63 students and researchers from 13 countries. This Camp was designed to support the preparation of (preferably new) teams to participate in RoCKIn@Home and RoCKIn@Work competitions, and featured guest lectures on vision-based pattern recognition, object and people detection, object grasping and manipulation, and Human-Robot Interaction in natural language.
- RoCKIn Field Exercise 2015, in Peccioli, Italy, at the ECHORD++ Robotics Innovation Facility, 18–22 March 2015: 42 participants divided in 9 teams (4 @Home, 5 @Work). The Field Exercise has been designed as a follow up of the previous RoCKIn Camp 2014, where most of the RoCKIn Competition 2014 best teams displayed their progresses and all participants improved their interaction with the RoCKIn scoring and benchmarking infrastructure.

6   Future Outlook: The European Robotics League

The novel European Robotics League (ERL[3]) competitions format has been introduced in the H2020 RockEU2 project. It aims to become a sustainable distributed format (i.e., not a single big event) which is similar to the for-mat of the European Football Champions League, where the role of national leagues is played by existing test beds (e.g., the RoCKIn test beds, but also the ECHORD++ project Robotics Innovation Facilities/RIFs), used as meeting points for "matches" where one or more teams visit the home team for a Local tournament. This format will exploit also arenas temporarily available during major competition events in Europe (e.g., RoboCup) allowing the realization of Major tournaments with more teams.

According to this new format, teams are scored in a given challenge for each tournament they participate to, and they get ranked based on scores accumulated over the year in their two best participations. The top ranked team(s) per Task and Functionality Benchmark are awarded prizes delivered during the European Robotics Forum in the year after. Travel support will be provided to selected teams based on criteria that will take into account research quality, financial needs and team technology readiness. Teams will be encouraged to arrive 1–2 weeks before the actual competition/event so to participate in integration weeks where the hosting institution provides technical support on using the local infrastructure (referee boxes, data acquisition and logging facility, etc.), ensuring a higher team technical readiness level (TTRL). TTRL concerns the ability of

---

[3] https://eu-robotics.net/robotics_league/index.html.

a team to have its robot(s) running without major problems, using modular software that ensures quick adaptation and composition of functionalities into tasks, and to use flawlessly the competition infrastructure, whose details may change from event to event.

Local tournaments will take place in currently available test beds at Instituto Superior Técnico premises in Lisbon, Portugal, at the ECHORD++ RIF in Scuola Superiore Sant'Anna, Peccioli, Italy, for ERL Service Robots (ERL-SR, former RoCKIn@Home); at Bonn-Rhein-Sieg University labs in Sankt Augustin, Germany, for both ERL-SR and ERL Industrial Robots (ERL-IR, former RoCKIn@Work). Major tournaments will be part of RoboCup2016 (Leipzig, Germany), and possibly RoboCup GermanOpen 2017 and the RoboCup PortugueseOpen in 2017. RockEU2 will provide a certification process to assess any new candidate test beds as RIFs for both challenges, based on the RoCKIn rulebook specifications and the implementation of the proper benchmarking and scoring procedures. This will enable the creation of a network of European robotics test beds having the specific purpose of benchmarking domestic robots, innovative industrial robotics applications and Factory of the Future scenarios.

ERL and the RoboCup Federation established an agreement that includes the sharing of tasks between the corresponding challenges in the two competitions, starting with different scoring systems, but that may possibly converge in the future. RoboCup is also starting to use benchmarking methods that were introduced during RoCKIn lifetime and that will be used in the ERL.

Acknowledgments. The RoCKIn project was funded under the EC Coordination Action contract no. FP7-ICT-601012. The RockEU2 project is funded under the EC Coordination Action contract no. H2020-ICT-688441.

References

1. Amigoni, F., Bastianelli, E., Berghofer, J., Bonarini, A., Fontana, G., Hochgeschwender, N., Iocchi, L., Kraetzschmar, G., Lima, P.U., Matteucci, M., Miraldo, P., Nardi, D., Schiaffonati, V.: Competitions for benchmarking: task and functionality scoring complete performance assessment. IEEE Robot. Autom. Mag. **22**(3), 53–61 (2015)
2. RoCKIn Deliverable D1.2: General evaluation criteria, modules and metrics for benchmarking through competition. http://rockinrobotchallenge.eu/rockin_d1.2.pdf
3. RoCKIn Deliverable D2.1.3: RoCKIn@Home Rule Book. http://rockinrobotchallenge.eu/rockin_d2.1.3.pdf
4. RoCKIn Deliverable D2.1.3: RoCKIn@Work Rule Book. http://rockinrobotchallenge.eu/rockin_d2.1.6.pdf
5. Shapley, L.S.: A value for n-person games. In: Kuhn, H.W., Tucker, A.W. (eds.) Contributions to the Theory of Games. Annals of Mathematical Studies, vols. II and 28, pp. 307–317. Princeton University Press, Princeton (1953)

Simulation Based Selection of Actions for a Humanoid Soccer-Robot

Heinrich Mellmann[✉], Benjamin Schlotter, and Christian Blum

Adaptive Systems Group, Department of Computer Science,
Humboldt-Universität zu Berlin, Berlin, Germany
{mellmann,schlottb,blum}@informatik.hu-berlin.de
http://naoth.de

Abstract. This paper introduces a method for making fast decisions in a highly dynamic situation, based on forward simulation. This approach is inspired by the decision problem within the RoboCup domain. In this environment, selecting the right action is often a challenging task. The outcome of a particular action may depend on a wide variety of environmental factors, such as the robot's position on the field or the location of obstacles. In addition, the perception is often heterogeneous, uncertain, and incomplete. In this context, we investigate forward simulation as a versatile and extensible yet simple mechanism for inference of decisions. The outcome of each possible action is simulated based on the estimated state of the situation. The simulation of a single action is split into a number of simple deterministic simulations – *samples* – based on the uncertainties of the estimated state and of the action model. Each of the samples is then evaluated separately, and the evaluations are combined and compared with those of other actions to inform the overall decision. This allows us to effectively combine heterogeneous perceptual data, calculate a stable decision, and reason about its uncertainty. This approach is implemented for the kick selection task in the RoboCup SPL environment and is actively used in competitions. We present analysis of real game data showing significant improvement over our previous methods.

1 Introduction

A highly dynamic environment requires a robot to make decisions quickly and with limited information. In the RoboCup scenario, the robot that is in possession of the ball needs to take action as quickly as possible before the opponent players get a chance to interfere. However, the particular situation might be very complex and many aspects like the robot's position on the field as well as the positions of the ball and obstacles need to be taken into account. This makes inferring a decision a complicated task. In this work we propose an inference method based on forward simulation to handle this complexity and ensure short reaction times at the same time. We focus in particular on the RoboCup scenario where the robot has to choose the best kick from several different possibilities, which provides the motivation for our approach.

© Springer International Publishing AG 2017
S. Behnke et al. (Eds.): RoboCup 2016, LNAI 9776, pp. 193–205, 2017.
https://doi.org/10.1007/978-3-319-68792-6_16

In the RoboCup community there have already been several attempts to implement similar methods. In particular [3,4] and [1] focus on a very similar task – the selection of the optimal kick. In [3], a probabilistic approach is used to describe the kick selection problem which is then solved using Monte Carlo simulation. In [4], the kick is chosen to maximize a proposed heuristic *game situation score* which reflects the goodness of the situation. In [1], the authors use an instance based representation for the kick actions and employ Markov decision process as an inference method. Internal forward simulation has already been successfully used as an inference method in robotics. In [2], the authors investigate navigation of robots in a dynamic environment. They use a simulation approach to envision movements of other agents and pedestrians to enable avoiding dynamic obstacles while moving towards a goal. In [5] a pancake baking robot is planning its actions using a full physical simulation of the outcome of possible actions.

For an effective decision, data from heterogeneous sources (e.g., visual percepts, ultrasound) needs to be combined. Often different filtering/modeling techniques are used for state estimation, which can make inference of decisions a difficult task. In particular, representation of uncertainty is problematic. As we will show, the simulation based approach can handle it easily.

The intuition behind a simulation-based approach is to *imagine* (or simulate) what would happen as the result of the execution of a particular action and then choose the action with the optimal (imagined/simulated) outcome. A potential issue with this approach is that the quality of the decision depends on the quality of the simulation, i.e., the model of the environment. For example in [5,6], the robots use complete fine-grained physical simulations for their decision-making. In contrast, we argue that the simulation itself can be quite coarse. To compensate for errors in the simulation, it is executed a number of times with varying initial conditions sampled according to the estimated state of the situation. Each of these realizations is evaluated individually and the overall decision for an action is then based on the distribution of the particular evaluations of the simulation. This is repeated for all possible actions (kicks) and the action with the best outcome distribution is chosen for execution.

We evaluate our approach based on labeled video and log data from real RoboCup competitions. The results show a significant improvement in comparison to our previous method.

The remainder of the paper is structured as follows. In the next section we discuss the action selection problem within the RoboCup domain. The main part of the paper consists of Sect. 3 and Sect. 4 where we describe the simulation and the evaluation-decision processes respectively. Our experimental findings are discussed in Sect. 5. Finally we conclude our findings in Sect. 6.

2   Action Selection Task in Robot Soccer

Consider the situation where a robot approaches the ball and needs to choose the right action from a fixed number of possibilities. In this study we assume the

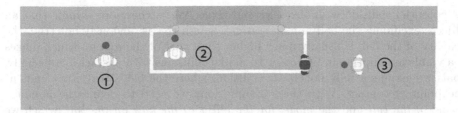

Fig. 1. Depictions of three different situations in which the best decision is not clear. The white robot is the robot having to take a decision on which (kick) action to perform while the blue robot is an opponent. The ball is depicted in red. (Color figure online)

following possible actions: four different kicks, namely kick right, left, forward short (dribbling) and forward long, and a turn around the ball towards the opponent goal. The last option is to fall back in case no kick is possible, or if no kick would improve the situation (Fig. 1).

To make an optimal decision different factors need to be taken into account. In our scenario we include estimated position of the robot on the field, position of the ball relatively to the robot, and obstacles in direct proximity. Each of these factors is modeled by a different probabilistic algorithm. We refer to the collective state estimated by these models as *situation state estimation.*

We approach this task using forward simulation. The outcome of each of the five actions is simulated using an estimated state of the situation, evaluated, and compared. The outcome of an action is described by the resulting position of the ball. Therefore, we need to model the interaction between the executing robot and the ball, the dynamics of the ball motion, and its possible interactions with the environment. In the following section these models will be discussed in detail.

3   Stochastic Forward Simulation

To be able to make decisions the robot needs an estimation of the state of the situation around it. In our case this state consists of the robot's position on the field, position of the ball relative to the robot, positions of the teammates and obstacles in close proximity. These particular aspects are usually estimated using various filtering techniques. In our case different independent probabilistic filters are involved, in particular particle filter for self localization and multi-hypothesis extended Kalman filter for the ball.

The task of the simulation process is to predict the state of the situation in case of the execution of a given action, e.g., kick. To do so, we need models for the effect of the action on the state of the situation, for the dynamics of particular objects and for interactions between the objects.

In general, an exhaustive physical simulation is a complicated and resource consuming process. To reduce complexity we make several assumptions. We focus only on simulating aspects involved in the action, i.e., the motion of the ball and its potential collision with obstacles and goals. We furthermore assume that all objects excluding the ball remain static. Though this is obviously not true, the velocity of the ball is usually much higher than that of the robots, which makes it a viable assumption in this case. To model collisions with obstacles, especially, goals we assume a fully nonelastic collision, where the ball's trajectory ends at the point of contact. With these assumptions we need to define the *dynamic model of the ball* and the *model for the effect of the kick on the ball*, which we discuss in the following two sections.

3.1   Ball Dynamics

To describe the dynamics of the ball motion we use a simple *rolling resistance* model which leads us to the following motion equation:

$$d(t) = -\frac{1}{2} \cdot g \cdot c_R \cdot t^2 + v_0 \cdot t \qquad (1)$$

where $d(t)$ is the distance the ball has rolled after the time $t > 0$, c_R is the rolling resistance coefficient and v_0 is the initial velocity of the ball after the kick. By solving $d'(t) = 0$ and putting the result in Eq. (1) the maximal rolling distance, i.e., the stopping distance of the ball, can readily be determined as

$$d_{max} = \frac{v_0^2}{2c_R \cdot g}. \qquad (2)$$

The parameters v_0 and c_R of this model have to be determined experimentally. It should be noted that v_0 depends mainly on the particular kick motion and c_R depends mainly on the particular carpet of the field, since the ball remains the same. Thus, v_0 has to be estimated once for each kick motion and c_R once for each particular carpet.

3.2   Kick-Action Model

The result of a kick can be described by the likelihood of the final ball location after its execution, i.e., positions where the ball is expected to come to a halt eventually. These positions can be estimated based on the dynamic model of the ball as described in Sect. 3.1 and the intended direction of the kick. We assume the direction of the ball motion α and the initial velocity v_0 of the kick behaving according to the Gaussian distribution. With this, the outcome of a kick action can be described as a tuple of initial velocity v_0, direction α, and corresponding standard deviations σ_v and σ_α:

$$a = (v_0, \alpha, \sigma_v, \sigma_\alpha) \in \mathbb{R}_+ \times [-\pi, \pi) \times \mathbb{R}_+ \times [-\pi, \pi) \qquad (3)$$

We predict the outcome of an action by sampling from the Gaussian distributions:

$$predict(a) := (d_{max}(\epsilon_v), \epsilon_\alpha) \in \mathbb{R}_+ \times [-\pi, \pi) \qquad (4)$$

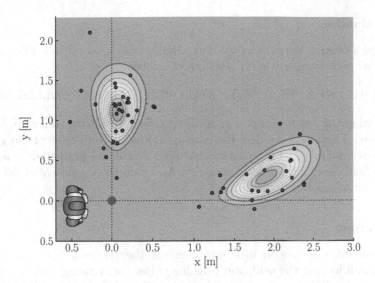

Fig. 2. Kick action model: distributions of the possible ball positions after a sidekick and the long kick forward with the right foot. Blue dots illustrate experimental data. (Color figure online)

where $\epsilon_v \sim N(v, \sigma_v)$ and $\epsilon_\alpha \sim N(\alpha, \sigma_\alpha)$. Note that the function $predict(\cdot)$ is non-deterministic. Figure 2 illustrates the resulting likelihood for the final ball positions for a kick forward and a sidekick left. The parameters are estimated empirically.

3.3   Simulating the Consequences of an Action

The action is simulated a fixed number of times. The resulting ball position of one simulation is referred to as a *sample*. The positions of the samples are generated according to the model introduced in Sect. 3.2. The algorithm checks for possible collisions with the goal box and if there are any, the kick distance gets shortened appropriately. Collisions with the obstacle model are handled the same way.

A *hypothesis* for the action $a \in \mathcal{A}$ is defined as a set of $n \in \mathbb{N}$ samples drawn from the model distribution of an action a as described in Sect. 3.2.

$$\mathcal{H}_a := \{p_i | p_i = predict(a), i = 1 \ldots n\} \subset \mathbb{R}_+ \times [-\pi, \pi) \qquad (5)$$

4   Action Selection

The implementation of the simulation algorithm is divided into three main steps: simulate the consequences for all actions, evaluate the consequences, and decide the best action. In this section we discuss these components in the case of the kick selection as described in the Sect. 3.

4.1 Evaluation

The samples of each hypothesis are individually evaluated by two different systems. First, each sample $h \in \mathcal{H}_a$ is assigned a label

$$label(h) \in \mathcal{L} := \{\text{INFIELD}, \text{OUT}, \text{GOALOPP}, \text{GOALOWN}, \text{COLLISION}\} \quad (6)$$

based on where on the field it is, e.g., inside the field, inside the own goal, outside the field etc. These labels reflect the corresponding discrete rules of the game.

In the second step, all samples labeled $INFIELD$ are evaluated by a scalar potential field encoding the team strategy. An example of a potential field used in our experiments is described closer in Sect. 4.3.

4.2 Decision

The overall decision has to take into account the trade-off between possible risks,e.g., ball leaving the field, and possible gains, e.g., scoring a goal, weighted by the chances of their occurrence. The estimation of those risks and gains can be done based on the individual ratings of the particular simulation results, i.e., samples. The likelihood of the occurrence of an event marked by a label $\lambda \in \mathcal{L}$ within a hypothesis $\mathcal{H}_a$ can be estimated as

$$p(\lambda|a) := \frac{|\{h \in \mathcal{H}_a | label(h) = \lambda\}|}{|\mathcal{H}_a|}. \quad (7)$$

For instance, the likelihood for scoring a goal with the action a can be written as $p(\text{GOALOPP}|a)$.

In our experiments we use a minimal two step decision process, whereby the actions that are *too risky* are discarded in the first step and the one with the highest gain is selected in the second. More precisely, we call an action *too risky* if there is a high chance for kicking the ball out of the field or scoring own goal. The set of actions with acceptable risk can be defined as:

$$\mathcal{A}_{acc} := \{a \in \mathcal{A} | p(\text{INFIELD} \cup \text{GOALOPP}|a) \geq T_0 \wedge p(\text{GOALOWN}|a) \leq T_1\} \quad (8)$$

with fixed thresholds T_0 and T_1 (in our experiments we used $T_0 = 0.85$ and $T_1 = 0$). Note that the cases indicated by OUT and $COLLISION$ are treated the same by this rule. From this set the actions with the highest likelihood of scoring a goal are selected

$$\mathcal{A}_{goal} := \text{argmax} \{p(\text{GOALOPP}|a)|a \in \mathcal{A}_{acc}\}. \quad (9)$$

In case that $\mathcal{A}_{goal}$ is empty the default action is always turn around the ball. In case $\mathcal{A}_{goal}$ contains more than one possible action, the best action is selected randomly from the set of actions with the maximal strategic value based on the potential field

$$a_0 \in \text{argmax}\{value(a)|a \in \mathcal{A}_{goal}\} \quad (10)$$

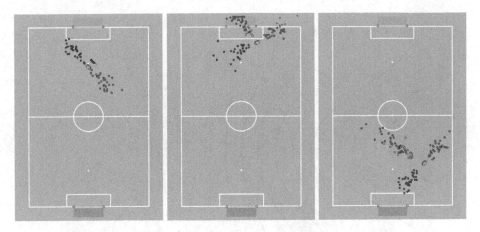

Fig. 3. Three examples for kick simulations. Each possible kick direction is simulated with 30 samples (different colors correspond to different kicks). Left: the short and long kicks are shortened due to collision with an obstacle. Middle: long kick is selected as the best action since it has the most samples result in a goal. Right: the best action is sidekick to the right – the other kicks are more likely to end up in a dangerous position for the own goal according to the potential field. (Color figure online)

with strategic values defined as

$$value(a) := \int_{\Omega} p(x|a) \cdot potential(x) \, \mathrm{d}x = \frac{1}{n} \sum_{i=0}^{n} potential(x_i) \qquad (11)$$

Figure 3 illustrates several situations with the corresponding simulated hypotheses and their evaluations.

4.3 Potential Field

A potential field assigns a value to each position of the ball inside the field. The values reflect the static strategy of the game and are used to compare possible ball positions in terms of their strategic value. For instance, the position a meter away in front of the opponent goal is obviously much better than the one in front of the own goal. In our experiments we use the following potential field:

$$P(x) = \underbrace{x^T \cdot \nu_{\mathrm{opp}}}_{\text{linear slope}} - \underbrace{N(x|\mu_{\mathrm{opp}}, \Sigma_{\mathrm{opp}})}_{\text{opponent goal attractor}} + \underbrace{N(x|\mu_{\mathrm{own}}, \Sigma_{\mathrm{own}})}_{\text{own goal repulsor}}, \qquad (12)$$

where $N(\cdot|\mu, \Sigma)$ is the normal distribution with mean μ and covariance Σ. It consists of three different parts: the linear slope points from the own goal towards the opponent goal and is modeling the general direction of attack; the exponential repulsor $N(x|\mu_{\mathrm{own}}, \Sigma_{\mathrm{own}})$ prevents kicks towards the center in front of own goal; and $N(x|\mu_{\mathrm{opp}}, \Sigma_{\mathrm{opp}})$ creates an exponential attractor towards the opponent goal.

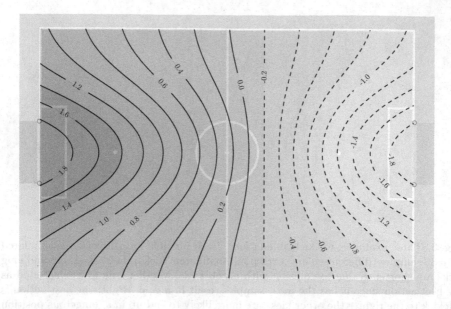

Fig. 4. Strategic potential field evaluating ball positions. Own goal is on the left (blue). (Color figure online)

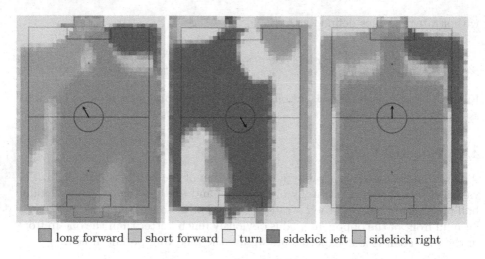

☐ long forward ☐ short forward ☐ turn ■ sidekick left ☐ sidekick right

Fig. 5. Resulting decisions based on different positions of the ball on the field and three different orientations of the robot. Different colors correspond to different decisions. The orientation of the robot is indicated by the arrow. Own goal is at the bottom, opponent at the top. (Color figure online)

The configuration used in our experiments is

$$\nu_{\text{opp}} = (-1/x_{\text{opp}}, 0)^{T} \tag{13}$$

with $x_{\text{opp}} = 4.5$ being the x-position of the opponent goal and

$$\mu_{\text{own}} = (-4.5, 0) \qquad\qquad \mu_{\text{opp}} = (4.5, 0) \qquad\qquad (14)$$

$$\Sigma_{\text{own}} = \begin{pmatrix} 3.375^2 & 0 \\ 0 & 1.2^2 \end{pmatrix} \qquad\qquad \Sigma_{\text{opp}} = \begin{pmatrix} 2.25^2 & 0 \\ 0 & 1.2^2 \end{pmatrix} \qquad (15)$$

for the repulsor and attractor respectively. All parameters are of unit m. Figure 4 illustrates the resulting potential field.

4.4 Kick Selection Visualization

Figure 5 illustrates the decisions made by the algorithm depending on the robot's position on the field with the ball in front of the robot for three different fixed orientations of the robot. Since the simulation it stochastic, the decision is repeated 20 times for each cell on the field.

5 Quantitative Analysis in Real Game Situations

In general evaluation of decision algorithms is difficult because they tend to behave differently in the isolated environment of the lab than under real conditions, e.g., during a soccer competition. In this section we present analysis of the simulation based action selection using human labeled combined video and log data from real games.

5.1 Methodology

Evaluation of algorithms in real robot soccer competition conditions is a challenging task. This is mainly because in a real game many factors affect the performance of the robot in a particular situation, e.g., robot executes a wrong kick because it is not localized correctly. To minimize the influence of side factors on the evaluation we need to observe what actually happened and the internal state of the robot at the same time.

For this purpose we recorded videos overlooking the whole field of the games during RoboCup competitions in 2015 alongside with log files recorded by each of the robots. Video recordings provide a ground truth of the situation while log data recorded by the robots provides the corresponding internal state. The log files contain perceptions and the behavior decision tree for every cognition cycle (33 ms). This allows us to extract the situations when the robot took a decision to kick.

The logs have been synchronized with video files and the extracted kick actions manually labeled. The labeling procedure has been performed with the help of the interface which had been designed specifically for this purpose. Figure 6 illustrates an example of a labeling session for the first half of the game with the team *NaoDevils* at the RoboCup 2015.

Fig. 6. Illustration of the labeling interface used to collect data regarding the quality of the kicks. At the bottom are time lines for each of the robots. Different actions are represented by buttons on the time line with different colors. On the right the robots estimated state is visualized, i.e., estimation of its position, ball model and obstacles. On the left are three categories of labels capturing the quality of the action. (Color figure online)

The labeling criteria consist of 15 distinct boolean labels in three categories: technical execution of the kick, e.g., robot did miss the ball; situation model (was the estimation of robots position on the field and the ball correct?); result of the action and strategic improvement of the situation (ball left the field, was moved closer to the opponent goal etc.).

5.2 Data Set

For our analysis we took a look at the games our team has played in two different competitions in 2015 – the *German Open 2015* (GO15) and *RoboCup 2015* (RC15). In both competitions our robots performed well – we reached the third place at the German Open and quarter finals at the RoboCup. At the GO15 we used our previous solution for action selection based on a manually adjusted heuristic decision tree and a potential field indicating the best direction towards the goal while at the RC15 the presented simulation based approach had been employed.

From GO15 a total of five game halves have been analyzed with: *ZKnipsers* (two halves, preliminaries); *HULKS* (first half, preliminaries); and *Nao Devils* (two halves, game for the 3rd place). And from RC15 we analyzed three complete games with: *RoboCanes* (two halves, preliminaries); *Nao Devils* (two halves, intermediate round); and *HTWK* (two halves, quarter finals). The selection of the games depends largely on the availability of the videos and log data.

5.3   Results

To single out the effect of the kick selection we focus on kicks where the robot was well *localized* (so it knew what it was doing) and kicks where executed successfully, i.e., the ball went in the intended direction and did not collide with opponent. In short: *successful* kicks are the ones which comply with our action model as described in Sect. 3.2. The top part of the Table 1 illustrates the numbers of the successful and failed kicks.

Our analysis has also revealed that a high percentage of the actions fail due to various reasons. The main reasons appear to be failure in the technical execution, e.g., the robot trips and doesn't kick the ball properly, and interference by opponent players. Both aspects are not part of the simulation and require further investigation. The Table 1 (**Failed execution**) summarizes the rates of the failed kicks split in these two cases. The higher opponent interference in the case of the new approach can be explained by the more challenging opponent teams at the RC15.

In the lover part of the Table 1 we summarize the evaluation of the the kick results according to the strategic improvement of the ball position as described in Sect. 5.1. The separation used here is very rough: +1 corresponds to the cases where the strategic position of the ball was clearly improved by the action, e.g., it was moved closer towards the opponent goal; −1 was given when the ball moved towards own goal or away from the opponent goal; and 0 when no improvement was visible, e.g., ball moved along the middle line. The results show that the new approach results in a higher rate of improvements (+1) and a lower rate of mediocre kicks (0), while the rate of cases where the position of the ball worsened (−1) remained at a comparable level.

Table 1. Analysis results of video material. The new algorithm shows a higher rate of strategic improvements (+1) and a lower rate of mediocre kicks (0). It is also about 5 times less likely to kick out at the opponent field line.

Algorithm	New		Old	
Total number of kicks	163		196	
Robot was localized	150	(92.02%)	165	(84.18%)
Successful execution	93	(57.06%)	153	(78.06%)
Failed execution	70		43	
Failed: opponent interference	33	(47.14%)	14	(32.56%)
Failed: technical failure	37	(52.86%)	29	(67.44%)
Successful execution + localized	86	(52.76%)	131	(66.84%)
+1	67	**(77.91%)**	88	(67.18%)
0	15	**(17.44%)**	39	(29.77%)
−1	4	(4.65%)	4	(3.05%)
Out at opponent goal line	1	**(1.16%)**	8	(6.11%)

Another important factor is the *number of times the ball leaves the field* because it results in a tactical disadvantage as the ball is replaced into the field. The penalty is especially large when the ball leaves on the opponent goal line, since the ball is then reset to the middle line. In this case we can see a significant improvement with the new approach as only one kick (1.16%) left the field at the opponent goal line in contrast to more than 6% (8 kicks) with the old solution.

In summary, the data shows that the new approach performs more robustly than our previous solution. The new algorithm is about 5 times less likely to kick out at the opponent field line (decrease by 81%) and 16% more likely to kick towards the opponent goal.

6 Conclusions and Future Work

We presented and discussed an action selection algorithm based on forward simulation. We discussed its application in the scenario of kick selection for robot soccer. This kick selection algorithm was successfully implemented and used in RoboCup competitions. The three main advantages of the presented approach are easy implementation and extensibility. Experimental data collected in real RoboCup games has shown that the algorithm performs very well and is an improvement over the algorithm used by our team up to now.

Our current effort focuses in particular on stepwise extension to simulating the ball approach and more dynamic evaluation. For instance, the potential field might reflect the influence regions of the own teammates based on their position, which would favor the kicks towards these regions and enable emergent passing.

At the present state the implemented method is limited to the selection of the kicks only. We believe that the true potential of the forward simulation can only unfold if extended to all areas of decision making like role decision, passing, positioning etc.

References

1. Ahmadi, M., Stone, P.: Instance-based action models for fast action planning. In: Visser, U., Ribeiro, F., Ohashi, T., Dellaert, F. (eds.) RoboCup 2007. LNCS (LNAI), vol. 5001, pp. 1–16. Springer, Heidelberg (2008). doi:10.1007/978-3-540-68847-1_1
2. Bordallo, A., Previtali, F., Nardelli, N., Ramamoorthy, S.: Counterfactual reasoning about intent for interactive navigation in dynamic environments. In: 2015 IEEE/RSJ International Conference on Intelligent Robots and Systems (IROS), pp. 2943–2950, September 2015
3. Dodds, R., Vallejos, P., Ruiz-del Solar, J.: Probabilistic kick selection in robot soccer. In: IEEE 3rd Latin American Robotics Symposium, LARS 2006, pp. 137–140, October 2006
4. Guerrero, P., Ruiz-del-Solar, J., Díaz, G.: Probabilistic decision making in robot soccer. In: Visser, U., Ribeiro, F., Ohashi, T., Dellaert, F. (eds.) RoboCup 2007. LNCS (LNAI), vol. 5001, pp. 29–40. Springer, Heidelberg (2008). doi:10.1007/978-3-540-68847-1_3

5. Kunze, L., Beetz, M.: Envisioning the qualitative effects of robot manipulation actions using simulation-based projections. Artif. Intell. (2015). http://www.sciencedirect.com/science/article/pii/S0004370214001544
6. Winfield, A.F.T., Blum, C., Liu, W.: Towards an ethical robot: internal models, consequences and ethical action selection. In: Mistry, M., Leonardis, A., Witkowski, M., Melhuish, C. (eds.) TAROS 2014. LNCS (LNAI), vol. 8717, pp. 85–96. Springer, Cham (2014). doi:10.1007/978-3-319-10401-0_8

Robust Tracking of Multiple Soccer Robots Using Random Finite Sets

Pablo Cano$^{(\boxtimes)}$ and Javier Ruiz-del-Solar

Department of Electrical Engineering, Advanced Mining Technology Center,
Universidad de Chile, Santiago, Chile
{pcano,jruizd}@ing.uchile.cl

Abstract. Having a good estimation of the robot-players positions is becoming imperative to accomplish high level tasks in any RoboCup League. Classical approaches use a vector representation of the robot positions and Bayesian filters to propagate them over time. However, these approaches have data association problems in real game situations. In order to tackle this issue, this paper presents a new method for building robot maps using Random Finite Sets (RFS). The method is applied to the problem of estimating the position of the teammates and opponents in the SPL league. Considering the computational capabilities of Nao robots, the GM-PHD implementation of RFS is used. In this implementation, the estimations of the robot positions and the robot observations are represented using Mixture of Gaussians, but instead of associating a robot or an observation to a given Gaussian, the weight of each Gaussian maintains an estimation of the number of robots that it represents. The proposed method is validated in several real game situations and compared with a classical EKF based approach. The proposed GM-PHD method shows a much better performance, being able to deal with most of the data association problems, even being able to manage complex situations such as robot kidnappings.

Keywords: World modeling · Multi-target tracking · Robot position estimation · Random Finite Sets

1   Introduction

As RoboCup progresses over the years, high-level skills become necessary to maintain a competitive level. Such skills are no longer restricted to the detection of field objects or to the self-localization of the robot players, but include team's skills based on the tracking (position estimation) of teammates and opponents. Examples of these skills are ball passing, adversaries' tracking and team's formation.

When the observability of the game and the players is not an issue to address, as in the case of the Small-size league, high- levels skills based on the tracking of the robot players have been already implemented (e.g. reactive coordination [1], and the analysis and learning of the opponent's strategies [2, 3]).

The situation in the Standard Platform League (SPL) is more complex given the restricted field of view of the robot´s camera and the low computational resources of the Nao robots; in this league the detection of other robots is not robust and the construction

© Springer International Publishing AG 2017
S. Behnke et al. (Eds.): RoboCup 2016, LNAI 9776, pp. 206–217, 2017.
https://doi.org/10.1007/978-3-319-68792-6_17

of a good map of obstacles/players is a difficult process. Current standard robot tracking systems maintain/update the robot estimations using Kalman filters (e.g. [4, 5]). However, in this tracking paradigm there is no clear solution of the data association problem, and several heuristics need to be used in order to eliminate and merge hypotheses.

In this context the main goal of this paper is to propose a new methodology for the robust tracking (position estimation) of multiple soccer robots using the Random Finite Sets (RFS) framework, which allows to overcome the drawbacks of current approaches. The proposed methodology is inspired in [6] where the term Probability Hypothesis Density (PHD) was introduced as the first moment of a point process. Then, the PHD filter is presented in [7] as a way to maintain hypotheses of multiple objects using sets instead of vectors to describe the object's states.

There are several works that use this new framework in the literature, concerning all kind of problems and subjects [8]. Principally, it is used in highly complex environments to track large amounts of features, which makes it very expensive computationally. But, in the SPL problem the number of features (robots) to detect rises to 10 in the worst case, which make it computationally tractable for a Nao robot's CPU.

The paper is organized as follows: in Sect. 2 the problem to resolve is described. Section 3 presents a brief introduction to RFS. Section 4 shows the implementation used in this work, and Sect. 5 the experimental results. Finally, conclusions are drawn in Sect. 6.

2 Problem Description: Data Association When Tracking Multiple Players in Robot Soccer

As already mentioned, knowing the position of the other robots in the field is relevant for implementing high-level soccer behaviors. In this work we will call *map of obstacles* to a map that a given player builds, and which includes the positions on the field of every other robot player, teammate or opponent (see Fig. 1). We will denote observations to the detections of these robots, and obstacles to the estimated position of these robots in the map.

Most of the existing methods used for estimating the map of obstacles employ a classical approach with a vector representation of the obstacles (robots), which are propagated over time using a Bayesian filter (e.g. an EKF filter). However, it has been demonstrated that the use of a vector representation of the obstacles has numerous drawbacks, mainly related to the data association between new and past observations (obstacles) [9]. Some examples of those problems are illustrated in Fig. 2: Fig. 2(a) shows a trivial case where the data association between two new observations (red crosses) and two obstacles (black crosses) is trivial. However, the data associations are not trivial in the cases illustrated in Fig. 2(b) and (c). First, Fig. 2(b) shows the case when two new measurements have a similar distance to the obstacle, in addition to be not very close to the obstacle (see the covariance of the obstacle representation). So, depending of the implemented data association strategy, this could end in one, two or three obstacles in the map. Figure 2(c) show a case where two obstacles are very close, so the new measurement could be associated with any of them, and leave the other with no update for that frame. For these cases, most of methods use heuristics to associate

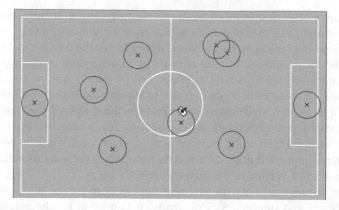

Fig. 1. Example of a map of obstacles. The white rectangle represents the robot which is building the map. The black crosses represent the robots/obstacles positions and the yellow circles the corresponding covariance of each representation. The lighted zone represents the Field of View of the camera. (Color figure online)

new measurements to the obstacles, or to create new obstacles if no association is made. But, in a highly dynamic environment as a robot soccer match, these methods may produce several bad associations or missed detections.

Finally, Fig. 2(d) describes a situation where no measurement is obtained for an obstacle inside the Field of View (FoV). For the classical approach, this is not different from an obstacle outside the FoV, and its only consequence is that the obstacles' covariance grows. So, depending of the speed of the covariance's growing (which maintain the obstacles outside the FoV), the obstacles inside the FoV will be maintained the same time that the others, although they do not receive any measurements.

3 Multi-target Tracking with Random Finite Sets

The main idea of the proposed methodology is to use *finite sets* instead of vectors for representing both observations and obstacles, which can encapsulate positions and quantity uncertainty. As has been widely demonstrated [7, 9, 10], the first moment of RFS, known as Probability Hypothesis Density (PHD), can be used to construct a filter which propagates the PHD of the map posterior instead of the map posterior itself.

3.1 PHD Filter

The PHD function v at a point represents the density of the expected number of obstacles occurring at that point of the state space (map). Therefore, a property of the PHD is that for any given region S of the map

$$\mathbb{E}[|M \cap S|] = \int_S v(m)dm \tag{1}$$

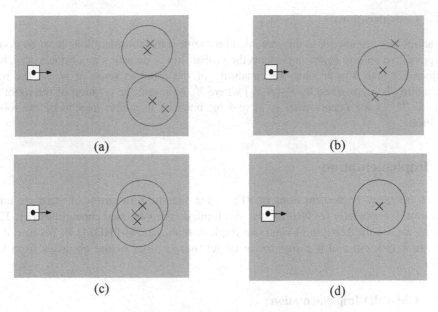

Fig. 2. The red crosses represent measurements of the sensor, black crosses represent the robots/obstacles positions and the yellow circles the corresponding covariance of each representation. (a) represents an easy case of data association, while (b) and (c) show more complex cases. (d) represents a case when an obstacle that should be detected by the robot is not sensed. (Color figure online)

where M represents the map RFS and $|\cdot|$ denotes the cardinality of a set. This means that, by integrating the PHD on any region S of the map, we obtain the expected number of obstacles in S [7].

The PHD filter considers the following two steps [7]:

- Prediction:

$$v_{k|k-1}(m) = v_{k-1}(m) + b_k(m) \tag{2}$$

where $b_k(m)$ represents the PHD of the new obstacles in time k.

- Update:

$$v_k(m) = v_{k|k-1}(m)\left[1 - P_D(m) + \sum_{z \in Z_k} \frac{P_D(m)g_k(z|m))}{c_k(z) + \int P_D(\xi)g_k(z|\xi)v_{k|k-1}(\xi)d\xi}\right] \tag{3}$$

where $P_D(m)$ represents the probability of detecting an obstacle at m, $g_k(z|m)$ represents the likelihood that z is generated by an obstacle at m at time k (i.e. the measurement likelihood) and $c_k(z)$ is the clutter intensity at time k.

3.2 Considerations

To adopt this framework to the presented problem, some considerations must be done. As presented before, $P_D(m)$ represents the probability of detecting an obstacle at m, but it does not take into account the capability of the robot to sense at m. So the real probability is represented by $P_D(m|X_k)$ where X_k represent the position of the robot in time k. The same occurs with g_k, c_k and b_k, because they also depend of the robot position.

4 Implementation

There are many implementations of RFS in the literature, but most of them are time consuming, especially for Nao robots with limited computational capabilities [11, 12]. Hence we use the Mixture of Gaussian implementation (GM-PHD) [13], because it is very time efficient and it allows to easily get the positions of the obstacles from the PHD.

4.1 GM-PHD Implementation

The main idea is to represent any RFS as a mixture of Gaussians. Therefore, both obstacles and detections are represented by Gaussians. But, to represent the position and number uncertainty of the obstacles present in the field, it is necessary to add a weight to every Gaussian. In this way their positions represent the multitude of location of obstacles in the map while their weights represent the number of obstacles in that given region. So, a PHD map is a Gaussian Mixture of the form,

$$v_{k-1}(m|X_{k-1}) = \sum_{j=1}^{J_{k-1}} \omega_{k-1}^{(j)} \mathcal{N}\left(m;\ \mu_{k-1}^{(j)},\ P_{k-1}^{(j)}\right) \qquad (4)$$

which is a mixture of J_{k-1} Gaussians, with $\omega_{k-1}^{(j)}$, $\mu_{k-1}^{(j)}$ and $P_{k-1}^{(j)}$ being their corresponding prior weights, means and covariances, respectively. The same form is used to represent the new obstacles at time k, $b_k(m|Z_{k-1}, X_{k-1})$, as

$$b_k(m|Z_{k-1},\ X_{k-1}) = \sum_{j-1}^{J_{b,k}} \omega_{k|k-1}^{(j)} \mathcal{N}\left(m;\ \mu_{k|k-1}^{(j)},\ P_{k|k-1}^{(j)}\right) \qquad (5)$$

where $J_{b,k}$ is the number of Gaussians in the new PHD at time k, Z_{k-1} is the vector of measurements at time $k-1$ and $\omega_{k|k-1}^{(j)}, \mu_{k|k-1}^{(j)}$ and $P_{k|k-1}^{(j)}$ determine the shape of the PHD of new obstacles. Therefore, the predicted PHD of the map, shown in (2) is also a Gaussian mixture

$$v_{k|k-1}(m|X_k) = \sum_{j=1}^{J_{k|k-1}} \omega_{k|k-1}^{(j)} \mathcal{N}\left(m;\ \mu_{k|k-1}^{(j)},\ P_{k|k-1}^{(j)}\right) \tag{6}$$

where $J_{k|k-1} = J_{k-1} + J_{b,k}$ are the number of Gaussians representing the union of the prior map PHD $v_{k-1}(m|X_{k-1})$, and the new obstacles PHD at time k. $\omega_{k|k-1}^{(j)}$, $\mu_{k|k-1}^{(j)}$ and $P_{k|k-1}^{(j)}$ represents the shape and form of the Gaussians of the prior map PHD if $j < J_{k-1}$ and the shape and form of the Gaussians of the new observations PHD otherwise.

So, the posterior PHD shown in (3) is also a Gaussian mixture of the form

$$v_k(m|X_k) = v_{k|k-1}(m|X_k)\left[1 - P_D(m|X_k) + \sum_{z \in Z_k} \sum_{j=1}^{J_{k|k-1}} v_{G,k}^{(j)}(z,\ m|X_k)\right] \tag{7}$$

where $v_{G,k}^{(j)}$ corresponds, according to the general PHD Filter update equation, to

$$v_{G,k}^{(j)}(z,\ m|X_k) = \omega_k^{(j)}(z|X_k)\mathcal{N}\left(m;\ \mu_{k|k}^{(j)},\ P_{k|k}^{(j)}\right) \tag{8}$$

$$\omega_k^{(j)}(z|X_k) = \frac{P_D(m|X_k)\omega_{k|k-1}^{(j)}q^{(j)}(z|X_k)}{c_k(z) + \sum_{i=1}^{J_{k|k-1}} P_D(m|X_k)\omega_{k|k-1}^{(i)}q^{(i)}(z|X_k)} \tag{9}$$

where $q^{(i)}(z|X_k) = \mathcal{N}\left(z;\ H_k\mu_{k|k-1}^{(i)},\ S_k\right)$ is the measurement likelihood. The components $\mu_{k|k}^{(i)}$ and $P_{k|k}^{(i)}$ can be obtained from the standard EKF update equations,

$$S_k^{(i)} = R_k + \nabla H_k P_{k|k}^{(i)} \nabla H_k^T \tag{10}$$

$$K_k^{(i)} = P_{k|k}^{(i)} \nabla H_k^T \left[S_k^{(i)}\right]^{-1} \tag{11}$$

$$\mu_{k|k}^{(i)} = \mu_{k|k-1}^{(i)} + K_k^{(i)}\left(z - H_k\left(\mu_{k|k-1}^{(i)}\right)\right) \tag{12}$$

$$P_{k|k}^{(i)} = \left[I - K_k^{(i)}\nabla H_k\right] P_{k|k-1}^{(i)} \tag{13}$$

with ∇H_k being the Jacobian of the measurement equation with respect to the obstacles estimated location.

4.2   Algorithm

In order to use the presented framework, it is necessary to create Gaussians according to the measurements of the robot's sensors. Therefore $b_k(m|Z_{k-1}, X_{k-1})$ is obtained from the measurements Z_{k-1} and the previous robot position X_{k-1}. The components of this Gaussians are determined according to

$$\omega_{b,k}^{(j)} = 0.01, \quad \mu_{b,k}^{(j)} = h^{-1}\left(z_{k-1}^j, X_{k-1}\right),$$

$$P_{b,k}^{(j)} = h'\left(\mu^{(j)}, X_{k-1}\right)R\left[h'\left(\mu^{(j)}, X_{k-1}\right)\right]^T$$

where h^{-1} is the inverse measurement equation, R is the measurement noise covariance and $h'\left(\mu^{(j)}, X_{k-1}\right)$ is the Jacobian of the measurement model function with respect to the Gaussian state, j. Therefore, the implementation initially considers all detections at time $k-1$ to be potential new features at time k.

Then, as every Gaussian is combined with every measurement to generate a new Gaussian, the numbers of Gaussians grow exponentially in every frame. That is why pruning and merging operations are necessary. Gaussians which are determined sufficiently close (through a Mahalanobis distance threshold) are merged into a single Gaussian. But this does not represent an elimination of an obstacle because one Gaussian can represent more than one obstacle by its weight; these values are added when two or more Gaussians are merged.

Figure 3 shows the pseudo code of the complete algorithm.

With this algorithm, the PHD of the map is obtained. Then to get the position of the obstacles in the map, it is necessary to evaluate every Gaussian's weight. If this values exceeds a given threshold, then the obstacle position is given by the Gaussian's mean vector, and it's added to a vector that represent the current map. Figure 4 shows this algorithm.

4.3   Application

Using the proposed methodology, it is obtained a representation of the obstacle map for the detection of soccer players (Nao robots) in the SPL league. To do this, the methodology is used as follows:

i. State space: in order to describe the obstacles in the field, the state space is a vector $p = (x, y)$ that represents positions on the field according to the center of the field as $(0, 0)$ of the coordinate system.

ii. Sensor: the used sensor is the Nao camera. This implies that transformations must be done in order to describe the measurements as positions on the field, using the camera's intrinsic and extrinsic parameters, as well as the position of the robot on the field. The detections are made with the same robot's detector provided in the B-Human Code Release 2014 [14].

iii. Probability of detection P_D: Given that the sensor is the camera of the robot, the probability of detection is given by the field of view of it and the position of the obstacle relative to the robot. This implies that P_D must be recalculated in every frame for all the Gaussians of the map.

iv. Moving obstacles: The movement of the obstacles is taken into account by growing the covariance of the mixture of Gaussians in every frame instead of adding a movement model into the prediction step.

//prediction step
// the parameters of the Map's MoG model ($v_{k-1}(m|X_{k-1})$) are modified
for $i = 1$ to J_{k-1} **do**
   //the obstacles may move -> covariance is increased
   $\mu_{k|k-1}^{(i)} = \mu_{k-1}^{(i)}, P_{k|k-1}^{(i)} = P_{k-1}^{(i)} + Q, \omega_{k|k-1}^{(i)} = \omega_{k-1}^{(i)}$
end for
//birth; new obstacles are added
generateNewGausians(Z_{k-1}, X_{k-1}) // equation (5)
$v_{k|k-1}(m|X_k) = \left\{ \mu_{k|k-1}^{(i)}, P_{k|k-1}^{(i)}, \omega_{k|k-1}^{(i)} \right\}_{i=1}^{J_{k|k-1}}$
//update step
for $i = 1$ to $J_{k|k-1}$ **do**
   calculate $P_D^{(i)}$
   $\omega_k^{(i)} = \left(1 - P_k^{(i)}\right)\omega_{k|k-1}^{(i)}$
end for
$N = 1$
for each z in Z_k
   for $i = 1$ to $J_{k|k-1}$ **do**
      calculate $H, S_k^{(i)}$ and $K_k^{(i)}$
      $\mu_k^{(N+i)} = \mu_{k|k-1}^{(i)} + K_k^{(i)}\left(z - \mu_{k|k-1}^{(i)}\right)$
      $P_k^{(N+i)} = \left[I - K_k^{(i)} H\right]P_{k|k-1}^{(i)}$
      $\tau^{(i)} = P_D^{(i)} \omega_{k|k-1}^{(i)} \left|2\pi S_k^{(i)}\right|^{-0.5} \times \exp\left(\left(z - \mu_{k|k-1}^{(i)}\right)\left[S_k^{(i)}\right]^{-1}\left(z - \mu_{k|k-1}^{(i)}\right)^T\right)$
   end for
   for $i = 1$ to $J_{k|k-1}$ **do**
      $\omega_k^{(N+i)} = \tau^{(i)} / \left(c(z) + \sum_{l=1}^{J_{k|k-1}} \tau^{(l)}\right)$
   end for
   $N = N + J_{k|k-1}$
end for
$J_k = N$
//updated map
$v_k(m|X_k) = \left\{ \mu_k^{(i)}, P_k^{(i)}, \omega_k^{(i)} \right\}_{i=1}^{J_k}$
prune $(v_k(m|X_k))$

Fig. 3. Pseudo code of the general algorithm that calculates the PHD that represent the map of obstacles.

```
M_k = [ ]
for i = 1 to J_k do
    if ω_k^(i) > thrld then
        M_k = [M_k μ_k^(i)]
    end if
end for
```

Fig. 4. Pseudo code of the algorithm that drawn obstacles according to the PHD of the map.

5   Results

In order to evaluate the proposed methodology several experiments with real Nao robots in a real SPL field were carried out. Given that we needed to measure the accuracy of the obstacle's map (i.e. robots map), a validation system consisting of a global vision system (camera over the field) for measuring the Ground Truth was implemented.

First, for very simple initial conditions, we carried out only one experiment in which a robot is placed in the center of the field and it observes three other static robots. The robot is moving its head all the time, and given its reduced field of view, at a given moment it is able to observe just one of the other robots and in some few cases two. The proposed GM-PHD based method is compared with a classical EKF based method. As expected, given the simplicity of the problem, both systems obtained an average error of about 20 cm in the position of the robots. Both methods run in real time, being the processing time of the GM-PHD method 0.13 ms, and the processing time of the EKF method 0.07 ms.

Secondly, the proposed GM-PHD based method and the classical EKF based method were compared in a set of experiments under a variety of more realistic and dynamic conditions, where the observer robot, i.e. the one that builds the map, moves as well as some of the observed robots. Figure 5 shows this set of experiments.

For the first experiment of this set, five static robots are placed on the field, and the observer robot performs a ready positioning, i.e. the robot walks from its starting position to their legal kick-off position. The observer robot moves its head from left to right all the time, hence the other robots are not inside the FoV in every frame. As can be seen in Fig. 5(a), the differences of the GM-PHD method and the classical EKF method, in term of a multi-tracking criteria, are notorious. While the GM-PHD approach correctly describes the presence of obstacles in most of the positions of the field, the classical one shows an incorrect number of obstacles for each real one. This is because the new observations are not correctly associated with the previous ones, due to the odometry errors and the non-constant observations; then new hypothesis are drawn incorrectly by the EKF method.

In the second experiment one moving robot observes five other robots; one moving robot and four static ones. The observer robot, while moves, observes the other moving robot occasionally, because it moves its head from left to right all the time. In Fig. 5(b)

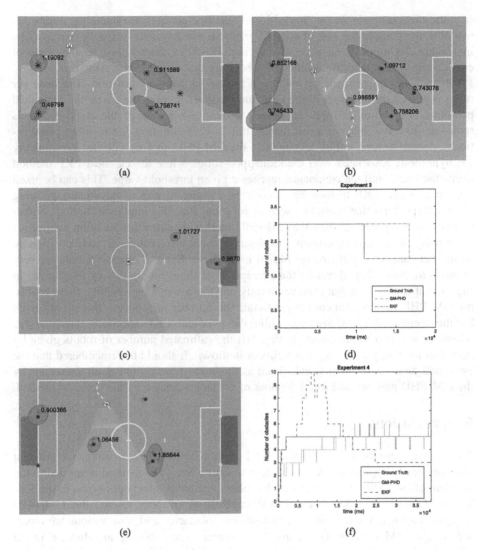

Fig. 5. Map building experiments under dynamic conditions. Four different situations are described in (a), (b), (c) and (e). In these diagrams the black asterisks represent the real position of the robots, obtained by the Ground Truth system; Blue crosses represent the robots' positions calculated by a EKF tracking method; The colored ellipses represent the robot estimations of the GM-PHD based method, and the associated number represents the weight of each Gaussian. The white dashed lines represent the trajectory of moving robots. (d)/(f) shows the estimated number of robots corresponding to situation (c)/(e). (Color figure online)

it can be seen that, when using the classical EKF approach, there are two wrongly detected robots placed in the previous path of the moving robot, in addition to the same error that occurs in the last experiment when more than one obstacle in the map is describing each real one. The GM-PHD method correctly relates these observations with the same obstacle. In fact, the GM-PHD method perfectly estimates the number of robots in the field. In the case of the EKF method, bad associations can be corrected by increasing the minimal distance of merging. But this can produce another type of errors, where detections from different robots are associated to the same one.

In the third experiment we analyze a typical kidnapping situation. The observer robot is placed in the center of the field and three static robot are placed in other field positions. The observer robot is looking around when one of the static robots is removed from the field (in a real match, this is very common due to robot penalizations). As can be seen in Fig. 5(c) and (d), the GM-PHD approach deletes very quickly the hypothesis associated with the kidnapped robot, while the classical EKF method keeps the track until the covariance reaches a given threshold value. This can be fixed for the classical EKF method by calculating a different rate of covariance growing when a hypothesis that should be seen is not seen. But, this implies including another heuristic to the process, while the GM-PHD method handles this situation naturally.

Finally, in the last experiment the observer robot also realizes a ready positioning while there are some static robots placed in the field. But two of these robots are very close from each other, therefore the perception of these robots is very inaccurate. In Fig. 5(e) it can be seen that even when only one Gaussian is representing these robots, the GM-PHD method can correctly estimate the number of robots in that place (given by the weight of the Gaussian), while the classical EKF approach fails due the odometry and perception errors. In Fig. 5(f) the estimated number of robots given by each method thought the entire experiment is shown. It should be remembered that the estimated number of robots is calculated as the sum of the weight of all Gaussians by the GM-PHD method, and as the number of obstacles created by the classical method.

6 Conclusions

This paper presents a new method for building obstacle maps using a consistent mathematically approach, known as Random Finite Sets. The method is applied to the problem of estimating the position of the robots, teammates and opponents, in the SPL league. Considering the computational capabilities of Nao robots, the GM-PHD implementation is used. In this implementation, obstacles and observations are represented using Mixture of Gaussians, but instead of associating an obstacle or an observation to a given Gaussian, the weight of each Gaussians maintains an estimation of the number of robots that it represents.

The proposed tracking method was validated in several real game situations, with moving robots, and compared with a classical EKF based approach. The proposed GM-PHD method showed a much better performance, being able to deal with most of the data association problems, even being able to manage complex situations such a robot kidnapping. Moreover, the method is able to run in real-time in the Nao robots (mean processing time is 0.13 ms; worse case processing time 0.3 ms).

Acknowledgments. The authors thank Constanza Villegas for her contributions to the development of this publication and the UChile Robotics Team for their general support. We also thank the B-Human SPL Team for sharing their code release, contributing the development of the Standard Platform League. This work was partially funded by FONDECYT Project 1161500.

References

1. Mendoza, J.P., Biswas, J., Cooksey, P., Wang, R., Klee, S., Zhu, D., Veloso, M.: Selectively reactive coordination for a team of robot soccer champions. In: Proceedings of AAAI-2016 (2016)
2. Trevizan, F.W.F., Veloso, M.M.M.: Learning opponent's strategies in the RoboCup small size league. In: Proceedings of AAMAS 2010 Workshop on Agents in Real-Time and Dynamic Environments, pp. 45–52, Toronto (2010)
3. Yasui, K., Kobayashi, K., Murakami, K., Naruse, T.: Analyzing and learning an opponent's strategies in the RoboCup small size league. In: Behnke, S., Veloso, M., Visser, A., Xiong, R. (eds.) RoboCup 2013. LNCS, vol. 8371, pp. 159–170. Springer, Heidelberg (2014). doi:10.1007/978-3-662-44468-9_15
4. Laue, T., Röfer, T.: Integrating simple unreliable perceptions for accurate robot modeling in the four-legged league. In: Lakemeyer, G., Sklar, E., Sorrenti, D.G., Takahashi, T. (eds.) RoboCup 2006. LNCS, vol. 4434, pp. 474–482. Springer, Heidelberg (2007). doi:10.1007/978-3-540-74024-7_48
5. Fabisch, A., Laue, T., Röfer, T.: Robot recognition and modeling in the RoboCup standard platform league. In: Pagello, E., Zhou, C., Behnke, S., Menegatti, E., Röfer, T., Stone, P. (eds.) Proceedings of the Fifth Workshop on Humanoid Soccer Robots in Conjunction with the 2010 IEEE-RAS International Conference on Humanoid Robots, pp. 65–70, Nashville, TN, USA (2010)
6. Goodman, I.R., Mahler, R.P.S., Nguyen, H.T.: Mathematics of Data Fusion. Springer, Dordrecht (1997). doi:10.1007/978-94-015-8929-1
7. Mahler, R.P.S.: A theoretical foundation for the stein-winter "probability hypothesis density (PHD)" multitarget tracking approach. In: Sensor and Data Fusion (2000)
8. Mahler, R.: A brief survey of advances in random-set fusion. In: 2015 International Conference on Control, Automation and Information Sciences (ICCAIS), pp. 62–67. IEEE (2015)
9. Mahler, R.P.S.: Statistical Multisource-Multitarget Information Fusion. Artech House, Inc., Norwood (2007)
10. Mahler, R.P.S.: Multitarget Bayes filtering via first-order multitarget moments. IEEE Trans. Aerosp. Electron. Syst. **39**, 1152–1178 (2003)
11. Vo, B.N., Singh, S., Doucet, A.: Sequential Monte Carlo methods for multi-target filtering with random finite sets. In: IEEE Transactions on Aerospace and Electronic Systems, pp. 1224–1245 (2005)
12. Vo, B.-N., Ma, W.-K.: The Gaussian mixture probability hypothesis density filter. IEEE Trans. Signal Process. **54**, 4091–4104 (2006)
13. Mullane, J.S., Vo, B.-N., Adams, M.D., Vo, B.-T.: Random Finite Sets for Robot Mapping & SLAM - New Concepts in Autonomous Robotic Map Representations. Springer, Heidelberg (2011). doi:10.1007/978-3-642-21390-8
14. Thomas, R., Laue, T., Judith, M., Bartsch, M., Batram, M.J., Arne, B., Martin, B., Kroker, M., Maaß, F., Thomas, M., Steinbeck, M., Stolpmann, A., Taddiken, S.: Team Report and Code Release 2013, pp. 1–194 (2014)

Adaptive Field Detection and Localization in Robot Soccer

Yongbo Qian$^{(\boxtimes)}$ and Daniel D. Lee

GRASP Lab, University of Pennsylvania, Philadelphia, PA 19104, USA
{yongbo,ddlee}@seas.upenn.edu
https://www.grasp.upenn.edu/

Abstract. Major rule updates for the RoboCup Standard Platform
League (SPL) in recent years pose significant perception challenges for
recognizing objects with similar color. Despite the frequent color changes
to goalpost, soccer ball and jerseys, the soccer field itself remains unaf-
fected, which makes green the only reliable color feature that can be
exploited. In this paper, we propose an efficient approach for adaptive
soccer field detection model utilizing NAO's two-camera system. Building
upon real-time image histogram analysis between top and bottom camera frames, the field color classifier is robust under inconsistent lighting
conditions, and can be further processed to generate field boundaries.
This approach could also be useful for other object detection modules
and robot's self-localization.

Keywords: Image histogram · Color segmentation · Boundary detection · Natural lighting · Self-localization

1 Introduction

The RoboCup soccer competition requires a robust and efficient perception system which should achieve accurate object detection and self-localization in real
time. However, due to the constrained nature of the computation on mobile
robots, vision has to run fast enough to provide real-time information while
leaving processing resources available to other autonomy algorithms. Moreover,
variable lighting conditions, frequent object occlusion and noise makes the problem even more challenging.

Similar to many other teams in the league, our team, the UPennalizers [1],
used to handle this problem using a manually defined color look-up table [2].
This method is well suited and efficient for image segmentation when object has
its unique color. Since everything except the field has been changed to white,
color-based segmentation becomes less effective to distinguish between different
objects. Furthermore, we are interested in having the robot eventually play soccer
outside with humans under natural lighting. This motivates us to develop a
new robust perception framework because the pre-defined color table lacks the
robustness when illumination varies.

S. Behnke et al. (Eds.): RoboCup 2016, LNAI 9776, pp. 218–229, 2017.
https://doi.org/10.1007/978-3-319-68792-6_18

As green becomes the only unique color cone we can leverage, wisely using it to detect static field becomes an important first step in perception, because it could provide contextual information for other objects. For example, performing ball and line detection only on the field could not only reduce the search region, but also yield to more accurate result. Similarly, goalpost detection could be more precise if the algorithm uses the fact that posts grow vertically onward the field boundary.

Using the field region to aid the detection of other objects is not a novel task in RoboCup. However, most teams generate field boundary with the pre-labeled green color. It is among our best interest to investigate real-time green feature analysis so that it could adapt to lighting changes. Berlin United 2015 [3] estimated the field color as a cubic area in the YUV color space, based on the assumption that both top and bottom images are mostly covered by the field. HTWK 2014 [4] detect field color through a peak detection in a 2D CbCr-Color-Histogram together with a fast search and region growing approach. This is also based on the same assumption which is not necessarily true all the time. To get rid of this assumption, HTWK 2015 [5] trained 300 different images from SPL events to extract the field color.

The teams from other leagues were also working towards illumination invariance techniques in RoboCup soccer. In the middle size league, Mayer et al. [6] suggested to use automated on-site vision calibration routines, along with improved color constancy algorithms and additional visual features aside of color to tackle the lighting variations. Sridharan and Stone [7] from the UT Austin Villa team proposed a color constancy method on Sony Aibo robots by comparing the color space distributions with the color cubes in the training samples using the KL-divergence measure.

Unlike the previous approaches, we present a simple yet efficient method in this work. This method considers a stronger assumption and does not require training images. As shown in Fig. 1, the two-camera system for NAO robot has its unique advantage allowing each camera performs different task. For example, as noticed in the previous games, the coverage of the bottom camera is always within the field because of the lower pitch angles; Therefore, we only need to implement field detection in the top camera image. This gives us

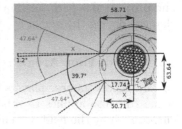

Fig. 1. Camera model for Alderbaran NAO robots [10]

the opportunity to pre-analyze the color distribution of bottom camera frames to find out the statistics information of green pixels and apply it to the top image. Now the task can be simply achieved by basic histogram smoothing, peak picking [8] and back projection techniques [9].

To complete the field detection module in our new perception framework, we then analyze the linear relations of the edge points to generate the field boundary. The boundary will re-define the search area for the detection of each object in top image, and also serves as a landmark feature in our particle filter to correct robot's orientation in localization. The object detection will still be performed in the whole bottom image. The detailed object detection mechanism is not within the scope of this paper, but will be mostly based on the edge and shape features of the non-green pixels on the field. The overall of this framework is shown in Fig. 2.

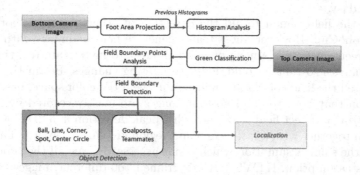

Fig. 2. Overview of the field detection module in perception framework

2 Field Color Detection

This section provides an overview of the field color detection method proposed in the perception framework. The approach utilizes the prior analysis of the color histogram of the robot foot area to segment the soccer field in top camera image using histogram back projection technique. Since the histogram analysis and projection is performed in real time, this method could adapt to the lighting changes during the game.

2.1 Robot Foot Area Projection

In any soccer games, players should stay on the field if not being penalized. Same rule also applies to robot soccer, meaning robot's feet should always be surrounded by the field, which is green carpet in this case. This provides a valid assumption which makes the foot area as our region of interest:

Assumption: the majority color within robot's foot area is green.

The correctness of this assumption depends on the definition of the foot area. It holds true for most of the positions on the field; however, when robot approaches to the field line, a large portion of white will also appear in the image, as shown in the Fig. 3 left. Assuming the resolution of the image I_{btm} from bottom camera is $w \times h$, based on camera's projective transformation [11], the width of line (around 5 cm) should not occupy more than $15\% \times h$ pixels. Here the robot foot area ROI is defined in I_{btm} as follows:

$$I_{btm(i,j)} \in ROI, \, if \, 0.625h \leqslant i \leqslant h, \, and \, 0.125w \leqslant j \leqslant 0.875w \quad (1)$$

The equation basically chooses the bottom 37.5% region of the image from bottom camera to be the foot area. This percentage is estimated by the logging data of a mock game. Larger values may include more white components, mostly ball and other robots' feet, while smaller foot area may be completely occupied by field lines, both risk holding against the assumption.

In addition, robot's head angle is constantly changing in order to keep track of the ball during the game. The defined ROI in the image may be projected to the ball, robot's own feet and jersey when kicking the ball (Fig. 3 middle), or robot's shoulder when head yaw value increases. Therefore, to complete the definition of foot area, the ROI will be discarded if when head pitch $\theta < -24.6°$ or head yaw $|\psi| > 65°$ in the corresponding frame. All the other cases are safe since robot will adjust its head angles to align the ball in the center of the image I_{btm} when the ball is getting close, so that the ball will not appear in the defined foot area if $\theta > -24.6°$.

Fig. 3. Left: the field of view of bottom camera when $\theta = 0$, $\psi = 0$; and the defined foot area ROI in I_{btm}. Middle: when $\theta = -24.6°$, ROI need to be discarded since field green may not be the majority color. Right: when $|\psi| = 65°$, ROI need to be discarded since robot's shoulder occupies the most of the region. (Color figure online)

2.2   Histogram Analysis

The green color of the soccer field may ideally have unique distribution over the G channel of the RGB color space. However, the field itself may not be lit evenly, for instance if lit by different spotlights or natural lighting, it could cause inconsistent apparent green across the field. Therefore, using an illumination invariant color space is important in order to eliminate the effect of varying green intensities. Here the RGB color space is transformed into normalized chromaticity coordinates, such that g chromaticity is:

$$g = \frac{G}{R + G + B} \tag{2}$$

The 1D histogram of the g chromaticity space will be used to extract the field feature from robot foot area ROI. Specifically, g can be quantized into n bins and the histogram bin set can be expressed as $Bin = [1, 2, \ldots, n]$. Each bin has a number of h_b pixels, where $b \in Bin$.

If the assumption that the majority color in the ROI is green stays true, the histogram should have a peak value $h_{b,max}$ which indicates that bin b consists of most pixels of field green. In order to further solidify the assumption, the histograms of five previous ROIs are combined. The values for the same bin can be simply added together. This essentially extends the ROI over the frames to minimize the non-green pixel distribution.

Note that five previous ROIs are not equivalent to five previous frames, since some frames might not pass the head angle check to have the valid ROI. Also, the images of ROIs for the previous frames will not be stored; instead, only the histograms of valid ROIs will be saved in a queue of size 5 for future processing. In this way, the algorithm can still run in a fast and efficient manner.

The histogram normalization is then performed on the new combined histogram H_b. This will obtain the probability that a pixel's g value is in bin b, given it is a pixel in the extended ROI. This distribution can be abbreviated as P_b:

$$P_b = \frac{H_b}{\sum_1^n H_b} \tag{3}$$

The bottom left histogram in Fig. 4 shows this probability distribution. Here n is set to be 32 in order to simplify the model. However, this histogram needs to be further processed to be representative for the whole field. First, a high pass filter, shown as the horizontal yellow line, is used to filter out the bins with low probability. The bins are discarded if the value is less than 30% of the peak value. The vertical yellow line is to remove the local maxima in the distribution. Based on the results of the proposed histogram model, the bins represent green pixels should be consecutive and the distribution of their values should be unimodal for global maxima, any local maxima is most likely to be another color.

$$P_b = 0 \quad if\ P_b < 0.3P_{b,max} \tag{4}$$

$$P_b = 0 \quad if\ P_b \neq P_{b,max} \quad and \quad P_{b-1} < P_b, P_{b+1} < P_b \tag{5}$$

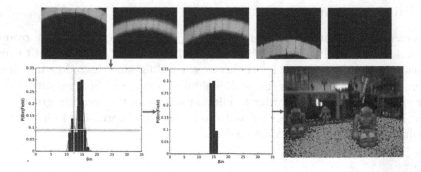

Fig. 4. Top: five consecutive valid ROIs in queue. Bottom Left: combined histogram for each ROI on top, further thresholding and filtering by yellow lines. Bottom Middle: histogram model for field feature. Bottom Right: green classification on I_{top}. (Color figure online)

After post-processing with filtering and thresholding techniques, the new histogram $\bar{P}_b$ with fewer bins (Fig. 4 bottom middle) becomes a valid model to represent field feature, since it should only contain the pixel information of field green.

2.3   Green Classification

The histogram model $\bar{P}_b$ will then be used to find the green pixels in the image I_{top} from top camera. Same quantization technique for the color space is performed. Essentially, a 32 bin 1D histogram of the g chromaticity space is calculated on I_{top}.

Here, a fast and efficient binary green classifier is more desired then the probabilistic green model, so the back projection process can be simplified. For all the non-zero bin b in $\bar{P}_b$, the pixels on I_{top} which are also in bin b are green. Bottom right plot in Fig. 4 masked the pixels classified as green on I_{top}. It is acceptable that the classification result is not completely precise, as long as it does not affect the formation of the field boundary.

Note that in this task, the parameters of both cameras need to be set the same so that the green pixels of two images could generally match. Although occasionally there were small inconsistencies between the cameras, but those slight differences did not affect the classification results in the experiments we performed.

As shown in Fig. 5, this field color detector approach is robust under inconsistent lighting conditions between multiple images. We also tested the algorithm

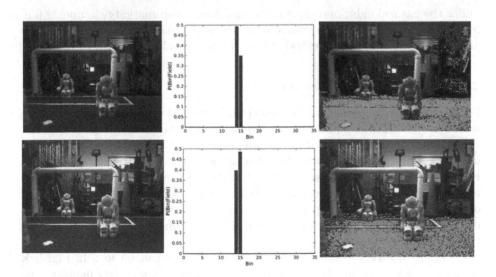

Fig. 5. When lighting changes during the game (top and bottom left), the peak value for histogram has a one-bin shift (top and bottom middle), and the green classification results are as expected (top and bottom right). (Color figure online)

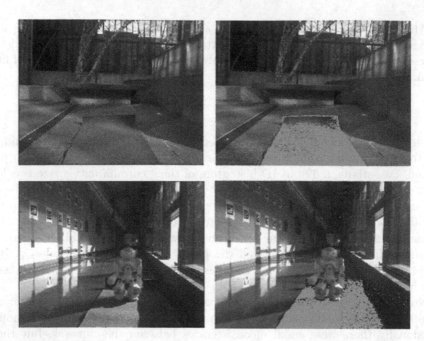

Fig. 6. The top and bottom scenes show that this field color detection approach works with inconsistent lighting conditions within the field, specifically under natural lighting which could cast shadows. (Color figure online)

under the natural light, and since the normalized g chromaticity channel is illumination invariant, the pixel values for green carpet under shadow and sunshine are similar; therefore, the method still works fairly well as shown in Fig. 6.

2.4 Experiments and Results

For the purpose of evaluating the perception rate and quality, different log files were recorded. Each log files contain 100 frames and was created when the basic robot behavior was performed in our lab environment. In order to simulate different lighting conditions, two different scenarios created, as seen in Fig. 5 (left). For comparison, the same set of log files was also evaluated upon other two methods: using the G channel in RGB (unnormalized G) as color space; and our traditional color look-up table method using Gaussian Mixture Model for color segmentation. The camera parameters and configuration of robot are set the same during the comparison.

One visualization example of those three methods can be seen in Fig. 7. It shows the green classification results for each method under two lighting conditions. Since green is classified in real time from the true green color around robot's foot area, both our proposed method (left) and the method using unnormalized G channel (middle) provide consistent results in various illuminations;

Fig. 7. The comparison of green classification results for three different methods on I_{top}, evaluated upon both dark (top) and bright (bottom) scene. (Color figure online)

Table 1. Field color detection rate of the proposed method compared to other two approaches.

Perception rate	Proposed method	Unnormalized G	Color-table
True positive rate	87.6%	68.1%	70.4%
False positive rate	1.4%	27.2%	7.5%

however, without using g chromaticity space, the classification cannot handle the inconsistent light within the field as well as the greenish background.

The traditional colortable-based method works well if the lighting condition does not change after the color was manually labeled (Fig. 7 top right). Given static nature of pre-defined color-table, it cannot work when lighting changed (bottom right). In that condition, Our method significantly out-performs the colortable based techniques.

The quantitative results are summarized in Table 1. The true positive rate is calculated from the percentage of correctly classified green pixels in the total green pixels for all the logging data, while the false positive rate is the percentage of incorrectly classified green pixels in total non-green pixels. Note that the log images were down-sampled to simplify the process of manually selecting and labeling the green area to obtain the ground truth. The results clearly show the necessity of normalizing G channel in color space, and the advantage of our proposed method over the color-table method.

3   Field Boundary Detection

Knowing the field boundaries helps robot limiting the search region for the objects of interest, which lead to improved detection speed and accuracy. The field boundary detection algorithm utilizes the field color classifier from the previous section to analyze the vertical scanlines and search linear relation of the green to non-green class transitions. HTWK [4] used RANSAC [13] algorithm to match the model of two straight lines, while B-Human 2013 [12] estimated the boundary by successively calculating the convex hull [14]. Our method here is a hybrid model which combines the advantages of both techniques.

3.1 Field Boundary Points

The first step of field boundary detection is to search for the possible points on the field edge. Since the valid field boundary points should always be below robot's horizon, we calculate the horizon line through robot's head angle transformation and top camera's projection. A top-down approach from the horizon to the bottom of the image is then adopted to build a score $S_{i,j}$ for each pixel i on the corresponding vertical

Fig. 8. Left: horizon line on the binary green classifier. Right: selected field boundary points on top camera image. (Color figure online)

scanline j. The policy is as follows: the score is initialized to 0 on the horizon line. A reward is added to $S_{i-1,j}$ for each $S_{i,j}$. If the $\text{Pixel}_{i,j}$ is classified as green, reward is set to be 1; otherwise reward is -1. Since the scan is downwards from non-field region to field, the pixel where the score is the lowest is then selected as the boundary point on that scanline.

The algorithm continues to perform on the next vertical scanline in the top camera image. Figure 8 left shows the horizon line on the binary green classifier. The selected field boundary points are marked as yellow spots in Fig. 8 right.

3.2 Convex Hull Filtering

In most cases, the field boundary points extracted from minimum score do not show clear linear relations. There are lots of false positive spots either due to the inaccuracy of green classification; or the objects on the field such as robots and ball which occlude part of the boundary. Those points need to be filtered out for further processing.

A filtering technique utilizing convex hull is performed on the raw field boundary points. Since most of the false boundary points are from the objects on the field, which are below the actual boundary, we calculate the upper convex hull from the raw boundary point set. For points not on the upper hull, associate them with upper hull edge formed by their 2-nearest neighbor vertices. The point far away from its corresponding edge is then removed. Figure 9 left shows the upper hull of the raw points; Fig. 9 middle shows the filtered boundary points.

3.3 RANSAC Line Fitting

In order to represent boundary points as boundary lines, a variant of RANSAC algorithm is implemented to fit the best line first. The algorithm randomly chooses two points in the filtered boundary points to form a line and check the distance between all the points and that line. If the distance is below a certain threshold, the corresponding point can be considered as an inlier. This process runs iteratively to maximize the number of inliers and find the best fit line to be a field boundary.

Fig. 9. Field boundary detection for both single boundary line case (top) and two lines case (bottom). The detection follows the sequence of building upper convex hull (left), filtering raw boundary points (middle) and line fitting using RANSAC (right).

The boundary points are not fitted by the first line might either because of noise, or the existence of a second boundary line. Therefore, the decision needs to be made carefully whether the second round of line fitting should be performed. If the percentage of the points left is above certain threshold, and nearly all of those points are distributed on the same side of the point set used to fit the first line, they are less likely to be just noise. A second round of RANSAC with smaller distance threshold is then performed on those points to match a secondary boundary line. The final step is to remove the lines above the intersection of two boundary lines to form a concrete field boundary. Figure 9 right shows the accurate line fitting for both single and two field boundary line(s).

4   Localization

The field boundary could be added as another vision-based landmark feature for robot's self-localization. As proposed from Schulz and Behnke [15], the approach utilizing the structure of field boundary and lines could be quite useful in robot's self-localization.

Currently, our localization algorithm [1] utilizes 200 particles to estimate the position state of the robot. A particle filter is implemented to track the continuous changes on the position, orientation and weight of each particle. Field boundary information can be included in the measurement update phase to adjust the particle state. Since the boundaries can be detected from far away, the position calculation may have large variance; therefore, field boundary detection will only correct particles' orientations and weights. If two boundaries can be detected, there are only four hypothesis of robot's orientation. If only one boundary can be seen and robot cannot see goal post at the same time, it is fair to assume that robot is facing the sideline. Combining with the body yaw value in the motion update phase, field boundaries can be extremely useful in determining robot's orientation. Figure 10 shows how field boundaries correctly update the particles' orientations.

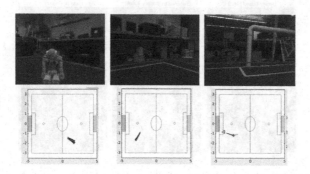

Fig. 10. Field boundary detection (top) and the corresponding positions and orientations of the particles (bottom). Using two boundary lines in the measurement update, and robot's body yaw in the motion update, particle filter tracks robot's direction (left and middle). Single boundary line could also serve as an additional landmark feature besides goal post to achieve more accurate localization (right).

5   Conclusion

We have presented an efficient approach for soccer field detection. Unlike other approaches that assume green is the majority color in both top and bottom images, we decrease the assumption region to robot's foot area, and utilizing head angles and previous frames to enhance the appearance of the green pixels. We analyze the histogram of g chromaticity space to find the threshold for top camera green classification. The binary field color classifier is then used to generate the field boundary using convex hull filtering and RANSAC line-fitting algorithms. We also briefly described how field boundary could help robot's self-localization.

The results indicate that our approach works adaptively on the field under variable lighting conditions and dynamic environment. Although it has been tested in our lab, we expect to fully examine the new perception framework built upon this field detection approach in real game scenario in RoboCup U.S Open 2016, and have the new system ready for the outdoor games in RoboCup 2016.

References

1. Qian, Y., He, Y., Han, Q., Poudel, S., Small, A., Lee, K., Lee, D.: RoboCup 2015 Standard Platform League Team Description Paper. Technical report (2015)

2. McGill, S.G., Yi, S.-J., Zhang, Y., Lee, D.D.: Extensions of a RoboCup soccer software framework. In: Behnke, S., Veloso, M., Visser, A., Xiong, R. (eds.) RoboCup 2013. LNCS, vol. 8371, pp. 608–615. Springer, Heidelberg (2014). doi:10.1007/978-3-662-44468-9_56

3. Mellmann, H., Krause, T., Ritter, C., Kaden, S., Hubner, T., Schlotter, B., Tofangchi, S.: Berlin United - Nao Team Humboldt Team Report 2015 - RC2. Technical report (2015)

4. Tilgner, R., Reinhardt, T., Kalbitz, T., Seering, S., Wunsch, M.: Team research report. Technical report (2014)

5. Tilgner, R., Reinhardt, T., Kalbitz, T., Seering, S., Wunsch, M.: Team research report. Technical report (2015)

6. Mayer, G., Utz, H., Kraetzschmar, G.K.: Playing robot soccer under natural light: a case study. In: Polani, D., Browning, B., Bonarini, A., Yoshida, K. (eds.) RoboCup 2003. LNCS, vol. 3020, pp. 238–249. Springer, Heidelberg (2004). doi:10.1007/978-3-540-25940-4_21

7. Sridharan, M., Stone, P.: Towards illumination invariance in the legged league. In: Nardi, D., Riedmiller, M., Sammut, C., Santos-Victor, J. (eds.) RoboCup 2004. LNCS, vol. 3276, pp. 196–208. Springer, Heidelberg (2005). doi:10.1007/978-3-540-32256-6_16

8. Kurugollu, F., Sankur, B., Harmanci, A.: Color image segmentation using histogram multithresholding and fusion. Image Vis. Comput. **19**(2001), 915–928 (2001)

9. Swain, M., Ballard, D.: Indexing via color histograms. In: Third International Conference on Computer Vision (1990)

10. NAO - Video camera specification. http://doc.aldebaran.com/2-1/family/robots/video_robot.html

11. Kofinas, N.: Forward and inverse kinematics for the NAO humanoid robot. Thesis (2012)

12. Röfer, T., Laue, T., Böockmann, A., Müller, J., Tsogias, A.: B-Human 2013: ensuring stable game performance. In: Behnke, S., Veloso, M., Visser, A., Xiong, R. (eds.) RoboCup 2013. LNCS, vol. 8371, pp. 80–91. Springer, Heidelberg (2014). doi:10.1007/978-3-662-44468-9_8

13. Fischler, M., Bolles, R.: Random sample consensus: a paradigm for model fitting with applications to image analysis and automated cartography. Thesis (2012)

14. Kriegel, H., Kroger, P., Zimek, A.: Outlier detection techniques. In: Tutorial at the 13th Pacific-Asia Conference on Knowledge Discovery and Data Mining (2009)

15. Schulz, H., Behnke, S.: Utilizing the structure of field lines for efficient soccer robot localization. Adv. Robot. **26**(14), 1603–1621 (2012)

Real-Time Visual Tracking and Identification for a Team of Homogeneous Humanoid Robots

Hafez Farazi[✉] and Sven Behnke

Autonomous Intelligent Systems, Computer Science Institute VI,
University of Bonn, Bonn, Germany
{farazi,behnke}@ais.uni-bonn.de
http://ais.uni-bonn.de

Abstract. The use of a team of humanoid robots to collaborate in completing a task is an increasingly important field of research. One of the challenges in achieving collaboration, is mutual identification and tracking of the robots. This work presents a real-time vision-based approach to the detection and tracking of robots of known appearance, based on the images captured by a stationary robot. A Histogram of Oriented Gradients descriptor is used to detect the robots and the robot headings are estimated by a multiclass classifier. The tracked robots report their own heading estimate from magnetometer readings. For tracking, a cost function based on position and heading is applied to each of the tracklets, and a globally optimal labeling of the detected robots is found using the Hungarian algorithm. The complete identification and tracking system was tested using two igus® Humanoid Open Platform robots on a soccer field. We expect that a similar system can be used with other humanoid robots, such as Nao and DARwIn-OP.

1 Introduction

Multi-target tracking is a well-known problem in computer vision, and has many applications, including traffic monitoring and automated surveillance. The aim of multi-target tracking is to automatically find objects of interest, assign a unique identification number to each, and to follow their movements over time. Multi-target tracking is fundamentally different to single-target tracking because of the difference in the state space model used for each. In particular, data association in situations of multiple detections with closely spaced and/or occluded objects makes multi-target tracking significantly more difficult. The expected number of visible targets is often unknown and may vary over time.

This work addresses a problem with an additional level of difficulty—the identification and tracking of multiple robots of identical appearance. Despite the lack of visual clues, our system is not only able to track each detected robot, but also to identify which robots are being tracked. This is done by generating a cost function for each tracklet, based on a motion model and the differences between the set of estimated and broadcasted headings of the robots. The output of the system, which is an estimation of the location and heading of each robot,

© Springer International Publishing AG 2017
S. Behnke et al. (Eds.): RoboCup 2016, LNAI 9776, pp. 230–242, 2017.
https://doi.org/10.1007/978-3-319-68792-6_19

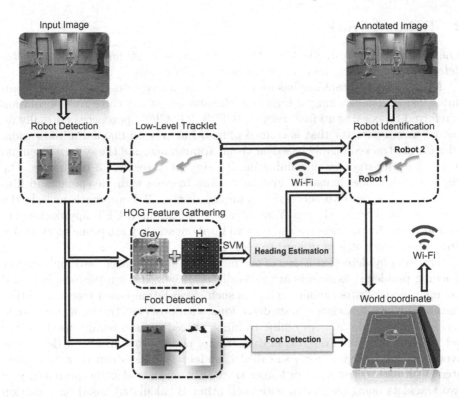

Fig. 1. Overview of our approach. After detection part, the heading of each robot is estimated based on proper HOG features. Using heading estimation and low-level tracklets observer finds and broadcasts the position of each robot.

is made available to the robots being observed, so that they may incorporate this into their own localization estimates, or use it for the generation of cooperative behaviors. Figure 1 gives an overview of our system.

The main contributions of this paper include:

1. The introduction of a novel pipeline to identify a set of homogeneous humanoid robots in an image.
2. The development of a high accuracy and low training time humanoid robot detection algorithm, based on a Histogram of Oriented Gradients descriptor.
3. A robust method for the estimation of the relative heading of a robot.
4. Experimental evidence that the proposed method can cope with long-term occlusions, despite a lack of visual differences between the tracked targets.
5. Demonstration that it is possible to track, identify and localize a homogeneous team of humanoid robots in real-time from another humanoid robot.

2   Related Work

The related work is divided into three categories, *multi-target tracking, robot detection and tracking* and *visual orientation estimation*.

Multi-target tracking has been studied for many years in the field of computer vision. The tracking of targets in the absence of any category information is referred to as category free tracking (CFT) [23]. CFT approaches normally do not require a detector that is trained offline, but rely on manual initialization. Objects are tracked mainly based on visual appearance, and the system attempts to track each target by discriminating it from other regions of the image. The visual target model is usually updated online to cope with viewpoint and illumination changes. Two successful examples of the CFT approach include the works of Allen et al. [1] and Yang et al. [21]. Although CFT approaches are computationally inexpensive and easy to implement, they are prone to excessive drift, after which it is very hard to recover.

Tracking by detection is one of the most popular approaches to multi-target tracking problems, as objects are naturally reinitialized when they are lost, and extreme model drifts cannot occur. As such, association based tracking (ABT) methods, which associate object detections with observed tracks, are proposed e.g. by Xing et al. [20]. An offline training procedure is generally used for the detection of objects of interest in each frame, and continuous object detections over time are linked to form so-called tracklets. Tracklets can then be associated with each other to form longer tracks. In most works, the probability of two tracklets being associated with each other is calculated based on a motion model and other criteria of visual similarity. The global tracklet association of highest probability is then computed using either the Hungarian algorithm [20], a Markov chain Monte Carlo method [22], or a Conditional Random Field [14].

Robot detection and tracking was done by Marchant et al. [13] using both visual perception and sonar data which was targeted for soccer environment. However, anthropomorphic design requirements in the Humanoid League prohibit teams from using sonar sensors. Many object detection approaches cannot be used for robot detection tasks due to the limitation in the onboard computer. Arenas et al. [3] detected Aibo robot and humanoid robots using the cascade of boosted classifiers, which is suitable for real-time applications. In another work Ruiz-Del-Solar et al. [15] proposed nested cascades of boosted classifiers for detecting legged robots. In addition to robot detection, gaze-direction of the robot is estimated based on Scale Invariant Feature Transform (SIFT) descriptor by Ruiz-Del-Solar et al. [16].

Visual orientation estimation of an object is often done by comparing projections of an accurate 3D model of the object to what is observed in the image, and finding the orientation that best matches the detected features [7]. These approaches work best only on simple backgrounds. Since the background in our application can be quite cluttered, and we do not wish to rely on the existence of an accurate 3D model of the detected robot, the most suitable approach for orientation estimation is through the use of image descriptors. Lin and Setiawan [11] proposed an orientation recognition system based on a SIFT descriptor [12], and a Support Vector Machine (SVM) classifier [5]. Shaikh et al. [18] proposed a template-based orientation estimation method for images of cars, based on the comparison of shape signatures.

3 Multi-target Tracking Formulation

We assume to have a collection of N humanoid robots of identical appearance that need to be identified and tracked by a further standing robot, or a stationary camera. In each camera frame, each of the robots can either be fully visible, partially visible, or not visible at all, and may be performing soccer actions such as walking, kicking and getting up. As such, the durations of partial or total lack of visibility may either be short or long. Each robot is equipped with a 9-axis inertial measurement unit (IMU), and the estimated absolute heading of the robot is broadcasted over Wi-Fi. The Wi-Fi communication between the robots is assumed to have delays, data loss, and even potentially connection loss for up to a few seconds. We use NimbRo network library [17] for Wi-Fi communication. Our objective is to detect, track and identify the N robots based solely on the captured images and the broadcasted heading information. Two igus® Humanoid Open Platform robots were used for the verification of the approach in this paper.

4 Vision System

4.1 Robot Detection

Although a number of pre-trained person detectors are available online, there is no detector for humanoid robots that can work out of the box. As such, we have designed, implemented and tested a robot detector that can robustly detect the igus® Humanoid Open Platform, although we expect the detector to work for other humanoid robot model as well, with the appropriate retuning and retraining. We evaluated five different methods for their suitability in our target domain before selecting and refining the most promising one. The methods were based, respectively, on color segmentation [8], adaptive object labeling [19], Haar wavelets [10], Local Binary Patterns [9], and Histograms of Oriented Gradients (HOG) [24]. The last of the five, a HOG feature descriptor used in the form of a cascade classifier was chosen based on criteria such as detection rate and training time. Although many RoboCup teams use a simple color segmentation approach to robot and obstacle detection, this approach is not safe in our case because we want to be able to distinguish the igus® Humanoid Open Platform from other objects on the field, such as the referee. Adaptive object labeling produced a relatively high rate of false positives, and it was nearly impossible to find a suitable threshold to work at all distances and in all situations. The method was also not able to deal well with occlusions. The Local Binary Pattern-based feature classifier also produced relatively poor results. However, the overall detection rates for the Haar wavelet and HOG cascading methods were found to be relatively good, and quite similar, but the former required a significantly longer time to train, so the latter was chosen.

Fig. 2. Robot detection results under various conditions.

In contrast to what is suggested for pedestrian detection [6], we do not feed the output of a multi-scale sliding window to a support vector machine (SVM) classifier. Instead, to save on computation time we use a cascade of rejectors with the AdaBoost technique to choose which features to evaluate in each stage, similar to what is suggested by Zhu et al. [24]. By using HOG features, we obtain a description of the visual appearance of the robot that is invariant to changes in illumination, position, orientation and background. As HOG is not rotation-scale invariant however, we artificially expand the number of positive images used for training by applying a number of transformations, also in part to minimize the required user effort in gathering the samples. These transformations include random rotations up to ±15°, mirroring, and the cutting of some parts of the sample image, in particular at the bottom, left and right, to emulate partial occlusion. Note that larger rotations of the images are not applied to allow the classifier to learn the shadow under the robot. This also has the positive effect of not detecting sitting or fallen robots, so that this discrete difference can be used in the identification phase to discern the robots. In our training of the igus® Humanoid Open Platform, we used a set of about 500 positive samples, 1000 negative samples, and a cascade classifier with 20 stages. The training time for the classifier was about 12 h on a standard PC.

As demonstrated in Fig. 2, this approach can detect the robot under various conditions, including while walking and kicking. The best detection results on the RoboCup field are at distances between 1 m and 5 m when the observer is not moving. After some post-processing, mainly related to non-maximum suppression, a bounding box for each detection is computed.

4.2   Heading Estimation

Given that all robots being detected in our application have the same visual appearance, estimation of the robot heading relative to the observer forms a primary cue to identify the robots, especially after long occlusions. To visually estimate the robot heading, we analyze the bounding boxes reported by the robot detector. We formulate the heading estimation problem as a multiclass classification problem by partitioning the full heading range into ten classes of size 36°, and use an SVM multiclass classifier with an RBF kernel.

The estimation is performed based on the output of a dense HOG descriptor on the upper half of the bounding box, the center position of the bounding box, and potential color features. The dense HOG features are used in the heading estimation to represent the visual features of each rotation class in the grayscale channel. Visual features of the robot are different depending on the position of the robot in the image. To address this issue, we pass the normalized position of the detected robot to our classifier. Many robots, including ours, have color features that can be used to help classify the robot heading. Hence, dense HOG features are also computed on the H channel, and the resulting feature vector is forwarded to the SVM classifier. To acquire the best possible results from the classifier, implemented using the LIBSVM library [4], all feature data is linearly scaled to the unit interval, and k-fold cross-validation and grid searching was used to find the best parameter set.

4.3   Foot Detection

Once a robot has been detected, it is desirable to be able to project the position of the robot to the egocentric world coordinates of the observing robot. For this to be reliable, a good estimate of the lowest part of the detected robot is required. Due to the non-maximum suppression in use, the bounding box often may not include all pixels of the robot feet. Due to the high sensitivity of the projection operation, especially when the robot is far from the observer, this causes significant errors in the estimated robot distance. To overcome this problem, we make the assumption that the robot is located on a surface of a mostly uniform known color. Starting from an appropriate region of interest, and using erosion, dilation and color segmentation techniques, we construct a segmented binary image such as the one in Fig. 3. A horizontal scan line scheme is then applied to improve the estimate of the bottom pixel of the robot. In more complicated cases, outside of the context of RoboCup, in which it is not possible to rely on a single predefined field color, one could use a background-foreground classification approach similar to the one proposed in [14]. After building a probability image, where each pixel contains the probability that it belongs to the background, our proposed method can be applied.

Fig. 3. Two non-green binary images for the detected robots in the left image. (Color figure online)

5   Tracking and Identification System

Many previous works in the area of tracking and identification are not suitable for our application, because they either work offline or are too computationally expensive. In this work, we propose a real-time two-step tracking system that first constructs low-level tracklets through data association, and then merges them into tracks that are labeled with a robot ID based on tracklet angle differences and the reported robot heading information. For the low-level tracking, we use greedy initialization, albeit with the assumption that the new tracklet should not be in the vicinity of another existing tracklet, in which case lazy initialization ensures that the detection is a robot and not a false positive. We use lazy deletion to cope with occlusion and false negatives.

5.1 Kalman Filter

Kalman filters are a state estimation technique for linear systems, with the general assumption that process and observation noise are Gaussian. Many researchers utilize Kalman filters as part of their object tracking pipeline, mainly due to its simplicity and robustness. Kalman filtering involves two main steps: Prediction and correction. In each cycle, a new location of the target is predicted using the process model of the filter, and in every frame where we detect a target, we update the corresponding Kalman filter with the position of the detection to correct the prediction. Using this approach, the target can still be tracked even if it is not detected or occluded. We use the constant acceleration model to derive the predictions in our model, in the one-dimensional case:

$$
\begin{aligned}
p_{k+1} &= p_k + \dot{p}_k \Delta T + \tfrac{1}{2}\ddot{p}_k \Delta T^2, \\
\dot{p}_{k+1} &= \dot{p}_k + \ddot{p}_k \Delta T, \\
\ddot{p}_{k+1} &= \ddot{p}_k,
\end{aligned}
\tag{1}
$$

where p_k, $\dot{p}_k$ and $\ddot{p}_k$ are the position, velocity and acceleration respectively at time step k. So, in our two-dimensional case the state vector becomes

$$
\boldsymbol{x}_k = \begin{bmatrix} h_k & v_k & \dot{h}_k & \dot{v}_k & \ddot{h}_k & \ddot{v}_k \end{bmatrix}^T,
\tag{2}
$$

where (h_k, v_k) is the position of the center of the robot in the image at time step k. The system model is then given by

$$
\boldsymbol{x}_{k+1} = \boldsymbol{\Phi} \boldsymbol{x}_k + \boldsymbol{w}_k,
\tag{3}
$$

where $\boldsymbol{w}_k \sim \mathcal{N}(\boldsymbol{0}, \boldsymbol{Q}_k)$ is zero mean Gaussian process noise with covariance $\boldsymbol{Q}_k$ and $\boldsymbol{\Phi}$ is the state transition matrix, derived from (1):

$$
\boldsymbol{\Phi} = \begin{bmatrix}
1 & 0 & \Delta T & 0 & \tfrac{1}{2}\Delta T^2 & 0 \\
0 & 1 & 0 & \Delta T & 0 & \tfrac{1}{2}\Delta T^2 \\
0 & 0 & 1 & 0 & \Delta T & 0 \\
0 & 0 & 0 & 1 & 0 & \Delta T \\
0 & 0 & 0 & 0 & 1 & 0 \\
0 & 0 & 0 & 0 & 0 & 1
\end{bmatrix}.
\tag{4}
$$

ΔT is the nominal time difference between two successive frames. In every frame where the robot is detected, the Kalman filter is updated using the coordinates of the center of the detected robot bounding box $\boldsymbol{z}_k = (\hat{h}_k, \hat{v}_k)$. The measurement model is given by

$$z_k = Hx_k + \vartheta_k, \tag{5}$$

where $\vartheta_k \sim \mathcal{N}(\mathbf{0}, R_k)$ is zero mean Gaussian measurement noise with covariance R_k and H is the measurement matrix

$$H = \begin{bmatrix} 1\ 0\ 0\ 0\ 0\ 0 \\ 0\ 1\ 0\ 0\ 0\ 0 \end{bmatrix}. \tag{6}$$

Given this system model, measurement model, and some initial conditions, the Kalman filter can estimate the state vector x_k at each time step together with its covariance Σ_k.

5.2   Data Association

In multi-target tracking, the problem of finding the optimal assignment between new target detections and existing tracklets, in such a way that each detection is assigned to at most one tracklet, is referred to as the data association problem. Assume that in the current frame we have n existing tracklets, and m new detections, where m is not necessarily equal to n. Let p_i denote the predicted position of the ith tracklet, and d_j denote the position of the jth detection. We construct the $n \times m$ cost matrix C, with entries given by

$$C_{ij} = \begin{cases} \|p_i - d_j\| & \text{if } \|p_i - d_j\| < D_{max}, \\ C_{max} & \text{otherwise}, \end{cases} \tag{7}$$

where $i = 1, \ldots, n$ and $j = 1, \ldots, m$, D_{max} is a distance threshold, and C_{max} is the length of the diagonal of the image in units of pixels. Using the cost matrix C, the optimal data association is calculated using the Hungarian algorithm.

5.3   Robot Identification

We modeled the problem of identifying the robots as a high-level data association problem. In each time step, we have n tracklets and r robots, where r is determined by the observer as the number of robots that are broadcasting their heading information over Wi-Fi. Each tracklet, in addition to a buffer T_{pos} of (x, y) pixel position values, incorporates a buffer of detected robot headings T_{rot}. Buffers R_{rot} of received absolute headings from the robots are also maintained. The previously calculated robot positions are also kept in a buffer R_{pos} of pixel position values. We wish to optimally assign each tracklet to at most one robot, based on the detected and received heading information Fig. 4. The core idea is to find the best tracklet assignments based on the average of the differences between the detected tracklet heading buffers and the broadcasted headings from the individual robots over a limited time range. We construct the $n \times r$ cost matrix G, with entries G_{ij} that relate to the cost of associating the ith tracklet with the jth robot:

$$\gamma = \begin{cases} \frac{r}{2\pi} \min\left\{ \left| R_{rot}^a[1] - R_{rot}^b[1] \right| : a < b,\ a,b \in 1,\ldots,r \right\} & \text{if } r \geq 2, \\ 0.5 & \text{otherwise,} \end{cases} \tag{8}$$

$$G_{ij} = \begin{cases} \frac{\gamma}{\pi D_i} \sum_{k=1}^{D_i} \left| T_{rot}^i[k] - R_{rot}^j[k] \right| + \frac{1-\gamma}{C_{max}} \left\| T_{pos}^i[1] - R_{pos}^j[1] \right\| & \text{if } D_i \geq \tau, \\ 2.0 & \text{otherwise,} \end{cases} \tag{9}$$

where τ is a minimum buffer size threshold, D_i is the number of elements in the buffers of the ith tracklet, and for example $T_{rot}^i[k]$ is the kth element of the T_{rot} buffer for the ith tracklet, where $k = 1$ corresponds to the most recently added value, and $k = D_i$ corresponds to the oldest value still in the buffer. Similarly, $R_{pos}^j[1]$ is the most recent (x,y) coordinate in the R_{pos} buffer for the jth robot. The interpolation factor γ determines, based on the minimum separation of the broadcasted robot headings, how much we should rely on differences in heading to associate the robots, and how much we should rely on differences in detected position. Once the cost matrix G has been constructed as described, the Hungarian algorithm is used to find the optimal robot-to-tracklet association. With that association, all information that is required to compute the egocentric world coordinates of the detected robots relative to the observer is available. Some low-pass filtering is performed on the final world coordinates to reduce the effects of noise, and produce more stable outputs.

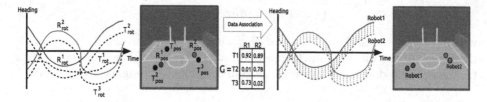

Fig. 4. Robot identification overview. We associate low-level tracklets with robots using comparison of heading and position.

6 Experimental Results

In our experiments, we used two igus® Humanoid Open Platform robots [2]. Each of them is equipped with a dual-core i7-4500U 2.4 GHz processor and a 720p Logitech C905 USB camera. On this hardware, the whole detection, tracking and identification pipeline takes around 50 ms, making it suitable for real-time applications. We performed four different tests to evaluate the proposed system. All tests were conducted on a RoboCup artificial grass field, and the results were manually evaluated for a subset of the frames by the user. The data that was used in the evaluation included varying lighting conditions, and partial, short term and long term occlusions. In the first experiment, we examined the output of the robot detection module by counting the number of successful detections and false positives. The second experiment tested the success rate of the foot detection. A detected position was declared successful if it was within a maximum of 8 pixels from the true bottom pixel of the robot. The third experiment tested the success rate and average error of the visual heading estimation, as compared to the ground truth heading output broadcasted by the corresponding robot. A success was declared if the angular deviation was under $18°$, half the size of the heading classes. In the final experiment, the robot identification output was verified by counting the proportion of frames in which the robot labels were correctly assigned. The results are summarized in Table 1. Note that in some of the experiments, we used a camera attached to a laptop, and in other experiments we used a further igus® Humanoid Open Platform. Figure 5 shows example results of detecting, tracking, identifying, and localizing two robots on the soccer field.

As an extension of the results, we conducted two further experiments where the final robot locations were broadcasted by the observer, and the robots used solely this localization information to walk to a predefined location on the field

Table 1. Robot detection, heading estimation, and identification results.

Test	Success rate	False positives	Average error	Frames
Robot detection	88%	7	–	1000
Foot detection	89%	–	–	932
Heading estimation	74%	–	17°	845
Robot identification	90%	–	–	932

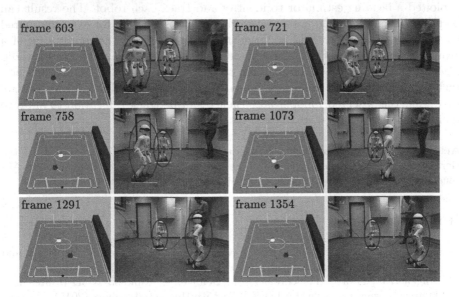

Fig. 5. Detection, tracking, and identification results obtained by our system.

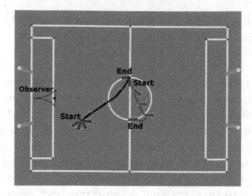

Fig. 6. Positioning experiment with blindfolded robots.

Fig. 6. A video of the expriment is available at our website[1] The cameras of the robots were covered to demonstrate that they were not using their own visual perception.

7   Conclusions

In this paper we proposed a real-time vision pipeline for detecting, tracking, and identifying a set of homogeneous humanoid robots, and gained promising results in experimental verification thereof. Unlike many other works, we could not use any visual robot differences to cope with partial or complete occlusions, so we exploited a heading estimator to identify and track each robot. The result can be used in many RoboCup and real-world scenarios, such as for example shared localization on a soccer field, external robot control, and the monitoring of a group of humanoid robots using a standard camera. As future work, we would like to extend the robot identification to use additional data association cues, such as for example if a robot has fallen down or left the field. Additionally, we would like the observed robots to use their resulting tracked location to improve their own localization.

Acknowledgment. This work was partially funded by grant BE 2556/10 of the German Research Foundation (DFG). The authors would like to thank Philipp All-geuer for help in editing the article and assisting in performing experimental tests.

References

1. Allen, J.G., Xu, R.Y., Jin, J.S.: Object tracking using camshift algorithm and multiple quantized feature spaces. In: Pan-Sydney Area Workshop (2004)
2. Allgeuer, P., Farazi, H., Schreiber, M., Behnke, S.: Child-sized 3D printed igus humanoid open platform. In: IEEE-RAS 15th Humanoid Robots (2015)

---

[1] Video link: https://www.ais.uni-bonn.de/videos/RoboCup_Symposium.2016.

3. Arenas, M., Ruiz-del-Solar, J., Verschae, R.: Detection of AIBO and humanoid robots using cascades of boosted classifiers. In: Visser, U., Ribeiro, F., Ohashi, T., Dellaert, F. (eds.) RoboCup 2007. LNCS, vol. 5001, pp. 449–456. Springer, Heidelberg (2008). doi:10.1007/978-3-540-68847-1_47
4. Chang, C.-C., Lin, C.-J.: LIBSVM: a library for support vector machines. ACM Trans. Intell. Syst. Technol. **2**, 1–27 (2011)
5. Cortes, C., Vapnik, V.: Support-vector networks. Mach. Learn. **20**, 273–297 (1995)
6. Dalal, N., Triggs, B.: Object detection using histograms of oriented gradients. In: Pascal VOC Workshop, ECCV (2006)
7. Dementhon, D.F., Davis, L.S.: Model-based object pose in 25 lines of code. Int. J. Comput. Vis. **15**(1–2), 123–141 (1995)
8. Farazi, H., Allgeuer, P., Behnke, S.: A monocular vision system for playing soccer in low color information environments. In: 10th Workshop on Humanoid Soccer Robots, IEEE-RAS International Conference on Humanoid Robots, Korea (2015)
9. Liao, S., Zhu, X., Lei, Z., Zhang, L., Li, S.Z.: Learning multi-scale block local binary patterns for face recognition. In: Lee, S.-W., Li, S.Z. (eds.) ICB 2007. LNCS, vol. 4642, pp. 828–837. Springer, Heidelberg (2007). doi:10.1007/978-3-540-74549-5_87
10. Lienhart, R., Maydt, J.: An extended set of haar-like features for rapid object detection. In: International Conference on Image Processing (ICIP) (2002)
11. Lin, C.-Y., Setiawan, E.: Object orientation recognition based on SIFT and SVM by using stereo camera. In: IEEE International Conference on Robotics and Biomimetics (ROBIO), pp. 1371–1376 (2008)
12. Lowe, D.G.: Object recognition from local scale-invariant features. In: 7th IEEE International Conference on Computer Vision (ICCV), pp. 1150–1157 (1999)
13. Marchant, R., Guerrero, P., Ruiz-del-Solar, J.: Cooperative global tracking using multiple sensors. In: Chen, X., Stone, P., Sucar, L.E., van der Zant, T. (eds.) RoboCup 2012. LNCS, vol. 7500, pp. 310–321. Springer, Heidelberg (2013). doi:10.1007/978-3-642-39250-4_28
14. Milan, A., Leal-Taixé, L., Schindler, K., Reid, I.: Joint tracking and segmentation of multiple targets. In: IEEE Conference on Computer Vision and Pattern Recognition (CVPR), pp. 5397–5406 (2015)
15. Ruiz-Del-Solar, J., Arenas, M., Verschae, R., Loncomilla, P.: Visual detection of legged robots and its application to robot soccer playing and refereeing. Int. J. Humanoid Rob. **7**(04), 669–698 (2010)
16. Ruiz-del-Solar, J., Verschae, R., Arenas, M., Loncomilla, P.: Play ball!. IEEE Robot. Automat. Mag. **17**(4), 43–53 (2010)
17. Schwarz, M.: NimbRo network library. Github (2015)
18. Shaikh, S.H., Roy, S., Chaki, N.: Recognition of object orientation from images. In: International Conference on Emerging Trends in Science, Engineering and Technology (INCOSET), pp. 260–263. IEEE (2012)
19. Wang, Z., Jiang, X., Xu, B., Hong, K.: An online multi-object tracking approach by adaptive labeling and Kalman filter. In: Conference on Research in Adaptive and Convergent Systems, pp. 146–151. ACM (2015)
20. Xing, J., Ai, H., Lao, S.: Multi-object tracking through occlusions by local tracklets filtering and global tracklets association with detection responses. In: IEEE Conference on Computer Vision and Pattern Recognition (CVPR) (2009)
21. Yang, C., Duraiswami, R., Davis, L.: Fast multiple object tracking via a hierarchical particle filter. In: 10th IEEE International Conference on Computer Vision (ICCV), pp. 212–219 (2005)

22. Yu, Q., Medioni, G., Cohen, I.: Multiple target tracking using spatio-temporal Markov chain monte carlo data association. In: IEEE Conference on Computer Vision and Pattern Recognition (CVPR). IEEE (2007)
23. Zhang, T., Ghanem, B., Liu, S., Ahuja, N.: Robust visual tracking via multi-task sparse learning. In: IEEE Conference on Computer Vision and Pattern Recognition (CVPR), pp. 2042–2049 (2012)
24. Zhu, Q., Yeh, M.-C., Cheng, K.-T., Avidan, S.: Fast human detection using a cascade of histograms of oriented gradients. In: IEEE Conference on Computer Vision and Pattern Recognition (CVPR), pp. 1491–1498 (2006)

Effective Multi-robot Spatial Task Allocation Using Model Approximations

Okan Aşık[✉] and H. Levent Akın

Department of Computer Engineering, Boğaziçi University, 34342 Istanbul, Turkey
{okan.asik,akin}@boun.edu.tr

Abstract. Real-world multi-agent planning problems cannot be solved using decision-theoretic planning methods due to the exponential complexity. We approximate firefighting in rescue simulation as a spatially distributed task and model with multi-agent Markov decision process. We use recent approximation methods for spatial task problems to reduce the model complexity. Our approximations are single-agent, static task, shortest path pruning, dynamic planning horizon, and task clustering. We create scenarios from RoboCup Rescue Simulation maps and evaluate our methods on these graph worlds. The results show that our approach is faster and better than comparable methods and has negligible performance loss compared to the optimal policy. We also show that our method has a similar performance as DCOP methods on example RCRS scenarios.

1 Introduction

Real-world multi-agent planning problems have a high complexity due to the *curse of dimensionality*. The number of agents also increases the complexity exponentially. Multi-agent planning can be defined as the coordination of a set of agents to get the highest possible reward from the environment they act in. Multi-agent planning has different categories, but in this work we consider only the centralized control of cooperative agents.

The spatial task allocation problem (SPATAP) is a subclass of multi-agent planning problems. In the SPATAP, a group of agents try to do the tasks which are spatially distributed to the environment. From the multi-agent planning perspective, the SPATAP has two important features; task interdependency, and agent interdependency. The tasks appear in the environment independently. Agents move in the environment without affecting each other. Despite these features, the SPATAP is still a complex multi-agent planning problem and cannot be solved using optimal algorithms as shown by Claes *et al.* [1].

SPATAP is formalized as a Multi-agent Markov Decision Process (MMDP). The state space is defined by the agent and the task positions. The agents either move in the environment (such as grid world) or take the action to do the task at the current location. The reward is defined according to the total task completion. The complexity of a SPATAP is determined by the state space and the action space. The optimal MMDP algorithm cannot solve SPATAP problems

© Springer International Publishing AG 2017
S. Behnke et al. (Eds.): RoboCup 2016, LNAI 9776, pp. 243–255, 2017.
https://doi.org/10.1007/978-3-319-68792-6_20

having non-trivial number of locations, agents, tasks and actions. There are two basic approaches to solve such complex MMDP problems; using approximate algorithms or approximate models. In this paper, we propose model approximations which are tailored for the SPATAPs.

The model approximation approach simplifies the given model and finds a solution for the simplified model as a proxy for the actual problem. The approximations aim to reduce the state space and action space of the actual problem. Claes et al. [1] propose a series of approximations for SPATAP planning. At every time step of the decision process, the method gets the current state of the actual problem and constructs a simpler model using the approximations. The algorithm calculates a policy for the simple model and the agents act on the actual decision process using the policy.

The approximations proposed by Claes et al. are subjective approximation, and phase approximation. The agent calculates the possible future positions of the agents by the assumption that they are the only agents in the environment. Then the agent can discount its own future reward according to the possibility of another agent being on that position. This removes the exponential complexity due to the number of agents in the state space. The agent assumes that a new task will not appear in the future. This also reduces the state space complexity due to the future tasks.

We extend the online planning framework of Claes et al. [1]. We first cluster tasks based on the distance between the tasks. Then, we first calculate the best cluster to go using the approximate model. Then, every agent plans only for the task in the assigned clusters. In these two levels of the planning, we apply subjective approximation and shortest-path pruning which removes the locations which are not on the shortest path between the agent and the tasks. We use Value Iteration [10] algorithm to calculate the best action, but we choose the planning horizon according to the time step required to reach k tasks.

We also generalize the SPATAP model from grid world to graph world where locations are represented by the vertices of a graph. We define Rescue Spatial Task Allocation Problem (Rescue-SPATAP) as an extension of SPATAP, and solve using SPATAP approximations. We show that the comparison with the optimal value not as good as pure SPATAP problems, but our method performs better than other algorithms including the SPATAP algorithm [1]. Finally, we apply our SPATAP approximations to RoboCup Rescue Simuation (RCRS) scenarios and have similar performance to Distributed Constraint Optimization (DCOP) methods of RMASBench [5].

2   Background

2.1   Multi-agent Markov Decision Process

A multi-agent Markov Decision Process (MMDP) is a mathematical formalization for the multi-agent planning in observable, but uncertain action environments.

Multiagent MDP is 5-tuple $\langle D, S, A, T, R \rangle$ where

- D is the set of agents,
- S is the finite set of states,
- A is the finite set of joint actions $(A_1 \times A_2 \times \ldots \times A_n)$,
- T is the transition function which assigns probabilities for transitioning from one state to another given a joint action,
- R is the immediate reward function.

We can solve an MMDP using the standard offline MDP planning algorithms such as value iteration [10]. The value iteration algorithm iteratively improves the estimation of the expected value of a state with the following Bellmann equation:

$$Q(s,a) = R(s,a) + \gamma \sum_{s' \in S} T(s,a,s')V(s') \tag{1}$$

$$V(s) = \max_{a \in A} Q(s,a) \tag{2}$$

s stands for a state, a stands for a joint action and γ stands for the discount value to determine how valuable future rewards are.

2.2   Rescue Spatial Task Allocation Problem

Spatial Task Allocation Problem (SPATAP) is introduced by Claes *et al.* [1]. SPATAP is defined on a location set where a set of different tasks appear on different locations. Agents have movement actions (to move from one location to another) and also task actions (required to carry out a specific task). We can think of a grid world where there are two or more cleaning robots. Cleaning tasks appear at different cells on the grid world. Agents are supposed to act for cleaning tasks as efficiently as possible. Although the allocation of agents to their closest tasks would seem to be the optimal, the authors prove that SPATAP is as hard as MMDP.

The original SPATAP formulation models tasks as independent. Emergence of a task at a location is independent of other locations. We introduce the Rescue Spatial Task Allocation Problem (Rescue-SPATAP) where tasks are defined as fires and dependent on their neighbors, which makes Rescue-SPATAP harder than SPATAP. In Rescue-SPATAP, the location of initial tasks/fires are fixed at the start of the process and new tasks only appear based on the vicinity of the current tasks. In the SPATAP formulation, every task has the same reward, but in Rescue-SPATAP, if the agent extinguishes a fire, it gets a reward proportional to the size of the building. We show that the online approximations proposed for SPATAPs are also applicable for Rescue-SPATAPs.

The RoboCup Rescue Simulator (RCRS) has four mobile agents: fire brigades, police forces, ambulances, and civilians. There are also three stationary center agents which provide a communication channel for fire brigades, polices, and ambulances. There are three types of tasks: rescuing the civilians, firefighting, and removing the blockades on the road. In this study, we target the firefighting problem, but our approach is also applicable for all RCRS tasks because they can be defined as spatial task allocation problem. The simulator uses a map of the city. The map defines buildings and roads. The simulator creates a disaster scenario by defining fire ignition points. Since only buildings are flammable, the dynamic tasks emerge as the buildings are catching fire. The ultimate aim is to develop an algorithm to effectively allocate agents to the buildings which are on fire.

We define a Rescue-SPATAP based on the RCRS. The problem is defined on a graph world. The graph world has two types of vertices; buildings and roads as already defined in the RCRS. In the RCRS, buildings have fire levels: *no fire, heating, burning, burnt, extinguished*. However, to reduce the complexity, we define only two states: *no fire*, and *burning*. We map the RCRS fire states to the graph world fire states as follows:

- *no fire* ← {*no fire, burnt, extinguished*}
- *burning* ← {*heating, burning*}

Since the fire simulator of the RCRS is quite complex to model [7], we model fire spreading as independent events where the building on fire affects the neighbor buildings' fire state. Every neighbor building in the vicinity of d meters will add p probability to change the state from *no fire* to *burning*. The agents move on the graph by choosing the neighbors of the vertex where the agent is on (same as RCRS). Also, the building the agent is on stays in *no fire* state. In RCRS, agents extinguish fires based on the size of the building and the water the agent has in its tank. However, we simplify the fire extinguishing behavior by that an agent extinguishes the fire of the building which the agent is on, regardless of other factors. The reward is defined as the ratio of the sum of the area of the buildings which are in *no fire* state to the area of all buildings.

3   Related Work

The teams in RoboCup Rescue Agent Simulation (RCRS) generally uses state-based strategies in behavioral agent frameworks[1]. The teams prefer agent frameworks which enable them to exploit typical scenarios. These agent frameworks let the teams fine tune their behaviors according to the cases arising over the trial-error periods. In a recent study, Parker *et al.* report the performance of decentralized coalition formation approach for RCRS [8]. The agents use a greedy algorithm with a utility function which is designed for different tasks. They compare static and dynamic coalition formation with heterogeneous agents. Due to the different characteristics of every RCRS scenario, they found that different approaches may work well for different scenarios.

In the literature, the RCRS problem is also modeled as a task allocation problem. The tasks constitute rescuing a civilian, firefighting, and clearing the

---

[1] http://roborescue.sourceforge.net/blog/2015/08/team-description-papers-tdps/.

blockades. The tasks are discovered over time and agents do not know all the tasks of the current state. This distributed dynamic task allocation problem is modeled as the distributed constraint optimization problem (DCOP) [11] and solved using state of the art DCOP algorithms such as MaxSum [3], and DSA [4]. Pujol-Gonzalez *et al.* improve the computational efficiency of MaxSum by introducing Binary MaxSum for RCRS [9]. They also introduce a method to integrate team coordination to DCOPs. The authors show that, by defining coordination variables for police forces and fire brigades, they are able to improve the performance. Although these approaches have reasonable performances, they require a lot of domain knowledge to design good utility functions with inter-team coordination variables. Our approach has inherent capacity to represent different agent types without changing the problem definition.

There are also attempts to solve fire task allocation problem with biologically-inspired methods [2]. They propose a new algorithm, called eXtreme-Ants, where agents are modeled as insects which have response thresholds for tasks that are modeled as stimulus. They show that the performance of the algorithm is comparable to DCOP methods.

RMASBench is an effort to provide a software repository to easily model RCRS as a DCOP and benchmark the different algorithms [5]. However, the current implementation requires the full state information of the simulation at every time step and the communication among DCOP agents isolated from RCRS. This hinders the application of the DCOP methods for RCRS. Also, modeling RCRS as task allocation problem neglects the dynamic nature of the problem and introduces the issue of designing good utility functions.

4   Methods

We model the firefighting task of the RoboCup Rescue Simulation (RCRS) as a Multi-agent Markov Decision Process (MMDP). We create an approximate MMDP model with single-agent, static task, shortest path pruning, task clustering, and online planning horizon approximations in our online planning framework.

The online planning framework gets the current state from the simulator (either Rescue-SPATAP simulator or RoboCup Rescue Simulator) and creates a new problem by clustering the near tasks together. Then, the approximations are applied to the clustered model to have less complex model. The policy for the approximated model is calculated using the Value Iteration [10] algorithm. We calculate the target of every agent by following the policies greedily to assign a cluster to every agent. Since we assigned a cluster to every agent, the model approximation and policy calculation is carried out considering only the tasks of the assigned clusters.

4.1   Hierarchical Planning by Task Clustering

Before applying any approximations to the actual model of the problem, we create clusters to further reduce the complexity. Since fires propagate from the initial ignition points, tasks appear as a cluster. Therefore, we introduce a distance based task clustering algorithm. The tasks which are closer to each other more than d meters belong to the same cluster. We assign a cluster for every agent by model approximations and value iteration algorithm. After every agent is assigned to a cluster, we plan only for the tasks which belongs to the agent's cluster.

To create a cluster, we iterate over all the burning buildings and compare the distance between the building and the buildings in a cluster. If the building is closer than d meters to one of the buildings which is in a cluster, the building is added to the cluster. The clustered buildings and their neighbors are removed. A new building for every cluster is created with the area equal to the sum of the area of the buildings in the cluster. Neighbors of the clustered buildings are also recreated as the neighbors of the cluster as seen in Fig. 1.

In the SPATAP, the actions are taken according to the calculated value function, but our approach calculates a priority order of tasks for every agent using the depth-first graph traversal algorithm on the value function (taking the agent position as the root).

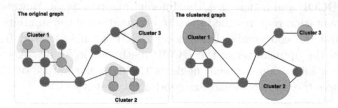

Fig. 1. The illustration of the task clustering. The initial graph (left) results in a clustered task graph (right).

4.2 Single-Agent Approximation

The state space of multi-agent planning has exponential complexity due to the number of agents. To reduce this complexity, we plan as a single agent by using other agents' positions as an indication of their policies. We calculate a policy for all agents as if they are the only agent in the environment. Then, for every agent we calculate the other agents' total effect which is called *presence mass* [1]. *Presence mass* is the probability distribution of other agents' positions on the graph world.

The *presence mass* can be calculated only if we know the policy of the agents. We calculate a policy for every agent based on their positions on the graph by assuming that they are the only agent on the world. We use this policy to have an idea about the most desirable action from the perspective of that agent. To reflect the uncertainty, we use this policy to calculate a Boltzmann distribution over actions for every state. We define a Boltzmann distribution over the state-action values (the expected cumulative reward when an action is taken in a state). This distribution defines the probability of choosing an action in a state.

The best response of the agent based on the *presence mass* of other agents can be computed by changing the discount factor (γ) of the Bellman equation (see Eq. 1). By changing the discount factor value, we can punish the actions resulting on a position where other agents have high *presence mass*. Therefore, we discount the future expected reward according to *presence mass* as proposed by [1]:

$$Q_i(s_i, a_i) = R(s_i, a_i) + \sum_{s_i' \in S_i} T(s_i, a_i, s_i') \left[(1 - f_i \, \text{pm}_i(s_i')) V_i(s_i') \right] \qquad (3)$$

$$\text{pm}_i(s_i') = \sum_{j \neq i} Pr(s_j = s_i' | s)$$

$$V_i(s_i) = \max_{a_i} Q_i(s_i, a_i)$$

Q_i denotes the expected total reward for the agent i if it is in state s_i, and takes the action a_i. V_i denotes the expected total reward for the agent i from the state s_i'. pm defines the *presence mass* of the other agents. The parameter f_i which is used to scale the future value is calculated as the ratio of maximum reward to the maximum value as suggested by [1].

4.3 Static Task Approximation

We also aim to reduce the exponential complexity due to the fire levels of buildings. Therefore, we use the approximation proposed by [1] and redefine the state space to include only the buildings that are in *burning* state. Claes *et al.* [1] propose this approximation for spatially distributed tasks where the occurrence of new tasks are independent. In the firefighting problem, there is the effect of neighbor buildings on the occurrence of new tasks. However, the propagation of fire on RCRS is slow such that we can plan considering only the buildings that are on fire without calculating their effects on their neighbors.

The deterministic actions and static task approximations on a graph world for a single agent MDP results in the following Bellman equation:

$$V(s) = \max_{s' \in N(s)} R(s') + \gamma V(s') \qquad (4)$$

s denotes the current state, s' the next state, N the neighbor function, γ is the discount factor and V stands for the value function. Since the actions are deterministic, reward function is only depended on the next state, s', and transition function (T) is removed (i.e. the action uniquely identifies the next state). Note that, we changed (s, a) term with s' since actions are deterministic. Every (s, a) term defines an s' (i.e. every action results in a single next state). N function defines the set of neighbor vertices of the given vertex (or state). This recursive equation will be calculated for h times with the initial values $V(s) = 0$ for h-horizon planning.

4.4 The Shortest Path Approximation

The tractability of the Bellman equation depends on the state space and the transition function (i.e. neighbors). If the agent does not move to the vertex which is in *burning* state, the state can only be identified by the position of the agent. If we remove the neighbors which will not be visited by the agent, we achieve to reduce the state space and also branching factor of the transition function. The value iteration algorithm propagates rewards from the goal state, in our case this is one of the vertices which is in the *burning* state.

We calculate the shortest path between the agent and the vertices that are in *burning* state, and also all possible *burning* vertex pairs. Since the actions are deterministic and tasks are static, the optimal policy will result in a movement of the agent on the shortest path from its own position to the one of the tasks.

4.5 Online Dynamic Planning Horizon

The running time of the value iteration algorithm for the finite horizon problems also depends on the planning horizon which determines the number of iterations of the algorithm. If we consider Rescue-SPATAP, we should plan according to the current time step of RCRS for the optimal performance. The RCRS simulation runs for 300 time steps. For example, if we are in 30th time step, we should construct our approximate model and plan with the value iteration for $300 - 30 = 270$ time steps. However, since we already approximated the problem, it might not increase the performance after a certain horizon. Therefore, we propose to determine the planning horizon based on the reachability of the vertices that are in *burning* state.

As shown by Claes *et al.* [1], if the agents plan only for the k closest tasks, the algorithm still has reasonable performance. In the value iteration algorithm, the reward propagates from the vertex that is in *burning* state since the agent gets higher reward when it can change the state of the vertex from *burning* to *no fire*. For example, we can consider a graph world with the initial state shown in Fig. 2. There are five vertices where the agent is located on the vertex 1 and the vertex 5 is in *burning* state. The agent should choose an action based on the values of the vertices 2 and 3. The three iterations of the value iteration algorithm for the example graph world can be seen in Fig. 2. The values of the vertices correspond to the states where the agent is on that vertex location. After the first and the second iterations of the algorithm, the agent cannot differentiate between the actions $A1$ and $A2$. However, after the third iteration of the algorithm, the agent

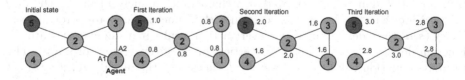

Fig. 2. Three iterations of the value iteration algorithm on a graph world.

can differentiate two vertices based on the value propagated to the vertex 2 and 3. In our small graph, three iterations of the algorithm is enough to differentiate two actions, but as the distance of the vertices that are in *burning* state increases, the minimum number of iteration of the algorithm will increase.

To calculate the planning horizon (i.e. the minimum number of iterations), we use the breath first graph traversal algorithm. We set the vertex of the agent as the root of the graph, and traverse the graph. When we find k numbers of *burning* vertices, we end the traversal and choose the last level of the tree as our planning horizon and remove the vertices which are not visited from our graph world.

5   Experiments and Results

We evaluate the effectiveness of our approach on the sampled graphs from RCRS maps. All the experiments are implemented using the BURLAP [6] library.

5.1   Comparison with the Optimal Policy

To measure the feasibility of our approach, we developed a Rescue-SPATAP simulator. We create 10 random scenarios having 8 buildings from five city graphs of RoboCup Rescue Simulation (RCRS), namely *Istanbul, Berlin, Eindhoven, Joao Pessoa*, and *Kobe*. The graph sampling can be seen as the random extraction of districts from a city map (see Fig. 3).

We define three random ignition points and two agents which are positioned on random locations. In the initial state, ignition buildings are in the *burning* state. The distance of the building to propagate the fire is $d = 50$ m and *burning* buildings add $p = 0.05$ probability to their neighbors' fire ignition. For example, if a building has 2 neighbor *burning* buildings, the probability of changing the state from *no fire* to *burning* will be $(0.05 + 0.05) = 0.1$. During all the experiments, we use the nearest *burning* building parameter as $k = 3$. Since we calculate the optimal policy for these simple graph worlds, we model agents' actions as deterministic to reduce the complexity. This assumption also complies with the RCRS in that the movement noise of agents is almost negligible, if we neglect the congestion of the roads.

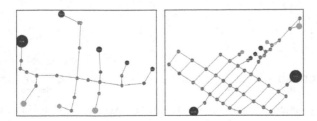

Fig. 3. Example sample graphs from Istanbul (left) and Kobe (right) maps having eight buildings (blue) and also road (gray) vertices. The yellow vertices denote the ignition points and the green vertices denotes the position of the agents. (Color figure online)

Table 1. The average reward per time step and its percentage with respect to the average optimal value

Random	SA	Greedy	SPATAP	SPATAP-Ext	Optimal
0.365 ± 0.154	0.623 ± 0.176	0.625 ± 0.189	0.621 ± 0.170	**0.654 ± 0.176**	0.712 ± 0.147
51.423%	87.56%	87.75%	87.15%	**91.88%**	100%

We show the average expected reward per time step over a horizon of 20 steps in Table 1. We present the results for random agent, single-agent approximation, greedy agent, SPATAP and SPATAP-Ext agents for 50 randomly generated scenarios and 100 samples for every scenario. Single-agent algorithm plans using the value iteration algorithm as if they were the only agent in the world and act this way. Greedy agent chooses to go to the closest vertex that is in *burning* state. Random agents choose random actions. SPATAP denotes the online approximations proposed by Claes *et al.* [1]. The online approximations proposed in this study as an extension to SPATAP is shown as SPATAP-Ext. For single-agent and SPATAP algorithms, we coordinate the selection of vertices when two agents are at the same position so that two agents do not choose the same best action. For greedy algorithm and SPATAP-Ext, we coordinate the choice of the target so that two agents do not go to the same target. We show that our approach is better than other algorithms. All the competing algorithms achieve 87% of optimal average reward, but the SPATAP-Ext achieves 92%.

5.2 Scalability

In Fig. 4a, we show the average reward per time step for scenarios having different number of buildings. These scenarios have five agents and three random ignition points. The values are averaged over 50 runs and every run is set for 50 horizon.

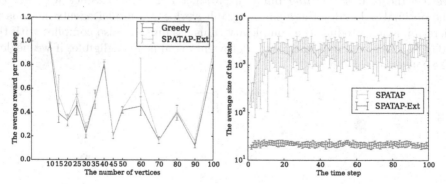

(a) The average reward per time step versus the number of vertices

(b) The average size of the state versus the time step

Fig. 4. Scalability comparison

We can see that SPATAP-Ext performs better or equal compared to Greedy algorithm. Depending on the ignition points, agents' positions and graph, the difference between two algorithms might increase or decrease.

Due to the approximations, we are able to have linear running time increases when the number of agents or the number buildings increases. The shortest path pruning and the dynamic planning horizon approximations result in further reduction in the size of the state space. We show the effect of these extensions in terms of the state space in Fig. 4b. Our approach reduces the state space by thousandfold compared to SPATAP only approximations. We use 10 runs of a sample scenario having 10 buildings and 2 agents.

5.3   RoboCup Rescue RMASBench

To benchmark SPATAP-Ext, we created 10 scenarios on the test map (having 37 buildings) of the RCRS. All of the scenarios[2] have five to ten ignition points, 8 agents in random positions and 100 horizon[3]. The agents do not act before the 20th time step of the simulation to ensure the propagation of the fire. The score of the RCRS at the end of the simulation is shown in Table 2. Since the fire propagation behavior is not randomized, we report results over a single run. This score represents the percentage of the damage on the city. We compare the performance of the SPATAP-Ext with DCOP algorithms (Greedy, DSA, BinaryMaxSum) of the RMASBench [5]. Although DCOP methods generally perform better than SPATAP-Ext, they have the advantage of well-tuned utility function. Another important factor affecting the performance of SPATAP-Ext is the assumption that a single agent can extinguish a fire in a single time step

Table 2. The comparison of the algorithms for 10 randomly created scenarios on the test map of RCRS.

Scenario	SPATAP-Ext	Greedy	DSA	BMS
1	0.875	0.866	**0.878**	0.866
2	0.796	**0.814**	0.805	0.801
3	0.821	**0.844**	**0.844**	**0.844**
4	0.776	0.798	0.798	**0.810**
5	0.746	0.814	**0.816**	**0.816**
6	0.840	**0.868**	0.865	0.867
7	0.872	**0.885**	0.874	0.874
8	0.729	0.738	0.731	**0.745**
9	**0.896**	0.890	0.890	0.890
10	0.881	0.881	**0.884**	0.881

---

[2] Test scenarios: https://github.com/okanasik/spatial_task_allocation.
[3] An example run can be seen here: https://youtu.be/nuj8s9aFAlg.

irrespective of the size of the building. This results in the distinct targets for every agent and increases the chances of the propagation of the fire. In RCRS, if more agents act to extinguish a fire, the faster the fire will be extinguished. When we analyze the results, we see that even DCOP greedy agent performs better than other methods, this suggest that reflex behavior is more important for such small maps.

To increase the performance of SPATAP-Ext agents on RCRS, we also create a set of buildings in unit sizes to enable more agents to extinguish the same building. Although this improved the performance, we see that agents are more likely to choose the closer buildings.

6   Conclusion

We show the application of online approximations for one of the challenging multi-agent planning problems. Our approach extends SPATAP framework with the introduction of the shortest path pruning, dynamic planning horizon and task clustering approximations for a harder problem Rescue-SPATAP. We show that our approach is better than Greedy approach and has similar performance to SPATAP, but requires less computation.

As a future work, we plan to extend this framework for heterogeneous agents to model whole RCRS problem. By introducing partial observability, communication, and decentralized planning, we plan to fully implement online planning framework for RCRS. We will also reduce the complexity by introducing macro-actions.

References

1. Claes, D., Robbel, P., Oliehoek, F.A., Tuyls, K., Hennes, D., van der Hoek, W.: Effective approximations for multi-robot coordination in spatially distributed tasks. In: Proceedings of the 14th International Conference on Autonomous Agents and Multiagent Systems, pp. 881–890 (2015)
2. Dos Santos, F., Bazzan, A.L.: Towards efficient multiagent task allocation in the robocup rescue: a biologically-inspired approach. Auton. Agent. Multi-agent Syst. **22**(3), 465–486 (2011)
3. Farinelli, A., Rogers, A., Petcu, A., Jennings, N.R.: Decentralised coordination of low-power embedded devices using the max-sum algorithm. In: Proceedings of the 7th International Joint Conference on Autonomous Agents and Multiagent Systems (AAMAS), pp. 639–646 (2008)
4. Fitzpatrick, S., Meertens, L.: Distributed coordination through anarchic optimization. In: Distributed Sensor Networks: A Multiagent Perspective, pp. 257–295 (2003)
5. Kleiner, A., Farinelli, A., Ramchurn, S., Shi, B., Maffioletti, F., Reffato, R.: Rmasbench: benchmarking dynamic multi-agent coordination in urban search and rescue. In: Proceedings of the 2013 International Conference on Autonomous Agents and Multi-agent Systems, AAMAS 2013, pp. 1195–1196. International Foundation for Autonomous Agents and Multiagent Systems, Richland (2013)

6. MacGlashan, J.: Burlap library (2016). http://burlap.cs.brown.edu
7. Nüssle, T.A., Kleiner, A., Brenner, M.: Approaching urban disaster reality: the ResQ firesimulator. In: Nardi, D., Riedmiller, M., Sammut, C., Santos-Victor, J. (eds.) RoboCup 2004. LNCS, vol. 3276, pp. 474–482. Springer, Heidelberg (2005). doi:10.1007/978-3-540-32256-6_42
8. Parker, J., Nunes, E., Godoy, J., Gini, M.: Exploiting spatial locality and heterogeneity of agents for search and rescue teamwork. J. Field Rob. **33**(7), 877–900 (2016). Wiley Online Library
9. Pujol-Gonzalez, M., Cerquides, J., Farinelli, A., Meseguer, P., Rodriguez-Aguilar, J.A.: Efficient inter-team task allocation in RoboCup rescue. In: Proceedings of the 14th International Conference on Autonomous Agents and Multiagent Systems, pp. 413–421 (2015)
10. Puterman, M.L.: Markov Decision Processes: Discrete Stochastic Dynamic Programming. Wiley, Hoboken (2014)
11. Scerri, P., Farinelli, A., Okamoto, S., Tambe, M.: Allocating tasks in extreme teams. In: Proceedings of the Fourth International Joint Conference on Autonomous Agents and Multiagent Systems, pp. 727–734. ACM (2005)

Using Monte Carlo Search with Data Aggregation to Improve Robot Soccer Policies

Francesco Riccio[(✉)], Roberto Capobianco, and Daniele Nardi

Department of Computer, Control and Management Engineering "Antonio Ruberti",
Sapienza University of Rome, Rome, Italy
{riccio,capobianco,nardi}@dis.uniroma1.it

Abstract. RoboCup soccer competitions are considered among the most challenging multi-robot adversarial environments, due to their high dynamism and the partial observability of the environment. In this paper we introduce a method based on a combination of Monte Carlo search and data aggregation (MCSDA) to adapt discrete-action soccer policies for a defender robot to the strategy of the opponent team. By exploiting a simple representation of the domain, a supervised learning algorithm is trained over an initial collection of data consisting of several simulations of human expert policies. Monte Carlo policy rollouts are then generated and aggregated to previous data to improve the learned policy over multiple epochs and games. The proposed approach has been extensively tested both on a soccer-dedicated simulator and on real robots. Using this method, our learning robot soccer team achieves an improvement in ball interceptions, as well as a reduction in the number of opponents' goals. Together with a better performance, an overall more efficient positioning of the whole team within the field is achieved.

Keywords: Policy learning · Reinforcement learning · Humanoid robots · Multi-robot systems

1 Introduction

Machine learning methods have been increasingly used in robotics to deal with uncertain and unstructured environments. In such scenarios, directly learning from data a (sub-)optimal set of parameters to generate robot behaviors is often more robust than hard coding them from prior knowledge. However, the variety of the problems and the lack of big amount of data still refrain researchers from the application of standard learning approaches to challenging domains such as RoboCup soccer competitions [5]. Here, in fact, manifold problems must be faced by a multi-robot system, such as coordination and decision making under partial observability of an adversarial and dynamic environment.

RoboCup soccer teams typically tackle competitions by deploying static behaviors for their robots. Here, each programmed agent executes a single policy

---

F. Riccio and R. Capobianco—These authors are contributed equally to the work.

© Springer International Publishing AG 2017
S. Behnke et al. (Eds.): RoboCup 2016, LNAI 9776, pp. 256–267, 2017.
https://doi.org/10.1007/978-3-319-68792-6_21

Fig. 1. MCSDA generates effective robot policies in a highly dynamic environment. (Color figure online)

that takes into account the state of the robot teammates, but does not change at run-time. However, during the game the partial observable environment discloses previously unavailable information, such as the strategy of the opponent team. On the one hand, predefined behavioral protocols cannot handle the newly available knowledge. Hence, the use of a learning approach to update each agent's current policy would be beneficial to the team performance. On the other hand, such information only consists of small portions of new data, that cannot be used without exploiting the structure of the domain and adequate machine learning methods.

In this paper, we specifically consider the setup proposed by the RoboCup Standard Platform League (SPL), where NAO robots compete in a 5-vs-5 soccer game (see Fig. 1). Our goal consists in generating a robot defender policy that adapts to the strategy of the opponent team. Such strategy is not known and, hence, makes the world dynamics unknown or difficult to model. The policy that we generate is composed of a discrete and limited set of actions, and it is at first instantiated to imitate an initial dataset of human (expert) deployed behaviors. To this end, we introduce Monte Carlo Search with Data Aggregation (MCSDA). Our algorithm uses a standard classifier to imitate expert actions given the current observation of a simplified representation of the game domain, modeled by the position and velocity of the ball in the field, as well as the player position. Since the classifier is trained over the distribution of observations and expert actions from multiple games, frequent patterns and main game areas can be exploited by the learned policy. Such policy is then improved by aggregating [11] the initial dataset with policy rollouts collected using simple Monte Carlo search [13]. While our algorithm strictly relates to state-of-the-art methods for reinforcement learning with unknown system dynamics [10] and recent applications to games like Go [12], the main novelty of this paper consists in the combination of these techniques, that allows to achieve good results on a partially observable, high dynamic robotic context. With this paper, in fact, we aim at showing that (1) the use of data aggregation together with Monte Carlo search is practical, effectively improves the learner's policy and preserves good properties, and (2) by adopting a simplified representation of the domain a good policy improvement can be obtained on complex and challenging robotic scenarios. The obtained results show improvements in the overall team performance, where the percentage of recovered ball and the number of won games increase with the number of MCSDA iterations.

The reminder of this paper is organized as follows. Section 2 provides an overview on the literature about policy learning and improvement, as well as strategy adaptation in the RoboCup context; Sect. 3 describes in detail the proposed approach introducing the MCSDA algorithm (Sect. 3.2). Finally, Sect. 4 describes the robot platform and the experimental setup together with the obtained results, while Sect. 5 concludes the paper with final remarks and future work.

2   Related Work

Policy learning is a very active area of research, due to its complexity and practical relevance. Reinforcement learning, Monte Carlo methods and imitation learning have been successfully applied in several contexts and domains. For example, in robotics Kober and Peters [6] use episodic reinforcement learning in order to improve motor primitives learned by imitation for a Ball-in-a-Cup task. Kormushev et al. [7], instead, encode movements with and extension of Dynamic Movement Primitives [4] initialized from imitation. Reinforcement learning is then used to learn the optimal parameters of the policy, thus improving the obtained performance. Differently, Ross et al. [11] propose a meta-algorithm for imitation learning (DAGGER), which learns a stationary deterministic policy that is guaranteed to perform well under its induced distribution of states. Their method, which strictly relates to a no-regret online learning approach, is then applied to learn some policies that can steer a car in a 3D racing game and can play Super Mario Bros., given input image features and corresponding expert demonstrations. The idea of applying policy learning on video-games has been recently used also by Mnih et al. [8], that present a deep agent (deep Q-network), that can use reinforcement learning to generate policies directly from high-dimensional sensory inputs. The authors test their algorithm on classic Atari 2600 games, achieving a level comparable to that of a professional human player across a set of 49 games. Similarly, Silver et al. [12] use deep "value networks" and "policy networks" to respectively evaluate board positions and select moves for the challenging game of Go. These neural networks are trained by a combination of supervised learning from human expert games, reinforcement learning and Monte Carlo tree search. The resulting program showed to be able to beat human Go champions and to achieve a performance beyond any previous expectation.

Building on the idea of adopting a combination of techniques similar to [12], our work mostly relates to the AGGREVATE and NRPI algorithms by Ross and Bagnell [10]. The former leverages cost-to-go information – in addition to correct demonstration – and data aggregation; the latter extends the idea of no-regret learners to Approximate Policy Iteration variants for reinforcement learning. However, differently from previous work our algorithm (MCSDA) uses shorter Monte Carlo roll-outs to evaluate policy improvements. By avoiding to always estimate the full cost-to-go of the policy MCSDA is more practical – and usable in robotics. Additionally, as explained in Sect. 3, the policy generated by our algorithm can be seen as a combination of expert and learned policies, allowing us to directly leverage results from [2].

Policy Adaptation in RoboCup
Policy classification and adaptation to the strategy of the opponent team is not a new idea in RoboCup competitions. For example, Han and Veloso [3] propose to employ Hidden Markov Models to detect opponents' behaviors, represented as game states. The authors first characterize the game state in terms of "behavioral-relevant state features" and then show how a cascade of HMMs is able to recognize different pre-defined robot behaviors. This idea has been further developed by Riley et al. [9], who propose a classification method for the opponents' behavior in a simulated environment. The authors first enable their agents to observe and classify the actions of the adversaries, and then to accordingly adapt their policy. More recently, Trevizan and Veloso [14] also address the problem of classifying opponents, and their strategies with respect to a set of behavioral components. Specifically, they are able to generalize and classify unknown opponents as combination of known ones. Yasui et al. [15] introduce a "dissimilarity function" to categorize opponent strategies via cluster analysis. The authors improve their team performance by analyzing logged data of previous matches and showing that team attacking strategies can be recognized and correctly classified. Finally, Biswas et al. [1] propose an opponent aware defensive strategies. In particular, once the state of the opponents is received, the robotic systems categorize the attacking robot as first and second level threats. Accordingly, the team displaces a variable number of defenders in order to prevent the opponent team to score.

It is worth remarking that all the aforementioned methods propose effective solutions to the problem of decision making in presence of adversaries. However, differently from our application of MCSDA on the RoboCup scenario – that uses only a small portion of the game-state and operates under unknown system dynamics, they operate in controlled environments, where full information is available. Additionally, while the MCSDA algorithm can be separately applied on each agent and automatically accounts for uncertainty, the described systems are usually centralized and do not consider uncertain outcomes. For these reasons, we consider our approach a valuable contribution also to the robotic and RoboCup community, where partially observable and highly dynamic scenarios need to be addressed.

3   Approach

The generation of our adaptive policy relies on standard machine learning methods. First, a classifier is used to imitate a sub-optimal expert policy and accordingly choose an action, given the current observation of the game domain. Then, the learned policy is improved by aggregating, in an online learning fashion, previous data with Monte Carlo policy rollouts. Throughout the learning process, the domain representation is simplified and it is reduced to the essential game elements – the position and velocity of the ball in the field.

3.1 Preliminaries

We present our learning problem using the Markov Decision Process notation, where S and A respectively represent a discrete set of states and actions, and $R(s)$ is the immediate reward obtained for being in state $s \in S$. R is assumed to be bounded in $[0, 1]$. In our learning setting not only we observe the reward function R, but also demonstrations of a sub-optimal policy π^* that aims at maximizing R and induces a state distribution d_{π^*}. Additionally, we assume the dynamics of the world to be unknown or to be accessible only through samples, due to its complexity. Those samples can be obtained by directly observing a policy executed in the world.

Our goal is to first find a policy $\hat{\pi}$ such that

$$\hat{\pi} = \arg \max_a \mathbb{E}_{s' \sim d_{\pi^*}}[s' \mid a, s], \tag{1}$$

and then to generate, at each iteration $i \in \{0, \ldots, N\}$, a new policy $\tilde{\pi}_i$ that improves $\tilde{\pi}_{i-1}$, with $\tilde{\pi}_0 = \hat{\pi}$. Such improvement is obtained by directly executing $\tilde{\pi}_{i-1}$ and aggregating the reward measured over several Monte Carlo simulations to the rewards at previous iterations. Note that, (1) as in previous work [2,10,11] we adopt a supervised learning approach to imitate and learn a policy, (2) since the chosen actions influence the distribution of states, our supervised learning problem is characterized by a non-i.i.d.[1] dataset.

3.2 Monte Carlo Search with Data Aggregation

We now present Monte Carlo Search with Data Aggregation – MCSDA, a modification of the AGGREVATE and NRPI algorithms by Ross and Bagnell [10] that (1) instead of the distribution of states induced by the expert, always uses the learned policy to roll-in and (2) rather than estimating the full cost-to-go of the policy, only uses shorter Monte Carlo roll-outs to evaluate policy improvements.

In its simplest form the algorithm takes as input a set $\mathcal{D}_e$ of state-action pairs obtained from expert demonstrations and proceeds as follows. First, MCSDA learns a classifier $\hat{\pi}$ by using $\mathcal{D}_e$ in order to imitate the expert. This is used to initialize our policy $\tilde{\pi}$. Then, during each iteration, the algorithm extends its dataset by (1) executing the previous policy $\tilde{\pi}$ and generating a state s_t at each time-step, (2) selecting for each s_t an action a_t that maximizes the expected value $V_p(s_t, a)$ of performing action a at the given state, (3) aggregating the new state-action pairs – at each time-step – to the previous dataset. Finally, the aggregated dataset is used to train a new classifier $\tilde{\pi}$ that substitutes the policy used at the previous iteration. The details of MCSDA are provided in Algorithm 1.

---

[1] Independent and identically distributed.

Algorithm 1. Monte Carlo Search with Data Aggregation (MCSDA).

Input: $\mathcal{D}_e$: dataset of state action pairs $\{s, a\}$ from expert demonstrations, N: number of iterations of the algorithm, K: number of Monte Carlo simulations, H: simulation steps.

Output: $\tilde{\pi}_N$: policy learned after N iterations of the algorithm.

```
1  begin
2  |   Train classifier π̂ on 𝒟ₑ to imitate the expert.
3  |   Set π̃₀ ← π̂.
4  |   Initialize 𝒟 ← 𝒟ₑ.
5  |   for i = 1 to N do
6  |   |   Set s₀ in some state from the initial state distribution D.
7  |   |   for t = 1 to T do
8  |   |   |   Get state sₜ by executing π̃ᵢ₋₁(sₜ₋₁).
9  |   |   |   𝒜 ← select or sub-sample (if needed) feasible actions in sₜ.
10 |   |   |   foreach a ∈ 𝒜 do
11 |   |   |   |   execute K Monte Carlo simulations of length H to estimate
                   Vₚ(sₜ, a).
12 |   |   |   end
13 |   |   |   Set aₜ ← arg max ₐ Vₚ(sₜ, a).
14 |   |   |   Set 𝒟 ← 𝒟 ∪ {sₜ, aₜ}.
15 |   |   end
16 |   |   Train classifier π̃ᵢ on 𝒟.
17 |   end
18 |   return π̃_N
19 end
```

By relying on data aggregation, MCSDA generates a sequence $\tilde{\pi}_1, \tilde{\pi}_2, \ldots, \tilde{\pi}_N$ of policies and preserves the main characteristics of algorithms like AGGREVATE – i.e., (1) it builds its dataset by exploring the states that the policy will probably encounter during its execution, (2) it can be interpreted as a Follow-The-Leader algorithm that tries to learn a good classifier over all previous data and (3) can be easily transformed to use an online learner by simply using the dataset in sequence. However, the implementation of MCSDA is more practical due to the reduced amounts of roll-outs generated from the Monte Carlo simulation. Additionally, our algorithm always performs the roll-in and the roll-out – after the one-step deviation – with the learned policy. Still, it is worth to notice that the learned policy is effectively generated from the mixture of sub-optimal expert policies and learner's experience from Monte Carlo simulations. Hence, expert policy actions will be likely executed at the beginning, while their execution probability will reduce with the number of iterations of the algorithm. This can be interpreted as combining the sub-optimal policy of the expert and the learned policy with a varying mixing parameter β that initially is equal to 1 – always uses the expert – and decreases over subsequent iterations of MCSDA. Consequently, we can rely on performances analogous to those presented by Chang et al. [2].

3.3 Using MCSDA to Improve Robot Soccer Policies

The application of MCSDA to the RoboCup context is not straightforward, but requires an additional modeling effort. First, in order to reduce the size of the problem, only the two-dimensional position $p_r = (x_r, y_r)$ of the robot, the position $p_b = (x_b, y_b)$ and velocity $v_b = (v_{xb}, v_{yb})$ of the ball in the field have been adopted to represent the game state and, hence, to build our learning dataset. Additionally, we generated the state-action pairs by considering the following subset of actions: stand (the robot does not move), move_up (the robot moves forwards), move_down (the robot moves backwards), move_left, move_right.

Given this reduced domain representation, as well as the goal of generating a robot policy that adapts to the game adversaries, we applied MCSDA to the RoboCup scenario by using the opponent team as our expert. To this end, first we created a simple heuristic-based classifier to recognize the opponents' actions with respect to the ball (i.e., we collected their policy) and, then, learned such policy in order to perform imitation. Note that at execution time the learned policy is mapped to our robots by considering their relative position with respect to the ball. In this work, such a mapping has been manually defined. This resolves

Fig. 2. Example of a full iteration of the Monte Carlo roll-outs: the robot evaluates all its actions, and selects the best one to maximize $V_p(s_t, a)$. In this example, the top-left sub-figure shows the world state at a given time t, and the current policy suggests the robot to execute move_left. Accordingly, the other sub-figures show the evolution of the world state after each roll-out extending the current policy until the horizon $H = 3$. The robot evaluates all the 5 actions: stand (top-center), move_up (top-right); move_down (bottom-left); move_left (bottom-center); move_right (bottom-right). In these figures, the blue arrow represents the chosen action for the current roll-out, while the purple arrows represent the movements of the robot according to the current policy. The yellow circle represents the point p_b used to compute the reward according to Eq. 2. (Color figure online)

situations where the opponent (expert) robot and our (learner) agent face the ball from opposite directions and, for example, the opponent's `move_left` action maps to `move_right` on our robot. Finally, Monte Carlo roll-outs have been executed as illustrated in Fig. 2 and using a reward function shaped as:

$$R(s) = \frac{\text{MAX\_FIELD\_DISTANCE} - |p_r - p_b|}{\text{MAX\_FIELD\_DISTANCE}}, \tag{2}$$

where MAX_FIELD_DISTANCE corresponds to the game-field diagonal. To run our Monte Carlo simulations, we used both a simplified simulator and a more complex one, provided by the B-Human RoboCup Team[2].

4   Experimental Evaluation

RoboCup is a dynamic adversarial environment where robots needs to adapt to the surroundings quickly and efficiently. For these reasons, the goal of this experimental section is to evaluate our learning approach in the short range after few number of simulation steps. The evaluation has been carried out through the B-Human soccer simulator entirely written in C++ with the middle-sized humanoid NAO robot. In this section, we test and validate the effectiveness of the two main phases of our approach: the continuous policy improvement via Monte Carlo roll-outs and the policy initialization via imitation learning. In our experiments we set the roll-out horizon $H = 3$. This value has been found to be a good trade-off between in-game performance improvement and usability of the approach. Extending the horizon, in fact, improves the player performance at the cost of more computational resources.

4.1   Policy Improvement

The goal of our learner is to improve its performance while playing against opponent robots and to decrease the number of opponent scores while intercepting as many balls as possible. According to Eq. 2, we can evaluate each action of our learner by considering the reward that the robot obtains during a match. Such a measurement expresses how good the learner is positioned within the field with respect to the ball. Therefore, we analyze the average reward of our agent as well as the number of ball interceptions and the final score of each match. Figure 3 reports the normalized average reward obtained by the learner during five regular games, after a different number of MCSDA iterations. On the y-axis is reported the obtained average reward.

Specifically, the learning defender features our MCSDA algorithm, while the non-learning defender has a fixed policy initialized at iteration zero. Such a baseline is a suitable comparison that allows us to quantify the improvements of our robot in terms of positioning with respect to its own initial policy. It is worth noticing that each reported match has been played with different policies generated at different iterations of MCSDA. Hence, each match represents a different

---

[2] https://www.b-human.de/.

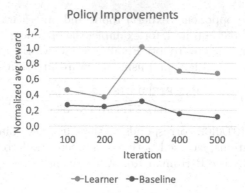

Fig. 3. Normalized average reward of the learner (*blue*) and baseline (*orange*) after different MCSDA iterations. (Color figure online)

configuration of the learner, where its actions are determined by a policy computed after 100, 200, 300, 400, 500 iterations of our algorithm. The plot shows a constant improvement with respect to our baseline and over previous configuration of its trained policy. It is worth remarking that the drop in performance between game 3 and 4 can be due to different factors affecting the game, such as player penalization and ball positioning rules. However, such drop has a marginal impact with respect to the previous improvements, and the performance of consequent matches remains constant.

Additionally, thanks to the nature of our testing environment, we are able to report more direct evaluation indices for our approach. To this end, we report the number of intercepted balls and the number of opponent scores. In particular, Fig. 4 shows the sum of intercepted balls of the two teams (learning and non-learning) on the same set of games as before, and Table 1 reports their final scores.

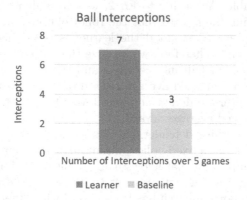

Fig. 4. Sum of intercepted ball over five matches after different MCSDA iterations. (Color figure online)

Table 1. The table reports the final scores of five matches after different MCSDA iterations.

Teams	MCSDA iterations				
	100	200	300	400	500
Learning	2	3	0	1	1
Non-learning	3	2	1	1	1

It is worth noticing that the number of intercepted balls of our learning agent (*green*) is more than twice the number of the opponent defender (*yellow*). Furthermore, the final results of the different matches promises an interesting profile: even though the learner does not win all of the matches, the number of opponent scores decreases as the learner refines its policy. Since MCSDA is applied only on defense robots, we do not achieve any improvement on the number of goals of our team. However, as expected, by increasing the number of iterations of our algorithm, the number of goals of the opponent team decreases.

4.2 Imitation Influence

Since our robots operate in dynamic environments the policy training process cannot be too long. Therefore, we need to restrict the search space for our learning process as much as possible. To this end, we generate an initial policy by running 100 matches with the only purpose of analyzing most probable positions and velocities of the ball, as well as opponents' positions within the field as introduced in Sect. 3.3.

In this case, we setup an experimental evaluation with the aim of studying the influence of our policy initialization on the overall MCSDA approach. In the setting shown in Fig. 5, the blue team deploys a robot learner featuring an

Fig. 5. Normalized average reward of the learner (*orange*) and the non-initialized policy learner (*purple*) during a match. (Color figure online)

initialized policy, while the red team deploys a learner with a non-initialized policy. In this test, we let the two defenders train their policies for 300 iterations. Afterwards, we select the two different policy profiles in order to play a regular match. Figure 5 shows the normalized averaged reward of the two learners: orange for the initialized policy, and purple for the not-initialized one. It is worth noticing that – as expected – an initialized policy significantly improves the learning process.

5   Discussion and Future Work

In this paper we presented MCSDA, an algorithm that strictly relates to recently developed approaches for policy improvement. We used and evaluated our method to generate better strategies for soccer defense in the RoboCup scenario. The application of MCSDA on this context allowed our robots to increase the number of ball interceptions, as well as to reduce the number of opponents' goals. Together with a better performance, an overall more efficient positioning of the defender player within the field has been achieved.

Contributions
The main contribution of this paper consists in the combination of data aggregation together with Monte Carlo search. The use of Monte Carlo search results in a practical algorithm, that allows a real-world implementation on a robot domain. By relying on data aggregation, instead, MCSDA preserves the main characteristics of algorithms like AGGREVATE and can be easily transformed to an online method. Finally, we also show that using MCSDA with a simplified representation of the domain a good policy improvement can be obtained on complex and challenging robotic scenarios.

Limitations and Future Work
Our algorithm still presents some limitations. In fact, even if Monte Carlo simulations make MCSDA practical, it requires expensive calls to a simulator and, hence, it has been applied to a single robot player. While simple simulators can be used, neither the online application of the algorithm, nor its use on a larger number of robots are straightforward. For this reason, as future work, we would like to adapt and test our algorithm to learn policies online and consequently apply the algorithm to the whole robot soccer team. Furthermore, we plan to perform additional studies on the performance guarantees that MCSDA can achieve.

References

1. Biswas, J., Mendoza, J.P., Zhu, D., Choi, B., Klee, S., Veloso, M.: Opponent-driven planning and execution for pass, attack, and defense in a multi-robot soccer team. In: Proceedings of the 2014 International Conference on Autonomous Agents and Multi-agent Systems, pp. 493–500. International Foundation for Autonomous Agents and Multiagent Systems (2014)

2. Chang, K.W., Krishnamurthy, A., Agarwal, A., Daume, H., Langford, J.: Learning to search better than your teacher. In: Proceedings of the 32nd International Conference on Machine Learning (ICML 2015), pp. 2058–2066 (2015)
3. Han, K., Veloso, M.: Automated robot behavior recognition applied to robotic soccer. In: Hollerbach, J.M., Koditschek, D.E. (eds.) Robotics Research, pp. 249–256. Springer, London (2000). doi:10.1007/978-1-4471-0765-1_30. Also in the Proceedings of IJCAI-99 Workshop on Team Behaviors and Plan Recognition
4. Ijspeert, A.J., Nakanishi, J., Schaal, S.: Trajectory formation for imitation with nonlinear dynamical systems. In: Proceedings of the 2001 IEEE/RSJ International Conference on Intelligent Robots and Systems, vol. 2, pp. 752–757. IEEE (2001)
5. Kitano, H., Asada, M., Kuniyoshi, Y., Noda, I., Osawa, E.: RoboCup: the robot world cup initiative. In: Proceedings of the First International Conference on Autonomous Agents, pp. 340–347. ACM (1997)
6. Kober, J., Peters, J.R.: Policy search for motor primitives in robotics. In: Advances in Neural Information Processing Systems, pp. 849–856 (2009)
7. Kormushev, P., Calinon, S., Caldwell, D.G.: Robot motor skill coordination with EM-based reinforcement learning. In: 2010 IEEE/RSJ International Conference on Intelligent Robots and Systems (IROS), pp. 3232–3237. IEEE (2010)
8. Mnih, V., Kavukcuoglu, K., Silver, D., Rusu, A.A., Veness, J., Bellemare, M.G., Graves, A., Riedmiller, M., Fidjeland, A.K., Ostrovski, G., et al.: Human-level control through deep reinforcement learning. Nature 518(7540), 529–533 (2015)
9. Riley, P., Veloso, M.: On behavior classification in adversarial environments. In: Parker, L.E., Bekey, G., Barhen, J. (eds.) Distributed Autonomous Robotic Systems 4, pp. 371–380. Springer, Tokyo (2000). doi:10.1007/978-4-431-67919-6_35
10. Ross, S., Bagnell, J.A.: Reinforcement and imitation learning via interactive no-regret learning. arXiv preprint arXiv:1406.5979 (2014)
11. Ross, S., Gordon, G.J., Bagnell, D.: A reduction of imitation learning and structured prediction to no-regret online learning. In: International Conference on Artificial Intelligence and Statistics, pp. 627–635 (2011)
12. Silver, D., Huang, A., Maddison, C.J., Guez, A., Sifre, L., van den Driessche, G., Schrittwieser, J., Antonoglou, I., Panneershelvam, V., Lanctot, M., et al.: Mastering the game of go with deep neural networks and tree search. Nature 529(7587), 484–489 (2016)
13. Tesauro, G., Galperin, G.R.: On-line policy improvement using Monte-Carlo search. In: NIPS, vol. 96, pp. 1068–1074 (1996)
14. Trevizan, F.W., Veloso, M.M.: Learning opponents strategies in the RoboCup small size league. In: Proceedings of the AAMAS, vol. 10. Citeseer (2010)
15. Yasui, K., Kobayashi, K., Murakami, K., Naruse, T.: Analyzing and learning an opponent's strategies in the RoboCup small size league. In: Behnke, S., Veloso, M., Visser, A., Xiong, R. (eds.) RoboCup 2013. LNCS, vol. 8371, pp. 159–170. Springer, Heidelberg (2014). doi:10.1007/978-3-662-44468-9_15

Cooperative Sensing for 3D Ball Positioning in the RoboCup Middle Size League

Wouter Kuijpers[1(✉)], António J.R. Neves[2], and René van de Molengraft[1]

[1] Departement of Mechanical Engineering, Eindhoven University of Technology, Eindhoven, The Netherlands
{w.j.p.kuijpers,m.j.g.v.d.Molengraft}@tue.nl
[2] IRIS Lab/IEETA/DETI, University of Aveiro, Aveiro, Portugal
an@ua.pt

Abstract. As soccer in the RoboCup Middle Size League (MSL) starts resembling human soccer more and more, the time the ball is airborne increases. Robots equipped with a single catadioptric vision system will generally not be able to accurately observe depth due to limited resolution. Most teams, therefore, resort to projecting the ball on the field. Within the MSL several methods have already been explored to determine the 3D ball position, e.g., adding a high-resolution perspective camera or adding a Kinect sensor. This paper presents a new method which combines the omnivision camera data from multiple robots through triangulation. Three main challenges have been identified in designing this method: *Inaccurate projections*, *Communication delay* and *Limited amount of data*. An algorithm, considering these main challenges, has been implemented and tested. Performance tests with a non-moving ball (static situation) and two robots show an accuracy of 0.13 m for airborne balls. A dynamic test shows that a ball kicked by a robot could be tracked from the moment of the kick, if enough measurements have been received from two peer robots before the ball exceeds the height of the robots.

1 Introduction

The Robot Soccer World Cup (RoboCup) Federation is an international organization which focuses on the promotion of robotics and Artificial Intelligence (AI) research, by offering a publicly appealing challenge: build robots that play soccer[1]. In the Soccer Middle Size League (MSL), robots of no more than 50 cm in diameter and 80 cm in height, play soccer in teams of five. At the moment of writing, 26 teams from all over the world compete in this league.

During a game of soccer, the position and velocity of the ball are of great importance. To detect the position of the ball, most teams have equipped their robots with a catadioptric vision system, which also serves a number of other purposes. Although this is not prescribed by the league, it has been widely adopted because of its price versus value as sensor. As soccer in the MSL starts

---

[1] RoboCup Homepage: http://www.robocup.org/.

© Springer International Publishing AG 2017
S. Behnke et al. (Eds.): RoboCup 2016, LNAI 9776, pp. 268–278, 2017.
https://doi.org/10.1007/978-3-319-68792-6_22

resembling human soccer more and more, the time the ball is airborne increases. Robots equipped with only a catadioptric vision system have a single camera, hence they will, generally, not be able to accurately observe depth due to limited resolution. Most teams, therefore, resort to projecting the ball on the field.

Figure 1 shows that projecting the ball (x_b, y_b, z_b) on the field leads to a false projection. The ball will be detected in position (x_p, y_p), where $x_p \neq x_b$ and $y_p \neq y_b$ when the ball is airborne. The positioning of the robot will benefit when the correct ball position (x_b, y_b), instead of the false projection is being used. With the height of the ball (z_b) it is possible to calculate where the ball bounces, at these locations the ball could be intercepted after a lob pass.

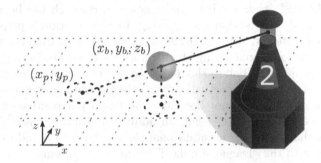

Fig. 1. A MSL robot detecting an airborne ball (x_b, y_b, z_b), creating a false projection (x_p, y_p).

This paper presents the design, implementation and testing of a new algorithm based on cooperative sensing and triangulation. Section 2 presents related research in the area of cooperative sensing and distributed sensor fusion. Section 3 presents the main challenges faced during the design and implementation of a multi-robot triangulation algorithm. Section 4 follows up on that by presenting the general structure of the algorithm. In this section special attention will be paid to how the previously defined challenges have been considered. Section 5 presents the results obtained during tests with the algorithm, results with a non-moving (static) and moving (dynamic) ball are presented. Section 6 concludes this paper with concluding remarks and recommendations for future work in this area.

2 Related Work

The topic of multi-robot tracking is one studied in many different applications and different communities as presented by [4]. To structure this broad field, [4] presents a unifying taxonomy to classify the various missions related to the topic. This paper presents a *Target Localization*-application. The application discussed here is characterized by (mostly) homogeneous teams of robots.[2] Target localization is also possible with heterogeneous teams as shown in [2].

---

[2] Some teams have equipped the goalkeeper with different or additional sensors [1].

An application using multiple sensors is presented in [7]. The part of the research presented in [7] focusing on stereo vision with catadioptric cameras is similar to the method presented here; triangulation. In this research the sensors are not connected to the same platform (robot), this fact makes the implementation of the triangulation algorithm more difficult because of data communication delay. This also shows from the research in [8], which researches cooperative map building in the context of autonomous vehicles. The vehicles are communicating via an IEEE 802.11n wireless interface, the data communication delay is taken into consideration by calculating and applying the coordinate offset. Although this method provides a solution in the context of autonomous vehicles, its results will deteriorate in an environment as dynamic as the MSL.

Within the MSL itself a substantial amount of research has been performed in the field of 3D ball detection and tracking. In [9] a solution is presented where aerial balls are detected using a front-facing perspective camera, the distance from the camera to the ball along the focal axis is calculated using the number of pixels occupied by the ball in the image. In [11] the robot is equipped with an additional front facing perspective camera, the measurement is combined with omnivision using triangulation. Instead of adding a perspective camera to the robot, [3,6] present a method using an additional Kinect sensor[3]. This paper presents a method in which no additional sensors have to be added and which is compatible with the "league standard" omnivision system.

3   Main Challenges

Before the design of the triangulation algorithm, a set of main challenges has been identified. Basically, the triangulation algorithm calculates the intersection of two lines, defined by the position of the robot (and its height) and the projection of the respective robot. The main challenges presented in this section, hinder the implementation of this 'simple' algorithm. The main challenges are: *Inaccurate projections*, *Communication delay* and *Limited amount of data*. In this section each challenge will be treated separately, elaborating on where it originates from and how it affects the triangulation of omnivision camera data.

3.1   Inaccurate Projections

The vision software is responsible for detecting the ball in the image captured by the camera in the catadioptric vision system. The exact structure of this software differs between teams, but frequently the main structure is comparable. The image captured is segmented based on colors, and from this blobs are identified. The blobs are ranked according to the probability of the blob being the ball, based on: the color of the ball, its size and shape. The position of the center of the blob in the image captured, is communicated to the rest of the system as the projection [10]. The projection might be inaccurate because of the limited resolution of the catadioptric vision system or because of motion blur e.g.

---

[3] Kinect: https://dev.windows.com/en-us/kinect.

The 'simple' algorithm presented at the start of this section, could rely on the calculation of the intersection of two lines. But due to the inaccuracies in projection, or in the localization of the robot, the lines of sight might not have an intersection. An algorithm searching for the intersection of the lines will therefore not suffice in this context.

3.2 Communication Delay

To be able to triangulate lines of sight, a robot requires the position and projection of at least one other robot, which means that the robots have to communicate information. Sharing information between robots induces additional delay on the information. To communicate, several teams in the MSL use the Real-time Data Base (RTDB) [5], where robots communicate via a distributed shared memory and an adaptive TDMA protocol for wireless communication.

If the effects of this additional delay would not be considered in the triangulation algorithm, lines of sight from different time instants might be triangulated. During a MSL game the ball can reach speeds of up to 11 m/s, with a communication delay of 20 ms, triangulating a different time instant introduces an error of 0.22 m into the triangulation algorithm. The effect of this error on the triangulated ball, depends on the positions of the robots relative to the ball and the height of the ball.

3.3 Limited Amount of Data

Aside from the delay on the data received from peers, the data from peers might also not be available at every time instant. If a peer, is not able to detect the ball because it is outside the field of view or the line of sight of the peer is obstructed by another robot, the ball is not detected by the peer and therefore not communicated. Secondly, the robot-robot communication will often not run at the same frequency as the acquisition of images by the vision system.

The combination of the two factors above might lead to time instants where no information or information from only one robot is available. It is desirable that the triangulation algorithm provides an output also at these time instants.

4 Triangulation Algorithm

In this section we propose a new triangulation algorithm, the emphasis here will be on how the main challenges, presented in the previous section, are considered in the design of the algorithm.

Figure 2 shows an example of a state of the triangulation algorithm. In this example, the current time is t_n and the algorithm represented executes on Robot 1. Robot 1 therefore has all position and projection information (represented by the circles) from itself, up to t_n. The information from the two other robots still has to arrive. Because of the communication delay, the data from Robot 2 is available up to t_{n-3} and data from Robot 3 is available up to t_{n-2}.

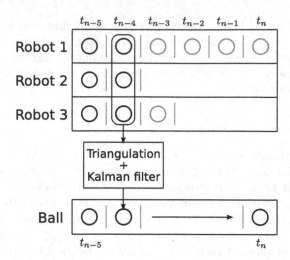

Fig. 2. An example of a state of the triangulation algorithm, used by three robots. The circles in the rows denoted by "Robot" represent communicated data, circles in the row denoted by "Ball" denote data regarding the state of the ball.

The proposed algorithm triangulates the most recent time instant where information from the most robots is available; in this case t_{n-4}. The algorithm applies triangulation to pairs of lines of sight. If more than two lines of sight are available (in the case of t_{n-4}) the lines of sight are triangulated pairwise, the results of these pairwise triangulations are combined by averaging. Pairwise triangulation has been chosen because the method for finding the minimum distance between two lines is one which is relatively easy and therefore more suitable to be implemented in a real-time system, compared to the method used for triangulating n lines. After triangulation, the 3D ball position is filtered by means of a Kalman filter. This results in a filtered 3D ball state at t_{n-4}. The state at t_{n-4}, in combination with the ball model, is used to determine the 3D ball state at t_n.

4.1 Inaccurate Projections

Due to inaccuracies in the projections, the lines of sight of the robots might not cross. Therefore, a minimum distance algorithm is in place. Figure 3(a) graphically represents the minimum distance algorithm. The lines $\overrightarrow{R_x P_x}$ and $\overrightarrow{R_y P_y}$ represent, respectively, the lines of sight of robot x and y. To find the minimum distance $\overrightarrow{n_{md}}$, the line $\overrightarrow{n}$ between two arbitrary points, one on each line, is parameterized

$$\overrightarrow{n} = \overrightarrow{n_0} + \overrightarrow{R_x P_x} s_1 - \overrightarrow{R_y P_y} s_2. \tag{1}$$

the minimum distance line $\overrightarrow{n_{md}}$ is perpendicular to both lines of sight, hence

$$\begin{cases} \overrightarrow{n} \cdot \overrightarrow{R_x P_x} = 0 \\ \overrightarrow{n} \cdot \overrightarrow{R_y P_y} = 0 \end{cases}. \tag{2}$$

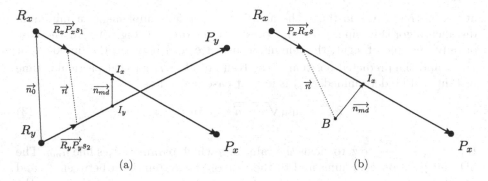

(a)   (b)

Fig. 3. Graphical representation of a minimum distance algorithm applied to: (a) two lines of sight (b) a line of sight and the predicted position of the Kalman filter.

Solving this system of equations yields a closed-form solution for the parameters s_1 and s_2, which are used to describe the intersection points I_x and I_y. The 3D ball position communicated to the rest of the system is in between I_x and I_y. This latter average can be replaced by a weighted average based on the length of e.g. $\overrightarrow{R_x P_x}$. The larger the distance between the robot and projection, the less accurate it will be.

4.2   Communication Delay

Due to the communication delay in the robot-robot communication, the arrival of information from peers is delayed. The proposed triangulation algorithm considers this effect by storing the information from the robots in a data buffer. The data buffer is graphically represented in the top of Fig. 2.

Triangulation on data from time instants in the past requires the storage of this information. The data buffer stores the information from the peer robots and the robot itself in this buffer, quantized to time instants defined by the execution times of the robot.

4.3   Limited Amount of Data

The data buffer could contain: no information or information from only a single robot. To find the 3D ball position, the 'simple' algorithm would require at least two lines of sight at a certain time instant.

In case no information from the robot itself and from its peers is available, the algorithm applies the model to the previous state to estimate the ball position at the current time instant. If the ball experiences disturbances: e.g. bouncing off other robots or being kicked by another robot this method will show serious deviations as these disturbances are not modeled.

In case only one robot detects the ball, it is not possible to obtain a 3D ball position using the 'simple' algorithm presented previously. It is, however, desirable to include the new information in the derivation of the 3D ball position

274 W. Kuijpers et al.

at the current time instant. The algorithm therefore implements a minimum distance algorithm similar to that presented before, see Fig. 3(b). In the case of only one line of sight, the minimum distance $\overrightarrow{n_{md}}$ between the line of sight $\overrightarrow{R_x P_x}$ and the predicted position of the Kalman filter B for that particular time instant will be determined. $\overrightarrow{n_{md}}$ is in that case defined as

$$\overrightarrow{n_{md}} = \min_s \sqrt{\overrightarrow{n} \cdot \overrightarrow{n}} = \min_s \overrightarrow{n} \cdot \overrightarrow{n}. \tag{3}$$

Equating $\frac{d(\overrightarrow{n} \cdot \overrightarrow{n})}{ds}$ to zero yields the value of s which parameterizes line $\overrightarrow{n_{md}}$. The 3D ball position communicated to the rest of the system is in between I_x and B. This latter average can be replaced by a weighted average based on e.g. the length of $\overrightarrow{R_x P_x}$. Note that this method assumes that the predicted position of the Kalman filter B is an accurate representation for the ball position, so the ball should not be affected by disturbances during the time, the prediction is made over.

5 Results

In this section a performance analysis of the algorithm will be presented, it consists out of two tests: static and dynamic. This section is structured accordingly.

5.1 Static Test

To validate the implementation of the algorithm and to quantify the accuracy of the algorithm in a static environment, a set of static tests is defined. The ball is positioned on 5 predefined (x, y) positions[4] which make up set $\mathcal{P}$:

$$\mathcal{P} = \{(0, 6.05), (0, 3.03), (0, 1.94), (1.5, 3.03), (-1.5, 3.03)\}. \tag{4}$$

For each position in $\mathcal{P}$, two different heights are used: the ball was placed on the field $z = 0.11\,\mathrm{m}$, and on a green box[5] $z = 0.42\,\mathrm{m}$. For each of the ball position (x, y, z), 200 measurements are logged and the mean error and standard deviations in the 200 measurements are determined. A photo during execution of $\mathcal{P}_3$ with $z = 0.42\,\mathrm{m}$, is presented in Fig. 4.

For each of the ball positions (x, y, z) the mean error and standard deviation within the measurement set is determined, the results are shown in Table 1. These results are also compiled into Fig. 5. In this figure the robot positions are denoted by a ×. The mean detected position is shown by the red and yellow dots, for each of the (ground truth) positions on the field; represented by the black dots. For the figure the detected ball positions have been quantized to two values of z: $z = 0.11\,\mathrm{m}$ and $z = 0.42\,\mathrm{m}$, presented in different plots.

---

[4] With respect to frame presented in: http://wiki.robocup.org/images/1/1a/MSL_WMDataStruct.pdf.

[5] A green box has been selected, to ensure that the actual detection of the ball by the vision module, is not affected by the presence of the box.

Fig. 4. Photo taken during the execution of $\mathcal{P}_3$ with $z = 0.42$ m, from the static tests.

Table 1. The mean error (μ) and standard deviation (σ) for both robots in the static test. ↑ represents $z = 0.42$ m and ↓ represents $z = 0.11$ m. The averages for all position are presented in the last row, denoted by $\mathbb{E}$.

		Robot 1		Robot 2	
		μ [m]	σ [cm]	μ [m]	σ [cm]
$\mathcal{P}_1$	↑	0.159	0.45	0.159	0.43
	↓	0.117	0.51	0.106	0.55
$\mathcal{P}_2$	↑	0.083	0.52	0.091	0.70
	↓	0.076	0.92	0.067	0.84
$\mathcal{P}_3$	↑	0.208	0.34	0.205	0.32
	↓	0.142	0.36	0.138	1.01
$\mathcal{P}_4$	↑	0.087	1.96	0.065	0.57
	↓	0.073	1.38	0.023	1.32
$\mathcal{P}_5$	↑	0.139	1.02	0.090	1.17
	↓	0.070	1.96	0.034	0.89
$\mathbb{E}$	↑	0.135	0.75	0.121	0.64
	↓	0.095	1.03	0.074	0.92

The analysis of the mean error table, shows that the mean error when the ball is lifted ($z = 0.42$ m) is always higher than when it is on the field ($z = 0.11$ m). The increase in (mean) error was probably caused by the less accurate detection of the ball. The ball will appear closer to the edge of the omnivision image, where the pixel density is less. The inaccuracy caused by the latter, combined with the other sources of inaccuracies mentioned in Subsect. 3.1 is also enlarged as the distance over which the ball is projected increases.

Evaluating the performance of the triangulation algorithm in the static situation shows a mean error of 0.13 m when the ball is airborne and 0.08 m when it is on the field. The standard deviation on the measurements is always lower than 2 cm. This performance is considered to be satisfactory for use in the MSL.

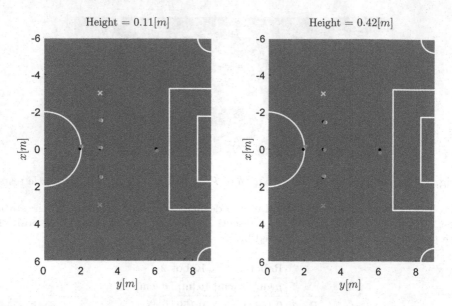

Fig. 5. Graphical representation of the results of the static test. The positions in (ground truth) set $\mathcal{P}$ are represented by black dots. The mean detected positions are represented by the red and yellow dots; corresponding to the robot, represented by the respective colored cross. (Color figure online)

5.2   Dynamic Test

To see if the triangulation algorithm is suitable for real-time 3D ball positioning by robots in the MSL, the algorithm has to be tested under dynamic game situations. The kick from a soccer robot has been selected as a dynamic event. The challenge that comes with tracking a kick, is the ball leaving the detectable space of the robots; the ball is not being detected when it exceeds the robot height. This means that before the ball leaves the detectable space of the robot, the triangulation algorithm has to have received enough measurements from peer-robots for its Kalman filter to have estimated the state accurately enough. If the state is estimated accurately, the point where it reenters the observable space can be calculated with decent accuracy. This subsection provides an analytic analysis of the dynamic tests. A photo of the setup is presented in Fig. 6.

The detected 3D ball positions from the robots without the ball (see Fig. 6) are presented in Fig. 7. The points in the figure represent the (filtered) triangulated balls, by the respective robots. The points are connected by lines to emphasize the sequence of points. Figure 7 shows that 8 samples are obtained from the moment the ball is kicked to the moment the ball leaves the observable space. The robots are positioned (x, y) at $(0, 2)$, $(0, 4)$ and $(-2, 3)$[6], where the latter robot is going to kick the ball.

---

[6] With respect to frame presented in: http://wiki.robocup.org/images/1/1a/MSL_WMDataStruct.pdf.

The initial state estimate x_0 represents a ball lying at the midpoint of the field. At the start of the experiment the Kalman filter is given some time to converge to the state presented in Fig. 6. These tests have been executed with a scalar matrix $Q = 1 \cdot I$, $R = 0.1 \cdot I$ and $P_0 = 1 \cdot I$. These matrices are used as tuning parameters for the Kalman filter, the results presented in Fig. 7 have been achieved after a rough tuning. The tuning of the Kalman filter in this case allows the Kalman filter to quickly converge to the actual ball trajectory after the kicking event, which was not included in the model. This, however, makes the estimation of the Kalman filter more susceptible to measurement inaccuracies, which can clearly be seen from the inaccuracies in the triangulated ball output.

Fig. 6. Photo of the setup of the dynamic test.

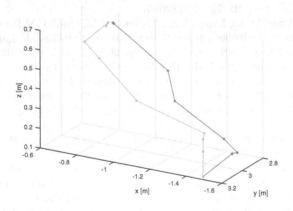

Fig. 7. The results of the dynamic test, where the ball trajectory, as detected by two robots (blue for the robot at $(0, 4)$ and orange for the robot at $(0, 2)$), is presented. The colored dots represent the detections of the ball. (Color figure online)

6 Conclusion and Future Work

This paper presents a method for 3D ball positioning in which no additional sensors have to be added and which is compatible with the "league standard" omnivision system. The algorithm was implemented on the robots of both team

CAMBADA and team Tech United. Static tests show that the error increases when the ball is airborne. An increase of ≈4 cm is observed if the ball is at a height of 0.42 cm compared to the situation where the ball is on the field. Dynamic tests show that it is difficult to track a kick from a robot. The Kalman filter has to react on the kick of the robot within samples, but it should not be susceptible to measurement inaccuracies.

The implementation on both teams is now directed towards testing. Before it is suitable for competition, the algorithm has to be integrated in the software more closely. For example: the projection of the ball can appear outside the field, both teams ignore the projection in this case. Tech United also employs Kinect sensors for ball detection, sensor fusion is therefore a point of attention as well.

References

1. Cunha, B., Neves, A.J.R., Dias, P., Azevedo, J.L., Lau, N., Dias, R., Amaral, F., Pedrosa, E., Pereira, A., Silva, J., Cunha, J., Trifan, A.: CAMBADA 2015: Team Description Paper (2015)
2. Dias, A., Almeida, J., Silva, E., Lima, P.: Multi-robot cooperative stereo for outdoor scenarios. In: 2013 13th International Conference on Autonomous Robot Systems, pp. 1–6. IEEE, April 2013
3. Neves, A.J.R., Trifan, A., Dias, P., Azevedo, J.L.: Detection of aerial balls in robotic soccer using a mixture of color and depth information. In: 2015 IEEE International Conference on Autonomous Robot Systems and Competitions, Aveiro, pp. 227–232 (2015)
4. Robin, C., Lacroix, S.: Multi-robot target detection and tracking: taxonomy and survey. Auton. Rob. **40**, 729–760 (2015)
5. Santos, F., Almeida, L., Lopes, L.S., Azevedo, J.L., Cunha, M.B.: Communicating among robots in the RoboCup middle-size league. In: Baltes, J., Lagoudakis, M.G., Naruse, T., Ghidary, S.S. (eds.) RoboCup 2009. LNCS, vol. 5949, pp. 320–331. Springer, Heidelberg (2010). doi:10.1007/978-3-642-11876-0_28
6. Schoenmakers, F., Koudijs, G., Lopez, C., Briegel, M., van Wesel, H., Groenen, J., Hendriks, O., Klooster, O., Soetens, R., Van De Molengraft, R.: Tech United Eindhoven Team Description 2013 - Middle Size League (2013)
7. Schönbein, M., Kitt, B., Lauer, M.: Environmental perception for intelligent vehicles using catadioptric stereo vision systems. In: ECMR, pp. 189–194 (2011)
8. Kim, S.-W., Chong, Z.J., Qin, B., Shen, X., Cheng, Z., Liu, W., Ang, M.H.: Cooperative perception for autonomous vehicle control on the road: motivation and experimental results. In: 2013 IEEE/RSJ International Conference on Intelligent Robots and Systems, pp. 5059–5066. IEEE, November 2013
9. Silva, J., Antunes, M., Lau, N., Neves, A.J.R., Lopes, L.S.: Aerial ball perception based on the use of a single perspective camera. In: Correia, L., Reis, L.P., Cascalho, J. (eds.) EPIA 2013. LNCS, vol. 8154, pp. 235–246. Springer, Heidelberg (2013). doi:10.1007/978-3-642-40669-0_21
10. Trifan, A., Neves, A.J.R., Cunha, B., Azevedo, J.L.: UAVision: a modular time-constrained vision library for soccer robots. In: Bianchi, R.A.C., Akin, H.L., Ramamoorthy, S., Sugiura, K. (eds.) RoboCup 2014. LNCS, vol. 8992, pp. 490–501. Springer, Cham (2015). doi:10.1007/978-3-319-18615-3_40
11. Voigtländer, A., Lange, S., Lauer, M., Riedmiller, M.: Real-time 3D ball recognition using perspective and catadioptric cameras. In: ECMR 2007, pp. 1–6 (2007)

Object Learning and Grasping Capabilities
for Robotic Home Assistants

S. Hamidreza Kasaei[1]([⊠]), Nima Shafii[1], Luís Seabra Lopes[1,2],
and Ana Maria Tomé[1,2]

[1] IEETA - Instituto de Engenharia Electrónica e Telemática de Aveiro,
Universidade de Aveiro, Aveiro, Portugal
{seyed.hamidreza,nima,lsl,ana}@ua.pt
[2] Departamento de Electrónica, Telecomunicações e Informática,
Universidade de Aveiro, Aveiro, Portugal

Abstract. This paper proposes an architecture designed to create
a proper coupling between perception and manipulation for assistive
robots. This is necessary for assistive robots, not only to perform manipulation tasks in reasonable amounts of time, but also to robustly adapt
to new environments by handling new objects. In particular, this architecture provides automatic perception capabilities that will allow robots
to, (i) incrementally learn object categories from the set of accumulated
experiences and (ii) infer how to grasp household objects in different
situations. To examine the performance of the proposed architecture,
quantitative and qualitative evaluations have been carried out. Experimental results show that the proposed system is able to interact with
human users, learn new object categories over time, as well as perform
object grasping tasks.

Keywords: Assistive robots · Object grasping · Object learning and
recognition

1 Introduction

Assistive robots are extremely useful because they can help elderly adults or
people with motor impairments to achieve independence in everyday tasks [3].
Elderly, injured, and disabled people have consistently put a high priority on
object manipulation [6]. On the one hand, a robot capable of performing object
manipulation tasks in domestic environments would be worthwhile. On the other
hand, this type of end-users expect robots to improve the task performance
and to robustly adapt to new environments by handling new objects. In other
words, it is not feasible to assume one can pre-program everything for assistive
robots. Instead, robots should infer and learn autonomously from experiences,
including feedback from human teachers. In order to incrementally adapt to new
environments, an autonomous assistive robot must have the abilities to process
visual information, infer grasp points and learn and recognize object categories
in a concurrent and interleaved fashion.

© Springer International Publishing AG 2017
S. Behnke et al. (Eds.): RoboCup 2016, LNAI 9776, pp. 279–293, 2017.
https://doi.org/10.1007/978-3-319-68792-6_23

However, several state of the art assistive robots employ traditional object grasping and object category learning/recognition approaches, often resorting to complete geometric models of the objects [9,16]. These traditional approaches are often designed for static environments in which it is viable to separate the training (off-line) and testing (on-line) phases. Besides, the knowledge of this kind of robots is static, in the sense that the representation of the known categories does not change after the training stage.

In this paper, a framework for assistive robots is presented which provides a tight coupling between object perception and manipulation. The approach is designed to be used by an assistive robot working in a domestic environment similar to the RoboCup @Home league environment. This work focuses on grasping and recognizing table-top objects. In particular, we present an adaptive object recognition system based on environment exploration and Bayesian learning. Moreover, the robot should manipulate detected objects while working in the environment.

The contributions presented here are the following: *(i)* an integrated framework for assistive robots that incorporates capabilities for object perception, learning and manipulation. *(ii)* unsupervised object exploration for constructing a dictionary of visual words for object representation using the Bag-of-Words model; *(iii)* open-ended learning of object category models from experiences; *(iv)* a data driven grasp pose detection approach for household objects including flat ones.

2 Related Work

Over the past decade, several researches have been conducted to develop assistive robots for motor impairments or elderly people that enable them to stay active and less dependent on others [3]. Jain et al. [6] presented an assistive mobile manipulator, EL-E, that can autonomously pick objects from a flat surface and deliver them to the user. Unlike our approach, the user provides a 3D location of the target object to the robot by pointing on the object with a laser pointer. In another work, a busboy assistive robot has been developed by Srinivasa et al. [14]. This work is similar to ours in that it integrates object perception and grasping for pick and place objects. However there are some differences. Their vision system is designed for detecting mugs only, while our perception system not only tracks the pose of different objects but also recognizes their categories.

Robotic grasping approaches are usually organized in three groups according to the knowledge available about objects: objects can unknown, known or familiar [1]. Grasping approaches for known objects typically use complete geometry of objects to improve grasp quality [1]. However, in real scenarios the complete knowledge about geometry and other properties of objects are not known in advance (objects are initially unknown). Thus, grasping approaches for unknown objects are needed. Hsiao et al. [5] proposed a data driven algorithm that searches among feasible top and side grasp candidates for unknown objects based on their partial view. Its advantage is that no supervised learning is required. In a similar approach [15] shows, a service robot is capable of grasping different household objects at the RoboCup @Home competition. However, unlike our approach, these grasp approaches are not able to grasp flat objects e.g., plates. Another goal in the field of assistive and service robots is to achieve interactive object category learning and recognition. Martinez et al. [11] described a fast and scalable perception system for object recognition and pose estimation.

In most of the proposed systems described above, training and testing are separate processes, which do not occur simultaneously. There are some approaches which support incremental learning of object categories. Hamidreza Kasaei et al. [7] and Oliveira et al. [13] approached the problem of object experience gathering and category learning with a focus on open-ended learning and human-robot interaction. They used instance-based learning approach to describe object categories whereas we employ a model based approach in which a Naive Bayes learning method is used.

3   Overall System Architecture

The overall system architecture is depicted in Fig. 1. It is a reusable framework and all modules were developed over Robot Operating System (ROS). The current architecture is an evolution of the architecture developed in previous work for object perception and open-ended perceptual learning [7,13]. The architecture consists of two memory systems, namely the *Working Memory* and the *Perceptual Memory*. Both memory systems have been implemented as a lightweight NoSQL database namely LevelDB developed by Google. *Working Memory* is used for temporarily storing and manipulating information and communications of all modules. A visual words dictionary, object representation data and object category knowledge are stored into the *Perceptual Memory*. The goal of the *Grasp Selection* is to extract a grasp pose (i.e. a gripper pose relative to the

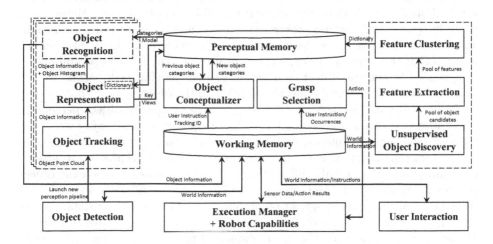

Fig. 1. Overall architecture of the proposed system

object) using the presented grasp approach (Sect. 7). The *Execution Manager* module receives the action and dispatches it to the robot platform as well as records success or failure information into the *Working Memory*.

The proposed architecture includes two perceptual learning components. The first component is concerned with building a visual words dictionary for object representation. The dictionary plays a prominent role because will be used for learning as well as recognition. The second component focuses on interactive object category learning and recognition. After constructing the dictionary, when the robot captures a scene, the first step is preprocessing, which employs three filtering procedures for removing unnecessary data. The *Object Detection* module is responsible for detecting objects in the scene. It creates a new perception pipeline for every detected object. Each pipeline includes *Object Tracking, Object Representation* and *Object Recognition* modules. The *Object Tracking* module estimates the current pose of the object based on a particle filter, which uses shape as well as color data [12]. The *Object Representation* module describes objects as histograms of visual words and stores them into the *Perceptual Memory*. A user can provide category labels for these objects via the *User Interaction* module [10]. Whenever the instructor provides a category label for an object, the *Object Conceptualizer* improves or creates a new object category model. In recognition situations, a probabilistic classification rule is used to assign a category label to the detected object. In the following sections, the characteristics of the object perception, learning and grasping modules are explained in detail.

4   Dictionary Construction

Comparing 3D objects by their local features would be computationally expensive. To address this problem, an approach for object representation is adopted in which objects are described by histograms of local shape features, as defined in Bag-of-Words models. A Bag-of-Words model requires a dictionary of visual words. Usually, the dictionary is created via off-line clustering of training data, while in open-ended learning, there is no predefined set of training data available at the beginning of the learning process. To cope with this limitation, we propose that the robot freely explores several scenes and collects several object experiences. In general, object exploration is a challenging task because of the dynamic nature of the world and ill-definition of the objects [4].

In the following, we used boolean expressions to specify object perception capabilities(see Eqs. 1 and 2). In both *object exploration* and *object detention* cases, we assume that interesting objects are on tables and the robot seeks to detect tabletop objects (i.e. C_{table}). On the one hand, to represent an object, it is important to store only different views, which is possible when the object is moved. On the other hand, storing all object views while the object is static would lead to unnecessary accumulation of highly redundant data. Hence, the C_{track} constraint is means the object candidate is already being tracked. Moreover, $C_{\text{instructor}}$ and C_{robot} are exploited to filter out object candidates corresponding to the instructor's body as well as robot's body. Accordingly, the resulting object candidates are less noisy and include only data corresponding to the objects:

$$\psi_{exploration} = C_{table} \wedge C_{track} \wedge \neg (C_{instructor} \vee C_{robot}) \qquad (1)$$

In our current setup, a table is detected by finding the dominant plane in the point cloud. This is done using a RANSAC algorithm. Extraction of polygonal prisms is used for collecting the points which lie directly above the table. Afterwards, an Euclidean Cluster Extraction algorithm is used to segment a scene into individual clusters. Every cluster that satisfy the exploration expression is selected. The output of this object exploration is a pool of object candidates. Subsequently, to construct a pool of features, spin-images are computed for the selected points extracted from the pool of object candidates. It should be noted that to balance computational efficiency and robustness, a downsampling filter is applied to obtain a smaller set of points distributed over the surface of the object. We use a PCL function to compute spin-images. Finally, the dictionary is constructed by clustering the features using the *k-means* algorithm. The centres of the N (i.e. $N = 90$) extracted clusters define the visual words, $\mathbf{w}_t$ ($1 \leq t \leq N$). Figure 2 shows the procedure of constructing a dictionary of visual words. A video of the system that a robot explores an environment[1] is available in: http://youtu.be/MwX3J6aoAX0.

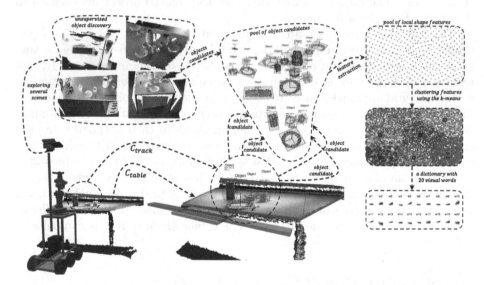

Fig. 2. The robot moves through an office to explore several scenes and extract tabletop objects to construct a dictionary of visual words.

---

[1] The ROS bag file used in this video was created by the Knowledge-Based Systems Group, Institute of Computer Science, University of Osnabrueck.

5 Object Detection and Representation

For fast processing of massive point clouds, two filters are used, namely distance filtering and downsampling [7]. Furthermore, knowledge of the positions of the arm joints relative to the camera pose is retrieved from the *Working Memory* and sensor data (i.e. points) corresponding to robot's body is filtered out from the original point cloud. After preprocessing, the next step is to find objects in the scene. The object detection module implements the following specification:

$$\psi_{\text{detection}} = C_{\text{table}} \wedge C_{\text{track}} \wedge C_{\text{size}} \wedge \neg (C_{\text{instructor}} \vee C_{\text{robot}} \vee C_{\text{edge}}) \quad (2)$$

The object detection uses a size constraint, C_{size}, to detect objects which can be manipulated by the robot. Moreover, a C_{edge} constraint is considered to filter out the segmented point clouds that are too close to the edge of the table. The object detection then assigns a new *Track ID* to each newly detected object and launches an object perception pipeline for the object candidate as well. The object detection pushes the segmented object candidates into the perception pipelines for subsequent processing steps.

The *Object Tracking* module is responsible for keeping track of the target object over time while it remains visible [12]. It receives the point cloud of the detected object and computes its geometric center of object view as the position of the object. The object tracking sends out the tracked object information to the *Object Representation* module.

The input to the object representation module is a point cloud of an object candidate **O**. The object representation module involves three main phases: keypoint extraction, computation of spin images for each keypoint and, finally, representing an object view as a histogram of visual words. For keypoint extraction, a voxelized grid approach is used to obtain a smaller set of points by taking only the nearest neighbor point for each voxel center [7]. Afterwards, the spin-image descriptor is used to encode the surrounding shape in each keypoint using the original point cloud. By searching for the nearest neighbor in the dictionary, each local shape is assigned to a visual word. Finally, each object is represented as a histogram of occurrences of visual words, $\mathbf{h} = [h_1 \; h_2 \ldots h_N]$, where the ith element of $\mathbf{h}$ is the count of the number features assigned to a visual word, $\mathbf{w}_i$. The obtained histogram of the given object is dispatched to the *Object Recognition* module and is recorded into the *Perceptual Memory* if it is marked as a key view.

6 Interactive Object Category Learning

Human-robot interaction is essential for supervised experience gathering, i.e. for instructing the robot how to perform different tasks. Particularly, an open-ended object learning and recognition system will be more flexible if it is able to learn new objects from a human user. For example, if the robot does not know how a *'Mug'* looks like, it may ask the user to show one. Such situation provides an opportunity to collect training instances from actual experiences of the robot and the system can incrementally update it's knowledge rather than retraining from scratch when a new instance is added or a new category is defined. The details of the interaction module and supervised object experience gathering is discussed in [10]. The *Object Conceptualizer* (category learning) module is activated when the instructor provides a category label for the object.

6.1   Object Conceptualizer

In this work, object category learning is a process of computing a Bayesian model for each object category. There are two reasons why Bayesian learning is useful for open-ended learning. One of them is the computational efficiency of Bayes approaches. In fact, the model can be incrementally updated when new information is available, rather than retrained from scratch. Second, open-ended systems usually have limited amount of memory available and therefore, it must involve experience management to prevent the accumulation of experiences. In Bayesian learning, new experiences are used to update category models and then the experiences are forgotten.

The probabilistic category model requires calculating the likelihoods of the object given the category k, $p(\mathbf{O}|C_k)$, and it is also parametrized by the prior probabilities $p(C_k)$. The likelihoods of objects in each category, $p(\mathbf{O}|C_k)$, cannot be estimated directly. To make it tractable, we assume that visual words of objects are independent given the category. Therefore, the $p(C_k)p(\mathbf{O}|C_k)$ is equivalent to the joint probability model $p(C_k, \mathbf{w}_1, \ldots, \mathbf{w}_n) = p(C_k)\ p(\mathbf{w}_1, \ldots, \mathbf{w}_n|C_k)$. The joint model can be rewritten using conditional independence assumptions:

$$p(C_k|\mathbf{w}_1, \ldots, \mathbf{w}_n) \propto p(C_k) \prod_{i=1}^{n} p(\mathbf{w}_i|C_k), \qquad (3)$$

where n is the size of the dictionary and $p(\mathbf{w}_i|C_k)$ is the probability of the visual word $\mathbf{w}_i$ occurring in an object of category k:

$$p(\mathbf{w}_i|C_k) = \frac{s_{ik} + 1}{\sum\limits_{j=1}^{n}(s_{jk} + 1)}, \qquad (4)$$

where s_{ik} is the number of times that word $\mathbf{w}_i$ was seen in objects from category C_k. On each newly seen object of this category with h_i features of type $\mathbf{w}_i$, the following update is carried out: $s_{ik} \leftarrow s_{ik} + h_i$. The prior probability of category k, $p(C_k)$, is estimated by dividing the number of seen objects from category k by the total number of seen objects in all categories.

6.2   Object Category Recognition

The last part of object perception is object category recognition. To classify an object $\mathbf{O}$, which is represented as a histogram of occurrences of visual words

$\mathbf{h} = [h_1, \ldots, h_n]$, the posterior probability for each object category $p(C_k|\mathbf{h})$ is considered as the object-category similarity (i.e. OCS(.)) and approximated using Bayes theorem as:

$$\text{OCS}(\mathbf{O}, C_k) = \frac{p(\mathbf{h}|C_k)p(C_k)}{p(\mathbf{h})}, \tag{5}$$

Since the denominator does not depend on C_k, it is constant and can be ignored. Equation 5 is re-expressed based on Eq. 3 and multinomial distribution assumption. In addition, to avoid underflow problems, the logarithm of the likelihood is computed:

$$\text{OCS}(\mathbf{O}, C_k) = \log p(C_k) + \sum_{i=1}^{n} h_i \, \log p(\mathbf{w}_i|C_k), \tag{6}$$

The category of the target object $\mathbf{O}$ is the one with highest likelihood. If, for all categories, the OCS(.) is smaller than a given threshold (e.g. CT = 0.75), then the object is classified as *Unknown*; otherwise, it is classified as the category that has the highest similarity. Consequently, object information including object recognition result, point cloud and global characteristics of the given object such as main axis, center and size of bounding box are written to the *Working Memory*, where the grasp selection module can fetch them to support object manipulation. *Grasp Selection* is triggered when a user instructs the robot to perform a task (e.x. *serve a meal*).

7   Grasp Methodology

In this work, we assume that it is possible to select suitable grasps pose for different household objects by only using partial object views. The grasp selection module retrieves the point cloud of a given object from working memory (see Fig. 1). The point cloud is then processed to determine an appropriate object's bounding box and reference frame. For constructing the object-centric reference frame, the vertical direction perpendicular to the table is assigned to the local z-axis since objects are assumed to be placed on a table. Principal Component Analysis (PCA) is used to compute the axes of minimum and maximum variance in the horizontal plane using points projected on the surface plane. The maximum variance axis is assigned to the x-axis. Although the result of PCA indicates the lines align to the eigen vectors, but the sign and direction of this line remains ambiguous to calculate x-axis. The direction of the x-axis is defined as the oposite direction to the origin of the arm base frame. Then, the bounding box of the object calculated along these axes is computed and the center of the bounding box is defined as the origin of the object's coordinate system. Since the object is only partially visible, the center of the object's bounding box is used as a proxy for the true center of mass. In this study, we use a set of heuristic grasp strategies. They are defined as follows:

Top grasp strategy: It is assumed that the object is only approached by the robot along the z-axis (perpendicular to the surface) while the gripper closing direction is aligned with the y-axis. Thus, in order to find the suitable grasp pose on the object, it is only needed to find the grasp position on x-axis. To do that, first, the object points are projected onto the xy-plane. Then, the points are clustered using equally sized intervals along x-axis. Each cluster indicates one grasp candidate. For each one, the maximum and the minimum of the positions of points along y-axis indicate the grasp width. In order to select a proper grasp candidate, since grasping around the center of mass of an object is preferable, the cluster around the origin is the first to be analyzed. This grasp minimizes the torque about the gripper axis due to the objects weight. If the grasp width of the selected candidate is larger than the width of the gripper (i.e. 12 cm), the other grasp candidates will be analyzed. The grasp candidates are then sorted based on how much their grasp width fits to the robot's palm. The size of palm of the JACO arm is 5 cm. Note, the grasp candidates that reach to the limits of the x-axis are rejected. Figure 3 (*left*) shows the process of the top grasps approach.

Fig. 3. The projected objects' points on the planes of the object bounding box (gray box) are analyzed to select the grasp pose (black square). The bad grasp poses (red squares) are rejected. (Color figure online)

Horizontal side grasp strategy: According to this grasp strategy, the object is approached in the horizontal plane, along the y-axis while negative y is used as approach direction and the gripper closing direction is aligned with the x-axis. In this case, the proper grasp position along z-axis should be found. To do that, first, object points are projected onto the xz-plane, then multiple grasp candidates are generated by sampling along the z-axis with equal interval size. Using a strategy similar to the one described for top grasps, the grasp candidates are analysed and one of them is selected. The grasp candidates located in the limits of the z-axis are also rejected. The process of the grasp selection using the horizontal side strategy is depicted in Fig. 3 (*center*).

Vertical side grasp strategy: In this strategy, the object is approached in the vertical plane along the y-axis. The approach direction is negative y and the gripper closing direction is aligned with the z-axis. This grasp strategy is designed to be used in grasping flat objects such as plates. In this strategy, the proper grasp position along x-axis should be inferred. To do that, first, the object's points are projected onto the xz-plane, then multiple grasp candidates are extracted by sampling along the y-axis with equal interval size. Like above strategies, the centered grasp candidate is selected if it fits inside the gripper. Otherwise, other grasp candidates are ranked as in the top grasp strategy.

Algorithm 1 rule of grasp strategy selection
---
if |z-axis| > |x-axis| and |z-axis| > |y-axis| then
    perform top grasp
else if |x-axis| > |z-axis| and |y-axis| > |z-axis| then
    perform vertical side grasp
else
    perform horizontal side grasp
end if

The grasp candidates located in the limits of the x-axis are also rejected. Figure 3 (*right*) shows the grasp selection process using vertical side grasp strategy. In our grasp methodology, first, one of the proposed grasp strategies is selected based on the size of the bounding box of the object. To do that the following rules are presented in Algorithm 1. Where |.| returns the size of object along an specific axis. Finally, the JACO arm robot is commanded to perform actions based on the selected grasp position and strategy. Inverse kinematic integrated from the JACO arm driver is used to control the end-effector pose goal. In a grasping scenario, first the robot is commanded to go to a pre-grasp position that is 0.2 cm behind the grasp pose along with the grasp orientation. The grasp orientation is given by grasp strategy. When the pre-grasp pose is reached, the robot approaches the grasp point and then closes the gripper. Afterwards, the height of the robot's end-effector in the arm-frame is recorded by the robot in working memory to be used as the desired height for placing the grasped object. Whenever the object is grasped, the robot picks up the object and navigates it to the predefined placing pose.

8 Experimental Results

Four types of experiments were performed to evaluate the proposed approach.

Table 1. Average object recognition performance (F1 measure) for different parameters

Parameters	VS			DS					IW		SL			
Values	0.01	0.02	0.03	50	60	70	80	90	4	8	0.02	0.03	0.04	0.05
Average F1	0.76	0.74	0.71	0.72	0.73	0.74	0.74	0.75	0.75	0.72	0.63	0.74	0.78	0.79

8.1 Off-line Evaluation of the Object Learning Approach

To examine the performance of different configurations of the proposed object learning approach (Sect. 6), a 10-fold cross validation scheme has been followed. For this purpose, an object dataset namely Restaurant Object Dataset [7] has been used which contains 339 views of 10 categories of objects. A total of 120 experiments were performed for different values of four parameters of the system, namely the voxel size (VS) which is related to number of keypoints extracted from each object view, the dictionary size (DS), the image width (IW) and support length (SL) of spin images. Results are presented in Table 1. The combination of parameters that obtained the best average F1 score was selected as the default system parameters. They are the following: $VS = 0.01$, $DS = 90$, $IW = 4$ and $SL = 0.05$. The results presented in Sects. 8.2 and 8.4 are computed using this configuration.

8.2 Open-Ended Evaluation

The off-line evaluation methodologies (e.g. k-fold cross validation, leave- one-out, etc.) are not well suited to evaluate open-ended learning systems, because they do not abide to the simultaneous nature of learning and recognition and those methodologies imply that the number of categories must be predefined. An evaluation protocol for open-ended learning systems was proposed in [2]. A *simulated teacher* was developed to follow the teaching protocol and autonomously interact with the system using three basic actions namely **teach**, used for teaching a new object category, **ask**, used to ask the system what is the category of an object view and **correct**, used for providing the system corrective feedback in case of misclassification. The idea is that, for each newly taught category, the simulated teacher repeatedly picks unseen object views of the currently known categories from a dataset and presents them to the system. It progressively estimates recognition performance of the system and, in case this performance exceeds a given threshold ($CT = 0.67$), introduces an additional object category. In this way, the system is trained and tested at the same time. Experiments were running the largest publicly available dataset namely RGB-D Object Dataset consisting of 250,000 views of 300 common household objects, organized into 49 categories [8].

When an experiment is carried out, learning performance is evaluated using several measures, including: (*i*) The number of learned categories at the end of an experiment (*TLC*), an indicator of **how much the system is capable of learning**; (*ii*) The number of question/correction iterations (*QCI*) required to learn those categories and the average number of stored instances per category (*AIC*), indicators of **time and memory resources required for learning**; (*iii*) Global classification accuracy (*GCA*), an F-measure computed using all predictions in a complete experiment, and the average classification accuracy (*ACA*), indicators of **how well the system learns**.

Since the order of introduction of new categories may have an effect on the performance of the system, ten experiments were carried out in which categories were introduced in random sequences. In the additional nine experiments, these categories were used again with different introduction sequences, which are reported in Table 2. By comparing all experiments, it is visible that

Table 2. Summary of experiments.

EXP#	#QCI	#TLC	#AIC	GCA (%)	ACA (%)
1	1257	49	8.16	79	83
2	1238	49	7.83	80	84
3	1227	49	7.65	81	84
4	1240	49	9.08	75	78
5	1236	49	7.95	80	83
6	1346	49	9.46	76	79
7	1293	49	9.02	77	81
8	1330	49	9.79	74	79
9	1336	49	9.55	75	78
10	1225	49	8.30	78	82

in the third experiment, the system learned all categories faster than other experiments. In the case of experiment 9, the number of iterations required to learn 49 object categories was greater than other experiments.

Figure 4 (*left*) shows the global classification accuracy as a function of the number of learned categories. In this figure we can see that the global classification accuracy decreases as more categories are learned. This is expected since the number of categories known by the system makes the classification task more difficult. Finally, Fig. 4 (*right*) shows the number of learned categories as a function of the protocol iterations. This gives a measure of how fast the learning occurred in each of the experiments.

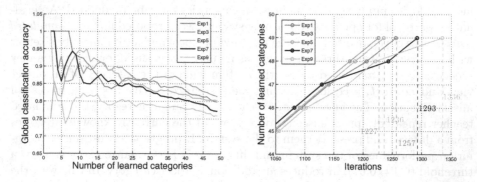

Fig. 4. System performance during simulated user experiments.

8.3   Grasp Evaluation

In order to evaluate the quality of the proposed grasp approach, a grasp scenario has been designed. In the grasp scenario, the JACO robot is instructed to pick-up an object using the proposed grasp methodology. After picking up the object, the robot carries the object to the placing position to see if the object slips due to bad grasp or not. A particular grasp is considered as success if the robot performed the scenario successfully. We analyzed the performance of our approach to grasp the household objects by evaluating the success rate. In our designed scenarios, 21 household objects were used which can be seen in Fig. 5.

As a testing scenario, the objects were placed in different orientations. In each experiment, an object was first put in the orientation shown by the object view in the Fig. 5 and robot tried to grasp it. Afterwards, we rotated the object about 60° for six times and repeated the scenario to test all viewpoints of the object. Therefore, each object was tested to be grasped by the robot 6 times, and 126 grasp trials were performed to complete the whole experiments. In these experiments, the robot could perform 111 successful grasps meaning that the overall success rate was about 88%. It was observed that the robot could grasp all objects by using the proposed strategies.

Fig. 5. The objects used as a test set to evaluate the proposed grasp approach.

8.4 System Demonstration

A *serve a meal* scenario has been designed to show all functionalities of the object recognition and grasping. In this demonstration, the system works in a scenario where a table is in front of the robot and a user interacts with the system. Note that, when the system starts, the set of categories known to the system is empty. In the session, a user presents objects to the system and provides the respective category labels. The user then instructs the robot to perform a *serve a meal* task (i.e. puts different restaurant objects on the table in front of the user). To achieve this task, the robot must be able to detect and recognize different objects and transport the objects to the predefined areas and completely serve a meal. For this purpose, the robot retrieves the world model information from the *Working Memory* including label and position of all active objects. The robot then chooses the object that is nearest to the arm's base and serves it to the user. A video of this session is available at: https://youtu.be/GtXBiejdccw. This small demonstration shows that the developed system is capable of detecting new objects, tracking and recognizing as well as manipulating objects in various positions.

9   Conclusion

In this paper, we presented an architecture designed to support a coupling between perception and manipulation for service robots. In particular, an interactive open-ended learning approach for acquiring 3D object categories and a data driven approach for object grasping have been presented, which enable robots to adapt to different environments and reason out how to behave in response to a complex task such as *serve a meal*. This paper also proposes unsupervised object exploration to construct the visual word dictionary and an incremental Bayesian learning approach for object category learning.

We have also tried to make the proposed architecture easy to integrate on other robotic systems. Our approach to object perception has been successfully tested on a JACO arm, showing the importance of having a tight coupling between perception and manipulation. For future work, we would like to investigate the possibility of improving performance of object grasping based on kinesthetic teaching and improving performance of object recognition using topic modelling.

Acknowledgement. This work was funded by National Funds through FCT project PEst-OE/EEI/UI0127/2016 and FCT scholarship SFRH/BD/94183/2013.

References

1. Bohg, J., Morales, A., Asfour, T., Kragic, D.: Data-driven grasp synthesis – a survey. IEEE Trans. Robot. **30**(2), 289–309 (2014)
2. Chauhan, A., Lopes, L.S.: Using spoken words to guide open-ended category formation. Cogn. Process. **12**(4), 341–354 (2011)
3. Ciocarlie, M., Hsiao, K., Jones, E.G., Chitta, S., Rusu, R.B., Şucan, I.A.: Towards reliable grasping and manipulation in household environments. In: Khatib, O., Kumar, V., Sukhatme, G. (eds.) Experimental Robotics. Springer Tracts in Advanced Robotics, vol. 79, pp. 241–252. Springer, Heidelberg (2014). doi:10.1007/978-3-642-28572-1_17
4. Collet, A., Xiong, B., Gurau, C., Hebert, M., Srinivasa, S.S.: Herbdisc: towards lifelong robotic object discovery. Int. J. Robot. Res. **34**(1), 3–25 (2015). doi:10.1177/0278364914546030
5. Hsiao, K., Chitta, S., Ciocarlie, M., Jones, E.G.: Contact-reactive grasping of objects with partial shape information. In: 2010 IEEE/RSJ International Conference on Intelligent Robots and Systems (IROS), pp. 1228–1235. IEEE (2010)
6. Jain, A., Kemp, C.C.: El-E: an assistive mobile manipulator that autonomously fetches objects from flat surfaces. Auton. Robot. **28**(1), 45–64 (2010)
7. Hamidreza Kasaei, S., Oliveira, M., Lim, G.H., Lopes, L.S., Tomé, A.M.: Interactive open-ended learning for 3D object recognition: an approach and experiments. J. Intell. Robot. Syst. **80**, 1–17 (2015)
8. Lai, K., Bo, L., Ren, X., Fox, D.: A large-scale hierarchical multi-view RGB-D object dataset. In: 2011 IEEE International Conference on Robotics and Automation (ICRA), pp. 1817–1824, May 2011
9. Leroux, C., Lebec, O., Ghezala, M.B., Mezouar, Y., Devillers, L., Chastagnol, C., Martin, J.C., Leynaert, V., Fattal, C.: ARMEN: assistive robotics to maintain elderly people in natural environment. IRBM **34**(2), 101–107 (2013)
10. Lim, G.H., Oliveira, M., Mokhtari, V., Hamidreza Kasaei, S., Chauhan, A., Seabra Lopes, L., Tome, A.: Interactive teaching and experience extraction for learning about objects and robot activities. In: 2014 RO-MAN: The 23rd IEEE International Symposium on Robot and Human Interactive Communication, pp. 153–160, August 2014
11. Martinez Torres, M., Collet Romea, A., Srinivasa, S.: Moped: a scalable and low latency object recognition and pose estimation system. In: IEEE International Conference on Robotics and Automation, (ICRA 2010), May 2010
12. Oliveira, M., Lim, G.H., Seabra Lopes, L., Hamidreza Kasaei, S., Tome, A., Chauhan, A.: A perceptual memory system for grounding semantic representations in intelligent service robots. In: Proceedings of the IEEE/RSJ International Conference on Intelligent Robots and Systems (IROS). IEEE (2014)
13. Oliveira, M., Lopes, L.S., Lim, G.H., Hamidreza Kasaei, H., Tomé, A.M., Chauhan, A.: 3D object perception and perceptual learning in the RACE project. Robot. Auton. Syst. **75**, 614–626 (2016). Part B
14. Srinivasa, S., Ferguson, D.I., Vande Weghe, M., Diankov, R., Berenson, D., Helfrich, C., Strasdat, H.: The robotic busboy: steps towards developing a mobile robotic home assistant. In: International Conference on Intelligent Autonomous Systems, pp. 2155–2162 (2008)

15. Stückler, J., Steffens, R., Holz, D., Behnke, S.: Efficient 3D object perception and grasp planning for mobile manipulation in domestic environments. Robot. Auton. Syst. **61**(10), 1106–1115 (2013)
16. Vahrenkamp, N., Do, M., Asfour, T., Dillmann, R.: Integrated grasp and motion planning. In: 2010 IEEE International Conference on Robotics and Automation (ICRA), pp. 2883–2888. IEEE (2010)

RGB-D-Based Features for Recognition of Textureless Objects

Santosh Thoduka[✉], Stepan Pazekha, Alexander Moriarty,
and Gerhard K. Kraetzschmar

Department of Computer Science, Bonn-Rhein-Sieg University of Applied Sciences,
Grantham-Allee 20, 53757 Sankt Augustin, Germany
{santosh.thoduka,stepan.pazekha,alexander.moriarty,
gerhard.kraetzschmar}@inf.h-brs.de

Abstract. Autonomous industrial robots need to recognize objects robustly in cluttered environments. The use of RGB-D cameras has progressed research in 3D object recognition, but it is still a challenge for textureless objects. We propose a set of features, including the bounding box, mean circle fit and radial density distribution, that describe the size, shape and colour of objects. The features are extracted from point clouds of a set of objects and used to train an SVM classifier. Various combinations of the proposed features are tested to determine their influence on the recognition rate. Medium-sized objects are recognized with high accuracy whereas small objects have a lower recognition rate. The minimum range and resolution of the cameras are still an issue but are expected to improve as the technology improves.

Keywords: Object recognition · Machine learning · Textureless objects · RGB-D data · Coloured pointclouds

1 Introduction

As industrial robots become increasingly autonomous there is a need for sophisticated perception capabilities. In controlled industrial settings where the environment is well described, perception tasks are simplified since assumptions can be made about the location of objects. As a result of assuming the object location is known, object recognition may not be required and object detection may be sufficient. However, with mobile robots, the same simplifications cannot be made since there is more uncertainty about the environment. Although the general locations of objects are known, the robot can no longer rely on being precisely localized in the environment. To compensate for this, there is a greater emphasis on performing complex perception tasks such as object recognition.

The availability of low cost RGB-D cameras has progressed research in 3D object recognition significantly. However, industrial objects pose a challenge for existing object recognition approaches due to their nature. Objects such as profiles, nuts, screws and bolts tend to be textureless, of homogeneous colour and,

© Springer International Publishing AG 2017
S. Behnke et al. (Eds.): RoboCup 2016, LNAI 9776, pp. 294–305, 2017.
https://doi.org/10.1007/978-3-319-68792-6_24

in some cases, quite small. Many are simple geometric shapes made of metal or plastic and often do not have particularly distinguishable features. There are also similarly shaped objects with only size or colour differentiating them. Existing state of the art 3D recognition algorithms rely on having sufficiently detailed point clouds of objects in order to extract features such as surface normals, colour gradients etc. For small objects, this is a challenge due to the minimum range of RGB-D cameras and their resolution.

RoboCup@Work [9] and RoCKIn@Work [4] are both robotic competitions which focus on mobile manipulation challenges relevant for small and medium sized industrial factory settings. In larger, traditional factories, machinery, service areas and robots can be fixed for long term production where the factory layout and production process is not expected to change frequently. In small factories settings, specifically Factories of the Future [1] which can adapt quickly and dynamically to meet production demands, a particular service area may serve multiple purposes through the production process. Service areas are locations where manipulation and perception tasks are performed. They are general purpose areas which may be shared with humans. As such, service areas can be cluttered and the location of objects on them not precisely known.

In RoboCup@Work, several tasks involve grasping objects that are placed on service areas among other objects. The objects need to be recognized and transported to different locations based on the task specification. In some cases, objects need to be inserted into containers or cavities. Some examples of the industrial objects used in the competition can be seen in Fig. 1.

Currently, this is the exact set of objects used, and there are no variations among each type.

The task of object recognition usually involves an offline training phase and an online recognition phase. In the training phase, representative samples of the objects are collected. For 3D recognition systems, this is typically point clouds of the objects taken from several views. Descriptive features are then extracted from the samples and used to train a classifier or save templates. During the recognition phase, an unknown object is segmented from the scene and the identical features are extracted from it. The features are then fed into the classifier or template matcher which returns the identifier of the best matched object from the previously trained objects.

As seen in Fig. 2, the point clouds generated by the RGB-D camera are noisy and does not capture all the small details of the objects. The small size and inadequately descriptive point clouds make the task of recognizing such objects a challenging one. For example, the large aluminium profile is only 10 cm x 4 cm x 4 cm, and the distance tube is 1 cm high with a radius of 1.6 cm. They are quite small in the field of view of the camera and the number of points that represent the object is quite low in some cases. In this paper, we focus on the extraction of descriptive features for textureless objects and test the approach using the objects in Fig. 1.

The paper is structured as follows: We review related work in Sect. 2, describe our approach in Sect. 3 and finally present the results in Sect. 4.

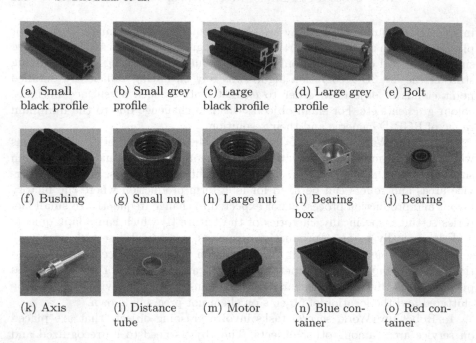

(a) Small black profile   (b) Small grey profile   (c) Large black profile   (d) Large grey profile   (e) Bolt

(f) Bushing   (g) Small nut   (h) Large nut   (i) Bearing box   (j) Bearing

(k) Axis   (l) Distance tube   (m) Motor   (n) Blue container   (o) Red container

Fig. 1. Object set used in the RoboCup@Work competition [3] (Color figure online)

2   Related Work

Object recognition using 3D point clouds can be broadly categorized into global and local feature-based methods. Global feature descriptors are computed for the entire object point cloud whereas local descriptors are calculated for individual points in the cloud. For example, the Point cloud library (PCL) [12] has implementations for local descriptors such as Point Feature Histogram (PFH), Radius-based Surface Descriptor (RSD), Signatures of Histograms of Orientations (SHOT) and global descriptors such as Viewpoint Feature Histogram (VFH), Ensemble of Shape Functions (ESF) and Global Fast Point Feature Histogram (GFPFH). These descriptors calculate relationships between points such as distances, angles of surface normals etc. and build histograms to represent the distribution of these relationships for each object. During the recognition phase, the stored descriptors are compared with descriptors calculated on the unknown scene and object using methods such as nearest neighbour search.

LINEMOD [5] is an example of a template-based recognition method. It provides a framework for combining different modalities to create a template. In the original implementation, colour gradients and surface normals were combined to form templates. The templates are later used to recognize and localize objects in an unknown scene.

In [15], a global descriptor called Viewpoint oriented Colour-Shape Histogram is described. The shape descriptors are based on the relationship between points and the centroid of the point cloud. Four features (two distances and two angles) for each point are measured and used to build the histogram.

In [7], the authors use colour descriptors, edge descriptors and shape descriptors as features for their fruit classifier. The shape descriptors include compactness, symmetry, local convexity and smoothness defined by Karpathy et al. [8], and image moment invariants defined by Hu [6].

Mustafa et al. [10] describe a multi-view object recognition system for a controlled industrial setting. They construct shape descriptors using 2D histograms of measures such as Euclidean distance, angles and normal distance between pairs of *texlets* (which describe local properties of a textured surface). Appearance descriptors are constructed using 2D histograms of the H and S components of texlet colour in the HSV colour space. Although they achieved a good recognition rate, small-sized objects were the cause of some of the miss-classifications.

The feature descriptors used in most of the methods tend to be bottom-up approaches. They try to capture a signature for objects using the distribution of features measured at the point level. In this paper, we describe global feature descriptors without using relations for individual points. Instead we try to capture the most salient features for an object by means of fitting bounding boxes, circles etc. Although some level of detail is still required in the point clouds, very small details are of less importance.

3   Approach

3.1   Segmentation

The service areas for RoboCup@Work tasks are flat surfaces on which objects are placed with a minimum distance of 2 cm between them [3]. The robot is positioned in front of the service area such that the arm-mounted 3D camera has a full or partial view of the workspace. A previously developed pipeline is used to detect the plane of the workspace, segment the points above the plane and cluster them based on Euclidean distance [2]. These point cloud clusters, which represent the objects on the workspace, form the input for the object recognition component developed here.

3.2   Data Collection

A set of point clouds for each object is collected for training and testing using the segmentation method explained above. Figure 2 shows some of the point clouds collected using an Asus Xtion PRO Live[1] RGB-D camera.

The objects are placed in various positions and orientations on the workspace while building the dataset. The camera is mounted on a stand at the approximate height and distance from the workspace as an arm-mounted camera on the robot. This allows the subsequently extracted features to be representative of all positions and orientations within the workspace. Hence, during runtime, the

---

[1] https://www.asus.com/3D-Sensor/Xtion_PRO/.

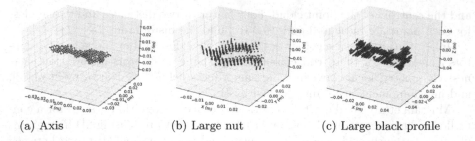

(a) Axis   (b) Large nut   (c) Large black profile

Fig. 2. Sample point clouds for (a) Axis (b) Large nut and (c) Large black profile

camera needs only to be approximately positioned in front of the workspace. The point clouds are translated to be centered at the origin and rotated such that the x, y and z axes align with the first three principal axes (retrieved using principal component analysis (PCA)) of the point cloud. This renders the extracted features invariant to the original pose of the object. Since the perceived colour of the objects is partially dependent on the lighting, it is expected that the point clouds are collected in the environment in which the objects will be used.

The set of point clouds used for training and testing are available online[2].

3.3   Features

Size and colour are the most salient features observable in point clouds. Additionally, circularity and the distribution of mass about the longitudinal axis also allow us to differentiate between a large set of various objects. Keeping this in mind, the following features are extracted from each object point cloud:

Bounding box. The oriented bounding box of the points is calculated and returns the length, width and height of the point cloud and hence describes the size of the object.

Colour. Since the colour of the objects are more or less homogeneous, only the mean and median colour are calculated. The red, green and blue channels of the colour component of each point are represented as a single floating point number as in PCL. The median and mean colour of the point cloud are calculated using this floating point representation.

Point cloud size. The number of points in the object point cloud is indicative of the size of the object but is also dependent on the distance of the object from the camera. However, since the distance of the camera from the objects does not change drastically, this feature is also considered.

---

[2] https://github.com/sthoduka/atwork_object_dataset.

Circularity. Although the bounding box captures the size of the object, it treats every object as a rectangular cuboid. Since cylindrical objects such as nuts, bearings and bushings are common in industrial settings, the circularity of an object is an important feature as well.

- **Mean circle radius:** In order to measure the circularity of an object, a circle is fit on the x-y plane of the point cloud based on the mean squared distance of all points from the centre. The radius of this circle is indicative of the size of the object.
- **Radial density distribution:** Points are projected onto 36 equal segments of the circle to form a radial histogram. This distribution describes how round an object is. As seen in Fig. 4, cylindrical objects (such as the nut) have a more uniform distribution whereas the distribution for longitudinal objects (such as the bolt) is more skewed along the principal axis. The radial density is calculated as

$$\frac{\sum_{j=1}^{N} \frac{k_j}{\max k}}{N} \tag{1}$$

where N is the number of bins in the histogram k.

A comparison of the radial density distribution for objects that are circular and non-circular in the X-Y plane is shown in Fig. 3.

- **Outlier/inlier error ratio:** The outlier error to inlier error ratio is calculated as

$$\frac{\frac{\sum_{j=1}^{N_o} dist(po_j)}{N_o}}{\frac{\sum_{k=1}^{N_i} dist(pi_k)}{N_i}} \tag{2}$$

where po and pi are the points outside and inside the circle, N_o and N_i are the sizes of each set of points and $dist(x)$ is the distance of point x from the circumference of the circle. This ratio measures the hollowness of the object, with objects such as the nuts having a higher ratio compared to the motor.

Distribution of mass along principal axis. Almost all of the longitudinal objects have an identical cross-section along their principal axis with the exception of the bolt and the axis. In order to differentiate these objects from the rest, the same circularity features, radius, radial density and outlier-inlier ratio, are calculated on eight slices along the principal axis. This adds an additional 24 features to the set.

Centre of mass offset. Another feature considered is the offset between the centre of mass and the geometric centre of the object. This offset is higher for objects such as the bolt and axis which are not symmetric about the y-z plane. Figure 5 visualizes the bounding box, the circle fit on the x-y plane and the circles fit on the slices. The thickness of the visualized circles is proportional to the radial density. Although the small black profile and the bolt are very similar

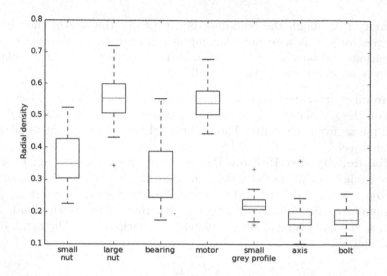

Fig. 3. Radial density distribution on the X-Y plane for cylindrical and non-cylindrical objects

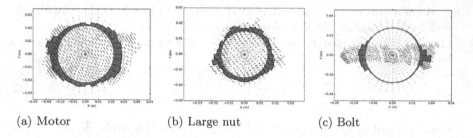

(a) Motor   (b) Large nut   (c) Bolt

Fig. 4. Radial density distribution for (a) Motor (b) Large nut and (c) Bolt

(similar bounding box, colour, mean circle radius etc.), the cap of the bolt is clearly identifiable by the larger circle compared to the similar-sized circles in the profile. Figure 6 shows the distribution of circle radii for the end slices and the remaining slices in the middle for the two objects. The larger range of radii for the bolt at the ends is likely to improve the classification between these two objects.

3.4   Training

A set of point clouds was collected for all objects in Fig. 1 and was split into training and test data. A total of 34 features was extracted from the training data set. Various combinations of features, as described in Sect. 4, were considered in order to compare the impact of the different features on the classification rate. The feature set was standardized and used to train a multi-class support vector machine (SVM) classifier [11] with a radial basis function kernel.

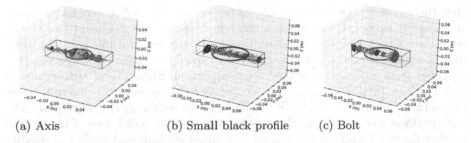

(a) Axis   (b) Small black profile   (c) Bolt

Fig. 5. Bounding box and mean circle features for (a) Axis (b) Small black profile and (c) Bolt

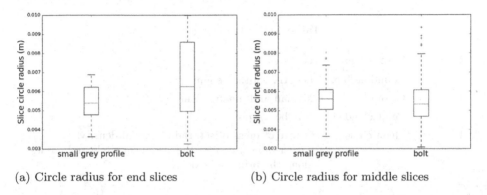

(a) Circle radius for end slices   (b) Circle radius for middle slices

Fig. 6. Differences in slice circle radii for small black profile and bolt

3.5 Testing

In order to test the classifier, feature vectors are calculated on the test data and input to the classifier which returns a list of probability estimates for each object. The object with the highest probability is selected and a threshold is applied to increase the confidence of classification. If the probability is below the threshold, the object is said to be unclassified.

4 Results

In order to test the effectiveness of different features on the classification rate, the features were split into four categories described in Table 1. Six different combinations of feature categories were used to create different classifiers. The results of the different classifiers are presented in Table 2. A probability threshold of 0.5 was used to discard low-probability classifications (indicated as *unclassified* objects). Although using the probability threshold reduces the overall true positive rate, it lowers the false positive rate as well. However, the consequence of an incorrect classification is not as easy to fix as not recognizing an object at all. For example, if the robot does not recognize an object, it can attempt to view the object from a different angle to try again. If the robot were to transport an incorrect object, it can cause a cascade of errors in subsequent tasks. The true positive rates for individual objects are presented in Table 3. In addition, the classification results using the local and global descriptor object recognition pipelines from PCL are presented for comparison. Signature of Histograms of OrienTations (SHOT) [13,14] with colour is used as the local descriptor and Ensemble of Shape Functions (ESF) [16] is used as the global descriptor. The poor performance of these methods is likely due to the small sizes of the clouds, making finding keypoints and the calculation of normals and surface properties harder. Since ESF does not consider colour, misclassifications between objects with only colour differences were considered correct.

Table 1. Feature categories

Category	Description	Features
A	Bounding box	Length, width, height
B	Colour	Median and mean colour
C	Point cloud size	Number of points
D	Mean circle	Centre of mass offset, radius, radial density, outlier-inlier ratio for the x-y mean circle and circles along the principal axis

Table 2. Overall classification results using different combinations of features.

Features	True positive rate	False positive rate	Unclassified
A, B	0.88	0.04	0.08
A, B, C	0.9	0.03	0.07
A, B, C, D	0.89	0.03	0.08
A, B, D	0.89	0.03	0.08
B, C, D	0.86	0.04	0.1
B, D	0.86	0.04	0.1

A - Bounding box, B - Colour, C - Point cloud size, D - Mean circle

The larger objects, such as the profiles, containers and bolts, are recognized with high accuracy. The small nut, bearing and distance tube have low classifications rates, likely due to their similarity. The misclassifications show that these are often confused with each other.

Introducing the mean circle features improves the recognition rate of the small nut, but marginally decreases the rate for the distance tube and bearing. The mean and median colour successfully classifies the identically shaped profiles and containers.

Table 3. True positive rates for individual objects.

Object	A, B	A, B, C	A, B, C, D	A, B, D	B, C, D	B, D	SHOT	ESF
Small black profile	0.99	0.99	1.0	0.99	0.95	0.95	0.73	0.5
Small grey profile	1.0	1.0	0.96	0.95	0.81	0.8	0.65	0.41
Large black profile	1.0	1.0	1.0	1.0	1.0	1.0	0.42	0.33
Large grey profile	1.0	1.0	1.0	1.0	1.0	1.0	0.06	0.51
Bolt	1.0	0.97	0.98	0.98	0.87	0.85	0.68	0.68
Bushing	0.88	0.89	0.89	0.89	0.83	0.84	0.52	0.16
Small nut	0.31	0.32	**0.48**	**0.5**	0.42	0.43	0.47	0.0
Large nut	0.99	0.99	0.97	0.97	0.96	0.96	0.98	0.77
Bearing box	1.0	1.0	1.0	1.0	1.0	1.0	0.17	0.23
Bearing	0.74	0.73	**0.65**	**0.65**	0.58	0.61	0.34	0.02
Axis	0.66	**0.8**	0.75	0.77	0.76	0.78	0.1	0.1
Distance tube	0.78	**0.91**	**0.77**	**0.75**	0.74	0.74	0.0	0.8
Motor	0.8	0.89	0.93	0.92	0.93	0.91	0.75	0.24
Red container	0.99	1.0	1.0	1.0	1.0	1.0	0.25	0.3
Blue container	1.0	1.0	1.0	0.99	0.99	0.99	0.94	0.4

A - Bounding box, B - Colour, C - Point cloud size, D - Mean circle, SHOT - Signature of Histograms of OrienTations, ESF - Ensemble of Shape Functions

It is surprising that the point cloud size significantly increases the recognition rate of objects such as the axis and distance tube. It is, however, the least generalisable feature since it is dependent on the camera resolution and distance between the object and camera.

It is observed that adding more features is not always better. Adding irrelevant features increases the likelihood that the classifier over-fits to the training data. This makes the classifier less generalisable and it performs poorly on new data. A minimal set of features that are able to distinguish between objects should be selected.

5   Conclusions and Future Work

The proposed features and classifier are able to identity some of the objects with a high accuracy, but perform poorly for some of the smaller objects. The features, although designed based on the objects defined for RoboCup@Work, are sufficiently general that they can be applied to objects of the same class as those presented here. However, if variations of the some object classes (such as profiles) are present, an additional classification method may be required to distinguish between variants. It is trivial to add more features to the classifier if there is a need. However, care must be taken not to over-fit the classifier to the training data. The addition of 2D image features such as corners, edges and contours is a possible improvement to this method. With the continuous improvement of RGB-D cameras, the quality of the point clouds are expected to improve as well. Consequently, the performance of the method is also likely to improve.

Acknowledgements. We gratefully acknowledge the continued support of the RoboCup team by the b-it Bonn-Aachen International Center for Information Technology and the Bonn-Rhein-Sieg University of Applied Sciences.

References

1. Factories of the Future. http://www.era.eu/attachments/article/129/FactoriesoftheFuture2020Roadmap.pdf (2013). Accessed 08 Mar 2016
2. Ahmed, S., Jandt, T., Kulkarni, P., Lima, O., Mallick, A., Moriarty, A., Nair, D., Thoduka, S., Awaad, I., Dwiputra, R., Hegger, F., Hochgeschwender, N., Sanchez, J., Schneider, S., Kraetzschmar, G.K.: b-it-bots RoboCup@Work team description paper. In: RoboCup. Leipzig, Germany (2016). https://mas-group.inf.h-brs.de/wp-content/uploads/2016/01/tdp_b-it-bots_atwork_2016.pdf
3. Carstensen, J., Hochgeschwender, N., Kraetzschmar, G., Nowak, W., Zug, S.: RoboCup@Work Rulebook Version 2016 (2016). http://www.robocupatwork.org/download/rulebook-2016-01-15.pdf. Accessed 08 Mar 2016
4. Dwiputra, R., Berghofer, J., Ahmad, A., Awaad, I., Amigoni, F., Bischoff, R., Bonarini, A., Fontana, G., Hegger, F., Hochgeschwender, N., Iocchi, L., Kraetzschmar, G., Lima, P., Matteucci, M., Nardi, D., Schiaffonati, V., Schneider, S.: The RoCKIn@Work challenge. In: Proceedings of 41st International Symposium on Robotics, ISR/Robotik 2014, pp. 1–6 (2014)
5. Hinterstoisser, S., Holzer, S., Cagniart, C., Ilic, S., Konolige, K., Navab, N., Lepetit, V.: Multimodal templates for real-time detection of texture-less objects in heavily cluttered scenes. In: 2011 IEEE International Conference on Computer Vision (ICCV), pp. 858–865. IEEE (2011)
6. Hu, M.K.: Visual pattern recognition by moment invariants. IRE Trans. Inf. Theory **8**(2), 179–187 (1962)
7. Jiang, L., Koch, A., Scherer, S.A., Zell, A.: Multi-class fruit classification using RGB-D data for indoor robots. In: 2013 IEEE International Conference on Robotics and Biomimetics (ROBIO), pp. 587–592. IEEE (2013)
8. Karpathy, A., Miller, S., Fei-Fei, L.: Object discovery in 3D scenes via shape analysis. In: 2013 IEEE International Conference on Robotics and Automation (ICRA), pp. 2088–2095. IEEE (2013)
9. Kraetzschmar, G.K., Hochgeschwender, N., Nowak, W., Hegger, F., Schneider, S., Dwiputra, R., Berghofer, J., Bischoff, R.: RoboCup@Work: competing for the factory of the future. In: Bianchi, R.A.C., Akin, H.L., Ramamoorthy, S., Sugiura, K. (eds.) RoboCup 2014. LNCS (LNAI), vol. 8992, pp. 171–182. Springer, Cham (2015). doi:10.1007/978-3-319-18615-3_14
10. Mustafa, W., Pugeault, N., Kruger, N.: Multi-view object recognition using viewpoint invariant shape relations and appearance information. In: 2013 IEEE International Conference on Robotics and Automation (ICRA), pp. 4230–4237. IEEE (2013)
11. Pedregosa, F., Varoquaux, G., Gramfort, A., Michel, V., Thirion, B., Grisel, O., Blondel, M., Prettenhofer, P., Weiss, R., Dubourg, V., Vanderplas, J., Passos, A., Cournapeau, D., Brucher, M., Perrot, M., Duchesnay, E.: Scikit-learn: machine learning in python. J. Mach. Learn. Res. **12**, 2825–2830 (2011)

12. Rusu, R.B., Cousins, S.: 3D is here: point cloud library (PCL). In: 2011 IEEE International Conference on Robotics and Automation (ICRA), pp. 1–4. IEEE (2011)
13. Tombari, F., Salti, S., Stefano, L.: Unique signatures of histograms for local surface description. In: Daniilidis, K., Maragos, P., Paragios, N. (eds.) ECCV 2010. LNCS, vol. 6313, pp. 356–369. Springer, Heidelberg (2010). doi:10.1007/978-3-642-15558-1_26
14. Tombari, F., Salti, S., Stefano, L.D.: A combined texture-shape descriptor for enhanced 3D feature matching. In: 2011 18th IEEE International Conference on Image Processing (ICIP), pp. 809–812. IEEE (2011)
15. Wang, W., Chen, L., Chen, D., Li, S., Kuhnlenz, K.: Fast object recognition and 6D pose estimation using viewpoint oriented color-shape histogram. In: 2013 IEEE International Conference on Multimedia and Expo (ICME), pp. 1–6. IEEE (2013)
16. Wohlkinger, W., Vincze, M.: Ensemble of shape functions for 3D Object Classification. In: 2011 IEEE International Conference on Robotics and Biomimetics (ROBIO), pp. 2987–2992. IEEE (2011)

Prioritized Role Assignment for Marking

Patrick MacAlpine$^{(\boxtimes)}$ and Peter Stone

Department of Computer Science, The University of Texas at Austin,
Austin, TX, USA
{patmac,pstone}@cs.utexas.edu

Abstract. This paper presents a system for marking or covering players on an opposing soccer team so as to best prevent them from scoring. A basis for the marking system is the introduction of prioritized role assignment, an extension to SCRAM dynamic role assignment used by the UT Austin Villa RoboCup 3D simulation team for formational positioning. The marking system is designed to allow for decentralized coordination among physically realistic simulated humanoid soccer playing robots in the partially observable, non-deterministic, noisy, dynamic, and limited communication setting of the RoboCup 3D simulation league simulator. Although it is discussed in the context of the RoboCup 3D simulation environment, the marking system is not domain specific and can readily be employed in other RoboCup leagues as prioritized role assignment generalizes well to many realistic and real-world multiagent systems.

1 Introduction

Coordinated movement among autonomous mobile robots is an important research area with many applications such as search and rescue and warehouse operations. The RoboCup 3D simulation soccer competition provides an excellent testbed for this line of research as it requires coordination among autonomous agents in a physically realistic environment that is partially observable, non-deterministic, noisy, and dynamic. The presence of adversarial opponent agents gives rise to the challenging coordination problem of how to cover or mark opponents so as to best prevent the opposing team from scoring. Agents must work together as a team to counteract their opponents' actions while maximizing their own game performance.

A common paradigm for specifying where players on a soccer field should move is the use of formations. Positioning players in a formation requires agents to coordinate with each other and determine where each agent should position itself on the field. The work in this paper focuses on role assignment—specifically tackling the problem of assigning interchangeable mobile robots to move to a set of target positions in a formation such that robots are present at their assigned positions in as little time as possible. Previous work on role assignment, and the basis for this work, is that of Scaleable Collision-avoiding Role Assignment with Minimal-makespan (SCRAM) role assignment functions [12]. SCRAM role assignment functions assign robots to target positions such that the makespan

© Springer International Publishing AG 2017
S. Behnke et al. (Eds.): RoboCup 2016, LNAI 9776, pp. 306–318, 2017.
https://doi.org/10.1007/978-3-319-68792-6_25

(time for all robots to reach their target positions) is minimized while avoiding collisions between robots. SCRAM only minimizes the completion time of the entire formation however, and does not take into consideration the possibility of some target positions being more important—and thus needing a robot to arrive at them sooner—than other potentially less important positions. Within the context of soccer we find it is often a high priority for a player to arrive as quickly as possible at a position for marking an opponent in a dangerous offensive location. Marking engenders the need for prioritized role assignment in which higher priority positions in a formation (those for marking opponents) are assigned to be reached by robots before lower priority positions.

Primary contributions of this paper are twofold. First, we introduce a new extension of SCRAM role assignment that allows for prioritization of roles. Second, we provide a detailed description and analysis of a marking system, incorporating prioritized role assignment, that we have implemented for use in the RoboCup 3D simulation domain.

The remainder of the paper is organized as follows. In Sect. 2 a description of the 3D simulation domain is given. Section 3 provides background information on SCRAM role assignment, while Sect. 4 introduces and motivates prioritized SCRAM role assignment. Section 5 details a marking system using prioritized role assignment, and analysis of the performance of the marking system is given in Sect. 6. Related work is discussed in Sects. 7 and 8 concludes.

2   Domain Description

The RoboCup 3D simulation environment is based on SimSpark [1], a generic physical multiagent system simulator. SimSpark uses the Open Dynamics Engine[1] (ODE) library for its realistic simulation of rigid body dynamics with collision detection and friction. ODE also provides support for the modeling of advanced motorized hinge joints used in the humanoid agents.

Games consist of 11 versus 11 agents playing on a 30 m in length by 20 m in width field. The robot agents in the simulation are modeled after the Aldebaran Nao robot,[2] which has a height of about 57 cm, and a mass of 4.5 kg. Each robot has 22 degrees of freedom: six in each leg, four in each arm, and two in the neck. In order to monitor and control its hinge joints, an agent is equipped with joint perceptors and effectors. Joint perceptors provide the agent with noise-free angular measurements every simulation cycle (20 ms), while joint effectors allow the agent to specify the speed and direction in which to move a joint.

Visual information about the environment is given to an agent every third simulation cycle (60 ms) through noisy measurements of the distance and angle to objects within a restricted vision cone (120°). Agents are also outfitted with noisy accelerometer and gyroscope perceptors, as well as force resistance perceptors on the sole of each foot. Additionally, agents can communicate with each other every other simulation cycle (40 ms) by sending 20 byte messages.

---

[1] http://www.ode.org/.

[2] http://www.aldebaran-robotics.com/eng/.

3   SCRAM Role Assignment

Given a desired team formation, such as the formation used by UT Austin Villa in Fig. 1, we need to map players to roles (target positions on the field). A naïve mapping having each player permanently mapped to one of the roles performs poorly due to the dynamic nature of the game. With such static roles an agent assigned to a defensive role may end up out of position and, without being able to switch roles with a teammate in a better position to defend, allow for the opponent to have a clear path to the goal.

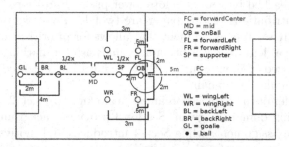

Fig. 1. Example formation where role positions are computed as offset positions from the ball.

A role assignment algorithm can be thought of as implementing a role assignment *function*, which takes as input the state of the world, and outputs a one-to-one mapping of players to roles. SCRAM role assignment functions [12] compute in polynomial time mappings from players to roles that both minimize the longest distance any agent has to travel (thereby minimizing the makespan or formation completion time) and avoid collisions between agents.

The SCRAM Minimum Maximal Distance Recursive (MMDR) function, which is a basis for the work in this paper, finds a mapping of agents to target positions which recursively minimizes the maximum distance that any agent travels. Let $\mathbb{M}$ be the set of all one-to-one mappings between agents and roles. If there are n agents and n target role positions, then there are $n!$ possible mappings $M \in \mathbb{M}$. Let the *cost* of a mapping M be the n-tuple of distances from each agent to its target, sorted in decreasing order. We can then sort all the $n!$ possible mappings based on their costs, where comparing two costs is done lexicographically. The lowest cost mapping is the one returned by MMDR. Sorted costs of mappings for a small example are shown in Fig. 2.

Proof that the MMDR role assignment function both minimizes the makespan and avoids collisions among agents, as well as $O(n^5)$ and $O(n^4)$ algorithms for computing MMDR, can be found in [12].

4   Prioritized SCRAM Role Assignment

It is not always the case that minimizing the makespan (completing a formation as fast as possible) is what is best for a team of robots. There are cases where

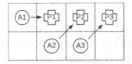

Fig. 2. Lowest lexicographical cost (shown with arrows) to highest cost ordering of mappings from agents (A1, A2, A3) to role positions (P1, P2, P3). Each row represents the cost of a single mapping.

1: $\sqrt{2}$ (A2→P2), $\sqrt{2}$ (A3→P3), 1 (A1→P1)
2: 2 (A1→P2), $\sqrt{2}$ (A3→P3), 1 (A2→P1)
3: $\sqrt{5}$ (A2→P3), 1 (A1→P1),   1 (A3→P2)
4: $\sqrt{5}$ (A2→P3), 2 (A1→P2), $\sqrt{2}$ (A3→P1)
5: 3 (A1→P3),   1 (A2→P1),   1 (A3→P2)
6: 3 (A1→P3), $\sqrt{2}$ (A2→P2), $\sqrt{2}$ (A3→P1)

it is preferable to have a subset of high priority role positions in a formation be reached by agents as soon as possible. One example of this is soccer where it is often desirable for players to arrive as fast as possible at positions for marking opponents in dangerous offensive locations. This section introduces a new extension to SCRAM role assignment allowing for subsets of role positions to be given different priorities.

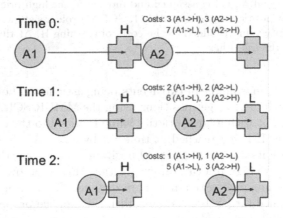

Fig. 3. Agents A1 and A2 being assigned and moving to the high priority (H) and low priority (L) target positions using the MMDR SCRAM role assignment algorithm.

Figure 3 shows an example of two agents being assigned to both high priority (H) and low priority (L) target positions using the MMDR SCRAM role assignment algorithm. As MMDR does not take into account priorities of different positions, the high priority position H will not be reached by an agent until time = 3 despite agent A2 starting only a distance of 1 from H.

To bias MMDR into producing an assignment that has agents reach all high priority positions as fast as possible we can add a large priority value P to costs for reaching all high priority positions. As long as P is greater than all possible distances to lower priority positions, MMDR will assign the closest agents to high priority positions before considering the assignment of agents to lower priority positions. This bias of MMDR assigning closer agents to higher priority positions is due to all costs to higher priority positions being greater and thus needing to be minimized before that of costs to lower priority positions.

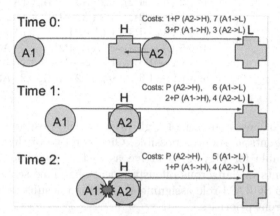

Fig. 4. Agents A1 and A2 being assigned and moving to the high priority (H) and low priority (L) target positions using the MMDR SCRAM role assignment algorithm, but with a large priority value P added to the costs of reaching H. At time = 2 agents A1 and A2 collide with each other.

Figure 4 shows an example of two agents being assigned to both high priority (H) and low priority (L) target positions using the MMDR SCRAM role assignment algorithm, but with a large priority value P added to the costs of reaching H. This results in H being reached at time = 1 by agent A2, but unfortunately later agent A1, on its way to its assigned position L, collides with A2. Assigning the closest agents to high priority target positions, and thereby no longer necessarily recursively minimizing the maximum distance that any agent must travel to reach its assigned target, breaks the collision avoidance property of MMDR.

To preserve collision avoidance, but still prioritize a subset of targets being reached as fast as possible, we can define a priority distance D around high priority targets for which agents within D distance of a target will not have the priority value P added to the cost of that target.

$$\mathrm{cost}(agent, target) = \begin{cases} |\overline{agent, target}| + \mathrm{P} & \text{if } |\overline{agent, target}| > \mathrm{D} \\ |\overline{agent, target}| & \text{otherwise} \end{cases}$$

Figure 5 shows an example of two agents being assigned to both high priority (H) and low priority (L) target positions using the MMDR SCRAM role assignment algorithm, but with a large priority value P added to the costs of reaching

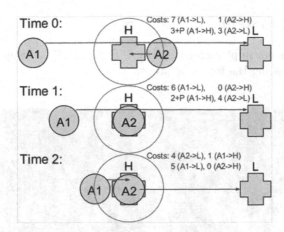

Fig. 5. Agents A1 and A2 being assigned and moving to the high priority (H) and low priority (L) target positions using the MMDR SCRAM role assignment algorithm, but with a large priority value P added to the costs of reaching H for any agents outside the priority distance of H (the purple circle). At time = 2 agents A1 and A2 switch targets due to agent A1 being within the priority distance of H.

H when agents are outside a priority distance D of H. This results in H being reached at time = 1 by agent A2, and then later when agent A1 gets within D of H agents A1 and A2 switch targets and avoid colliding.

Defining a priority distance D causes agents to arrive within a distance D of all high priority targets as fast as possible. Although agents might not arrive exactly at the high priority targets in as little time as possible, this is often fine for many applications including marking in soccer. When marking a player does not need to be right next to an opponent, but just within a close enough distance to the opponent to be able to react quickly and prevent the opponent from receiving the ball. Assuming D is not too large, should a player come within D distance of an opponent who is already being marked by a teammate, it should then be safe for the players to switch who is marking the opponent.

Augmenting MMDR with a large P priority value and D priority distance for high priority positions extends SCRAM role assignment to allow for prioritization of targets. The collision avoidance property of SCRAM, based on the triangle inequality and fully explained in [12], is still preserved with prioritization as any agents within D distance of a high priority target will switch targets before they collide.

It is possible to have multiple subsets of targets with different priorities, or a hierarchy of prioritization, by assigning different P values to different subsets of targets. An example of this is given later in Sect. 5.3 for which a highest priority target is given a priority value of P_s, and other high priority targets are given a priority value of P_m, where $P_s \gg P_m$.

5   Marking System

The marking system implemented by the UT Austin Villa team is a sequential process encompassing the following steps:

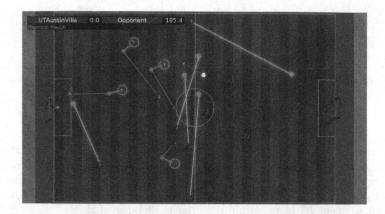

Fig. 6. Steps of the marking system. The white dot is the ball. Step 1 (Deciding Who to Mark): Opponent agents selected to be marked are circled in yellow. Step 2 (Selecting Roles for Marking): Green dots represent target formation positions with purple dots representing target formation positions that have been selected to be replaced by the orange dot marking positions. Step 3 (Assigning Roles): Orange lines represent agents assigned to marking positions, light blue lines represent agents assigned to target formation positions, and the red line shows the agent assigned to go to the ball. (Color figure online)

1. Decide which players to mark
2. Select which roles to use for marking purposes
3. Use prioritized role assignment to assign players to positions

Each of these steps (shown in Fig. 6), as well as additional details of the marking system, are described in the following subsections.

5.1   Deciding Who to Mark

The first step in the marking system is to decide which if any opponents should be marked (those opponents considered to be in dangerous offensive positions). The decision on whether or not to mark an opponent is heuristic based and uses the following rules:

1. Opponent is close enough to take a shot on goal
2. Opponent is not the closest opponent to the ball
3. Opponent is not too close to the ball
4. Opponent is not too far behind the ball

The first rule suggests that an opponent is in a dangerous scoring position. As we always send one player to the ball (the *onBall* role in Fig. 1), the second and third rules prevent marking of opponents when we should already have a player moving toward their positions. The fourth rule is due to very few teams passing the ball backwards. Figure 6 shows opponent agents selected to be marked circled in yellow.

5.2 Selecting Roles for Marking

The next step is to select which formation role positions should be given up in favor of having agents who would otherwise be assigned to those roles instead move to marking role positions. Marking role positions are calculated as the position 1.5 m from a marked opponent along the line from that opponent to the center of our goal (shown in orange in Fig. 6). The selection of formation positions to replace with marking positions is determined by using the Hungarian algorithm [4] to compute the minimum sum of distances matching between all formation and marking positions in a bipartite graph. This matching results in the closest formation positions to marking positions being replaced by the marking positions that they are nearest. If there are ever more marking positions than available formation positions then some marking positions will be matched to dummy nodes in the bipartite graph and not be assigned to an agent.

Figure 6 shows the result after selecting formation positions to be used as marking role positions with the formation positions selected drawn in purple, and those not selected and still being used drawn in green.

5.3 Assigning Roles

Agents are assigned to marking positions and formation positions (Fig. 6 shows these assignments in orange and light blue respectively) using prioritized SCRAM role assignment discussed in Sect. 4. Marking positions are considered higher priority than formation positions, and use a priority value $P_m = 100$ and a priority distance $D_m = 3$. Additionally, when a teammate is kicking the ball, a couple of players are assigned to high priority kick anticipation position roles near the location where the ball is being kicked to [10]. Kick anticipation roles are given the same priority value and distance as marking roles.

There are several roles in Fig. 1 that are never reassigned to be marking roles. The *goalie* role is always assigned to a single agent designated as the goalie who is allowed to dive and block a ball when an opponent takes a shot on goal. The *onBall* role is always assigned to the agent closest to the ball as it is that agent's job to gain possession of the ball. The *supporter* role is also very important as the *supporter* is in a critical position right behind the ball should the *onBall* role agent lose possession of the ball. The *supporter* is considered a higher priority role than marking roles, and thus uses a priority value $P_s = 10000$ along with a priority distance $D_s = 1.5$. All P and D values were chosen experimentally.

5.4 Coordination

In order for agents on a team to assume correct positions on the field they all must coordinate and agree on which mapping of agents to roles to use. If every agent had perfect information of the locations of the ball and its teammates this would not be a problem as each could independently calculate the optimal mapping to use. Agents do not have perfect information, however, and are limited to noisy measurements of the distance and angle to objects within a restricted vision cone (120°). To synchronize their assigned roles agents using a voting coordination system as described in [9].

Coordination can become more difficult if an opponent is standing in a position right on the borderline of whether or not the opponent should be marked. To prevent thrashing between different role assignments in such a situation, opponents who are currently being marked must move at least .25 m outside a mark-able position on the field before they will stop being marked. Also, to prevent thrashing between different selections of formation positions to use for marking, a selection is never changed (assuming the cardinality of matchings are the same) unless the new selection's matching's sum of distances is at least one meter less than the previous selection's matching's sum of distances.

6 Results and Analysis

After the 2015 RoboCup competition was over we played 1000 games of our team's released binary against all teams' released binaries (this includes playing against ourselves) and found that only the UTAustinVilla and FCPortugal teams' binaries were able to score over 100 goals against our released binary [11]. Both the UTAustinVilla and FCPortugal teams created set plays allowing them to score quickly off kickoffs which empirically we found to be the source of the majority of the goals that they scored against our released binary (74.5% of goals for UTAustinVilla and 78.2% of goals for FCPortugal)

To test the effectiveness of our marking system using prioritized role assignment we played 1000 games against both the UTAustinVilla and FCPortugal teams' released binaries using the marking system (Prioritized Marking). We also played 1000 games against both teams without using marking (No Marking) as well as with marking but using normal non-prioritized SCRAM role assignment (Marking No Prioritization). Results of the number of goals against scored by opponents can be seen in Table 1, and an analysis of the scoring percentage of opponents' set plays is shown in Table 2.

Table 1 shows a dramatic drop in the number of goals scored by opponents when using marking. There is also a small decrease in the number of goals against when using prioritized SCRAM instead of non-prioritized SCRAM for marking. Table 2 reveals the source of the reduction in goals against as using marking almost completely eliminates the opponents' abilities to score on kickoff set plays. FCPortugal's kickoff (shown in Figs. 7, 8 and 9) consists of a player first passing the ball backwards on the kickoff to a waiting player who then passes the ball forward to a teammate running forward to a dangerous offensive position

Table 1. Number of goals against when playing 1000 games against the released binaries of UTAustinVilla and FCPortugal from RoboCup 2015.

Opponent	No marking	Marking no prioritization	Prioritized marking
UTAustinVilla	1525	336	319
FCPortugal	230	40	37

Table 2. Scoring percentage of opponents' set plays when playing 1000 games against the released binaries of UTAustinVilla and FCPortugal from RoboCup 2015.

Set play	No marking	Marking no prioritization	Prioritized marking
UTAustinVilla Kickoff	48.31	0.16	0.16
FCPortugal Kickoff	6.22	0.06	0.06
UTAustinVilla Corner Kick	15.97	12.31	7.59

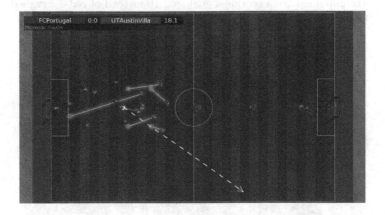

Fig. 7. Not marking against FCPortugal kickoff. Dashed white line shows trajectory of ball during pass. Not marking allows for an opponent to run forward and receive a pass in an open position to score a goal (blue 10 is not marked). (Color figure online)

on the side of the field. UTAustinVilla's kickoff and corner kick set plays are described in [11]. Although the numbers in Table 2 do not show an advantage in using prioritized SCRAM over non-prioritized SCRAM against kickoffs, we have seen some instances such as in Fig. 8 where not using prioritization is harmful. Prioritized SCRAM does however show an advantage against UTAustinVilla's corner kick set plays. Videos of set plays and marking are available online.[3]

---

[3] http://www.cs.utexas.edu/~AustinVilla/sim/3dsimulation/AustinVilla3DSimulatio nFiles/2016/html/marking.html.

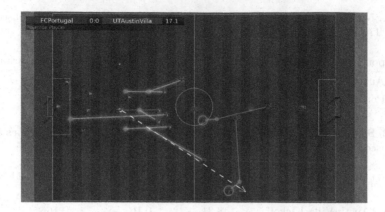

Fig. 8. Marking, but not prioritized, against FCPortugal kickoff. Dashed white line shows trajectory of ball during pass. Not using prioritization with marking results in a player assigned to mark an opponent being too far away from that assigned opponent to prevent the opponent from scoring a goal (red 10 instead of red 3 assigned to mark blue 10). (Color figure online)

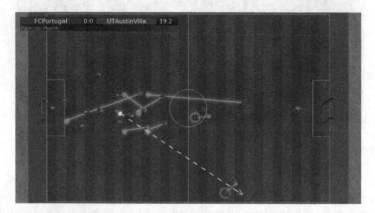

Fig. 9. Prioritized marking against FCPortugal kickoff. Dashed white line shows trajectory of ball during pass. Prioritized marking prevents opponents from receiving a pass in an open position to score a goal (red 3 marking blue 10). (Color figure online)

Overall using marking, and to a greater extent using marking with prioritized SCRAM role assignment, provides a considerable defensive advantage when playing soccer against opponents who use set plays. The average goal difference across 1000 games when playing against UTAustinVilla with prioritized marking improved to 0.657 ($\pm$0.028) from $\sim$0 without marking, and this same number against FCPortugal improved to 2.530 ($\pm$0.040) with prioritized marking from 2.476 ($\pm$0.043) without marking. We also played 1000 games against the other ten teams' released binaries from RoboCup 2015, none of which we knew to use passing for set plays, and found no measurable difference in goals against or game performance when using marking versus those teams.

7 Related Work

While there has been considerable research focused on role assignment in the 2D soccer simulation domain (for example by Stone and Veloso [15] and Reis et al. [14]), relatively little outside of [2] has been published on this topic in the more physically realistic 3D soccer simulation environment [2], as well as related work in the RoboCup Middle Size League (MSL) [6], rank positions on the field in order of importance and then iteratively assign the closest available agent to the most important currently unassigned position until every agent is mapped to a target location. Previous approaches to marking in 2D simulated soccer have included using a fuzzy logic inference system [8], a pareto-optimal approach that attempts to maximize the total prevented threat of opponents while minimizing the total time needed to move to positions [5], and opponent modeling [3]. In the RoboCup Small Size League (SSL) teams have computed threat levels of opponents when deciding who to mark [7,13]. The work presented in this paper differs from the mentioned previous work as it takes into account real-world concerns and movement dynamics, such as the need for avoiding collisions of robots, when assigning players to mark opponents.

8 Conclusion

We have introduced a new extension of SCRAM role assignment that allows for prioritization of roles. This prioritized role extension to SCRAM has been incorporated into a marking system that is very effective in defending against set plays used by teams within the RoboCup 3D simulation domain. Ongoing work includes improving the heuristics in our marking system for identifying who to mark, as well as possibly adding different priorities for different marking positions. A promising direction for future work is to apply SCRAM prioritized role assignment to applications outside of marking and RoboCup such as general patrol and coverage tasks.

Acknowledgments. This work has taken place in the Learning Agents Research Group (LARG) at UT Austin. LARG research is supported in part by NSF (CNS-1330072, CNS-1305287), ONR (21C184-01), and AFOSR (FA9550-14-1-0087). Peter Stone serves on the Board of Directors of, Cogitai, Inc. The terms of this arrangement have been reviewed and approved by UT Austin in accordance with its policy on objectivity in research.

References

1. Boedecker, J., Asada, M.: Simspark-concepts and application in the RoboCup 3D soccer simulation league. In: Autonomous Robots, pp. 174–181 (2008)
2. Chen, W., Chen, T.: Multi-robot dynamic role assignment based on path cost. In: 2011 Chinese Control and Decision Conference (CCDC), pp. 3721–3724, May 2011

3. Habibi, J., Younesy, H., Heydarnoori, A.: Using the opponent pass modeling method to improve defending ability of a (Robo)Soccer simulation team. In: Polani, D., Browning, B., Bonarini, A., Yoshida, K. (eds.) RoboCup 2003. LNCS, vol. 3020, pp. 543–550. Springer, Heidelberg (2004). doi:10.1007/978-3-540-25940-4_50

4. Kuhn, H.W.: The Hungarian method for the assignment problem. Naval Res. Logistics Q. **2**(1–2), 83–97 (1955)

5. Kyrylov, V., Hou, E.: Pareto-optimal collaborative defensive player positioning in simulated soccer. In: Baltes, J., Lagoudakis, M.G., Naruse, T., Ghidary, S.S. (eds.) RoboCup 2009. LNCS (LNAI), vol. 5949, pp. 179–191. Springer, Heidelberg (2010). doi:10.1007/978-3-642-11876-0_16

6. Lau, N., Lopes, L., Corrente, G., Filipe, N.: Multi-robot team coordination through roles, positionings and coordinated procedures. In: IEEE/RSJ International Conference on Intelligent Robots and Systems (IROS 2009), pp. 5841–5848, October 2009

7. Li, C., Xiong, R., Ren, Z., Tang, W., Zhao, Y.: ZJUNlict: RoboCup 2014 small size league champion. In: Bianchi, R.A.C., Akin, H.L., Ramamoorthy, S., Sugiura, K. (eds.) RoboCup 2014. LNCS (LNAI), vol. 8992, pp. 47–59. Springer, Cham (2015). doi:10.1007/978-3-319-18615-3_4

8. Li, X., Chen, X.: Fuzzy inference based forecasting in soccer simulation 2D, the RoboCup 2015 soccer simulation 2D league champion team. In: Almeida, L., Ji, J., Steinbauer, G., Luke, S. (eds.) RoboCup 2015. LNCS (LNAI), vol. 9513, pp. 144–152. Springer, Cham (2015). doi:10.1007/978-3-319-29339-4_12

9. MacAlpine, P., Barrera, F., Stone, P.: Positioning to win: a dynamic role assignment and formation positioning system. In: Chen, X., Stone, P., Sucar, L.E., Zant, T. (eds.) RoboCup 2012. LNCS (LNAI), vol. 7500, pp. 190–201. Springer, Heidelberg (2013). doi:10.1007/978-3-642-39250-4_18

10. MacAlpine, P., Depinet, M., Liang, J., Stone, P.: UT Austin villa: RoboCup 2014 3D simulation league competition and technical challenge champions. In: Bianchi, R.A.C., Akin, H.L., Ramamoorthy, S., Sugiura, K. (eds.) RoboCup 2014. LNCS (LNAI), vol. 8992, pp. 33–46. Springer, Cham (2015). doi:10.1007/978-3-319-18615-3_3

11. MacAlpine, P., Hanna, J., Liang, J., Stone, P.: UT Austin villa: RoboCup 2015 3D simulation league competition and technical challenges champions. In: Almeida, L., Ji, J., Steinbauer, G., Luke, S. (eds.) RoboCup 2015. LNCS (LNAI), vol. 9513, pp. 118–131. Springer, Cham (2015). doi:10.1007/978-3-319-29339-4_10

12. MacAlpine, P., Price, E., Stone, P.: SCRAM: scalable collision-avoiding role assignment with minimal-makespan for formational positioning. In: Proceedings of the Twenty-Ninth AAAI Conference on Artificial Intelligence (AAAI-15), January 2015

13. Mendoza, J.P., Biswas, J., Zhu, D., Wang, R., Cooksey, P., Klee, S., Veloso, M.: CMDragons 2015: coordinated offense and defense of the SSL champions. In: Almeida, L., Ji, J., Steinbauer, G., Luke, S. (eds.) RoboCup 2015. LNCS (LNAI), vol. 9513, pp. 106–117. Springer, Cham (2015). doi:10.1007/978-3-319-29339-4_9

14. Reis, L.P., Lau, N., Oliveira, E.C.: Situation based strategic positioning for coordinating a team of homogeneous agents. BRSDMAS 2000. LNCS, vol. 2103, pp. 175–197. Springer, Heidelberg (2001). doi:10.1007/3-540-44568-4_11

15. Stone, P., Veloso, M.: Task decomposition, dynamic role assignment, and low-bandwidth communication for real-time strategic teamwork. Artif. Intell. **110**(2), 241–273 (1999)

MRSLaserMap: Local Multiresolution Grids for Efficient 3D Laser Mapping and Localization

David Droeschel[(✉)] and Sven Behnke

Autonomous Intelligent Systems, Computer Science, University of Bonn,
Bonn, Germany
{droeschel,behnke}@ais.uni-bonn.de

Abstract. In this paper, we present a three-dimensional mapping system for mobile robots using laser range sensors. Our system provides sensor preprocessing, efficient local mapping for reliable obstacle perception, and allocentric mapping with real-time localization for autonomous navigation. The software is available as open-source ROS-based package and has been successfully employed on different robotic platforms, such as micro aerial vehicles and ground robots in different research projects and robot competitions. Core of our approach are local multiresolution grid maps and an efficient surfel-based registration method to aggregate measurements from consecutive laser scans. By using local multiresolution grid maps as central data structure in our system, we gain computational efficiency by having high resolution in the near vicinity of the robot and lower resolution with increasing distance. Furthermore, local multiresolution grid maps provide a probabilistic representation of the environment—allowing us to address dynamic objects and to distinguish between occupied, free, and unknown areas. Spatial relations between local maps are modeled in a graph-based structure, enabling allocentric mapping and localization.

1 Introduction

In recent years, robotic competitions, such as RoboCup or the DARPA Robotics Challenge[1] (DRC), became increasingly popular. They foster robotics research by benchmarking robotic systems in standardized test scenarios. When integrating robot systems for such competitions, limited resources are one of the main constraints. For instance, recently, Micro Aerial Vehicles (MAVs), such as quadrotors, have gained attention in the robotics community. While being attractive for their wide range of applications, their size and weight limitations pose a challenge realizing cognitive functions—such as autonomous navigation—since onboard memory and computing power are limited. To meet these restrictions, efficient algorithms and data structures are key. We developed our mapping system for the purpose of efficient online mapping and successfully employed it in multiple research projects and robotic competitions. Input to our method are measurements of a continuously rotating 3D laser scanner.

---

[1] http://www.theroboticschallenge.org/.

© Springer International Publishing AG 2017
S. Behnke et al. (Eds.): RoboCup 2016, LNAI 9776, pp. 319–326, 2017.
https://doi.org/10.1007/978-3-319-68792-6_26

In order to gain both memory and runtime efficiency, we build local multiresolution grid maps with a high resolution close to the sensor and a coarser resolution farther away. Compared to uniform grids, local multiresolution leads to the use of fewer grid cells without loosing information and, consequently, results in lower computational costs. Furthermore, it corresponds well to the sensor measurement characteristics in relative distance accuracy and measurement density.

Measurements are aggregated in grid cells and summarized in surface elements (surfels) that are used for registration. Our registration method matches 3D scans on all resolutions concurrently, utilizing the finest common resolution available between both maps.

The system aggregates sparse sensory data from a 3D laser scanner to a dense environment representation used for obstacle avoidance and simultaneous localization and mapping (SLAM) as shown in Fig. 1. While being developed in our previous works [1,2], it has been successfully applied for autonomous outdoor [3] and indoor [4] navigation of MAVs. Furthermore, it has been used on our mobile manipulation robot Momaro during the DRC—supporting operators with a dense environment representation and localization—and during the DLR SpaceBot Camp 2015 to allow for autonomous navigation in rough terrain.

In conjunction with this paper, our software *MRSLaserMap* is published open-source[2], making it available to other researchers and RoboCup teams in order to facilitate developing robotic applications, contributing to the system, and for comparing and reproducing results. This paper gives an overview of the software architecture to ease integration of the system and presents results from different data sets which we also made publicly available[3].

2   Related Work

Different publicly available frameworks for laser-based mapping exist. In the context of RoboCup, mostly 2D approaches are used for mapping and localization. For example, in the RoboCup@Home league, where navigation in planar environments is sufficient, *GMapping* [5] is popular. In contrast, the RoboCup Rescue league necessitates navigation in uneven terrain and approaches such as *Hector Mapping* [6] are used. While a variety of 3D SLAM approaches exist [7–11], maintaining high run-time performance and low memory consumption is an issue.

Hornung et al. [8] implement a multiresolution map based on octrees (OctoMap). Ryde and Hu [12] use voxel lists for efficient neighbor queries. Both of these approaches consider mapping in 3D with a voxel being the smallest map element. The 3D-NDT [13] discretizes point clouds in 3D grids and aligns Gaussian statistics within grid cells to perform scan registration.

---

[2] https://github.com/AIS-Bonn/mrs_laser_map.
[3] http://www.ais.uni-bonn.de/laser_mapping.

Fig. 1. Results of our mapping system facilitating autonomous navigation of an MAV. Sparse laser scans (a) are aggregated in a local multiresolution grid map (b) by registering surfels (c). The resulting allocentric map (d) of the scene (e).

In contrast to the mentioned approaches, our mapping system is divided into an efficient local mapping—with constant runtime and memory consumption— and a graph-based allocentric mapping module, which allows for online mapping by leveraging local mapping results.

3   Key Components

The key components of our system have been published in our previous work and will therefore be addressed only briefly. The reader is referred to [1] for details on local multiresolution grid maps and the surfel-based registration method and to [2] for the allocentric mapping.

3.1   Local Multiresolution Grid Map

The assembled 3D point clouds are accumulated in a robot-centric grid map with increasing cell sizes from the robot center. It consists of multiple robot-centric 3D grid maps with different resolutions, called levels. Each grid map is embedded in the next level with coarser resolution and double cell length.

Each level is composed of circular buffers holding the individual grid cells. Multiple circular buffers are interlaced to obtain a map with three dimensions. The length of the circular buffers depends on the resolution and the size of the map. In case of a translation of the robot, the circular buffers are shifted whenever necessary to maintain the egocentric property of the map. In case of a translation equal or larger than the cell size, the circular buffers for respective dimensions are shifted. For sub-cell-length translations, the translational parts are accumulated and shifted if they exceed the length of a cell.

In each grid cell, individual measurements are stored along with occupancy probability and a surface element (surfel). A surfel summarizes its attributed points by their sample mean and covariance. Point measurements of consecutive 3D scans are stored in fixed-sized circular buffers, allowing for point-based data processing and facilitating efficient nearest-neighbor queries. Surfels store statistics about the surface that is mapped. The occupancy probability is used to determine if a cell is free, occupied, or unknown—accounting for uncertainty in the measurements and dynamic objects.

Similar to [8] we use a beam-based inverse sensor model and ray-casting to update the occupancy of a cell. For every measurement in the 3D scan, we update the occupancy information of cells on the ray between the sensor origin and the endpoint with an approximated 3D Bresenham algorithm [14].

3.2 Surfel-based Registration

Aggregating measurements from consecutive time steps necessitates a robust and reliable estimate of the sensor motion. To this end, newly acquired scans are aligned with the so far aggregated map by means of scan registration. We use our surfel-based registration method, which has been designed for this data structure. It leverages the multiresolution property of the map and gains efficiency by summarizing 3D points to surfels that are used for registration. Measurements from the aligned 3D scan replace older measurements in the map and update the occupancy information.

3.3 Simultaneous Localization and Mapping

Modeling the environment in a topological graph structure consisting of nodes, which are connected by edges, allows us to map larger environments and localize the robot in an allocentric frame. Nodes are individual local multiresolution grid maps from different view poses. They are connected by edges, which are spatial constraints from aligning these local maps with each other. Loop-closure is triggered by adding spatial constraints between close-by view poses. We use the g^2o framework [15] to optimize the graph.

4   Software Architecture

Our system is implemented in C++ using ROS and divided in three modules as shown in Fig. 2. Each module is capsuled in a separate ROS nodelet, running in the same nodelet manager—ensuring fast inter-process communication.

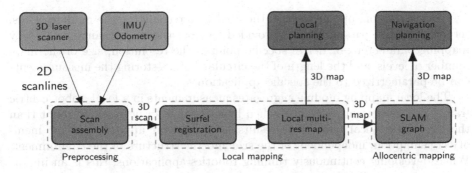

Fig. 2. Overview of our mapping system. The measurements are preprocessed to assemble a 3D scan. The resulting 3D point cloud is used to estimate the transformation between the current scan and the map. Registered scans are stored in a local multiresolution grid map. Local maps are registered against each other in a SLAM graph

4.1   Preprocessing

When using 3D laser scanners that provide a scan from multiple 2D scan lines—for instance by rotating an off-the-shelf 2D laser scanner—the individual 2D scans need to be assembled to a 3D scan. For this purpose, we provide the *scan assembler* nodelet. Since the sensor is moving during acquisition, we undistort the individual 2D scans in two steps.

First, measurements of individual 2D scans are undistorted with regards to the rotation of the 2D laser scanner around the sensor rotation axis. Using spherical linear interpolation, the rotation between the acquisition of two scan lines is distributed over the measurements.

Second, the motion of the robot during acquisition of a full 3D scan is compensated. To estimate robot motion, different sensors can be used, e.g., wheel odometry, visual odometry, or measurements from an inertial measurement unit (IMU). The interface for motion sensors is generalized to the ROS transform library and can be parametrized.

4.2   Local Mapping

The local mapping module is the central component of the system. It aggregates consecutive 3D scans in a local multiresolution grid map by aligning them with our efficient surfel-based registration method.

Standard ROS point cloud messages are expected as input to the module and are be published as output for the dense representation of aggregated scans. Furthermore, the map is published in a custom ROS message to the allocentric mapping module. To provide local planners with information about occupied, free, and unknown areas, the grid structure is published as well. Finally, the estimated motion between consecutive 3D scans, i.e., the recovered transformation from the registration method, is published in a ROS transform to correct odometry drift relative to the local map.

During mission, operators need the ability to reconfigure the module. Thus, service calls and parameters are provided to reset the map, change occupancy mapping parameters, or delete specific points. The resolution, size of the map, number of levels, and the length of the circular buffers storing the measurements can be parametrized to the specific application.

The local mapping module aggregates measurements in a local, robot-centric frame, i.e., measurements vanish when being farther away from the robot than the size of the local map. This results in a constant upper-bound for memory consumption, independent of the size and the structure of the environment. When developing continuously running robotics applications, this is an important property.

4.3   Allocentric Mapping

The local mapping module can be used in combination with the allocentric mapping module to map larger environments and track the robot pose in an allocentric frame. The module stores copies of local maps in a graph structure as nodes, connected by edges. After every scan update of the local mapping module, the current local map is registered to the graph by aligning it to a reference node. The reference node is a pointer to the last tracked local map and is updated if other nodes are closer to the current pose or a new node is added. A new node and the corresponding edge to the reference node is added to the graph if the robot moved sufficiently far. Edges are also added between close-by nodes that are not in temporal sequence. After adding an edge, graph optimization is triggered.

To visualize the allocentric map over a limited network connection, we implemented a visualization nodelet that is able to run off-board on a different computer. Data transmission between the allocentric mapping nodelet and the visualizer is compressed and incremental—only transmitting newly added nodes. When no node was added, optimized edges and the current tracked pose are transmitted, allowing to update the off-board graph structure.

Similar to the local mapping module, this module also provides the ability to reconfigure. Graph structures can be reset and parameters controlling when new nodes are added can be set.

5   Evaluation

Our system has been evaluated on different MAV platforms, e.g., for autonomous outdoor navigation and mapping as shown in Fig. 1. Furthermore, it has been deployed on our mobile manipulation robot Momaro during the DLR SpaceBot Camp 2015 and the DARPA Robotics Challenge as shown in Fig. 3. In our previous work [16] we evaluated the runtime and registration accuracy of the local mapping and registration system. The evaluation shows that our method is considerably more accurate and efficient than state-of-art methods.

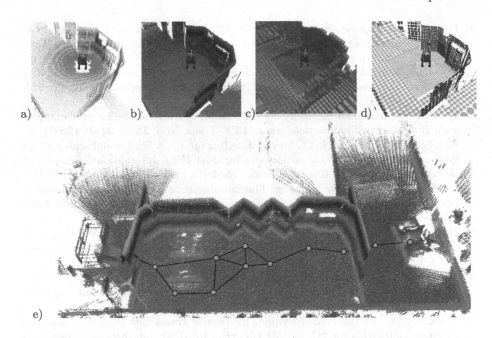

Fig. 3. Results of our mapping system on our mobile manipulation robot Momaro. The data has been acquired during the DRC. Sparse laser scans (a) are aggregated in a local multiresolution grid map (b + c) by registering surfels (d). The resulting allocentric map (e) shows graph structure, consisting of nodes (gray discs) and edges (black lines).

6 Conclusion

In this paper, we present MRSLaserMap, an efficient system for laser-based online mapping and localization. The implementation is publicly available as open-source project to facilitate research and the building of 3D robot navigation functionalities for other groups and RoboCup Teams.

Acknowledgments. This work has been supported by the European Union's Horizon 2020 Programme under Grant Agreement 644839 (CENTAURO) and grant BE 2556/7-2 of German Research Foundation (DFG).

References

1. Droeschel, D., Stückler, J., Behnke, S.: Local multi-resolution representation for 6D motion estimation and mapping with a continuously rotating 3D laser scanner. In: IEEE International Conference on Robotics and Automation (ICRA) (2014)
2. Droeschel, D., Stückler, J., Behnke, S.: Local multi-resolution surfel grids for MAV motion estimation and 3D mapping. In: Proceeding of the International Conference on Intelligent Autonomous Systems (2014)

3. Droeschel, D., Nieuwenhuisen, M., Beul, M., Holz, D., Stückler, J., Behnke, S.: Multilayered mapping and navigation for autonomous micro aerial vehicles. J. Field Rob. (JFR) **33**(4), 451–475 (2016)
4. Nieuwenhuisen, M., Droeschel, D., Beul, M., Behnke, S.: Autonomous navigation for micro aerial vehicles in complex GNSS-denied environments. J. Intell. Rob. Syst. 1–18 (2015)
5. Grisetti, G., Stachniss, C., Burgard, W.: Improved techniques for grid mapping with Rao-Blackwellized particlefilters. IEEE Trans. Rob. **23**(1), 34–46 (2007)
6. Kohlbrecher, S., von Stryk, O., Meyer, J., Klingauf, U.: A flexible and scalable slam system with full 3D motion estimation. In: 2011 IEEE International Symposium on Safety, Security, and Rescue Robotics (SSRR), pp. 155–160, November 2011
7. Nüchter, A.: 3D Robotic Mapping: The Simultaneous Localization and Mapping-problem with Six Degrees of Freedom. Springer, Heidelberg (2008). doi:10.1007/978-3-540-89884-9
8. Hornung, A., Wurm, K.M., Bennewitz, M., Stachniss, C., Burgard, W.: OctoMap: an efficient probabilistic 3D mapping framework based onoctrees. Auton. Robots **34**, 189–206 (2013)
9. Elseberg, J., Borrmann, D., Nüchter, A.: 6DOF semi-rigid SLAM for mobile scanning. In: IEEE/RSJ International Conference on Intelligent Robots and Systems (IROS) (2012)
10. Maddern, W., Harrison, A., Newman, P.: Lost in translation (and rotation): fast extrinsic calibration for 2D and 3D LIDARs. In: IEEE International Conference on Robotics and Automation (ICRA), May 2012
11. Anderson, S., Barfoot, T.D.: Towards relative continuous-time SLAM. In: IEEE International Conference on Robotics and Automation (ICRA) (2013)
12. Ryde, J., Hu, H.: 3D mapping with multi-resolution occupied voxel lists. Auton. Robots **28**, 169–185 (2010)
13. Stoyanov, T., Magnusson, M., Andreasson, H., Lilienthal, A.J.: Fast and accurate scan registration through minimization of the distance between compact 3D NDT representations. Int. J. Rob. Res. **31**(12), 1377–1393 (2012)
14. Amanatides, J., Woo, A.: A fast voxel traversal algorithm for ray tracing. In: In Eurographics 1987, pp. 3–10 (1987)
15. Kuemmerle, R., Grisetti, G., Strasdat, H., Konolige, K., Burgard, W.: G2o: a general framework for graph optimization. In: IEEE International Conference on Robotics and Automation (ICRA) (2011)
16. Razlaw, J., Droeschel, D., Holz, D., Behnke, S.: Evaluation of registration methods for sparse 3D laser scans. In: 2015 European Conference on Mobile Robots (ECMR). IEEE (2015)

Robust Collision Avoidance for Autonomous Mobile Robots in Unknown Environments

Muhannad Mujahed$^{(\boxtimes)}$, Dirk Fischer, and Bärbel Mertsching

GET Lab, University of Paderborn, Pohlweg 47-49, 33098 Paderborn, Germany
{mujahed,fischer,mertsching}@get.uni-paderborn.de
http://getwww.uni-paderborn.de/

Abstract. This paper presents a new collision avoidance method for mobile robots operating in unknown cluttered environments. The proposed method computes the steering angle based on the location of all obstacles surrounding the robot, not just the closest one. Hence, our technique is capable of generating smooth robot trajectories, particularly for unstructured environments. Moreover, the stability of the robot's motion is improved by providing a smoother bridge between avoiding obstacles and approaching the goal. Oscillations occurring in narrow corridors are reduced by considering the distribution of obstacles to both sides of the direction of motion. Simulation and experimental results are presented to demonstrate the performance of the proposed approach.

1 Introduction

Nowadays, applications such as exploration, search and rescue, or mining require autonomous mobile robots to perform difficult or dangerous tasks without human intervention. In such applications, the environment is usually unknown and changes over time. Moreover, unpredictable obstacles may block the robot's trajectory during mission operations. In order to guarantee a safe navigation in these environments, it is necessary to incorporate the sensory perceptions within the motion planning and the control loop. By this means, robots can detect environmental changes and re-plan dynamically to reach a goal safely. This is achieved by reactive obstacle avoidance navigation techniques.

The earlier obstacle avoidance methods for mobile robots as well as for manipulators were based on the concept of Artificial Potential Field APF (e.g. [1,2]). Within this concept, obstacles exert a repulsive force while the target asserts an attractive force onto the robot. The vector sum of these forces determines the steering angle. APF methods are considered fast and computationally efficient. However, failure to find an oscillation-free motion and getting stuck in local minima are well-known problems in these methods. Recent works try to overcome such drawbacks, such as [3], by using a modified Newton method, and [4], by employing a family of 2D smooth vector fields.

Other common techniques add constraints, coming from physical limitations and sensory data, to the velocity space, and choose the speed that maximizes an objective function and satisfies all constraints. The Dynamic Window [5,6] and

© Springer International Publishing AG 2017
S. Behnke et al. (Eds.): RoboCup 2016, LNAI 9776, pp. 327–338, 2017.
https://doi.org/10.1007/978-3-319-68792-6_27

Curvature Velocity [7, 8] are popular methods that follow this strategy. Despite the fact that these methods drive the robot faster with smoother behavior, they are unsuitable for cluttered environments as they fail to drive robots in between closely spaced obstacles. Moreover, they still can be trapped in local minima.

Several methods are based on the concept of Velocity Obstacles VO [9, 10] or Inevitable Collision States ICS [11, 12]. These methods perform collision avoidance by identifying the set of robot's velocities/states that may cause collision at a future time, and choose velocities outside of this set. A VO variant, RVO [13, 14], deals with the problem of cooperative obstacle avoidance. Although these methods explicitly consider the velocity of obstacles, they assume known or predictable future of the scene which is hard to achieve in real applications [15]. Additionally, it is difficult to determine the suitable time horizon for VO-based techniques, particularly in cluttered environments [16].

The Nearness-Diagram ND approach [17] and its improved version ND+ [18] use a "divide and conquer" strategy to identify the current navigational situation and then generate the corresponding motion law. These methods can successfully drive the robot in dense and cluttered environments and avoid local trap situations. The Smooth Nearness-Diagram SND method [19] was then developed enhancing the smoothness of the paths generated by ND+. Unfortunately, SND can be trapped in narrow corridors if one of its sides has a large number of obstacle points compared to the other. The Closest Gap CG method [20] addresses this problem by providing a stricter deviation against the nearest obstacles and by considering the ratio of threats on the both sides of the robot's heading.

The above mentioned ND variants avoid collisions with nearby obstacles using an idea inspired from the APF concept, which is likely to cause an oscillatory robot motion in narrow passages. This may also lead to longer trajectories and more execution time. The Tangential Closest Gap TCG [21] was then developed solving this drawback by integrating two concepts: the Closest Gap for extracting openings surrounding the robot and the Tangential Escape [22] for reactive collision avoidance navigation. A similar approach [23] solves this problem by taking into account the angular width of the chosen gap, as seen by the robot, and the closest obstacle in collision with the path towards this gap. This approach has been enhanced in [24] by considering all colliding obstacle points.

In this paper, we introduce the TCG+ navigation approach which is an enhancement of the TCG method. Compared to the TCG, our new approach takes into account the location of all close obstacle points in determining the steering angle, rather than the closest one. As a consequence, a smoother robot motion is achieved. Furthermore, the TCG+ provides a smoother bridge between avoiding obstacles (circumnavigating an obstacle) and approaching the goal (satisfying the leaving condition), resulting in a more stable behavior. Considering the distribution of obstacles to both sides of the direction of motion reduces oscillations occurring in narrow passages. The ability to generate smooth and stable robot trajectories reduces the possibility of wheel skidding over ramps, and thus is extremely beneficial in performing RoboCup rescue missions. The TCG+ is deployed as the reactive layer for our autonomous robot GETbot in the RoboCup Rescue Robot League competitions.

This paper presents the TCG+ reactive collision avoidance method design in Sect. 2. In Sects. 3 and 4, we show and discuss the simulation and experimental results. Subsequently, in Sect. 5 the performance of the proposed TCG+ approach is evaluated. Finally, Sect. 6 highlights our conclusions.

2 Reactive Collision Avoidance Technique

This section presents the TCG+ collision avoidance method for mobile robots operating in unknown cluttered environments which serves as a reactive planner in a hybrid navigation system. The TCG+ approach works as follows: first, the sensory data is analyzed to determine the structure of obstacles surrounding the robot. Based on this analysis, an instantaneous waypoint which makes progress towards the goal is located in a collision-free area as described in Sect. 2.2. The location of the waypoint is then adjusted to avoid nearby obstacles as explained in Sect. 2.3.

2.1 Definitions and Notations

The robot and goal locations are denoted by $\mathbf{p}_r$ and $\mathbf{p}_g$, respectively. The robot is wrapped into a circle whose radius is denoted by R. A scan point is denoted by $\mathbf{p}_i$, $i = 1, \ldots, n$. The polar coordinates of $\mathbf{p}_i$ are denoted by (r_i, θ_i).

For any two angles (θ_1, θ_2), the minimum angular distance between them is dist $(\theta_1, \theta_2) = \min (\text{dist}_c (\theta_1, \theta_2), \text{dist}_{cc} (\theta_1, \theta_2))$, where $\text{dist}_c (\theta_1, \theta_2) = (\theta_1 - \theta_2) \bmod 2\pi$ and $\text{dist}_{cc} (\theta_1, \theta_2) = (\theta_2 - \theta_1) \bmod 2\pi$.

In order to normalize an angle θ to the range $[-\pi, \pi[$, a projection function is defined as:

$$\text{proj}(\theta) = ((\theta + \pi) \bmod 2\pi) - \pi \tag{1}$$

Assume that $a < b$, a saturation function is defined as:

$$\text{sat}_{[a,b]}(x) = \begin{cases} a, & \text{if } x \leq a \\ x, & \text{if } a < x < b \\ b, & \text{if } x \geq b \end{cases} \tag{2}$$

2.2 Locating a Waypoint

If the direct path towards the goal is blocked[1], it is required to drive the robot towards an intermediate goal, referred to as a *waypoint*, rather than towards the goal itself. Locating the waypoint $\mathbf{p}_{cg}$ is based on studying the distribution of obstacles surrounding the robot: First, the sensory data is searched for gaps which indicate potential free areas where the robot fits through. Several methodologies can be found in the literature for extracting gaps (e.g. [17,20]). Here, we follow the CG method [20] due to its simplicity and computational efficiency. The

---

[1] The direct path towards the goal is blocked if the line segment connecting the robot to it intersects an obstacle in the configuration space.

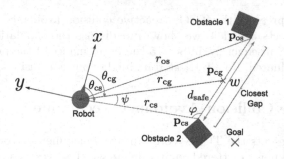

Fig. 1. Locating the closest gap waypoint.

navigable gap closest to the goal, called *closest gap*, is then selected to navigate through. At each time instance, the gap is characterized by two points (sides), one of them is closer to the goal than the other. We refer to it by $\mathbf{p}_{cs}$ and the other by $\mathbf{p}_{os}$ (see Fig. 1). In general, $\mathbf{p}_{cg}$ is located on the line segment connecting $\mathbf{p}_{cs}$ to $\mathbf{p}_{os}$ in such a way that a safe distance d_{safe} is preserved between $\mathbf{p}_{cg}$ and $\mathbf{p}_{cs}$ as the robot moves towards the closest gap. The value of d_{safe} is set to half of the width of the gap. However, when the gap is wide enough, it is better to limit d_{safe} so that the resultant trajectory is shorter:

$$d_{safe} = \begin{cases} R + D_s, & \text{if } \|\mathbf{p}_{cs} - \mathbf{p}_{os}\| > 2(R + D_s) \\ \frac{1}{2}\|\mathbf{p}_{cs} - \mathbf{p}_{os}\|, & \text{otherwise} \end{cases} \tag{3}$$

where D_s is a suitable clearance to be maintained between the robot and $\mathbf{p}_{cs}$.

Let θ_{cs} and θ_{os} be the angles between the x-axis of the robot and $\mathbf{p}_{cs}$ and $\mathbf{p}_{os}$, respectively, and r_{cs} the distance between $\mathbf{p}_r$ and $\mathbf{p}_{cs}$. The polar coordinates of $\mathbf{p}_{cg}$ are defined as follows:

$$\theta_{cg} = \begin{cases} \text{proj}\,(\theta_{cs} - \psi), & \text{if } \theta_{cs} > \theta_{os} \\ \text{proj}\,(\theta_{cs} + \psi), & \text{otherwise} \end{cases} \tag{4}$$

$$r_{cg} = \sqrt{d_{safe}^2 + r_{cs}^2 - 2d_{safe}r_{cs}\cos(\varphi)} \tag{5}$$

with φ and ψ are defined by:

$$\varphi = \arccos\left(\frac{w^2 + r_{cs}^2 - r_{os}^2}{2wr_{cs}}\right) \tag{6}$$

$$\psi = \arccos\left(\frac{r_{cg}^2 + r_{cs}^2 - d_{safe}^2}{2r_{cg}r_{cs}}\right) \tag{7}$$

where r_{os} is the distance to $\mathbf{p}_{os}$.

2.3 Obstacle Avoidance Method

While driving the robot towards $\mathbf{p}_{cg}$, the TCG+ will adjust the trajectory by rotating $\mathbf{p}_{cg}$ by an angle Γ temporarily in order to avoid the risk of collision with nearby obstacles. In [21], the rotation angle is computed so that the robot takes the direction of the tangent to the closest obstacle point. In case of unstructured environments, the position of this point may change rapidly resulting in an abrupt change in the robot's trajectory. Sharp turns may also occur due to the transition from following an obstacle boundary to resuming the progress towards the goal and vise versa. The proposed approach solves these drawbacks by using all nearby obstacle points in computing the rotation angle. It also balances the transition between avoiding obstacles and approaching the goal.

The key idea of the TCG+ is the computation of the rotation angle caused by each of N obstacle points considered as a hazard while driving the robot towards $\mathbf{p}_{cg}$. An obstacle point $\mathbf{p}_i$ is a hazard if the distance to it measured from the robot boundary is less than D_s and the angular distance between $\mathbf{p}_{cg}$ and $\mathbf{p}_i$, relative to the laser scanner coordinate system is less than $\frac{\pi}{2}$, i.e.:

$$\|\mathbf{p}_r - \mathbf{p}_i\| \leq R + D_s \wedge \text{dist}(\theta_{cg}, \theta_i) \leq \frac{\pi}{2} \tag{8}$$

The TCG+ method considers dividing the workspace into two subspaces; one is to the right of the robot's direction of motion (to the right of $\overrightarrow{\mathbf{p}_r\mathbf{p}_{cg}}$) while the other is to the left. A hazard $\mathbf{p}_i$ located in any of the two subspaces causes a rotation angle (γ_i) to $\mathbf{p}_{cg}$ based on its position, the position of $\mathbf{p}_{cg}$, and the clearance to obstacles located on the other subspace. Assume that the subspace including $\mathbf{p}_i$ is denoted by S_i and the other is $\hat{S}_i$. We consider the clearance to the obstacle point closest to the robot's boundary $\hat{\mathbf{p}}_c$, among those falling in $\hat{S}_i$, since it poses the highest risk.

$$\hat{\mathbf{p}}_c = \underset{\mathbf{p}}{\text{argmin}}\|\mathbf{p} - \mathbf{p}_r\|, \quad \mathbf{p} \in \hat{S}_i \tag{9}$$

The value of γ_i is determined so that $0.5\,\|\mathbf{p}_i - \hat{\mathbf{p}}_c\|$ is maintained to whichever of $\mathbf{p}_i$ and $\hat{\mathbf{p}}_c$ is closer to the robot boundary. By this means, the clearance to obstacles is maximized as the robot moves towards $\mathbf{p}_{cg}$. Moreover, oscillations occurring in narrow openings due to changing the location of the closest obstacle are reduced. If $\hat{S}_i$ doesn't contain any hazard, γ_i is set in such a way that the robot points parallel to the tangent of $\mathbf{p}_i$:

$$\gamma_i = \begin{cases} \text{sat}_{[0,\chi]}\left(\text{dist}\left(\zeta, \theta_{cg}\right)\right)\beta - \chi\beta, & \text{if } |\zeta - \theta_{cg}| \leq \pi \\ \chi\beta - \text{sat}_{[0,\chi]}\left(\text{dist}\left(\zeta, \theta_{cg}\right)\right)\beta, & \text{otherwise} \end{cases} \tag{10}$$

with ζ, β and χ are given by:

$$\zeta = \begin{cases} \theta_i, & \text{if no hazard falls in } \hat{S}_i \\ \theta_{\min}, & \text{otherwise} \end{cases} \tag{11}$$

$$\beta = \begin{cases} 1, & \text{if } \zeta \geq \theta_{cg} \\ -1, & \text{otherwise} \end{cases} \tag{12}$$

$$\chi = \begin{cases} \frac{\pi}{2}, & \text{if no hazard falls in } \hat{S}_i \\ \arcsin\left(\frac{\frac{1}{2}\|\mathbf{p}_i - \hat{\mathbf{p}}_c\|}{r_{\min}}\right), & \text{otherwise} \end{cases} \tag{13}$$

where θ_{min} and r_{min} denote the angle and distance to whichever of $\mathbf{p}_i$ and $\hat{\mathbf{p}}_c$ is closer to the robot's boundary, respectively, and θ_i the angle towards $\mathbf{p}_i$. The value of β determines the correct direction of escaping towards the closest gap. Having a closer look at Eq. (10), it is apparent that the value of γ_i becomes 0 if the angular distance between ζ and θ_{cg} gets greater than χ (a leaving condition). Notice that if no hazard falls in $\hat{S}_i$ and $\mathbf{p}_i$ is the obstacle point closest to the robot, the effect of (10) is analogous to the *virtual rotation angle* from [21].

Hazards falling within the right subspace cause *positive rotation angles*, while hazards falling in the left subspace cause *negative rotation angles*. The average positive and negative rotation angles are computed separately. This is to assign the same weight (relative importance) to hazards located on both sides of the direction of motion, even if one side has a large number of hazards compared to the other. In this regard, we avoid the problem of movement close to obstacles (or even hitting obstacles in narrow corridors) falling on the side with fewer hazards (see [20] for more details). Let N_{pos} and N_{neg} represent the number of hazards causing positive and negative rotation angles, respectively. The average positive and negative rotation angles are then defined as follows:

$$\Gamma_{pos} = \frac{\sum_{i=1}^{N_{pos}} \gamma_i}{N_{pos}}, \quad \gamma_i > 0 \tag{14}$$

$$\Gamma_{neg} = \frac{\sum_{i=1}^{N_{neg}} \gamma_i}{N_{neg}}, \quad \gamma_i < 0 \tag{15}$$

Finally, the rotation angle Γ is defined as the average of Γ_{pos} and Γ_{neg}:

$$\Gamma = \frac{\Gamma_{pos} + \Gamma_{neg}}{2} \tag{16}$$

The location of the waypoint after rotating it by Γ is denoted by $\tilde{\mathbf{p}}_g$ and computed as follows:

$$\tilde{\mathbf{p}}_g = \begin{bmatrix} \cos(\Gamma) & \sin(\Gamma) \\ -\sin(\Gamma) & \cos(\Gamma) \end{bmatrix} \mathbf{p}_{cg} \tag{17}$$

The TCG+ method considers limiting the robot's speed based on the distance to nearby obstacles [20,21]:

$$v_{cut} = \sqrt{1 - \text{sat}_{[0,1]}\left(\frac{D_{vs} - r_c}{D_{vs}}\right)} \cdot v_{max} \tag{18}$$

where D_{vs} is a parameter that determines how much the speed is limited, v_{max} the maximum linear speed of the robot, and r_c the distance towards the obstacle point closest to the robot boundary.

For driving the robot towards $\tilde{\mathbf{p}}_g$, we use the same motion commands proposed in the TCG method [21]:

$$v = k_{brake} \, v_{cut} \cos(\tilde{\theta}_g) \tag{19}$$

$$w = \text{sat}_{[-w_{max}, w_{max}]}\left(k_{max} \tilde{\theta}_g + \frac{v \sin(\tilde{\theta}_g)}{\tilde{r}_g}\right) \tag{20}$$

where $\tilde{r}_g$ and $\tilde{\theta}_g$ are the distance and angle towards $\tilde{\mathbf{p}}_g$, respectively, and w_{max} the maximum angular speed of the robot. The value of k_{brake} in (19) is set to $\tanh(\tilde{r}_g)$, if $\tilde{\mathbf{p}}_g = \mathbf{p}_g$ (to ensure smooth braking while reaching the goal), and to 1 otherwise. The parameter k_{max} in (20) is used to limit the angular speed of the robot. Having in mind that the maximum angular velocity in (20) corresponds to $\frac{\partial w}{\partial \theta_g} = 0$, the value of k_{max} can be defined as follows:

$$k_{max} = \frac{w_{max} - \frac{1}{2}k_{beak}v_{cut}}{\frac{\pi}{4}} \tag{21}$$

3 Simulations

In this section, the differences in the behavior of the TCG and TCG+ methods are demonstrated using the stage robot simulator. They were implemented using the Robot Operating System (ROS) [25]. The simulated robot has a rectangular shape (0.52 m, 0.48 m) and works in a differential-driven mode. The maximum velocities were set to (0.5 m/s, 1.0 rad/s) while the safe distances (D_s, D_{vs}) were set to (0.7 m, 0.9 m). The sensing system adopted is a laser scanner which delivers 1100 measurements over 360° and covering a range of 10 m.

For these simulations, two environments with many narrow and curved passages were created, mimicking unstructured environments, as shown in Fig. 2.

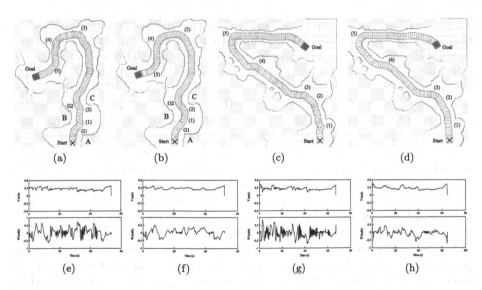

Fig. 2. Simulations. (a, b) Path followed by (a) TCG and (b) TCG+ methods in scenario 1. (c, d) Path followed by (c) TCG and (d) TCG+ in scenario 2. (e, f) Translational and rotational velocities versus time for (e) TCG and (f) TCG+ in scenario 1. (g, h) Translational and rotational velocities versus time for (g) TCG and (h) TCG+ in scenario 2.

The route chosen by the TCG method in the first scenario is shown in Fig. 2a. At the starting point, the leaving condition is fulfilled since the angular distance between the closest obstacle (on the side labeled A here) and $\mathbf{p}_{cg}$ (falling within gap G1 created by A and B obstacles) exceeds $\pi/2$. In such a case, the robot navigates directly towards $\mathbf{p}_{cg}$. While navigating through G1, the distance to side B obstacles gets less than the distance to side A obstacles and $\mathbf{p}_{cg}$ gets inside gap G2 created by B and C obstacles. At this moment, the angular distance between the closest obstacle and $\mathbf{p}_{cg}$ is less than $\pi/2$. Therefore, the robot moves parallel to the tangent of side B obstacles until having fulfilled the leaving condition. This behavior continues until having passed all gaps. The frequent transition between following an obstacle boundary and resuming the progress towards $\mathbf{p}_{cg}$, and the quick variation in the location of the closest obstacle cause rapid changes in the steering angle. This can be interpreted from the large spikes visible in the velocity profile shown in Fig. 2e. The behavior of the TCG method in the second scenario is roughly similar to that of the first one as depicted in Figs. 2c and g.

By applying the proposed TCG+ approach, the robot managed to navigate both obstacle courses much smoother than the TCG method as can be seen from Figs. 2b and d. For example, see the trajectories of both methods at the points labeled 1–5 in Figs. 2a, b, c and d. We have confirmed our visualization by plotting the recorded motion commands versus time in Figs. 2f and h.

4   Experimental Results

The simulation results have been confirmed using our rescue mobile robot GET-bot, a skid-steering Pioneer 3-AT equipped with two laser scanners and an onboard computer. One laser scanner is located at the front of the robot while the other is located at the back. The front laser scanner is a Hokuyo UTM-30LX having an angular resolution of $0.25°$ and a field of view of $270°$ with a maximum range of 30 m. The rear scanner is a Hokuyo URG-04LX having an angular resolution of $0.35°$ and a field of view of $240°$ covering 5.6 m. We merged the range data acquired from both laser scanners to get a $360°$ field of view. The robotic platform is rectangular (0.52×0.48 m) with non-holonomic constraints. The maximum robot speeds (v_{max}, w_{max}) are 0.7 m/s and 2.4 rad/s, respectively. The safe distances (D_s, D_{vs}) were set to (0.7 m, 0.9).

Next, we outline two experiments carried out using GETbot where the goal was the only information provided to the robot in advance[2]. For the first experiment, we created an environment similar to the RoboCup Rescue Arena as shown in Fig. 3a. Notice that a stable and smooth navigation in such arena reduces the possibility of wheel skidding over ramps, and therefore of great importance in rescue missions. The maximum robot velocities (v_{max}, w_{max}) were limited to (0.5 m/s, 1.0 rad/s), since moving fast over ramps is risky. The route chosen for the second experiment contained places where the room available to maneuver

---

[2] Videos of both experiments are available at: http://getwww.uni-paderborn.de/research/videos/tcgplus.

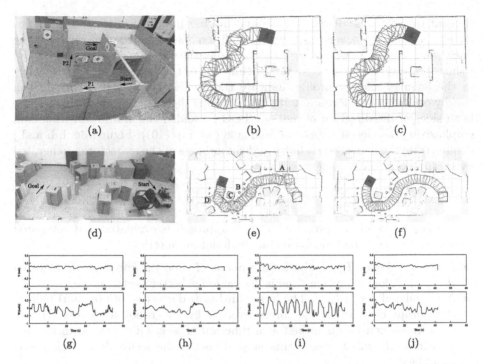

Fig. 3. Experiments. (a) Experimental setup for scenario 1. (b, c) Path followed by (b) TCG and (c) TCG+ in scenario 1. (d) Experimental setup for scenario 2. (e, f) Path followed by (e) TCG and (f) TCG+ in scenario 2. (g, h) Velocities versus time for (g) TCG and (h) TCG+ in scenario 1. (i, j) Velocities versus time for (i) TCG and (j) TCG+ in scenario 2.

is reduced as shown in Fig. 3d. Therefore, the maximum velocities were limited to (0.4 m/s, 0.8 rad/s). Both experiments have been carried out using the implementation of the TCG and TCG+ methods.

The trajectories followed by the TCG method in experiments 1 and 2 are shown in Figs. 3b and e, respectively. The robot was able to traverse the courses of both experiments and reach the goal. However, sharp changes in the direction of motion occurred. For example, see the trajectory while traveling through the starting area (passage P1) and while leaving the passage labeled P2 in Fig. 3b. The behavior was much worse in the second experiment as the motion was oscillatory almost during the complete mission as shown in Fig. 3e. Moreover, the robot moved close to the obstacles labeled A - D in the figure. This is due to the fact that the environment is composed of very narrow passages with different obstacle shapes and sizes rather than straight walls (maze-like environment) as in the first experiment. These frequent changes in the direction of motion are a result of performing obstacle avoidance based only on the closest obstacle point. In tight passages, the location of this point quickly varies as the robot moves. Moreover, the robot was switching between moving in the direction of the tangent to the closest obstacle boundary and moving directly towards $\mathbf{p}_{cg}$. The latter occurred whenever the leaving condition was satisfied. We recorded the linear and angular velocities over the course of the experiments. Figures 3g and i show these velocities plotted versus time where the large spikes, particularly in the angular velocity profile, indicate the oscillatory motion. By taking all nearby obstacles into account and by considering the distribution of obstacles to both sides of the direction of motion, TCG+ avoided this limitation while still emphasizing the closest threat on each side (see Eq. (10)). Figures 3c, f, h and j demonstrate the increased stability and smoothness of the trajectories generated by the proposed TCG+ method.

5   Evaluation

The performance of the proposed TCG+ approach is evaluated and compared to that of the TCG method based on the following metrics:

- Execution Time (T_{tot}). The total amount of time the robot needs to reach the goal. A low execution time is desirable for better performance.
- Accumulated Jerk (J_{acc}). The jerk (third time derivative of position) reflects the abrupt changes in the forces exerted by the robot actuators. Hence, smoothness can be quantified as a function of jerk. Given the translational velocity of the robot at each time step, we define the accumulated jerk metric as follows:

$$J_{acc} = \frac{1}{T_{tot}} \int_0^{T_{tot}} [\ddot{v}(t)]^2 \, dt \qquad (22)$$

Having less accumulated jerk is desirable as it indicates less oscillatory, more stable, and smoother behavior.
- Average Bending Energy (B_{avg}). The bending energy is a measure of the energy requirement of the robot motion, and thus can be used to assess the smoothness of the trajectory. Given the curvature k at any point along a trajectory, the average bending energy is given by [26]:

$$B_{avg} = \frac{1}{n} \int_{x_0}^{x_n} k^2(x) \, dx \qquad (23)$$

where

$$k(x) = \frac{f''(x)}{(1 + (f'(x))^2)^{\frac{3}{2}}} \, dx \qquad (24)$$

A low B_{avg} is preferred as it is an indication of an increased smoothness.

Based on the aforementioned metrics, a performance evaluation of the TCG+ approach was performed. Table 1 shows the results obtained for the simulations and experiments presented in Sects. 3 and 4. A significant improvement in the performance of the TCG+ over the TCG can be observed in all tests conducted. We believe that this enhancement is due to the fact that the TCG+ calculates Γ based on the location of all nearby obstacles and balances the transition between avoiding obstacles and approaching the goal. It also considers the distribution of obstacles to both sides of the direction of motion.

Table 1. Performance evaluation of the TCG and TCG+ methods.

Sim.	Method	T_{tot}	J_{acc}	B_{avg}	Exp.	Method	T_{tot}	J_{acc}	B_{avg}
1	TCG	54	0.543	0.176	1	TCG	44	0.155	0.935
	TCG+	**51**	**0.073**	**0.071**		TCG+	**42**	**0.018**	**0.101**
2	TCG	67	0.517	0.229	2	TCG	54	0.221	4.192
	TCG+	**64**	**0.071**	**0.049**		TCG+	**41**	**0.036**	**0.237**

6   Conclusions

This paper presents the TCG+ navigation approach for reactive obstacle avoidance. The TCG+ adapts the earlier developed Tangential Closest Gap method by making use of all close obstacle points in determining the motion direction and by providing a smoother bridge between obstacle avoidance and goal approach. The trajectories generated by the TCG+ are smoother and more stable when compared to those generated by the TCG. Additionally, taking into account the distribution of obstacles to both robot sides reduces oscillations in narrow corridors occurring in the TCG method. Simulation and experimental results demonstrated the effectiveness of the proposed approach.

References

1. Khatib, O.: Real-time obstacle avoidance for manipulators and mobile robots. Int. J. Robot. Res. **5**, 90–98 (1986)
2. Rezaee, H., Abdollahi, F.: Adaptive artificial potential field approach for obstacle avoidance of unmanned aircrafts. In: 2012 IEEE/ASME International Conference on Advanced Intelligent Mechatronics, (Kachsiung), pp. 1–6, July 2012
3. Ren, J., McIsaac, K.A., Patel, R.V.: Modified newtons method applied to potential field based navigation for nonholonomic robots in dynamic environments. Robotica **26**, 117–127 (2008)
4. Panagou, D.: Motion planning and collision avoidance using navigation vector fields. In: 2014 IEEE International Conference on Robotics and Automation, (Hong Kong, China), pp. 2513–2518, May 2014
5. Fox, D., Burgard, W., Thrun, S.: The dynamic window approach to collision avoidance. IEEE Robot. Aut. Mag. 4(1), 23–33 (1997)
6. Seder, M., Petrovic, I.: Dynamic window based approach to mobile robot motion control in the presence of moving obstacles. In: IEEE International Conference on Robotics and Automation (ICRA), (Roma, Italy), pp. 1986–1991, April 2007
7. Simmons, R.: The curvature-velocity method for local obstacle avoidance. In: IEEE International Conference on Robotics and Automation (ICRA), (Minnosota, USA), pp. 3375–3382, April 1996
8. Shi, C., Wang, Y., Yang, J.: A local obstacle avoidance method for mobile robots in partially known environment. Robot. Auton. Syst. **58**, 425–434 (2010)
9. Fiorini, P., Shiller, Z.: Motion planning in dynamic environments using velocity obstacles. Int. J. Rob. Res. **17**, 760–772 (1998)

10. Wu, A., How, J.P.: Guaranteed infinite horizon avoidance of unpredictable, dynamically constrained obstacles. Aut. Rob. **32**(3), 227–242 (2012)
11. Fraichard, T., Asama, H.: Inevitable collision states - a step towards safer robots? Adv. Robot. **18**(10), 1001–1024 (2004)
12. Lawitzky, A., Nicklas, A., Wollherr, D., Buss, M.: Determining states of inevitable collision using reachability analysis. In: IEEE/RSJ International Conference on Intelligent Robots and Systems (USA), pp. 4142–4147, September 2014
13. Berg, J., Lin, M.C., Manocha, D.: Reciprocal velocity obstacles for real-time multi-agent navigation. In: IEEE International Conference on Robotics and Automation (ICRA), (Pasadena, CA), pp. 1928–1935, May 2008
14. Bareiss, D., Berg, J.: Generalized reciprocal collision avoidance. Int. J. Robot. Res. **34**, 1501–1514 (2015)
15. Jin, J., Kim, Y., Wee, S., Gans, N.: Decentralized cooperative mean approach to collision avoidance for nonholonomic mobile robots. In: IEEE International Conference on Robotics and Automation, (USA), pp. 35–41, May 2015
16. Shiller, Z., Sharma, S.: High speed on-line motion planning in cluttered environments. In: IEEE/RSJ International Conference on Intelligent Robots and Systems (IROS), (Vilamoura, Portugal), pp. 596–601, October 2012
17. Minguez, J., Montano, L.: Nearness diagram (ND) navigation: collision avoidance in troublesome scenarios. IEEE Trans. Robot. Autom. **20**(1), 45–59 (2004)
18. Minguez, J., Osuna, J., Montano, L.: A "divide and conquer" strategy based on situations to achieve reactive collision avoidance in troublesome scenarios. In: IEEE International Conference on Robotics and Automation, pp. 3855–3862 (2004)
19. Durham, J.W., Bullo, F.: Smooth nearness-diagram navigation. In: IEEE/RSJ International Conference on Intelligent Robots and Systems (IROS), (Nice, France), pp. 690–695, September 2008
20. Mujahed, M., Fischer, D., Mertsching, B., Jaddu, H.: Closest Gap based (CG) reactive obstacle avoidance navigation for highly cluttered environments. In: IEEE/RSJ International Conference on Intelligent Robots and Systems (IROS), (Taipei, Taiwan), pp. 1805–1812, October 2010
21. Mujahed, M., Jaddu, H., Fischer, D., Mertsching, B.: Tangential closest Gap based (TCG) reactive obstacle avoidance navigation for cluttered environments. In: IEEE International Symposium on Safety, Security, and Rescue Robotics (SSRR), (Linköping, Sweden), pp. 1–6, October 2013
22. Ferreira, A., Pereira, F.G., Vassallo, R.F., Sarcinelli-Filho, M., Bastos-Filho, T.F.: An approach to avoid obstacles in mobile robot navigation: the tangential escape. SBA. Sociedade Brasileira de Automatica **19**, 395–405 (2008)
23. Mujahed, M., Fischer, D., Mertsching, B.: Safe Gap based (SG) reactive navigation for mobile robots. In: European Conference on Mobile Robots (ECMR), (Barcelona, Spain), pp. 325–330, June 2013
24. Mujahed, M., Fischer, D., Mertsching, B.: Smooth reactive collision avoidance in difficult environments. In: IEEE Conference on Robotics and Biomimetics (ROBIO), (Zhuhai, China), pp. 1471–1476, December 2015
25. Quigley, M., Conley, K., Gerkey, B.P., Faust, J., Foote, T., Leibs, J., Wheeler, R., Ng, A.Y.: ROS: an open-source robot operating system. In: ICRA Workshop on Open Source Software (2009)
26. Munoz, N., Valencia, J., Londono, N.: Evaluation of navigation of an autonomous mobile robot. In: Proceedings of International Workshop on Performance Metrics for Intelligent Systems Workshop (PerMIS), pp. 15–21 (2007)

Robots as Individuals in the Humanoid League

Maike Paetzel[1]([✉]), Jacky Baltes[2], and Reinhard Gerndt[3]

[1] Uppsala Univeristy, 75105 Uppsala, Sweden
maike.paetzel@it.uu.se
[2] University of Manitoba, Winnipeg, MB R3T 2N2, Canada
jacky@cs.umanitoba.ca
[3] Ostfalia University of Applied Sciences, 38304 Wolfenbüttel, Germany
r.gerndt@ostfalia.de
http://bit-bots.de, http://www.cs.umanitoba.ca/~jacky,
http://www.wfwolves.de

Abstract. Having the goal of winning against the human world champions in soccer in 2050 in mind, the Humanoid League is facing the challenges of having to increase field and robot size until the sizes of regular fields and regular players are reached in the year 2040. The next major step is foreseen for the year 2020, when minimum robot size will increase by 50%, the number of robots per team will increase and the field size will fourfold. All three aspects will have a crucial impact. For the organizers, it will become increasingly hard, if not impossible at some point, to make arrangements for up to six fields at the RoboCup venue. For the participants, sustaining a team of ever increasing robots, in size and numbers will be a similar challenge. We believe that the 2050 goal can only be achieved if a new scheme of competition of individual robots, playing with others, can be found. Then, teams could focus on a single robot. To encourage this, we propose to revise the competition scheme, moving away from participating with a team of robots to participating with a single robot, that preserves the competitive element of ranking performance of individual robots and awarding trophies. This paper is intended to spark a discussion of a rule change to encourage participation of single robots in the Humanoid League and still contribute to reaching the 2050 goal.

1 Introduction

According to the Humanoid League Proposed Roadmap [6] released in 2014, by 2020 the field size should be increased significantly and duration of the matches should be doubled, the number of players increased from 4 to 6 and the minimum robot height increased from 40 cm to 60 cm. Figure 1 shows the evolution of field and robot sizes over the coming years. The increase of the number of robots would increase the necessary investment by 50%. Furthermore, often larger robots will have to be developed and built.

The larger size and number of robots will also increase the effort to participate in events, e.g. for logistics. This will also be the case for the organizers of events,

© Springer International Publishing AG 2017
S. Behnke et al. (Eds.): RoboCup 2016, LNAI 9776, pp. 339–346, 2017.
https://doi.org/10.1007/978-3-319-68792-6_28

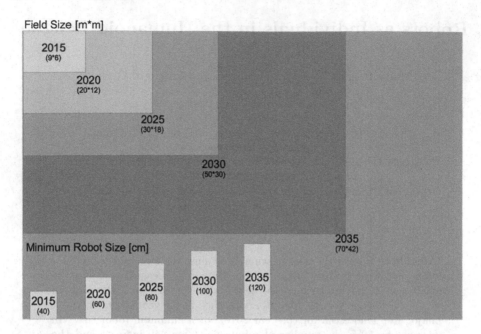

Fig. 1. HL roadmap for field and robot sizes.

which would have to fourfold the size of fields. Even though there is foreseen to be only a single class of robots, which means the division in Kid, Teen and Adult Size will be obsolete, if the number of teams still is the same, this will not reduce the number of fields required. Actively reducing the number of teams would not support reaching the goal of the 2050 game. In view of the very high challenges an increase of the number of teams would be advisable. However, with ever increasing investments and cost this may not be within reach. The league already faces stagnation of the number of teams participating in the Humanoid League. We believe that one main reason is that teams fear both the cost as well as the Hardware and Software challenges connected to larger robots.

Currently, a team is usually based in one university, so this university has to provide the whole budget and researchers working in the team. As the budget and manpower in all research institutes is limited, we believe that the key to mastering the challenges of the 2050 goal is to

(a) lower the barrier for participation, e.g. to a single robot and
(b) foster a closer cooperation and collaboration between the teams, e.g. by means of a common inter-robot communication [1].

This cooperations can be shaped very differently: Teams can jointly develop a new Hardware platform sharing costs and workload, but it is also possible that a team consists of different robots from different Universities if each University can only afford to build a very limited number of robots. In any case, a pre-requirement to building a successful joint team lays in the ability of the robots to communicate with each other. The Humanoid League does not provide a common communication protocol and attempts by teams to provide such a framework did only become accepted regional. An example for such a communication protocol the *mitecom* protocol developed by team FUmanoids [8], which is used by many teams in Europe.

In this paper we suggest a new playing scheme that allows to award individual robots based on their performance within a cooperative game as soccer. We review the state of the art of such a challenges in real sport and in other leagues of the RoboCup and based on this we sketch potential approach rule sets for the Humanoid League.

2   Performance Indicators in Human and RobotSport Disciplines

We shortly present the state of the art in human sport disciplines and in other hardware soccer leagues. In human sport disciplines we are faced with a similar challenge. Identifying the 'importance' of a player for the team play or overall is a challenging task. This task ranges from identifying the 'Most Valuable Player' of a game, over highest performers of a season to determining the 'value' of a player. Soccer coaches are faced by this challenge for a long time in order to identify suitable players for games, for specific trainings or for transfer to other teams. Typically they observe players during training and during games and rate performance in a number of categories, like 'technical ability', 'tactical awareness', 'physical fitness', and 'personal attitude'. Categories typically are further subdivided into individual aspects, e.g. dribbling, passing and heading [5]. A shortcoming of many catalogues of performance aspects is the lack of universal applicability for all players of a team. This becomes immediately obvious if strikers and goal keepers are considered and also holds for any other specialized position like midfield and defense. The individual aspects are then rated and can be aggregated to single number. However, this kind of assessment requires a considerable effort. Transferred to a competition situation, it would require to have many referees, preferably one per player, to watch and record performance with respect to the catalogue of relevant aspects.

Some human sport disciplines like Basketball count the number of activities related to offense and defense activities. Highly prominent aspects are scored points and assists, to help another player to score. These aspects are typically less subjective than those relevant for coaching. However, there still are specialized players, such that a comparison of all players of a team can not be based on indicators that are in any way related to specific aspects. A highly condensed performance indicator is the number of goals or points scored and goals suffered. Many leagues use this very objective scheme to determine the ranking of teams within leagues. Some disciplines, e.g. ice hockey, try to rank their players according to their contribution to scoring and suffering goals without necessary having to be immediately involved in it.

Another ranking scheme, observable in human sport business is auctioning players for transfer to other teams. Assuming a perfect market situation, auctions would reveal the true price of a player and thus allow a ranking of players. The underlying theory of auctions is described in numerous publications related to game theory, e.g. [4].

The Standard Platform League (SPL) [9] can be considered the closest to the Humanoid League due to the Hardware similarity. The SPL introduced a Drop-In competition in 2014. The main purpose was encouraging the development of robots which are *"good teammates and play well with a team composed of drop-in players from a variety of teams"*. All teams participating in the main tournament have to participate in the SPL Drop-In challenge. Additional teams to only compete in this challenge may be selected. This is very important as it allows teams to get started in a RoboCup competition without being able to provide a full team of robots. In the SPL Drop-In competition the same game rules as in the regular games are applied, with some exceptions like not having a coaching robot, a designated goal keeper and timeouts. The scoring is a mixture of the game score for a team and a score per robot assigned by human referees. The robots are constantly rated, based on positive and negative team play and once for the entire game based on the overall positioning and game participation. A separate award is given to the best player after a number of Drop-In games have been played.

The Middle Size league [7] has a Technical Challenge called *Cooperative Mixed-Team Play* in which teams need to demonstrate the team play of at least 90 seconds between two or more robots from different teams. The activity to demonstrate is not fixed in the rules.

3   Player-Centered Competition Approach

The core of the new approach to reduce costs for participants and organizers is a robot centered assessment, i.e. all results of a gameplay have to be broken down to and awarded to individual robots. In order to account for granularity of the scoring mechanism, a number of games with robot teams assembled from different robots for each game are required. This would result in a series of Drop-In games with possibly changing teammates for every game. The question remaining is, how many games are required and how are results allocated to individual robots.

3.1   Goal-Based Ranking

A very simplistic goal-based approach would be to have a counter for every robot to count goals scored while being member of a team with +1 and goals suffered with −1. A high score would thus be an indicator of a good and successful team play. The approach does not require a specific refereeing overhead and is based on objective measures. It would award a equal share of the goal to every single player, even if not immediately involved in the scoring action.

A respective statement would hold for goals suffered. The thought model would be an incapable player whilst the other one scores or prevents goals being rewarded an equal share. However, with a number of games in changing configurations of team mates, the teams with lower-performing players are expected to be less successful and thus any player insufficiently contributing will have a lower score. The number of games to reliably make the difference obvious depends on the number of team mates and the actual performance gap. Team mates could be allocated randomly or by a fixed scheme to assure as many different team configurations as possible.

3.2   Auction-Based Ranking

A very basic auctioning situation often can be observed when children assemble their teams by interchanging selection of team mates by team leaders. Team members selected first typically are considered more 'valuable' than others. Any goals scored and suffered by the team can then be weighted with the reciprocal position of selection (first selection = highest weight). This approach, however, requires the team leaders to base their choices upon objective judgement of the individual performance and is generally prone to collusions. Choices will also reflect a specific strategy of the team leader. Since the team leader needs to have an incentive for making the decision to the best of his or her abilities, he or she should be considered as the first selection. As with the previously presented approach, a number of games need to be played. In order to have equal opportunities for every participating university, every group needs to be team leader once. Therefore the number of games needs to be fixed to the number of participating groups divided by two.

3.3   Referee-Based Ranking

The SPL Drop-In Challenge can be easily adapted to the Humanoid League rules and serve as a basis for the new award scheme for individual robots. As a start, the game time should be shortened to only one 10 min half with no timeout and pushing rules applied and no dedicated goal keeper as in the SPL. Whichever defending robot reaches the goal area first is considered the current goal keeper. The illegal defense rule then applies to all robots entering afterwards. All other goal keeper specific rules do not apply during the Drop-In games, which among others means that the goal keeper does not have special protection from being touched by other players in the goal area.

The main improvement over the SPL Drop-In challenge we suggest is the introduction of a set of objective rules for judging the performance of a specific robot. We aim to have only one additional referee per team for the entire challenge to not add too much overhead for the teams to provide referees (Fig. 2). The referee for a team provides the player-specific score for all robots playing for one team. The robot specific score will be added to the average game result to determine the overall score of a robot. We acknowledge that the *referee-based ranking* might become difficult over time, when speed and intensity of game play evolves. By that time it would be desirable to have an automated referee assistant system to help judging the proposed rules.

Fig. 2. Refereeing duty during HL game.

We propose the following set of rules which shall be judged constantly during the game. For every positive game play the robot receives one point, for every negative game play one minus point.

Positive game play:

- **Successful pass of the ball to a team mate:** A pass is considered successful if the ball stops in a radius of 30 cm around a team mate or if a team mate can take the ball in move.
- **Successful receiving of a pass:** A pass is considered successfully received if a team mate passes the ball and the receiving robot touches the ball in move or within 10 s after it stopped.
- **Intercept an opponents shot:** If an opponent passes the ball and the robot either touches the ball in move or withing 10 s after it stopped and before another robot of the opponents team could touch the ball.
- **Man-marking:** A robot positions itself in between the opponent currently in possession of the ball and another opponent who is not already marked by another robot.
- **Position to receive a pass:** A robot positions itself between the opponent goal and the robot of its own team currently in possession of the ball without being marked by an opponent, or the reasonable attempted to resolve the situation of being marked by an opponent.

Negative game play:

- **Pushing team mates:** A robot touches another robot from its own team for longer than 1 s. If only one robot was actively walking towards the team mate, only this robot will receive a negative score. If both were actively walking towards each other, both will receive a negative score. A negative score is not given if the touching was caused by at least one robot falling.
- **Steeling the ball from teammates:** A robot kicks or attempt to kick the ball if it is in front of a teammate, within a range of 20 cm and the teammate focuses the ball with the camera.
- **Illegal defense:** In addition to the 30 s penalty the robot will receive a negative score for this move.
- **Illegal attack:** In addition to the 30 s penalty the robot will receive a negative score for this move.
- **Incapable player** and **Request for pickup/Request for service:** To encourage teams to build robust robots, in addition to the time penalty the robot will receive a negative score for each of the moves. This also means if a team requests a pickup and extends it to a request of service, the robot will receive -2 points for this combined move.

There is no overall game performance or positioning rated by the referees, as we believe this is already covered by the sum of the specific rules.

4 Discussion

The three approaches presented in this paper are all based on the idea of judging the play of individual robots during multiple games in different team compositions. This idea is different from regular human team sport events, where teams on the level of world championships are announced in advance and remain mostly constant throughout the tournament. The players then have the chance to practice together and develop a team game strategy beforehand, which often becomes an important factor for winning. We could potentially adapt our approaches to having fixed teams for a tournament and announcing those in advance. However, as most teams are located far away from each other, we believe that it would remain difficult for teams to train together for financial and logistical reasons and most of the training would still be performed on the tournament. In addition, developing a game strategy is still possible in our proposed approaches, as the teams compositions will be announced at least some hours in advance, which gives the teams time to adapt to the new circumstances.

All proposed approaches support specialization of team players. Teams are highly encouraged to develop different game behaviors for goal keepers, defenders and strikers as the robot's team mates might themselves have different specializations. In order to perform well in teams with all kinds of robots with different abilities, each robot must be able to switch roles accordingly.

Whichever approach for ranking is followed, having a common team communication protocol for the robots will be advantageous and thus foster its use.

It could be based on one of the existing team communication protocols shared between teams in the league. One possibility is the *mitecom* protocol from team FUmanoids, which is popular among European RoboCup teams. In the SPL, it has already been shown that teams could adapt to a common team communication protocol without causing major complications. We therefore aim to discuss the requirements for such a protocol with all teams during the next world championships and then publish a team communication protocol shortly afterwards so teams have enough time to convert their own team communication.

In general, as the teams can focus on one or two robots in terms of hardware maintenance and the joint teams will highly encourage teams to share software and ideas with others, we believe that all of our proposed approaches would lead to an increase in the overall game performance within the league.

5 Conclusions

Drop-In games address the issue of ever increasing effort and cost for contributing to the RoboCup Humanoid league. Teams can participate with a single robot only and thus the entry barrier will be lowered for new universities.

Since there are many questions yet to solve, e.g. the number of games that need to be played for a robust ranking result, Drop-In games should be introduced as a technical challenge for a start. With the gained experience, the Humanoid League may gradually adopt the Drop-In approach as a general scheme to address the challenges of the 2050 soccer game between humans and robots as a research community and still preserve the competitive element.

References

1. Gerndt, R., Seifert, D., Baltes, J., Sadeghnejad, S., Behnke, S.: Humanoid robots in soccer. IEEE Rob. Autom. Mag. **22**(3), 147–154 (2015)
2. Robocup Humanoid League: Results for Robocup (2015). Web page: https://www.robocuphumanoid.org/hl-2015/results/. Accessed 11 Apr 2015
3. Humanoid League Technical Committee: Robocup soccer humanoid league rules and setup - for the 2015 competition in hefei. Technical report, RoboCup (2015)
4. Dixit, A.K., Nalebuff, B.J.: The art of strategy (2008)
5. Turner, T.: How to assess soccer players without skill tests. www.gaasa.org/ftpfiles/AssessPlayers.pdf. Accessed 25 Mar 2016
6. N.N. Humanoid league proposed roadmap. www.robocuphumanoid.org/wp-content/uploads/HumanoidLeagueProposedRoadmap.pdf. Accessed 25 Mar 2016
7. N.N. Middle size robot league rules and regulations (2016). http://wiki.robocup.org/images/0/0f/Robocup-msl-rules-2016.pdf. Accessed 25 Mar 2016
8. N.N. Mixed team communication protocol. https://github.com/fumanoids/mitecom. Accessed 25 Mar 2016
9. N.N. RoboCup standard platform league (NAO) Rule Book (2015). www.tzi.de/spl/pub/Website/Downloads/Rules2015.pdf. Accessed 25 Mar 2016

RAFCON: A Graphical Tool for Task Programming and Mission Control

Sebastian G. Brunner$^{(\boxtimes)}$, Franz Steinmetz$^{(\boxtimes)}$, Rico Belder,
and Andreas Dömel

Robotics and Mechatronics Center (RMC) of the German Aerospace Center (DLR),
Oberpfaffenhofen, Wessling, Germany
{sebastian.brunner,franz.steinmetz,rico.belder,andreas.domel}@dlr.de

Abstract. There are many application fields for robotic systems including service robotics, search and rescue missions, industry and space robotics. As the scenarios in these areas grow more and more complex, there is a high demand for powerful tools to efficiently program heterogeneous robotic systems. Therefore, we created RAFCON, a graphical tool to develop robotic tasks and to be used for mission control by remotely monitoring the execution of the tasks. To define the tasks, we use state machines which support hierarchies and concurrency. Together with a library concept, even complex scenarios can be handled gracefully. RAFCON supports sophisticated debugging functionality and tightly integrates error handling and recovery mechanisms. A GUI with a powerful state machine editor makes intuitive, visual programming and fast prototyping possible. We demonstrated the capabilities of our tool in the SpaceBotCamp national robotic competition, in which our mobile robot solved all exploration and assembly challenges fully autonomously. It is therefore also a promising tool for various RoboCup leagues.

1 Introduction

Managing the heterogeneous modules (e.g. navigation, vision, manipulation etc.) of a robot is challenging, as the scenarios in common robotic application fields like household and industries grow more and more complex. In this work, we thus focus on how complex tasks can be programmed and how all subsystems of a robot orchestrated at a central instance using visual programming and hierarchical state machines.

For solving complex tasks, one approach is to semantically specify the robot and its environment in a planning domain on which a task planner can be used to infer all steps for reaching a certain goal, which is also specified in the planning domain. PDDL [13] is a common solution for such planning problems and is often used in service robotic scenarios [12]. Such planners often suffer from over- or under-constraint models and fail if a real world failure cannot be represented

---

S.G. Brunner and F. Steinmetz have contributed equally to this work.

© Springer International Publishing AG 2017
S. Behnke et al. (Eds.): RoboCup 2016, LNAI 9776, pp. 347–355, 2017.
https://doi.org/10.1007/978-3-319-68792-6_29

in their environment model [4]. Furthermore, they have a much higher computational footprint. Therefore, they are not suited for many real-world tasks, e.g. industrial scenarios.

Alternatively, state machines [11] often come into play to specify the behavior of the robot in a more bottom-up like approach (see [5,9,14]). The robotic system is always in a certain state and proceeds to the next state depending on internal or external events. As classical state machines have problems coping with complex scenarios, powerful dialects were invented like *statecharts* [8] and *SyncCharts* [1]. They augment a classical state machine with hierarchy and concurrency concepts, preemption handling, error recovery and data management. Our state machine dialect uses and adapts many of these features and is furthermore based on *flowcharts* in regards of its eventless design.

Specifically for programming robotic tasks, there exist many tools. Next to well-designed solutions for educational purposes like *Scratch* [17] or *NXT-G* [10] from LEGO Mindstorms, all tools designed for real world robots suffer from certain problems. For some tools, maintenance and support was canceled, e.g. *ROS Commander* [14], *RobotFlow* [7] or *MissionLab* [2], others do not offer their code to the open source community, like *Gostai Studio* [3], or do not provide a graphical editor, such as *SMACH* [4].

Therefore, we developed RAFCON, a visual programming tool, allowing for the creation of hierarchical state machines. It is written in Python, as the language is interpreted, easy to learn and can be integrated with software modules of other languages. RAFCON was created completely from scratch. It is inspired by the flow control tool *Bubbles*, which has been developed at our institute some years ago [20]. Before starting with the implementation, experienced roboticist of our institute elaborated a long list of requirements. The key advantages of our tool are the novel visualization supporting state machines of several hundreds of states (see Sect. 4), powerful error recovery mechanisms, sophisticated debugging functionalities and usability and intuitiveness to allow for fast prototyping.

Furthermore, RAFCON enables collaborative state machine development. During the SpacebotCamp 2016[1], we successfully used RAFCON as both an autonomous task control software on a mobile robot as well as part of a mission control center setup with powerful remote monitoring and control capabilities. The mission in the SpacebotCamp included autonomous exploration and localization on a moon-like terrain, as well as object detection and assembly, all within a 60 min time limit (see Fig. 1). Thereby, many challenges had to be tackled that are also common e.g. in the RoboCup Rescue League.

The paper is structured as follows: At first we explain the core framework in Sect. 2. The following Sect. 3 describes all important components of the GUI. After proofing the capabilities of our task programming tool in the case study in Sect. 4, we will summarize our results and future work in Sect. 5.

---

[1] http://s.dlr.de/ura7.

Fig. 1. The left figure shows the state machine for the SpaceBotCamp, in which we took part with our Lightweight Rover Unit (LRU, [19]). On the right, the LRU is depicted while it mounts a blue container onto the red base station. (Color figure online)

2   Core Framework

The core of the RAFCON framework mainly consists of the *state machine* and the *execution engine*. Hereby, next to the logical flow, also data flow concepts are supported. All of these concepts are described in the following.

State machine: A state machine contains an execution engine and a *root state* that is the starting point of the execution. State machines are hierarchical, meaning that there are states that can contain child states.

State: The states of a state machine are the instances at which actions take place (Moore machine). There are four different types of states:

- *Execution states* are the essential states as they contain a user-defined function called `execute`, which is written in Python code. This `execute` function serves as connection to other middleware. These states cannot have any children.
- *Hierarchy states* group several child states. Each hierarchy state has a fixed *start state* that defines the entry point of the state.
- *Concurrency states* also group several child states, however all of these child states are evaluated concurrently, i. e. in parallel. The subtype *preemptive concurrency state* stops all child states, as soon as one child state has finished its execution, while a *barrier concurrency state* waits for all child states to finish.
- *Library states* are intended to reuse state machines. They simply wrap a whole state machine.

Outcome: Each state has two or more outcomes. As the name implies, these elements define the possible exit statuses of a state. Mandatory outcomes are *aborted*, in case an error occurred in the state, and *preempted*, for which the state was preempted from outside.

Transition: States are connected via transitions. A transition starts at an outcome and either ends in a sibling state or in an outcome of a parent state. If a state ends with a certain outcome, the transition connected to that outcome is followed to determine the next state.

Data port: Next to outcomes, states can also have *input data ports* and *output data ports*. They correspond to parameters respectively return values of functions. Data ports have a name, type and default value.

Data flow: Data ports of the same type can be connected using data flows. Thereby, the value assigned to the source ports gets forwarded to the target port.

Execution engine: The execution engine runs a state machine, starting at the root state. If a hierarchy state is reached, the execution goes down in the hierarchy to the defined start state. The execution can split up, if a concurrency state is executed. The hierarchy is went back up, if a transition is reached that goes from a child to its parent state. For execution states, the values assigned to the input data ports are forwarded to the `execute` function that can contain arbitrary code. The function can also assign values to the output data ports and defines the outcome of the state.

Many features of the engine help in debugging and testing even complex state machines. The engine supports continuous and step mode. `execute_backwards` function. One can also command the engine to start execution at an arbitrary state. During the execution, a state machine can be changed on the fly. Finally, the execution can be controlled from a separate host, which is especially useful for mobile robots.

3   Graphical User Interface

The graphical user interface, shown in Fig. 2, is the most prominent feature of RAFCON. The central widget, the *Graphical State Machine Editor*, is the part of the GUI that renders RAFCON unique amongst other (visual) task programming tools. Next to the creation of state machines, this GUI enables the user to execute and monitor the state machine, also from remote. The GUI design was developed in cooperation with professional interface designers[2].

Concerning task engineering, visual programming is in our opinion superior to textual languages in this context due to several reasons: First of all, the overview and the understanding of a state machine is increased as the user builds a mental model [15] of it. Beyond that, the logic and data flows are visualized separately, which gives a clear view on the data handling and routing. Furthermore, visual programming is more intuitive. All this improves the speed of state machine creation.

---

[2] Interaktionswerk, https://interaktionswerk.de/.

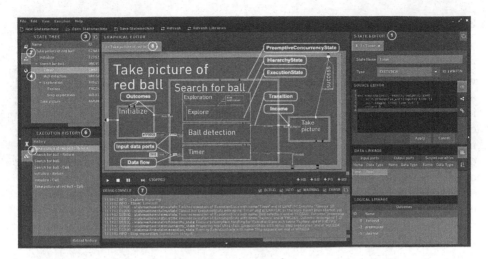

Fig. 2. An example state machine visually programmed in RAFCON. An autonomous agent explores a unknown environment until it localizes a red ball or stops because a timer preempts the execution. (Color figure online)

3.1 GUI Layout

The GTK+ widget toolkit was used to implement the GUI. A model-view-controller architecture is used for the GUI in order to communicate with the core. Thus, the core and the GUI are clearly separated. The four *Gestalt principles* [6] closure, similarity, continuity and proximity are heavily used to enhance information retrieval. A modular and flexible layout is achieved by making all sidebar tabs detachable, scalable and foldable.

All the different components of the GUI can be seen in Fig. 2. The right sidebar shows the *state editor* (1). It lists all details of a state, like name, descriptions, ports and connections and offers functionality to modify all of these properties. Execution states have in addition a source view to edit their `execute` function.

The left sidebar features many widgets with different purposes. A *Library manager* (2) organizes all library states in a clear fashion for easy reuse. The *State machine tree* (3) shows the structure of the state machine in a tree and can be used to explicitly select and navigate to a certain state. (4) is the *Global variable manager* managing all global variables, (5) shows the *Modification history* of all changes performed to the a state machine under construction and the *Execution history* (6) keeps track of all states during an execution including the context data.

The sidebar (7) at the bottom is the *Logging View*. Here all output of the executed states, the core and the GUI is collected and can be filtered by their logging level.

3.2   Graphical Editor

As already mentioned, the Graphical State Machine Editor is the most sophisticated element of the GUI. A clear visualization of complex state machines with highly nested hierarchies (see Sect. 4) is a big challenge. We implemented a mature navigation solution that is often experienced in digital maps. Zooming into the state machine (e.g. with the mouse wheel) reveals more of the details of lower hierarchy levels, while zooming out hides their details. The panning mechanism enables the user to translate the view to another position. Thus, the different hierarchy levels can be shown in varying degrees of detail, depending on the states the user is interested in.

The editor can also be used for direct interaction with the state machine for e.g. handling states, creating connections with via-points, copying and pasting of states and moving logic and data ports along the state border. Different view modes help the user to focus on the kind of information he is interested.

4   Case Study

In November 2015, the DLR Space Administration organized the SpaceBot-Camp 2016 with the aim to stimulate research and innovations in autonomous space robotic scenarios. The mission of the competition was to explore a rough, unknown terrain with a mobile robot, to localize and pick up two objects and finally to assemble those objects on a base station located on a crushed stone hill top, shown in Fig. 1. Next to having no uplink to the robot for the majority of the time, and complete communication blackouts for two occasions, there was also a constant two second communication delay. Concerning these restrictions, a highly autonomous behavior was required from the LRU robot [18] to solve the challenge in less than 60 min.

Our robot accomplished all tasks in only half of the given time limit. Hereby, RAFCON played a central role in autonomously orchestrating all modules of the system, like navigation, manipulation and vision. An abstract overview of this system architecture is shown in Fig. 3.

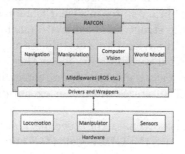

Fig. 3. The architecture in the SpaceBotCamp, in which RAFCON is coordinating the main software modules of our mobile robot.

RAFCON enabled us to collaboratively define the first two hierarchies of the overall state machine in the beginning. Subsequently, the state machine could be clearly divided into several sub-state-machines that were programmed by different developers. All in all, our final state machine consisted of more than 750 states and more than 1200 transitions. The maximum depth, i. e. number of hierarchies, was eight. This is a high number, considering the rather high-level nature of the used states.

During competition runtime, a ground station team was allowed to monitor the robot. Hereby, we were able to observe the current status of the state machine execution remotely. Therefore, several ground stations operators could subscribe to the state machine running on the robot and were supplied with status data of the state machine. This included the current execution point(s) and the values of data ports. Thus, an operator for navigation could observe the correct behavior of the robot during navigation, a manipulation expert could examine correct object assembly and an operator for computer vision could keep track of the detection and pose estimation procedures.

5   Conclusions

The visual programming tool RAFCON, presented in this paper, fills a gap in the robot programming domain. While for example ROS [16] unifies the communication in a heterogenous system, there is currently no graphical tool at hand for using that communication. RAFCON seamlessly integrates with ROS or other middlewares to orchestrate the different components in a way that they together perform a certain task. Our tool features a clear programming interface (API) that can be used for programmatic state machine generation or the integration with a logical planner. The state machine concept allows to quickly alter the execution by simply reconnecting some transitions. For this, no deep programming skills as required, as the GUI allows for intuitive visual programming.

Therefore, RAFCON is an ideal tool for mission control that can be used in different RoboCup competitions, for example the Logistics or Rescue League. This has been proved in the SpaceBotCup, in which similar requirements compared to the mentioned RoboCup leagues had to be met. A video of RAFCON is presented on https://www.youtube.com/watch?v=35dUykJandU.

We are constantly improving RAFCON and planning to release it as open source by the end of the year via GitHub. By then, the documentation will be finished and the implementation be stable.

Acknowledgment. This work has been funded by the Helmholtz-Gemeinschaft Germany as part of the project RACELab, by the Helmholtz Association, project alliance ROBEX, under contract number HA-304 and by the European Commission under contract number FP7-ICT-608849-EUROC.

References

1. André, C.: SyncCharts: a visual representation of reactive behaviors. Rapp. de Recherche TR95-52 Université de Nice-Sophia Antipolis (1995)
2. Arkin, R.: Missionlab v 7.0 (2006). http://www.cc.gatech.edu/ai/robot-lab/research/MissionLab
3. Baillie, J.C., Demaille, A., Hocquet, Q., Nottale, M., Tardieu, S.: The urbi universal platform for robotics. In: First International Workshop on Standards and Common Platform for Robotics (2008)
4. Bohren, J., Cousins, S.: The SMACH high-level executive [ROS news]. IEEE Rob. Autom. Mag. **4**(17), 18–20 (2010)
5. Bohren, J., Rusu, R.B., Jones, E.G., Marder-Eppstein, E., Pantofaru, C., Wise, M., Mösenlechner, L., Meeussen, W., Holzer, S.: Towards autonomous robotic butlers: lessons learned with the PR2. In: Robotics and Automation (ICRA), 2011 IEEE International Conference on, pp. 5568–5575 (2011)
6. Chang, D., Dooley, L., Tuovinen, J.E.: Gestalt theory in visual screen design: a new look at an old subject. In: Proceedings of the Seventh World Conference on Computers in Education Conference on Computers in Education: Australian Topics, vol. 8, pp. 5–12. Australian Computer Society, Inc (2002)
7. Côté, C., Létourneau, D., Michaud, F., Valin, J.M., Brosseau, Y., Raïevsky, C., Lemay, M., Tran, V.: Code reusability tools for programming mobile robots. In: Intelligent Robots and Systems (IROS), IEEE/RSJ International Conference on, pp. 1820–1825 (2004)
8. Harel, D.: Statecharts: a visual formalism for complex systems. Sci. Comput. Program. **8**(3), 231–274 (1987)
9. Jentzsch, S., Riedel, S., Denz, S., Brunner, S.: TUMsBendingUnits from TU Munich: RoboCup 2012 logistics league champion. In: Chen, X., Stone, P., Sucar, L.E., van der Zant, T. (eds.) RoboCup 2012. LNCS, vol. 7500, pp. 48–58. Springer, Heidelberg (2013). doi:10.1007/978-3-642-39250-4_5
10. Kelly, J.F.: LEGO MINDSTORMS NXT-G Programming Guide. Apress, New York City (2010)
11. Krithivasan, K.: Theory of Automata, Formal Languages and Computation. New Age International (P) Ltd., New Delhi (2014). ISBN (10): 81-224-2334-5. ISBN (13): 978-81-224-2334-1
12. Leidner, D., Borst, C., Hirzinger, G.: Things are made for what they are: solving manipulation tasks by using functional object classes. In: Humanoid Robots (Humanoids), 12th IEEE-RAS International Conference on, pp. 429–435 (2012)
13. Mcdermott, D., Ghallab, M., Howe, A., Knoblock, C., Ram, A., Veloso, M., Weld, D., Wilkins, D.: PDDL - the planning domain definition language. Tech. Rep, Yale Cent. Comput. Vis. Control (1998)
14. Nguyen, H., Ciocarlie, M., Hsiao, K., Kemp, C.: ROS commander (ROSCo): behavior creation for home robots. In: Robotics and Automation (ICRA), 2013 IEEE International Conference on, pp. 467–474 (2013)
15. Navarro Prieto, R., Cañas, J.J.: Are visual programming languages better? The role of imagery in program comprehension. Int. J. Hum Comput Stud. **54**(6), 799–829 (2001)
16. Quigley, M., Conley, K., Gerkey, B., Faust, J., Foote, T., Leibs, J., Wheeler, R., Ng, A.Y.: ROS: an open-source robot operating system. In: ICRA Workshop on Open Source Software, vol. 3 (2009)

17. Resnick, M., Maloney, J., Monroy Hernández, A., Rusk, N., Eastmond, E., Brennan, K., Millner, A., Rosenbaum, E., Silver, J., Silverman, B., et al.: Scratch: programming for all. Commun. ACM **52**(11), 60–67 (2009)
18. Schuster, M., Brand, C., Brunner, S., Lehner, P., Reill, J., Riedel, S., Bodenmüller, T., Bussmann, K., Büttner, S., Dömel, A., Friedl, W., Grixa, I., Hellerer, M., Hirschmüller, H., Kassecker, M., Marton, Z.C., Nissler, C., Rueß, F., Suppa, M., Wedler, A.: The LRU rover for autonomous planetary exploration and its success in the SpaceBotCamp challenge. In: Submitted to IEEE International Conference on Autonomous Robot Systems and Competitions (ICARSC) 2016 (2016)
19. Wedler, A., Rebele, B., Reill, J., Suppa, M., Hirschmüller, H., Brand, C., Schuster, M., Vodermayer, B., Gmeiner, H., Maier, A., Willberg, B., Bussmann, K., Wappler, F., Hellerer, M.: LRU-Lightweight Rover Unit. In: ASTRA (2015)
20. Widmoser, H.: Interaction planning for collaborative human-robot assembly tasks. Master's thesis, TU München (2012)

Communication-Less Cooperation Between Soccer Robots

Wei Dai, Qinghua Yu, Junhao Xiao$^{(\boxtimes)}$, and Zhiqiang Zheng

College of Mechatronics and Automation,
National University of Defense Technology, Changsha, China
weidai_nudt@foxmail.com, junhao.xiao@ieee.org
junhao.xiao@hotmail.com, http://nubot.trustie.net/

Abstract. This paper focuses on communication-less multi-robot cooperation, particularly, we present our research results on ball passing between MSL soccer robots without communication. Under this condition, the robots cannot share localization with teammates using wireless communication. Therefore, a novel method of color recognition is applied to recognize and localize the other robots. According to the positions of the teammates and obstacles, the robot that dribbles will find the best point for passing and the other robot will adjust its position and state for receiving. Two experiments are designed to test the localization accuracy with the front camera system. Finally, the method is evaluated under the 2015 MSL technique challenge rule, which proves the effectivity of the proposed method.

Keywords: Multi-robot cooperation · Communication-less cooperation · Soccer robots · RoboCup middle size league

1 Introduction

The robotic soccer system is a complicated multi-robot system, like human soccer teams, the robots have to accomplish a series of actions by cooperation with each other. As known, precise cooperation depends on stable communication among robots. However, no commonly used communication method is prone to limited bandwidth and communication distance. And the defect is especially terrible in the complex electromagnetic environment such as the RoboCup venue [1, 2].

In this work, we focus on cooperation without communication between soccer robots. In the current MSL matches, robots achieve cooperation using wireless communication. For example, in a simple passing cooperation, the robot which is dribbling the ball has to know the position of its teammate which is ready for receiving. As a matter of fact, the robot cannot obtain the information in real time stably because of communication interference and delay, which may lead to failure of cooperation. Hence, researches have been attempting to improve the cooperation mechanism in multi-robot systems under unreliable communication. Most work focus on the improvement of communication protocols or cooperation strategy, but these methods fails when the communication is interrupted. To deal with this problem, we have

S. Behnke et al. (Eds.): RoboCup 2016, LNAI 9776, pp. 356–367, 2017.
https://doi.org/10.1007/978-3-319-68792-6_30

designed a method to enable communication-less cooperation between robots. Based on the proposed mechanism, each robot will be able to make decisions according to the data that collected by its own sensor.

The rest of the paper is organized as follows. In Sect. 2, the related work is shortly overviewed. Section 3 gives a formal description of the problem. In Sect. 4, the proposed method is detailed. Experiments and results, together with a field of report during RoboCup 2015 is presented in Sect. 5. Section 6 concludes the paper and discusses the future research directions.

2 Related Work

In the field of distributed multi-robot system, cooperation is a hot research topic. Moreover, wireless is the most common way of communication in the cooperation, but at the same time, wireless communication is always susceptible. There are two ways to improve the cooperation reliability in the distributed multi-robot system.

Improve the reliability of communication. Most of the time, the failure of cooperation is caused by communication delay. Therefore, Wang et al. attempt to improve the reliability with Predict-Fuzzy logic communication [3] and later adopt a hybrid communication protocol [4] for multi-robot cooperation. Alexander et al. propose a new wireless communication protocol [5] by combining WNet [6] with multicast instead of unicast.

Improve the cooperation strategy. When the delay cannot be reduced or eliminated effectively, the cooperation strategy will be improved to adapt to the communication with delay. Gao et al. compensate the state estimation error caused by a delay in the measurements which are predicted in advance [7]. Rekleitis et al. present an algorithm for the complete coverage of free space by a team of mobile robots with the line-of-sight communication [8]. Meng et al. speed up the reconnection procedure for the strategies, implicit communication through vision sensors is proposed to establish a movement plan to recover the explicit communication [9]. And Tyler et al. adopt an effective task allocation method for multi-robot cooperation, in order to deal with the sporadic and unreliable communication [10].

To the best of our knowledge, pioneer research on communication-less cooperation started very early in the nineties of last century [11, 12], however, the method cannot deal with complex multi-robot systems such as MSL.

3 Problem Formulation

In this paper, all experiments are conducted on our NuBot MSL soccer robot platform [13, 14], and the algorithm is implemented under the open source Robot Operating System (ROS) [15], which is becoming the *de facto* standard of robotic software. As one league with the longest history among RoboCup, lots of scientific and technical progresses have been achieved in MSL, and its games are becoming more and more fluent and fierce. Therefore, in recent years, the MSL final has been serving as the grand finale of RoboCup, which gives the opportunity to all audiences and participants to enjoy the game together.

Besides competitions, MSL also conducts two challenges every year, i.e., the Technique Challenge and Scientific/Engineering Challenge, which encourages new technique and scientific progress and push MSL to step forward towards the RoboCup Grand Challenge. The research presented here is motivated by the MSL Technique Challenge 2015, which stays unchanged in the coming RoboCup 2016 Leipzig, Germany.

The challenge asks the question "whether the MSL soccer robots are able to make passes without communication?" [16]. It is played in a 12 m x 8 m MSL field made of artificial grass (smaller than the normal field of 18 m x 12 m) and carried out by two active robots. During the challenge, wireless communications must be disconnected for all the robots, and the field APs (Access Point) should also be shut down. At the beginning, two robots are placed manually on the field in advance, and the ball is placed on one penalty spot of the field. Furthermore, two black obstacles, which are similar in size to a MSL robot, are placed at random positions. The robots should be placed as one on each side of the field, so does the obstacles, as shown in Fig. 1(a). The robot which is on the same side with the ball has to detect the ball and grab it, then dribble it for 1 m at least. Afterwards, the robot has to pass the ball to the other robot. After a successful pass, the robots are required to swap their field side, during the swap, the ball should also be dribbled to the other field side, as shown in Fig. 1(a). In the below, the coordinate system of the field defined in Fig. 1(b) will be used, i.e., the whole field is divided into two parts named *my_field* and *opp_field* respectively.

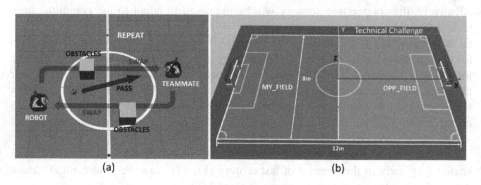

Fig. 1. (a) The rough process and (b) the field of the technical challenge

4   Problem Solution

The flow chart of the proposed solution is illustrated in Fig. 2. At first, the passer robot catches the ball and locates the receiver robot with its front camera. Then revise its position for passing considering the ball and obstacles. At the same time, the receiver robot will adjust its pose to receive. After accomplishing a round of passing, they have to swap their position and restart a new round. The four steps will be explained in the next subsections.

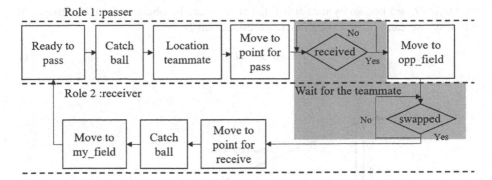

Role 1 :passer

Fig. 2. Flow chart of the proposed communication-less bass passing

4.1 Locating the Teammate with a Color Card

Due to the difficulties of the omnidirectional vision system in distinguishing between teammates and obstacles (all black that demanded in the MSL rules), we have equipped a front camera to each robot. Moreover, in order to recognize the teammates, two color cards have been placed at the front of the robot, as shown in Fig. 3.

In MSL, color cards are originally used for audiences and referees to distinguish between the two teams in the competitions. Here, they represent the difference between the teammate and obstacles, which could be recognized by color segmentation [17, 18] from images of the front camera. A modified color look-up table segmentation method has been employed [19], which is efficient and accurate, a typical segmentation result has been drawn in Fig. 3.

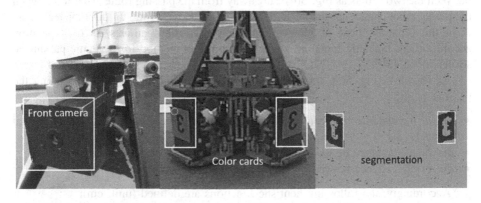

Fig. 3. The color cards (segmentation) and the front camera (Color figure online)

In order to locating the teammate, a trigonometric method has been utilized, considering the height of the front camera and the color card is known in advance. As showed in Fig. 4, the vertical distance from the ground to the front camera D_F and to the target D_T are known by measuring, the angle α can be obtained from the image. In this way, we can obtain a rough distance estimation D by:

$$D = \tan \alpha \times (D_F - D_T) \tag{1}$$

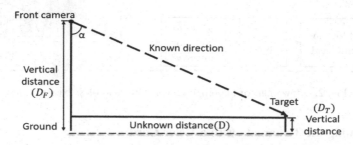

Fig. 4. Sketch of trigonometric relation

4.2 Point for Passing

After catching the ball, the passer robot can pass directly at the current position without considering the two obstacles. However, this may lead to two unexpected situations: Firstly, the robot cannot find the teammate which is in the back of the obstacles; secondly, the ball may be blocked on the way to the opponent field. Therefore, a better point should be selected for passing to raise the success rate of cooperation.

On the choice of the passing point, the principle is to make sure that the passer robot can see the receiver robot and the effectual obstacles (obstacle is effectual when it between the two robots as Fig. 5(b)) stay away from the passing route. Therefore, when the passer robot cannot see the receiver robot, it will move a little bit until the teammate is in the camera's field of view. Then the passer robot adjusts its own position according to a heuristic function, which is a common method for dynamic passing in soccer robots [20].

As shown in Fig. 5(a), three distances have been considered for determining the passing point:

- **dis_a:** the distance between the effectual obstacle and the passing route (ineffectual obstacle: $dis\_a \rightarrow +\infty$)
- **dis_b:** the distance between the passing point and the current position
- **dis_c:** the distance between the receiver robot and the passing point.

Accordingly, the following heuristic functions are defined (unit: cm):

$$h_a(p) = \begin{cases} 0 & dis\_a \leq 50 \\ (dis\_a - 50)/150 & 50 < dis\_a < 200 \\ 1 & dis\_a \geq 200 \end{cases} \tag{2}$$

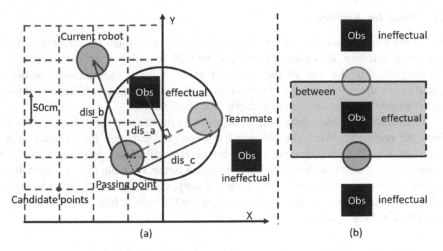

Fig. 5. (a) Three distances in the heuristic function (b) effectual obstacle

In other words, the distance between the obstacle and the robot within the scope of *(50, 200)* is linearly mapped to *(0, 1)*. When the distance is less than 50 cm, $h_a(p)$ is set to 0. And it will be set to 1 when the distance is larger than 200 cm. The value of $h_a(p)$ represent the influence of the corresponding obstacle and the $h_a(p)$ are multiple as the same number of obstacles.

$$h_b(p) = \begin{cases} (300 - dis\_b)/200 & 100 \le dis\_b \le 300 \\ 0 & else \end{cases} \tag{3}$$

According to the rule, the robot must dribble the ball for at least 1 m, while at the same time longer distance dribbling means less reliable. As a result, the distance between the candidate passing point and the robot within the scope of *(100, 300)* is linearly mapped to *(0, 1)*, leaving 0 for other distances, as shown in (3).

$$h_c(p) = \begin{cases} (400 - dis\_c)/300 & 100 \le dis\_c \le 400 \\ 0 & else \end{cases} \tag{4}$$

According to experiments using the front camera, the color card can be well recognized at the distance between 100 cm to 400 cm. Therefore, the *dis_c* related part is defined as in (4).

To determine the passing point, a series of candidates in the same side with a interval of 50 cm, as showed in Fig. 5(a), are evaluated according to $h(p)$. The best point for passing is that with the maximal $h(p)$.

$$h(p) = 0.5 * \sum h_a(p) + 0.25 * h_b(p) + 0.25 * h_c(p) \tag{5}$$

where the weights are experimental tuned, according to the performance of passing.

4.3   Point for Receiving

Due to the localization error, if the receiver robot doesn't adjust the position and state on its own initiative, it is difficult to receive the ball. In our strategy, the receiver robot will keep face to the ball all the time and grabs it when the ball rolls across the centerline. In the whole process of cooperation, the receiver robot will keep its position near the middle circle, where is conducive for receiving.

As mentioned above, there is also an obstacle on the opponent field, which may block the receiving. When the obstacle has been placed within the effective area as shown in Fig. 5(a), the receiver robot should also adjust its position to avoid the influence of the obstacle. Since the receiver robot doesn't dribble the ball, its point for receiving is chosen from some static points simply according to the effectual obstacle and the current position of passer robot (cannot see the ball) or ball (can see the ball), as detailed in Tables 1 and 2.

Table 1. Adjust position according to the effectual obstacles (x: cm)

passer_pos	receiver_pos
passer_pos.x > 0	*receiver_pos.x = −200*
passer_pos.x < 0	*receiver_pos.x = 200*

Table 2. Adjust position according to the effectual obstacles (y: cm)

obstacle_pos	passer_pos (not see ball) | ball_pos (see ball)	receiver_pos
obstacle_pos.y > 50	*anywhere*	*receiver_pos.y = −150*
obstacle_pos.y < −50		*receiver_pos.y = 150*
else	*passer_pos.y > 0 | ball_pos.y > 0*	*receiver_pos.y = 150*
	else	*receiver_pos.y = −150*

There are two special cases: Firstly, if there is no effectual obstacle around the receiver robot, it will maintain unmoved; secondly, when $-50 \leq obstacle\_pos.y$ 50 and the receiver robot cannot see the ball neither the passer robot, it will maintain unmoved too. Actually, the passer robot will try to find the receiver robot in such a situation.

4.4   Swapping the Position

According to the rules, the robots have to swap their positions after accomplishing a round of passing. Positions of the ball and the robot have been used as a flag that divides the different stages of swapping.

As shown in Table 3 and Fig. 1(a), the robot selects the next action according to its position and the ball position. In this way, robots can swap their positions and repeat the cooperation.

Table 3. Different stages of swapping (start with *ball_pos.x < 0*)

ball_pos	robot_pos	status of robot
ball_pos.x < 0	*robot_pos.x < 0*	*kick ball and wait for the teammate receives ball*
ball_pos.x > 0	*robot_pos.x < 0*	*move to opp_field*
ball_pos.x > 0	*robot_pos.x > 0*	*wait for the teammate (dribbler) moves to my_field*
ball_pos.x < 0	*robot_pos.x > 0*	*ready to receive ball and enter the next round*

5 Experiments

In order to evaluate the method of cooperation, we have designed three experiments. Sections 5.1 and 5.2 test the performance of teammate localization with the influence of distance, angle and relative velocity. Section 5.3 draws experiments under the rules of technical challenge, and makes comparisons against another method.

5.1 Influence of Distance and Angle

Two robots have been placed on the field without any obstacles, one (observer) is static on the point *(0, 0)* and facing front, the other one (observed) is placed at different points as Table 4 lists and facing observer. The purpose of this experiment is to test the performance of the color card based localization method with respects to distance and angle.

Table 4. Different points where observed robot placed

Points (cm)	X: 100–250		
Y: −100–100	*(100, −50)*	*(200, −80)*	*(250, −100)*
	(100, 0)	*(200, 0)*	*(250, 0)*
	(100, 50)	*(200, 80)*	*(250, 100)*

The result is shown in the following Fig. 6, each point has three positions:

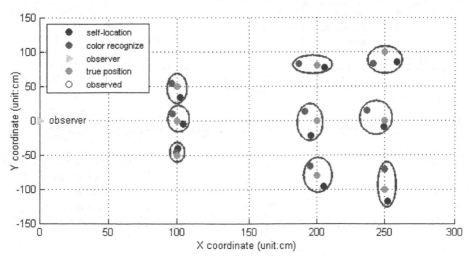

Fig. 6. Different positions of each point (Color figure online)

- **Blue:** observed own self-localization result using the omnidirectional vision system;
- **Red:** observed location by color recognition of the observer;
- **Green:** ground truth.

According to the results, the distances between three positions have an error less than 30 cm. According to the maneuvering characteristics of our NuBot robots, the error is acceptable, as the receiver robot would be able to catch the coming ball with its motion reaction. Furthermore, it could be seen that the error between red and green points has the tendency to increase along with the distance, but relative stable in the angle. On the other hand, the error between blue and green points is randomized according to the distance and angle.

5.2   Influence of Relative Velocity

In most of the time, the robots are in motion when cooperating with others. This experiment is intended to test the performance of the method when the robots are moving. Two robots have been placed on the field without any obstacles. Then robot1 (observed) moves along the straight line between *(100, −200)* and *(100, 200)*, and robot2 (observer) moves along the line between *(−100, −200)* and *(−100, 200)*. The velocity of robot1 is twice as robot2. First stage: they start from $y = -200$ at the same time until robot1 reach *(100, 200)*. Second stage: robot1 turn back and robot2 keeps moving to *(−100, 200)*. There are three movement trajectories recorded separately in the two stages and displayed in Fig. 7.

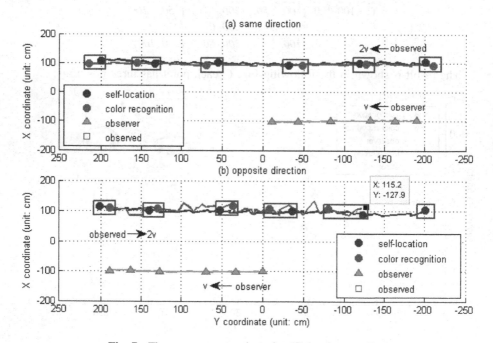

Fig. 7. Three movement trajectories (Color figure online)

- **Blue:** recorded by robot1 (self-location)
- **Red:** recorded by robot2 (color recognition)
- **Green:** recorded by robot2 (self-location)

From the results, the key factor for localization accuracy is not simply the distance between two robots, but also their relative velocity. As can be seen, when the two robots move along with the same direction and the relative velocity is v ($v \approx 1$ m/s), the error between blue and red locus is acceptable. However, if the relative velocity is increased to $3\,v$, the localization error will be terrible or even failed, as Fig. 7(b) represents. When they move along with the opposite direction, the red locus undulated seriously and disappear when observed robot $y < -127.9$. Under this condition, the cooperation will be irresponsible.

5.3 Influence of Obstacles

In order to evaluate the performance with regards to obstacles, two robots have been placed on each field, and then make passing with obstacles or without obstacles, respectively. Furthermore, the obstacles have been placed in the effective area:

- *Two robots make passing in current positions after grabbing ball;*
- *Two robots adjust their positions according to the obstacles as the above methods.*

Finally, we do 20 times passing experiments and record the success rate of passing and maximum times of seriate passing. The result is shown in Fig. 8:

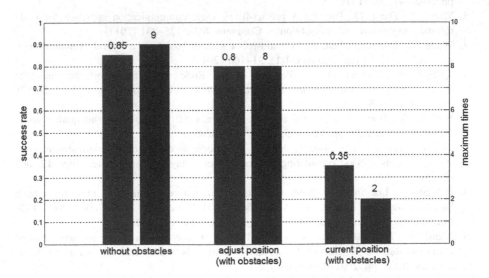

Fig. 8. Make passing with obstacles or without obstacles

It can be seen, the success rate decreases markedly without adjusting the position considering the obstacles. Furthermore, the passing is insensitive to obstacles if the robots adjust their positions. The maximum times of seriate passing have the similar trend as the success rate, which means that the swapping method is valid. Actually, our team has won the second place in the MSL technical challenge of RoboCup 2015.

6 Discussion and Conclusions

In this work, we focused on cooperation without communication between soccer robots. This paper is mainly about two issues: how to recognize and localize the receiver robot and how to pass the ball to it. The former concerns with machine vision, while the latter involves cooperation strategy. As a result, we proposed method for communication-less cooperation based on color card recognition, and a new passing strategy. Under the condition of a low relative velocity and a short distance between two robots, the success rate can reach a high level.

In further research, we are looking to achieve a longer distance cooperation based on other sensors, such as the RGB-D camera Kinect. With depth information, we hope more communication-less cooperation ways can be established.

References

1. http://www.robocup2015.org/
2. Kitano, H., Asada, M., Kuniyoshi, Y., Noda, I., Osawa, E.: RoboCup: the robot world cup initiative. In Proceedings of the First International Conference on Autonomous Agents, pp. 340–347, ACM (1997)
3. Wang, T., Dang, Q., Pan, P.: A predict-fuzzy logic communication approach for multi robotic cooperation and competition. J. Commun. 6(3), 225–231 (2011)
4. Wang, T., Dang, Q., Pan, P.: A multi-robot system based on a hybrid communication approach. Stud. Media Commun. 1(1), 91–100 (2013)
5. Tiderko, A., Bachran, T., Hoeller, F., et al.: RoSe — a framework for multicast communication via unreliable networks in multi-robot systems. Robot. Auton. Syst. 56(12), 1017–1026 (2008)
6. Bachran, T., Bongartz, H.J., Tiderko, A.: A framework for multicast and quality based forwarding in manets, pp. 120–125, Acta Press (2005)
7. Wei, G., Jian, Y., Ju, L., Bo, X., Junwei, Y.: Cooperative location of multiple unmanned surface vessels (USVs) considering communication delay. J. Harbin Eng. Univ. 12, 003 (2013)
8. Rekleitis, I., Lee-Shue, V., New, A.P., et al.: Limited communication, multi-robot team based coverage. In: Robotics and Automation, 2004. Proceedings. ICRA 2004. 2004 IEEE International Conference on. IEEE, vol. 4, pp. 3462–3468 (2004)
9. Meng, Y., Nickerson, J.V., Gan, J.: Multi-robot aggregation strategies with limited communication. In: Intelligent Robots and Systems, 2006 IEEE/RSJ International Conference on. IEEE, pp. 2691–2696 (2006)
10. Tyler, G., John, A.: Effective task allocation for evolving multi-robot teams in dangerous environments (2013)
11. Genesereth, M.R., Ginsberg, M.L., Rosenschein, J.S., Cooperation without communication. In: The National Conference on AI, Philadelphia, PA, pp. 51–57. August 1986
12. Arkin, R.C.: Cooperation without communication: multiagent schema-based robot navigation. J. Robot. Syst. 9(3), 351–364 (1992)

13. Xiao, J., Lu, H., Zeng, Z., et al.: NuBot team description paper 2015. In: Proceedings of RoboCup (2015)
14. Xiong, D., Xiao, J., Lu, H., Zeng, Z., Yu, Q., Huang, K., Yi, X., Zheng, Z.: The design of an intelligent soccer-playing robot. Ind. Robot: Int. J. **43**(1), 91–102 (2016)
15. Quigley, M., Conley, K., Gerkey, B., Faust, J., Foote, T., Leibs, J., Wheeler, R., Ng, A.Y.: ROS: an open-source robot operating system. In: ICRA Workshop on Open Source Software, vol. 3, no. 3.2, p. 5 (2009)
16. http://wiki.robocup.org/images/3/3f/Msl-rules_2015.pdf
17. Ferman, A.M., Tekalp, A.M., Mehrotra, R.: Robust color histogram descriptors for video segment retrieval and identification. IEEE Trans. Image Process. **11**(5), 497–508 (2008)
18. Gönner, C., Rous, M., Kraiss, K.-F.: Real-time adaptive colour segmentation for the robocup middle size league. In: Nardi, D., Riedmiller, M., Sammut, C., Santos-Victor, J. (eds.) RoboCup 2004. LNCS, vol. 3276, pp. 402–409. Springer, Heidelberg (2005). doi:10.1007/978-3-540-32256-6_33
19. Liu, F., Lu, H., Zheng, Z.: A modified color look-up table segmentation method for robot soccer. In: Proceedings of the 4th IEEE LARS/COMRob, vol. 7 (2007)
20. Bruce, J., Zickler, S., Licitra, M., et al.: CMDragons: dynamic passing and strategy on a champion robot soccer team. In: Robotics and Automation, 2008. ICRA 2008. IEEE International Conference on IEEE, pp. 4074–4079 (2008)

Decentralized Reinforcement Learning Applied to Mobile Robots

David L. Leottau[1]([⊠]), Aashish Vatsyayan[2], Javier Ruiz-del-Solar[1], and Robert Babuška[2]

[1] Advanced Mining Technology Center, Department of Electrical Engineering, Universidad de Chile, Av. Tupper 2007, Santiago, Chile
dleottau@ing.uchile.cl
[2] Delft Center for Systems and Control, Delft University of Technology, 2628 CD Delft, The Netherlands

Abstract. In this paper, decentralized reinforcement learning is applied to a control problem with a multidimensional action space. We propose a decentralized reinforcement learning architecture for a mobile robot, where the individual components of the commanded velocity vector are learned in parallel by separate agents. We empirically demonstrate that the decentralized architecture outperforms its centralized counterpart in terms of the learning time, while using less computational resources. The method is validated on two problems: an extended version of the 3-dimensional mountain car, and a ball-pushing behavior performed with a differential-drive robot, which is also tested on a physical setup.

Keywords: Multiagent learning · Decentralized control · Reinforcement learning · Robot soccer

1 Introduction

Reinforcement learning (RL) has been increasingly used to learn complex behaviors for robots in the real world [1,2]. One of the main challenges is the large number of training trials required, especially in systems with many state and action variables [3]. For such problems, distributed reinforcement learning can be used to address this issue [4]. For instance, in mobile robotics, a common high-level motion command is the desired velocity vector (e.g.: $[v_{right}, v_{left}]$ for a differential robot, or $[v_x, v_y, v_\theta]$ for an omnidirectional robot). If each component of this vector is handled individually, a distributed control scheme can be applied. By taking care of the coordination among the agents, it is possible to use decentralized methods [5] to learn behaviors which require these motion commands, taking an advantage of parallel computation and other benefits of multiagent systems (MAS) [4,6].

In Decentralized Reinforcement Learning (DRL), a problem is decomposed in several learning tasks, or sub-problems, whose information and resources are managed separately and these tasks work together toward a common goal. In

S. Behnke et al. (Eds.): RoboCup 2016, LNAI 9776, pp. 368–379, 2017.
https://doi.org/10.1007/978-3-319-68792-6_31

systems with multidimensional action spaces, each individual action variable is handled by a separate agent.

In this paper we propose to use DRL for mobile robots, where each component of the desired velocity vector (e.g.: $[v_l, v_w]$, linear and angular speed for the particular case of a differential-drive robot) is learned by a separate agent. Since most of the MAS works reported in the literature do not address or validate MultiAgent Learning (MAL) algorithms with multiple-state, stochastic, and real world problems [4], our goal is to show that MAS are also applicable to real-world problems like robotic platforms, by using a DRL architecture. Thereby, two separate problems are considered. The first is an extended version of the three dimensional mountain car (3DMC) [7], which is a common RL test bed. The second is a ball-pushing behavior, a soccer task performed with a differential-drive robot in a noisy and stochastic setting, which is also tested with a physical setup. Both validation problems are modeled and implemented by using a Centralized RL (CRL) and a DRL architecture, in order to compare and analyse both approaches.

The main contribution of this paper is twofold: first, we propose a DRL scheme for learning individual behaviors in the context of mobile robots; second, we compare CRL with DRL on two different validation problems. To the best of our knowledge, this is the first decentralized architecture for learning on mobile robot platforms, along with a comparison with the centralized RL counterpart.

The remainder of this paper is organized as follows: Sect. 2 gives a brief introduction to DRL, Sect. 3 introduces the control problems, Sect. 4 presents and analyses the experimental results, Sect. 5 presents the related work, and Sect. 6 concludes the paper and outlines future work.

2 Decentralized Reinforcement Learning

In DRL, the learning problem is decomposed into several sub-problems which as learned in parallel by separate agents. The MAS perspective yields several potential advantages if the problem is approached with decentralized learners and the coordination is taken care of [4]:

- The learning speed might be higher compared to a centralized agent which has to search an exponentially larger action space.
- The state space can be reduced if not all the state information is relevant to all the learning agents.
- Different algorithms, models or configurations can be used independently by the different agents.
- Memory and processing time requirements are smaller.
- Parallel or distributed computing implementations are suitable.

A DRL scheme also has several challenges which must be efficiently solved in order to take advantage of aforementioned MAS benefits. Agents have to coordinate their individual behaviors towards a coherent and desired joint behavior. The formulation of a good DRL modeling and learning goal is a difficult problem [4].

3 Validation Problems

In order to validate the DRL approach, two different problems have been selected: the 3-Dimensional mountain car (3DMC), a canonical and already reported RL test-bed [7]; and the ball-pushing behavior, a noisy and stochastic real world application, which is performed with the MiaBotPro [8] differential-drive robot, and tested on a physical setup. These problems allow us to carry out a comparative analysis between a DRL scheme and its CRL counterpart. For the case of DRL implementations, both problems are modeled with two RL agents, no explicit coordination mechanism, or MAL algorithm; so, indirect coordination will emerge between the two independently learning agents.

3.1 Three-Dimensional Mountain Car

Centralized modeling: An under-powered car has to move to its goal state [7]. The slope of the mountain is shown in Fig. 1. The state has four continuous-valued features: $x, \dot{x}, y, \dot{y}$. The positions (x, y) have the range of $[-1.2, 0.6]$ and the speeds $(\dot{x}, \dot{y})$ are constrained to $[-0.07, 0.07]$. The agent selects from five actions: {Neutral, West, East, South, North}. West and East modify $\dot{x}$ by -0.001 and +0.001 respectively, while South and North modify $\dot{y}$ by -0.001 and $+0.001$ respectively. On each time step $\dot{x}$ is updated by $0.025(\cos(3x))$ and $\dot{y}$ is updated by $-0.025(\cos(3y))$ due to gravity. The goal state is $x \geq 0.5 \, and \, y \geq 0.5$. The agent begins at rest at the bottom of the hill. The reward is -1 for each time step until the goal is reached, at which point the episode ends and the reward is 0. The episode also ends, and the agent is reset to the start state, if the agent fails to find the goal within 5000 time steps.

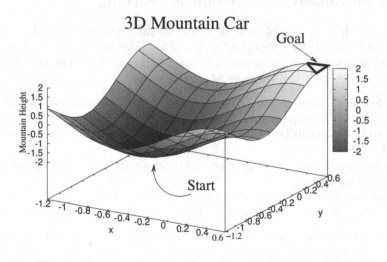

Fig. 1. 3D mountain car surface. Figure adopted from [7].

Proposed decentralized modeling: In the original 3D mountain car problem, a centralized approach is followed. The original 5 actions modeling (CRL-5a) make it impossible for the car to turn or perform a diagonal move at each time step. In order to make this problem fully decentralized, more realistic, and challenging, we have extended the action space by incorporating four more actions: {NorthWest, NorthEast, SouthWest, SouthEast}. Since the car is now able to move on x and y axes at the same time, $\dot{x}$, and $\dot{y}$ updates must be multiplied by $1/\sqrt{2}$ for these new four actions because of the diagonal moves. The decentralized approach employs two independent agents: $agent^x$ whose action space is $\{Neutral, West, East\}$, and $agent^y$ whose action space is $\{Neutral, South, North\}$. The learning task then be seen as two independent, parallel sub-tasks, $agent^x$ trying to reach the east top, and $agent^y$ trying to reach the north top.

Performance index: The evolution of the learning process is evaluated by measuring and averaging 25 runs. The performance index is the cumulative reward per episode, where $-5,000$ is the worst case, and zero the best, though unreachable case.

RL algorithm and optimized parameters: SARSA(λ) with Radial Basis Function (RBF) approximation with ϵ-greedy exploration is implemented for these experiments [1]. The exploration rate ϵ is decayed by 0.99 at the end of each learning episode. The following parameters are obtained after the hill climbing optimization procedure: learning rate (α), eligibility traces decay factor (λ), and exploration probability (ϵ). These parameters are detailed in Table 2 for each implemented scheme. Additionally, the number of Gaussian RBF cores per feature were also optimized: 9 cores to x and y, 6 cores to $\dot{x}$ and $\dot{y}$, and a standard deviation per core $1/2 \cdot |feature_{max} - feature_{min}|/nCores$.

A summary of the three implemented cases is shown below:

- *CRL Original model (CRL-5a):*
  Actions: {Neutral, West, East, South, North}
  Global reward function: $r = 0$ if goal, $r = -1$ otherwise
  Joint state vector: $[x, \dot{x}, y, \dot{y}]$
- *CRL Extended model (CRL-9a):*
  Actions: {Neutral, West, NorthWest, North,
  NorthEast, East, SouthEast, South, SouthWest}
  Global reward function: $r = 0$ if goal, $r = -1$ otherwise
  Joint state vector: $[x, \dot{x}, y, \dot{y}]$
- *Decentralized RL model (DRL):*
  Actions $agent^x$: {Neutral, West, East},
  Actions $agent^y$: {Neutral, South, North}
  Individual reward functions:
  $r_x = 0$ if $x \geq 0.5$, $r_x = -1$ otherwise; $r_y = 0$ if $y \geq 0.5$, $r_y = -1$ otherwise
  Joint state vector: $[x, \dot{x}, y, \dot{y}]$

3.2   Ball-Pushing

We are considering the ball-pushing behavior [9], a basic robot soccer skill [2] similar to [10,11], where a differential robot player attempts to push the ball and score a goal. The MiaRobot Pro is considered for this implementation (See Fig. 2. In the case of a differential robot, the complexity of this task comes from its non-holonomic nature, limited motion and accuracy, and especially from the highly dynamic and non-linear physical interaction between the ball and the robot's irregular front shape. The description of the desired behavior will use the following variables: $[v_l, v_w]$, the velocity vector composite by linear and angular speeds; a_w, the angular acceleration; γ, the robot-ball angle; ρ, the robot-ball distance; and, ϕ, the robot-ball-target complementary angle. These variables are shown in Fig. 2 at left, where the center of the goal is located in $\oplus$, and a robot's egocentric reference system is considered with the x axis pointing forwards.

RL procedure is carried out episodically. After a reset, the ball is placed in a fixed position 20 cm in front of the goal, the robot is set on a random position behind the ball and the goal. The successful terminal state is reached if the ball crosses the goal line. If robot leaves the field is also considered a terminal state. The RL procedure is carried out in a simulator and the bests learned policy obtained between the 25 runs for the CRL and DRL implementations are directly transferred and tested on the MiaBot Pro robot on the experimental setup.

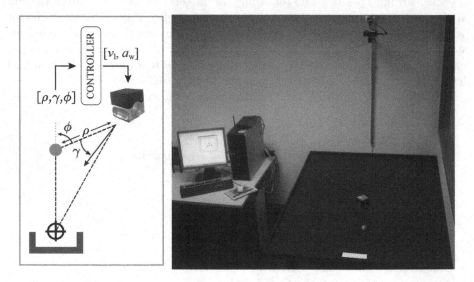

Fig. 2. Definition of variables for the ball-pushing problem (left), and, a picture of the implemented experimental setup (right).

Centralized modelling: For this implementation, proposed control actions are twofold $[v_l, a_w]$, the requested linear speed and the angular acceleration, where $A^{a_w} = [positive, neutral, negative]$. Our expected policy is to move fast and push the ball towards the goal. That means: to minimize ρ, γ, ϕ; and to maximize v_l. Thus, this centralized approach considers all possible actions combinations $\mathcal{A} = A^{v_l} \cdot A^{a_w}$ and learns $[v_l, a_w]$ actions, from the observed joint state $[\rho, \gamma, \phi, v_w]$, where $[v_w = v_{w(k-1)} + a_w]$. States and actions are detailed in Table 1.

Table 1. Description of state and action spaces for the DRL modeling of the ball-pushing problem

Joint state space: $S = [\rho, \gamma, \phi, v_w]^T$			
Feature	Min.	Max.	N.Cores
ρ	0 mm	1000 mm	5
γ	−45 deg	45 deg	5
ϕ	−45 deg	45 deg	5
v_w	−10 deg/s	10 deg/s	5
Decentralized action space: $A = [v_l, a_w]$			
Agent	Min.	Max.	N.Actions
v_l	0 mm/s	100 mm/s	7
a_w	−2 deg/s^2	2 deg/s^2	3
Centralized action space: $A = [v_l \cdot a_w]$			
$A_T = A^{v_l} \cdot A^{a_w} = 5 \cdot 3 = 15$ actions			

Decentralized modelling: Differential robot velocity vector can be split in two independent actuators, right and left wheel speeds $[v_r, v_l]$ or linear and angular speeds $[v_l, v_w]$. To keep parity with the centralized model, our decentralized modelling considers two single agents for learning v_l and a_w in parallel as it is depicted in Table 1. In this way, the *ball-pushing* behavior can be decomposed in two sub-task, *ball-shooting* and *ball-goal-aligning*, which are performed respectively by $agent^{v_l}$ and $agent^{a_w}$. The joint state vector $[\rho, \gamma, \phi, v_w]$ is identical to the one proposed for the centralized case.

A common reward function is considered for both CRL and DRL implementations, it is shown in expression (1), where P_{bg} is the distance where the ball crossed goal line with respect to the center of the goal, $gpSize = 75\,mm$ is the distance from the center of the goal to the post, $K = 10$ is a constant gain, and *max* features are normalization values taken from Table 1.

$$R(s) = \begin{cases} K \cdot (1.1 - |P_{bg}|/(gpSize)) & \text{if goal} \\ -(\rho/\rho_{max} + \gamma/\gamma_{max} + \phi/\phi_{max}) & \text{otherwise} \end{cases} \quad (1)$$

Performance index: The evolution of the learning process is also evaluated by measuring and averaging 25 runs. Percentage of scored goals across trained episodes is considered as performance index:

$\%ofScoredGoals = scoredGoals/Episode$, where $scoredGoals$ are the amount of scored goals until the current training $Episode$. Final performance is also measured running again a thousand episodes with the best policy (between 25) obtained per each tested scheme.

RL algorithm and optimized parameters: A RBF SARSA(λ) algorithm with softmax action selection is implemented for these experiments [1]. Boltzman exploration temperature is decayed as:

$\tau = \tau_0 \cdot exp(-dec \cdot episode/maxEpisodes)$, where $episode$ is the current episode index and $maxEpisodes = 1000$ trained episodes per run. Thereby, the following parameters are optimized: learning rate (α), eligibility traces decay factor (λ), Boltzman exploration initial temperature (τ_0), and exploration decay factor (dec). Obtained values after optimization are listed in Table 1. Furthermore, number of discretized actions for the linear velocity are optimized obtaining $A^{v_l} = 5$ for the CRL scheme and $A^{v_l} = 7$ for the DRL.

4 Experimental Results and Analysis

4.1 Three-Dimensional Mountain Car

Figure 3 shows a performance comparison between: the original implementation of 3DMC proposed at [7], CRL-5a; the extension of that original problem where 9 actions are considered, CRL-9a; and a decentralized scheme, DRL; It is important to remember that a better performance tends from negative to zero. Table 2 shows the averaged final performance of the last 100 episodes. Our results for CRL-5a (red dotted line in Fig. 3) converges considerably faster than results presented in [7], it can be due to parameter optimization, and because we have implemented a RBF approach instead CMAC for continuous states generalization. CRL-9a converges slower than the original one as it is expected because of the augmented action space. Notice that DRL speeds-up convergence and outperforms both centralized schemes. From error bars in Fig. 3, it can be noticed that asymptotic performance is similar between the three implementations. Thereby, the most noticeable result is the fact that the DRL scheme is able to learn faster than CRL ones without loosing performance. Expressing learning speed as a *time to threshold* as it is presented in Table 2, DRL is two times faster than CRL-5a and it has a better performance in around 15 units. Further, DRL is almost three times faster than CRL-9a, its direct centralized counterpart, showing an outperform of around 35 units.

Regarding computational resources, from optimized parameters definition in Sect. 3.1, the DRL scheme uses two Q functions which consume $2 \cdot 9 \cdot 6 \cdot 9 \cdot 6 \cdot 3 = 17496$ memory cells, versus $9 \cdot 6 \cdot 9 \cdot 6 \cdot 9 = 26244$ of its CRL-9a counterpart; DRL consumes 1/3 less memory. Moreover, we have measured the elapsed time of both learning process along the 25 performed runs, the DRL took 0.62 h, being 1.56 times faster than CRL-9a, which took 0.97 h. These times are referential, experiments were performed with an Intel(R)Core(TM)i7-4774CPU@3.40Ghz with 4 GB in RAM. Notice than even for this simple problem with only two agents, there is a considerable memory consumption and processing time saving.

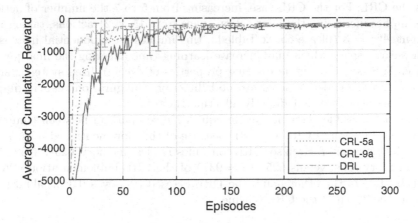

Fig. 3. 3DMC learning evolution plots. Results are averaged across 25 learning runs and error bars show the standard deviation (Color figure online).

Table 2. 3D mountain car parameters, final performances, and convergence time.

Approach	Optimized parameters	Final performance	Time to Th. †
DRL	$\alpha = 0.2, \lambda = 0.95, \epsilon = 0.06$	-205.49	71
CRL-5a	$\alpha = 0.25, \lambda = 0.95, \epsilon = 0.06$	-221.47	146
CRL-9a	$\alpha = 0.2, \lambda = 0.95, \epsilon = 0.06$	-240.91	195

†Time to threshold [12] is defined for this case as the number of episodes to achieve or overcome by first time a performance of -240.91.

4.2 Ball-Pushing

Figure 4 presents learning evolution plots and Table 3 shows the best policy final performances. Notice that learning evolution plots achieves lower performances than final performance presented in Table 3. It is because the performance of learning evolution plots is affected by the poor performance during early learning episodes, meanwhile final performance presented in the table is measured by using the best policy during the whole test. The DRL scheme sped-up learning time and improved the CRL final performance by 15%. If a time to threshold of 37.98% is considered (the best performance achieved by CRL during the learning process shown in Fig. 4), it can be said that the DRL scheme learns more than twice as fast as the CRL scheme, achieving this threshold in 441 learning episodes. It can be also noticed from error bars during early episodes, where they do not overlaps between them.

As it was mentioned in Sect. 3.2, number of discretized actions for the linear velocity were optimized obtaining $A^{v_l} = 5$ for the CRL scheme and $A^{v_l} = 7$ for the DRL. Notice that the DRL implementation allows a finer discretization than the CRL. For the CRL case, increasing from 5 to 7 the number of actions of v_l implies increasing the joint action space from 15 to 21 actions, taking into account $A^{a_w} = 3$ (please check Table 1), this implies an exponential increasing in the search space which may increase learning time affecting the final performance. This is one of the interesting properties of decentralized systems, since agents are independents, separate modellings or configurations can be implemented per agent without directly affecting the others.

It is not possible carrying out an equitative comparison between computational consumption of CRL vs. DRL because of the aforementioned 5 vs. 7 discretized actions for v_l. Even so, DRL consumes 1/3 less memory, $625 \cdot 7 + 625 \cdot 3 = 6250$ memory cells, versus $625 \cdot 15 = 9375$ of the CRL implementation (Please see Table 1). On the other hand, the DRL elapsed time was 0.36 h, almost the same as the 0.34 h of the CRL scheme.

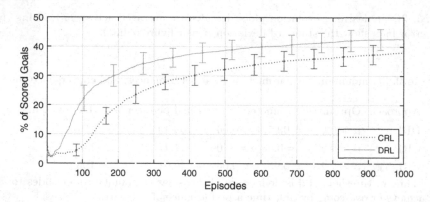

Fig. 4. Ball-pushing learning evolution plots. Results are averaged across 25 learning runs and error bars show the standard deviation.

4.3 Ball-Pushing: Physical Setup

An experimental setup is implemented in order to test learned policies onto a physical setup, which is shown in Fig. 2 at right. The differential drive robot Miabot Pro is used, it is a small cube with a size of $75 \times 75 \times 75$ mm and a weight of 0.55 kg. It has two wheels which are driven by two electro motors. The robot is connected via Bluetooth to a central computer close to the robot soccer platform which is $1.5\,\mathrm{m} \times 1\,\mathrm{m}$. A web camera above the platform provides position and orientation of the robot, ball, and goal. This central vision system operates at 30 frames per second. The robot position is identified by color segmentation

Table 3. Ball-pushing optimized parameters and best policy final performances of the simulated and real setup

Approach	Optimized parameters	Performance sim. (%)	Performance real (%)
DRL	$\alpha = 0.3$, $\lambda = 0.9$, $\tau_0 = 1$, $dec = 10$	75.28	68.57
CRL	$\alpha = 0.5$, $\lambda = 0.9$, $\tau_0 = 2$, $dec = 7$	62.15	57.14

and thresholding. The color patch on the robot make this approach convenient due to its simple nature and ease of implementation. The state observation is processed from the vision system, while speed of the wheels are transmitted through Bluetooth from the computer. These speeds are computed from the Q tables by using a greedy search policy.

The best learned policy obtained between the 25 runs carried out by simulation for the CRL and DRL implementations are directly transferred and tested on the MiaBot Pro robot on the experimental setup. The robot was positioned in seven different positions trying to cover the whole state space, and 10 trials were run from each position. The results from these experiments can be seen in Table 3, where performance is presented in percentage of success to score a goal considering the seventy attempts.

It can be seen from the Table 3 that DRL performs on average 11.43% better than CRL. Simulation and physical setup performances are similar which validates simulation experiments and results.

Some experiments for centralized and decentralized RL were recorded and can be seen in [13]. In this video it can be seen that actions are a bit abrupt, it is because of no smoothing or extrapolation of the discrete actions where carried out, policies were transferred directly from Q functions to the physical robot. Also, cases where the mark of the robot or some tracker was lost in the vision system were disregarded. These aspects should be improved for future implementations, however, the porpoise of this work is more focused to compare CRL and DRL approaches, than achieving an optimal performance.

5   Related Work

A multiagent RL application for the multi-wheel control of a mobile robot is presented in [14]; the robot's platform is decomposed into driving modules agents that are trained independently, in order to provide energy consumption optimization. In [15], the DRL of the soccer ball-dribbling behavior is accelerated by using transfer knowledge, there, each component of the omnidirectional biped walk (v_x, v_y, v_θ) is learned in parallel with single agents working on a multi-agent task. Similar to [9], where some layered learning strategies are studied and one of them involves the DRL of individual behaviors in the context of soccer robotics.

In [5], definitions of centralized and multiagent learning approach for reinforcement learning are presented. Both learning strategies are tested on a 2-link manipulator, and compared in terms of performance, convergence time, and computational resources. In [3], a distributed RL architecture is presented to learn the inverse kinematics of a 3-link-planar robot and the SCARA robot; experimental results have shown that it is not necessary that the decentralized agents perceive the whole state space in order to learn a good global policy. A multiagent influence RL approach is presented in [16], this uses agent's influences to estimate learning error between them; it has been validated with a multi-joined robotic arm.

6 Conclusions

This paper has proposed a decentralized reinforcement learning architecture for implementing behaviors with a mobile robot, where the individual components of the commanded velocity vector are learned in parallel by separate agents working in a multiagent task.

Two validation problems have been modeled and implemented: an extended version of the three dimensional mountain car, and a ball-pushing behavior performed with a differential-drive robot, which has been also tested on a physical setup. A DRL and its CRL counterpart scheme has been implemented for the two validation problems in order to compare and analyze strengths, weaknesses and properties of the DRL proposed framework.

Experimental results have evidenced that with less computational resources, and non direct coordination mechanism, DRL implementations have shown better performances and faster learning times than their CRL counterparts for all the implemented experiments. This empirically demonstrate that benefits of MAS are also applicable to more complex and real world problems like robotic platforms. It opens the door to explore applications with higher dimensional action spaces where a CRL scheme could not be easily implementable, like snake robots, multi-link robotic arms, omni-directional mobile robots, multi-rotor aerial vehicles, etc. Moreover, evaluating MAL algorithms with cooperation and coordination between agents is part of our ongoing schedule.

Acknowledgment. This work was partially funded by FONDECYT under Project Number 1161500. David Leonardo Leottau was funded under grant CONICYT-PCHA/Doctorado Nacional/2013-63130183. The authors would like to thank Technical University of Delft for providing the resources to test the learnt policies on an experimental setup.

References

1. Sutton, R., Barto, A.: Reinforcement Learning: An Introduction. MIT Press, Cambridge (1998)
2. Riedmiller, M., Gabel, T., Hafner, R., Lange, S.: Reinforcement learning for robot soccer. Auton. Robots **27**(1), 55–73 (2009)

3. Martin, J., Lope, H.D.: A distributed reinforcement learning architecture for multi-link robots. In: 4th International Conference on Informatics in Control, Automation and Robotics, ICINCO 2007. Number 3, Angers, Francia, pp. 192–197 (2007)
4. Busoniu, L., Babuska, R., De-Schutter, B.: A comprehensive survey of multiagent reinforcement learning. IEEE Trans. Syst. Man Cybern. Part C Appl. Rev. **38**(2), 156–172 (2008)
5. Busoniu, L., Schutter, B.D., Babuska, R.: Decentralized reinforcement learning control of a robotic manipulator. In: Ninth International Conference on Control, Automation, Robotics and Vision, ICARCV 2006, 5–8 December, Singapore, pp. 1–6. IEEE (2006)
6. Stone, P., Veloso, M.: Multiagent systems: a survey from a machine learning perspective. Auton. Robot. **8**(3), 1–57 (2000)
7. Taylor, M.E., Kuhlmann, G., Stone, P.: Autonomous transfer for reinforcement learning. In: The Autonomous Agents and Multi-agent Systems Conference (AAMAS), Number May, Estoril, Portugal, pp. 283–290 (2008)
8. Systems, M.: Miabotpro manual (2016)
9. Leottau, D.L., Ruiz-del-Solar, J., MacAlpine, P., Stone, P.: A study of layered learning strategies applied to individual behaviors in robot soccer. In: Almeida, L., Ji, J., Steinbauer, G., Luke, S. (eds.) RoboCup 2015. LNCS (LNAI), vol. 9513, pp. 290–302. Springer, Cham (2015). doi:10.1007/978-3-319-29339-4_24
10. Takahashi, Y., Asada, M.: Multi-layered learning system for real robot behavior acquisition. In: Kordic, V., (ed.) Cutting Edge Robotics, Number pp. 357–375, July 2005 (2004)
11. Emery, R., Balch, T.: Behavior-based control of a non-holonomic robot in pushing tasks. In: Proceedings 2001 ICRA. IEEE International Conference on Robotics and Automation (Cat. No.01CH37164), vol. 3, pp. 2381–2388. IEEE (2001)
12. Taylor, M., Stone, P.: Transfer learning for reinforcement learning domains: a survey. J. Mach. Learn. Res. **10**, 1633–1685 (2009)
13. Vatsyayan, A.: Video: centralized and decentralized reinforcement learning of the ball-pushing behavior (2016). https://youtu.be/pajMkrf7ldY
14. Dziomin, U., Kabysh, A., Golovko, V., Stetter, R.: A multi-agent reinforcement learning approach for the efficient control of mobile robot. In: 2013 IEEE 7th International Conference on Intelligent Data Acquisition and Advanced Computing Systems (IDAACS), vol. 2, pp. 867–873. IEEE (2013)
15. Leottau, D.L., Ruiz-del-Solar, J.: An accelerated approach to decentralized reinforcement learning of the Ball-Dribbling behavior. In: AAAI Workshops, Austin, Texas USA, pp. 23–29 (2015)
16. Kabysh, A., Golovko, V., Lipnickas, A.: Influence learning for multi-agent system based on reinforcement learning. Int. J. Comput. **11**(1), 39–44 (2012)

Searching Objects in Known Environments: Empowering Simple Heuristic Strategies

Ramon Izquierdo-Cordova[1], Eduardo F. Morales[1(✉)], L. Enrique Sucar[1],
and Rafael Murrieta-Cid[2]

[1] Instituto Nacional de Astrofísica, Óptica y Electrónica (INAOE),
Luis Enrique Erro No. 1, 72840 Tonantzintla, Pue, Mexico
{izquierdocr,emorales,esucar}@inaoep.mx
[2] Centro de Investigación en Matemáticas, A.C. (CIMAT),
Jalisco S/N, Col. Valenciana, 36023 Guanajuato, Gto, Mexico
murrieta@cimat.mx

Abstract. We consider the problem of exploring a known structured environment to find an object with a mobile robot. We proposed a novel heuristic-based strategy for reducing the traveled distance by first obtaining an exploration order of the rooms in the environment and then, searching for the object in each room by positioning the robot through a set of viewpoints. For the exploration order we proposed a heuristic based on the distance from the robot to the room, the probability of finding the object therein and the room area; integrated in a $O(n^2)$ complexity greedy algorithm that selects the next room. The experimental results show an advantage of the proposed heuristic over other methods in terms of expected traveled distance, except for full search which has a complexity of $O(n!)$. For the exploration within each room, we integrate the localization of horizontal flat surfaces with the generation of poses. With the set of poses, a similar heuristic establishes the exploration order that guides the robot path inside the room. The evaluation of the set of poses shows an average coverage of the flat surfaces of more than 90% when it is configured with an overlap of 40%. Experiments were performed with a real robot using three objects in a six-room environment. The success rate for the robot finding the object is 86.6%.

Keywords: Service robots · Object search

1 Introduction

A desirable skill of a service robots is to assist people by fetching and carrying objects that they require, even if they do not have precise information about the place where to find the object. The robot must then make decisions about the strategy to explore the environment and find the object as quickly as possible. To find an object, given a map of the environment, the robot has to decide in which order to traverse the map and how to search for objects in each place, as depicted in Fig. 1.

© Springer International Publishing AG 2017
S. Behnke et al. (Eds.): RoboCup 2016, LNAI 9776, pp. 380–391, 2017.
https://doi.org/10.1007/978-3-319-68792-6_32

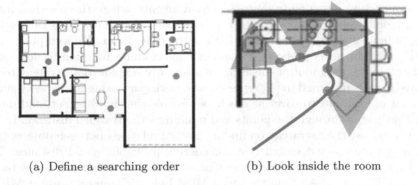

(a) Define a searching order   (b) Look inside the room

Fig. 1. To find an object the robot must first decide (a) an order to explore the rooms, and then (b) choose and visit a set of viewpoints inside the room.

We present a two-step object search strategy that uses a novel heuristic to determine the exploration order of a set of rooms and information about horizontal flat surfaces existing in the environment to complete an exploration route inside each room. The first step is based on the probability that the object is in the room, the room area, and the distance from the robot current position to each room. For the exploration in each room, it is proposed the integration of horizontal flat surfaces in the robot map for pose generation. With the set of poses, heuristics based on distances and visible areas guide the robot path inside the room. Experiments were performed with a real robot to search three different objects in a six-room environment, achieving a success rate of 86.6%.

2   Related Work

Searching objects in known environments requires, among others aspects, to define an exploration strategy, to plan and execute the routes according to the exploration strategy, and to recognize the object. Previous work addresses some of these aspects. Robot localization and object search are considered in [12], where a robot moves to unexplored 2D areas creating new nodes in a navigation graph representing the environment. The search path is calculated with a nearest-room-first strategy. With the same goal of finding the shortest path, a 3D exploration strategy is described in [11], where harmonic functions lead the robot to exploration boundaries. An alternative approach is presented in [1] where a robot explores and gathers information about the scene to determine the room in which it is located.

In [10] the authors assume that the robot has a map of the environment represented as 2D polygonal maps. To find routes that minimize the search time, the environment is decomposed into convex sections. A two-level heuristic looks, in the first level, for an order of exploration along sections based on a uniform probability density function which characterizes the object location. In the second level, individual segments are refined using the calculus of variations.

This approach is extended in [5] to 3D environments, where the search is made with a mobile robot equipped with a robotic arm of seven degrees of freedom having a limited scope camera placed at the top of its hand. A decomposition of the 3D environment is proposed in convex regions and a function to determine whether to move the robot or the arm. An alternative exploration strategy based on three steps is proposed in [4]: represent the workspace using Minkowsky sums, find a set of locations to cover as much as possible the environment, and find a route that passes through the points and minimizes the traveled distance. In [2], the authors base their strategy on finding a set of relations between objects that minimizes the expected search cost considering probability and distance. The work in [8] selects a group of locations where the object is supposed to be, based on probabilities obtained from the Open Mind Indoor Common Sense (OMICS) database. An exploration order of all rooms in the group is obtained based on Euclidean distances. A planner-independent formulation is presented in [13], in which the object search problem knowing the probability of the object being in a determined place is defined formally as a Stochastic Shortest Path. Three different algorithms to find the shortest route are proposed.

This work focuses on finding an exploration order in a known domestic environment given a probability distribution for the position of the object over the rooms, and the subsequent problem of finding a set of poses inside each room and a route for visiting them. In contrast to previous work, we propose a very efficient and simple heuristic to determine the room exploration order, which gives results close to the optimal solution. Additionally, we integrated the room exploration technique and the object search approach inside each room, and implemented the complete method in a real mobile robot.

3   Determining the Exploration Order

When exploring a set of rooms for searching an object several elements can be considered. If we want to minimize time, we could go to the closest places first. If we have information that the object has a good chance of being in a certain room, we could visit that room first as it gives us a higher chance of success. An additional element to take into account is the area of the room, since exploring a large room takes longer than a small one. Our proposed heuristic function seeks to balance the search criteria leveraging the strengths of simple strategies.

3.1   Heuristic Approach

Given a map of the environment with rooms on the map, $R_1, R_2, \ldots, R_n$, previously tagged by a user, our problem consists of finding an order to visit the n rooms, to minimize the expected time to find the object. Assuming that the robot moves at a constant velocity, this is equivalent to minimizing the expected traveled distance. We assume the robot can obtain $P_1, P_2, \ldots, P_n$ probabilities of finding the object in the locations; has information of the area of each room, $A_1, A_2, \ldots, A_n$; and can compute $d_1, d_2, \ldots, d_n$, the respective distances from the current position of the robot to each of the rooms. We define the proposed heuristic function as:

$$H(R_i) = \frac{P_i}{d_i\sqrt{A_i}} \tag{1}$$

Since the value of the heuristic is only used to select which room will be explored next, the area and distance values do not need to be normalized. Finally, to obtain the full order we use the greedy *BestLocalRatio* algorithm based on the previous heuristic (see Algorithm 1), where the best room to search is selected using Eq. 1, and from that room the next best room is selected. The process continues until all the rooms have been selected.

Algorithm 1. Best Local Ratio

Require: *RoomList*
Ensure: *ExploringOrderList*
1: *ExploringOrderList* ← *empty*
2: **repeat**
3:     **for all** *Room* in *RoomList* and not in *ExploringOrderList* **do**
4:         Compute heuristic in formula (1)
5:     **end for**
6:     Select *Room_i* with the maximum heuristic value
7:     Add *ExploringOrderList* ← *Room_i*
8: **until** |*RoomList*| = |*ExploringOrderList*|
9: **return** *ExploringOrderList*

3.2 Alternative Strategies

Determining the exploration order with the minimum expected time (distance) is NP-Hard [10], so several authors have proposed finding a solution through heuristics. In this work we have selected four alternative approaches, illustrated in Fig. 2. Five strategies are compared against the proposed heuristics in our experiments. Two use simple heuristics: nearest room and most probable room, and the other three try to minimize the expected distance traveled by the robot:

$$E(d) = \sum_{i=1}^{n} \left(D_i + \sqrt{A_i} \right) P_i, \tag{2}$$

where n is the number of rooms or nodes, P_i is the probability of finding the object in room i and D_i is the accumulated distance from the starting point of the robot to room i following the route through all rooms $j(j < i)$. i and j are room indexes according to the exploration order being evaluated. This equation is based on [10], adding the term $\sqrt{A_i}$ as an estimate to take into account the distance that the robot has to travel inside each room.

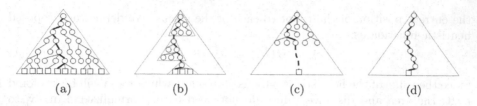

Fig. 2. A qualitative illustration of the exploration trees for the different strategies: (a) exhaustive search, (b) dominant strategies heuristic, (c) Monte-Carlo based methods, (d) greedy algorithms.

Exhaustive Search. A complete search in all possible orders is performed using the algorithm described in [6]. The route with the smallest expected value of distance of all possible paths that go through all rooms is selected. This method has a computational complexity $O(n!)$. Even using linear programming methods, the best existing algorithm has a complexity $O(n^2 2^n)$ [3].

Dominating Strategies Heuristic. For constructing the full path the room with the highest value using P_i/d_i is selected, where P_i is the probability of finding the object in room i, and d_i is the distance. After selecting the room with the highest value, a breath-first exploration is performed from that node until it reaches a depth of $\log n$ nodes, avoiding expanding those nodes that are not strictly dominant. The partial route with the shortest expected value of distance according to Eq. 2 is selected. This procedure is repeated until a full path is completed [10]. It has a computational complexity of $O(n^3 \log n)$.

Monte-Carlo Based Search. An exploration of the search tree is made until it reaches a predefined depth. In the experiments a depth of 10 nodes was used. From the leaf nodes in the expanded subtree, complete routes are constructed by randomly choosing nodes. These routes are used to evaluate the expected distance normalizing its value to $[0,1]$ with the formula $1/(1+E(d))$. Generating several random routes for each leaf node gives an estimation of the quality of the sub-route from the starting node to that leaf node. For determining the end node of the subtree to complete the random route it is used the Upper Confidence Bound for Trees (UCT) [7], that consists of evaluating from the root node in the exploration tree, which one is the best child.

Nearest and Most Probable Room. These two strategies use the greedy algorithm so they keep a computational complexity of $O(n^2)$. The nearest room strategy selects the closest room, while the most probable room strategy selects the most likely place. The results show that despite being extremely simple strategies, they get excellent results in special conditions.

4   Exploration Inside the Room

Getting the minimum set of poses to cover a polygon when the robot has limited visibility is a complex problem [9]. In order to reduce complexity, we have used a method based on randomly generating a set of N poses. Once we have the random set, each pose is evaluated to select those ones which observe the largest portion of the flat surfaces in the room (see Algorithm 2).

Algorithm 2. Pose Generator

Require: N = Number of randomly poses to generate
Ensure: *PosesList*
 1: Randomly generate N poses
 2: Delete unreachable poses
 3: **for all** pose in *PosesList* **do**
 4:    Compute *Visible Area*
 5: **end for**
 6: Delete pose with no *Visible Area*
 7: **for all** pair of poses in *PosesList* **do**
 8:    **if** pair is *nearby* **then**
 9:      Delete pose in pair with less *Visible Area*
10:    **end if**
11: **end for**
12: **for all** pair of poses in *PosesList* **do**
13:    **if** pair is *redundant* **then**
14:      Delete pose in pair with less *Visible Area*
15:    **end if**
16: **end for**
17: **return** *PosesList*

Unlike related work, our algorithm observes a surface from different viewpoints but not looking for complete reconstruction. For object search it is only important to see if the object can be recognized. We have a configurable control to re-observe flat surfaces as much as it is required depending on the conditions of the environment. The clutter condition can be determined based on the number and spatial distribution of objects on flat surfaces.

Once the robot is inside a room, the pose generation algorithm determines a set of poses for the robot for looking for the object (assumed to be over a flat surface), as well as a route to visit all the selected poses, or until the object is found. We use: (i) the *field of view (FOV)*, the maximum angle at which the sensor is capable of perceiving the observable world and (ii) the *depth of field (DOF)*, the space in front of the focus plane, between the first and last points acceptably sharp. When we intersect FOV with DOF we obtain what is known as *sensor visibility cone*. Since in this work the object search is supposed to be in a two-dimensional space, the visibility cone will be framed by a circular trapeze, but to facilitate geometric calculations we use a simple trapeze.

The pose generator algorithm randomly generates poses and then eliminates those that can not be reached by the robot. The next step eliminates poses that do not have a visible area in flat surfaces. The next filter compares each pair of poses and removes one of each pair considered as *nearby* poses. The pose of the pair that is kept is that one with the largest visible area. If the angle and the distance differences between two pairs of poses are lower than the given thresholds U_α and U_d, then they are considered *nearby*. A third filter eliminates *redundant* poses. Two poses are considered *redundant* if the intersection of their observed areas is larger than a proportion of the visibility cone of the object recognizer. This ratio, which we call overlap threshold, is a given value U_t, $0 \leq U_t \leq 1$. Finally, the algorithm delivers a set of poses that are reachable by the robot and observe the largest proportion of flat surfaces existing in the environment while the amount of overlap over the visibility area of different poses is controlled.

Once we have a set of poses to explore the environment, we must now decide how to go through them in order to find the object as fast as possible. The problem is similar to the traveling salesman problem, so we propose and compare three heuristic strategies to visit the set of poses:

Nearest Pose (NP). Assuming that the robot moves at a constant speed, the entire route is planned iteratively selecting the pose that has the shortest distance from the current one.

Largest Visible Surface Pose (LVSP). The idea behind this strategy is that a flat surface with the largest area is more likely to contain the searched object. The set of poses is grouped according to the flat surface they observe and each group is then sorted according the nearest pose. The group of poses with observations to the largest flat surface are visited first.

In Room Best Local Ratio (IRBLR). We use a similar strategy to *BestLocalRatio* that considers distances and visible areas. Since we assume equal probabilities to find the object in each flat surface, our heuristic takes the form: $H(R_i) = \frac{1}{d_i \sqrt{A_i}}$, being d_i the distance from the last pose to the new one, and A_i the visible area of pose i.

5 Experiments

We performed experiments to evaluate the performance of the proposed algorithms and show experimental tests with a real robot.

5.1 Room Order

To evaluate the strategies for the exploration order of rooms, a database of maps was created from real home plans divided in categories according to the number of rooms in each map. The selection includes small homes with three rooms to big residences with thirteen rooms. For each category, five different maps are considered. In total 55 home plans were tested (Fig. 3). Each map is labeled manually by the user, selecting a point within each room, and then automatically creating a complete graph with distances between each of the rooms.

Objects in real world have almost as many probability distributions as the number of them. Instead of selecting specific objects for testing, we chose several probability distributions to evaluate the exploration strategies and see how

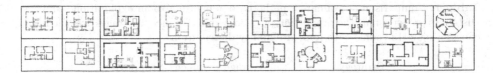

Fig. 3. Some of the maps tested in the experiments.

these differences affect the results. The distributions considered are: a uniform distribution; a normal distribution ($\mu = 0.5$, $\sigma^2 = 1.0$); a gamma probability distribution ($\kappa = 2.0$, $\theta = 0.2$); and an exponential distribution ($\lambda = 6.5$).

Although the objective is to minimize the expected time to find the object, we use instead the expected distance, assuming a constant speed for the robot. We decided to use as measure of distance the ratio over the optimal expected distance (Eq. 2) obtained with the exhaustive search strategy. This measure allows us to compare between maps with different distances between their rooms and even between maps with different numbers of rooms. Our simulation experiments were evaluated computing values of the expected distance as described in Eq. (2). All evaluated strategies compute only orders, and paths are computed by the same planning algorithm for all strategies.

Figure 4 illustrates the average expected distance for maps containing from 3 to 13 rooms, five maps for each size, for each one of the probability distributions

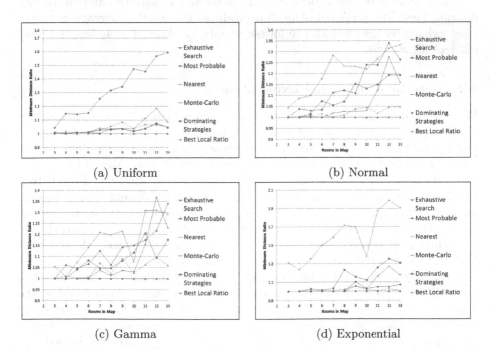

Fig. 4. Comparison of exploration strategies for real maps between 3 and 13 rooms using as reference the optimal expected distance. The probability of finding the object follows different distributions over the rooms.

Table 1. Comparison of evaluated methods to generate a room exploration sequence. Distances are shown as the proportion of the optimal distance. Averages are calculated considering 3–13 rooms with four probability distributions.

Strategy	Average distance wrt optimum	Std. dev.
Exhaustive search	1.0000	0.0000
Best Local Ratio	1.0281	0.0222
Monte-Carlo	1.0621	0.0900
Dominant strategies	1.0845	0.0678
Most probable	1.1523	0.1030
Nearest	1.2506	0.1188

used for object locations. The nearest room strategy produces values of expected distance close to the optimal values when the probabilities are equal between rooms (uniform distribution) but it has the worst results when the difference between probabilities is large (exponential distribution). The opposite case is presented with the most probable strategy. However, the proposed strategy being a combination of these two simple heuristics, produces expected distances close to the optimal values for all the distributions.

Table 1 shows average expected distances for all the map sizes and probability distributions. The proposed algorithm produces the smallest average distances after exhaustive search with the lowest variability. Also, it is among the most efficient algorithms.

5.2   Pose Generation and Exploration

We evaluated the quality of the set of generated poses considering the percentage of coverage of existing flat surfaces in the map and the percentage of the total visible area observed from more than one pose. We use a fixed number of poses (1000) because the rooms have similar areas, but it is possible to take into account the area of each room. We varied the overlap threshold from 0 to 1 in 0.2 increments and tested pose generation in seven different rooms. Results are summarized in Table 2. As expected, there is a relation between coverage and overlap. With a robust object recognizer and/or an almost-free-occlusion environment, it is desirable to have low overlap, with a threshold between 0.2 and 0.4, and a larger value in scenarios with more occlusions.

We compare the three strategies (NP, LVSP and IRBLR) to visit the set of poses. The evaluation metric used is the expected distance to be traveled by the robot. We assume an uniform distribution about the object location over every flat surface. Then the likelihood of a pose is given by the amount of visible area from that pose. The metric that evaluates the path over n poses is defined as:

$$E(d) = \sum_{i=1}^{n} (D_i P_i), \tag{3}$$

Table 2. Evaluation of the set of poses generated with Algorithm 2 in terms of percentages of coverage and overlap of the total flat surfaces when we change the overlap threshold.

	Coverage (%)		Overlap (%)	
	Average	Std. dev.	Average	Std. dev.
0.0	61.44	30.57	0.00	0.00
0.2	86.49	15.47	1.64	3.05
0.4	91.99	8.68	9.88	11.52
0.6	91.29	12.45	55.81	25.87
0.8	93.27	11.51	96.32	43.21
1.0	96.59	4.07	101.25	39.70

where D_i is the accumulated distance from the starting position of the robot to the pose i and P_i is the value of the visible area of the pose i normalized by the total area of all existing flat surfaces in the room.

Finding distances for all pairs of the complete set of poses has a high computational cost, so we use the Euclidean distance to speed up the process of generating paths. We generate five sets of different poses for each of the seven rooms in the environment. Some rooms contain one or two flat surfaces while the large room, which is the union of the other six, contains nine. For each strategy a path for each of the sets of poses is created and evaluated with the expected distance, Eq. 3. The results are shown in Fig. 5. In the rooms *bathroom, bedroom* and *study* there is just one flat surface, so that strategies do not differ in their traveled distances, while in the rest of the rooms with at least two flat surfaces, a slight advantage for the IRBLR method can be observed.

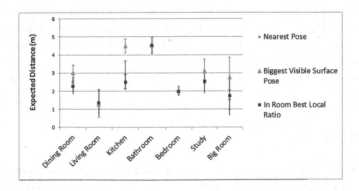

Fig. 5. Comparison of expected distances produced by the strategies to visit a set of poses that search for an object within a room.

5.3   Real Mobile Robot

We conducted experiments with a real robot searching for three different objects: *coke can, remote control* and *mug* in an environment similar to an apartment with 6 rooms. The room in which the objects were located was randomly generated following certain probability distribution for each object, and the flat surface for the object was selected according to each surface area. We located the object in the flat surface with a random pose using a uniform distribution. The robot started from a fixed initial position. We used a differential two wheeled Peoplebot platform equipped with a laser for navigation and a Kinect sensor for object recognition. As recognition algorithm we used *Tabletop* [14] configured with default parameters due to its good recognition performance, but specially for its capacity to recognize flat surfaces.

Table 3 summarizes the results. The robot has a success rate for the three objects of 86.6%. Although the average search times may seem high for the size of the environment, it should be noted that in the case of the *coke can* and *remote control* it includes the cases where the objects were not found and the whole path was traveled. In general, the locations of objects are concentrated in the first two most probable rooms according to the probability distribution.

Table 3. Results from five searches with three objects located at different positions in each repetition. *No object* corresponds to the whole path of the six rooms and is presented for comparison.

Success/trials	Coke can		Mug		Remote ctrl		No object	
	4/5		5/5		4/5		5	
	Avg	Stdev	Avg	Stdev	Avg	Stdev	Avg	Stdev
Time (min)	6.69	5.03	2.41	1.73	5.31	4.20	11.696	0.652
Distance (m)	22.59	16.03	7.85	5.61	20.85	14.91	39.549	3.023
Turns (degrees)	5251.00	3688.16	1809.00	1198.94	3722.40	3006.01	9155.222	757.460
Planned poses	16.40	9.81	8.40	4.62	12.00	10.07	27.333	1.581
Reached poses	13.00	10.65	4.20	3.42	9.20	7.36	23.889	2.421
Visited rooms	3.40	2.41	1.60	0.55	2.40	1.52	6.00	0.00

6   Conclusions

We proposed a novel heuristic-based strategy for a mobile robot to search for an object in a known environment based on a two-step approach. Firstly, obtaining an exploration order of the rooms in the environment based on a novel heuristic which takes into account the probability, the distance and the area of the rooms. And secondly, searching for the object in each room by randomly generating poses that are filtered and that observe flat surfaces in the environment. Additionally, we propose a heuristic method for visiting the set of poses based on distance and visible area. We implemented the proposed methods in a real robot and evaluated the integrated approach in a realistic environment. The experimental results with the real robot give evidence that the proposed approach can be used in object search applications with service robots. As future work we will develop strategies to determine the probabilities of different objects being in certain room in a home environment based on the Web and incorporate information of where objects were previously found using a Bayesian approach.

References

1. Aydemir, A., Pronobis, A., Gobelbecker, M., Jensfelt, P.: Active visual object search in unknown environments using uncertain semantics. IEEE Trans. Robot. **29**(4), 986–1002 (2013)
2. Aydemir, A., Sjöö, K., Folkesson, J., Pronobis, A., Jensfelt, P.: Search in the real world: active visual object search based on spatial relations. In: IEEE International Conference on Robotics and Automation (ICRA), pp. 2818–2824. IEEE (2011)
3. Bellman, R.: Dynamic programming treatment of the travelling salesman problem. J. ACM (JACM) **9**(1), 61–63 (1962)
4. Cabanillas, J., Morales, E.F., Sucar, L.E.: An efficient strategy for fast object search considering the robot's perceptual limitations. In: Kuri-Morales, A., Simari, G.R. (eds.) IBERAMIA 2010. LNCS, vol. 6433, pp. 552–561. Springer, Heidelberg (2010). doi:10.1007/978-3-642-16952-6_56
5. Espinoza, J., Sarmiento, A., Murrieta-Cid, R., Hutchinson, S.: Motion planning strategy for finding an object with a mobile manipulator in three-dimensional environments. Adv. Robot. **25**, 1627–1650 (2011)
6. Heap, B.: Permutations by interchanges. Comput. J. **6**(3), 293–298 (1963)
7. Kocsis, L., Szepesvári, C.: Bandit based Monte-Carlo Planning. In: Fürnkranz, J., Scheffer, T., Spiliopoulou, M. (eds.) ECML 2006. LNCS, vol. 4212, pp. 282–293. Springer, Heidelberg (2006). doi:10.1007/11871842_29
8. Kunze, L., Beetz, M., Saito, M., Azuma, H., Okada, K., Inaba, M.: Searching objects in large-scale indoor environments: a decision-theoretic approach. In: IEEE International Conference on Robotics and Automation (ICRA), pp. 4385–4390 (2012)
9. Rourke, J.O., Supowit, K., et al.: Some NP-hard polygon decomposition problems. IEEE Trans. Inf. Theor. **29**(2), 181–190 (1983)
10. Sarmiento, A., Murrieta-Cid, R., Hutchinson, S.: An efficient motion strategy to compute expected-time locally optimal continuous search paths in known environments. Adv. Robot. **23**, 1533–1560 (2009)
11. Shade, R., Newman, P.: Choosing where to go: complete 3D exploration with stereo. In: IEEE International Conference on Robotics and Automation (ICRA), pp. 2806–2811. IEEE (2011)
12. Sjö, K., Gàlvez-López, D., Paul, C., Jensfelt, P., Kragic, D.: Object search and localization for an indoor mobile robot. J. Comput. Inf. Technol. **17**, 67–80 (2009)
13. Trevizan, F., Veloso, M.: Finding objects through stochastic shortest path problems. In: Proceedings of the International Conference on Autonomous Agents and Multi-agent Systems, pp. 547–554. International Foundation for Autonomous Agents and Multiagent Systems (2013)
14. Willow Garage and ROS Community: ORK - Object Recognition Kitchen (2011). https://github.com/wg-perception/object_recognition_core

A Deep Learning Approach for Object Recognition with NAO Soccer Robots

Dario Albani$^{(\boxtimes)}$, Ali Youssef, Vincenzo Suriani, Daniele Nardi,
and Domenico Daniele Bloisi

Department of Computer, Control, and Management Engineering,
Sapienza University of Rome, via Ariosto, 25, 00185 Rome, Italy
{albani,youssef,nardi,bloisi}@diag.uniroma1.it,
suriani.1347908@studenti.uniroma1.it

Abstract. The use of identical robots in the RoboCup Standard Platform League (SPL) made software development the key aspect to achieve
good results in competitions. In particular, the visual detection process is
crucial for extracting information about the environment. In this paper,
we present a novel approach for object detection and classification based
on Convolutional Neural Networks (CNN). The approach is designed to
be used by NAO robots and is made of two stages: image region segmentation, for reducing the search space, and Deep Learning, for validation. The proposed method can be easily extended to deal with different
objects and adapted to be used in other RoboCup leagues. Quantitative
experiments have been conducted on a data set of annotated images captured in real conditions from NAO robots in action. The used data set
is made available for the community.

Keywords: Robot vision · Deep Learning · RoboCup SPL · NAO
robots

1 Introduction

Starting from 2008, the RoboCup Standard Platform League (SPL) involves
Aldebaran NAO as the common robot for the competitions. Due to the limited
computational power available, Computer Vision techniques adopted by the different teams are mostly based on color segmentation approaches. The success
of those solutions has been facilitated by special expedients, for example the
use of a red ball, controlled illumination, and yellow coloured goals. However,
the current trend in using more and more realistic game fields, with white goal
posts, natural light, and a ball with black and white patches, as well as person-
alized jersey shirts, imposes the adoption of robust detection and classification
methods, which can deal with a more realistic and complex environment.

In this paper, we propose a method for validating the results provided by
color segmentation approaches. In particular, we present a novel algorithm for
merging an adaptive segmentation procedure with a Deep Learning based validation stage, which exploits Convolutional Neural Networks (CNN). Our approach

© Springer International Publishing AG 2017
S. Behnke et al. (Eds.): RoboCup 2016, LNAI 9776, pp. 392–403, 2017.
https://doi.org/10.1007/978-3-319-68792-6_33

is designed to work in scenes with changes in the lighting conditions that can affect significantly the robot perception. The segmentation procedure follows a color based approach with a mechanism for automatically adapting the exposure and white balance parameters of the camera. The validation step consists in a supervised image classification stage based on CNN.

The main contributions of this paper are: (i) A dynamic white balance and exposure regularization procedure; (ii) A Deep Learning based validation step; (iii) A novel fully annotated data set, containing images from multiple game fields captured in real conditions. We present quantitative results obtained with different network architectures, from the simplest one (three layers) to more complex ones (five layers). To test and train our networks, we have created a specific data set, containing 6,843 images, coming from the upper camera of different NAO robots in action. The data set is fully annotated and publicly available.

The rest of the paper is organized as follows. Section 2 presents an overview of the object detection methods presented during the last years of Robocup competition together with a survey of the recent Deep Learning classification approaches. Section 3 contains the details of our method. The data set for training and testing is described in Sect. 4, while the quantitative experimental results are reported in Sect. 5. Conclusions are drawn in Sect. 6.

2   Related Work

The RoboCup 2050 challenge consists in creating a team of fully autonomous humanoid robot soccer players able to win a real soccer game against the winner of the FIFA World Cup. To deal with such a difficult goal, it is necessary to develop a vision system that is able to provide all the environmental information necessary to play soccer on a human level [3]. This means that: (1) a pure color based approach cannot be a feasible solution for the RoboCup 2050 challenge and (2) solutions able to provide articulated information about the scene are needed. In particular, the presence of different views and varying color information produced by the camera of a moving robot makes recognition a hard task, which cannot be solved with *ad hoc* solutions.

In this section, we briefly discuss the specific techniques currently used in the RobocCup SPL and then we provide an overview of more general, recent Deep Learning methods developed in the Computer Vision field.

The method described in [6] exploits color similarities for ball and goal recognition. The recognition routine is invariant to illumination changes and it is not computationally expensive, making it suitable for real-time applications on NAO robots. The detection of the objects (lines, ball, penalty marks, and goal posts) is obtained by merging geometrical (line detection and curve fitting [13]) and color information [12,17]. In addition, the ball motion model is combined with contextual information [3] to enhance the performance of the ball tracker and to carry out event understanding.

In the attempt of developing more accurate human-like vision system, recent approaches tend to work on the middle level of features, where the low level features are aggregated in order to increase scene understanding [1,10]. Convolutional Neural Network (CNN), as a hierarchical model based on low level features, has showed impressive performance on image classification [9], object detection [2], and pedestrian detection [11]. In the group of CNN based methods, DetectorNets [16] and OverFeat [15] perform the object detection on a coarse set of sliding-windows. On the other hand, R-CNN [4,5] works on the extraction of proposal regions, over the entire image at multiple scales, to be classified using a support vector machine (SVM) trained on CNN features.

Recognition approaches use machine learning methods based on powerful models to address the large number of object categories present in general scenes. Deep Models outperformed hand-engineering features representation in many domains [8]. For example, a Deep Learning model based on large and depth network (5 convolution layers and 3 fully connected ones) described in [9] performed image classification on the ImageNet ILSVRC-2010 data set better than the previous state-of-the-art methods. Moreover, single object detection based on deep Convolutional Neural Network [2] demonstrate to be more effective on ILSVRC-2012 and DeepMultiBox data sets with respect to previous object localization approach, thanks to the capacity of handling the presence of multiple instances of the same object in the processed image.

Here, our aim is to combine fast color segmentation techniques already in use in the SPL with more computationally demanding classification methods, in order to use CNN for NAO robot detection, even in presence of a limited hardware. We believe that the adoption of Deep Learning techniques adds an additional level of robustness to the NAO vision system and can lead to the use of context information for higher-level computation, e.g., behaviours.

3   Proposed Approach

Our functional architecture is shown in Fig. 1, where the CNN block is placed at the end. In our case, the use of CNN for classification purposes is important to obtain a validation of the extracted image regions, carried out in the initial part of the pipeline. It is worth noting that, even if Deep Learning procedures spread across various research fields thanks to the release of powerful and cheap hardware (e.g., GPUs for gaming), running those procedures on less advanced hardware (e.g., the ATOM CPU offered by the NAO platform) can overwhelm

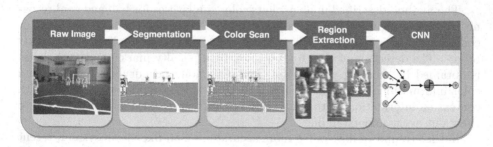

Fig. 1. Our pipeline for the deep learning NAO detection module.

the available computation power. As a possible approach for Deep Learning techniques to work on NAOs, we propose to have a pre-processing step that allow to reduce the amount of information to be tested by the CNN. In other words, we want to reduce the possible search space. This reduction is provided by the Segmentation, Color Scan, and Region Extraction functions in the pipeline.

During the last few years, different papers proposed solutions for using Deep Learning also for object detection without being able to merge it with a classification step [2,16]. Our method adopts the same approach, i.e., detection followed by classification, with the difference that the detection process does not involve Deep Learning techniques.

Segmentation. The input for the pipeline is an RGB image acquired by the camera of the robot at each cycle. The image is converted to the HSI (Hue, Saturation, and Intensity) color space and is processed to extract regions according to their color. In particular, all the regions that fall inside a given range on the Hue channel are replaced by the corresponding color (see step 2 in Fig. 1). A dynamic update of the white balance and the exposure is used to cope with possible illumination changes (e.g., light from windows) and to increase the robustness to lightning changes. To keep the acquisition rate of the camera consistent with real-time applications, the update of the camera settings is limited to once per second.

The adaptive camera setting update procedure is initialized with values calculated on contextual information. For the white balance, our approach uses the *green world assumption* (Assumption 1) to set the initial values.

Assumption 1. Given an input image, it is possible to establish an horizon line (knowing the robot structure) and to segment the part of the image placed below the horizon according to a neighbours color clustering procedure. The biggest segmented regions is green-coloured.

Nevertheless, there are cases in which the above assumption does not hold (e.g., the robot is looking outside the field border or another robot is standing close to the camera). To deal with possible inconsistencies, we use a threshold that allows for discarding images that present large variations in the Hue values with respect to the previously received images. Equation 1 illustrates the details of the white balance update procedure, where $max(.)$ and $min(.)$ represent the pixels with higher and lower Hue values, respectively.

$$wb_{t1} = (\frac{max(H_{t0}^n) - min(H_{t1}^n)}{n}) \cdot 100 \tag{1}$$

H_{ti}^n is the average value in the set H of n pixels coming from the images captured at time ti. Thus, wb_{t1} represents the variation in percentage over the Hue channel of the green region extracted according to Assumption 1.

Algorithm 1 shows the validation procedure for the pixels belonging to the set H, while Fig. 2 contains an example where the region selection process is applied for white balancing. The procedure for updating the camera exposure

396   D. Albani et al.

Algorithm 1. Validation

1: **procedure** VALIDATEREGIONS($Regions, H_{average}^{t_{i-1}}$)
2:     $H_{low} \leftarrow 60°$ ▷ high boundary for green
3:     $H_{high} \leftarrow 120°$ ▷ low boundary for green
4:     **for all** r **in** $Regions$ **do**
5:         $H_{avg}^{r,t_i} \leftarrow average(r)$
6:         **if** $(H_{avg}^{t_{i-1}} - H_{avg}^{r,t_i}) < threshold$ **then**
7:             $append(r, Accepted)$
8:             $H_{avg}^{t_i} \leftarrow H_{avg}^{t_i} + H_{avg}^{r,t_i}$ ▷ update H_{avg} for comparisons at time t_{i+1}
9:         **end if**
10:    **end for**
11:    **return** $Accepted, H_{avg}^{t_i}$
12: **end procedure**

---

is carried out by sampling green pixels from the image below the robot horizon line (thus avoiding possible outliers or strong sources of illumination). A mask with fixed weights (see Fig. 3) is used to compare samples from each region and to compute an overall value that is then tested against a predefined threshold. Such threshold is based on samples collected every 4 s and stored in memory. If a significant variation in the intensity of the current pixels with respect to the average of the stored ones is detected, then the camera exposure parameter is re-calculated accordingly.

Color Scan. Once the image has been corrected for possible changes in the illumination conditions, the next step is to scan it for detecting color changes. Our approach is based on the work presented in [13]. Due to the introduction of the realistic ball (a ball with black and white patches) in the SPL matches, the focus is on white-coloured areas: Regions with a sufficient number (i.e., greater than a fixed threshold) of white pixels are grouped together.

Fig. 2. Region selection process for white balance compensation.

Fig. 3. Adaptive exposure compensation according to the robot's interest areas (Color figure online).

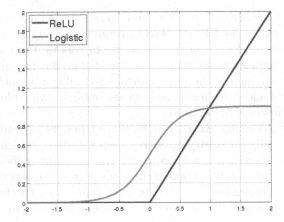

Fig. 4. The ReLU $f(x) = max(0, x)$ and the logistic function $f(x) = \frac{1}{1+\exp(-x)}$. Thanks to [18] for the original image.

Region Extraction. The image of a NAO robot in standing position can be enclosed in a rectangular bounding box with a larger height with respect to the width, while the image of a ball can be enclosed in a square. Therefore, regions are extracted and fed to a pre-trained Convolutional Neural Network.

CNN. Different CNNs have been tested to obtain a good trade-off between accuracy and computational load. A first CNN presents three layers, being the smallest and thus the fastest. Other networks reach up to five layers, as presented in [9]. Although inner parameters may change, all the convolutional layers present the same inner structure: Convolutional, Pooling, and Normalization layers. For limiting the computational needs, we have decided to use a single-scale CNN and to avoid more complex structures, such as multi-scale CNN.

As suggested by Zeiler et al. in [18], to allow non-linearity for the CNNs, we use a rectified linear unit (ReLU) as shown in Fig. 4. The ReLU replaces the traditional neuron's activation function, it is not affected by the gradient vanishing problem (as for sigmoid and tanh function) and it offers high efficiency even without pre-training. To implement the networks, we have used the open source framework TensorFlow[1], recently released by Google Brain. TensorFlow is a Deep Learning framework similar to other frameworks like Caffe or Torch.

4 Dataset Description

To properly train the recognition network, a big amount of data from a real scenario is needed. The creation of a data set is not trivial, since it may contain images taken in varying conditions, and it requires accurate ground-truth annotations. Due to the lack of a public data set concerning the RoboCup SPL

---

[1] tensorflow.org.

environment, we have decided to collect and share a set of images taken from different real fields, called the **SPQR NAO image data set.** We strongly believe that the introduction of supervised techniques in robotic platforms like NAOs can lead to great improvements also in scientific fields that lie outside the soccer competitions. To encourage the development of similar approaches from other authors, we have decided to made the data set publicly available at: www.diag. uniroma1.it/~labrococo/?q=node/6.

The SPQR NAO image data set is built over images captured by different players (i.e., NAO robots) in varying environments. Indeed, the images have been captured during tests made on fields subject to natural and artificial illumination at the same time, thus different areas of the scene may be subject to high contrast and differences in brightness. A particular mention goes to the Multi-Sensor Interactive Group from the University of Bremen, which provided a part of the images in the data set.

All the images in the data set are annotated and have been processed accordingly to a pre-sampling phase, where images that are temporally adjacent have been discarded. Three different classes, namely *ball*, *nao*, and *goal*, have been considered for the ground-truth data. All the annotations are provided in a text file named "annotations.txt" that contains one annotation per line. Annotations entries are divided into *ImageName*, *UpperRightCorner*, *BottomLeftCorner*, *Class*. *ImageName* is the full image name, including the extension. The *Class* information is set accordingly to the three above listed classes. The remaining two parameters are the image coordinates of the upper-left and bottom-right corners of the bounding box that wraps the corresponding object. The origin of the image coordinates is placed in the upper-left corner. Since more than one object is usually present in an image, bounding boxes could overlap. Figure 5 shows an example of the annotations available.

Fig. 5. One of the annotated images from the SPQR NAO image data set.

5   Experimental Results

This section contains the quantitative experimental results obtained by our method. It is worth noting that, due to the lack of publicly available data sets containing images captured by NAO in real SPL matches, we were not able to compare our results with other methods. For such a reason, we have decided to make publicly available our data set in order to provide other authors a way for comparing their results with ours.

During a typical SPL match, the robots can capture a number of different objects (both in the field and from outside). Moreover, in addition to the other NAOs, also humans may be present on the field (e.g., the referees and the audience). Thus, we trained our networks to generate a binary classification between the two classes "NAO robot" and "not-NAO robot". It is worth noting that, for this task, CNN based approaches are very powerful and, as shown in rest of this section, optimal results have been achieved. However, the computational cost required by a CNN based approach can be a problem. The aim of this work is to investigate the possibility of reducing the computational requirements to be compatible with the limited hardware of the NAO robots.

5.1   Dynamic Exposure and White Balance

The initial manual camera calibration constitutes a very restrictive limit for any robotic applications. The NAO vision system is not very robust to illumination variations and the two auto-white balance and auto-exposure available options can drastically influence the performance. The above considerations led us to consider the environment lighting conditions as one of the most influencing factor during a match.

Changes in the camera settings requires a non-trivial recovery of the stable conditions. Figure 6 shows the dynamic compensation of the camera settings as

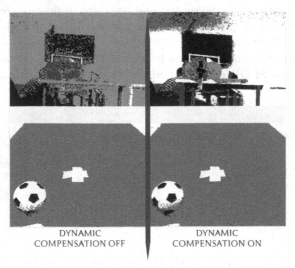

Fig. 6. Dynamic exposure and white balance results.

previously explained. The raw and the segmented image in the first column do not present any dynamic update, while those in the second column do. The comparison between the two is straightforward and, when enabled, the dynamic procedure allows to continuously adapt the parameters to environmental changes, still maintaining real-time performance (25 frames per second).

5.2   CNN Training and Evaluation

We trained our classifier on the SPQR NAO image data set, where original annotations have been subject to the data augmentation process proposed by Sermanet and LeCun in [14]. 24,236 overlapping crops are extracted and labelled with the *nao* class. More than a single crop could derive from an annotations; such crops present at max 0.5 Jaccard overlap similarity as shown in Eq. 2, where A and B are defined as different crops.

$$J(A, B) = \frac{|A \cap B|}{|A \cup B|} \tag{2}$$

37,156 negatives are then extracted from the remaining part of the image.

Evaluation has been made by using an independent and non augmented subset of 1000 images coming from the SPQR NAO image data set.

5.3   CNN Results

We have tested three different architectures as shown in Fig. 7, starting from a three inner-layers networks up to a five inner-layers. In all of the proposed networks, the learning rate present a decay factor and the Adagrad online optimization has been applied [7]. The same kernel [5, 5] has been used for every convolutional layer; dropout is not present. The output of the first convolutional layer present a depth of 64, the second and the third, if present, respectively 128 and 384. We use $SAME$ padding with a stride of $[1, 1, 1, 1]$ for the convolutional layer and $[1, 3, 3, 1]$ for the pooling.

First, we present quantitative results for the three tested networks. These are computed over the SPQR data set and reported in Table 1. Meaningful results

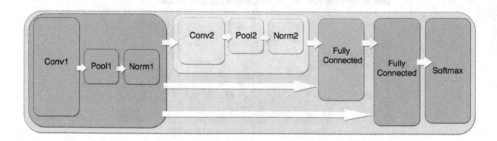

Fig. 7. Overview of the three proposed architectures.

Table 1. Quantitative results on the SPQR NAO image data set. Results are expressed in terms of accuracy and frames per second (FPS)

Architecture	Accuracy (%)	FPS
3-Layers	100	14–22
4-Layers	100	13–20
5-Layers	100	11–19

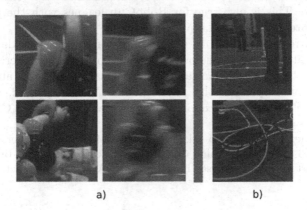

a)   b)

Fig. 8. Examples of the samples used for testing. (a) Four correctly classified positives labelled as NAO class. (b) Two correctly classified negatives. Images courtesy of the B-human team.

about the execution time come from tests ran on the NAO platform. Due to the lack of computational power, all the process not related to the proposed work were disabled during this phase. Last column of Table 1 reports the results for the number of images processed per second over the NAO. The time spent for the evaluation of a single image via the relative network is approximately 7 seconds if the whole network has to be initialized.

Results from Table 1 shows a perfect accuracy on all the tested networks. Such results do not come unexpected because of the simplicity of the classification task and of its domain of application (see Fig. 8). On the other hand, the analysis of the computational load results show margin for real-time applications.

6   Conclusions

We have presented a Deep Learning method for NAO detection to be used in the RoboCup Standard Platform League. In particular, our pipeline contains two main stages: (1) a pre-processing step to segment the image, in order to reduce the search space; (2) a validation phase based on the Convolutional Neural Networks (CNN), which is useful to confirm that the extracted regions actually contains objects of interest.

An important contribution of this work is the creation of a novel data set, called SPQR NAO image data set. The data set, containing images captured from NAOs in action on a regular field, is fully annotated and publicly available.

The proposed approach performs very well under a pure accuracy point of view. However, applicability problems arise when considering the computational time even with a binary classification. Even if the NAO platform is limited in computational power and not feasible for reaching a high frame rate, we believe that Deep Learning techniques have to be considered to deal with the Robocup 2050 challenge. This is also true for RoboCup leagues with the possibility of exploiting greater computational power.

We are currently working on using simpler networks outside the existing frameworks that may reduce the overall execution time. Moreover, we are planning to extend the classification task to more classes and to be able to classify also other objects typical of this environment. As future work, we intend to develop a complete object detection procedure based on custom CNN.

Acknowledgment. We wish to acknowledge the Multi-Sensor Interactive Systems Group Faculty 3 - Mathematics and Computer Science University of Bremen for providing a big part of the images used in the SPQR NAO image data set.

References

1. Dalal, N., Triggs, B.: Histograms of oriented gradients for human detection. In: Computer Vision and Pattern Recognition, vol. 1, pp. 886–893 (2005)
2. Erhan, D., Szegedy, C., Toshev, A., Anguelov, D.: Scalable object detection using deep neural networks. In: Computer Vision and Pattern Recognition, pp. 2155–2162 (2014)
3. Frese, U., Laue, T., Birbach, O., Röfer, T.: (A) vision for 2050-context-based image understanding for a human-robot soccer match. ECEASST **62** (2013)
4. Girshick, R.: Fast R-CNN. In: Proceedings of the International Conference on Computer Vision (ICCV) (2015)
5. Girshick, R., Donahue, J., Darrell, T., Malik, J.: Rich feature hierarchies for accurate object detection and semantic segmentation. In: Proceedings of the IEEE Conference on Computer Vision and Pattern Recognition (CVPR) (2014)
6. Härtl, A., Visser, U., Röfer, T.: Robust and efficient object recognition for a humanoid soccer robot. In: Behnke, S., Veloso, M., Visser, A., Xiong, R. (eds.) RoboCup 2013. LNCS, vol. 8371, pp. 396–407. Springer, Heidelberg (2014). doi:10.1007/978-3-662-44468-9_35
7. Duchi, J., Hazan, E., Singer, Y.: Adaptive subgradient methods for online learning and stochastic optimization. J. Mach. Learn. Res. **12**, 2121–2159 (2011)
8. Jia, Y., Shelhamer, E., Donahue, J., Karayev, S., Long, J., Girshick, R., Guadarrama, S., Darrell, T.: Caeff: convolutional architecture for fast feature embedding. In: Proceedings of the 22nd ACM International Conference on Multimedia, MM 2014, pp. 675–678 (2014)
9. Krizhevsky, A., Sutskever, I., Hinton, G.E.: Imagenet classi cation with deep convolutional neural networks. In: Advances in Neural Information Processing Systems 25, pp. 1106–1114 (2012)

10. Lienhart, R., Kuranov, A., Pisarevsky, V.: Empirical analysis of detection cascades of boosted classifiers for rapid object detection. In: Michaelis, B., Krell, G. (eds.) DAGM 2003. LNCS, vol. 2781, pp. 297–304. Springer, Heidelberg (2003). doi:10.1007/978-3-540-45243-0_39
11. Ouyang, W., Wang, X.: Joint deep learning for pedestrian detection. In: Computer Vision (ICCV), pp. 205–2063 (2013)
12. Röfer, T.: Region-based segmentation with ambiguous color classes and 2-D motion compensation. In: Visser, U., Ribeiro, F., Ohashi, T., Dellaert, F. (eds.) RoboCup 2007. LNCS, vol. 5001, pp. 369–376. Springer, Heidelberg (2008). doi:10.1007/978-3-540-68847-1_37
13. Röfer, T., Laue, T., Richter-Klug, J., Schünemann, M., Stiensmeier, J., Stölpmann, A., Stowing, A., Thielke, F.: B-Human team report and code release (2015). http://www.b-human.de/downloads/publications/2015/CodeRelease2015.pdf
14. Sermanet, P., Eigen, D., Zhang, X., Mathieu, M., Fergus, R., LeCun, Y.: Overfeat: Integrated recognition, localization and detection using convolutional networks. CoRR, abs/1312.6229 (2013)
15. Sermanet, P., LeCun, Y.: Traffc sign recognition with multi-scale convolutional networks. In: The 2011 International Joint Conference on Neural Networks (IJCNN), pp. 2809–2813 (2011)
16. Szegedy, C., Toshev, A., Erhan, D.: Deep neural networks for object detection. In: Advances in Neural Information Processing Systems 26, pp. 2553–2561 (2013)
17. Volioti, S., Lagoudakis, M.G.: Histogram-based visual object recognition for the 2007 four-legged robocup league. In: Darzentas, J., Vouros, G.A., Vosinakis, S., Arnellos, A. (eds.) SETN 2008. LNCS, vol. 5138, pp. 313–326. Springer, Heidelberg (2008). doi:10.1007/978-3-540-87881-0_28
18. Zeiler, M.D., Ranzato, M., Monga, R., Mao, M.Z., Yang, K., Le, Q.V., Nguyen, P., Senior, A.W., Vanhoucke, V., Dean, J., Hinton, G.E.: On rectified linear units for speech processing. In: IEEE International Conference on Acoustics, Speech and Signal Processing, ICASSP, pp. 3517–3521 (2013)

Impact Force Reduction Using Variable Stiffness with an Optimal Approach for Falling Robots

Juan Calderon[1,3](✉), Gustavo A. Cardona[4], Martin Llofriu[2],
Muhaimen Shamsi[2], Fallon Williams[2], Wilfrido Moreno[1],
and Alfredo Weitzenfeld[2]

[1] Department of Electrical Engineering, University of South Florida,
Tampa, FL, USA
juancalderon@mail.usf.edu, wmoreno@usf.edu
[2] Department of Computer Science and Engineering, University of South Florida,
Tampa, FL, USA
aweitzenfeld@usf.edu
[3] Department of Electronic Engineering, Universidad Santo Tomás, Bogota,
Colombia
[4] Department of Electrical and Electronics Engineering,
Universidad Nacional de Colombia, Bogota, Colombia
gacardonac@unal.edu

Abstract. The work described in this paper is focused on the reduction
of the impact force exerted by the ground on a falling humanoid robot.
It proposes the use of a variable stiffness in the arms's motors to prevent
damages. The proposed work is applicable when the falling prevention
techniques fail or when falling is unavoidable. This work proposes the
generation of variable stiffness in a motor through the optimal design of
a PID controller. The variation of the Q matrix in a LQR controller produces different levels of motor stiffness. The proposed variable stiffness is
tested in a Darwin OP Robot. The performance of the proposed design
is evaluated using the estimation of the impact force. Results show an
impact force reduction on falling motions by means of stiffness variation.

Keywords: Variable stiffness · Optimal control · Humanoid robot ·
Falling robot

1   Introduction

In the last decades many research institutes, companies and academic initiatives
have focused their efforts in the research and production of humanoids robots.
Some academic initiatives such as RoboCup [1] have set soccer robot as their
main goal, but this objective is just one topic in the bigger scope covered by
RoboCup. The three main robotics areas are education, search & rescue and
soccer. The first one is focused on the research on improving search and rescue
of victims in disaster zones using robots. The second area relates to education,
where the main objective is to introduce high school students and children into

© Springer International Publishing AG 2017
S. Behnke et al. (Eds.): RoboCup 2016, LNAI 9776, pp. 404–415, 2017.
https://doi.org/10.1007/978-3-319-68792-6_34

the fascinating world of science and robotics [2]. Finally, the soccer is focused on the development of wheeled robots [3] with small size and middle size leagues and humanoid robots with kid, teen, and adult size leagues. The soccer initiative is approached by different research fields such as artificial intelligent [4], computer vision [5], and locomotion skills. Darpa [6] encourages the development of humanoid robots that collaborate in the rescue of human casualties in hazardous areas. The Darpa Humanoid Challenge proposes different tasks, which are focused on the design and improvement of humanoid robots with new skills and applications in the real world. To achieve a so-called humanoid-robot interaction in the real world, improving skills such as walking, running, jumping is a must. To improve these locomotion skills, it is necessary to keep the robot balanced while it performs different movements. With the purpose of keeping balance, Vukobratovic and Borovac introduced in [7] the use of Center of Mass (CoM) and Zero Moment Point (ZMP) as a reference points to perfom balance control. Aditionally, Kajita et al. [8] proposed the inverted pendulum model as a reduced dynamic model for humanoid robots, thus simplifying the design of balance control systems for these robots. However, sometimes the balance control fails and the robot falls. Then it is necessary to answer a new question: what does a robot have to do when falling is unavoidable? Some authors describe different kinds of a possible solution to this problem. The consensus is that the main goal is to prevent or diminish damage at the moment of hitting the ground.

Previous works try to reduce the impact force through the use of different aproaches such as: the design of movement sequences inspired by martial arts [9], falling simulation used by the animation industry [10], mechanical additions in the contact zones of the robot [11] and the use of variable stiffness in motors located in the arms [12]. The present paper proposes an idea similar to the latter approach, but it includes a new method to generate low stiffness in the arms motors. This method uses an optimal control approach to calculate the PID parameters. This paper is organized as follows: Sect. 2 presents related work; Sect. 3 presents the impact reduction strategy; Sect. 4 presents experiments and results; while Sect. 5 presents the final conclusions.

2   Related Work

Falling robots have become one of the most interesting research topics recently. It tries to minimize the damage in the robot joints and it even tries to protect the important parts such as chest and head where the processors, cameras and batteries are usually located. Some previous works propose different ways to reduce the impact force in falling robots, such as fall prediction, fall sequences generation, reducing the shock force exerted in the ground impact, mechanical improvements, and manipulation of joint stiffness. One of the most important steps in the study on the falling robot is to predict and detect when the robot is falling [14]. Karsen and Wirsen [15] predict fall events using principal component analysis. The most popular technique to reduce the damage on the robot at the moment of impact is to take inspiration from what the human reaction would be in different falling scenarios. Fujiwara et al. [9] take decisions based in martial arts or more specifically judo techniques, while also trying to reduce the angular momentum. Ruiz-del Solar [16] uses a similar approach based in Japanese martial arts skills, but he adds another concept based on the idea of keeping the Center of Mass (COM) as low as possible to reduce the impact force on the joints. Wilken et al. [11] propose an algorithm for a diving motion in a goalkeeper robot. This algorithm optimizes the falling time and defines the movement trajectory according to the direction and velocity of the ball. Ha et al. [10] is focused in another interesting approach of the falling motion field. It consists on the use of technics from animation to reduce impact forces in falling bodies. Hu and Liu [17] also show other kind of research to reduce the damage in humanoid falls. They propose an algorithm focused on the dissipation of the momentum in the initial phase of the fall. They do so by using multiple contact points with the ground, thus splitting the impact force through various contact points. They validated their algorithm using physics simulation software and a BioloidGp humanoid robot. Wilken et al. [11] study the case of a goalkeeper robot, they propose to add mechanical improvements to the more exposed parts, susceptible to damage due to falls, such as the hip and the upper limbs. The goal is to enlarge the lifespan of the joints. Thus they propose the use of springs to recover the target position of the joints, and the addition of something padded to dampen the shock as well. Pratt et al. [18] propose the idea that full stiffness is not always the best way to work. They make a mathematical study about the effect of low stiffness in a robotic joint and how to control it. Additionally, they list several cases in which low stiffness has a good performance, such as: stable force control, lowering reflecting inertia, less damages during unexpected contact and shock tolerance. Shock tolerance and unexpected contact are the two main arguments in favor of the use of variable stiffness in the present work.

Other works use low stiffness to save energy or reduce impact forces. Elibol et al. [19] make a study about the performance variation of the walking process of a humanoid robot using different joint stiffness values. Calderon et al. [20] propose a statistic algorithm to compute the low stiffness value required for the robot to perform a stand up movement correctly, while reducing energy consumption by lowering each joint's stiffness value.

An earlier work related with this paper is presented by Calderon et al. [21]. They propose the variation of the ankle and knee stiffness value throughout the different stages of a jumping process for a humanoid robot. They indicate when it is necessary to decrease or increase the proportional gain, but they do not provide a method to estimate the P value in a control system. The present work uses a similar approach than that depicted by Calderon et al. in [22,23] where they propose a complete control method to perform a vertical jump movements in a legged robot. Additionally, they depicted a fuzzy method to estimate the low stiffness required to reduce the impact force in the landing phase of the vertical jump. In a similar way the present work proposes a method to estimate the stiffness value when the robot is falling. A preliminary version of this work was presented at SoutheastCon (2016) in Cardona et al. [12]. They proposed a fuzzy logic method to calculate the low stiffness value with the aim to reduce the impact force when a humanoid robot is falling. This new version includes an improved method to calculate the desired low stiffness according with an estimation of the impact force and impact velocity. The low stiffness is reached through the calculation of the motor control gains using an optimal approach. Additionally the optimal gains are transformed to an optimal PID to allow the implementation in a PID controlled actuator robot, in this case a Darwin robot. The current work is the improvement proposed in the future work section in Cardona et al. [12].

3   Impact Reduction Strategy

The impact force reduction strategy is based on the use of low stiffness in the arm motors of the humanoid robot. The proposed strategy is inspired in real human behavior. When humans are falling, they try to protect their chest and head using their hands and arms. Consquently, the most common fracture in human fall accidents are the wrist, arm, or clavicule. According to Ruiz-del Solar [16] in human accidents is very common to break the bones, but in humanoid robots the links are particularly strong and the impact force affects the joints, breaking the motors. Using the last two ideas. Once the robot detects that it is falling, it moves its arms to the front position trying to protect the head and chest from the impact force. But, with this movement the robot is putting at risk the integrity of the arm motors. To protect the motors, the stiffness of every arm motor is decreased, affecting the gains of the motor control system. The control gains are calculated using an optimal (LQR) approach and these values are redesigned to implement in the PID control of the Darwin Robot motors. As mentioned in the last section, this work bases the impact reduction strategy in the motor stiffness variation using a LQR approach. Thus, this section is divided into three parts. The first one is the mathematical model of the electrical motor. The second one is the formulation of the optimal control system, and finally the calculation of PID constants from the LQR, according with the requirements of the robotic platform.

3.1   Electrical Motor Model

Since most actuators of actual robots are electric motors, the present work uses the mathematical model of a typical electric motor for the controller design. The characteristic equation of the electrical motor is presented in Eq. 1

$$\frac{\theta(s)}{V_{in}(s)} = \frac{K_t G_r}{s\Big((Js+b)(Ls+R)+K_t K_b\Big)} \tag{1}$$

where, V_{in} is the input voltage, θ is angular position, L is the armature inductance, R is the armature resistance, b is the motor viscous friction constant, J is the moment of the inertia of the rotor, K_t is the motor torque constant, Gr is gear ratio, and K_b is the electromotive force constant.

3.2 Linear Quadratic Regulator

The Linear Quadratic Regulator (LQR) optimal control has been widely studied over decades with a broad range of applications. It minimizes the error in
the state variable trajectories of a system while requiring the minimum control
energy. The objective to use LQR is to generate a variable stiffness effect in
the actuator (electric motor) as it will be explained ahead. LQR is based in the
minimization of the performance index as shown by Eq. 2.

$$ J = \int_0^\infty \left[x^T(t)Qx(t) + u^T Ru(t) \right] dt \tag{2} $$

where Q and R are the penalization matrices for state variables error and control
signal, respectively. The relation between Q and R determines what is more
important between the minimization of state error or the control energy. Thereby,
the present work proposes to determine the stiffness of the motors using the Q
matrix. When Q has large values, the motor position error is penalized. Then,
the motor tries to keep the position against any disturbance (high stiffness).
Otherwise, if Q has small values, a certain position error is allowed, generating
low stiffness in the motor. The feedback control law is defined by 3.

$$ u(t) = -R^{-1}B^T Px(t) = -Kx(t) \tag{3} $$

where, K is known as the Kalman gain and it is defined as $K = R^{-1}BP$ and
P is a symmetric positive defined matrix and it is a solution of the Continuous
Algebraic Riccatti Equation defined by 4.

$$ A^T P + PA - PBR^{-1}P + Q = 0 \tag{4} $$

Here, A and B are the matrices of the state space description of the plant
(motor), Q is symmetric positive semi-definite weighted matrix, and R is a constant matrix. Using the Riccati Equation, the feedback gains can be calculated
and the design of the control system can be performed. However, the system performance depends of the adequate selection of the Q matrix. The next section
explains how to calculate Q based on a desired model and how to tune a PID
using the LQR approach.

3.3 Optimal PID

PID is a control system widely used around the world. For the current case,
this paper tries to provide a method to vary the stiffness in a motor using PID,
with an optimal approach. The variable stiffness is used to reduce the impact
force in falling robots, as previously mentioned. The design of optimal PID is
based in the works presented by [24,25]. Where they first proposed a PID design
using LQR approach, but the selection of the Q matrix was not defined. The
second one designs the PID using LQR and provides a method to determine the
Q values, based on the characteristic polynomial of the desired behavior. The

current work assumes the designs of PID as a LQR optimal control design, where the error is the state variables and the optimal state-feedback gains are the PID parameters (K_p, K_i, and K_d). The Fig. 1 shows the typical PID configuration, where $r(t)$ is the desired actuator position.

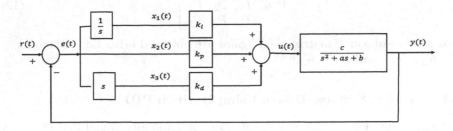

Fig. 1. PID controller for second order system

The PID and the second order plant (motor) are defined by 5 and 6 respectively.

$$G(s) = \frac{c}{s^2 + as + b} = \frac{y(s)}{u(s)} \tag{5}$$

$$u(s) = e(s)\left(\frac{K_i}{s} + K_p + K_d s\right) \tag{6}$$

Now, the state variables are defined as 7.

$$x_1 = \int e(t)dt, x_2 = e(t), x_3 = \frac{de(t)}{dt} \tag{7}$$

For the feedback design, the external desired set-point does not affect the controller design and it is possible to assume $r(t) = 0$, thus $e(t) = -y(t)$. This is a common assumption in the standard regulator design. Assuming $r(t) = 0$ the transfer function can be expressed as 8.

$$\frac{Y(s)}{U(s)} = \frac{c}{s^2 + as + b} = \frac{-E(s)}{U(s)} \tag{8}$$

Now the relation between $U(s)$ and $E(s)$ is written in the time domain and shown in 9.

$$\ddot{e}(t) + a\dot{e}(t) + be(t) = -cu(t) \tag{9}$$

replacing 8 in 9 the relation between $u(t)$ and $y(t)$ is expressed in terms of the state variables as 10.

$$\dot{x}_3 + ax_3 + bx_2 = -cu(t) \tag{10}$$

finally, using 7 and 10 the state space formulation is depicted in 11.

$$\begin{bmatrix} \dot{x}_1 \\ \dot{x}_2 \\ \dot{x}_3 \end{bmatrix} = \begin{bmatrix} 0 & 1 & 0 \\ 0 & 0 & 1 \\ 0 & -b & -a \end{bmatrix} \begin{bmatrix} x_1 \\ x_2 \\ x_3 \end{bmatrix} + \begin{bmatrix} 0 \\ 0 \\ -c \end{bmatrix} u(t); \quad A = \begin{bmatrix} 0 & 1 & 0 \\ 0 & 0 & 1 \\ 0 & -b & -a \end{bmatrix}, B = \begin{bmatrix} 0 \\ 0 \\ -c \end{bmatrix} \tag{11}$$

Now it looks as a standard state-space representation $\dot{x} = Ax(t) + Bu(t)$ where A and B are shown by 11. Then, using Eq. 4 the Riccatti Equation Solution can be applied using A and B from the 11 and P is defined as a 3×3 symmetric matrix as depicted in 12.

$$P = \begin{bmatrix} P_{11} & P_{12} & P_{13} \\ P_{21} & P_{22} & P_{23} \\ P_{31} & P_{32} & P_{33} \end{bmatrix} \tag{12}$$

Using the results of P matrix, the K gains are obtained using Eq. 3 where $K_1 = K_i$, $K_2 = K_p$, and $K_3 = K_d$.

3.4 Variable Stiffness Design Using Optimal PID

In order to develop variable stiffness in a motor using an optimal PID design, it is necessary to establish a desired transfer function according with the desired performance. Usually the desired function is determined according with requirements of settling time, overshoot and rise time among others. However, for the present case those parameters can be defined according to the normal performance of the motor in common robot activities like walk.

The idea of this point is to set up a standard point where the motor stiffness will be defined as a normal stiffness. Starting from this point a low and high stiffness will be defined. Thus, the desired function is defined as a third order system, which characteristic polynomial has three roots defined by $(s + \alpha_1)$, $(s + \alpha_2)$, and $(s + \alpha_3)$. The objective of this section is to design a PID controller, starting from the desired performance using optimal approach. The PID transfer function is defined as shown by 13

$$G_{PID}(s) = k_p + \frac{k_i}{s} + k_d s \tag{13}$$

Following the method described by [25], Q and P matrices are defined as shown by 14 and 12 respectively.

$$Q = \begin{bmatrix} q_1 & 0 & 0 \\ 0 & q_2 & 0 \\ 0 & 0 & q_3 \end{bmatrix} \tag{14}$$

According with the optimal conditions, where P has to be a solution of the Riccati Eq. 4. The values of Q can be set in terms of motor transfer function coefficients and the roots of the desired polynomial characteristic equation. The Q values are depicted by 15-17.

$$q_1 = \frac{R\alpha_1^2\alpha_2^2\alpha_3^2}{c^2} \tag{15}$$

$$q_2 = \frac{R\left(\alpha_1^2\alpha_2^2 + \alpha_1^2\alpha_3^2 + \alpha_3^2\alpha_2^2 - b^2\right)}{c^2} \tag{16}$$

$$q_3 = \frac{R\left(\alpha_1^2 + \alpha_2^2 + \alpha_3^2 - a^2 + 2b\right)}{c^2} \tag{17}$$

Once Q has been defined, the Riccati equation is applied using 4 and the P matrix is obtained. The solution of the Riccati equation can be found using numerical methods or mathematical software as Matlab. Now, the optimal PID constants are computed using 18.

$$K_i = R^{-1}cP_{13}; \qquad K_p = R^{-1}cP_{23}; \qquad K_d = R^{-1}cP_{33} \qquad (18)$$

Because the optimal PID gains were calculated using a characteristic polynomial of the desired transfer function with the usual performance parameters, the stiffness in the motor is assumed as a usual stiffness. But, based on this design, it is possible to calculate a new set of optimal PID gains. These new gains can produce a high or low stiffness from the usual stiffness perspective. The low and high stiffness can be designed scaling the Q_{usual} matrix by a ρ factor as shown by 19.

$$Q_{new} = \rho Q_{usual} \qquad (19)$$

where ρ is a scalar parameter, for $\rho > 1$ a high stiffness is obtained and $0 < \rho < 1$ the low stiffness will be reached by the motor. Finally with the Q_{new} defined, it is necessary to solve the Riccati equation for Q_{new} and get the P values to calculate the new PID control gains.

4   Experiment and Results

In order to perform experiments of the falling protection, a Darwin Op Humanoid Robot was chosen. This robot was used because it is one of the most popular humanoid robots in RoboCup and its actuators are used along the different leagues, such as Humanoid soccer, rescue, junior, and @home. The robot is 45.5 cm high, 3 kg weight, and it has 20 Degrees of Freedom (DoF). The motor actuators are Dynamixel MX-28, having an absolute encoder resolution of 4,096, stall torque of 31.6 kg-cm and programmable PID control. The last characteristic is the most important, because the present work proposes an optimal PID to generate variable stiffness. The proposed method depends of the transfer function of the motor to design the PID. Since there is not enough information about the motor model, a reduced model is proposed, as shown in Fig. 2. Where G_o is the internal model of the electrical motor. For the sake of simplicity, some variables were set to zero, such as target velocity $(\dot{\theta}_d)$, K_i and K_d. According with the manufacturer's specifications if $\dot{\theta}$ is zero, the feedback loop of velocity control is disabled. So that the internal model just depends of the proportional gain (K_p). The proposed model is a second order system as depicted by 1 and shown in Fig. 2. It was estimated using the "Ident Tool Box" from Matlab. The obtained constants are $a = 106.1$, $b = 3$, and $c = 1319$ with $K_p = 16$. This model is affected by the nonlinearity of the saturation function. This function is the operation voltage limit of the motor. This reduced model works with K_p values less than 64 and position error less than 1000, which is not a problem for the proposed method, as it is used in situation where the position error is close to zero and the system is trying to keep the set point.

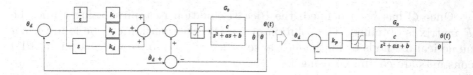

Fig. 2. Reduced motor model

The other important parameters of the proposed method are the roots of the characteristic equation of the desired behavior. In this case $a_1 = -238$, $a_2 = -79$, and $a_3 = -8.5$. The method can now be applied using the transfer function and desired roots established.

The experiment consists of running several trials of the falling robot with different values of ρ. The robot is standing up and it is pushed from back to front, then it moves its arms to the safe position. The new values of PID according with ρ are programmed in the elbow and shoulder motors. Figure 3 shows a motion sequence of the experiment.

Fig. 3. Motion sequence of the experiment

At the end of the motion sequence in Fig. 3, the reader can observe how the arms are displaced from the safe position and the impact between the robot body and the ground is reduced.

Figure 4 shows the position of the center of mass (CoM) of the robot in five different trials. Every trial has different values of ρ, for these cases $\rho = 0.05, 0.1, 0.3, 1$, and 3.

Other important parameter used to measure the ground impact force is the displacement (d) of the CoM in the impact moment. Figure 4 shows how d increases as ρ is reduced.

The average impact force can be estimated using 20, where d is inversely proportional to the impact force. V_l is the impact velocity and m is the robot mass.

$$F_{i-avg} = \frac{\frac{1}{2}mV_l^2}{d} \qquad (20)$$

The results of the Impact force, impact velocity, and CoM displacement are depicted in Table 1. Table 1 depicts the results of the five trials shown by Fig. 4.

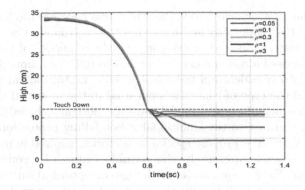

Fig. 4. Center of mass position with different ρ values

Table 1. Experiment results

ρ	Impact velocity (m/s)	Distance (d) (cm)	Impact Force (N)	Impact reduction (%)
0.05	1.78	7.61	60.44	86.8
0.1	1.72	4.34	98.84	78.52
0.3	1.75	1.79	248.07	41.60
1	1.72	1.54	278.55	39.46
3	1.69	0.9	460.14	0

Results show how the displacement (d) increases according to the decrements of ρ. The impact force is reduced with smaller values of ρ and it rises with large values of ρ. This highlights the importance of the stiffness variation to reduce the impact force. The low stiffness generates large values of displacement and a significant reduction of the impact force.

5 Conclusions

The reduction of the impact force in a falling robot was achieved using a variable stiffness approach. This work illustrates how the reduction of the stiffness in the motor can help to reduce the impact force. The stiffness variation is performed through the design of a PID controller. Additionally, the coefficients of the PID are calculated using a LQR design. The proposed design of the PID controller was tested using a Darwin OP humanoid robot, and several trials with different parameters were performed. The results were satisfactory showing a reduction of ground impact force of up to 86%. The stiffness variation was proposed in terms of the Q matrix variation using a modulating coefficient, ρ. Low stiffness is reached with $0 < \rho < 1$ and high stiffness is generated using $\rho > 1$. According with experiments low stiffness allows for the reduction of the impact force through the center of mass displacement. Nevertheless, it is necessary to take into account that as ρ gets close to 0, the stiffness is becomes too low. Then, the arms don't stop the robot body and it crashes to the ground. The estimation of the motor parameters was performed using a reduced model of the Dynamixel MX-28. The proposed algorithm can be applied to full size robots, but it is necessary to take into consideration the robot weight, mathematical model of the arm motors, and the type of control system used in the motor. If the controller is not a PID, a different control model must be designed, based in calculated LQR values. In contrast to the traditional robot falling protection algorithms, the present work does not propose special trajectories inspired in martial arts or animation technologies. Alternately, the variable stiffness is proposed in terms of a LQR design. Future work includes the use of optimization theory to generate variable stiffness. Additionally, the proposed algorithm could be joined to trajectory generation algorithms to complement each other.

Acknowledgments. This work is supported in part at USF by NSF-CRCNS grant #1429937, "A replay-driven model of spatial sequence learning in the Hippocampus-PFC network using reservoir computing".

References

1. Kitano, H., Asada, M., Kuniyoshi, Y., Noda, I., Osawa, E.: Robocup: the robot world cup initiative. In: Proceedings of the First International Conference on Autonomous Agents, pp. 340–347. ACM, February 1997
2. Calderon, J.M., Rojas, E.R., Rodriguez, S., Baez, H.R., Lopez, J.A.: A robot soccer team as a strategy to develop educational iniciatives. In: Latin American and Caribbean Conference for Engineering and Technology, Panama City, Panama (2012)
3. Rodriguez, S., Rojas, E., Perez, K., Lopez, J., Baez, H., Calderon, J.M.: STOxs 2013 Team Description Paper (2013)
4. Quintero, C., Rodríguez, S., Pérez, K., López, J., Rojas, E., Calderón, J.: Learning soccer drills for the small size league of robocup. In: Bianchi, R.A.C., Akin, H.L., Ramamoorthy, S., Sugiura, K. (eds.) RoboCup 2014. LNCS, vol. 8992, pp. 395–406. Springer, Cham (2015). doi:10.1007/978-3-319-18615-3_32
5. Perez-Hernandez, A.K., Gomez-García, A., Rojas-Martínez, E.R., Rodríguez-Rojas, C.S., López-Jiménez, J., Calderón-Chavez, J.M.: Edge detection algorithm based on fuzzy logic theory for a local vision system of robocup humanoid league. Tecno Lóg. **30**, 33–50 (2013)
6. DARPA: DARPA Robotics Challenge. DARPA, January 2015. http://www.theroboticschallenge.org/
7. Vukobratović, M., Borovac, B.: Zero-moment point thirty five years of its life. Int. J. Humanoid Robot. **1**(1), 157–173 (2004)
8. Kajita, S., Nagasaki, T., Kaneko, K., Yokoi, K.: A hop towards running humanoid biped. In: Proceedings of the 2004 IEEE International Conference on Robotics and Automation, ICRA 2004 (2004)
9. Fujiwara, K., Kanehiro, F., Kajita, S., Kaneko, K., Yokoi, K., Hirukawa, H.: UKEMI: falling motion control to minimize damage to biped humanoid robot. In IROS, pp. 2521–2526, October 2002

10. Ha, S., Ye, Y., Liu, C.K.: Falling and landing motion control for character animation. ACM Trans. Graph. (TOG) **31**(6), 155 (2012)
11. Wilken, T., Missura, M., Behnke, S.: Designing falling motions for a humanoid soccer goalie. In: Proceedings of the 4th Workshop on Humanoid Soccer Robots (Humanoids 2009), pp. 79–84 (2009)
12. Cardona, G., Moreno, W., Weitzenfeld, A., Calderon, J.: Reduction of impact force in falling robots using variable stiffness. In: Conference SoutheastCon (2016)
13. Ogata, K., Terada, K., Kuniyoshi, Y.: Real-time selection and generation of fall damage reduction actions for humanoid robots. In: Humanoids 2008, Daejeon, Korea, pp. 233–238 (2008)
14. Renner, R., Behnke, S.: Instability detection and fall avoidance for a humanoid using attitude sensors and reflexes. In: 2006 IEEE/RSJ international conference on Intelligent robots and systems, pp. 2967–2973. IEEE (2006)
15. Karssen, J.G.D., Wisse, M.: Fall detection in walking robots by multi-way principal component analysis. Robotica **27**(2), 249–257 (2009)
16. Ruiz-del Solar, J., Moya, J., Parra-Tsunekawa, I.: Fall detection and management in biped humanoid robots. In: IEEE International Conference on Robotics and Automation (ICRA), pp. 3323–3328 (2010)
17. Ha, S., Liu, C.K.: Multiple contact planning for minimizing damage of humanoid falls. In: 2015 IEEE/RSJ International Conference on Intelligent Robots and Systems (IROS). IEEE (2015)
18. Pratt, G.A., Williamson, M.M., Dillworth, P., Pratt, J., Wright, A.: Stiffness isn't everything. In: Khatib, O., Salisbury, J.K. (eds.) Experimental Robotics IV. LNCIS, vol. 223, pp. 253–262. Springer, Heidelberg (1997). doi:10.1007/BFb0035216
19. Elibol, E., Calderon, J., Weitzenfeld, A.: Optimizing energy usage through variable joint stiffness control during humanoid robot walking. In: Behnke, S., Veloso, M., Visser, A., Xiong, R. (eds.) RoboCup 2013. LNCS, vol. 8371, pp. 492–503. Springer, Heidelberg (2014). doi:10.1007/978-3-662-44468-9_43
20. Calderon, J.M., Elibol, E., Moreno, W., Weitzenfeld, A.: Current usage reduction through stiffness control in humanoid robot. In: 8th Workshop on Humanoid Soccer Robots, IEEE-RAS International Conference on Humanoid Robots (2013)
21. Calderon, J.M., Llofriu, M., Moreno, W., Weitzenfeld, A.: Soft landing in jumping robot using compliant motor capability. In: Workshop Get in Touch! Tactile & Force Sensing for Autonomous, Compliant, Intelligent Robots, ICRA 2015, Seattle, Washington (U.S.A.), 26–30 May 2015
22. Calderón, J.M., Moreno, W., Weitzenfeld, A.: Fuzzy variable stiffness in landing phase for jumping robot. In: Snášel, V., Abraham, A., Krömer, P., Pant, M., Muda, A.K. (eds.) Innovations in Bio-Inspired Computing and Applications. AISC, vol. 424, pp. 511–522. Springer, Cham (2016). doi:10.1007/978-3-319-28031-8_45
23. Calderon, J.M., Moreno, W., Weitzenfeld, A.: Impact force reduction using fuzzy variable stiffness in a jumping robot. J. Netw. Innov. Comput. **4**, 152–163 (2016)
24. Das, S., et al.: LQR based improved discrete PID controller design via optimum selection of weighting matrices using fractional order integral performance index. Appl. Math. Model. **37**(6), 4253–4268 (2013)
25. Yu, G.-R., Hwang, R.-C.: Optimal PID speed control of brush less DC motors using LQR approach. In: 2004 IEEE International Conference on Systems, Man and Cybernetics, vol. 1. IEEE (2004)

Robust Multi-modal Detection of Industrial Signal Light Towers

Victor Mataré, Tim Niemueller$^{(\boxtimes)}$, and Gerhard Lakemeyer

Knowledge-Based Systems Group, RWTH Aachen University, Aachen, Germany
{matare,niemueller,gerhard}@kbsg.rwth-aachen.de

Abstract. Introducing robots to provide flexible logistics in a smart factory and cohabitation of robot workers and human operators will require robots to recognize and interpret the same cues in the environment as humans do. In this paper, we describe a novel method to detect machine light signal towers as one such cue that are frequently seen on production machines. It uses color information to determine basic regions of interest and applies a number of spatial constraints to make it robust against many common disturbances. As an option, the algorithm can use laser data for machine-specific reduction of the search space for a speed up by an order of magnitude providing fast, accurate, and robust detection. It recognizes the respective activation states and even blinking lights.

1 Introduction

Industrial manufacturing is expected to change considerably in the near future – a paradigm shift often called Industry 4.0 [1]. Part of this vision are *smart factories*, context-aware facilities that can take into account information like object positions or machine status [2]. They provide *manufacturing services* that can be combined efficiently in (almost) arbitrary ways. This challenge is modeled by the *RoboCup Logistics League (RCLL)* [3].

Fig. 1. Illustration of recognition and noise. (Color figure online)

While some factories will be designed according to this vision with networked machinery, even more existing facilities will be incrementally upgraded for economic reasons, requiring the robots to adapt to existing machines, and to work safely alongside humans [4,5]. The light signals used in the RCLL are industry-standard parts[1] that are often used to indicate a machine's status, e.g. when it is about to run out of material, or whether it is currently safe for a human to perform certain operations. Being able to visually recognize these is important

---

[1] Similar to http://www.werma.com/en/s_c1006i2580/K37_cable_24VAC/DC_GN/YE/RD/69811075.html.

© Springer International Publishing AG 2017
S. Behnke et al. (Eds.): RoboCup 2016, LNAI 9776, pp. 416–427, 2017.
https://doi.org/10.1007/978-3-319-68792-6_35

even in the presence of a network to communicate that very information, for example to prevent misunderstandings between humans and robots in case of a signal or network failure.

In this paper, we describe a novel method that uses a coarse (yet expressive and very efficient) color model to search for relevant regions of interest (ROI) of the light colors red, yellow, and green. These regions are then filtered by a number of spatial constraints to eliminate typical false positives like colored reflections on metal parts of the machine. A machine-specific laser-based detection of the signal tower can be used to reduce the image search space considerably, providing an order of magnitude speed-up while increasing reliability. Eventually, the detected ROIs for the three colors are analyzed for their activation state (cf. Fig. 1) and for temporal relations to detect blinking lights.

In the following Sect. 2 we briefly describe the RCLL and the problem of light signal tower detection. In Sect. 3 we highlight some related work before describing the method in detail in Sect. 4. We provide evaluation results in Sect. 5 before we conclude in Sect. 6.

2 RoboCup Logistics League and Signal Light Towers

RoboCup [6] is an international initiative to foster research in the field of robotics and artificial intelligence. Besides robotic soccer, RoboCup also features application-oriented leagues which serve as common testbeds to compare research results. Among these, the industry-oriented RoboCup Logistics League[2] (RCLL) tackles the problem of production logistics in a smart factory. Groups of three robots have to plan, execute, and optimize the material flow and deliver products according to dynamic orders in a simplified factory. The challenge consists of creating and adjusting a production plan and coordinating the group [3].

A game is split into two major phases. In the *exploration phase*, the robots must determine the positions of machines assigned to their team and recognize and report a combination of marker and light signal state. During the *production phase*, the robots must transport workpieces to create final products according to dynamic order schedules which are announced to the robots only at run-time, while the machines indicate their status with light signals.

Machines in the RCLL are represented by Festo's Modular Production System (MPS) stations, each equipped with a red/yellow/green *signal light tower*. For example, in Fig. 2 a robot approaches a ring station, where the signal tower is on the front left corner of the station.

Fig. 2. Robot approaching a ring station. (Color figure online)

2 RoboCup Logistics website: http://www.robocup-logistics.org.

The distinctive feature of this vision problem is the presence of *active light sources* with an extreme variation in brightness which far exceeds the sensitivity range of our consumer-grade cameras.

To be able to detect blinking states, we have to recognize both lit and unlit signals, but depending on ambient light, unlit signals may be captured as almost all black while lit signals are captured as mostly white (cf. Fig. 3). Another problem is the fact that the individual red/yellow/green segments are not optically separated internally, for example, a lit red segment will always make parts of an unlit yellow segment appear red. In combination with extensive and *unpredictable background clutter* (cf. Fig. 3) coming from colorful reflections on shiny machine parts, colorfully dressed spectators and other objects, false positives become a major problem. Since individual segments are made of a transparent material with a fluted surface, the use of many light emitting sensors like a Kinect is infeasible. The use of stereo cameras is made difficult since the amount of textures is low if the region of a color is mostly a bright spot if the light is turned on, or the remainder of the image too dark if tuned down.

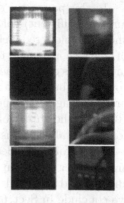

Fig. 3. Actual light signals vs. environment clutter. (Color figure online)

3   Related Work

Automatic detection of roadside traffic lights is a related field in particular for autonomous driving. Ziegler et al. describe the challenges posed by a long real-world overland journey [7] under urban and rural conditions at daytime. While it is in principle possible to work around the whole issue by broadcasting traffic signal states over radio, this would require major infrastructure investments [8].

A common practice is to build a database containing features of known intersections to assist locating a traffic signal within a camera image [7,8]. The required data are gathered on a special mapping run of the routes. Fairfield and Urmson generate a detailed prior map that contains a global 3D pose estimate of every traffic signal [8]. Ziegler et al. create a manually labeled 2D visual feature database [7]. During autonomous driving, these hints are then used to limit the search space for the classifier that detects the red, yellow and green lights.

Such approaches do not cover some of the typical problems outlined in Sect. 2 and do not use a second sensor that allows to reduce the problem space.

Another approach in the RCLL has been to reduce camera exposure and contrast until only lit signals would create a saturated output [9]. A drawback of this approach is that this makes the camera unusable for other tasks.

Color detection has been a long-standing issue in RoboCup. In other leagues like the Standard Platform League, lookup tables were sufficient while constant lighting was provided [10]. These methods generally cannot capture the dynamic range with active light sources. Edge and color segmentation have been used to detect vertically stacked color-coded landmarks [11]. While somewhat similar in shape, they did not change during the game and had no temporal dependencies.

4 Multi-modal Light Signal Detection

Image processing is performed as a sequence of operations forming a processing pipeline that is depicted in Fig. 4. A *classifier* takes an input image and determines *regions of interest (ROI)* by detecting colors along a grid with pixels of relevant colors according to *similarity color models*. An assembly stage combines ROIs of different colors according to some spatial constraints. Additionally, based on the detection of the flat side panel of the MPS (cf. Fig. 2) by means of a 2D laser scanner, the ROIs can be further constrained by an estimate of the expected position within the image. This combination of different sensors makes this a multi-modal approach which significantly reduces the search space and the chance of false positives. Distance-based tracking ensures that consecutive frames are accepted for small movements. A brightness classifier detects lit/unlit signal segments in the determined ROIs and temporal aggregation is performed to detect blinking signals.

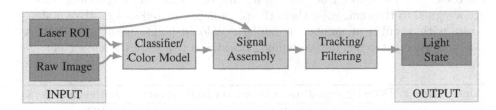

Fig. 4. A model of the processing pipeline. (Color figure online)

In the following we will detail the major components of the pipeline which has been implemented using the computer vision framework in Fawkes [12].

4.1 Color Model

The color model is responsible for deciding whether an input color matches a certain reference color. The used color model has been ported from the VLC video player[3]. It works directly with the YUV colorspace that is produced natively by most webcams, thus eliminating colorspace conversion. In the YUV colorspace, the *luminance* (roughly conforms to the concept of brightness) information is encoded entirely in the Y dimension, while the color value (*chrominance*) is a 2D vector in the UV plane. The saturation of a color then corresponds to the length of the UV vector.

Normalizing the two color vectors by their saturation and computing the length of the difference vector then

Fig. 5. Sector of the UV plane recognized by the color model. (Color figure online)

---

[3] Based on VLC's (http://www.videolan.org) color threshold filter (colorthres.c).

gives a reasonable similarity measure: $\delta_{UV} = |\, |\mathbf{r}| \cdot \mathbf{c} - |\mathbf{c}| \cdot \mathbf{r} \,|$, where $\mathbf{r} = (u_r, v_r)^T$ is the reference color, $\mathbf{c} = (u_c, v_c)^T$ is the input color, and δ_{UV} is the scalar color difference. Specifying a threshold on δ_{UV} then allows us to decide whether some pixel from the camera image matches a given color within a certain tolerance. Along with a threshold on $|\mathbf{c}|$ and on δ_Y, such a color model describes a subset of the UV space (similar to Fig. 5) that extends through a portion of the Y dimension. Multiple such color models can be combined into a multi-color model that contains all shades we expect to see e.g. in the red light in a signal tower.

4.2 Classifier

A classifier takes an input image and outputs regions of interest. The color classifier used in this work takes a color model that ascribes a principal color to a pixel color and a scanline grid. The classifier then analyzes each crossing of the grid. If the pixel is found to belong to a known color class, it considers the direct 5×5 neighborhood. Only if a sufficient number of neighboring pixels are assigned to the same color class, the pixel is considered as a positive match. Areas with a sufficient number of similarly colored points result in a ROI. A post-processing step merges overlapping or adjacent ROIs of the same color.

Algorithm 1. Detect a signal tower based on ROIs returned by the classifiers.

Input: R_1, R_0: sets of red on/off ROIs, G_1, G_0: sets of green on/off ROIs,
          S: the set of previously detected signals
Output: $S \cup T$ where T are detections in current image

1: $l \leftarrow$ GET_LASER_ROI(); $T \leftarrow \varnothing$
2: **for all** $(R, G) \in \{R_0, R_1\} \times \{G_0, G_1\}$ **do**
3:     $T \leftarrow T \cup$ CREATE_LASER_SIGNAL(R, G, l)
4: **end for**
5: **if** $T \neq \varnothing$ **then**
6:     $T \leftarrow \{\arg\max_{t \in T}$ MATCH_QUALITY($\mathbf{t}, l$)$\}$
7: **else**
8:     **for all** $(r, g) \in R_0 \cup R_1 \times G_0 \cup G_1$ **do**
9:         $T \leftarrow T \cup$ RED_GREEN_MATCH(r, g)
10:     **end for**
11: **end if**
12: **if** $S = \varnothing$ **then return** T **end if**
13: **for all** $t \in T$ **do**
14:     $\mathbf{s}, dist \leftarrow$ CLOSEST_MATCH_BY_DISTANCE(S, t)
15:     **if** $dist \leq cfg_{max\_jitter}$ **then**
16:         UPDATE_STATE($\mathbf{s}, \mathbf{t}$)
17:     **else**
18:         $S \leftarrow S \cup t$
19:     **end if**
20: **end for**
21: **return** S

4.3 Signal Assembly

In the signal assembly, we compose a signal of the ROIs denoting enabled or disabled green (G_1 and G_0) and red (R_1 and R_0) signal lights which have been determined by the classifier described above. Algorithm 1 depicts the overall approach: first, it is tried to determine if ROIs can be found that fit into a laser-based ROI (ll. 1–4). If this succeeds, only the best matching ROI combination is kept (ll. 5–6), otherwise a full search on the image is performed (ll. 7–11). If no previous detections exist the algorithm returns the detected signals (l. 12). For the remaining candidates, a distance-based tracking is performed (ll. 13–20). States of previous detections are updated if a new detection is spatially close (ll. 14–17) or just added otherwise (l. 18).

Red/Green Matching. A crucial part is the matching of red and green ROIs that are spatially related such that they can represent a light signal. The input ROIs can be of the full image, or constrained to a laser-based ROI (see next section). We limit the search for the signal to red and green ROIs since the yellow light may appear to change color if the lights above or below are lit. Depending on the environment—which might contain arbitrary colorful objects that match the reference colors—the color classifier can return any number of rectangular ROIs, some of which may be part of the signal we are looking for. Algorithm 2 shows the procedure. First, GEOM_OK checks the width and vertical position of the green ROI, and the horizontal alignment of both ROIs:

> **function** GEOM_OK(r, g)
> > **return whether** width$(g) \leq cfg_{max\_width} \wedge \text{top}(g) > cfg_{green\_horizon}$
> > $\wedge \ \text{center}_x(g) \text{ - center}_x(r) \leq cfg_{x\_align\_threshold}$
> **end function**

Any (r, g) pair that does not satisfy this constraint cannot possibly be part of one signal tower, so it is skipped (ll. 2 and 18). A pair that passes is then checked for a special case that can occur due to the extreme brightness of the red and green lights (ll. 3 and 4). The used webcams have an acrylic lens cover that easily gathers a slight haze from dust and wiped-off fingerprints, often causing lit signals to create a colored bloom around the actual light source. The result is a ROI that does contain the signal light, but which is overly large. Whether a ROI ρ_1 is affected by bloom is determined in relation to another ROI ρ_2:

> **function** FIX_BLOOM(ρ_1, ρ_2)
> > **if** [width-ratio$(\rho_1, \rho_2) > cfg_{max\_width\_ratio}$
> > > $\wedge \ \text{aspect-ratio}(\rho_1) \leq cfg_{max\_aspect\_ratio}$
> > > $\wedge \ 0 < \text{vspace}(\rho_1, \rho_2) < 1.5 \cdot \text{height}(\rho_2)]$ **then**
> > > left$(\rho_1) \leftarrow$ left(ρ_2)
> > > width$(\rho_1) \leftarrow$ width(ρ_2)
> > > bottom$(\rho_1) :=$ top$(\rho_2) -$ height(ρ_2)
> > **end if**
> **end function**

If bloom is detected, the geometry of the ROI that is likely not or less-affected by bloom is used to improve the geometry. After this, another constraint tests if the vertical space between r and g is sufficient to fit a similarly-sized yellow ROI in between (VSPACE-OK). If this constraint is violated, the (r, g) pair is skipped. Otherwise the two ROIs are aligned well enough horizontally and a similarly-sized gap for a yellow ROI exists in between. If these are still too dissimilar in width (l. 6), the width of both is set to the mean width while preserving the center position (l. 7–9). If a pair of red and green ROIs ran through this process, we assume both must be part of the same signal tower, and generate a yellow ROI y that fits in between (l. 11–14).

Laser-Assisted ROI Pre-processing If the position of the MPS table could be detected with the 2D laser scanner, a bounding box can be estimated in which the colored ROIs are to be expected (cf. pink box in Fig. 6). We call this rectangular region the *laser ROI* or *l*. Within *l*, we can expect to find (almost) no clutter, which allows us make additional assumptions, as described in Algorithm 3. For example, we can now handle overexposure (Fig. 6) by simply merging the broken-down red or green ROIs into one (Lines 2 and 3). If the red or green light is switched off, large parts of it may appear in a very dark shade

---

Algorithm 2. Return ROI tuple (r, y, g) if r and g fit all constraints

---

1: **function** RED_GREEN_MATCH(r, g)
2:     **if** $r \neq \varnothing \wedge g \neq \varnothing \wedge$ GEOM_OK(r, g) **then**
3:         FIX_BLOOM(r, g)
4:         FIX_BLOOM(g, r)
5:         **if** VSPACE-OK(r, g) **then**
6:             **if** $\neg(1/cfg_{max\_width\_ratio} \leq$ width-ratio$(r, g) \leq cfg_{max\_width\_ratio})$ **then**
7:                 $\delta_w \leftarrow$ width$(g) -$ width(r)
8:                 left$(g) \leftarrow$ left$(g) + \delta_w/2$
9:                 width$(g) :=$ width$(g) + \delta_w/2$
10:            **end if**
11:            left$(y) \leftarrow$ mean(left(r), left(g))
12:            width$(y) \leftarrow$ mean(width(r), width(g))
13:            height$(y) \leftarrow$ mean(height(r), height(g))
14:            top$(y) \leftarrow$ bottom$(r) + 1/2($top$(g) -$ bottom$(r) -$ height$(y))$
15:            **return** (r, y, g)
16:        **end if**
17:    **end if**
18:    **return** $(\varnothing)$
19: **end function**

Terminology: left(ρ) denotes the left border of a ROI ρ, so right$(\rho) =$ left$(\rho) +$ width(ρ), top(ρ) denotes the top border of ρ, bottom$(\rho) =$ top$(\rho) +$ height(ρ); vspace(ρ_1, ρ_2) is the amount of vertical space between ρ_1 and ρ_2: top$(\rho_2) -$ bottom(ρ_2), and mean(a, b) is the arithmetic mean value of a and b. The function aspect-ratio(ρ) returns width$(\rho)/$height(ρ) if width$(\rho) >$ height(ρ), and height$(\rho)/$width(ρ) otherwise, so that for any ρ, aspect-ratio$(\rho) \geq 1$. width-ratio(ρ_1, ρ_2) simply returns width$(\rho_1)/$width(ρ_2), so it can be used to determine which one is wider than the other.

Algorithm 3. Generate a ROI tuple (r, y, g) from R and G that lies within l.

```
 1: function CREATE_LASER_SIGNAL(R, G, l)
 2:     r_m ← [⋃ R] ∩ l
 3:     g_m ← [⋃ G] ∩ l
 4:     if r_m ≠ ∅ ∧ [b_r ← CLASSIFY_BLACK(above(r_m))] ≠ ∅ then
 5:         δ_y ← top(r_m) − bottom(b_r)
 6:         if −δ_y > height(r_m) then
 7:             δ_y ← −height(r_m)
 8:         end if
 9:         top(r_m) ← bottom(b_r)
10:         height(r_m) ← height(r_m) + δ_y
11:     end if
12:     if g_m ≠ ∅ ∧ [b_g ← CLASSIFY_BLACK(below(g_m))] ≠ ∅ then
13:         δ_y ← top(g_m) − bottom(b_g)
14:         if δ_y > 0 then
15:             height(g_m) ← height(g_m) + δ_y
16:         end if
17:     end if
18:     s ← RED_GREEN_MATCH(r_m, g_m)
19:     if s ≠ ∅ then
20:         return s
21:     else if r_m ≠ ∅ ∧ g_m ≠ ∅ then
22:         e_r ← |1 − height(r_m)/width(l)|
23:         e_g ← |1 − height(g_m)/width(l)|
24:         if height(g_m) > width(l) ∧ e_g > e_r then
25:             FIX_HEIGHT(g_m, r_m)
26:         else if height(r_m) > width(l) ∧ e_r > e_g then
27:             FIX_HEIGHT(r_m, g_m)
28:         end if
29:         return RED_GREEN_MATCH(r_m, g_m)
30:     else if r_m ≠ ∅ then
31:         g, y ← CREATE_ROIs_FROM_RED(r_m)
32:         return (r_m, y, g)
33:     else if g_m ≠ ∅ then
34:         r, y ← CREATE_ROIs_FROM_GREEN(g_m)
35:         return (r, y, g_m)
36:     end if
37: end function
```

The union $\rho_1 \cup \rho_2$ is defined as the ROI ρ_m that contains both ρ_1 and ρ_2; the intersection $\rho_1 \cap \rho_2$ is the ROI that is contained in both ρ_1 and ρ_2 (which might be the empty ROI).

that does not have enough saturation to discriminate it from other, unwanted objects. In this case, the merged ROI may still not cover the full area of the signal light, but we also do not suffer from bloom. Since we do not expect black clutter (T-shirts, black machine parts etc.), we can look for the black socket (l. 12) or the black cap on top (l. 4). If the "black" classifier is successful, r_m or g_m may be improved using the respective black ROIs (ll. 5–10 and 13–16).

In the case of green, we only extend g_m (i.e. δ_y must be positive), since an unlit green signal part often turns out so dark as to appear black.

After this pre-processing the red/green matching algorithm is tried once with r_m and g_m (l. 18). If this succeeds, we have successfully obtained a tuple (r_m, y, g_m) that covers the full signal tower and can be passed on for tracking, brightness classification and blinking detection. If the red/green matching fails while both r_m and g_m are defined, one of the two ROIs might be blown up because of bloom, and can be improved if the other one does not suffer from bloom. Since the width of both r_m and g_m is limited to the width of the laser ROI l, we can estimate how badly bloom affects a ROI by its aspect ratio (ll. 22–23). The height of a bloom-affected ROI can then be improved in relation the ROI that is less affected (ll. 24–28).

Fig. 6. Laser ROI (pink rectangle), over-exposed lights (Color figure online)

After this, the Red/Green matching is tried once more with improved r_m or g_m. If this fails again, we give up on the current combination of ROI sets.

Apart from the case where we were able to obtain both r_m and g_m, we also handle cases where one of the two is missing (ll. 33–35). If, e.g., there is only a red ROI r_m, matching green and yellow ROIs can be generated. In this case a black ROI b that might have been found can be used to estimate the overall height of the color ROIs. Eventually, three similarly sized ROIs should be found.

4.4   Tracking, State Detection, and Filtering

After ROIs have been determined, distance-based tracking is performed. A resulting ROI tuple denoting a signal tower is matched against previous detections based on their distance and a maximum threshold (algorithm 1, ll. 14–16).

To determine the activation states, the brightness of the respective ROIs is evaluated. ROIs of high brightness are considered to be active lights. This information is stored in a circular buffer. The buffer length is determined by the number of frames that can be processed per second and the maximum blinking frequency in the RCLL, which is 2 Hz. The light state is considered to be unknown, as long as the buffer is not completely filled. Once filled, the number of on/off transitions is counted. If this is larger than 1, the specific light is blinking.

Additionally, a confidence value is produced based on the visibility of the signal tower. A positive value for this visibility history denotes consecutive positive sightings, negative values how many images the signal tower could not be detected. The value immediately turns negative on failed detections and is not step-wise decremented.

A filtering stage can be used that performs outlier removal, i.e., if the light signal is not visible for a short time the old state is assumed to still be valid. Additionally, the visibility history is used to explicitly state that a signal is unknown if the value is below a given threshold.

5   Evaluation

The approach has been evaluated in terms of run-time and detection rates. The experiments were conducted on the actual robot that features an additional laptop (cf. Fig. 2) with a Core i7-3520M CPU and 8 GB of RAM.

Figure 7 shows the *run-time* per frame as 1-second averages (30 images), without (a) and with (b) laser-based ROI pre-processing. During each run, the situation was modified twice after 20 and after 40 s, each time introducing more background clutter. Overall, the classifier requires the largest amount of processing time. After introducing more clutter, this part requires more processing time (to be expected with more pixels classified as red or green), as does the ROI assembly stage, since more ROIs are produced and are tried to be combined to a signal tower. Enabling the laser-assisted ROI pre-processing considerably reduces the overall processing time due to search space reduction for the classifier. The ROI assembly stage takes longer since it now requires additional classifier runs for the black cap and socket. The occasional outliers in (b) are due to the laser-line detection not converging and falling back to full-image classification.

Table 1 shows the *detection rate* from running the image processing pipeline on an actual robot detecting signals on an MPS in three situations posing typical problems. For each situation, the robot moved to four nearby locations facing the MPS and took 30 images. This was done for all valid light signal combinations (no blinking). Figure 8 shows example images for each dataset. Three different configurations were used. The pipeline was run without and with the laser-based ROI pre-processing. Finally, filtering was enabled. Blind search incurs high run-time and mediocre detection results (first macro column). Using the laser-based ROI vastly reduces the search space, increasing the detection rate considerably (second macro column). This is improved even further using the filtering and outlier removal (last macro column). With conservative settings requiring a high confidence, this results in virtually no false detections in actual games.

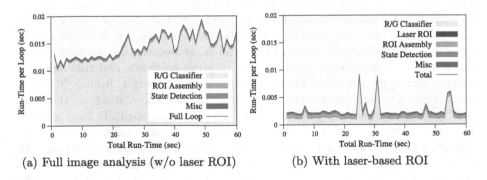

(a) Full image analysis (w/o laser ROI)   (b) With laser-based ROI

Fig. 7. Run-time data during live detection with and without a laser ROI. The Y axis denotes the time since system start, the X axis shows the run-time of the algorithm in 1 s averages stacked by sub-components.

Table 1. Results after applying the approach in three situations (cf. Fig. 8), each with seven signal combinations and from four different positions in front of the MPS; we give True (T) and false (F) positives (P) and negatives (N) (T/N omitted in this test), and detection rate.

Op. Mode	w/o Laser ROI			w/Laser ROI			Filtered (w/LR)		
Dataset ▷	DS 1	DS 2	DS 3	DS 1	DS 2	DS 3	DS 1	DS 2	DS 3
# T/P	310	350	604	708	764	692	495	463	393
# F/P	49	271	152	137	102	175	25	21	7
# F/N	509	245	112	23	0	1	0	0	0
Rate (%)	35.71	40.42	69.59	81.57	88.22	79.72	95.19	95.66	98.25

(a) DS 1: green background clutter and reflection. (b) DS 2: some clutter, red shines into yellow light. (c) DS 3: good conditions, no clutter.

Fig. 8. Example images from the datasets used in the detection rate evaluation. (Color figure online)

6   Conclusion

Integrating robots into human working areas will require recognizing cues that were designed for human consumption, such as light signal towers which are mounted to many machines in factories. In this paper, we have presented a novel approach to detect such towers and recognize the respective signal states. The algorithm encodes detailed human knowledge (collected in several RCLL competitions) that deals with typical problems that arise, for instance due to reflections of the lights on metal machine parts, or because colored light shines into adjacent lights when illuminated. To improve efficiency and robustness, a multi-modal approach has been chosen combining detection from a 2D laser scanner and a camera image. To use the algorithm in a new situation, the main modification required is providing a new mapping from such 2D laser scanner data to a region of interest in the image. The evaluation results show that the algorithm performs at a high speed allowing real-time light tower detection with a very good detection rate yielding only a negligible number of false readings.

An implementation of the algorithm is available as part of the Fawkes software stack release[4] for the RCLL [12]. The datasets and evaluation scripts are available on the project website.[5]

---

[4] https://www.fawkesrobotics.org/p/rcll2015-release/.
[5] https://www.fawkesrobotics.org/p/rcll-signal-vision.

Acknowledgments. T. Niemueller was supported by the German National Science Foundation (DFG) research unit *FOR 1513* on Hybrid Reasoning for Intelligent Systems (https://www.hybrid-reasoning.org).

References

1. Kagermann, H., Wahlster, W., Helbig, J.: Recommendations for implementing the strategic initiative INDUSTRIE 4.0. Final Report, Platform Industrie 4.0 (2013)
2. Lucke, D., Constantinescu, C., Westkämper, E.: Smart factory - a step towards the next generation of manufacturing. In: 41st CIRP Conference on Manufacturing Systems and Technologies for the New Frontier (2008)
3. Niemueller, T., Ewert, D., Reuter, S., Ferrein, A., Jeschke, S., Lakemeyer, G.: RoboCup logistics league sponsored by festo: a competitive factory automation testbed. In: Behnke, S., Veloso, M., Visser, A., Xiong, R. (eds.) RoboCup 2013. LNCS, vol. 8371, pp. 336–347. Springer, Heidelberg (2014). doi:10.1007/978-3-662-44468-9_30
4. Andersen, R.H., Solund, T., Hallam, J.: Definition and initial case-based evaluation of hardware-independent robot skills for industrial robotic co-workers. In: 41st International Symposium on Robotics (2014)
5. Angerer, S., Strassmair, C., Staehr, M., Roettenbacher, M., Robertson, N.M.: Give me a hand - the potential of mobile assistive robots in automotive logistics and assembly applications. In: IEEE International Conference on Technologies for Practical Robot Applications (TePRA) (2012)
6. Kitano, H., Asada, M., Kuniyoshi, Y., Noda, I., Osawa, E.: Robocup: the robot world cup initiative. In: 1st International Conference on Autonomous Agents (1997)
7. Ziegler, J., Bender, P., Schreiber, M., Lategahn, H., Strauss, T., Stiller, C., Dang, T., Franke, U., Appenrodt, N., Keller, C.G., Kaus, E., Herrtwich, R.G., Rabe, C., Pfeiffer, D., Lindner, F., Stein, F., Erbs, F., Enzweiler, M., Knöppel, C., Hipp, J., Haueis, M., Trepte, M., Brenk, C., Tamke, A., Ghanaat, M., Braun, M., Joos, A., Fritz, H., Mock, H., Hein, M., Zeeb, E.: Making bertha drive - an autonomous journey on a historic route. IEEE Intell. Transp. Syst. Mag. **6**(2), 8–20 (2014)
8. Fairfield, N., Urmson, C.: Traffic light mapping and detection. In: International Conference on Robotics and Automation (ICRA) (2011)
9. Jentzsch, S., Riedel, S., Denz, S., Brunner, S.: TUMsBendingUnits from TU Munich: RoboCup 2012 logistics league champion. In: RoboCup Symposium (2012)
10. Barrett, S., Genter, K., He, Y., Hester, T., Khandelwal, P., Menashe, J., Stone, P.: UT Austin Villa 2012: standard platform league world champions. In: Chen, X., Stone, P., Sucar, L.E., Zant, T. (eds.) RoboCup 2012. LNCS (LNAI), vol. 7500, pp. 36–47. Springer, Heidelberg (2013). doi:10.1007/978-3-642-39250-4_4
11. Murch, C.L., Chalup, S.K.: Combining edge detection and colour segmentation in the four-legged league. In: Australasian Conference on Robotics and Automation (2004)
12. Niemueller, T., Reuter, S., Ferrein, A.: Fawkes for the RoboCup logistics league. In: Almeida, L., Ji, J., Steinbauer, G., Luke, S. (eds.) RoboCup 2015. LNCS (LNAI), vol. 9513, pp. 365–373. Springer, Cham (2015). doi:10.1007/978-3-319-29339-4_31

Selecting the Best Player Formation for Corner-Kick Situations Based on Bayes' Estimation

Jordan Henrio[1(✉)], Thomas Henn[1], Tomoharu Nakashima[1],
and Hidehisa Akiyama[2]

[1] Osaka Prefecture University, Osaka, Japan
{jordan.henrio,thomas.henn}@cs.osakafu-u.ac.jp,
tomoharu.nakashima@kis.osakafu-u.ac.jp
[2] Fukuoka University, Fukuoka, Japan
akym@fukuoka-u.ac.jp

Abstract. In the domain of RoboCup 2D soccer simulation league, appropriate player positioning against a given opponent team is an important factor of soccer team performance. This work proposes a model which decides the strategy that should be applied regarding a particular opponent team. This task can be realized by applying preliminary a learning phase where the model determines the most effective strategies against clusters of opponent teams. The model determines the best strategies by using sequential Bayes' estimators. As a first trial of the system, the proposed model is used to determine the association of player formations against opponent teams in the particular situation of corner-kick. The implemented model shows satisfying abilities to compare player formations that are similar to each other in terms of performance and determines the right ranking even by running a decent number of simulation games.

Keywords: Soccer simulation · Strategy selection · Bayes' estimation · Earth mover's distance · Hierarchical clustering

1 Introduction

One of the essential parts in developing a team in the RoboCup 2D soccer simulation league is to design an effective strategy or method that outperforms opponent teams. Player formation is one of the most important aspects in the strategy design as it gives the guidelines of the decision making during the game. The player formations are generally designed according to a given opponent team. However, this tasks is labourious since the search space can be really large depending on the set-play the formation is associated with. In addition, selecting the best strategy regarding unknown opponents is one of the most challenging task of this league.

On the other hand, it is not necessary to create a specialized player distribution against each of all opponents as it is possible that some of them are similar

© Springer International Publishing AG 2017
S. Behnke et al. (Eds.): RoboCup 2016, LNAI 9776, pp. 428–439, 2017.
https://doi.org/10.1007/978-3-319-68792-6_36

regarding particular features. By using this fact, it is possible to cluster similar opponents together and then look for the most effective strategy against this group.

This research proposes a model which groups similar opponent teams together during a learning stage and determines the most effective player formation for each cluster by using sequential Bayes' estimations. Then, during a real game the system classify the current opponent among one of the determined clusters and apply the strategy that has been estimated to be the best regarding the resulting classification.

2 Related Work

The task of recognizing the opponent strategy in order to apply an appropriate counter action has been already addressed in previous researches. For example, the works of Visser *et al.* [1] and Drücker *et al.* [2] propose a system for recognizing opponent's formations and then apply a counter formation. This is done by using an artificial neural network that is able to classify data among 16 formation classes and then apply the counter formation especially designed against each class. Classified data are a representation of the field as a grid expressing the formation of the opponent. Riley and Veloso [3] also proposed a method performing opponent classification by using a grid representation of the field. However, the grid is used for displacement and location of objects instead of just observing the structures of formations. Also, they used a decision tree instead of neural networks.

However, this paper focuses on how to select the best player formation regarding a particular cluster rather than the issue of how build clusters. The selection issue is a well know problem in probability, often named as the k-armed bandit problem. This problem has been already addressed in the context of simulated soccer game by Bowling *et al.* [4]. They proposed to apply an algorithm that selects the most effective and available team plans during particular situations. The most effective plan is the one that minimizes the regret which is the amount of additional reward that could have been received by behaving optimally. The work presented in this paper is similar in the sense that we also focus on a method which selects the best choice in a particular situation. However, the situation is considered to be a particular opponent team in a particular event of the game and not a particular state of the environment. Doing so allows us to focus on more precise effectiveness measurement functions.

3 Proposed Model

As a solution, we propose to use a simple model as shown in Fig. 1. This system takes a label of cluster of opponent teams' as an input parameter and returns the best strategy to apply. However, it is difficult to estimate the best strategy among the ones we have in hand. For this reason the proposed model consists of two modules, *Learner* and *Selector*.

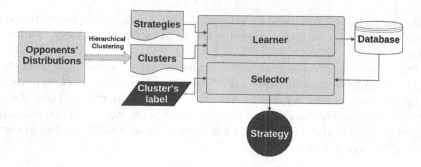

Fig. 1. Proposed model

The *Learner* part works in offline mode. It takes a set of clusters as an input parameter. Clusters are obtained by applying hierarchical clustering on opponent teams' distributions before the *Learner* works. Then, its role is to learn against each cluster, by looking at the set of strategies that we have already developed, which one is the most appropriate. This decision is done by performing statistical analysis on simulated games by using the different strategies as it is explained in Sect. 5. Once the learner is able to decide which strategy we should apply regarding a particular cluster of opponent teams, it inserts the cluster-strategy pair in a database.

The *Selector* part works in online mode. It takes the resulting classification of the current opponent team as input. Then, by using the estimations done by the learner it can directly return the best strategy to apply.

As a first trial of this system, the proposed model was used to determine which corner-kick formations should be used against particular clusters of opponent teams from JapanOpen competitions. This championship is the RoboCup yearly meeting within Japan.

4 Opponents Clustering

4.1 Team Distributions

At a general level the system groups opponent teams by similarity in the player formation. In order to understand the player formation, the distribution of the players is used. In this paper, offensive corner-kick formations were designed regarding the defensive formation of the opponent. Therefore, this work suggests to build such player distribution representing the defense of the opponent by considering locations of players over the corner-kick area. As a way to represent the opponent player distributions, the system designs a partition of the corner-kick area of the field as shown in Fig. 2. This partition is totally arbitrary, but shows how opponent players are spread in this area during their defensive corner-kick situations. Resulting distributions represent the number of players in each of the 18 blocks in the area of interest (the so-called attacking third). Also, an additional

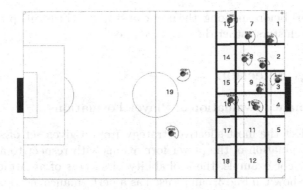

Fig. 2. 19 blocks of the partitioned soccer field

block representing the remaining part of the field is considered. For example, Fig. 2 shows eleven opponents in their defensive corner-kick formation. By analyzing this defense player formation, the resulting distribution would be written as the following 19-dimensional integer vector: $[1, 0, 1, 0, 0, 0, 1, 2, 1, 1, 0, 0, 1, 0, 0, 1, 0, 0, 2]$.

If we consider a rougher partition of the field, the player distributions would tend to be the same regardless the opponent team. For instance, let us consider the extreme case where the grid is only constitued of one cell. By doing so, any team would be represented by the 1-dimensional integer vector. Conversely, a finer partition would make the player distributions become much more different from each other.

4.2 Clustering Process

Once all opponents' distributions are determined, the degree of similarity between each possible pair is analyzed in order to generate a distance matrix. The distances between distributions are computed by using the Earth Mover's Distance (EMD) [5] method. EMD provides a pseudo metric measure between two probability distributions. It can handle vectors with different dimensionalities and weighted features. The measurement process is expressed as a transportation problem where one distribution is the supplier and the other the customer. The cost between the supplier and customer is related to the distance between features of the two distributions which are computed by using a ground distance such as the euclidean distance. This is an advantage of using EMD since we can evaluate how much two formations of players are different by using a ground distance that makes sense in the case of soccer field. Also, the possibility to consider weighted features could become an advantage in future work since it is possible to give more importance to certain parts of the formations.

It is possible to apply hierarchical clustering on the resulting distance matrix in order to determine clusters of similar opponent teams. This process merges the pairs with the smallest distance together until all the opponents belong to a single cluster. By using a threshold representing the maximum distance accepted between clusters before merging, the user can stop the clustering process and then obtain several clusters rather than a single one.

5   Strategy Selection

5.1   Performance Evaluation of Player Formations

In order to select the most effective strategy from a given set of strategies, the performance evaluation of the player formations with respect to a success metric is required. For example, the probability of success of an attack following a corner-kick as shown in Fig. 3, can be used as a performance metric. However, the RoboCup 2D soccer simulation league introduces randomness in the way the players interact with the environment. Each player receives imperfect and noisy information from his virtual sensors. As a result, two soccer games with the exactly same teams can differ significantly. Therefore, evaluating player positioning performance is a challenging task. There is a lot of variance when trying to estimate a success metric. Thus, it is necessary to run a large number of soccer games in order to estimate one player formation's performance with enough precision.

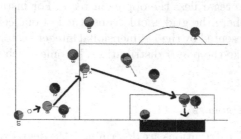

Fig. 3. Example of an actions' chain for a corner-kick which leads to a successful score

In order to sort each player formation with respect to the others, the difference in means between the probability of successful corner-kick distributions of each player formation's simulation is considered.

5.2   Sequential Bayes' Estimation

Bayes' theorem is stated as in (1):

$$p(\theta|D) = \frac{p(D|\theta)P(\theta)}{p(D)}, \tag{1}$$

where $p(\theta|D)$ is called the posterior, $p(D|\theta)$ is likelihood, $p(\theta)$ the prior and $p(D)$ is the evidence which stands as a normalizing constant. It is calculated as expressed in (2):

$$p(D) = \int p(D|\theta)p(\theta)d\theta, \tag{2}$$

where θ represents the value of the parameter to estimate, in our case that is the probability of the success of an attack following a corner-kick. D corresponds to the new data extracted at the moment of applying the theorem. The purpose of the Bayes' theorem is to update the prior belief $p(\theta)$ we have about the value of θ using new data D. The posterior distribution $p(\theta|D)$ will then correspond to our updated belief in the different possible values of θ.

It is possible to sequentially update the parameters by applying Bayes' theorem each time one or more simulations are over by using the previous posterior as the prior for the next computation of the posteriors.

Obviously, according to the success metric used by the system, the results of one experience (successful corner-kicks observed within one game), the likelihood follows a binomial law as in (3):

$$p(X = k) = C_k^n \theta^k (1 - \theta)^{n-k}, \tag{3}$$

where n is the number of total corner-kicks observed during the simulated game, k the number of successful corner-kicks observed and θ the probability of an offensive corner-kick to be successful by using the player formation.

Navarro and Perfors [6] have demonstrated that the posterior distribution of a beta-binomial distribution is also a beta-distribution. Thus, if you consider the probability of getting a successful corner-kick by using a particular formation of players, the posterior distribution after observing k successes over the total n corner-kicks can be expressed as in (4):

$$p(\theta|k, n) \sim B(a + k, n - k + b) \tag{4}$$

where B denotes the beta distribution, a and b are the parameters coming from the prior distribution and θ is the probability of a successful attack following a corner-kick which is the parameter we want to estimate. This fact simplifies computations since it is possible to represent the performance of a player formation by a Beta distribution and then after running a game, construct a new Beta distribution by giving the number of corner-kicks and the number of observed successes.

5.3   Player Formations Comparisons

A difference distribution is used to determine whether one player formation is better than another or whether additional simulations are required to be sure. For this purpose, the system begins by computing the Highest Density Interval (HDI) [7] which is the interval that spans most of the mass of the distribution (say 95%) such that every point inside the interval has a higher probability than any point outside the interval.

To compare the performance of two player distributions in the attack case (let us say Distributions 1 and 2), the probability of success of Distributions 1 and 2 is considered, defined as p_1 and p_2, respectively. Assume that a posterior distribution for each of those probabilities is obtained. In this case, by calculating all of the possible values of $p_1 - p_2$, it is possible to obtain a distribution of the difference of $p_1 - p_2$. HDI is used instead of the posteriors in order to simplify the computation of this calculation.

Then, there are three possible scenarios as follows. Preliminary, let us define $[u, v] = \{x \in \mathbb{R} | u \leq x \leq v\}$ to be the HDI of the resulting distribution $p_1 - p_2$. The first possible case is when $u \geq 0$, which means $p_1 - p_2 > 0 \Rightarrow p_1 > p_2$. Naturally, the opposite case is also possible, $p_1 - p_2 < 0 \Rightarrow p_1 < p_2$, which happens when $v \leq 0$. Another possible sketch is that $[u, v] = \{x \in \mathbb{R} | w \leq u \leq x \leq v \leq z\}$ where w and z are around 0 which is equivalent to saying that $p_1 = p_2$ for all practical purposes. The $[w, z] = [-0.015, +0.015]$ interval is used in this paper. If the two player formations are deemed equal or when the maximum number of simulations is reached, the player formation with less variance is considered as better than the other.

6   Experiments

6.1   Opponents Clustering

First experiments involved 12 teams participating in Japan Open competitions, as well as two versions of Agent2D [8] which does not participate in any competitions, but are used by most of the participants as the starting point of team development. Three clusters were created by the hierarchical clustering. The second cluster is the most populated among the three ones because it represents the teams using a player formation similar (if not the same) to that of Agent2D, which constitutes probably their implementation starting point. On the other hand, the third cluster included only the team Ri-one_B 2015 that is too far to be merged with any other clusters.

6.2   Association Learning

In order to experiment the abilities of the learner, we used three corner-kick formations that were already implemented in our team. Additionally, a special script was used. This script runs simulations which only perform corner-kick situations. Generally, 37 corner-kicks are executed during one simulation, but this number can vary from one run to another due to the randomness present in simulations. As first experiment, 10 simulations per strategy were simulated before comparing pairs of player formations and a beta distribution with parameters 2 and 2 (i.e., Beta(2, 2)) was used to represent our prior beliefs.

The results of our first experiment are shown in Fig. 4, the probability density functions of each player formation against each cluster. It can be seen that each cluster is associated with a different player formation. Excepted the pair (1, 3) for the first cluster (Fig. 4a), all pairs can be easily ranked. Then, the most effective player formation can be determined with certainty. However, the HDI of almost all distributions is quite large, thus a precise probability of success cannot be provided.

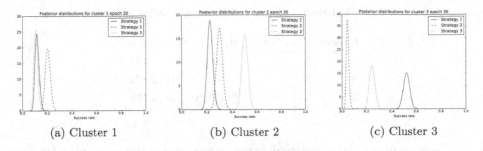

(a) Cluster 1   (b) Cluster 2   (c) Cluster 3

Fig. 4. Posterior distributions for each cluster, by running $M = 10$ simulations

In order to improve estimations about the player formations' probability of success, a second experiment was conducted and simulations were generated by blocks of 60 games. That is, 60 games for each player formation were conducted every time the performance is compared. Figure 5 shows the resulting probability density functions of the player formation. As expected, curves became finer and tended to be centered to the true probability of their respective player formation. Also, the pairs which were difficult to differentiate after the first experiment, can now be well ordered.

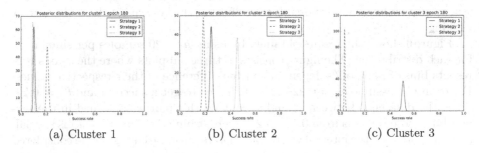

(a) Cluster 1   (b) Cluster 2   (c) Cluster 3

Fig. 5. Posterior distributions for each cluster, by running $M = 60$ simulations

Table 1 provides a summary of the second experience. It shows the final associated player formation for each cluster. Also, it indicates the HDI of the selected player formation. Finally, it gives the ratio of the best player formation's distribution mean over the second best's.

6.3   System Validation

The proposed method in this paper estimates the probability of success of offensive player formations against given opponent teams. In other words, the parameter θ of a binomial distribution is estimated. However, it is legitimate to wonder about the correctness of the estimations.

Table 1. Results summary of the second experiment.

Cluster	Distribution	HDI	Ratio
1	2	[0.203, 0.237]	1.787
2	3	[0.531, 0.571]	2.073
3	1	[0.471, 0.512]	2.179

The experiment in this section puts player formations aside and evaluates how well our method can differentiate probability distributions with parameters close together. Additionally, it estimates how many simulations are required to draw trustful conclusions about the ranking of offensive player formations regarding their success probability.

Player formations are substitued by a set of randomly generated parameters θ. Then, a simulation of n offensive corner-kicks by using a particular formation is substitued by n sampling from a binomial distribution parameterized by one of the randomly generated θ values. Notice that the system knows the generated parameters and is able to order them. Afterwards, as in the parameter estimation method, by feeding the Bayesian estimator with the number k of successes over the n samples the system updates prior beliefs about the parameters and tries to estimates the value of the randomly generated parameters. Actually, since the true values are known, it is possible to verify that the system gets back the correct ranking.

Figure 6 shows the results obtained by using $n = 20$ samples per simulation for each distribution. The figure consists of three subplots where the x-axis represents bins of pairs of θs depending on the difference of their respective values. For example, assume $\theta_1 = 0.22$ (22% of chance to get a success) and $\theta_2 = 0.24$. Since the difference between θ_1 and θ_2 is 0.02, this pair is contained in the second bin whose range is from 0.1 to 0.2. The first bin (the one in black) is special, since it represents the interval where parameters are close enough to be considered

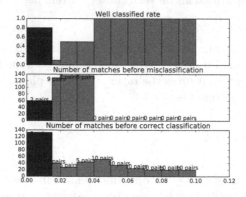

Fig. 6. System's validation by blocks of 20 samples

equal. The number of generated parameters was done in such a way that each bin contains ten pairs of parameters.

The first subplot shows the rate of well ordered pairs in each bin. According to this plot, the system can perfectly rank pairs with a difference greater than 0.04 and this accuracy decreases as the distances between parameters increase. In this subplot the correct ranking inside the first bin is not really important since it contains pairs that are considered to be equal.

The second and third subplots show the number of correctly ranked (respectively uncorreclty ranked) pairs in each bin and the number of sampling steps before drawing conclusion (y-axis). As indicated in the first subplot, the ranking is perfect for any pairs contained in the bin whose range is greater than 0.04. Furthermore, at most fifty samples were required to obtain such results and this number decreases as the distances increase. However, the system has difficulties to rank pairs with difference less than 0.04.

Figure 7 shows the performance evaluation by using $n = 60$ samples per simulation for each distribution. Actually, increasing this number improves the accuracy since the system is able to rank prefectly pairs with at least a difference of 0.03 by requiring at most eighty samples. These two experiments show that increasing the number of samples increase the accuracy. On the other hand, since the data that the player receives is biased and because of the rarity of corner-kick event occurence during one single game, a deviation of 4% of success probability between two formations is not so significant. For this reason, in the particular case of selecting the best strategy for offensive corner-kicks, estimating the formations' parameter by running only 20 simulations is enough.

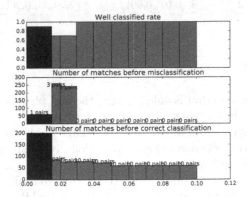

Fig. 7. System's validation by blocks of 60 samples

6.4   Cluster Validation

It could be also interesting to look at the performance of each player formation in the clusters. While some teams have been considered as similar in terms of defensive player formations, it does not exclude the possibility of disparities among the teams of the same cluster since results of actions are not affected by player positioning only. Proper agents' skills are an equally important factor.

In order to verify the quality of association according to each opponent team, another alternative of the algorithm was applied. This one is nearly the same as the standard version, but rather than trying to estimate the effectiveness of each player formation against the clusters, the system estimates it against every team individually.

Table 2 summarizes the teams whose the most effective strategy is not the same as the one estimated against the cluster which they belong. As a reminder, Cluster 1 counts three teams and Cluster 2 counts ten teams. Regarding the team Ri-one_A 2015 (Cluster 1), Distribution 1 seems to be better than Distribution 2 which is the one associated to its cluster. However, the error seems to be much more serious, according to the team A_TSU_BI-2014 (Cluster 2) since Distribution 2's mean is slightly more than three times better than the selected formation's (Distribution 3) mean. In fact, this association error is not significant during a game against Ri-one_A 2015. On the other hand, performing games against A_TSU_BI-2014 with the wrong strategy would affect the results of games since there is roughly 20% more chance to get a success by using the formation associated to Distribution 2 rather than the one selected (Distribution 3).

Table 2. Difference between expected performances in cluster.

Team	Cluster	Selected (Dist./HDI)	Best option (Dist./HDI)	Ratio
Ri-one_A 2015	1	2/[0.13, 0.16]	1/[0.23, 0.27]	1.73
A_TSU_BI- 2014	2	3/[0.07, 0.09]	2/[0.23, 0.26]	3.28

7   Conclusion

In this research, a system that is able to select the best player formation in corner-kick situations regarding a group of teams was developed. This decision is taken by doing sequential Bayes' estimations from the results of several games. The model does not create effective offensive player formations, but instead indicates the best that we have already in hand.

The results are satisfying since the system is able to rank correctly player formations with at least a difference of 4% of success probability by proceeding only 20 simulations. Furthermore, it is possible to increase the precision of the system by getting more data. However, by doing so the learning time would increase considerably. Additionally, it is quite impossible to feel a difference during one game, since during a true match the number of corner-kicks that happen is very low. This is why such an error rate is acceptable.

On the other hand, there is a possibility of disparities inside the clusters. As explained earlier, if the difference between player formations is only 4% there is actually no real difference in terms of final results of one game due to the rare occurence of corner-kicks executed during a standard game. But if a player formation is not designed to be the best and is actually three times better than the selected one, difference could be observed regarding final results. These disparities are due to the fact that during the clustering process only the positions of opponents are considered and not the defensive skills of the team. Then, another clustering criterion can be considered for better performance.

Finally, while the first trials selected player formations for corner-kicks only it is possible to use it for any situation of the game, at the condition to have a criterion for opponents clustering and a success metric for data observations. Furthermore, it is possible to extend this system in order to build strategies, i.e. sets of player formations that cover any situation, rather than selecting the best player formation according to a particular situation. In this case opponents would not be in only one cluster, but in several clusters, one for each situation. However, such a learning process seems difficult to realize since a very large number of standard games is required, ones which do not simulate only one kind of situation, in order to see enough every kind of situations and hope to obtain good approximations of each player formation.

References

1. Visser, U., Drücker, C., Hübner, S., Schmidt, E., Weland, H.-G.: Recognizing formations in opponent teams. In: Stone, P., Balch, T., Kraetzschmar, G. (eds.) RoboCup 2000. LNCS, vol. 2019, pp. 391–396. Springer, Heidelberg (2001). doi:10.1007/3-540-45324-5_44
2. Drücker, C., Hübner, S., Schmidt, E., Visser, U., Weland, H.-G.: Virtual werder. In: Stone, P., Balch, T., Kraetzschmar, G. (eds.) RoboCup 2000. LNCS, vol. 2019, pp. 421–424. Springer, Heidelberg (2001). doi:10.1007/3-540-45324-5_51
3. Riley, P., Veloso, M.: On behavior classification in adversarial environments. In: Parker, L.E., Bekey, G., Barhen, J. (eds.) Distributed Autonomous Robotic Systems 4, pp. 371–380. Springer, Heidelberg (2000). doi:10.1007/978-4-431-67919-6_35
4. Bowling, M., Browning, B., Veloso, M.: Plays as effective multiagent plans enabling opponent-adaptive play selection. In: Proceedings of International Conference on Automated Planning and Scheduling (ICAPS 2004) (2004)
5. Rubner, Y., Tomasi, C., Guibas, L.J.: The earth mover's distance as a metric for image retrieval. Int. J. Comput. Vis. **40**, 99–121 (2000)
6. Navarro, D., Perfors, A.: An introduction to the beta-binomial model. In: COMPSCI 3016: Computational Cognitive Science (2012)
7. Kruschke, J.K.: Doing Bayesian Data Analysis: A Tutorial Introduction with R and BUGS. Academic Press/Elsevier, Cambridge (2010)
8. Akiyama, H., Nakashima, T.: HELIOS base: an open source package for the RoboCup soccer 2D simulation. In: Behnke, S., Veloso, M., Visser, A., Xiong, R. (eds.) RoboCup 2013. LNCS, vol. 8371, pp. 528–535. Springer, Heidelberg (2014). doi:10.1007/978-3-662-44468-9_46

Standard Rescue Tasks Based on the Japan Virtual Robotics Challenge

Masaru Shimizu[1], Masayuki Okugawa[2], Katsuji Oogane[3], Yoshikazu Ohtsubo[4], Tetsuya Kimura[5], Tomoichi Takahashi[6(✉)], and Satoshi Tadokoro[7]

[1] Chukyo University, Nagoya, Japan
shimizu@sist.chukyo-u.ac.jp
[2] Aichi Institute of Technology, Toyota, Japan
okugawa@aitech.ac.jp
[3] Niigata Institute of Technology, Kashiwazaki, Japan
koogane@mce.niit.ac.jp
[4] Kinki University, Higashi-osaka, Japan
ohtsubo@mech.kindai.ac.jp
[5] Nagaoka University of Technology, Nagaoka, Japan
kimura@mech.nagaokaut.ac.jp
[6] Meijo University, Nagoya, Japan
ttaka@meijo-u.ac.jp
[7] Tohoku University, Sendai, Japan
tadokoro@rm.is.tohoku.ac.jp

Abstract. Robotic technology can be effectively used in the inspection and maintenance of aging social infrastructure. The capabilities of these robots are similar to those required for disaster response robots. This paper presents the concepts and outlines of the Japan Virtual Robotics Challenge (JVRC). The tasks in this challenge were designed based on the Sasago tunnel disaster, in which ceiling panels fell over 130 m as a result of the release of the anchor bolts from the walls over time. Lessons from JVRC indicate that service robots can function as first responders, and that disaster rescue tasks have much in common with every day maintenance tasks. Standard tasks for robots are proposed and one scenario is demonstrated to show its validity. We hope that the application of robots used for everyday maintenance can improve the availability of robots at disaster scenes.

Keywords: Rescue robot · Standard task · Service robot · Maintenance

1 Introduction

Disasters can occur at anytime and anywhere around the world. When a disaster strikes, the long period of time taken for emergency inspection of social infrastructure and its hindrance to quick recovery is always highlighted. Since the damage and malfunction of social infrastructure has an adverse effect on human life and civil society, both preventive maintenance and quick recovery are important for disaster prevention.

© Springer International Publishing AG 2017
S. Behnke et al. (Eds.): RoboCup 2016, LNAI 9776, pp. 440–451, 2017.
https://doi.org/10.1007/978-3-319-68792-6_37

Any social infrastructure that is over 50 years old experiences serious problems because of the limited lifespan of concrete structures. Although periodic inspection of major infrastructure is conducted, it is still insufficient to ensure the detection of abnormalities or signs of rapid deterioration. Additionally, there are some areas where it is difficult to perform human inspection. The Sasago tunnel accident in Japan was such a case [15]. The anchor bolts were being forced out from the walls over time and ceiling panels had fallen by over 130 m.

Robotics is being applied for different purposes in social infrastructure of various fields. The ICARUS project in EU and NEDO Robot White Paper 2014 are examples of the application of robotics in the fields of infrastructure, construction and civil engineering, factory plant maintenance, agriculture, disaster response, and nuclear energy [5,9]. If robots that perform maintenance tasks of social infrastructure can also be adapted to act as first responders at disaster sites, it would increase their range of applications.

The Japan Virtual Robotics Challenge (JVRC) was held at October 7–10, 2015 [6]. Eight teams participated and their robots (six humanoids, one with crawler, and a hybrid of a humanoid and crawler) performed seven tasks. The concept of the tasks was based on the idea of search and rescue operations conducted by robots, and robots conducting inspection tasks share many of their characteristics. In this paper, a list of standard tasks from the lessons of JVRC is proposed tasks that robots can perform as first responders during emergencies. The following section describes the background of social infrastructure inspection and a history of rescue robots. The outline of the JVRC with tunnel disasters and the idea of an "equivalent task" are introduced in Sect. 3. Sections 4 and 5 contain lessons learnt from the JVRC and describe standard rescue tasks in case of future emergencies.

2   Rescue Robots and Their History of Competitions

Many projects on rescue tasks and robots have been promoted in the form of robotics competition (Table 1). Their purposes range from search-and-rescue operations at disaster sites to inspections of social infrastructure and oil platforms. The RoboCup Rescue [11], DARPA Robotics Challenge (DRC) [3] in US, and ARGOS Challenge in France [1] are a few such examples. They have concrete targets that open up to the areas or fields wherein robots were used in real life, such as the Hanshin-Awaji earthquake, the September 11 attacks at the World Trade Center, and the Fukushima Daiichi Nuclear Plant in 2011. The validity of these projects has been recognized internationally [7].

In 1980s, the possibility of accidents caused by aging social infrastructure was pointed out in US [10] and disasters related with social infrastructures have been reported around the world recently. In order to prevent the accident from the aging accidents, periodical inspection and constant maintenance are considered to be important. Perform inspection and maintenance tasks urge to work at narrow and closed areas, e.g., pipe lines, bridges, and inside of hazardous facilities. Robot technology have been applied to tasks where human are difficult to access the places and hard do perform. Those task are in the same

Table 1. History of rescue robot competition and test field

Year	Title of competition	Target		Field	Background case
		Operation	Robot		
1997	Disaster city	Rescue	Land/air	Standardization	Oklahoma City bombing (1995)
1998	RoboSub		Sea		
2000	RoboCup rescue	Rescue	Land/air	Real	Hanshin-Awaji Earthquake(1995)
2005	Robotics test	Facility	Field/facility	Land	Real filed
2006	ELROB		Land/air		
2008	Roboboat		Sea		
2011	Guardian centers	Rescue	Land/sea/air	Real field	
2012	ICARUS	Rescue	Land/sea/air		Earthquakes in l'Aquila, Haiti
2013	DARPA	Rescue	Land	Real/simulation	Fukushima nuclear disaster
2013	euRathlon	Rescue	Land/sea/air		Fukushima nuclear disaster
2014	ARGO challenge	Survey	Land	Real field	
2015	JVRC	Maintenance/ rescue	Land	Simulation	Sasago tunnel ceiling accident

ones in disaster response application, e.g., inspection of damaged places and flammable/hazardous areas [4].

3   Overview of Japan Virtual Robotics Challenge

3.1   Background and Scenario

The JVRC is a robotics competition involving the use of computer simulations. It is part of a collaborative project between the US and Japan, organized by the New Energy and Industrial Technology Development Organization (NEDO). The participants in JVRC developed control software for robots that were provided by the organizer or were designed by the participants themselves. The participants remotely operate their robots by using the Choreonoid robot simulator and compete in various tasks [2,8].

The Sasago tunnel disaster was chosen as the scenario for the tasks in the JRVC. The reason for the collapse of ceilings was that they were suspended by bolts that eventually became loose. It is believed that regular checks for signs of deterioration would have prevented the ceiling from falling. The tasks involve the design of periodic safety checks via visual inspection and hammering test and rescue operations during disasters.

The scenario is as follows: an earthquake caused the tunnel wall to collapse onto moving vehicles, causing a crash, which in turn led to a massive pileup of following vehicles. The affected vehicles included a tanker and a large truck. The tanker overturned and the truck scattered its cargo across the roadway. A few of the victims remained trapped inside their vehicles. The maintenance of the tunnel facilities is required to be performed by robots.

3.2   Outline of Tasks

Table 2 shows a list of tasks included in the JVRC. There are two categories: ordinary tasks and rescue tasks. Ordinary tasks are typical inspection tasks that involve visual inspection and a hammering test (Fig. 1). Both tasks, and especially the hammering test, are difficult to recreate in a simulation as they

Table 2. Task of JVRC

Id	Purpose	Images
O1	Visual Inspection Check for cracks on the tunnel wall and road	
O2	Hammering test Check the conditions of fastener components and damaged wall	
R1	Vehicle Inspection Check the vehicles and surrounding conditions for vehicle damage, leaking fuel and survivors outside vehicles	
R2	Traverse Obstacles Traverse obstacles, or in the confined space formed by obstacles	
R3	Vehicle Inspection using Tools Investigate condition inside the vehicle by using tools	
R4	Secure the Route Remove the obstacles from the specified route to secure the route	
R5	Support Fire Extinguishing Use equipments in "Road tunnel emergency facility installation standards".	

overhead view of tunnel before accident:

Fig. 1. Two inspection tasks: vision inspection and hammering test.

are; therefore, their equivalent tasks were created. These equivalent tasks are explained in the following section.

O1: Visual Inspection

This task represents the visual inspection of cracks, swelling, and leakage in the walls and roads of the tunnel. It is given by the figures in O1 in Table 2. A tunnel is approximately 3.6 m wide and inspection targets are placed on the tunnel wall at heights up to 2.4 m.

After inspection, the condition of the cracks must be reported in the form of an Inspection Report [14].

O2: Hammering Test

This test is used to inspect the condition of the parts of the fastener and the damaged wall by hammering the parts or close to the damaged area. The sound produced by hammering reflects the difference between normal areas and the areas that need to be repaired. The figures in Table 2 show that a fan is installed on the tunnel roof with the help of fasteners. Target areas for inspection are located near the fastener components.

The report of the condition of the components must be prepared in the same format as O1.

R1: Vehicle Inspection

Sometimes vehicles are overturned in tunnel accidents. This makes it necessary to check for someone in the vehicle or investigate the possibility of oil being spilled outside. The situations vary depending on whether the vehicle is a standard or large car, the tires are in contact with the road, etc.

R2: Traversing Obstacles

After an accident, the roads are filled with fallen objects. Exploring the tunnel requires one to go through the area filled with debris or to squeeze into conned spaces formed by obstacles. Obstacles in the left diagram of Table 2 consist of $40 \, \text{cm}^2$ blocks with a $15°$ ramp[1]. The diagram on the right is the confined space through which some robots are required to crouch down to pass.

R3: Vehicle Inspection using Tools

Tools must be used to check the inside of the vehicle for people who may be trapped inside. These tools include spreaders and ladders, which are used in everyday situations.

---

[1] This field is composed of the specified used in DRC.

In case the overturned vehicle is a large car, there are two kinds of tasks to undertake. One scenario involves climbing the ladder and identifying the target through the upper window. The other is to investigate through the upper window without using a ladder.

R4: Secure the Route

It is necessary to remove obstacles from the road to secure the route for smooth evacuation and rescue operations. In Table 2, the obstacles are represented by L-shaped bars and blocks whose size and weight are variable. The obstacles over the route are targets to be removed, and the routes are the obstacles are designated by color.

R5: Support Fire Extinguishing

Facilities for extinguishing fires are installed in a tunnel. This task involves utilizing the facilities to extinguish fires instead of relying on human effort. It begins with opening the box, pulling out the hose, removing the nozzle, connecting the nozzle to the hose, and finally opening the valve.

3.3 Equivalent Tasks for Inspection

When a robot performs the hammering test, it moves its end effector to the specified position, manipulates the effector along a specified direction relative to the test object, and collects sound when the end effector hits the target. The series of moves can be simulated. However, it does not seem to represent the function of the hammering test in actual inspection tasks. Instead, the test is replicated to a more feasible level that evaluates the equivalent of this basic inspection function. The basic task is to maintain control over the robot.

The equivalent tasks in the JVRC include the visual inspection of targets consisting of QR codes and a pipe[2]. Figure 2 shows the target and snapshots of robots executing O1 and O2. The QR code is attached at the bottom of the

Fig. 2. Image of inspection target as equivalent task in O1 and O2: QR code in the pipe (left), a robot inspecting a target on the wall of tunnel (center), and performing a hammering test (right).

---

[2] The same structure of pipe star or visual target used in RoboCup Rescue Robot League.

pipe, and the robot is required to move its end effector along the pipe without making contact. The size of the QR codes and the pipe length can be changed to modify the difficulty of the task.

3.4 Comparisons to DRC Tasks and Result

The DRC was inspired by the Fukushima-Daiichi nuclear accident in Japan in 2011. In this challenge, humanoid robots were supposed to follow the following eight instructions in a simulation and in the real world instead of humans.

Vehicle: Drive and exit utility vehicle
Terrain: Walk across rough terrain
Ladder: Climb industrial ladder with 60–70° inclination
Debris: Remove debris from doorway
Door: Open series of doors with lever door handle
Wall: Cut through wall by using tools
Valve: Locate and close leaking valves
Hose: Carry and connect fire Hose.

The design of the JVRC tasks is based on the concept that ordinary tasks and rescue tasks have a lot in common with elementary robotic tasks, even though robots for ordinary tasks are designed with suitability in mind. Table 3 shows the common points between the tasks of the DRC and the JVRC. Ordinary tasks O1 and O2 and inspection task R1 are not in the DRC. The ordinary tasks are thought to be one category of service robots such as RoboCup@Home. The tasks of service robots include manipulation and object recognition at the conditions of everyday environment. Further, the vehicle task in the DRC has no corresponding task in JVRC.

Table 4 shows the scores of the top four teams in the competition. All robots, except one ranked below the top four teams, got no points in R5. The winning team was a centaur-type robot, in which the upper body was a humanoid and

Table 3. Comparison between the tasks of JVRC and DRC

	R1	R2	R3	R4	R5
Vehicle					
Terrain		√			
Ladder			√		
Debris				√	
Door					
Wall		√			
Valve					√
Hose					√

Table 4. Scores of the top four robots in JVRC

	Robot type	O1	O2	R1	R2	R3	R4	R5	Total
1	Centaur	57	6	59	85	10	54	-	271
2	Humanoid	20	6	64	54	10	29	-	182
3	Humanoid	29	12	62	15	10	30	-	158
4	Crawler	18	0	17	61	0	30	-	126

the lower body was a crawler-type robot. Figure 3 shows the centaur-type robot and a humanoid robot pull the hose from the box in the R5 task. The second and third places went to humanoid robots who participated in the DRC. In the fourth place was a crawler-type robot with one manipulator. Whereas the robots of the other three teams were simulated models, the robot of the top team was a combination of parts of a real humanoid robot and a real crawler. This was the only robot that was not a simulation.

Fig. 3. A centaur-type and humanoid robots pulling the hose from the box in R5.

4 Proposal of Standard Rescue Tasks

4.1 Types of Robot

The tasks of JVRC are redesigned from typical rescue tasks; service robots involved in maintaining and inspecting social structures would be first responders to emergencies. At Fukushima, exploration inside buildings was an urgent issue in the aftermath of the disaster. At present, various kinds of robots are in operation, and plans are being made to use them in the decommissioning of nuclear plants [13]. Various kinds of services and tasks have been developed with the use of drones, including delivery services and bridge inspection. Decommission and service tasks have a lot in common with maintenance and inspection tasks.

4.2 Standard Rescue Task as First Resonder Function

Disaster scenes include a variety of cases, and different scenes require different functions and operations of rescue robots. The following four tasks are proposed as elemental tasks highly similar to inspection tasks.

1. Quick exploration of a changed area after disaster: Exploration and the associated map generation of the scene following the disaster are important tasks for rescue robots. These two tasks are the main topics of rescue leagues. For service robots used in maintaining social structures, maps of structures are used

every day. At disaster sites, the information required concerns the changes in
the scene that have occurred due to the accident. Robots are assessed on how
efficiently and completely they can explore and report on the damaged area,
given a map of the scene from prior to the disaster.

2. Sensor monitoring task:

In addition to map generation, sensor data are used to detect victims, gas
leakages, res, and other important features of the scene. Robots are required
to report the data to the operators either on line or offline. The data consist
of time, place and sensing information. The sensing data are either raw or
recognition data. Figure 4 shows three pictures of a QR code. A program will
commonly read Fig. 4(a) correctly, and not read Fig. 4(b) and (c). The three
pictures are an example of a sensing task requirement, and QR code mark
sensing is proposed as the second task.

3. Manipulation task:

Figure 4(c) shows an example of how something like a cable or dirt on a mark
can prevent code recognition. If this were encountered by a human worker,
he/she would get rid of the cable, or wipe off the dirt in order to read the code.
Simple manipulation functions that are used in maintenance tasks widen the
rescue task, as the task R4 from JVRC indicates.

4. Action in dark and confined spaces:

Inspection of anchor bolts in tunnels is an example of dark places where
flashlights are typically used to light the space. Falling furniture, ceilings or
other obstructions are caused by accidents and these result in confined spaces
for robots to operate. The traverse of these confined space in R2 of JVRC is
thought to be an energy consuming task for robots.

(a) readable QR image. (b) an distorted image. (c) blobby or blocked image.

Fig. 4. QRcode marks.

4.3   New Scenario Containing the Standard Task

In 2014, a new challenge was proposed to demonstrate the potential of the
RoboCup rescue league (RSL) in minimizing losses during disasters [12]. They
uploaded the CAD data of Portmesse Nagoya; the venue of RoboCup 2017.
Figure 5(a) and (b) shows the overview of Portmesse Nagoya and a 3D model of
Hall No. 1 with the exhibition hall.

Using the CAD data, more concrete rescue scenarios can be created than the scenarios used presently at RSL competitions. The following scenario is such a case; during an emergency, a robot travels through a hall toward an exit. This situation is motivated from R4 task of JVRC. The task of the robot is to check on damage in the center of the hall. Two blocks that have fallen in the corridor are observed from the exit. After dealing with these obstructions, the robot is required to continue past and explore the area further.

(a) An overvie of Portmesse Nagoya. (b) 3D CAD model of Hall 1 with display.

Fig. 5. RoboCup 2017 venue: Portmesse Nagoya

The activity consists of two standard tasks; quick exploration and manipulation tasks. Figure 6(a) shows screenshots of JVRC that robots pulls a rod to go their goals. Figure 6(b), (d) and (d) show areas near an entrance in Portmesse

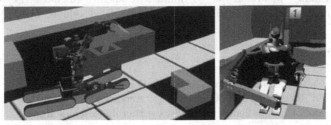

(a) robots pulling a rod to secure the route.

(b) corridor with two blocks. (c) one block is removed. (d) cleared corridor.

Fig. 6. Clearing spaces task to perform next tasks.

Nagoya Hall 1. The rescue robot pushing a block to the side, and proceeding to the center of the hall of the hall for further exploration. This demonstration shows a combination of standard, realistic tasks in inspection, maintenance, and rescue scenarios.

5 Conclusions

In this paper, tasks of robots at rescue and maintenance sites are compared and discussed. In 2015, the JVRC competition was held and the competition tasks were designed based on the maintenance tasks of social infrastructures. As with the maintenance of social infrastructure, in which robots are already being used, plans are being made to use robots to inspect areas not easily accessible by humans. These tasks have many similarities with rescue tasks, which DRC employed as target tasks. The concept of equivalent tasks is introduced in simulations and the tasks were used in the JVRC. From the lessons of the JVRC, new standards for tasks are proposed, and one simulation task is demonstrated to show the possibility of creating more realistic scenarios for RSL.

We hope these tasks can be used to broaden the functional standards for robots.

Acknowledgment. The work was supported by NEDO Grant for international research, development and RoboCup Fund. The authors acknowledge to Adam Jacoff (NIST) for his advice and comments for JVRC task development from the viewpoint of standard performance test method of the response robots. We also appreciate insightful discussions with IRS-U (Captain Kennichi Makabe) from the viewpoint of the disaster responders. Finally, we would like to thank to Souichiro Suzuki (AIT) and Takumi Ohta (NUT) for their dedicate effort of the task model development in JVRC.

References

1. ARGOS Challenge. http://www.argos-challenge.com/. Accessed 22 Feb 2016
2. Choreonoid. http://www.choreonoid.org/. Accessed 22 Feb 2016
3. DARPA Robotics Challenge. http://www.theroboticschallenge.org/. Accessed 22 Feb 2016
4. Disaster City. https://teex.org/Pages/about-us/disaster-city.aspx. Accessed 17 May 2016
5. ICARUS. http://www.fp7-icarus.eu/project-overview
6. Japan Virtual Robotics Challenge. http://www.jvrc.org/en/index.html. Accessed 22 Feb 2016
7. Murphy, R.R.: Disaster Robotics. The MIT Press, Cambridge (2014)
8. Nakaoka, S.: Choreonoid: extensible virtual robot environment built on an integrated GUI framework. In: Proceedings of the 2012 IEEE/SICE International Symposium on System Integration (SII2012) (2012)
9. NEDO Robot White Paper. http://www.nedo.go.jp/library/robot_hakusyo.html. Accessed 22 Feb 2016. (in Japanese)
10. Choate, P., Walter, S.: America in Ruins: The Decaying Infrastructure. Duke University Press, Durham (1983)

11. R.R. Rescue. http://wiki.robocup.org/wiki/Robot_League. Accessed 22 Feb 2016
12. Takahashi, T., Shimizu, M.: How can the RoboCup rescue simulation contribute to emergency preparedness in real-world disaster situations? In: Bianchi, R.A.C., Akin, H.L., Ramamoorthy, S., Sugiura, K. (eds.) RoboCup 2014. LNCS, vol. 8992, pp. 295–305. Springer, Cham (2015). doi:10.1007/978-3-319-18615-3_24
13. TEPCO. http://www.tepco.co.jp/en/decommision/index-e.html. Accessed 22 Feb 2016
14. The Ministry of Land, Infrastructure. Transport and tourism, periodic inspection guide for road tunnel (2014). (in Japanese)
15. Tsuji, M., et al.: Learning from accident: ceiling fall accident of Sasago tunnel in Chuo expressway. Mon. Fire Fighting **35**(4), 1–11 (2013)

Virtually Adapted Reality and Algorithm Visualization for Autonomous Robots

Danny Zhu[✉] and Manuela Veloso

Computer Science Department, Carnegie Mellon University,
Pittsburgh, PA 15213, USA
dannyz@cs.cmu.edu

Abstract. Autonomous mobile robots are often videotaped during operation, whether for later evaluation by their developers or for demonstration of the robots to others. Watching such videos is engaging and interesting. However, clearly the plain videos do not show detailed information about the algorithms running on the moving robots, leading to a rather limited visual understanding of the underlying autonomy. Researchers have resorted to following the autonomous robots algorithms through a variety of methods, most commonly graphical user interfaces running on offboard screens and separated from the captured videos. Such methods enable considerable debugging, but still have limited effectiveness, as there is an inevitable visual mismatch with the video capture. In this work, we aim to break this disconnect, and we contribute the ability to overlay visualizations onto a video, to extract the robot's algorithms, in particular to follow its route planning and execution. We further provide mechanisms to create and visualize virtual adaptations of the real environment to enable the exploration of the behavior of the algorithms in new situations. We demonstrate the complete implementation with an autonomous quadrotor navigating in a lab environment using the rapidly-exploring random tree algorithm. We briefly motivate and discuss our follow-up visualization work for our complex small-size robot soccer team.

1 Motivation and Introduction

Imagine watching a mobile autonomous robot, or a video of one, as it moves about and performs some task in the world, and trying to infer what it intends to accomplish. Seeing such a robot can be interesting, but only a tiny amount of the information contained in and used by the algorithms that control the robot is actually available in this way.

Having some means to expose this hidden state of robots in an intuitive manner is valuable for both the developers of the robots and for other observers. Typical debugging and information displays show some abstract version of the state on a screen, ranging in level of detail from simple text output to two-dimensional displays to full three-dimensional renderings of the robot. Such displays can be informative, but there remains a visual mismatch with reality: any display is

© Springer International Publishing AG 2017
S. Behnke et al. (Eds.): RoboCup 2016, LNAI 9776, pp. 452–464, 2017.
https://doi.org/10.1007/978-3-319-68792-6_38

still disjoint from the actual view of the robot itself. By merging the depictions of the real robot and the debugging information, we can break this disconnect and obtain a much better view of the progress of the algorithm. We contribute the ability to create a view of a robot in motion that takes a plain video and combines it with logs made during execution by adding extra drawings on top of the video; these drawings depict extra information to give direct insight into the execution of the algorithm.

In this work, we chose to demonstrate these drawing techniques using navigation in a two-dimensional environment with a quadrotor, which is shown in Fig. 1. We define sets of obstacles in the space and instruct the quadrotor to fly between specified points while avoiding the obstacles. We take visualizations generated by the control algorithms and draw them with the correct perspective and occlusion onto a video of the quadrotor such that they appeared in the video to be markings on the ground. The quadrotor is controlled by algorithms intimately tied to the robot's location and the space around it, but with a great deal of computation going on to produce the result at each step which cannot be understood solely from the original video. Creating augmented visualizations is especially helpful when working with robots such as quadrotors, which have the capability to move in ways that humans cannot follow.

Besides revealing internal details of the planning done by the robot, we also demonstrate the creation and display of virtual adaptations of the real environment, in the form of obstacles which are present only virtually; without the integrated display that we provide, there would be no way to see such items in their context relative to the execution of the algorithm.

A primary motivation of our work comes from our experience with CMDragons, our robot soccer team for the RoboCup Small Size League (SSL) [12,13]; we have created similar visualizations for our SSL team. The control programs of teams in the SSL are complex, with hierarchical architectures containing dozens of subcomponents, each making decisions based on the state of the world 60 times per second. While videos of SSL are interesting to watch, the fast pace and small game objects can make it difficult to tell in detail what is happening on the field at any given moment. In Fig. 2, we show a typical frame from a video of an SSL game, along with the result of adding our drawings on top of it.

2   Related Work

The visualization we present here is closely related to augmented reality, which is, broadly, the inclusion of virtual objects in the view of a real 3-D environment. Augmented reality has seen a wide variety of uses, both in relation to robotics and otherwise; it allows for enhancement of a user's view of reality by providing additional information that would not otherwise be available. Azuma [2] listed a variety of uses of augmented reality, including those for medicine, manufacturing, robotics, entertainment, and aircraft control. One common use of augmented reality within robotics is to provide enhanced interfaces for teleoperated robots. Kim [10] described an interface for controlling a robotic arm that could overlay

Fig. 1. The quadrotor we used to demonstrate our visualization, alongside its protective hull, which is used for safety when flying indoors. The colored pattern on top is not normally part of the hull; we used it for tracking (see Sect. 5). (Color figure online)

Fig. 2. Left: a plain frame from a video of the SSL. Right: an example visualization created based on that frame. Robots of the two teams are surrounded by circles of different colors, and other drawings generated by our team code are projected onto the field as well. (Color figure online)

3-D graphics onto a live video view of the arm. The interface provided a view of the predicted trajectory of the arm, allowing for much easier control in the presence of signal delay between the operator and the arm. Our work shares the 3-D registration and drawing that are common to augmented reality systems, although most definitions of augmented reality require an interactive or at least live view, which we do not currently provide. Amstutz and Fagg [1] developed a protocol for communicating robot state in real time, along with a wearable augmented reality system that made use of it. They demonstrated an example application that overlaid information about nearby objects onto the user's view, one that showed the progress of a mobile robot navigating a maze, and one that showed the state of a robotic torso. Though they focused mainly on the protocol aspect, their work has very similar motivations and uses to ours.

Other recent work has also involved using augmented reality overlays to aid in the understanding of the behavior of autonomous robots. Chadalavada et al. [6] demonstrated a robot that projected its planned future path on the ground in front of it. They found that humans in the robot's vicinity were able to plan smoother trajectories with the extra information, and gave the robot much higher ratings in attributes such as predictability and reliability, verifying that describing an agent's internal state is valuable for interacting with humans. Collett [7] developed a visualization system similar to the one described here, but we focus on combining the drawing with the ability to display and animate details of the future plan of the robot, rather than the low-level sensor and state information from the robot.

Animation has long been an invaluable tool for understanding algorithms. In algorithm animation, the changes over time in the state of a program are transformed into a sequence of explanatory graphics. Done well, such a presentation can explain the behavior of an algorithm much more quickly than words. BALSA [4] is an influential early framework for algorithm animation. It introduced the idea of "interesting events," which arise from the observation that not every single operation in an algorithm should necessarily be visualized. In BALSA, an algorithm designer inserts calls to special subroutines inside the algorithm; when execution of the algorithm reaches the calls, an interesting event is logged, along with the parameters to the call. The designer then writes a separate renderer that processes the log of interesting events into an actual animation to display.

We are performing a form of algorithm animation here, but with an unusual focus: most animations are designed with education in mind and delve into the details of an abstract algorithm, rather than being integrated with a physical robot. Additionally, the typical lifecycle of an algorithm being executed on a mobile autonomous robot is different from the standalone algorithms that are usually animated. In most animations, a single run of the algorithm from start to finish results in an extended, and each interesting event corresponds to some interval of time within it. For an autonomous robot, algorithms are instead often run multiple times per second, with each run contributing a tiny amount to the behavior of the robot, and it makes sense for each frame of an animation to depict all the events from one full run. An example of this kind of animation comes from the visual and text logging systems employed by teams in the RoboCup Small Size League, a robot soccer league. The algorithms behind the teams in the league consist of many cooperating components, each with its own attendant state and computations running 60 times per second. As a result, understanding the reasons behind any action that the team takes can be challenging, necessitating the development of powerful debugging tools in order for a team to be effective. For text-based log data, Riley et al. [14] developed the idea of "layered disclosure," which involves structuring output from an autonomous control algorithm into conceptual layers, which correspond to high- and low-level details of the agent's state. Teams have also developed graphical logging in tandem with the text output: the algorithms can output lists of objects to draw, and we can view both this drawing output and text output either in real time or in a replay fashion. The existence of these tools speaks to the need for informative debugging and visualization when dealing with autonomous agents.

3 Pipeline

The overall sequence of events in creating the visualizations we demonstrate is as follows. First, we record a video of the robot or robots while the algorithm is running. During execution, each run of the algorithm saves a sequence of interesting events to a file, along with the current time.

Then we manually annotate certain aspects of the video to enable the rendering to be done: the time at which the video started, which allows each frame of the video to be corresponded with the interesting events from the appropriate run of the algorithm, and the ground and image coordinates of at least four points on the ground in the video, which allows any point in the ground coordinates (with which the algorithm) works to be translated into the corresponding coordinates in the video. We only need to mark points on the ground plane because we are only drawing points within it.

Finally, we combine the video, the interesting events, and the annotations to produce one output video containing both the video recording and extra information. During this stage, each frame of the video of the real robot is associated with the events from the most recent run of the algorithm. Each event is then transformed into zero or more appropriate drawing primitives, which are overlaid onto the frame as described in Sect. 4.

4 Rendering

To take the descriptive information generated by the algorithm and draw it convincingly on the video, we need two key pieces of information for each frame: the set of pixels in the frame that should be drawn on, and the transformation from the ground coordinates used by the algorithm into video pixel coordinates.

4.1 Masking

We were flying our quadrotor above an SSL playing field, and we wanted to draw only on the field surface, not on top of the quadrotor or any obstacles on the field. In order to do so, we need to detect which pixels in the video are actually part of the field in each frame. Since the majority of the field is solid green, a simple chroma keying (masking based on the color of each pixel) mostly suffices. We convert the frame to the HSV color space, which separates hue information into a single channel, making it more robust to lighting intensity changes and well-suited for color masking of this sort. We simply took all the pixels with hue values within a certain fixed range to be green field pixels, providing an initial estimate of the mask.

To account for the field markings, which are not green, we applied morpho-logical transforms [15] to the mask of green pixels. The idea is that the markings form long, thin holes in the green mask, and there are no other such holes in our setup; therefore, a dilation followed by an erosion with the same structuring element (also known as a closing) fills in the field markings without covering any other pixels. We also applied a small erosion beforehand to remove false positives from the green chroma keying. The structuring elements for all the operations were chosen to be iterations of the cross-shaped 3×3 structuring element, with the number of iterations chosen by hand.

4.2 Coordinate Transformation

Since we are only concerned with a plane in world space, we need a homography to give the desired coordinate transformation, if we assume an idealized pinhole camera [8]. A pinhole camera projects the point (x, y, z) in the camera's coor-dinate system to the image coordinates $\left(\frac{x}{z}, \frac{y}{z}\right)$, so the coordinates (u, v) are the image of any point with coordinates proportional to $(u, v, 1)$. Suppose that the ground coordinates $(0, 0)$ correspond to the coordinates $\boldsymbol{q}$ in the camera's coor-dinate system, and that $(1, 0)$ and $(0, 1)$ correspond to $\boldsymbol{p}_x$ and $\boldsymbol{p}_x$ respectively. Then, for any x and y, the ground coordinates (x, y) correspond to the camera coordinates

$$x\,\boldsymbol{p}_x + y\,\boldsymbol{p}_y + \boldsymbol{q} = \begin{pmatrix} \boldsymbol{p}_x & \boldsymbol{p}_y & \boldsymbol{q} \end{pmatrix} \begin{pmatrix} x \\ y \\ 1 \end{pmatrix}.$$

Thus, multiplying by the matrix $\begin{pmatrix} \boldsymbol{p}_x & \boldsymbol{p}_y & \boldsymbol{q} \end{pmatrix}$ takes ground coordinates to the corresponding image coordinates; the resulting transformation is a homog-raphy. There are well-known algorithms to compute the homography that best fits a given set of point or line correspondences. We used the function for this purpose, findHomography, from the OpenCV library [3].

We primarily used a stationary camera; for such videos, we manually anno-tated several points based on one frame of the video and used the resulting homography throughout the video. We used intersections of the preexisting SSL field markings as easy-to-find points with known ground coordinates. We also implemented a line-tracking algorithm similar to the one by [9], which allows some tracking of the field with a moving camera.

4.3 Drawing

Finally, with the above information at hand, drawing the desired shapes is straightforward. To draw a polygon, we transform each vertex individually according to the homography, which gives the vertices of the polygon as it would appear to the camera. Since a homography maps straight lines to straight lines, the polygon with those vertices is in fact the image of the original polygon. Then we fill in the resulting distorted polygon on the video, only changing pixels that are part of the field mask. We used crosses and circles (represented as many-sided polygons) as primitives. Figure 3 shows an example of an frame from the output video, along with the image created by drawing the same primitives directly in a 2-D image coordinate system, and Fig. 4 demonstrates the stages involved in drawing each frame.

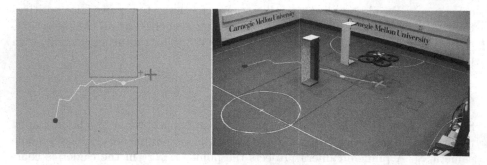

Fig. 3. Left: A 2-D visualization generated from the interesting events of one run of the RRT, using a domain based on physical obstacles. Right: The result of drawing that visualization onto the corresponding frame from the video of the real robot.

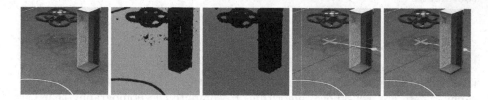

Fig. 4. The stages in processing each frame of a video to overlay the virtual drawings. From left to right: (1) the original frame, (2) the raw green mask, (3) the mask, after morphological operations, (4) the result of drawing without taking the mask into account, and (5) the drawing, masked appropriately. (Color figure online)

5   Quadrotor Navigation

As our testbed for demonstrating this merged visualization, we used the rapidly-exploring random tree (RRT) algorithm [11] to navigate a quadrotor around sets of virtual and real obstacles.

5.1   The RRT Algorithm

The RRT algorithm finds a path from a start state to a goal state within some state space, parts of which are marked as obstacles and are impassable. The most basic form of the algorithm consists of iterating the following steps, where the set of known states is initialized to contain only the given start state:

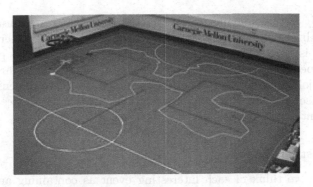

Fig. 5. The visualization generated from the RRT running with a domain consisting of entirely virtual obstacles.

1. generate a random state r
2. find the closest known state c to r
3. extend c toward r, creating e
4. if e is directly reachable from c, add e to the set of known states, recording that c is its parent.

The iteration terminates when a state is found sufficiently close to the goal state. The entire path is then constructed by following the chain of parents to the start state.

The simplest state space for an RRT consists of the configuration space of the robot, with dynamics ignored; states are connected simply by drawing lines in the space. Although this is a great simplification, it is straightforward in concept and implementation, and often leads to sufficiently good results.

Since the quadrotor can accelerate in any direction without yawing to face it, we chose to ignore orientation and take states to be the locations within a rectangular region on the ground. As is typical for kinematic RRTs, the random state generation simply chooses a location uniformly at random within the set of configurations and the metric is Euclidean distance between locations.

A common optimization used with RRTs is to simplify the returned path by skipping directly from the start state to the last state in the path which is directly reachable from it [5]. This causes the robot to navigate directly toward the first turn on the path; without it, the randomness of the RRT means that the first step in the path may take the robot in widely varying directions between timesteps. After each run of the RRT, the quadrotor attempts to fly toward the point resulting from this optimization.

5.2   Obstacle Domains

For simplicity of implementation, our obstacles consisted only of straight line segments (which can be used to build polygonal obstacles). Some of the domains were based on real objects, as shown in Fig. 3, while some were purely virtual, as shown in Fig. 5.

The purely virtual domains provide a particularly interesting use case for our kind of visualization. Without this augmented display, the perceived behavior of the robot is hard to explain: it simply follows a convoluted path while in apparently open space. As always, information about the algorithm can still be displayed disjointly from the quadrotor itself, e.g., in a two-dimensional visualization on a screen, but the combined animation provides reduced indirection and a more intuitive presentation.

5.3 Interesting Events

Conceptually, we think of each interesting event as containing an event type, the possibilities for which are described below, along with a list of parameters, whose meanings depend on the type.

Most of the interesting events during one full run of the RRT roughly correspond to the individual steps of the iteration. They fall into the following categories:

- the generation of a random state,
- the addition of a new known state,
- the addition of a state to the final path, and
- the computation of the first state of the simplified path.

For the first and last category, the parameters simply contain the coordinates of the state in question; for the second and third, the parameters contain the coordinates of the state and its parent.

We also treat the following items as events in that they represent information that is useful for monitoring the algorithm and can lead directly to drawings; although they are perhaps not "events" in the usual sense:

- the locations of the obstacles,
- the start state (i.e., the current position of the robot),
- the goal state, and
- the acceleration command sent to the quadrotor.

After the fact, during the processing of the video, we can choose which of the types of events to include in the processing of the video, and how to depict each one. In the examples shown here, we draw lines from the first simplified state to its parent (which is the start state), and from all subsequent states in the path to their parents. We also distinguish the first simplified state and goal state with circles and the start state with a cross. The acceleration command is depicted with a smaller cross whose position is offset from the start state by a vector proportional to the acceleration. Finally, the obstacles are drawn as red lines in every frame.

5.4 Sensing and Planning

In order to provide high-quality tracking of the quadrotor's position, we attached an SSL-Vision [16] pattern to the top of the quadrotor. SSL-Vision uses overhead cameras to track the locations of specific colored patterns; it is typically used for the RoboCup SSL, which has robots solely on the ground, but is flexible enough to track the pattern without modification despite the tilting of the quadrotor and the increase in perceived size due to its altitude.

The main control loop executes each time sensor data are received from the quadrotor, which occurs at approximately 15 Hz. Using the position of the camera and the reported altitude from the sensor data, it computes a true position above the ground. (Since SSL-Vision is intended for robots at fixed heights, the position it reports is actually the intersection of the line from the camera to the quadrotor with a horizontal plane at the robot height.) We estimate the current velocity of the quadrotor by performing a linear fit over the last five observed positions.

At each iteration, the planner runs the RRT from the current position to the current goal to generate a new path through the environment. Only the first position in the optimized path is relevant; the controller attempts to fly the quadrotor toward that position.

Since the obstacles in the state space are virtual, it may happen that the quadrotor moves across an obstacle, between states that are not supposed to actually be connected. When this happens, the planner ceases normal path planning and moves the quadrotor back to the point where the boundary was crossed, to simulate being unable to move through the obstacle. In this case, the last valid point is shown with a red cross, as in Fig. 6.

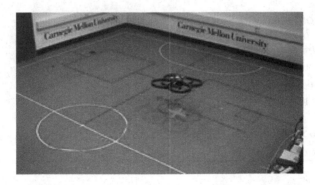

Fig. 6. The visualization generated when the quadrotor has executed an impossible move across an obstacle. The target point is the circle in the top corner, but navigation cannot continue until the quadrotor returns a point reachable from the red cross. (Color figure online)

5.5   Control

There remains the problem of actually moving the quadrotor to the target point. The quadrotor accepts pitch and roll commands, which control the horizontal acceleration of the quadrotor, as well as yaw and vertical speed commands, which we use only to hold the yaw and altitude to fixed values. Since acceleration can only be changed by rotating the whole body of the quadrotor, there is latency in the physical response, compounded by the latency in the vision system and communication with the quadrotor.

Thus we need to supply acceleration commands that allow the quadrotor to move smoothly to a desired point in the face of latency and unmodeled dynamics. Since the low-level control was not the focus of this work, we simply devised the *ad hoc* algorithm shown in Algorithm 1. It takes the displacement to the target from a projected future position of the quadrotor, computes a desired velocity which is in the direction of the displacement, and sets the acceleration to attempt to match that velocity. The perpendicular component of the velocity difference is more heavily weighted, since we considered it more important to get moving in the right direction than at the right speed.

Algorithm 1. The algorithm used to control the quadrotor. The current location of the quadrotor is denoted by *loc*, its velocity by *vel*, and the target point by *target*; we define $\text{proj}_u v$ to be the projection of v onto u and $\text{bound}(v, l) = \frac{v}{\|v\|} \cdot \min(l, \|v\|)$.

$\Delta t_{loc} = 0.3\,\text{s}$
$\Delta t_{vel} = 0.5\,\text{s}$
$vel_{max} = 1000\,\text{mm/s}$
$a_{max} = 1500\,\text{mm/s}$
$\Delta t_{acc}^{\|} = 0.8\,\text{s}$
$\Delta t_{acc}^{\perp} = 0.5\,\text{s}$
function CONTROL(*loc, vel, target*)
 $loc_{fut} \leftarrow loc + \Delta t_{loc} \cdot vel$
 $\Delta loc \leftarrow target - loc_{fut}$
 $vel_{des} \leftarrow \text{bound}\left(\frac{\Delta loc}{\Delta t_{vel}}, vel_{max}\right)$
 $\Delta vel \leftarrow vel - vel_{des}$
 $\Delta vel_{\|} \leftarrow \text{proj}_{vel_{des}} \Delta vel$
 $\Delta vel_{\perp} \leftarrow \Delta vel - \Delta vel_{\|}$
 return $\text{bound}\left(\frac{\Delta vel_{\|}}{\Delta t_{acc}^{\|}} + \frac{\Delta vel_{\perp}}{\Delta t_{acc}^{\perp}}, a_{max}\right)$
end function

---

6 Conclusions and Future Work

In this paper, we demonstrated a means of visualizing the algorithms controlling an autonomous robot that intuitively depicts the relationship between the robot's state and the environment around it. We overlaid drawings generated based on the navigation algorithms for a quadrotor such that they appear to be part of the environment itself.

We intend to extend and generalize the implementation of the interesting event handling and drawing to other domains. A first step in that direction is the SSL drawings discussed previously; we have implemented the equivalent drawings for the SSL, but for the moment, the two systems are disparate and ad hoc, and we would like to unify the representations and interfaces involved.

We would also like to improve the interactivity of the system as a whole; although the video processing already occurs at faster than real time, equipment limitations mean we need to stop recording before beginning processing. We are interested in allowing the robot to respond to actions by a human viewing the visualization, such as changing the target point or the set of obstacles, creating a closed loop system between human and robot that incorporates both physical and virtual elements.

For now, the capabilities of our system with regards to the input video are also limited: we require a background that is amenable to chroma keying in order to perform the pixel masking. More advanced computer vision techniques could reduce or remove the need for this condition.

References

1. Amstutz, P., Fagg, A.H.: Real time visualization of robot state with mobile virtual reality. In: The IEEE International Conference on Robotics and Automation, Proceedings of ICRA 2002, vol. 1, pp. 241–247. IEEE (2002)
2. Azuma, R.T.: A survey of augmented reality. Presence **6**(4), 355–385 (1997)
3. Bradski, G.: OpenCV. Dr. Dobb's J. Softw. Tools (2000)
4. Brown, M.H., Sedgewick, R.: A system for algorithm animation, vol. 18. ACM (1984)
5. Bruce, J., Veloso, M.: Real-time randomized path planning for robot navigation. In: IEEE/RSJ International Conference on Intelligent Robots and Systems, vol. 3, pp. 2383–2388. IEEE (2002)
6. Chadalavada, R.T., Andreasson, H., Krug, R., Lilienthal, A.J.: That's on my mind! Robot to human intention communication through on-board projection on shared floor space. In: European Conference on Mobile Robots (ECMR) (2015)
7. Collett, T.H.J.: Augmented reality visualisation for mobile robot developers. Ph.D. thesis, University of Auckland (2007)
8. Forsyth, D.A., Ponce, J.: Computer Vision: A Modern Approach. Prentice-Hall, Englewood Cliffs (2003)
9. Hayet, J.-B., Piater, J., Verly, J.: Robust incremental rectification of sports video sequences. In: British Machine Vision Conference (BMVC 2004), pp. 687–696 (2004)
10. Kim, W.S.: Virtual reality calibration and preview/predictive displays for telerobotics. Presence: Teleoper. Virtual Environ. **5**(2), 173–190 (1996)
11. LaValle, S.M.: Rapidly-exploring random trees: a new tool for path planning. Technical report 98–11, Iowa State University (1998)
12. Mendoza, J.P., Biswas, J., Cooksey, P., Wang, R., Klee, S., Zhu, D., Veloso, M.: Selectively reactive coordination for a team of robot soccer champions. In: The Thirtieth AAAI Conference on Artificial Intelligence, Proceedings of AAAI 2016 (2016)
13. Mendoza, J.P., Biswas, J., Zhu, D., Wang, R., Cooksey, P., Klee, S., Veloso, M.: CMDragons 2015: coordinated offense and defense of the SSL champions. In: Almeida, L., Ji, J., Steinbauer, G., Luke, S. (eds.) RoboCup 2015. LNCS, vol. 9513, pp. 106–117. Springer, Cham (2015). doi:10.1007/978-3-319-29339-4_9

464   D. Zhu and M. Veloso

14. Riley, P., Stone, P., Veloso, M.: Layered disclosure: revealing agents' internals. In: Castelfranchi, C., Lespérance, Y. (eds.) ATAL 2000. LNCS, vol. 1986, pp. 61–72. Springer, Heidelberg (2001). doi:10.1007/3-540-44631-1_5
15. Serra, J.: Image Analysis and Mathematical Morphology. Academic Press Inc., Cambridge (1983)
16. Zickler, S., Laue, T., Birbach, O., Wongphati, M., Veloso, M.: SSL-vision: the shared vision system for the RoboCup small size league. In: Baltes, J., Lagoudakis, M.G., Naruse, T., Ghidary, S.S. (eds.) RoboCup 2009. LNCS, vol. 5949, pp. 425–436. Springer, Heidelberg (2010). doi:10.1007/978-3-642-11876-0_37

Champion Papers

RoboCup 2016 Best Humanoid Award Winner Team Baset Adult-Size

Mojtaba Hosseini[✉], Vahid Mohammadi, Farhad Jafari,
and Esfandiar Bamdad

Humanoid Robotic Laboratory, Robotic Center, Baset Pazhuh Tehran Company,
No. 383, Jalale-ale-ahmad Ave., P.O. Box 14636-75871, Tehran, Iran
hmojtaba89@gmail.com, ebamdad@basetp.com
http://robot.basetp.com

Abstract. This document introduces the team Baset as the champion of Humanoid adult-size league in RoboCup 2016 and describes the hardware, software and electrical design of Baset adult-size robot platform which is designed based on previous achievements of team Baset Adult-Size [1] and Baset Teen-Size [2] robots. Some methods have been explained to adapt to the changes in the rules of RoboCup 2016 and win the adult-size league, including acceleration based walk engine with smooth and fast strides, soft jump motion, perception of real soccer ball, particle filter based localization, path planning, ball handling and fast trajectory using Gaussian filters, a behavior system which decreases the time of scoring a goal considerably, and the changes in the hardware which results in more stable movements of the robot.

1 Introduction

Team Baset, consisting of four team members working on different aspects of the humanoid robots, has started its researches since 2014 at Baset Pazhuh Tehran[1] company. This team participated in the RoboCup competitions and ranked 1st in Teen-Size and 3rd in Kid-Size leagues, and introduced the first Teen-Kid humanoid robot platform in RoboCup 2014. Following that year, team Baset ranked 2nd in soccer competitions and 1st in the technical challenges in RoboCup 2015 adult-size league. After one year of experience in the adult-size league, team Baset participated in the RoboCup 2016 adult-size humanoid league and ranked 1st in both the soccer competitions and the technical challenges and consequently has been awarded the Louis Vuitton cup as the best humanoid robot of that year. The results of team Baset in RoboCup 2016 competitions are presented in Table 1, comparing them to the teams that ranked second.

The high weight and size of adult-size humanoid robots limit their speed, agility, and their ability to play soccer for long periods. The rules of RoboCup 2016 limits the time during which the robots can score a goal as a penalty kick with two randomly placed obstacles on the field. Thus, the robots have to act fast to score a goal. An adult-size robot should be able to handle the ball fast, avoid obstacles, and shoot toward

---

[1] Baset Pazhuh Tehran is a well know company in electronic instruments such as measurement and alarm units. http://www.basetp.com.

© Springer International Publishing AG 2017
S. Behnke et al. (Eds.): RoboCup 2016, LNAI 9776, pp. 467–477, 2017.
https://doi.org/10.1007/978-3-319-68792-6_39

the opponent's goal. To achieve that, it needs to localize itself on the field, generate a quick and confident trajectory toward the ball and find exact position of the obstacles on the field. In this paper, we describe our approach to address these constraints and overcome the slowness attribute of adult-size robots. In Sect. 2, the hardware and electronics of Baset robot, and hardware related methods used to increase robot's stability is described. In Sect. 3.1, the methods to achieve a smooth, stable, and fast walk engine, and also the jump motion, is explained. In Sects. 3.2 and 3.3, respectively, the methods to perceive the standard soccer ball and the localization is described. Finally, in Sect. 3.4 the new behavior system used during RoboCup 2016 competitions is explained.

By the methods described in this document, Baset robot could follow the rules and despite the mentioned limitations, could act with high agility keeping its balance without falling down and score goal in less than 90 s.

Table 1. Results of team Baset in RoboCup 2016 competitions compared to others (https://www.robocuphumanoid.org/hl-2016/results/#adult)

Adult-size soccer	Baset 1st	Sweaty 2nd	Technical challenges	Baset 1st	HuroEvolutionAD 2nd
Plays	6	6	Push recovery	10	5
Wins	6	2	Goal kick	10	7
Scored goals	15	5	High jump	10	–
Received goals	1	3	High kick	7	7

2 Hardware and Electronics

The most important aspect to construct the structure of Baset robot was its weight because the robot's agility depends heavily on its total weight. The initial design of the robot weighed approximately 16 kg which decreased to 13.5 kg by making some changes on the upper-body structure and the thickness of links before RoboCup 2016, and make all the mechanical parts out of aluminum. The 13.5 kg weight of the robot is significantly low considering the total of 28 MX-106[2] actuators and robot's 145 cm height. The full configuration of Baset robot is shown in Table 2.

The structure of Baset adult-size platform is a parallel design with 6 degrees of freedom on each leg, which is depicted in Fig. 1. In order to achieve both speed and power, the total of 13 actuators has been used to construct each leg, 4 actuators working together in each knee joint, depicted in the Fig. 1 top-right, 2 actuators working together alongside external power transfer gears in each hip-roll and ankle-roll joints, depicted in the Fig. 1 down-right, and 1 actuator alongside an external gear in each hip-yaw joint.

[2] MX-106 is a powerful actuator produced by Robotis. www.robotis.us/dynamixel-mx-106r.

Table 2. Hardware configuration of Baset adult-size robot

Weight	13.5 kg	
Height	145 cm	
DOF	18	
Actuators	Mx-106, Mx-64, Mx-28	
Camera	Logitech C905 640 × 480 @ 30 fps	
Battery	Li-Po 3Cells/6400 mAh	
Controllers	Low level controller	Main controller
Computer	BeagleBone Black Rev C [5]	Intel NUC [4]
OS	Ubuntu 14.04	Windows 10
Sensors	IMU[a] via I2C	Camera via USB

[a]Inertial Measurement Unit

Thanks to the decreased weight of the robot and fast actuators, Baset robot was the only adult-size robot that could actually jump in the technical challenges. Results of which are shown in Table 1.

Two controllers, one for high level processes such as image processing, and one for low level tasks such as controlling and synchronizing actuators on every joint has been used. A model of low level controller and power controller board is depicted in Fig. 2. The low-level controller, using BeagleBone Black[3] with Ubuntu operating system, produces all the required information about sensors and actuators, and makes the data available for the main controller through the communication interface over Ethernet using UDP protocol for an uninterrupted and fast response.

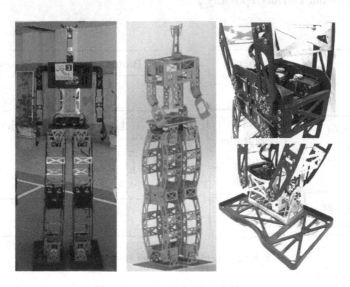

Fig. 1. Baset adult-size platform

---

[3] BeagleBone Black is an industrial board with ARM processor. https://beagleboard.org/black.

Fig. 2. Robot's low level controller and power board designed by team Baset

Using Ubuntu, as a non-real-time operating system for the low-level controller, makes it easier and faster to develop and debug software on it, but it has a disadvantage that it's not possible to control half-duplex RS-485 direction pins in real-time, which is needed to achieve a fast communication speed with actuators. In order to deal with this issue, a MAX13488E[4] IC is used to take the responsibility of controlling the direction automatically in real-time. As shown in Fig. 3, in order to achieve the fastest communication speed with actuators, 3 individual RS-485 ports, one for each leg and one for upper-body joints have been used. The reason is that a single bus is not suitable to communicate with too many actuators. Baset robot's electronic schematics are available freely on our GitHub repository[5].

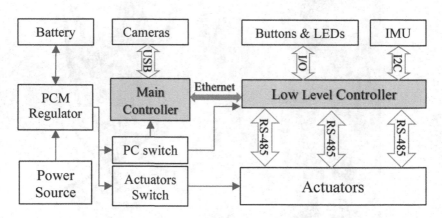

Fig. 3. Electrical design of Baset robot

---

[4] https://www.maximintegrated.com/en/products/interface/transceivers/MAX13488E.html.
[5] https://github.com/farhadjafari/Humanoid/.

3 Software

3.1 Walk Engine and Motion Control

A fast communication interface over Ethernet has been developed in order to access the whole or partial data of objects on low level controller board, such as forward kinematics of all joints, and use them for the walk engine and static motions.

The parallel structure of Baset robot using multiple actuators for each joint, made us develop algorithms for a stable and fast walking system [3] for RoboCup 2016, which is based on the previous success of team Baset on Adult-Size and Teen-Size robots. The algorithm controls the proportional gain of actuators relatively to each foot's Z trajectory. Figure 4 depicts the Z trajectory of robot's left foot and the P-Gains of its actuators during two full strides. As depicted in Fig. 4, the lowest gains are used when the robot puts its foot on the ground, and the highest gains are used when the whole weight of the robot is on the supporting leg. Compared to the swinging foot, higher gains are used for the supporting leg. Following this approach, the robot is now capable of switching supporting foots smoothly by putting each foot on the ground using lower P-Gains which decreases the foot's impact intensity on the field. The decreased impact intensity increases the life time of the actuators significantly and helps the robot to walk smoothly with lower noise using smoother strides. While the strides are smoother, due to the high P-Gains set on the supporting leg, as well as higher stability on the field, the maximum forward walking speed reached to 50 cm/s.

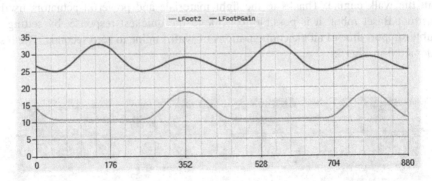

Fig. 4. P-Gains (green) relative to left foot's Z trajectory (orange) (Color figure online)

The new developed walk engine accepts acceleration for forward, sideward, and rotation. The acceleration defines the robot's tendency to change the speed and direction of its current walking state every moment. The higher acceleration values help the robot to be more agile whenever it is required (e.g. when dribbling the ball) and the lower values helps the robot to walk with high confidence without worrying about changing direction on a high-speed walk. The behavior system decides whether to use the higher acceleration values or the lower ones in each situation.

The new walk engine also accepts multiple configurations and can linearly combine them to provide custom configuration depending on the robot's situation and state on the field. The combination is linear and every parameter in each configuration is combined with the same parameter in the other configurations, resulting a new configuration which is between the pre-defined configurations. One configuration is for ball handling and has the minimum, yet working, time period for strides and lower amplitudes of Z axis movement of each foot. The other configuration is specialized for the fastest and the most stable omnidirectional walking without handling the ball. The last configuration is specialized for the goal keeper which increases sideward movement and acceleration to help the goalkeeper walk immediately on the desired direction. Other configurations have been used for technical challenges. The behavior system combines these configurations during the match in accordance with the situation. When the robot is not handling the ball, it combines dribbling and fast-walking configurations depending on the ball's distance to the robot, helping the robot walk fast and confident when it's far from the ball and perform quick and agile actions when dribbling the ball. The system also uses the goalkeeper configuration when the robot acts as a goalkeeper. Due to the smooth linear changes in these configurations, the robot doesn't act abnormally on the field and the average balance of the robot is maintained. The high confident walking system with high speed played a major role in winning the RoboCup 2016 adult-size competitions.

The high weight and size of adult-size robots forces many teams to considerably increase the double support time of the walking system. It's obvious that during double support time, on which both feet are touching the field, no actions can be requested from the walk engine. Thanks to the light materials and powerful actuators used to construct Baset robot, it is possible to achieve the quickest response, by setting the double support time of all the configurations of walk engine to zero seconds. The result is depicted in Fig. 5.

Fig. 5. Walking with zero second double support time

The static motion generator controls proportional gains just like the walk engine system. To design a motion, depending on the pressure and strike on each joint, custom gains can be used, making it possible to design a jump motion. As shown in Fig. 6, Baset robot could jump about 3.4 cm during technical challenges. The high jump challenge is defined in RoboCup 2015 rules[6] as the time that the robot terminates

---

[6] http://www.robocuphumanoid.org/wp-content/uploads/HumanoidLeagueRules2015-06-29.pdf.

ground contact and stays in the air. The jump time is measured with a special device provided by the league. In order to make the jump motion we had to make sure that the mechanical structure of the robot could provide both the speed and the power. Thus, the knees constructed with 4 actuators working together in parallel, which is depicted in Fig. 1 top-right. To generate the jump motion, first the upper parts from the knee joints are moved upward while increasing both the speed and P-Gains of each foot, then after reaching the highest position, the lower parts of each leg are moved upward which lets the robot terminate the ground and make the jump. Then, while decreasing the speed and P-Gains of both feet, the robot lands on the ground with the lowest possible P-Gains set to the actuators. Therefore, the robot can jump without getting hurt.

Fig. 6. Jump motion for 3.4 cm during the technical challenges, RoboCup 2016

3.2   Perception

In Humanoid adult-size league detecting the obstacles and the opponent's goal keeper plays a major role to win the competition. To locate each object in real self-coordinating system, the DH parameters and extrinsic camera matrix provided by motion module has been used. Lines are detected by a customized low computational cost method using RANSAC algorithm [6].

To calibrate the cameras, the chessboard calibration method [7], provided by OpenCV, has been used.

Ball Perception. The standard soccer ball has been used in the adult-size league since RoboCup 2015. In order to perceive the ball, using a growing color table and a simple contour detection algorithm [8, 9] on the binary image after removing white lines, the potential spots are detected first. Then these spots are compared to the ball and a confidence value is calculated.

To determine how much each spot resembles the ball, three algorithms have been used. Each algorithm calculates the confidence value using its specific Gaussian filter which reduces the effect of noises. By combining these confidence values according to their importance, each spot's overall likelihood to be a ball is calculated. A sample of detected ball is depicted in Fig. 7. The algorithms used to calculate the confidence of each spot are as following:

- The size of the spot is compared to the size of the real ball.
- The best matching circle is detected using OpenCV Hough Circle Transform [10] and its radius is compared to the actual ball's radius.
- Using Correlation Histogram Comparison algorithm [11] with 32 bins, all three HSV color channels of the spot is compared to the previously trained colors of the real ball. This algorithm output has more importance than the other two when combining them to get the overall confidence.

There is an ongoing research in the team Baset to use stereo camera's depth image to achieve more robust ball perceptions.

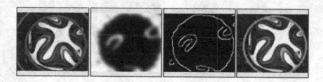

Fig. 7. Ball perception

3.3 Localization

A good and robust localization method is the key to succeed in the humanoid league. To localize the robot, the Sample Importance Resampling method has been used due to its simplicity and low computational cost.

The localization problem has been solved by using 110 particles, which are living by the probability proportional to their weights. For calculating each particles' weight, a Gaussian function has been used on distance and orientation [12].

The sensor-reset technique [13] has been used in order to solve the global localization problem. This method solves the kidnaped robot problem by spreading 10 random particles in the field. For tracking the robot's position, the dead reckoning data provided by the motion module has been used. The motion module gathers all the required information from each joint, such as current position and speed, and keeps track of the robot's current speed and acceleration. It also provides camera's position and orientation toward the robot's ground contact. Localization output is depicted in Fig. 8.

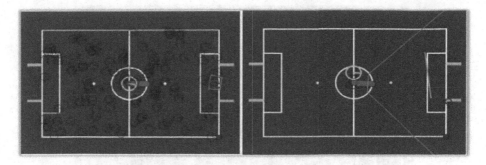

Fig. 8. Initial particles (left) and after conversion to one location (right)

3.4 Behavior

The adult-size league has customized rules compared to the other size classes. A team takes a penalty shoot and has up to 150 s to score a goal. The ball is placed behind the robot which is faced the opponent goal. Then the robot starts the penalty from the center of the field, while two obstacles are randomly positioned on the opponent's field. The robot has to reach the ball, dribble it to the opponent's field while avoiding any touches with the obstacles, and shoot the ball toward the goal. Touching the obstacles finishes the penalty chance. The opponent team uses its robot as the goal keeper during each penalty shoot. After each penalty, the teams replace the roles and the penalty shoot continues for 5 strikes for each team in a normal match.

Because the adult-size robots are big and usually heavy, they can't move as agilely as teen-size and kid-size robots. Thus, they have to act smart to score a goal during the limited time they have which underscores the importance of the behavior that the robot follows.

The robot's camera has limited field of view while the obstacles can be placed near the robot forcing it to spend reasonable time scanning the field in order to find the obstacles exact position. To deal with this issue, the robot does not search for obstacles at first, instead it starts to find the ball as soon as the game starts then walks behind the ball. As shown in Fig. 9, when the robot is behind the ball in its own field, due to the obstacles long distance to the robot, by looking toward the opponent's goal, both obstacles will be within the field of view of the camera and there won't be necessary to scan the field to detect the obstacles. Therefore, the time to find the obstacles on the field is reasonably decreased.

Thanks to the perfect omnidirectional walking capability of Baset robot, it is possible to follow a trajectory which considers robot's yaw angle on the field as a parameter. To produce the trajectory, three Gaussian filters have been used which determine the sideward, forward, and rotation speed of walking system. These filters use the ball position toward the robot which is produced by the robot's vision system all the time as the input. A linear relationship between rotation speed and forward or sideward speed is used by which the higher value of rotation speed decreases both forward and sideward speeds. This way the robot moves toward the ball with a short

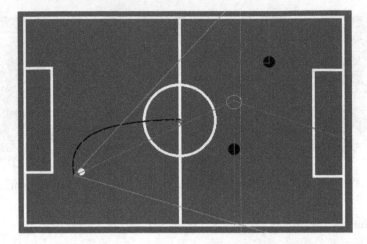

Fig. 9. Robot's behavior. Black curve indicates robot's trajectory toward ball, and gray lines on that curve indicate robot's direction on the field. Yellow lines show the camera's field of view. Red circle is the place to which the robot shifts the ball then shoots it toward opponent's goal. Violet segments of lines indicate the gaps between obstacles and field lines. (Color figure online)

trajectory considering robot's angle on the field and can handle the ball without losing its own desired direction. A sample of resulting trajectory is depicted in Fig. 9 with black curve.

The robot, after walking behind the ball and finding the obstacles, considers the three free gaps made by obstacles and selects the one which is bigger and also needs less time for the robot to pass through (red circle on Fig. 9). Then, it shifts the ball there. As the robot is always maintaining its desired direction while handling the ball, when it reaches the ball, it has already aimed the opponent's goal and moved one of its feet behind the ball. Otherwise, if the desired direction of the robot or the location of the ball toward it's foot is not obtained, the robot will spend extra time to fulfill it. Then it shoots the ball toward the opponent's goal.

4   Conclusion

In this paper, we provided our approaches and methods which let us win the humanoid adult-size league in RoboCup 2016 competitions. We first described our robust hardware and electronic devices which helped the robot play for long periods. Then we described the walk engine that controls P-Gains of actuators and accepts acceleration as a parameter. We also described how we obtained agile walking system by zeroing the double support time, how we could make a jump motion, how we perceived the real soccer ball and localized on the field, and finally described the behavior system of the robot to play the adult-size soccer.

During the competition, our robot proved to be the most stable one without even falling once. We demonstrated that an adult-size robot can play real soccer instead of penalty shoots using the high walking speed and stability. We also demonstrated the capability of jump motion for the first time in the adult-size league.

For further researches, we are updating the mono vision of the robot with a stereo camera. The provided information from the stereo camera is going to be used to perceive the obstacles and the opponent's robot as well as the ball more accurately, and to record the visual odometry of the robot's head in three dimensions. Afterwards, a fusion between robot's walking pedometer and the visual odometry of camera is going to be used to enhance the robot's localization accuracy. We are also planning to make our robots play real soccer in the adult-size league more efficiently in the future.

References

1. Mohammadi, V., Hosseini, M., Jafari, F., Farazi, H., Bamdad, E.: Baset Adult-Size 2015 Team Description Paper
2. Farazi, H., Hosseini, M., Mohammadi, V., Jafari, F., Rahmati, D., Bamdad, E.: Baset Teen-Size 2014 Team Description Paper (2014)
3. Hosseini, M., Mohammadi, V., Jafari, F., Bamdad, E.: Baset Adult-Size 2016 Team Description Paper
4. Intel NUC Mini Personal Computers. http://www.intel.com/content/www/us/en/nuc/overview.html
5. BeagleBone Black development platform. http://www.beagleboard.org/BLACK
6. Fischler, M.A., Bolles, R.C.: Random sample consensus: a paradigm for model fitting with applications to image analysis and automated cartography. Commun. ACM **24**(6), 381–395 (1981)
7. Camera Calibration with OpenCV. http://docs.opencv.org/doc/tutorials/calib3d/camera_calibration/camera_calibration.html
8. Suzuki, S.: Topological structural analysis of digitized binary images by border following. Comput. Vis. Graph. Image Process. **30**(1), 32–46 (1985)
9. OpenCV Official Documentation Site. http://docs.opencv.org/modules/imgproc/doc/structural_analysis_and_shape_descriptors.html?highlight=findcontours#findcontours
10. Hough Circle Transform by OpenCV. http://docs.opencv.org/2.4/doc/tutorials/imgproc/imgtrans/hough_circle/hough_circle.html
11. Histogram Comparison Algorithms by OpenCV. http://docs.opencv.org/2.4/doc/tutorials/imgproc/histograms/histogram_comparison/histogram_comparison.html
12. Strasdat, H., Bennewitz, M., Behnke, S.: Multi-cue localization for soccer playing humanoid robots. In: Lakemeyer, G., Sklar, E., Sorrenti, Domenico G., Takahashi, T. (eds.) RoboCup 2006. LNCS, vol. 4434, pp. 245–257. Springer, Heidelberg (2007). doi:10.1007/978-3-540-74024-7_21
13. Coltin, B., Veloso, M.: Multi-observation sensor resetting localization with ambiguous landmarks. Auton. Robots **35**(2–3), 221–237 (2013)

RoboCup 2016 Humanoid TeenSize Winner NimbRo: Robust Visual Perception and Soccer Behaviors

Hafez Farazi[✉], Philipp Allgeuer, Grzegorz Ficht, André Brandenburger, Dmytro Pavlichenko, Michael Schreiber, and Sven Behnke

Autonomous Intelligent Systems, Computer Science, University of Bonn, Bonn, Germany
{farazi,pallgeuer}@ais.uni-bonn.de, behnke@cs.uni-bonn.de
http://ais.uni-bonn.de

Abstract. The trend in the RoboCup Humanoid League rules over the past few years has been towards a more realistic and challenging game environment. Elementary skills such as visual perception and walking, which had become mature enough for exciting gameplay, are now once again core challenges. The field goals are both white, and the walking surface is artificial grass, which constitutes a much more irregular surface than the carpet used before. In this paper, team NimbRo TeenSize, the winner of the TeenSize class of the RoboCup 2016 Humanoid League, presents its robotic platforms, the adaptations that had to be made to them, and the newest developments in visual perception and soccer behaviour.

1 Introduction

In the RoboCup Humanoid League, there is an ongoing effort to develop humanoid robots capable of playing soccer. There are three size classes—KidSize (40–90 cm), TeenSize (80–140 cm), and AdultSize (130–180 cm). Note that the overlap in size classes is intentional to facilitate teams to move up to higher size classes.

The TeenSize class of robots started playing 2 vs. 2 games in 2010, and a year later moved to a larger soccer field. In 2015, numerous changes were made in the rules that affected mainly visual perception and walking, namely:

- the green field carpet was replaced with artificial grass,
- the field lines are only painted on the artificial grass, so they are highly variable in appearance and no longer a clear white,
- the only specification of the ball is that it is at least 50% white (no longer orange), and
- the goal posts on both sides of the field are white.

Our approach to addressing these rule changes in terms of perception are given in Sect. 3.1.

© Springer International Publishing AG 2017
S. Behnke et al. (Eds.): RoboCup 2016, LNAI 9776, pp. 478–490, 2017.
https://doi.org/10.1007/978-3-319-68792-6_40

Fig. 1. The igus® Humanoid Open Platform, Dynaped and team NimbRo. (Color figure online)

In this year's RoboCup, we used our fully open-source 3D printed robots, the igus® Humanoid Open Platform [1], and the associated open-source ROS software. Furthermore, we revived one of our classic robots, Dynaped, with the same ROS software, by upgrading its electronics and PC and developing a new communications scheme for this to work. This was done in such a way that the robot hardware in use was completely transparent to the software, and abstracted away through a hardware interface layer. More details are given in Sect. 2. Both platforms are shown in Fig. 1, along with the human team members.

2   Robot Platforms

2.1   Igus Humanoid Open Platform

RoboCup 2016 was the first proper debut of the latest addition to the NimbRo robot soccer family—the igus® Humanoid Open Platform, shown on the left in Fig. 1. Although an earlier version of the robot had briefly played in 2015, 2016 was the first year where the platform constituted an integral part of the NimbRo soccer team. Over the last three years, the platform has seen continual development, originating from the initial NimbRo-OP prototype, and seven robots of three generations have been constructed. The igus® Humanoid Open Platform is 92 cm tall and weighs only 6.6 kg thanks to its 3D printed plastic exoskeleton design. The platform incorporates an Intel Core i7-5500U CPU running a full 64-bit Ubuntu OS, and a Robotis CM730 microcontroller board, which electrically interfaces the twelve MX-106R and MX-64R RS485 servos. The CM730 incorporates 3-axis accelerometer, gyroscope and magnetometer sensors, for a total of 9 axes of inertial measurement. For visual perception, the robot is equipped with a Logitech C905 USB camera fitted with a wide-angle lens. The robot software is based on the ROS middleware, and is a continuous evolution of the ROS software that was written for the NimbRo-OP. The igus® Humanoid Open Platform is discussed in greater detail in [1].

2.2   Upgraded Dynaped

Dynaped, shown in the middle in Fig. 1, has been an active player for team NimbRo since RoboCup 2009 in Graz, Austria. Through the years, Dynaped

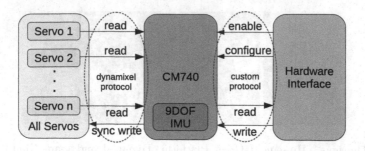

Fig. 2. Dynaped's custom communication scheme

has played both as a goalie and a field player during numerous competitions, contributing to the team's many successes. Dynaped's competition performance and hardware design, including features like the effective use of parallel kinematics and compliant design, contributed to NimbRo winning the Louis Vuitton Best Humanoid Award in both 2011 and 2013.

In 2012, our focus of development shifted towards the development of an open platform—the NimbRo-OP prototype, later followed by the igus® Humanoid Open Platform. Because of platform incompatibilities and a severe electrical hardware failure during RoboCup 2015, we decided to upgrade Dynaped to the newer ROS software, in a way that is transparently compatible with the igus® Humanoid Open Platform. The upgrade included both hardware and software improvements. In terms of hardware, Dynaped has been equipped with a modern PC (Intel Core i7-5500U CPU), a new CM740 controller board from Robotis, and a vision system as in the igus® Humanoid Open Platform, consisting of the same camera unit and 3D-printed head.

To adapt Dynaped to the new ROS software framework, a number of modifications had to be made. Thanks to the modularity of our software, only the low-level modules needed a specific reimplementation, while all of our high-level functionality that contributed to the success during RoboCup 2016 could be used untouched. At first glance, the only fundamental difference seems to be the utilisation of parallel kinematics, leading to the loss of one degree of freedom, but in fact, quite importantly, Dynaped still uses the older Dynamixel actuators. The used Dynamixel EX-106 and RX-64 have very similar physical properties to the MX-106 and MX-64 used in the igus® Humanoid Open Platform, but they lack a bulk read instruction, which is essential for allowing fast communications with multiple actuators with a single instruction. This limitation greatly reduces the control loop frequency, as each actuator needs to be read individually. This increases the latencies with each added actuator to the bus. To reduce these delays, Dynaped utilises a custom firmware for the CM740, which no longer acts merely as a passthrough from the PC to the servos. Instead, it communicates with both sides in parallel (see Fig. 2). On the actuator side, the CM740 queries all registered devices on the Dynamixel bus in a loop. Communications with the PC are performed using an extension of the original Dynamixel protocol,

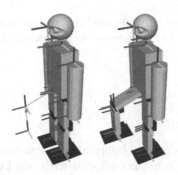

Fig. 3. Serial to parallel kinematic translation. Left: before translation, virtual chain visible. Right: after translation. (Color figure online)

which allows the use of the same, well-developed error handling as our original firmware, as well as having the option to still use the CM740 as a passthrough device. The CM740-PC protocol has been extended by four new instructions:

- Configure extended packet communication,
- Enable extended packet communication,
- Send extended packet, and
- Receive extended packet.

To start the custom communication scheme, the hardware interface first sends a configuration packet containing a list of servo ID numbers, along with their respective model types. This informs the CM740 which servo registers it needs to keep reading from and writing to. Typically, these registers correspond to position, torque, and controller gain data. The read packets contain the most recent data from all of the Dynamixel devices, with an indication of how many times it has been read from since the last packet. The write packets include the current position setpoints and compliance values for the servos. In Dynaped's case, the packet transmission frequency is 100 Hz, which allows all devices on the Dynamixel bus to be read at least once before a new read packet is sent. This transfer rate would not be achievable on Dynaped's hardware with the traditional request-response transmission paradigm.

Creating a model with parallel kinematics and using it in the hardware interface proved to be another challenge, as ROS does not natively support this. In order to translate between the serial and parallel kinematics, the created model has two sets of leg kinematic chains, a virtual serial one and the true parallel one that is actuated. The virtual kinematic chain receives the commands as-is from the motion modules, which the hardware interface then translates for the parallel chain (see Fig. 3) before sending a command to the actuators. In order to recreate the state of the parallel joints when reading out positions from the actuators, virtual joints have been added in order to offset the next link in the kinematic chain by the same angle that the joint has rotated. With these modifications, the robot can be seen as an igus® Humanoid Open Platform robot by the software, and thanks to our modular design approach, no robot-specific changes had to be done to any motion modules, or other higher level parts of our code.

3   Software Design

3.1   Visual Perception

The primary source of perceptual information for humanoid robots on the soccer field is the camera. Each robot is equipped with one Logitech C905 camera, fitted with a wide-angle lens that has an infrared cut-off filter. The diagonal field of view is approximately 150°. The choice of lens was optimised to maximise the number of usable pixels and minimise the level of distortion, without significantly sacrificing the effective field of view. Our vision system is able to detect the field boundary, line segments, goal posts, QR codes and other robots using texture, shape, brightness and colour information. After identifying each object of interest, by using appropriate intrinsic and extrinsic camera parameters, we project each object into egocentric world coordinates. The intrinsic camera parameters are pre-calibrated, but the extrinsic parameters are calculated online by consideration of the known kinematics and estimated orientation of the robot. Although we have the kinematic model of both robot platforms, some variations still occur on the real hardware, resulting in projection errors, especially for distant objects. To address this, we utilised the Nelder-Mead [2] method to calibrate the position and orientation of the camera frame in the head. This calibration is crucial for good performance of the projection operation from pixel coordinates to egocentric world coordinates, as demonstrated in Fig. 4. As a reference, the raw captured image used to generate the figure is shown in the left side of Fig. 5. More details can be found in [3].

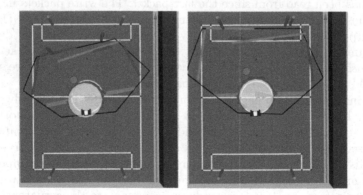

Fig. 4. Projected ball, field line and goal post detections before (left) and after (right) kinematic calibration. (Color figure online)

Fig. 5. Left: a captured image with ball (pink circle), field line (light blue lines), field boundary (yellow lines), and goal post (dark blue lines) detections. Right: distant ball detection on RoboCup 2016 field. (Color figure online)

Field Detection: Although it is a common approach for field boundary detection to find the convex hull of all green areas directly in the image [4], more care needs to be taken in our case due to the significant image distortion. The convex hull may include parts of the image that are not the field. To exclude these unwanted areas, vertices of the connected regions are first undistorted before calculating the convex hull. The convex hull points and intermediate points on each edge are then distorted back into the raw captured image, and the resulting polygon is taken as the field boundary. An example of the final detected field polygon is shown in Fig. 5.

Ball Detection: In previous years of the RoboCup, most teams used simple colour segmentation and blob detection-based approaches to find the orange ball. Now that the ball has a pattern and is mostly white however, such simple approaches no longer work effectively, especially since the lines and goal posts are also white. We extend [5], our approach is divided into two stages. In the first stage, ball candidates are generated based on colour segmentation, colour histograms, shape and size. White connected components in the image are found, and the Ramer-Douglas-Peucker [6] algorithm is applied to reduce the number of polygon vertices in the resulting regions. This is advantageous for quicker subsequent detection of circle shapes. The detected white regions are searched for at least one third full circle shapes within the expected radius ranges. Colour histograms of the detected circles are calculated for each of the three HSV channels, and compared to expected ball colour histograms using the Bhattacharyya distance. Circles with a suitably similar colour distribution to the expected one are considered to be ball candidates.

In the second stage of processing, a dense histogram of oriented gradients (HOG) descriptor [7] is applied in the form of a cascade classifier, with use of the AdaBoost technique. Using this cascade classifier, we reject those candidates that do not have the required set of HOG features. The aim of using the HOG

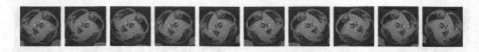

Fig. 6. Ball detection tracking data augmentation extending one positive sample (leftmost) to ten, by applying rotations and mirroring operations.

descriptor is to find a description of the ball that is largely invariant to changes in illumination and lighting conditions. The HOG descriptor is not rotation invariant, however, so to detect the ball from all angles, and to minimise the user's effort in collecting training examples, each positive image is rotated by $\pm 10°$ and $\pm 20°$ and mirrored horizontally, with the resulting images being presented as new positive samples, as shown in Fig. 6. Greater rotations are not considered to allow the cascade classifier to learn the shadow under the ball. The described approach can detect balls with very few false positives, even in environments cluttered with white, and under varying lighting conditions. In our experiments, we observed detection a FIFA size 3 ball up to 4.5 m away with a success rate above 80% on a walking robot, and up to 7 m away on a stationary robot, as shown in the right side of Fig. 5. It is interesting to note that our approach can find the ball in undistorted and distorted images with the same classifier.

Field Line and Centre Circle Detection: Due to the introduction of artificial grass in the RoboCup Humanoid League, the field lines are no longer clearly visible. In past years, many teams based their line detection approaches on the segmentation of the colour white [4]. This is no longer a robust approach due to the increased number of white objects on the field, and due to the visual variability of the lines. Our approach is to detect spatial changes in brightness in the image using a Canny edge detector on the V channel of the HSV colour space. The V channel encodes brightness information, and the result of the Canny edge detector is quite robust to changes in lighting conditions.

A probabilistic Hough line detector [8] is used to extract line segments of a certain minimum size from the detected edges. The minimum size criterion helps to reject edges from white objects in the image that are not lines. The output line segments are filtered in the next stage to avoid false positive line detections where possible. We verify that the detected lines cover white pixels in the image, have green pixels on either side, and are close on both sides to edges returned by the edge detector. The last of these checks is motivated by the expectation that white lines, in an ideal scenario, will produce a pair of high responses in the edge detector, one on each side of the line. Ten equally spaced points are chosen on each line segment under review, and two normals to the line are constructed at each of these points, of approximate 5 cm length in each of the two directions. The pixels in the captured image underneath these normals are checked for white colour and green colour, and the output of the canny edge detector is checked for a high response. The number of instances where these three checks succeed are independently totalled, and if all three counts exceed the configured thresholds, the line segment is accepted, otherwise the line segment is rejected.

In the final stage, similar line segments are merged together to produce fewer and bigger lines, as well as to cover those field line segments that might be partially occluded by another robot. The final result is a set of line segments that relate to the field lines and centre circle. Line segments that are under a certain threshold in length undergo a simple circle detection routine, to find the location of the centre circle. In our experiments, we found that this approach can detect circle and line segments up to 4.5 m away.

Localisation on the Soccer Field: Localisation of the robot on the soccer field—the task of estimating the 3D pose (x, y, θ) of the robot—is performed using the field line, centre circle and goal post detections. Each component of the 3D pose is estimated independently. To estimate the θ component, we use the global heading information from the magnetometer, and maintain an internal correction term based on the angular deviation between the expected and detected orientations of the white lines. This approach does not rely on having an accurate magnetometer output, and in experiments was able to correct deviations up to 30° coming from the magnetometer. Using the estimated θ, which is normally quite exact, we can rotate every vision detection to align with the global field coordinate system. The detected line segments can thereby be classified as being either horizontal or vertical field lines. In each cycle of the localisation node, we use the perception information and dead-reckoning walking data to update the previously estimated 2D location. For updating 2D location, we distinguish x and y component using estimated θ. The y component of the localisation is updated based on the y components of the detected centre circle, goal posts and vertical field lines. With the assumption that the robot is always inside the field lines, the vertical sidelines can easily be differentiated and used for updates. The x component of the localisation is analogously updated based on the x components of the detected centre circle, goal posts and horizontal field lines. The horizontal lines belonging to the goal area are discriminated from the centre line by checking for the presence of a consistent goal post detection, centre circle detection, and/or further horizontal line that is close and parallel. This approach can easily deal with common localisation difficulties, such as sensor aliasing and robot kidnapping. In contrast to some other proposed localisation methods for soccer fields, this method is relatively easy to implement and very robust. Our experiments indicate that the mean error of our localisation is better than what was reported in both [4,9].

3.2   Bipedal Walking

Motivated by the changed game environment at the RoboCup competition— the chosen application domain for our own use of the igus® Humanoid Open Platform—the gait generation has been adapted to address the new challenge of walking on artificial grass. The use of a soft, deformable and unpredictable walking surface imposes extra requirements on the walking algorithm. Removable rubber cleats have been added at the four corners underneath each foot of the robot to improve the grip on the artificial grass. This also has the effect that the

486   H. Farazi et al.

ground reaction forces are concentrated over a smaller surface area, mitigating at least part of the contact variability induced by the grass.

The gait is formulated in three different pose spaces: joint space, abstract space, and inverse space. The *joint space* simply specifies all of the joint angles, while the *inverse space* specifies the Cartesian coordinates and quaternion orientations of each of the limb end effectors relative to the trunk link frame. The *abstract space* is a representation that was specifically developed for humanoid robots in the context of walking and balancing [10]. The abstract space reduces the expression of the pose of each limb to parameters that define the length of the limb, the orientation of a so-called limb centre line, and the orientation of the end effector. Simple conversions between all three pose spaces exist.

The walking gait in the ROS software is based on an open loop central pattern generated core that is calculated from a gait phase angle that increments at a rate proportional to the desired gait frequency. This open loop gait extends the gait of our previous work [11]. The central pattern generated gait begins with a configured halt pose in the abstract space, then incorporates numerous additive waveforms to the halt pose as functions of the gait phase and commanded gait velocity. These waveforms generate features such as leg lifting, leg swinging, arm swinging, and so on. The resulting abstract pose is converted to the inverse space, where further motion components are added. The resulting inverse pose is converted to the joint space, in which form it is commanded to the robot actuators. A pose blending scheme towards the halt pose is implemented in the final joint space representation to smoothen the transitions to and from walking.

A number of simultaneously operating basic feedback mechanisms have been built around the open loop gait core to stabilise the walking. The PID-like feedback in each of these mechanisms derives from the fused pitch and fused roll [12] state estimates and works by adding extra corrective action components to the central pattern generated waveforms in both the abstract and inverse spaces, namely arm angle, hip angle, continuous foot angle, support foot angle, CoM shifting, and virtual slope. The corrective actions are illustrated in Fig. 7. The step timing is computed using the capture step framework [13], based on the lateral CoM state [14].

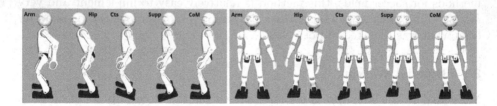

Fig. 7. The implemented corrective actions in both the sagittal (left image) and lateral (right image) planes, from left to right in both cases the arm angle, hip angle, continuous foot angle, support foot angle, and CoM shifting corrective actions. The actions have been exaggerated for clearer illustration.

Overall, the feedback mechanisms were observed to make a significant difference in the walking ability of the robots, with walking often not even being possible for extended periods of time without them. The feedback mechanisms also imparted the robots with disturbance rejection capabilities that were not present otherwise. Reliable omnidirectional walking speeds of $21\,\mathrm{cm\ s^{-1}}$ were achieved on an artificial grass surface of blade length $32\,\mathrm{mm}$. Over all games played at RoboCup 2016, none of the five robots ever fell while walking[1] in free space. Only strong collisions with other robots caused falls from walking Igus robot s could quickly recover using keyframe get-up motions [15].

3.3 Soccer Behaviours

Given the current game state, as perceived by the vision system, the robots must autonomously decide on the higher-level actions to execute in order to try to score a goal. For this we use a two-layered hierarchical finite state machine (FSM), that has a tailor-made custom implementation for RoboCup soccer. The upper layer is referred to as the *game FSM*, and the lower layer is referred to as the *behaviour FSM*. Given the current required playing state of the robot, the former is responsible for deciding on a suitable higher-level action, such as for example "dribble or kick the ball to these specified target coordinates", and based on this higher-level action, the latter is responsible for deciding on the required gait velocity, whether to kick or dive, and so on.

In the order of execution, a ROS interface module first abstracts away the acquisition of data into the behaviours node, before this data is then processed, refined and accumulated into a so-called sensor variables structure. This aggregates all kinds of information from the vision, localisation, RoboCup game controller, team communications and robot control nodes, and precomputes commonly required derived data, such as for example the coordinates of the currently most intrusive obstacle, whether the current ball estimate is stable, and/or how long ago it was last seen. This information is used to decide on the appropriate game FSM state, such as for example *default ball handling, positioning*, or *wait for ball in play*, which is then executed and used to compute standardised game variables, such as for example *kick if possible* and *ball target*. These game variables, along with the sensor variables, are then used by the behaviour FSM to decide on a suitable state, such as for example *dribble ball, walk to pose* or *go behind ball*. The execution of the required behaviour state then yields the required low-level action of the robot, which is passed to the robot control node via the aforementioned ROS interface module, completing the execution of the soccer behaviours.

3.4 Human-Robot Interfaces

Despite being designed to operate autonomously, our robots still need suitable human-robot interfaces to allow them to be configured and calibrated. For the

---

[1] Video: https://www.youtube.com/watch?v=9saVpA3wIbU.

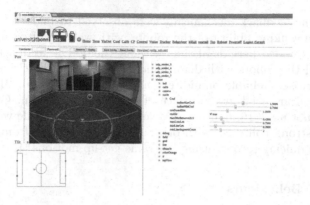

Fig. 8. A screenshot of the web application used to help calibrate the robot.

lowest and most fundamental level of control and operation, each robot can be launched and configured directly on the command line inside SSH sessions directly on the robot PC. This allows the greatest amount of freedom and flexibility in launching ROS nodes and checking their correct operation, but is also a complex and time-consuming task that is prone to errors and requires in-depth knowledge of the robot and software framework.

To overcome these problems, a web application was developed for the robot (see Fig. 8), with the robot PC as the web server, to allow standard web browsers of all devices to connect to the robot for configuration and calibration. This operates at a higher level of abstraction than the command line, and allows users to perform all common tasks that are required when operating the robot. This makes routine tasks significantly quicker and easier than on the command line, and avoids problems altogether such as hangup signals and resuming command line sessions. By exploiting the client-server architecture of web applications and the highly developed underlying web protocols, the connection is very robust, even over poor quality wireless network connections, and of low computational cost for the robot as most processing is implemented on the client side. The web application, amongst many other things, allows the user to start, stop and monitor ROS nodes, displays all kinds of status information about the robot, allows dynamic updates to the configuration server parameters, shows the processed vision and localisation outputs, allows various calibration and system services to be called, and allows the pose of the head to be controlled manually.

During operation, whether managed over the command line or the web server, the robot can be visualised using the RQT GUI, and dynamically reconfigured using the configuration server. This requires a live network connection to the robot for communication purposes. To configure the robot instantaneously, and without the need for any kind of network connection, a QR code detector has been implemented in the vision module. With this feature, arbitrary reconfiguration tasks can be effectuated due to the great freedom of data that can be robustly encoded in a QR code. QR codes can conveniently be generated on mobile devices, also for example with a dedicated mobile application, and shown to the robot at any time. The robot plays a short tune to acknowledge the QR code, serving as auditory feedback that the QR code was detected and processed.

4   Conclusions

In this paper, we described our platforms and approaches to playing soccer in the Humanoid TeenSize class. During RoboCup 2016, we successfully demonstrated that our robots could robustly perceive the game environment, make decisions, and act on them. Our team NimbRo TeenSize aggregated a total score of 29:0 over five games. We have released our hardware[2] and software[3] to GitHub with the hope that it is beneficial for other teams and research groups.

Acknowledgements. We acknowledge the contributions of igus® GmbH to the project, in particular the management of Martin Raak towards the robot design and manufacture. This work was partially funded by grant BE 2556/10 of the German Research Foundation (DFG).

References

1. Allgeuer, P., Farazi, H., Schreiber, M., Behnke, S.: Child-sized 3D Printed igus Humanoid Open Platform. In: Proceedings of 15th IEEE-RAS International Conference on Humanoid Robots (Humanoids), (Seoul, Korea) (2015)
2. Nelder, J.A., Mead, R.: A simplex method for function minimization. Comput. J. **7**(4), 308–313 (1965)
3. Farazi, H., Allgeuer, P., Behnke, S.: A monocular vision system for playing soccer in low color information environments. In: 10th Workshop on Humanoid Soccer Robots, IEEE-RAS International Conference on Humanoid Robots (Korea) (2015)
4. Laue, T., De Haas, T.J., Burchardt, A., Graf, C., Röfer, T., Härtl, A., Rieskamp, A.: Efficient and reliable sensor models for humanoid soccer robot self-localization. In: Fourth Workshop on Humanoid Soccer Robots, pp. 22–29 (2009)
5. Schulz, H., Strasdat, H., Behnke, S.: A ball is not just orange: using color and luminance to classify regions of interest
6. Ramer, U.: An iterative procedure for the polygonal approximation of plane curves. Comput. Graph. Image Process. **1**(3), 244–256 (1972)
7. Dalal, N., Triggs, B.: Object detection using histograms of oriented gradients. In: Pascal VOC Workshop, ECCV (2006)
8. Matas, J., Galambos, C., Kittler, J.: Robust detection of lines using the progressive probabilistic hough transform. Comput. Vis. Image Underst. **78**, 119–137 (2000)
9. Schulz, H., Behnke, S.: Utilizing the structure of field lines for efficient soccer robot localization. Adv. Rob. **26**(14), 1603–1621 (2012)
10. Behnke, S.: Online trajectory generation for omnidirectional biped walking. In: Proceedings of 2006 IEEE International Conference on Robotics and Automation (ICRA) (2006)

---

[2] Hardware: https://github.com/igusGmbH/HumanoidOpenPlatform.
[3] Software: https://github.com/AIS-Bonn/humanoid_op_ros.

11. Missura, M., Behnke, S.: Self-stable omnidirectional walking with compliant joints. In: 8th Workshop on Humanoid Soccer Robots, Humanoids (2013)
12. Allgeuer, P., Behnke, S.: Fused angles: a representation of body orientation for balance. In: International Conference on Intelligent Robots and Systems (IROS) (2015)
13. Missura, M., Behnke, S.: Balanced walking with capture steps. In: Bianchi, R.A.C., Akin, H.L., Ramamoorthy, S., Sugiura, K. (eds.) RoboCup 2014. LNCS, vol. 8992, pp. 3–15. Springer, Cham (2015). doi:10.1007/978-3-319-18615-3_1
14. Allgeuer, P., Behnke, S.: Omnidirectional bipedal walking with direct fused angle feedback mechanisms. In: Proceedings of 16th IEEE-RAS International Conference on Humanoid Robots (Humanoids), (Cancún, Mexico) (2016)
15. Stückler, J., Schwenk, J., Behnke, S.: Getting back on two feet: reliable standing-up routines for a humanoid robot. In: IAS, pp. 676–685 (2006)

Rhoban Football Club: RoboCup Humanoid Kid-Size 2016 Champion Team Paper

Julien Allali, Louis Deguillaume, Rémi Fabre, Loic Gondry, Ludovic Hofer,
Olivier Ly, Steve N'Guyen, Grégoire Passault, Antoine Pirrone,
and Quentin Rouxel[✉]

Rhoban Football Club Team, LaBRI, University of Bordeaux, Bordeaux, France
quentin.rouxel@labri.fr

Abstract. For its fifth participation to the RoboCup Kid-Size Humanoid League, the Rhoban Football Club reached the first place of the competition in 2016 in Leipzig. This competition aims at opposing teams of small autonomous humanoid robots in real soccer games. Implementation of complex mechanics, electronics and software systems is needed. In this paper, we summarize and describe some distinctive parts of our architecture. Going from our foot pressure sensors, our open-source alternative Dynamixel firmware, the use of kinematics models, the odometry and camera calibration to our perception system as well as simple but effective team play strategies.

1 Introduction

Within the RoboCup competition, the Humanoid League[1] gathers the community of custom humanoid robots playing soccer. Unlike in the Standard League, the robots are built by the teams (mechanics, electronics, software) constrained by humanoid morphology and *human-like* sensors (no lidar, infra-red, laser, ultrasonic, ...). The Humanoid League is divided in three sub-leagues according to the robot's height: Kid-Size (40 cm to 90 cm), Teen-Size (80 cm to 140 cm) and Adult-Size (130 cm to 180 cm). For budgetary and practical reasons, the Kid-Size League gathers more teams (17 in 2016) than the other two (4 and 8 in 2016). During Kid-Size games, two teams of four fully autonomous humanoid robots are playing an adapted soccer version. The field size is 6 m by 9 m and the ground is made of artificial grass with white lines, white goal posts. The ball is at least 50% white.

The Rhoban team is a young small research group in robotics from the LaBRI, a computer science laboratory of the University of Bordeaux, France. It was founded by Olivier Ly in 2010 and is mainly interested in mobile robots, in particular legged and humanoid robots. Our main research activities target motion control and locomotion, including quadruped gaits, kick synthesis, walking control and learning odometry and planning.

---

[1] RoboCup Humanoid League rules: https://www.robocuphumanoid.org/materials/rules/.

© Springer International Publishing AG 2017
S. Behnke et al. (Eds.): RoboCup 2016, LNAI 9776, pp. 491–502, 2017.
https://doi.org/10.1007/978-3-319-68792-6_41

Our interest in the RoboCup Kid-Size is motivated by the very challenging competition along with the great community. The autonomous soccer Humanoid League is a well suited game to address state of the art locomotion and perception questions while allowing for mechatronic innovations. We support the emphasis of the competition on robustness and real world applications of robotics methods.

From our very first participation in the RoboCup in the Kid-Size league in 2011, we learned the importance of mechanical and electronics robustness which led to our second participation in 2013 where we managed to score our first goals. But only after a complete redesign of the walk and the vision system, we were able to reach the quarters in 2014. Then in 2015 – with the new rules including artificial grass – we achieved the third place while beginning to redesign our core software architecture. For our first time, we had the possibility to work on some more "advanced" components such as foot pressure sensors, localization and odometry estimation from a kinematic model. All these developments eventually led us to the first place in 2016, after we finished the redesign of our core architecture along with numerous improvements of our system.

In the following, we describe specific technical points on our RoboCup 2016 architecture that could be interesting to share with the community. First, Sect. 2 presents distinctive hardware foot pressure sensors and the choice of industrial camera. Section 3 describes our optimized electronics custom router board and our alternative Dynamixel open-source firmware. Finally Sect. 4 outlines our major software components: the complete kinematics model, the odometry and camera calibration, the vision pipeline and the localization particle filter, our user interface tools, the team play and high level strategies and finally our monitoring tool.

2   Hardware

2.1   Foot Pressure Sensors

Our major hardware specificity is the use of strain gauge based force sensors in the robot's feet [8]. The device takes advantage of the cleats that were added by many teams when switching from flat carpets to 3 cm artificial grass in 2015. Our feet have a rectangular support polygon while getting all the contact forces with the ground through four points. Each of these points is linked to the core of the foot by a mechanical bar with strain gauges glued on it. It forms a resistor network whose values vary according to the mechanical deformations. See Fig. 1 of an overview of the device.

We designed a custom electronic board that features amplifiers and a small microcontroller that is able to communicate directly through the Dynamixel serial bus, allowing daisy chaining with the last ankle motor and thus simplifying hardware integration. The strain gauges are low-cost off-the-shelf components easy to find on the market. The mechanical and electronic designs are open-source [10].

The strain gauges measure the normal component of the ground reaction force at each point of the cleats, which allows to compute the center of pressure

Fig. 1. An overview of our feet devices, below view (on the left) and top view (on the right)

(CoP) of the robot. The latter is the point P on the ground where the moment of the ground reaction forces vanishes [11]. It is then defined as:

$$P = \frac{\sum_i F_i J_i}{\sum_i Fi}$$

where F_i and J_i are respectively the force measured and the position of the ith gauge. It is the geometric barycenter of the cleat positions with measured forces as weight.

We use these sensors to enhance the walking stability, tackling the problem of lateral balance. This was already discussed in [4, 7]. They proposed a capture step approach, using the data from the motor encoders and from the inertial measurement unit to estimate the position and speed of the center of mass. The inverted pendulum model is then used to predict and adjust the support swap timing and position. Our approach has similarities since we also have a nominal trajectory for the center of pressure that is compared with the one we estimate using the sensor. A threshold ensures that the mass is transferred to the other foot during support swing, and pauses the move if it does not[2].

We assessed the efficiency of this method using the setup shown in Fig. 2. A 1 Kg mass is attached to a 1.9 m rope and is dropped repeatedly on the robot at 0.5 and 0.6 m. This setup is similar to one of the challenge of the kid-size league named *push recovery*. The experimental results are summarized in Table 1.

Table 1. Push recovery tests with and without the stabilization loop enabled.

	Stabilisation enabled		Stabilisation disabled	
	Fall	No-fall	Fall	No-fall
50 cm	1	19	15	5
60 cm	9	11	14	6

---

[2] This behavior can be seen in action in the video: https://youtu.be/avJI_cBuMm0.

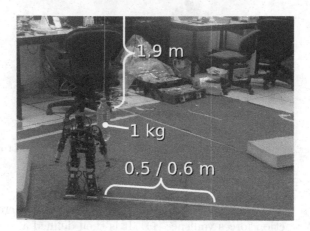

Fig. 2. Benchmark setup for the lateral perturbation rejection tests.

2.2 Cameras and Lenses

In 2016 we decided to switch from standard webcams to small industrial cameras (See3CAM_11CUG from e-con Systems). This change was mainly driven by our need to minimize the motion blur thanks to a global shutter. Moreover, the extended control over the camera's parameters also allows for a slightly better color perception. Another strategy that has proved quite convenient is the ability to use a relatively wide angle lens (about 100° field of view). This wide field of view is oriented vertically, which allows the robot to see both its feet and the opponent goal in most cases but with the cost of a high image distortion.

Unfortunately during the competition we observed that the camera's USB 3.0 interface provoked interference with the WiFi of our robots. This problem seems to be well established now [1] and for the next year we plan to change our cameras once more.

3   Electronics and Firmware

3.1   Custom Electronics Board

While all the high-level logic is executed in the robot embedded computer (Compulab Fitlet), the low-level communication with the Dynamixel servo- motors and sensors is managed by a custom "router" board. This board is driven by a STM32 microcontroller (72 MHz 32 bit Cortex-M3 Arm) and is aimed at optimizing the communication between servo-motors (Dynamixel TTL or RS485 bus), sensors (I2C or SPI) and the embedded computer via USB2 (Fig. 3).

This optimization is firstly done by separating the serial servo-motor bus in three independent physical buses: one per leg and one for the upper body – the router board dealing with the three buses in parallel. Moreover, a pseudo "SYNC-READ" command is implemented. This command asks for multiple values to be read in one packet. This packet is actually processed by the microcontroller, which issues standard read commands sequentially, parallelizing communication through the three physical buses, and thus increasing the communication speed.

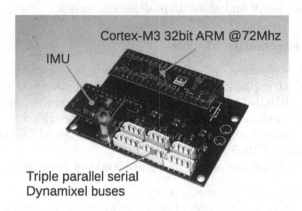

Fig. 3. Our custom board to handle device communications.

When the robot is walking, a complete cycle, which includes a write and a read on all its devices takes less than 10 ms.

3.2 Dynaban Alternative Firmware for Dynamixel

A currently ongoing open-source project is the Dynaban custom firmware[3] for Dynamixel servo-motors. The aim of this project is to release to the community a working open-source implementation of the Dynamixel firmware in order to increase our control over the actuation. For example, a feed forward control has been implemented to improve the position's tracking accuracy and was originally presented in [2]. This controller makes use of polynomial position and torque trajectories continuously sent ahead of time. This firmware has been successfully tested (only in a standard mode without feed forward) during the whole RoboCup 2016 competition on one of our Sigmaban robot.

4   Software

Our entire code base is implemented in C++11 and currently has the following architecture:

---

[3] Dynaban project: https://github.com/RhobanProject/Dynaban.

- The low-level[4] thread is running the serial bus communication.
- The motion thread updates the models from low-level data, runs the team play and the game controller services, updates high level states and finally computes the walk and head motions.
- The perception thread sequentially reads a frame from the camera, extracts the ball, goal posts and field features and then runs the localization particle filter to update ball and absolute position estimation.

4.1 Robot Kinematics Models

An important component of our architecture is a complete geometric and kinematics model implemented on top of the Rigid Body Dynamics Library (RBDL[5]). The RBDL C++ library is developed by Martin Felis (Heidelberg University) and implements the classical algorithms described in [3]. The model of the robot is directly exported from the Computer-Aided Design (CAD) software to a standard URDF[6] file.

Three different instances of the model are used and presented in the following:

- "Goal model": motor's target positions,
- "Current model": state of the robot estimated from current values of sensors,
- "Past model": state of the robot slightly delayed.

The goal model is only considering the 20 joint degrees of freedom (DoFs). The current and past models are also considering the support state (left or right foot) and a 5 DoFs $(x, y, yaw, pitch, roll)$ floating base located at the center of the supporting foot.

"Goal" model: The goal model is used to represent the desired joint state of the robot. Analytical Inverse Kinematics (IK) is implemented for the leg (6 DoFs) and for the head (2 DoFs). The leg IK allows to design a walk and kick motion in Cartesian space by specifying the trunk and flying foot position and orientation. The head IK is used to control the neck yaw and pitch motors in order to target any given point in the Cartesian egocentric frame at the center of the camera's image.

"Current" model: The estimation of the current state of the robot is based on motor encoders, the Inertial Measurement Unit (IMU) and the foot pressure sensors. Firstly, the pressure sensors are measuring the weight on each foot. The foot with the highest weight is considered as the current support foot and is fixed on the ground. The IMU has 3 accelerometers and 3 gyroscopes filtered by a AHRS system[7] implemented on the embedded computer. This filter provides

---

[4] RhAL Rhoban low-level library: https://github.com/Rhoban/RhAL.
[5] C++ Rigid Body Dynamics Library: http://rbdl.bitbucket.org/.
[6] XML Unified Robot Description Format: http://wiki.ros.org/urdf.
[7] Open-Source Razor IMU AHRS filtering: https://github.com/ptrbrtz/razor-9dof-ahrs.

pitch and roll Euler angles of the robot's trunk. In addition, a simple integration of the Z gyroscope provides an absolute yaw estimation. This yaw estimation is obviously drifting but has proven to be quite accurate on small time scale. Typically, the drift is about 5° after 30 s of robot manipulation. To estimate the robot state, the IMU is considered exact. Given the joint positions, the orientation of the support foot on the ground is set such that the trunk orientation matches the IMU computed roll, pitch and yaw angles. The possible discrepancy between the IMU and motor positions accounts for the soft ground and the mechanical backlash.

Finally, the estimated state of the robot is also used to evaluate the odometry. The estimation of the robot's self relative motion is a very important ingredient of the localization process. At each step, the relative displacement between the new and the old support foot position is integrated. It comes out that the use of the foot pressure sensors instead of relying only on the feet kinematics is important to achieve accurate results. The accuracy of the odometry is further improved through a calibration process detailed in the Sect. 4.2.

"Past" model: The past model is used to provide a history of the model state at any point in the past. All the low-level data are stored for a fixed period of time and can be used to rebuild a model of the robot state in the past. In particular, this system is useful for the vision and localization components as images can take a few hundred milliseconds to be processed. It is then necessary to have access to a complete state of the model at the moment the image was taken.

This model is mainly used for the localization of the Cartesian egocentric position of an object on the ground at a given position on the image. And secondly, the prediction of the expected ball radius in pixels at a given position on current image, which is a strong criteria for ball or goal post false positive rejection.

It is to be noted that all these models allow for the external features (ball, goal post...) to be stored in the world absolute reference frame, taking into account the robot's displacement. For instance, even if the localization or ball detection process runs at low frequency, the walk controller always could have access to a fresh and updated ball relative position being patched up by the odometry integration and model kinematics.

4.2 Odometry and Camera Calibration

Instead of relying on classical visual odometry as many other teams do in RoboCup SPL [5], our odometry estimation is based on a simple kinematics integration and a good support foot detection. In addition, the accuracy of the estimation is improved through a calibration process coming from our previous work [9].

The idea is to account for model errors and sliding ground contacts by learning a corrective model. The original work uses a motion capture setup and a non parametric non linear Locally Weighted Linear Regression (LWPR) method to learn a corrective function of the robot's relative displacement at each step.

The original motion capture setup is not convenient to deploy on a field during the competition. Therefore, the full motion of the robot can not be measured and the calibration process has been simplified for the RoboCup context. Instead of the LWPR regression, a classical linear model is fitted. The robot is manually driven between two known points on the field several times (6 runs were used). During each run, all low-level data are recorded and the robot is driven such as all walk directions (forward, backward, lateral steps) are explored. Then, the robot's displacements are replayed off-line and a black-box optimization algorithm (CMA-ES [6][8]) is applied to find the parameters of the model. The optimization tries to minimise the error between the simulated robot final position (under current odometry correction) and actual known robot's displacement. With this procedure, the odometry accuracy typically achieves a drift of about 20 cm for a displacement of 2.5 m forward, which was sufficient for our needs.

Another issue requiring a frequent calibration concerns the deformation of mechanical parts. In particular, a deformation of the neck part holding the camera can result in a large distance estimation error of external objects. A discrepancy up to $5°$ on the kinematics orientation between the trunk and the camera has been detected during the competition.

Here, the calibration is done by aiming the camera at known points on the ground. A correction of the geometry between the camera and the trunk of the robot is then computed by comparing the measured and expected positions of these known points.

It is to be noted that these calibration procedure had to be repeated daily during the competition.

4.3   Vision Flexible Architecture

The real RoboCup environment being only known at the beginning of the competition, the algorithms used to detect key features often need to be adapted or even modified entirely on site.

In order to allow for a quick prototyping, we represent our vision algorithm as a directed acyclic graph of independent filters. The topology of the graph and all the parameters of the filters are stored in XML configuration files which can easily be modified. The vision core system is then able to instantiate on the fly, OpenCV filters or custom algorithms based on this file. Basic monitoring and parameters updates are available online, without requiring any interruption of the program. Modifications of the topology of the graph require changes in the configuration file, but they do not require compilation. In order to reduce the computational burden of embedded vision, most of the filters heavily use regions of interest, detecting the areas susceptible to contain useful information in downscaled images.

---

[8] CMA-ES C++ library: https://github.com/beniz/libcmaes.

The consistency and guaranty of continuous improvement of the vision algorithm is ensured by a benchmark process which uses manually tagged images and compares them with the results of our algorithm. This allows us to run non-regression tests to validate our modifications.

This setup allowed us to quickly adapt during the first few days and all along the competition. We were able to experiment several approaches in parallel and to choose the best one based on the benchmark results. Moreover, the quick development time also allowed us to produce different independent algorithms to detect the ball and the goals and also to work on different conditions in order to be aggregated by the particle filter.

4.4   Localization with Particle Filter

In order to estimate the position of the robot on the field, we use a 3-dimensional particle filter in which each particle represents an estimate of the position and the orientation of the robot on the field. This filtering method allowed us to aggregate observations from different sources.

As observations, we used measurement of a magnetic compass, the goal posts, the borders and the corners of the field area. Since the measurements provided by the magnetic compass are particularly noisy, we only use it as a binary information, mainly to help disambiguation the field symmetry. Visual observations are scored according to the angle between the camera to the theoretical position vector and camera to the estimated position vector.

Since it was not possible for us to get rid of false positives, we decided to impose a minimum score on the potential of the particles given visual observations. This value was chosen according to the false positive rate which was provided by our benchmark system.

The mutation of the particles at each step was divided into two parts: controlled mutation based on odometry; and exploration. This system heavily relies on the corrected odometry which allows to strongly reduce the exploration strength.

Due to the limited computational power, we were forced to use a maximum of 1000 particles, which is quite small considering the size of the 3D state space. In order to face this problem, we introduced more a priori knowledge with special particle distributions which are used to reset the filter after specific game events such as kick-off or robot services. Likewise, the cases where the robot falls were handled by adding an uniform noise on all the particles and by using a random orientation.

For development and debugging, we can generate images summarizing the results of the detection and the current state of the particle filter (see Fig. 4).

4.5   User Interface and Configuration Tool

Being able to easily and very quickly debug and tweak some parameters on the robot is an essential element of the RoboCup competition. Our experience led us to the conclusion that a command line interface was far more efficient than a

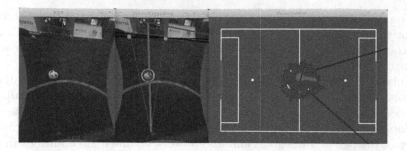

Fig. 4. The result of the vision and localisation processes. The tagged image in the middle is showing the ball estimated position and radius, goal post bases, goal center direction, field borders estimation in black and the horizon line in blue (Color figure online)

graphical one. So in order to fit our needs we developed the open-source project RhIO[9] (Rhoban Input Output Library).

This is a lightweight client-server library targeted to be integrated into existing code in order to monitor, debug and configure a running process in real time. The main user interface is a bash-like shell with a folder-file architecture. The project is described more deeply in [10]. Note that the network protocol used relies on TCP and can not be used for monitoring during games.

4.6   Team Play

Compared to the RoboCup Standard Platform League, our team play is still very basic. Nevertheless, some simple and easy-to-implement robot coordination have proven to be quite effective to improve game quality.

Our robots are continuously listening and broadcasting messages at 3 Hz on the WiFi UDP. The packets are containing the:

- robot's unique id,
- ball position in egocentric frame and quality estimation,
- absolute position on the field and estimation quality,
- high level state (for monitoring),
- software errors (for monitoring).

The ball and field quality is an estimation between 0 and 1 of the confidence over the computed position provided by the particle filter.

Based on these information, our first team play strategy has been running since the RoboCup 2014 in João Pessoa. It implements a simple ball *mutex* area. There is a hierarchy among the robots according to their knowledge of the ball position. This system gives the priority to play the ball to the closest robot while the others keep a specific fixed exclusion distance from the ball. Note that the exclusion radius parameter is slightly different for each team member in order to prevent two side attackers to lay on the same circle.

---

[9] RhIO Project: https://github.com/rhoban/rhio.

So when the main attacker falls, loses the ball or fails, he either indicates no ball detection (zero quality) or stops broadcasting. Therefore, the next closer side attacker takes the ball lock and tries to recover the ball possession. The last feature of this simple behavior is that side teammates are following the main attacker, resulting in nice grouped progression on the field. However, this simple strategy does not explicitly prevent the teammates from colliding. An actual avoidance system still need to be implemented.

Another team play strategy which was only implemented during the very end of the RoboCup 2016 competition is the ball position sharing. When a robot is unsuccessfully looking for the ball during a fixed period of time and if another team member is localized and knows where the ball is with a sufficiently high quality, these information are shared. For example, this allows lost attackers to come back in defence when the goalie is detecting a nearby approaching ball.

4.7   Monitoring

By listening to the UDP broadcasts, an external software is able to monitor the robots internal state during the games. As shown in Fig. 5, we can see robots localization on field, ball estimated position, high level behaviors state as well as software errors. For example, this allow to clearly know that a Dynamixel cable or the USB camera is disconnected after a fall. The rules allow in some conditions to remove a robot temporary from the game. Monitoring has proven to be an important feature during games and allows for a better pick-up or service management of the robots. Typically, a malfunctioning robot or a lost robot failing to recover a proper localization can be picked up and re-initialized on the field's border after a fixed among of time.

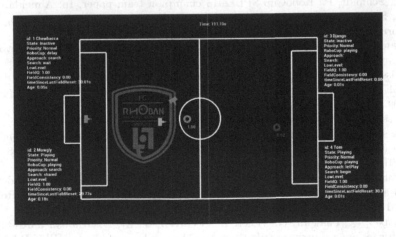

Fig. 5. Monitoring viewer showing in real time the robots state from UDP broadcast

5   Conclusion

As always, a lot of points are calling for improvements. We will pursue our inspection of small industrial cameras and comparison of wide versus narrow field of view lenses for RoboCup vision. A better tracking accuracy could be expected if our walk and kick motions were taking advantage of the new Dynaban feed forward controller. Concerning the software, a more automatic and faster camera calibration procedure would be more convenient to encompass the slow mechanical deformation. The major task for the localization process next year will be to break the field symmetry without the absolute magnetic orientation and still improve its accuracy. Either by recognizing our own goalie or either by detecting external features outside the field with a great caution to avoid moving spectators. Finally, an accurate localization and other robots detection are the last perception requirements to begin to develop real high level strategies similar to the NAOs in Standard Platform League. The Kid-Size league may not be that far from seeing ball passes between robots of the same team.

References

1. USB 3.0* radio frequency interference impact on 2.4 GHz wireless devices. Tech. rep. Intel Corporation (2012)
2. Fabre, R., Rouxel, Q., Passault, G., N'Guyen, S., Ly, O.: Dynaban, an open-source alternative firmware for dynamixel servo-motors. In: Symposium RoboCup 2016: Robot World Cup XX (2016)
3. Featherstone, R.: Rigid Body Dynamics Algorithms. Springer, Heidelberg (2014). doi:10.1007/978-1-4899-7560-7
4. Graf, C., Röfer, T.: A closed-loop 3D-LIPM gait for the robocup standard platform league humanoid. In: 5th Workshop on Humanoids Soccer Robots, Nashville, TN, USA (2010). http://www.humanoidsoccer.org/ws10/program.html
5. Hall, B., Harris, S., Hengst, B., Liu, R., Ng, K., Pagnucco, M., Pearson, L., Sammut, C., Schmidt, P.: RoboCup SPL 2015 champion team paper. In: Almeida, L., Ji, J., Steinbauer, G., Luke, S. (eds.) RoboCup 2015. LNCS, vol. 9513, pp. 72–82. Springer, Cham (2015). doi:10.1007/978-3-319-29339-4_6
6. Hansen, N., Ostermeier, A.: Completely derandomized self-adaptation in evolution strategies. Evol. Comput. 9(2), 159–195 (2001)
7. Missura, M., Behnke, S.: Lateral capture steps for bipedal walking. In: 2011 11th IEEE-RAS International Conference on Humanoid Robots (Humanoids), pp. 401–408. IEEE (2011)
8. Passault, G., Rouxel, Q., Hofer, L., N'Guyen, S., Ly, O.: Low-cost force sensors for small size humanoid robot. In: 2015 IEEE-RAS 15th International Conference on (Video Contribution) Humanoid Robots (Humanoids), pp. 1148–1148. IEEE (2015). https://youtu.be/_d7Phe0qois
9. Rouxel, Q., Passault, G., Hofer, L., N'Guyen, S., Ly, O.: Learning the odometry on a small humanoid robot. In: 2016 IEEE International Conference on Robotics and Automation (ICRA). IEEE (2016)
10. Rouxel, Q., Passault, G., Hofer, L., N'Guyen, S., Ly, O.: Rhoban hardware and software open source contributions for robocup humanoids. In: IEEE-RAS International Conference on Humanoid Robots Proceedings of 10th Workshop on Humanoid Soccer Robots. Seoul, Korea (2015)
11. Sardain, P., Bessonnet, G.: Forces acting on a biped robot. Center of pressure-zero moment point. IEEE Trans. Syst. Man Cybern. Part A Syst. Humans 34(5), 630–637 (2004)

B-Human 2016 – Robust Approaches for Perception and State Estimation Under More Natural Conditions

Thomas Röfer[1,2]([✉]), Tim Laue[2], and Jesse Richter-Klug[2]

[1] Deutsches Forschungszentrum für Künstliche Intelligenz,
Cyber-Physical Systems, Enrique-Schmidt-Str. 5, 28359 Bremen, Germany
thomas.roefer@dfki.de
[2] Fachbereich 3 – Mathematik und Informatik, Universität Bremen,
Postfach 330 440, 28334 Bremen, Germany
tlaue@uni-bremen.de

Abstract. In 2015 and 2016, the RoboCup Standard Platform League's major rule changes were mostly concerned with the appearance of important game elements, changing them towards a setup that is more similar to normal football games, for instance a black and white ball and white goals. Furthermore, the 2016 *Outdoor Competition* was held in a glass hall and thus under natural lighting conditions. These changes rendered many previously established approaches for perception and state estimation useless. In this paper, we present multiple approaches to cope with these challenges, i. e. a color classification for natural lighting conditions, an approach to detect black and white balls, and a self-localization that relies on complex field features that are based on field lines. This combination of perception and state estimation approaches enabled our robots to preserve their high performance in this more challenging new environment and significantly contributed to our success at RoboCup 2016.

1 Introduction

B-Human is a joint RoboCup team of the University of Bremen and the German Research Center for Artificial Intelligence (DFKI). The team was founded in 2006 as a team in the Humanoid League, but switched to participating in the Standard Platform League in 2009. Since then, we participated in seven RoboCup German Open competitions, the RoboCup European Open, and eight RoboCups and only lost four official games. As a result, we won all German Open and European Open competitions, the RoboCups 2009, 2010, 2011 and 2013. This year, we won the main (indoor) competition and became the runner-up in the newly introduced outdoor competition.

The rules of the competition are changed every year to make the task more challenging and to work towards the RoboCup Federation's 2050 goal. In the past two years, these changes mostly concerned the appearance of the environment, making it look more like a human football environment. In 2015, the yellow goals were replaced by white ones and it 2016, a black and white ball

© Springer International Publishing AG 2017
S. Behnke et al. (Eds.): RoboCup 2016, LNAI 9776, pp. 503–514, 2017.
https://doi.org/10.1007/978-3-319-68792-6_42

replaced the previously used orange one. In addition, over both years, almost all restrictions regarding jersey colors have been removed, too. This combination of changes has made simplistic and purely color-based approaches such as "detect the orange spot" or "find yellow rectangles" useless as most unique color assignments do not exist anymore. Furthermore, to evaluate the performance under natural lighting, the *Outdoor Competition 2016* was held in a glass hall, requiring the adaptiveness of image preprocessing algorithms. In addition, this competition had one more challenging aspect: walking on artificial grass. We solved all vision-related challenges sufficiently well, but were less successful regarding a robust walking implementation, which ultimately resulted in losing the outdoor final. However, we still scored more goals (18) outdoors than all of our seven competitors together (17).

This paper mainly focuses on our vision system and the impact it had on ball localization and self-localization. The robustness of these components strongly contributed to our success. For instance, we were the only team in the competition that never got a *leaving the field* penalty.[1] In comparison, the average number of *leaving the field* calls was 35.45 times per team (5.8 per team per game), which either meant that the robots were delocalized or they were chasing a false ball they detected outside the field.

This paper is organized as follows: Sect. 2 describes our image preprocessing approach, which is capable of handling natural lighting, followed by the algorithms required to detect the new black and white ball in Sect. 3. Finally, the new complex field features, which make the perception of the white goals unnecessary, and their impact on self-localization are presented in Sect. 4.

2   Image Preprocessing

In the Standard Platform League, all teams use the same robot model, the *SoftBank Robotics NAO*. The NAO is equipped with two cameras – one located in the forehead and one in the chin – that are the major source of information about the environment. Processing these images is the most time-consuming task performed on the robot, because they consist of a large amount of data. Before 2016, the basic principle of our vision system was to reach real-time performance, i.e. to process 60 images per second, by analyzing only a fraction of the pixels available. The selection was based on the perspective under which the camera that took the image observed the environment and the expected size objects would have in the different parts of the image. This approach is still followed in our current system, but there are now preprocessing steps that consider the whole image. To keep the real-time performance, the amount of data to process was reduced by using a smaller image resolution and processing was accelerated by employing the SIMD (*single instruction multiple data*) instructions of NAO's processor.

---

[1] Actually, we got two, but both were the result of human errors, as we confirmed from analyzing video footage and log files.

2.1   NAO's Camera Images

NAO's cameras provide images in the YUV 4:2:2 color space. In this format, two neighboring pixels have separate brightness values (Y), but share the same color information (U and V). This format is a little bit cumbersome to handle, because it always requires a distinction between whether a pixel is the left or the right one of a pair that share the color channels. Therefore in the past, we have acquired images that were twice the resolution than we actually needed. We interpreted two neighboring pixels as a single one, ignoring the second Y channel, and skipped every second row to keep the aspect ratio. As a result, the images were used as if their format would be YUV 4:4:4. However, for using SIMD instructions, it is important to process as much data as possible with a single instruction. Therefore, having an unused Y channel is not desirable. In addition, color information has become less and less important in the Standard Platform League, because most color coding was removed from the setup during the recent years. Hence, it is important to keep the resolutions we used before for brightness information, i. e. 640×480 pixels for the upper camera and 320×240 pixels for the lower one, but the color information can be sparser.

2.2   The YHS2 Image Format

As a result, the YUV 4:2:2 format now appears to be a reasonable compromise, which reduces the amount of data to process by a factor of two. However, its data layout is still impractical. Therefore, the original image (cf. Fig. 1a) is split into two dedicated images: a gray-scale image (cf. Fig. 1b) and a color-classified image (cf. Fig. 1c). The color-classified image assigns one of the following classes to each pixel: *field*, *white*, *black*, and *other*[2]. These two images are used by all further image processing steps instead of the original image. Both images are generated together in a single pass using the SSE3[3] instruction set of NAO's Intel Atom CPU. The gray-scaled image simply consists of all Y values. The color-classified image needs the actual color classification as well as an optional color conversion. A suitable candidate for lighting-independent color classification is the HSI (*hue*, *saturation*, *intensity*) color space. Unfortunately, an implementation of a correct conversion to the HSI color space takes about 7 ms for the whole upper image. This is why we implemented a color conversion to the *YHS2* format[4] instead. It follows roughly the same idea, but requires significantly less computation time. In *YHS2*, a vector that is created from the U and V channels describes the *H*ue (cf. Fig. 1e) as its angle as well as the *S*aturation (cf. Fig. 1d) as its length divided by the luminance component *Y*. The color classification is performed in two steps. First, it is decided, whether a pixel is saturated or not. If the hue value of a saturated pixel is inside a specific range (normally something greenish), it is classified as *field*, otherwise as *other*. An unsaturated pixel is categorized by

---

[2] Saturated, but not green, i. e. not the field color.

[3] Unfortunately, the AVX extensions are not supported by the NAO's CPU.

[4] The *YHS2* conversion is inspired by a discussion found in the internet at http://forum.doom9.org/showthread.php?t=162053.

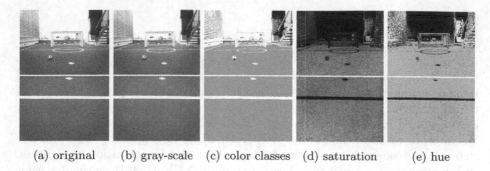

(a) original   (b) gray-scale   (c) color classes   (d) saturation   (e) hue

Fig. 1. Examples of upper and lower camera images in different formats (Color figure online)

its Y value as either being *black* or *white*. The whole classification takes 4 ms for the upper camera image and only 1 ms for the lower one.

2.3 Basic Feature Detection

The colored images are used by the subsequently executed modules to find initial cues – the so-called *spots* – that indicate interesting features. In a first step, the images are subsampled by traversing precomputed scan-lines to build regions of the same color class. In advance, an initial coarse grid is used to detect the field's boundary, i. e. the polygon that encompasses the green field. This is done to avoid further calculations within areas outside the field (where we do not expect any objects relevant for the game).

After regions have been found, the detection of the lines – which provide the base for all field elements that we currently consider – is realized by fitting white regions via linear regression over their field coordinates. In parallel it is also tried to fit a mid circle into the field coordinates of sets of short white line elements. For this purpose, linear regression is used, too. In case of field lines hitting or crossing each other in an approximately right angle, a field line intersection is detected. Each intersection is either classified as *L*, *T*, or *X*, according to its appearance.

Finally, penalty marks are detected by searching for small white areas which are surrounded by field color. If too much black is found inside the area, it will be discarded, as it might also be a ball.

3 Detecting the Black and White Ball

The introduction of the black and white ball is the major new challenge in the Standard Platform League in 2016. Until the RoboCup 2015, the ball was orange and rather easy to detect. In particular, it was the only orange object on the field. The new ball is mainly white with a regular pattern of black patches, just as a miniature version of a regular soccer ball. The main problem is that the field lines, the goals, and the NAO robots are also white. The latter even have several round plastic parts and they also contain grey parts. Since the ball is often in the vicinity of the NAOs during a game, it is quite challenging to avoid a large number of false positives.

Playing with a normal soccer ball has also been addressed in the Middle Size League (MSL), e. g. [3,5]. However, the robots in the MSL are typically not white and they are equipped with more computing power than the NAO is, e. g. Martins et al. [8] presented a ball detection that requires 25 ms at a resolution of 640 × 480 pixels on a Intel Core 2 Duo 2 running at 2 GHz. In contrast, the solution presented here is on average more than ten times faster running on an Intel Atom at 1.6 GHz, which allows our robots to process all images that their cameras take.

We use a multi-step approach for the detection of the ball. First, the vertical scan lines our vision system is mainly based on are searched for ball candidates. Then, a contour detector fits ball contours around the candidates' locations. Afterwards, fitted ball candidates are filtered using some general heuristics. Finally, the surface pattern inside each remaining candidate is checked. Furthermore, the ball state estimation has been extended by some additional checks to exclude false positives that cannot be avoided during image processing.

3.1 Searching for Ball Candidates

Our vision system scans the image vertically using scan lines of different density based on the size that objects, in particular the ball, would have in a certain position of the image. To determine ball candidates, these scan lines are searched for sufficiently large gaps in the green that also have a sufficiently large horizontal extension and contain enough white (cf. Fig. 2a). Candidates that are significantly inside of a detected robot are discarded. In addition, the number of candidates is reduced by only accepting ones that are sufficiently far away from other candidates.

3.2 Fitting Ball Contours

As the position of a ball candidate is not necessarily in the center of an actual ball, the area around such a position is searched for the contour of the ball as it would appear in this part of the image given the intrinsic parameters of the camera and its pose relative to the field plane. The approach is very similar to the detection of objects in 3-D space using a stereo camera system as described by Müller et al. [9], but we only use a single image instead. Thereby, instead of searching a 3-D space for an object appearing in matching positions in two images at the same time, only the 2-D plane of the field is searched for the ball to appear in the expected size in a single camera image. For each ball candidate, a contrast-normalized Sobel (CNS) image of the surrounding area is computed (cf. Fig. 2b). This contrast image is then searched for the best match with the expected ball contour (cf. Fig. 2c). The best match is then refined by adapting its hypothetical 3-D coordinates (cf. Fig. 2d).

 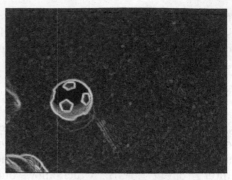

(a) Vertical scan lines and a detected ball candidate (the cross). Parts of the robot's body are ignored (bottom left).

(b) Contrast-normalized Sobel image. The colors indicate the directions of the gradients.

(c) Visualization of the search space for the ball contour. The actual search is only performed around the ball candidate, but in single pixel steps in both dimensions.

(d) The contour with the highest response (green) and the sample grid to check the ball pattern (pixels classified as black are shown in red, white pixels in blue).

Fig. 2. The main steps of the ball detection (Color figure online)

3.3 Filtering Ball Candidates

The fitting process results in a measure, the *response*, for how well the image matches with the contour excepted at the candidate's location. If this value is below a threshold, the ball candidate is dropped. The threshold is dynamically determined from the amount of green that surrounds the ball candidate. On the one hand, the less green is around the candidate, the higher the response must be to reduce the amount of false positives inside robots. However, if a ball candidate is completely surrounded by green pixels and the response was high enough to exclude the possibility of being a penalty mark, the ball candidate is accepted right away, skipping the final step described below that might be failing if the ball is rolling quickly. All candidates that fit well enough are processed in descending order of their response. As a result, the candidate with the highest response that also passes all other checks will be accepted. These other checks include that the ball radius found must be similar to the radius that would be expected at that position of the image.

3.4   Checking the Surface Pattern

For checking the black and white surface pattern, a fixed set of 3-D points on the surface of the ball candidate are projected into the image (cf. Fig. 2d). For each of these pixels, the brightness of the image at its location is determined. Since the ball usually shows a strong gradient in the image from its bright top to a much darker bottom half, the pixels are artificially brightened depending on their position inside the ball. Then, Otsu's method [10] is used to determine the optimal threshold between the black and the white parts of the ball for the pixels sampled. If the average brightnesses of both classes are sufficiently different, all pixels sampled are classified as being either black or white. Then, this pattern is looked up in a pre-computed table to determine whether it is a valid combination for the official ball. The table was computed from a 2-D texture of the ball surface considering all possible rotations of the ball around all three axes and some variations close the transitions between the black and the white parts of the ball.

3.5   Removing False Positives Before Ball State Estimation

The major parts of B-Human's ball state, i. e. position and velocity, estimation remained unchanged for many years and consist of a set of Kalman filters. However, the introduction of the new black and white ball required the addition of a few more checks. In previous years, the number of false positive ball perceptions has been zero in most games. Hence, the ball tracking was implemented as being as reactive as possible, i. e. every perception was considered. Although the new ball perception is quite robust in general, several false positives per game cannot be avoided due to the similarity between the ball's shape and surface and some robot parts. Therefore, there must be multiple ball perceptions within a certain area and within a maximum time frame before a perception is considered for the state estimation process. This slightly reduces the module's reactivity but is still fast enough to allow the execution of ball blocking moves in a timely manner. Furthermore, a common problem is the detection of balls inside robots that are located at the image's border and are thus not perceived by our software. A part of these perceptions, i. e. those resulting from our teammates, is excluded by checking against the communicated teammate positions.

3.6   Results

The approach allows our robots to detect the ball in distances of up to five meters with only a few false positive detections. Figure 3 shows the statistics of how well the ball was seen by different teams in terms of how long ago the ball was seen

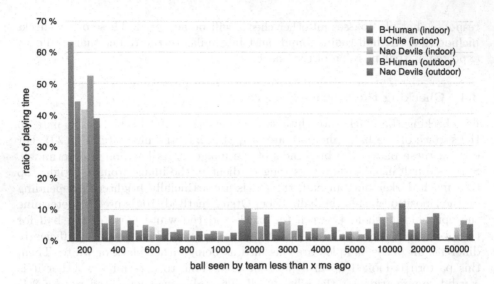

Fig. 3. Analysis of the team communication data of the indoor semifinal B-Human vs. UChile Robotics Team, the quarterfinal Nao Devils Dortmund vs. UT Austin Villa (UT Austin Villa is missing in this chart, because they did not broadcast their team communication.), and the outdoor final B-Human vs. Nao Devils Dortmund (Color figure online)

by the team, i. e. the robot that saw it most recently. The statistics was created from some of the log files recorded by the TeamCommunicationMonitor [11] at RoboCup 2016 that were made available at the website of the league. Since the teams analyzed were some of the best in the competition[5], it is assumed that the number of false positive ball detections, which would also result in low numbers, is negligible. Although the chart in Fig. 3 suggests that the ball detection worked better indoors, it actually benefited from the good lighting conditions in the outdoor competition. However, since our robots were only walking slowly and fell down quite often, the average distance to the ball was a lot higher, which impeded the perception rate. In a rather dark environment, as on Field A in the indoor competition, balls with lower responses had to be accepted in order to detect the ball at all. This resulted in more false positive detections, in particular in the feet of other robots, because they are also largely surrounded by green.

The runtime is determined by the number of ball candidates that are found. For instance, the log file of player number 2 from the second half of the final shows that the search for ball candidates took 0.135 ms on average and took never longer than 0.816 ms. Computing the CNS image for the candidates took 0.285 ms on average and reached a maximum of 5.394 ms. Checking these candidates took 0.951 ms on average, but sometimes took significantly longer.

---

[5] The third-placed Nao-Team HTWK was not analyzed, because they only provided binary information in the standard communication's field *ballAge*.

The maximum duration reached was 10.604 ms. As it rarely happens that the processing of images from the upper and the lower camera take long in subsequent frames, the frame rate was basically 60 Hz all the time.

4 Complex Field Features and Self-localization

In the past, B-Human used goals as a dominant feature for self-localization. When the field was smaller and the goal posts were painted yellow, they were easy to perceive from most positions and provided precise and valuable measurements for the pose estimation process. In particular the sensor resetting part, i. e. the creation of alternative pose estimates in case of a delocalization, was almost completely based on the goal posts perceived. In 2015, we still relied on this approach, using a detector for the white goals [11]. However, as it turned out that this detector required too much computation time and did not work reliably in some environments (requiring lots of calibration efforts), we decided to perform self-localization without goals but by using complex field features derived from certain constellations of perceived field lines.

4.1 Field Features

The self-localization always used field lines, their crossings, and the center circle as measurements. Since 2015, these features are complemented by the perception of the penalty marks. All these field elements are distributed over the whole field and can be detected very reliably, provided a constant input of measurements in most situations.

Built upon this, the perception of a new category of measurements, the so-called *field features*, has been implemented. They are created by combining multiple basic field elements in a way that a robot pose (in global field coordinates) can be derived directly (the handling of the field symmetry, which leads to actually two poses, is described in the following section). The currently computed features are: the penalty area, the center circle (including the center line that provides the direction), the field corners, the center corners (where the center line touches the outer field lines, cf. Fig. 4a), and the goal frame on the floor. Some of these features can be determined by different field element constellations, e. g. the penalty area can be derived from a subset of its corners as well as from a penalty mark and the penalty area's line next to it (cf. Fig. 4b). All considered lines are preprocessed by classifying them in short and long lines and by determining their relation to the field border (if available). The crossings of the lines are categorized as $L/T/X$ on the one hand and in *big/small* on the other hand. In this context, *big* means that it is a crossing that results from the intersection of two long lines, such as field corners perceived from a longer distance.

Overall, this approach provides a much higher number of reliable pose estimates than the previous goal-based approach, as the field lines on which it is based can be seen from many perspectives and have a more robust context

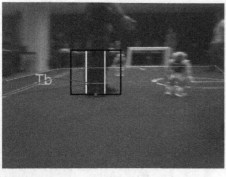 

(a) Center corner: two long field lines intersect and represent a big T (marked Tb).

(b) Penalty area: a penalty mark and a close line allow the detection of this area.

Fig. 4. Two examples for field features, both are depicted as blue lines. (Color figure online)

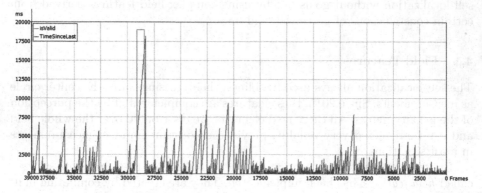

Fig. 5. Detected field features of one robot during the second half of the 2016 SPL final. The blue plot shows the elapsed time since the last feature was detected. The red line marks a period of time during which the robot's camera perspective was invalid, making feature detection impossible. It can be seen that there was never a period of time longer than nine seconds during which no field feature was detected. On average, a field feature was seen every 668 ms. (Color figure online)

(straight white lines surrounded by green carpet) than the noisy unknown background of goal posts. An example of the continuous perception of field features is plotted in Fig. 5.

4.2 Localization Resetting

The self-localization is based on a particle filter [4] with a low number of particles that each include an Unscented Kalman filter (UKF) [6]. Both approaches are straightforward textbook implementations [12], except for some adaptions to handle certain RoboCup-specific game states, such as the positioning after returning from a penalty. Field features can be used as measurements for these filters but not as a perception of relative landmarks. Instead, an artificial measurement of a global pose is generated, reducing the translational error in both dimensions as well as the rotational error at once. Furthermore, no data association – in contrast to the basic field elements that are not unique – is required.

However, particles only cover the state space very sparsely. Therefore, to recover from a delocalization, it is a common approach to perform *sensor resetting*, i. e. to insert new particles based on recent measurements [7]. The field features provide exactly this information and thus are used by us for creating new particles. As false positives can be among the field features, e. g. caused by robot parts overlapping parts of lines and thereby inducing a wrong constellation of elements, an additional filtering step is necessary. All robot poses that can be derived from recently observed field features are clustered and only the largest cluster, which also needs to contain a minimum number of elements, is considered as a candidate for a new sample. This candidate is only inserted into the sample set in case it significantly differs from the current robot pose estimation.

To resolve the field's symmetry when handling the field features, we use the constraints given by the rules (e. g. all robots are in their own half when the game state switches to *Playing* or when they return from a penalty) as well as the assumption that the alternative that is more compatible to the previous robot pose is more likely than the other one. This assumption can be made, as no teleportation happens in real games. Instead, most localization errors result from situations in which robots lose track of their position and accumulate translational and rotational errors.

Self-localization without goals has already been realized by other teams, starting with Robo Eireann in 2011 [13]. There have also been different solutions for resolving the field's symmetry, e. g. by observing the field's surrounding, an approach that has been used by the two-time world champion UNSW Australia [2] who successfully use a visual compass [1]. However, our recent developments in localization and perception – along with a growing number of robots that have a z-axis gyroscope – enabled us to reduce the number of *Leaving the Field* penalties from 15 (in seven games during RoboCup 2015) to basically zero (in eleven games during the RoboCup 2016). This is a result that – as mentioned in Sect. 1 – significantly outperforms all other teams during a real competition.

5   Conclusion

In this paper, we have presented our vision and state estimation approaches that helped us to cope with the recent changes of the league's environment and significantly contributed to our success at RoboCup 2016. The analysis of data recorded during that competition shows that our robots have been able to frequently see important elements of the game, i. e. the new ball as well as complex field features. This enabled our robots to show great performances during games in the indoor competition as well as in the outdoor competition, in which we scored more goals than all other teams together. Furthermore, in contrast to all other teams, our robots never accidentally left the field. This indicates a very robust self-localization as well as no false ball positives outside the field. Overall, our system is ready for upcoming competitions, which are supposed to be held under more natural lighting conditions than the past ones.

References

1. Anderson, P., Hengst, B.: Fast monocular visual compass for a computationally limited robot. In: Behnke, S., Veloso, M., Visser, A., Xiong, R. (eds.) RoboCup 2013. LNCS, vol. 8371, pp. 244–255. Springer, Heidelberg (2014). doi:10.1007/978-3-662-44468-9_22
2. Ashar, J., et al.: RoboCup SPL 2014 champion team paper. In: Bianchi, R.A.C., Akin, H.L., Ramamoorthy, S., Sugiura, K. (eds.) RoboCup 2014. LNCS, vol. 8992, pp. 70–81. Springer, Cham (2015). doi:10.1007/978-3-319-18615-3_6
3. Coath, G., Musumeci, P.: Adaptive arc fitting for ball detection in RoboCup. In: APRS Workshop on Digital Image Analyzing, pp. 63–68 (2003)
4. Fox, D., Burgard, W., Dellaert, F., Thrun, S.: Monte-Carlo localization: efficient position estimation for mobile robots. In: Proceedings of the Sixteenth National Conference on Artificial Intelligence, pp. 343–349, Orlando, USA (1999)
5. Hanek, R., Schmitt, T., Buck, S., Beetz, M.: Towards RoboCup without color labeling. In: Kaminka, G.A., Lima, P.U., Rojas, R. (eds.) RoboCup 2002. LNCS, vol. 2752, pp. 179–194. Springer, Heidelberg (2003). doi:10.1007/978-3-540-45135-8_14
6. Julier, S.J., Uhlmann, J.K., Durrant-Whyte, H.F.: A new approach for filtering nonlinear systems. In: Proceedings of the American Control Conference, vol. 3, pp. 1628–1632 (1995)
7. Lenser, S., Veloso, M.: Sensor resetting localization for poorly modelled mobile robots. In: Proceedings of the 2000 IEEE International Conference on Robotics and Automation (ICRA 2000), vol. 2, pp. 1225–1232, San Francisco, USA (2000)
8. Martins, D.A., Neves, A.J., Pinho, A.J.: Real-time generic ball recognition in RoboCup domain. In: Proceedings of the 3rd International Workshop on Intelligent Robotics, IROBOT, pp. 37–48 (2008)
9. Müller, J., Frese, U., Röfer, T.: Grab a mug - object detection and grasp motion planning with the NAO robot. In: Proceedings of the IEEE-RAS International Conference on Humanoid Robots (HUMANOIDS 2012), pp. 349–356, Osaka, Japan. IEEE (2012)
10. Otsu, N.: A threshold selection method from gray-level histograms. IEEE Trans. Syst. Man Cybern. 9(1), 62–66 (1979)
11. Röfer, T., Laue, T., Richter-Klug, J., Stiensmeier, J., Schünemann, M., Stolpmann, A., Stöwing, A., Thielke, F.: B-Human team description for RoboCup 2015. In: RoboCup 2015: Robot Soccer World Cup XIX Preproceedings. RoboCup Federation, Hefei, China (2015)
12. Thrun, S., Burgard, W., Fox, D.: Probabilistic Robotics. MIT Press, Cambridge (2005)
13. Whelan, T., Stüdli, S., McDonald, J., Middleton, R.H.: Efficient localization for robot soccer using pattern matching. In: Hähnle, R., Knoop, J., Margaria, T., Schreiner, D., Steffen, B. (eds.) ISoLA 2011. CCIS, pp. 16–30. Springer, Heidelberg (2012). doi:10.1007/978-3-642-34781-8_2

UT Austin Villa: RoboCup 2016 3D Simulation League Competition and Technical Challenges Champions

Patrick MacAlpine[⊠] and Peter Stone

Department of Computer Science, The University of Texas at Austin, Austin, USA
{patmac,pstone}@cs.utexas.edu

Abstract. The UT Austin Villa team, from the University of Texas at Austin, won the 2016 RoboCup 3D Simulation League, winning all 14 games that the team played. During the course of the competition the team scored 88 goals and conceded only 1. Additionally the team won the RoboCup 3D Simulation League technical challenge by winning each of a series of three league challenges: free, keepaway, and Gazebo running challenge. This paper describes the changes and improvements made to the team between 2015 and 2016 that allowed it to win both the main competition and each of the league technical challenges.

1 Introduction

UT Austin Villa won the 2016 RoboCup 3D Simulation League for the fifth time in the past six years, having also won the competition in 2011 [1], 2012 [2], 2014 [3], and 2015 [4] while finishing second in 2013. During the course of the competition the team scored 88 goals and only conceded 1 along the way to winning all 14 games the team played. Many of the components of the 2016 UT Austin Villa agent were reused from the team's successful previous years' entries in the competition. This paper is not an attempt at a complete description of the 2016 UT Austin Villa agent, the base foundation of which is the team's 2011 championship agent fully described in a team technical report [5], but instead focuses on changes made in 2016 that helped the team repeat as champions.

In addition to winning the main RoboCup 3D Simulation League competition, UT Austin Villa also won the RoboCup 3D Simulation League technical challenge by winning each of the three league challenges: free, keepaway, and Gazebo running challenge. This paper also serves to document these challenges and the approaches used by UT Austin Villa when competing in the challenges.

The remainder of the paper is organized as follows. In Sect. 2 a description of the 3D simulation domain is given. Section 3 details changes and improvements to the 2016 UT Austin Villa team (including those for marking, getting open, tuning kick selection for height, indirect kick set plays, and directional kicks), while Sect. 4 analyzes the contributions of these changes in addition to the overall performance of the team at the competition. Section 5 describes and analyzes the league challenges that were used to determine the winner of the technical challenge, and Sect. 6 concludes.

© Springer International Publishing AG 2017
S. Behnke et al. (Eds.): RoboCup 2016, LNAI 9776, pp. 515–528, 2017.
https://doi.org/10.1007/978-3-319-68792-6_43

2   Domain Description

The RoboCup 3D simulation environment is based on SimSpark [6], a generic physical multiagent system simulator. SimSpark uses the Open Dynamics Engine (ODE) library for its realistic simulation of rigid body dynamics with collision detection and friction. ODE also provides support for the modeling of advanced motorized hinge joints used in the humanoid agents.

Games consist of 11 versus 11 agents playing two 5 min halves of soccer on a 30 × 20 m field. The robot agents in the simulation are modeled after the Aldebaran Nao robot, which has a height of about 57 cm, and a mass of 4.5 kg. Each robot has 22° of freedom: six in each leg, four in each arm, and two in the neck. In order to monitor and control its hinge joints, an agent is equipped with joint perceptors and effectors. Joint perceptors provide the agent with noise-free angular measurements every simulation cycle (20 ms), while joint effectors allow the agent to specify the speed/direction in which to move a joint.

Visual information about the environment is given to an agent every third simulation cycle (60 ms) through noisy measurements of the distance and angle to objects within a restricted vision cone (120°). Agents are also outfitted with noisy accelerometer and gyroscope perceptors, as well as force resistance perceptors on the sole of each foot. Additionally, agents can communicate with each other every other simulation cycle (40 ms) by sending 20 byte messages.

In addition to the standard Nao robot model, four additional variations of the standard model, known as heterogeneous types, are available for use. These variations from the standard model include changes in leg and arm length, hip width, and also the addition of toes to the robot's foot. Teams must use at least three different robot types, no more than seven agents of any one robot type, and no more than nine agents of any two robot types.

The 2016 RoboCup 3D Simulation League competition included a couple key changes from the previous year's competition. The first of these was a rule change to make previously direct kick-ins—awarded to the opposing team when a player is the last to touch the ball before it goes out of bounds over the sideline—indirect (another player other than the player who took the kick must touch the ball before a goal can be scored). This rule was put in place to encourage both passing and teamwork, and to make the rules for kick-ins more similar to their equivalent in human soccer of indirect throw-ins. Coupled with this rule change, and also to match human soccer, an indirect kick is awarded to the opposing team if a player taking a kick (direct or indirect) touches the ball twice in a row.

The second change to the RoboCup 3D Simulation League was to add an automated referee for calling charging fouls. Players are deemed to have committed a charging foul, and are beamed outside the field of play as punishment, if when colliding with an opposing player their force (velocity component in the direction of the opposing player) exceeds a tunable threshold. Charging is not called on a player if the player has recently touched the ball—thus deemed to be going for the ball—or if two players are charging into each other at the same time. Calling charging fouls improves play by reducing the number of collisions while at the same time better matching the rules of human soccer.

3   Changes for 2016

While many components contributed to the success of the UT Austin Villa team, including dynamic role assignment [7] and an optimization framework used to learn low level behaviors for walking and kicking via an overlapping layered learning approach [8], the following subsections focus only on those that are new for 2016. A performance analysis of these components is provided in Sect. 4.1.

3.1   Marking

During the 2015 RoboCup competition it was noticed that teams had developed good kicking/passing abilities, and then were exploiting these abilities through set plays by passing the ball to open teammates in good positions to take a shot on goal. To counteract set plays, UT Austin Villa developed and employed a marking system for the 2016 RoboCup competition to cover and defend against opponents in dangerous offensive positions from receiving passes.

The marking system implemented by the UT Austin Villa team is a sequential process encompassing the following three steps:

1. Decide which players to mark
2. Select which roles to use for marking purposes
3. Use prioritized role assignment to assign players to positions.

In the first step, hand-coded heuristics are used to decide which opponents are in dangerous offensive positions and should be marked. Next, from the team's default formation positions, computed as offset positions from the ball using Delaunay triangulation [9], a set of formation positions are selected to be replaced with positions needed for marking. The set of formation positions to be replaced, computed by the Hungarian algorithm [10], is that which minimizes the sum of distances between positions for marking and the formation positions that are being replaced by the marking positions. Finally, prioritized role assignment [11], an extension of SCRAM role assignment [7], is used to assign agents to move to the team's desired role positions (both those for formation and marking purposes). A full description of the marking system can be found in [11].

3.2   Getting Open

In 2015 UT Austin Villa optimized variable distance kicks [4] that allow for the ball to be kicked different distances in one meter increments. These kicks provide passing options as robots can select from many potential targets to kick the ball to. Each potential kick location is given a score according to Eq. 1, and the location with the highest score is chosen as the location to kick the ball to. Equation 1 penalizes kick locations that are farther from the opponent's goal, penalizes kicks that have the ball end up near opponents, and also rewards kicks for landing near a teammate. All distances in Eq. 1 are measured in meters.

$$\texttt{score}(location) = \begin{array}{l} -\|centerOfOpponentGoal - location\| \\ \forall opp \in Opponents, -\max(25 - \|opp - location\|^2, 0) \\ + \max(10 - \|closestTeammateToTarget - location\|, 0) \end{array} \tag{1}$$

Ideal locations for kicking the ball are those near a teammate who is in an offensive and open (no opponents are close by) position on the field to receive a pass and take a shot on goal. New for the RoboCup 2016 competition, rather than waiting for a teammate to broadcast a location the ball is going to be kicked to, and only then moving to that position [3], a robot assuming the center forward or striker role [2] in the team's formation moves toward the position that it calculates its teammate closest to the ball is anticipated to potentially kick the ball to using Eq. 1. As Eq. 1 gives higher values for locations away from opponents, this behavior results in the striker dynamically moving to open offensive positions on the field rather than the previous behavior of standing at a fixed location relative to the ball—possibly close to opponents marking that player—as it waits to hear from a teammate where the ball might next be kicked.

3.3 Tuning Kick Selection for Height

In addition to allowing for more precise passing, variable distance kicks [4] are also useful for taking shots on goal. Generally speaking, the greater the distance a kick travels the longer and higher the ball may travel in the air, and possibly over the goal, when shooting. During the 2015 RoboCup competition, to try and prevent accidentally shooting the ball over the goal, kicks for shooting on goal were limited to those traveling no more than 7 m in distance beyond the goal line. Despite this attempt at limiting the distance for kicks when shooting, a number of shots still missed their target by flying above the goal.

Table 1. The maximum forward distance measured across 100 kicks for different kick types (kicks for different distances) during which the ball is above the height of the goal. All values are in meters.

Kick type (distance in meters)	10	11	12	13	14	15	16	17	18	19	20
Max above goal height distance	4.00	4.50	6.25	10.50	6.00	7.50	8.75	9.75	10.50	15.50	16.00

For the 2016 RoboCup competition, the UT Austin Villa team took a more calibrated approach to preventing shots from going over the goal. Instead of estimating 7 m as the difference between a kick's distance and the maximum forward distance the ball can travel at a height above the goal for all kick types, the maximum forward distance the ball is above the height of the goal was directly measured across 100 kick attempts for each kick type. Table 1 shows these measurements for different kicks for an agent with a type four body model (an agent with the standard Nao model but with toes added). Using these measurements, the kick with maximum power that will not fly above the goal—the kick with the maximum distance, but whose forward above goal height distance is less than the ball's distance to the goal—is selected when shooting on goal.

From the data in Table 1 it can be seen that there is not a constant offset difference between the distance of a kick and the maximum forward distance that the ball can be above the height of the goal. Furthermore, as for many of the kick types this difference is less than the 7 m estimated value used during the 2015 competition, it is not surprising that shots went over the goal during last year's competition.

3.4   Indirect Kick Set Plays

With this year's rule changes (outlined in Sect. 2) making kick-ins indirect, and double touches on kicks result in an indirect free kick for the opposing team, it becomes practical to use set plays for indirect kicks. During indirect kicks the team switches to a formation shown in Fig. 1, where three players are spread in a line across the field near the halfway line, and another three players are spread in a line across the field in a more forward offensive position. The player taking the kick, now with more options from the formation as to which teammate to pass the ball to, chooses to kick the ball to the best location as decided by Eq. 1 in Sect. 3.2. The player taking the kick also waits 10 s from the start of an indirect kick before kicking the ball so as to give its teammates time to move to their assigned positions in the indirect kick formation.

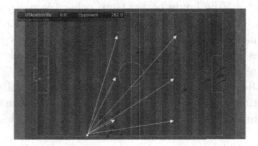

Fig. 1. Indirect kick formation for set plays during a kick-in. Yellow lines represent potential passes to teammates in the formation. (Color figure online)

3.5   Directional Kicks

Directional kicks incorporating inverse kinematics created for the 2011 competition [1], but whose use was later discontinued due to poor performance, were reintroduced and integrated into agents with a type four body model (the standard Nao model but with toes added) using overlapping layered learning [8]. Unlike a standard forward kick, where an agent must take the time to line up behind the ball in the direction that it is to be kicked, directional kicks allow for an agent to quickly approach and kick the ball from multiple angles and relative ball positions (example ball positions and kick directions are shown in Fig. 2).

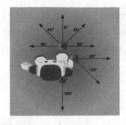

Fig. 2. Possible directions to kick the ball with respect to the placement of the ball at *a*, *b*, and *c* (left image). Agent with its back to the goal taking a shot before scoring at RoboCup 2016 using a 180° "hook" kick where the ball is pulled backward and then kicked behind the agent (right images).

4   Main Competition Results and Analysis

In winning the 2016 RoboCup competition UT Austin Villa finished with a perfect record of 14 wins and no losses.[1] During the competition the team scored 88 goals while only conceding 1. Despite finishing with a perfect record, the relatively few number of games played at the competition, coupled with the complex and stochastic environment of the RoboCup 3D simulator, make it difficult to determine UT Austin Villa being better than other teams by a statistically significant margin. At the end of the competition, however, all teams were required to release their binaries used during the competition. Results of UT Austin Villa playing 1000 games against each of the other eight teams' released binaries from the competition are shown in Table 2.

UT Austin Villa finished with at least an average goal difference greater than 1.8 goals against every opponent. Additionally UT Austin Villa only lost 4 games out of the 8000 that were played in Table 2 with a win percentage

Table 2. UT Austin Villa's released binary's performance when playing 1000 games against the released binaries of all other teams at RoboCup 2016. This includes place (the rank a team achieved at the 2016 competition), average goal difference (values in parentheses are the standard error), win-loss-tie record, and goals for/against.

Opponent	Place	Avg. goal diff.	Record (W-L-T)	Goals (F/A)
FUT-K	2	1.809 (0.036)	888-3-109	1872/63
FCPortugal	3	2.431 (0.040)	954-1-45	2452/21
BahiaRT	4	3.123 (0.040)	985-0-15	3123/0
magmaOffenburg	5	3.921 (0.049)	996-0-4	3926/5
KgpKubs	8	7.728 (0.046)	1000-0-0	7729/1
ITAndroids	6	9.022 (0.053)	1000-0-0	9024/2
HfutEngine3D	9	10.192 (0.056)	1000-0-0	10192/0
Miracle3D	7	11.126 (0.059)	1000-0-0	11126/0

---

[1] Full tournament results can be found at https://robocup.info/xml/RC2016_SS3D_tournament.xml.

greater than 88% against all teams. This shows that UT Austin Villa winning the 2016 competition was far from a chance occurrence. The following subsection analyzes some of the components described in Sect. 3 that contributed to the team's dominant performance.

4.1 Analysis of Components

1000 games were played between a version of the UT Austin Villa team with marking (Sect. 3.1) turned off and each of the RoboCup 2016 teams' released binaries. Only the top three teams from the competition showed any appreciable difference in the number of goals scored against the team without marking when compared to the same team with marking (no other teams were able to score more than 6 goals even with marking turned off). Results against the top three teams are shown in Table 3. Against all three teams the average goal difference went down when not using marking. Additionally both the number of goals against, and the percentage of goals scored off set plays,[2] increased drastically without marking. These results show marking provides a substantial defensive improvement, and furthermore is very effective in defending against set plays.

Table 4 shows the average goal difference achieved by the following different versions of the UT Austin Villa team when playing 9000 games against all teams at RoboCup 2016 (1000 games against each opponent).

UTAustinVilla Released binary (no directional kicks).

NoGettingOpen Agent assigned to striker role does not try and get open.

Table 3. Average goal difference and goals against (with percentage of goals against scored off set plays in parentheses) achieved by versions of the UT Austin Villa team with and without marking when playing 1000 games against the top three teams at RoboCup 2016.

Opponent	Average goal difference		Goals against (set play %)	
	Marking	No marking	Marking	No marking
UTAustinVilla	0.001	−0.336	290 (18.62%)	667 (61.67%)
FUT-K	1.809	1.613	63 (25.40%)	288 (66.67%)
FCPortugal	2.431	2.361	21 (23.81%)	160 (81.88%)

Table 4. Average goal difference achieved by different versions of the UT Austin Villa team when playing 9000 games against all teams at RoboCup 2016 (1000 games against each opponent).

UTAustinVilla	NoGettingOpen	NoKickHeightTuning	NoIndirectKickSetPlays	DirectionalKicks
5.484	5.430	5.331	5.459	3.815

---

[2] Goals within 20 s of corner kicks, 25 s of kick-ins and indirect free kicks, and 35 s from start of kickoffs. Times reduced by 5 s against UTAustinVilla opponent.

NoKickHeightTuning Kick selection not tuned for height when shooting.
NoIndirectKickSetPlays No indirect kick set plays.
DirectionalKicks Uses directional kicks.

As the removal of most components in Table 4 decreased average goal difference, these components were beneficial to the team. Having the player assigned to the striker role move to get open (Sect. 3.2) slightly improves performance and additionally increased the average number of goals scored against all opponents from 5.476 to 5.526. Tuning which kick is selected when taking a shot based on height (Sect. 3.3) also increased the average goal difference. This improvement is likely due to no longer kicking the ball over the goal as the average shot scoring percentage against all opponents increased from 29.69% without tuning to 32.05% with kick height tuning: the ability to kick the ball with just the right amount of power such that it flies into the goal—but not over it—is a valuable skill during games. While using indirect kick set plays (Sect. 3.4) showed only a very slight increase in average goal difference, the average scoring percentage on indirect kicks jumped from 27.10% to 34.78% when using set plays.

The only change that hurts performance is the use of directional kicks. It was known during the competition that choosing to pass the ball with a directional kick instead of using a longer kick to take a shot on goal decreased performance, and so directional kicks were disabled during the semifinals and finals rounds. Directional kicks do however increase the average number of pass attempts in a game from 13.020 to 15.838, and they raise the average possession (a teammate is closer than any opponent to the ball) percentage time from 56.71% to 59.81%. Directional kicks may become more useful if teams' goalie behaviors improve resulting in the need to be more selective when choosing when to shoot on goal.

4.2   Additional Tournament Competition Analysis

To further analyze the tournament competition, Table 5 shows the average goal difference for each team at RoboCup 2016 when playing 1000 games against

Table 5. Average goal difference for each team at RoboCup 2016 (rows) when playing 1000 games against the released binaries of all other teams at RoboCup 2016 (columns). Teams are ordered from most to least dominant in terms of winning (positive goal difference) and losing (negative goal difference).

	UTA	FUT	FCP	mag	Bah	ITA	Kgp	Mir	Hfut
UTAustinVilla	—	1.809	2.431	3.921	3.123	9.022	7.728	11.126	10.192
FUT-K	−1.809	—	0.708	2.424	1.477	6.692	5.799	8.795	7.535
FCPortugal	−2.431	−0.708	—	0.756	1.022	4.343	5.127	7.204	5.535
magmaOffenburg	−3.921	−2.424	−0.756	—	0.154	3.624	4.080	5.908	4.742
BahiaRT	−3.123	−1.477	−1.022	−0.154	—	3.416	4.661	6.067	4.556
ITAndroids	−9.022	−6.692	−4.343	−3.624	−3.416	—	0.163	1.939	1.096
KgpKubs	−7.728	−5.799	−5.127	−4.080	−4.661	−0.163	—	0.253	1.391
Miracle3D	−11.126	−8.795	−7.204	−5.908	−6.067	−1.939	−0.253	—	0.800
HfutEngine3D	−10.192	−7.535	−5.535	−4.742	−4.556	−1.096	−1.391	−0.800	—

all other teams at RoboCup 2016. It is interesting to note that the ordering of teams in terms of winning (positive goal difference) and losing (negative goal difference) is strictly dominant—every opponent that a team wins against also loses to every opponent that defeats that same team. Relative goal difference does not have this same property, however, as a team that does better against one opponent relative to another team does not always do better against a second opponent relative to that same team. UT Austin Villa is dominant in terms of relative goal difference, however, as UT Austin Villa has a higher goal difference against each opponent than all other teams against the same opponent.

5 Technical Challenges

For the third straight year there was an overall technical challenge consisting of three different league challenges: free, keepaway, and Gazebo running challenge. For each league challenge a team participated in points were awarded toward the overall technical challenge based on the following equation:

$$\texttt{points}(rank) = 25 - 20 * (rank - 1)/(numberOfParticipants - 1)$$

Table 6. Overall ranking and points totals for each team participating in the RoboCup 2016 3D Simulation League technical challenge as well as ranks and points awarded for each of the individual league challenges that make up the technical challenge.

Team	Overall		Free		Keepaway		Gazebo running	
	Rank	Points	Rank	Points	Rank	Points	Rank	Points
UTAustinVilla	1	**75**	1	**25**	1	**25**	1	**25**
FCPortugal	2	48.33	2	20	4	10	2	18.33
magmaOffenberg	3	41.67	3	15	3	15	3	11.67
FUT-K	4	30	5	5	2	20	4	5
BahiaRT	5	15	4	10	5	5	—	—

Table 6 shows the ranking and cumulative team point totals for the technical challenge as well as for each individual league challenge. UT Austin Villa earned the most points and won the technical challenge by taking first in each of the league challenges. The following subsections detail UT Austin Villa's participation in each league challenge.[3]

5.1 Free Challenge

During the free challenge, teams give a five minute presentation on a research topic related to their team. Each team in the league then ranks the top five

---

[3] Videos of the keepaway and Gazebo running challenges can be found at http://www.cs.utexas.edu/~AustinVilla/sim/3dsimulation/#2016challenges.

presentations with the best receiving 5 votes and the 5th best receiving 1 vote. Additionally several respected research members of the RoboCup community outside the league vote, with their votes being counted double. The winner of the free challenge is the team that receives the most votes. Table 7 shows the results of the free challenge in which UT Austin Villa was awarded first place.

Table 7. Results of the free challenge.

Team	Votes
UTAustinVilla	**37**
FCPortugal	35
magmaOffenburg	33
BahiaRT	31
FUT-K	14

UT Austin Villa's free challenge submission[4] was on the team's marking system [11] discussed in Sect. 3.1. The FC Portugal team presented research on a learning algorithm, originally designed to learn a parameterized kick for kicking the ball different distances [12], to also allow for the ball being at different relative positions with respect to the robot. The magmaOffenburg team divulged work on learning a kick while walking in raw actuator space [13]. The BahiaRT team discussed an extension to their existing defensive system [14], and the FUT-K team talked about their approach to preventing long passes by the opponent.

5.2 Keepaway Challenge

In the course of the keepaway challenge,[5] a group of three agents on one team attempts to maintain possession and keep the ball away from a single opponent agent for as long as possible. Additionally, the ball must be kept within a slowly shrinking square area on the field, which is eventually reduced in size to zero after five minutes. During a keepaway task attempt, if the opponent agent touches the ball, or the ball leaves the allowed keepaway area on the field, a keepaway attempt is considered over, and the time that has passed from the beginning of the attempt is recorded as the score for that attempt.

UT Austin Villa created two formations for use in the keepaway challenge shown in Fig. 3. In the first formation, agents align themselves in a triangle shape. The agent on the ball waits until the opponent gets near, and then that agent passes the ball to the teammate for which the angle between the opponent and teammate as measured from the ball is the largest (the ball is passed to the teammate with the least chance of the opponent intercepting the pass). In the

---

[4] Free challenge entry descriptions available at http://chaosscripting.de/files/competitions/RoboCup/WorldCup/2016/3DSim/freeChallenge/.

[5] Details and framework for the keepaway challenge at https://github.com/magmaOffenburg/magmaChallenge#keep-away-challenge.

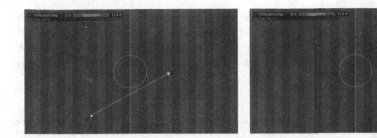

Fig. 3. Keepaway challenge triangle (left image) and square (right image) formations. Red box is keepaway area. Yellow lines show where ball will next be passed. Blue line shows agent movement using second level kick anticipation (moving to new position in formation once pass has occurred). (Color figure online)

second formation, agents assume a square shape with teammates in position to receive a pass at 90° angles to the ball. The same passing strategy as used with the triangle formation is used with the square formation, but with the addition that kick anticipation [4] is extended to the second level—a player anticipates and runs to the location of a second pass from the location that the next (first) pass is broadcast as going to by the player kicking the ball—so that teammates will be in their designated formation positions after a pass has occurred. Which formation to use is chosen randomly at the beginning of a keepaway attempt.

Table 8. Time in seconds for each of the teams competing in the keepaway challenge.

Team	Attempt 1	Attempt 2	Attempt 3	Average of best two attempts
UTAustinVilla	**235.39**	**152.56**	**223.55**	**229.47**
FUT-K	108.95	38.04	140.09	124.52
FCPortugal	35.40	33.04	80.78	58.09
magmaOffenburg	35.76	20.86	24.86	30.31
BahiaRT	17.50	17.26	13.52	17.38

Table 8 shows the results of the keepaway challenge where teams were ranked by the average time of a team's best two out of three attempts. UT Austin Villa won the challenge with an average time of over three minutes. Each of UT Austin Villa's keepaway attempt times were greater than all other teams' attempts.

5.3 Gazebo Running Challenge

Ongoing work within the RoboCup community is the development of a plugin[6] for the Gazebo [15] robotics simulator to support the RoboCup 3D Simulation League. As such, a challenge[7] was held where robots attempt to walk forward as

---

[6] https://bitbucket.org/osrf/robocup3ds.

[7] Framework for running the Gazebo running challenge at https://github.com/magmaOffenburg/magmaChallenge.

fast as possible for 20 s in the Gazebo simulator without falling. In preparation for the challenge UT Austin Villa optimized fast walking parameters for the team's omnidirectional walk engine [16] within the Gazebo simulator using the CMA-ES algorithm [17]. Walk engine parameters were optimized for 300 generations of CMA-ES with a population size of 150.

Table 9. Speed in meters per second for each of the teams competing in the Gazebo running challenge.

Team	Run 1	Run 2	Run 3	Run 4	Run 5	Average
UTAustinVilla	**1.01**	**1.20**	**1.03**	**1.20**	**1.16**	**1.12**
FCPortugal	0.62	0.59	0.67	0.63	0.61	0.63
magmaOffenberg	0.44	0.26	0.43	0.44	0.40	0.39
FUT-K	0.00	0.00	0.00	0.00	0.00	0.00

Results of the Gazebo running challenge are shown in Table 9. Each participating team performed five running attempts and were scored by the average forward walking speed across all attempts. UT Austin Villa won the challenge with all five of the team's runs having a speed of over 1 m/s. Each of UT Austin Villa's running attempt speeds were greater than all other teams' attempts.

6   Conclusion

UT Austin Villa won the 2016 RoboCup 3D Simulation League main competition as well as all technical league challenges.[8] Data taken using released binaries from the competition show that UT Austin Villa winning the competition was statistically significant. The 2016 UT Austin Villa team also improved dramatically from 2015 as it was able to beat the team's 2015 champion binary by an average of 0.561 ($\pm$0.029) goals across 1000 games.

In an effort to both make it easier for new teams to join the RoboCup 3D Simulation League, and also provide a resource that can be beneficial to existing teams, the UT Austin Villa team has released their base code [18].[9] This code release provides a fully functioning agent and good starting point for new teams to the RoboCup 3D Simulation League (it was used by the new KgpKubs team at the 2016 competition). Additionally the code release—which was awarded second place for the HARTING Open Source Prize at RoboCup 2016—offers a foundational platform for conducting research in multiple areas including robotics, multiagent systems, and machine learning.

---

[8] More information about the UT Austin Villa team, as well as video highlights from the competition, can be found at the team's website: http://www.cs.utexas.edu/~AustinVilla/sim/3dsimulation/#2016challenges.

[9] Code release at https://github.com/LARG/utaustinvilla3d.

Acknowledgments. This work has taken place in the Learning Agents Research Group (LARG) at UT Austin. LARG research in 2016 is supported in part by grants from NSF (CNS-1330072, CNS-1305287), ONR (21C184-01), and AFOSR (FA9550-14-1-0087). Peter Stone serves on the Board of Directors of Cogitai, Inc. The terms of this arrangement have been reviewed and approved by UT Austin in accordance with its policy on objectivity in research.

References

1. MacAlpine, P., Urieli, D., Barrett, S., Kalyanakrishnan, S., Barrera, F., Lopez-Mobilia, A., Ştiurcă, N., Vu, V., Stone, P.: UT Austin Villa 2011: a champion agent in the RoboCup 3D soccer simulation competition. In: Proceedings of the 11th International Conference on Autonomous Agents and Multiagent Systems (AAMAS 2012) (2012)
2. MacAlpine, P., Collins, N., Lopez-Mobilia, A., Stone, P.: UT Austin Villa: RoboCup 2012 3D simulation league champion. In: Chen, X., Stone, P., Sucar, L.E., van der Zant, T. (eds.) RoboCup 2012. LNCS, vol. 7500, pp. 77–88. Springer, Heidelberg (2013). doi:10.1007/978-3-642-39250-4_8
3. MacAlpine, P., Depinet, M., Liang, J., Stone, P.: UT Austin Villa: RoboCup 2014 3D simulation league competition and technical challenge champions. In: Bianchi, R.A.C., Akin, H.L., Ramamoorthy, S., Sugiura, K. (eds.) RoboCup 2014. LNCS, vol. 8992, pp. 33–46. Springer, Cham (2015). doi:10.1007/978-3-319-18615-3_3
4. MacAlpine, P., Hanna, J., Liang, J., Stone, P.: UT Austin Villa: RoboCup 2015 3D simulation league competition and technical challenges champions. In: Almeida, L., Ji, J., Steinbauer, G., Luke, S. (eds.) RoboCup 2015. LNCS, vol. 9513, pp. 118–131. Springer, Cham (2015). doi:10.1007/978-3-319-29339-4_10
5. MacAlpine, P., Urieli, D., Barrett, S., Kalyanakrishnan, S., Barrera, F., Lopez-Mobilia, A., Ştiurcă, N., Vu, V., Stone, P.: UT Austin Villa 2011 3D simulation team report. Technical report AI11-10, The University of Texas at Austin, Department of Computer Science, AI Laboratory (2011)
6. Boedecker, J., Asada, M.: Simspark–concepts and application in the robocup 3D soccer simulation league. In: SIMPAR-2008 Workshop on the Universe of RoboCup Simulators, Venice, Italy, pp. 174–181 (2008)
7. MacAlpine, P., Price, E., Stone, P.: SCRAM: scalable collision-avoiding role assignment with minimal-makespan for formational positioning. In: Proceedings of the Twenty-Ninth AAAI Conference on Artificial Intelligence (AAAI 2015) (2015)
8. MacAlpine, P., Depinet, M., Stone, P.: UT Austin Villa 2014: RoboCup 3D simulation league champion via overlapping layered learning. In: Proceedings of the Twenty-Ninth AAAI Conference on Artificial Intelligence (AAAI 2015) (2015)
9. Akiyama, H., Noda, I.: Multi-agent positioning mechanism in the dynamic environment. In: Visser, U., Ribeiro, F., Ohashi, T., Dellaert, F. (eds.) RoboCup 2007. LNCS (LNAI), vol. 5001, pp. 377–384. Springer, Heidelberg (2008). doi:10.1007/978-3-540-68847-1_38
10. Kuhn, H.W.: The hungarian method for the assignment problem. Nav. Res. Logist. Q. **2**, 83–97 (1955)
11. MacAlpine, P., Stone, P.: Prioritized role assignment for marking. In: RoboCup 2016: Robot Soccer World Cup XX. LNAI. Springer, Heidelberg (2016)
12. Abdolmaleki, A., Simoes, D., Lau, N., Reis, L.P., Neumann, G.: Learning a humanoid kick with controlled distance. In: RoboCup 2016: Robot Soccer World Cup XX. LNAI. Springer, Heidelberg (2016)

13. Dorer, K., Kurz, V.: Learning a kick while walking in raw actuator space (2016)
14. da Silva, C., Soares, A., Argollo, E., Simões, M.A.C., Frias, D., de Souza, J.R.: Módulo cooperativo de defesa para um time de futebol de agentes humanoides autônomos. In: XIII Workshop de Trabalhos de Iniciação Científica e Graduação da Escola Regional de Computação Bahia - Alagoas - Sergipe (2015)
15. Koenig, N., Howard, A.: Design and use paradigms for gazebo, an open-source multi-robot simulator. In: Intelligent Robots and Systems (IROS) (2004)
16. MacAlpine, P., Barrett, S., Urieli, D., Vu, V., Stone, P.: Design and optimization of an omnidirectional humanoid walk: a winning approach at the RoboCup 2011 3D simulation competition. In: Proceedings of the Twenty-Sixth AAAI Conference on Artificial Intelligence (AAAI 2012) (2012)
17. Hansen, N.: The CMA Evolution Strategy: A Tutorial (2009). http://www.lri.fr/~hansen/cmatutorial.pdf
18. MacAlpine, P., Stone, P.: UT Austin Villa robocup 3D simulation base code release. In: RoboCup 2016: Robot Soccer World Cup XX. LNAI. Springer, Heidelberg (2016)

Disruptive Innovations in RoboCup 2D Soccer Simulation League: From Cyberoos'98 to Gliders2016

Mikhail Prokopenko[1]([⊠]) and Peter Wang[2]

[1] Complex Systems Research Group, Faculty of Engineering and IT,
The University of Sydney, Sydney, NSW 2006, Australia
`mikhail.prokopenko@sydney.edu.au`
[2] Data Mining, CSIRO Data61, PO Box 76, Epping, NSW 1710, Australia

Abstract. We review disruptive innovations introduced in the RoboCup 2D Soccer Simulation League over the twenty years since its inception, and trace the progress of our champion team (Gliders). We conjecture that the League has been developing as an ecosystem shaped by diverse approaches taken by participating teams, increasing in its overall complexity. A common feature is that different champion teams succeeded in finding a way to decompose the enormous search-space of possible single and multi-agent behaviours, by automating the exploration of the problem space with various techniques which accelerated the software development efforts. These methods included interactive debugging, machine learning, automated planning, and opponent modelling. The winning approach developed by Gliders is centred on human-based evolutionary computation which optimised several components such as an action-dependent evaluation function, dynamic tactics with Voronoi diagrams, information dynamics, and bio-inspired collective behaviour.

1 Introduction

> Agent Smith: "You can't win, it's pointless to keep fighting!
> Why, Mr. Anderson? Why do you persist?"
> Neo: "Because I choose to."
>
> The Matrix Revolutions.

The first official RoboCup was held in 1997, proposing a new benchmark for Artificial Intelligence (AI) and robotics. Incidentally, another classical AI challenge was successfully met in May 1997 when IBM Deep Blue defeated the human world champion in chess. By design, RoboCup and chess differ in a few key elements: environment (static vs dynamic), state change (turn-taking vs real-time), information accessibility (complete vs incomplete), sensor readings (symbolic vs non-symbolic), and control (central vs distributed) [1]. These differences are

S. Behnke et al. (Eds.): RoboCup 2016, LNAI 9776, pp. 529–541, 2017.
https://doi.org/10.1007/978-3-319-68792-6_44

emphasised in the RoboCup 2D Soccer Simulation League [2], which quickly gained prominence, becoming one of the largest RoboCup leagues.

In this league, two teams of 12 fully autonomous software programs (called "agents") play soccer in a two-dimensional virtual soccer stadium (11 player agents and 1 coach agent in each team), with no remote control. Each player agent receives relative and noisy input from its virtual sensors (visual, acoustic and physical) and may perform some basic actions in order to influence its environment, e.g., running, turning and kicking the ball. The coach agent receives perfect input but can communicate with the player agents only infrequently and through a fairly limited channel. The ability to simulate soccer matches without physical robots abstracts away low-level issues such as image processing and motor breakages, allowing teams to focus on the development of complex team behaviours and strategies for a larger number of autonomous agents [3,4].

A simulated game lasts just over 10 min on average, and is played over a small network of computer workstations which execute the code in parallel. Each simulation step takes merely a tenth of a second, during which the entire sensorymotor cycle takes place within an agent: starting with receiving new sensory inputs from the simulator, proceeding to updating the internal memory, to evaluating possible choices, to sending the chosen action back to the simulator. The main challenge for each agent is to derive the best possible action to execute at any specific time, while facing unexpected actions of the opposing agents.

Over 20 years, the RoboCup community has developed the open-source 2D simulator and visualisation software which currently, with various packaged utilities and basic agent libraries, contains nearly a million lines of code. During this period, the League and the participating teams have undergone several transitions each of which eventually expanded the level of agents' intelligence and their behavioral complexity. In this paper we attempt to trace not only the ten-year long progress of our own team from its first implementation (Cyberoos; participated between 1998 and 2003) to the RoboCup-2016 champion team (Gliders; competed first in 2012), but also put this trace in the context of the twenty-year long evolution of the Sim2D League itself.

The conjecture we put forward is that the League has been developing as an ecosystem with an increasing complexity shaped by different approaches taken by participating teams. Furthermore, this evolving ecosystem has experienced a series of salient transitions leading to emergence of qualitatively new properties in the intelligence exhibited by the agents. By a transition we do not mean a mere extension of some simulated capabilities, such as the introduction of goalkeepers, heterogeneous player types, or a coach language. Instead, we associate a transition with a specific methodological advance which played the role of a *disruptive innovation*, with wide-spread consequences affecting the entire "ecosystem", for example, a release of standard libraries, and so on. We use the term "disruptive innovation" in a broad sense to indicate an innovation that creates a new ecosystem (by analogy with a new market or value network), eventually disrupting an existing system, displacing established structures and relationships.

2   A Simulated World

The foundation supporting the evolution of the League is undoubtedly the construction of the soccer server itself, providing a centralised world model with several key features, enhanced over the following years:

- distributed client/server system running on a network and producing fragmented, localised and imprecise (noisy and latent) information about the environment (virtual soccer field) [5,6];
- concurrent communication with a number of autonomous agents [7];
- heterogeneous sensory data (visual, auditory, kinetic) without a global vision, and limited range of basic commands/effectors (turn, kick, dash, . . .) [8];
- asynchronous perception-action activity and limited window of opportunity to perform an action [9];
- autonomous decision-making under constraints enforced by teamwork (collaboration) and opponent (competition) [10];
- conflicts between reactivity and deliberation [11].

The only restriction that was imposed from the outset is that participants should "never use central control mechanisms to control a team of agents" [12].

A crucial feature making this simulated world an evolving "ecosystem" is the availability of binaries (and sometimes the source code) of participating teams, contained within an online team repository. The repository is updated after each annual RoboCup competition, allowing the participants to improve their teams with respect to the top teams of the previous championships. These improvements diversify the teams' functionality and explore the immense search-space of possible behaviours in the quest for optimal solutions. This process results in a co-evolution of the teams, raising the overall competition level.

3   Partial Automation of Development Efforts

"AT Humboldt" from Humboldt University, Germany became the first champion of the League at RoboCup-1997 (Nagoya, Japan). The team used a combination of reactive and planning systems, successfully deploying its agents within the simulated world.

The following couple of years passed under the domination of "CMUnited" team from Carnegie Mellon University (USA) which took the championship in 1998 (Paris, France) and 1999 (Stockholm, Sweden). One of the key reasons for this success was the development of several tools partially automating the overall effort, such as an offline agent training module, and layered disclosure: a technique for disclosing to a human designer the specific detailed reasons for an agent actions (in run-time or retroactively). Layered disclosure made it possible to inspect the details of an individual player's decision-making process at any point [13], becoming in our view the first disruptive innovation in the League. Together with the offline agent training module, it clearly exemplified the power of automation in accelerating the development effort—precisely because it enabled the design effort to reach into a larger part of the search-space by encoding more diverse behaviours.

It is important to point out that there were other novelties introduced by CMUnited-98 and CMUnited-99, such as "single-channel, low-bandwidth communication", "predictive, locally optimal skills (PLOS)", "strategic positioning using attraction and repulsion (SPAR)", etc. [13], but we believe that it is the partial automation of the software development that became the *disruptive* innovation. It has led to a wide-spread adoption of several debugging, visualising, log-playing, log-analysing, and machine learning tools.

4   Configurational Space

A number of new teams in 2000 utilised the code base of the 1999 champions, CMUnited-99: it provided code for interaction with the soccer server, skills, strategies, and debugging tools in a variety of programming languages [14]. The champion of RoboCup-2000 held in Melbourne, Australia, "FC Portugal" from University of Aveiro and University of Porto, extended this code base with a systematic approach to describing team strategy, the concepts of tactics, formations and player types, as well as the situation based strategic positioning, the dynamic positioning and role exchange mechanisms [11,15].

The generic innovation underlying these mechanisms comprised the ability to configure diverse single- and multi-agent behaviours. The range of these behaviours span from active (ball possession) to strategic (ball recovery), from formations to tactics, and from individual skills to team strategies. Such diversity resulted in a considerable configurational flexibility displayed by the winning team, significantly increasing the software development productivity, and more importantly, expanding the extent of the available behavioural search-space.

Not surprisingly, the expansion brought about by the larger configurational capacity was further exploited by the introduction of a standard coach language [16] enabling high-level coaching with explicit definition of formations, situations, player types and time periods, and resulting in a high-level coordination of team behaviour. In other words, a disruptive innovation again was delivered by a method which allowed to access deeper regions of the available search-space.

Team "TsinghuAeolus" from Tsinghua University, China, which won the next two championships (RoboCup-2001 in Seattle, USA, and RoboCup-2002 in Fukuoka), focussed specifically on increasing the agents' adaptability via a novel online advice-taking mechanism [17]. The configurational space was extended by a task-decomposition mechanism that assigned different parts of the task to different agents.

A major boost to the League was provided by the partial release of the source code of the next champion, team "UvA Trilearn" from University of Amsterdam, The Netherlands, which won RoboCup-2003 in Padua, Italy [18]. This release resulted in a standardisation of many low-level behaviours and world model, effectively "locking in" the configurational space attained by that time, and motivating several teams to switch their code base to UvA Trilearn base.

5   Cyberoos: 1998–2003

At this stage we take a brief look at our first team, Cyberoos, which participated in RoboCup competitions between 1998 and 2003. The Cyberoos'98 team took 3rd place in the 1998 Pacific Rim RoboCup competition [19], while Cyberoos'2000 were 4th in the Open European RoboCup-2000 [9]. Despite these regional successes, the team's best result at the world stage was a shared 9th place which Cyberoos repeatedly took at the RoboCup competitions in 2000, 2001, 2002 and 2003, never reaching the quarter-finals [20–23]. In hindsight, the main reason for this lack of progress was an oversight of the main tendency driving the innovations in the League: the exploration of the search-space due to the automation of the development efforts and the standardisation of the configurational space.

Instead, the approach taken by Cyberoos focussed on self-organisation of emergent behaviour within a purely reactive agent architecture [21]. Only during the later years the Cyberoos architecture diversified, and included semi-automated methods that quantified the team performance in generic information-theoretic terms [22, 23]. This approach focussed on measuring the behavioural and belief dynamics in multi-agent systems, offering a possibility to evolve the team behaviour, optimised under a universal objective function, within the framework of information-driven self-organisation [24–26]. However, this framework has started to take a functional shape only a few years later, after the time when the Cyberoos team effort stopped in 2003.

6   Search-Space Decomposition

The next decade of RoboCup championships witnessed an intense competition between three teams: "Brainstormers" from University of Osnabrück, Germany, "WrightEagle" from University of Science and Technology of China, and "HELIOS" from Fukuoka University and Osaka Prefecture University, Japan. Brainstormers became champions three times: in 2005 (Osaka, Japan), 2007 (Atlanta, USA), and 2008 (Suzhou, China); WrightEagle came first an incredible six times: in 2006 (Bremen, Germany), 2009 (Graz, Austria), 2011 (Istanbul, Turkey), 2013 (Eindhoven, The Netherlands), 2014 (Joao Pessoa, Brazil) and 2015 (Hefei, China); and HELIOS succeeded twice: in 2010 (Singapore) and 2012 (Mexico City, Mexico).

6.1   Machine Learning

Brainstormers' effort focussed on reinforcement learning methods aiming at a universal machine learning system, where the agents learn to generate the appropriate behaviors to satisfy the most general objective of "winning the match". Unfortunately, as has been acknowledged [27], "even from very optimistic complexity estimations it becomes obvious, that in the soccer simulation domain, both conventional solution methods and also advanced today's reinforcement learning techniques come to their limit – there are more than $(108 \times 50)^{23}$ different states and more than $(1000)^{300}$ different policies per agent per half time".

The high dimensionality of the search space motivated Brainstormers to use a multilayer perceptron neural network [27]: a feedforward artificial neural network which utilises a supervised learning technique called backpropagation for training the network. Rather than developing a universal learning system, Brainstormers succeeded in decomposing the problem into a number of individual behaviours (e.g., NeuroKick, NeuroIntercept, NeuroHassle) and tactics (e.g., NeuroAttack2vs2, NeuroAttack3vs4, NeuroAttack7vs8), learned with supervised learning techniques.

Recently, there has been some renewed interest in backpropagation networks due to the successes of deep learning. In our view, the potential of reinforcement learning methods in RoboCup has not yet been fully realised, and deep learning may yet to become a disruptive innovation for the Simulation league.

6.2 Automated Planning

WrightEagle team addressed the challenges of (i) high dimensionality of the search space and (ii) the limited computation time available in each decision cycle, by using Markov Decision Processes (MDPs). The developed framework decomposes a given MDP into a set of sub-MDPs arranged over a hierarchical structure, and includes heuristics approximating online planning techniques [28]. WrightEagle approach abandoned "the pursuit of absolute accuracy" and divided the continuous soccer field into the discrete space, further subdividing it into the players' control areas according to geometric reachability. The resultant structure enables automated planning, accelerating the search process and extending the search depth [28].

6.3 Opponent Modelling

"HELIOS" team [29,30] followed a similar path, targeting a decomposition of the problem space in developing an unsupervised learning method based on Constrained Delaunay Triangulation (CDT) [31]. A Delaunay triangulation for a set P of points in a plane is a triangulation $\mathcal{D}(\mathcal{P})$ such that no point in P is inside the circumcircle of any triangle in $\mathcal{D}(\mathcal{P})$ (in CDT the circumcircle of some triangles contains other triangles' vertices). The method divides the soccer field into a set of triangles, which provide an input plane region for Neural Gas (NG) and Growing Neural Gas (GNG) methods. Specifically, the set P_b of N points represents specifically chosen positions of the ball on the field, while sets P_i describe the sets of coordinates of each player $1 \leq i \leq 11$, so that there is a bijective correspondence between P_b and each of P_i. Moreover, when the ball takes any position within a triangle of $\mathcal{D}(P_b)$, each player's position is computed in a congruent way within $\mathcal{D}(P_i)$. During offline experiments or even during a game, the behaviour of the opponent, for example, the players' motion, directions of the passes, and the overall team formations, can be mapped, analysed and categorised [29,30].

It is evident that the main reason behind the recurrent successes of all three champion approaches is a dynamic decomposition of the problem space and its subsequent efficient exploration. This innovation goes beyond a simple standardisation of low-level behaviours within a rich but static configurational space, by employing automated learning and planning methods in a dynamic search.

7   Standardisation of "Hardware"

An influential disruptive innovation arrived in 2010, when HELIOS team released a major update of their well-developed code base [32]:

- *librcsc-4.0.0*: a base library for the RoboCup Soccer Simulator (RCSS);
- *agent2d-3.0.0*: a base source code for a team;
- *soccerwindow2-5.0.0*: a viewer and a visual debugger program for RCSS;
- *fedit2-2.0.0*: a team formation editor for *agent2d*.

This resulted in nearly 80% of the League's teams switching their code base to agent2d over the next few years. One may think of this phenomenon as a standardisation of the simulated hardware, freeing the effort to improving the higher-level tactical behaviours.

8   Gliders (2012–2016): Fusing Human Innovation and Artificial Evolution

We turn our attention to our champion team which won RoboCup-2016 (Leipzig, Germany): Gliders [33–37]. Gliders2012 and Gliders2013 reached the semi-finals of RoboCup in 2012 and 2013; Gliders2014 were runner-ups in 2014; Gliders2015 finished third in RoboCup-2015, and Gliders2016 (a joint effort of the University of Sydney and CSIRO) became world champions in 2016.

RoboCup-2016 competition included 18 teams from 9 countries: Australia, Brazil, China, Egypt, Germany, Iran, Japan, Portugal and Romania. Gliders2016 played 23 games during several rounds, winning 19 times, losing twice and drawing twice, with the total score of 62:13, or 2.70:0.57 on average. In the two-game semi-final round, Gliders2016 defeated team CSU_Yunlu from Central South University (China), winning both games with the same score 2:1. The single-game final against team HELIOS2016 (Japan) went into the extra time, and ended with Gliders2016 winning 2:1. The third place was taken by team Ri-one from Ritsumeikan University (Japan).

The 2016 competition also included an evaluation round, where all 18 participating teams played one game each against the champion of RoboCup-2015, team WrightEagle (China). Only two teams, the eventual finalists Gliders2016 and HELIOS2016, managed to win against the previous year champion, with Gliders defeating WrightEagle 1:0, and HELIOS producing the top score 2:1.

The Gliders team code is written in C++ using *agent2d-3.1.1* [32], and fragments of source code of team MarliK released in 2012 [38].

In order to optimise the code, the Gliders development effort over the last five years involved *human-based evolutionary computation* (HBEC): a set of evolutionary computation techniques that rely on human innovation [39,40].

In general, evolutionary algorithms search a large space of possible solutions that together form a population. Each solution is a "genotype": a complex data structure representing the entire team behaviour encoded through a set of "design points". A design point can be as simple as a single parameter (e.g., risk tolerance in making a pass), or as complicated as a multi-agent tactical behaviour (e.g., a conditional statement describing the situation when a defender moves forward to produce an offside trap).

Some design points are easy to vary. For instance, a formation defined via Delaunay Triangulations $\mathcal{D}(P_b)$ and $\mathcal{D}(P_i)$, $1 \leq i \leq 11$, is an ordered list of coordinates, and varying and recombining such a list can be relatively easily automated. Other design points have an internal structure and are harder to permute. For example, a conditional statement describing a tactic has a condition and an action, encoded by numerous parameters such as positional coordinates, state information, and action details. Once such a statement (a design point) is created by human designers, its encoding can be used by evolutionary algorithms. However, the inception of the tactic needs creative innovation in the first place, justifying the hybrid HBEC approach.

The HBEC solutions representing team behaviours are evaluated with respect to their fitness, implemented as the average team performance, estimated over thousands of games for each generation played against a specific opponent. Some solutions are retained and recombined (i.e., the members of the population live) and some are removed (i.e., die) through selection. Importantly, the evolutionary process is carried out within different landscapes (one per known opponent), and typically results in different solutions evolved to outperform specific opponents. In order to maintain coherence of the resultant code, each design point is implemented with a logical mask switching the corresponding part of the genotype on and off for specific opponents (determined by their team names). This is loosely analogous to epigenetic programming [41].

The approach is aimed at constantly improving performance from one artificial "generation" to another, with team designers innovating and recombining behaviours while the fitness landscape and the mutations are for the most part automated. The performance of Gliders was evaluated on several supercomputer clusters, executing on some days tens of thousands of the experimental runs with different behaviour versions. It would be a fair estimate that the number of such trials is approaching 10 million. The overall search-space explored by the HBEC includes variations in both Gliders behaviour and opponent modelling. The approach incorporates disruptive innovations of the past years, including the standardisation of simulated "hardware" and several effective search-space decompositions.

Specific variations included (i) action-dependent evaluation function, (ii) dynamic tactics with Voronoi diagrams, (iii) information dynamics, and (iv) bio-inspired collective behaviour.

The approach introduced in Gliders2012 [33] retained the advantages of a single evaluation metric (implemented in *agent2d* [32]), but diversified the evaluation by considering multiple points as desirable states. These desirable states for action-dependent evaluation are computed using Voronoi diagrams which underlie many tactical schemes of Gliders.

Starting from 2013, Gliders utilised information dynamics [42–47] for tactical analysis and opponent modelling. This analysis involves computation of information transfer and storage, relating the information transfer to responsiveness of the players, and the information storage within a team to the team's rigidity and lack of tactical richness.

The constraints on mobility, identified by the information dynamics, were investigated and partially overcome with bio-inspired collective behaviour [36]. Gliders2015 utilise several elements of swarm behavior, attempting to keep each player's position as close as possible to that suggested by a specific tactical scheme, while incorporating slight variations in order to maximise the chances of receiving the pass and/or shooting at the opponent's goal. This behaviour increased the degree of coherent mobility: on the one hand, the players are constantly refining their positions in response to opponent players, but on the other hand, the repositioning is not erratic and the players move in coordinated ways.

These directions were unified within a single development and evaluation framework which allowed to explore the search-space in two ways: translating human expertise into new behaviours and tactics, and exhaustively recombining them with an artificial evolution, leveraging the power of modern supercomputing. This fusion, we believe, produced a disruptive innovation on its own, providing the winning edge for Gliders.

9 Conclusion

In this paper we reviewed disruptive innovations which affected advancement of the RoboCup 2D Soccer Simulation League over the twenty years since its inception, and placed the progress of our champion team in this context. It is important to realise that the neither of these processes has been linear, and many ideas have been developing along a spiral-shaped trajectory, resurfacing over the years in a different implementation. For example, the utility of evolutionary computation supported by supercomputing has been suggested as early as 1997, when a simulated team was developed with the agents whose high-level decision making behaviors had been entirely evolved using genetic programming [48]. Yet the complexity of the domain proved to be too challenging for this approach to gain a widespread adoption at that time.

Without an exception, all the winning approaches combined elements of some automation (debugging, machine learning, planning, opponent modelling, evolutionary computation) with human-based innovation in terms of a decomposition of the search-space, providing various configurations, templates and structures. Is there still a way toward a fully automated solution, when the agents learn or evolve to play a competitive game without a detailed guidance from human designers, but rather by trying to satisfy a universal objective ("win a game")?

On the one hand, the ability to run a massive number of simulated games on supercomputing clusters producing replicable results will only strengthen in time [4], and so may lend some hope in meeting this challenge positively. On the other hand, the enormous size and dimensionality of the search-space would defy any unstructured exploration strategy. A methodology successfully resolving this dilemma may not only provide an ultimate disruptive innovation in the League, but also provide a major breakthrough in the general AI research.

Acknowledgments. Several people contributed to Cyberoos and Gliders development over the years. Marc Butler, Thomas Howard and Ryszard Kowalczyk made exceptionally valuable contributions to Cyberoos' effort during 1998–2002 [9,19–21]. We are grateful to Gliders team members Oliver Obst, particularly for establishing the tournament infrastructure supporting the team's performance evaluation on CSIRO Accelerator Cluster (Bragg), and Victor Jauregui, for several important insights on soccer tactics used in Gliders2016 [37]. We thank David Budden for developing a new self-localisation method introduced in Gliders2013 [34,49] as well as contributing to the analysis of competition formats [4], and Oliver Cliff for developing a new communication scheme adopted by Gliders from 2014 [35]. The overall effort has also benefited from the study quantifying tactical interaction networks, carried out in collaboration with Cliff et al. [46]. We are thankful to Ivan Duong, Edward Moore and Jason Held for their contribution to Gliders2012 [33]. Gliders team logo was created by Matthew Chadwick.

References

1. Asada, M., Kitano, H., Noda, I., Veloso, M.: RoboCup: today and tomorrow - what we have have learned. Artif. Intell. **110**, 193–214 (1999)
2. Kitano, H., Tambe, M., Stone, P., Veloso, M.M., Coradeschi, S., Osawa, E., Matsubara, H., Noda, I., Asada, M.: The RoboCup synthetic agent challenge 97. In: Kitano, H. (ed.) RoboCup 1997. LNCS, vol. 1395, pp. 62–73. Springer, Heidelberg (1998). doi:10.1007/3-540-64473-3_49
3. Budden, D., Wang, P., Obst, O., Prokopenko, M.: Simulation leagues: analysis of competition formats. In: Bianchi, R.A.C., Akin, H.L., Ramamoorthy, S., Sugiura, K. (eds.) RoboCup 2014. LNCS (LNAI), vol. 8992, pp. 183–194. Springer, Cham (2015). doi:10.1007/978-3-319-18615-3_15
4. Budden, D.M., Wang, P., Obst, O., Prokopenko, M.: Robocup simulation leagues: enabling replicable and robust investigation of complex robotic systems. IEEE Robot. Autom. Mag. **22**(3), 140–146 (2015)
5. Noda, I., Stone, P.: The RoboCup soccer server and CMUnited clients: implemented infrastructure for MAS research. Auton. Agent. Multi-Agent Syst. **7**(1–2), 101–120 (2003)
6. Haker, M., Meyer, A., Polani, D., Martinetz, T.: A method for incorporation of new evidence to improve world state estimation. In: Birk, A., Coradeschi, S., Tadokoro, S. (eds.) RoboCup 2001. LNCS (LNAI), vol. 2377, pp. 362–367. Springer, Heidelberg (2002). doi:10.1007/3-540-45603-1_44

7. Stone, P., Veloso, M.: Task decomposition, dynamic role assignment, and low-bandwidth communication for real-time strategic teamwork. Artif. Intell. **110**(2), 241–273 (1999)
8. Riley, P., Stone, P., Veloso, M.: Layered disclosure: revealing agents' internals. In: Castelfranchi, C., Lespérance, Y. (eds.) ATAL 2000. LNCS, vol. 1986, pp. 61–72. Springer, Heidelberg (2001). doi:10.1007/3-540-44631-1_5
9. Butler, M., Prokopenko, M., Howard, T.: Flexible synchronisation within RoboCup environment: a comparative analysis. In: Stone, P., Balch, T., Kraetzschmar, G. (eds.) RoboCup 2000. LNCS, vol. 2019, pp. 119–128. Springer, Heidelberg (2001). doi:10.1007/3-540-45324-5_10
10. Stone, P., Riley, P., Veloso, M.: Defining and using ideal teammate and opponent models. In: Proceedings of the Twelfth Annual Conference on Innovative Applications of Artificial Intelligence (2000)
11. Reis, L.P., Lau, N., Oliveira, E.C.: Situation based strategic positioning for coordinating a team of homogeneous agents. BRSDMAS 2000. LNCS, vol. 2103, pp. 175–197. Springer, Heidelberg (2001). doi:10.1007/3-540-44568-4_11
12. Noda, I., Suzuki, S., Matsubara, H., Asada, M., Kitano, H.: Robocup-97: the first robot world cup soccer games and conferences. AI Mag. **19**(3), 49–59 (1998)
13. Stone, P., Riley, P., Veloso, M.: The CMUnited-99 champion simulator team. In: Veloso, M., Pagello, E., Kitano, H. (eds.) RoboCup 1999. LNCS (LNAI), vol. 1856, pp. 35–48. Springer, Heidelberg (2000). doi:10.1007/3-540-45327-X_2
14. Stone, P., Asada, M., Balch, T., Fujita, M., Kraetzschmar, G., Lund, H., Scerri, P., Tadokoro, S., Wyeth, G.: Overview of Robocup-2000. In: Stone, P., Balch, T., Kraetzschmar, G. (eds.) RoboCup 2000. LNCS, vol. 2019, pp. 1–29. Springer, Heidelberg (2001). doi:10.1007/3-540-45324-5_1
15. Reis, L.P., Lau, N.: FC Portugal team description: RoboCup 2000 simulation league champion. In: Stone, P., Balch, T., Kraetzschmar, G. (eds.) RoboCup 2000. LNCS, vol. 2019, pp. 29–40. Springer, Heidelberg (2001). doi:10.1007/3-540-45324-5_2
16. Reis, L.P., Lau, N.: COACH UNILANG - a standard language for coaching a (Robo) soccer team. In: Birk, A., Coradeschi, S., Tadokoro, S. (eds.) RoboCup 2001. LNCS, vol. 2377, pp. 183–192. Springer, Heidelberg (2002). doi:10.1007/3-540-45603-1_19
17. Jinyi, Y., Ni, L., Fan, Y., Yunpeng, C., Zengqi, S.: Technical solutions of tsinghuaeolus for Robotic soccer. In: Polani, D., Browning, B., Bonarini, A., Yoshida, K. (eds.) RoboCup 2003. LNCS (LNAI), vol. 3020, pp. 205–213. Springer, Heidelberg (2004). doi:10.1007/978-3-540-25940-4_18
18. Kok, J.R., Vlassis, N., Groen, F.: UvA Trilearn 2003 team description. In: Polani, D., Browning, B., Bonarini, A., Yoshida, K. (eds.) CD RoboCup 2003. Springer, Heidelberg (2003)
19. Prokopenko, M., Kowalczyk, R., Lee, M., Wong, W.Y.: Designing and modelling situated agents systematically: Cyberoos98. In: Proceedings of the PRICAI-98 Workshop on RoboCup, pp. 75–89 (1998)
20. Prokopenko, M., Butler, M., Howard, T.: On emergence of scalable tactical and strategic behaviour. In: Stone, P., Balch, T., Kraetzschmar, G. (eds.) RoboCup 2000. LNCS (LNAI), vol. 2019, pp. 357–366. Springer, Heidelberg (2001). doi:10.1007/3-540-45324-5_39
21. Prokopenko, M., Wang, P., Howard, T.: Cyberoos 2001: Deep behaviour projection agent architecture. In: Birk, A., Coradeschi, S., Tadokoro, S. (eds.) RoboCup 2001. LNCS, vol. 2377, pp. 507–510. Springer, Heidelberg (2002). doi:10.1007/3-540-45603-1_70

22. Prokopenko, M., Wang, P.: Relating the Entropy of joint beliefs to multi-agent coordination. In: Kaminka, G.A., Lima, P.U., Rojas, R. (eds.) RoboCup 2002. LNCS (LNAI), vol. 2752, pp. 367–374. Springer, Heidelberg (2003). doi:10.1007/978-3-540-45135-8_32

23. Prokopenko, M., Wang, P.: Evaluating team performance at the edge of chaos. In: Polani, D., Browning, B., Bonarini, A., Yoshida, K. (eds.) RoboCup 2003. LNCS (LNAI), vol. 3020, pp. 89–101. Springer, Heidelberg (2004). doi:10.1007/978-3-540-25940-4_8

24. Nehaniv, C., Polani, D., Olsson, L., Klyubin, A.: Evolutionary information-theoretic foundations of sensory ecology: channels of organism-specific meaningful information. In: da Fontoura Costa, L., Müller, G.B. (eds.) The 10th Altenberg Workshop in Theoretical Biology 2004 - Modeling Biology: Structures, Behavior, Evolution, Konrad Lorenz Institute for Evolution and Cognition Research, Altenberg, Austria, pp. 9–11 (2005)

25. Prokopenko, M., Gerasimov, V., Tanev, I.: Measuring spatiotemporal coordination in a modular robotic system. In: Rocha, L., Yaeger, L., Bedau, M., Floreano, D., Goldstone, R., Vespignani, A., (eds.) Artificial Life X: Proceedings of The 10th International Conference on the Simulation and Synthesis of Living Systems, Bloomington IN, USA, pp. 185–191 (2006)

26. Prokopenko, M., Gerasimov, V., Tanev, I.: Evolving Spatiotemporal coordination in a modular robotic system. In: Nolfi, S., Baldassarre, G., Calabretta, R., Hallam, J.C.T., Marocco, D., Meyer, J.-A., Miglino, O., Parisi, D. (eds.) SAB 2006. LNCS (LNAI), vol. 4095, pp. 558–569. Springer, Heidelberg (2006). doi:10.1007/11840541_46

27. Riedmiller, M., Gabel, T., Trost, F., Schwegmann, T.: Brainstormers 2D - team description 2008. In: RoboCup 2008: Robot Soccer World Cup XII; CD (2008)

28. Zhang, H., Chen, X.: The decision-making framework of WrightEagle, the RoboCup 2013 Soccer simulation 2D league champion team. In: Behnke, S., Veloso, M., Visser, A., Xiong, R. (eds.) RoboCup 2013. LNCS, vol. 8371, pp. 114–124. Springer, Heidelberg (2014). doi:10.1007/978-3-662-44468-9_11

29. Akiyama, H., Noda, I.: Multi-agent positioning mechanism in the dynamic environment. In: Visser, U., Ribeiro, F., Ohashi, T., Dellaert, F. (eds.) RoboCup 2007. LNCS (LNAI), vol. 5001, pp. 377–384. Springer, Heidelberg (2008). doi:10.1007/978-3-540-68847-1_38

30. Akiyama, H., Shimora, H.: Helios 2010 team description. In: RoboCup 2010: Robot Soccer World Cup XIV; CD (2010)

31. Chew, L.P.: Constrained delaunay triangulations. Algorithmica 4(1–4), 97–108 (1989)

32. Akiyama, H.: Agent2D Base Code (2010). http://www.rctools.sourceforge.jp

33. Prokopenko, M., Obst, O., Wang, P., Held, J.: Gliders 2012: tactics with action-dependent evaluation functions. In: RoboCup 2012 Symposium and Competitions: Team Description Papers, Mexico City, Mexico, June 2012 (2012)

34. Prokopenko, M., Obst, O., Wang, P., Budden, D., Cliff, O.: Gliders 2013: tactical analysis with information dynamics. In: RoboCup 2013 Symposium and Competitions: Team Description Papers, Eindhoven, The Netherlands, June 2013 (2013)

35. Prokopenko, M., Obst, O., Wang, P.: Gliders 2014: dynamic tactics with Voronoi diagrams. In: RoboCup 2014 Symposium and Competitions: Team Description Papers, Joao Pessoa, Brazil, July 2014 (2014)

36. Prokopenko, M., Wang, P., Obst, O.: Gliders 2015: opponent avoidance with bio-inspired flocking behaviour. In: RoboCup 2015 Symposium and Competitions: Team Description Papers, Hefei, China, July 2015 (2015)

37. Prokopenko, M., Wang, P., Obst, O., Jaurgeui, V.: Gliders 2016: integrating multi-agent approaches to tactical diversity. In: RoboCup 2016 Symposium and Competitions: Team Description Papers, Leipzig, Germany, July 2016 (2016)
38. Tavafi, A., Nozari, N., Vatani, R., Yousefi, M.R., Rahmatinia, S., Pirdir, P.: MarliK 2012 soccer 2D simulation team description paper. In: RoboCup 2012 Symposium and Competitions: Team Description Papers, Mexico City, Mexico (2012)
39. Kosorukoff, A.: Human based genetic algorithm. In: 2001 IEEE International Conference on Systems, Man, and Cybernetics, vol. 5, pp. 3464–3469. IEEE (2001)
40. Cheng, C.D., Kosorukoff, A.: Interactive one-max problem allows to compare the performance of interactive and human-based genetic algorithms. In: Deb, K. (ed.) GECCO 2004. LNCS, vol. 3102, pp. 983–993. Springer, Heidelberg (2004). doi:10.1007/978-3-540-24854-5_98
41. Tanev, I., Yuta, K.: Epigenetic programming: genetic programming incorporating epigenetic learning through modification of histones. Inf. Sci. **178**(23), 4469–4481 (2008)
42. Lizier, J.T., Prokopenko, M., Zomaya, A.Y.: Information modification and particle collisions in distributed computation. Chaos **20**(3), 037109 (2010)
43. Wang, X.R., Miller, J.M., Lizier, J.T., Prokopenko, M., Rossi, L.F.: Quantifying and tracing information cascades in swarms. PLoS One **7**(7), e40084 (2012)
44. Ay, N., Bernigau, H., Der, R., Prokopenko, M.: Information-driven self-organization: the dynamical system approach to autonomous robot behavior. Theor. Biosci. **131**, 161–179 (2012)
45. Lizier, J.T., Prokopenko, M., Zomaya, A.Y.: Coherent information structure in complex computation. Theor. Biosci. **131**, 193–203 (2012)
46. Cliff, O.M., Lizier, J.T., Wang, X.R., Wang, P., Obst, O., Prokopenko, M.: Towards quantifying interaction networks in a football match. In: Behnke, S., Veloso, M., Visser, A., Xiong, R. (eds.) RoboCup 2013. LNCS (LNAI), vol. 8371, pp. 1–12. Springer, Heidelberg (2014). doi:10.1007/978-3-662-44468-9_1
47. Lizier, J.T., Prokopenko, M., Zomaya, A.Y.: A framework for the local information dynamics of distributed computation in complex systems. In: Prokopenko, M. (ed.) Guided Self-Organization: Inception. ECC, vol. 9, pp. 115–158. Springer, Heidelberg (2014). doi:10.1007/978-3-642-53734-9_5
48. Luke, S.: Genetic programming produced competitive soccer softbot teams for RoboCup 97. In: Koza, J.R., Banzhaf, W., Chellapilla, K., Deb, K., Dorigo, M., Fogel, D.B., Garzon, M.H., Goldberg, D.E., Iba, H., Riolo, R.L., (eds.) Proceedings of the 3rd Annual Genetic Programming Conference, Morgan Kaufmann, pp. 214–222 (1998)
49. Budden, D., Prokopenko, M.: Improved particle filtering for pseudo-uniform belief distributions in robot localisation. In: Behnke, S., Veloso, M., Visser, A., Xiong, R. (eds.) RoboCup 2013. LNCS (LNAI), vol. 8371, pp. 385–395. Springer, Heidelberg (2014). doi:10.1007/978-3-662-44468-9_34

Tech United Eindhoven Middle Size League Winner 2016

Ferry Schoenmakers, Koen Meessen, Yanick Douven, Harrie van de Loo,
Dennis Bruijnen, Wouter Aangenent, Bob van Ninhuijs, Matthias Briegel,
Patrick van Brakel, Jordy Senden, Robin Soetens, Wouter Kuijpers,
Joris Reijrink, Camiel Beeren, Marjon van 't Klooster$^{(\boxtimes)}$, Lotte de Koning,
and René van de Molengraft

Eindhoven University of Technology, Den Dolech 2, P.O. Box 513,
5600 Eindhoven, MB, The Netherlands
techunited@tue.nl
http://www.techunited.nl/

Abstract. The Tech United Eindhoven Mid-size league (MSL) team
won the 2016 Championship in Leipzig. This paper describes the main
progress we made in 2016 which enabled this success. Recent progress in
software includes improved perception methods using combined omnivision of different robots and integrating the Kinect v2 camera onto the
robots. To improve the efficiency of shots at the opponents' goal, the
obstacle detection is improved. During the tournament new defensive
strategies were developed as an answer to the advanced attacking strategies that were seen during the round robins. Several statistics of matches
during the tournament show the overall performance of Tech United at
RoboCup 2016.

Keywords: RoboCup soccer · Middle-size league · Cooperative
sensing · Multi-network extension · Kinect

1 Introduction

Tech United Eindhoven represents the Eindhoven University of Technology during Robocup championships. The team participates in the Mid-size league and
the RoboCup@Home league and consists of PhD, MSc, BSc students and former TU/e students, with academic staff members of different departments. The
team started participating in the Middle-Size League 2006. In 2011 the service
robot AMIGO was added to the team to participate in the RoboCup@Home
league. Knowledge acquired in designing our soccer robots was extensively used
in creating a service robot.

This paper starts with a short introduction on our robot hardware and software platform in Sect. 2, and elaborates next on the main software improvements
we created to be able to win the 2016 Robocup competition.

Section 3 describes improvements in the area of perception. It starts with the
explanation of a method to attain 3D ball information by combining 2D ball

© Springer International Publishing AG 2017
S. Behnke et al. (Eds.): RoboCup 2016, LNAI 9776, pp. 542–553, 2017.
https://doi.org/10.1007/978-3-319-68792-6_45

information from multiple robots. Section 3.2 continues on 3D ball perception and explains the integration of a Kinect v2 on our robots to get a full 3D image of the environment. Section 3.3 describes the last perception improvement and provides details on an improved obstacle detection method using omnivision images. In Sect. 4 our defensive strategy is described which was modified during the tournament. It also describes the penalty blocking strategy of our goalkeeper which in the end provided us the world-championship.

The last Sect. 5 elaborates on the tournament results, match results, as well as match statistics.

2 Robot Platform

Our robots have been named TURTLEs (acronym for Tech United RoboCup Team: Limited Edition). The platform is driven by three omni-directional wheels and contains an omnivision camera on top for localization. The software on the robot is executed on an industrial Beckhoff pc running Linux.

2.1 Hardware

The current hardware is based on the generation of 2009 with several small re-designs to improve ball-handling and robustness, see Fig. 1. Development of these robots started in 2005. During tournaments and numerous demonstrations, this generation of soccer robots has proven to be evolved in a very robust platform. The schematic representation published in the second section of our team description paper of 2014 [4] covers the main outline of our robot design. For 2016 a re-design of the upper body of the robot has been performed to integrate Kinect v2 cameras and create a more robust frame for the omni-vision unit on top of the robot. This prevents the need for recalibration of mirror parameters when the top of the robot is hit by a ball. A detailed list of hardware specifications, along with CAD files of the base, upper-body, ball handling and shooting mechanism, has been published on a ROP wiki.[1]

2.2 Software

The software on the robots is divided in three main processes: Vision, Worldmodel and Motion. These process communicate with each other through a real-time database (RTDB) designed by the CAMBADA team [7]. The vision process is responsible for environment perception using omni-vision images and provides the location of the ball, obstacles and the robot itself. The worldmodel combines the ball, obstacle and robot position information provided by vision with data acquired from other team members to get a unified representation of the world. The motion process is based on a layered software model with from top to bottom the strategy defining high-level team strategy based on worldmodel

---

[1] http://www.roboticopenplatform.org/wiki/TURTLE.

Fig. 1. Fifth generation TURTLE robots, with on the left-handside the goalkeeper robot.

information. The second layer consists of actions which are executed by roles which are deployed on the turtles. These actions use a limited set of basic skills such as shoot, dribble with ball or just drive. The lowest level of the motion process contains the motion control of the robot actuators.

Inter-robot communication is based on UDP multicast communication at a fixed message rate of 25 Hz. The communication application sends a small selection of records from the real-time database written by the three main processes. The communicated information is used by the worldmodel of all robots and to execute multi-robot strategy such as passing. Further, the information can be received by any base-station next to the field for diagnostic purposes.

3   Improved Perception

The ball and obstacle perception of the robots have been improved in three ways, this section is structured according to these three improvements. In Sect. 3.1 an algorithm on 3D ball position estimation is described. Section 3.2 describes the implementation of the Kinect image processing, and the integration in the robot using RTDB. Section 3.3 elaborates on obstacle detection using omni-vision images.

3.1   3D Ball Position Estimation Using Cooperative Sensing

This research has been executed together with the CAMBADA team from Aveiro, Portugal [8]. To detect the position of the ball, most teams have equipped their robots with a catadioptric vision system, also known as *omnivision* [1,2,5]. Currently, the ball position is estimated by projecting the ball found in the 2D image on the field in the x-y plane, assuming that the ball is always on the ground when seen by the omni-vision. Finding a way to obtain the 3D ball position (x_b, y_b, z_b) enables the robot to follow the correct ball position in x-y

plane. Moreover, the height (z_b) of the ball serves a purpose by enabling the interception of lob passes [2]. Cooperative sensing can be used to determine the ball position in three dimensions by triangulation of omnivision camera data. This is graphically represented in Fig. 2(a). Here, P_1 and P_2 are the projected ball positions estimated by respectively robot 1 and 2, P_{ball} is the actual ball position.

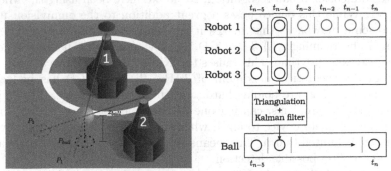

(a) Graphical representation of om- (b) A schematic representation of
nivision camera data triangulation. the triangulation algorithm.

Fig. 2. 3D ball position estimation using multi-robot triangulation.

3.1.1 Algorithm Structure

A schematic representation of the triangulation algorithm is presented in Fig. 2(b). Every execution, the new information from the robot itself and its peers is stored into a buffer, quantized to time instants defined by the executions. The state of the algorithm as presented in Fig. 2(b) is at time t_n, information from peers is delayed by the robot-robot communication. For triangulation, the algorithm selects a time instant at which information from multiple robots is available. In the case of the state represented in Fig. 2(b), t_{n-4} is selected. The available 2D ball projections at this time instant are triangulated and the obtained 3D ball position is filtered with a Kalman filter, which combines this new measurement with the model of the ball. This yields a (filtered) 3D ball position at time instant t_{n-4} which is then fast-forwarded in time to t_n using the model of the ball.

3.1.2 Results

The algorithm presented in Fig. 2(b) has been implemented on the robots. Two kinds of tests have been executed: with a static ball and with a moving ball. Tests with a static ball show that the average accuracy obtained with the algorithm is 10.6 cm. Note that the mapping from camera coordinates to robot coordinates has not been calibrated specifically for this test. During the tests with a moving ball an attempt was made to track the position of the ball from the moment it was kicked by a robot (12 m/s). To be able to get a good estimation of the ball position when the ball has exceeded the height of the robot, the state of the Kalman filter has to be converged before this moment. To accommodate this, enough samples from peer robots have to be received. Calculations show that if the robot-robot communication is performed at 40 Hz this is satisfied.

3.2   Integration Kinect v2 Camera

For three-dimensional ball recognition, so far we have been using the Microsoft Kinect v1. While this device poses a great addition to the omnivision unit, it also has some drawbacks that makes it unreliable and suboptimal. There are four main shortcomings: (i) The CCD has low sensitivity, hence we need to increase the exposure time. This causes the Kinect to shoot video at only 15 Hz, instead of the theoretical maximum of 30 Hz. (ii) The CCD has bad quality colors, making color thresholding hard, and tuning cumbersome. (iii) There are many robustness problems, causing one of the image streams to drop out, or causing the complete device to crash when mounted on a robot. And (iv) The depth range is limited to 6 m. This means that a full speed ball at 12 m/s arrives 0.5 s after the first possible detection.

A possible solution to the Kinect v1's shortcomings is the Kinect v2 [3]. It has a higher quality CCD with better color quality and improved sensitivity. It is therefore easier to find the ball in the color image, and it can always run at 30 Hz. The depth range has increased to 9 m, giving the goalkeeper more time to react. Early tests also have not shown any dropouts of the device or its video streams.

For processing the increased amount of data from the Kinect v2, a GPU is required. The robot software runs on an industrial computer, which does not have a GPU, nor can it be extended to include one. Therefore, a dedicated GPU development board, the Jetson TK1 [6], is used to process all the data from the Kinect. This board incorporates a 192-core GPU and a quad-core ARM CPU, which is just enough to process all data coming from one Kinect. The board runs Ubuntu 14.04 with CUDA for easy parallel computation. This enables us to offload some of the graphical operations to the GPU.

First, the video stream data is processed on the GPU. The ball is then detected using the following steps:

1. The color image is registered to the depth image, i.e. for each pixel in the depth image, the corresponding pixel in the color image is determined.
2. Color segmentation is performed on the color image using a Google annotated database that contains the chance of an RGB value belonging to a color.
3. A floodfill algorithm is performed for blob detection (CUDA).
4. The blobs are sorted based on their size/distance ratio and width/height ratio:

$$p = \left[1 + \alpha(w - h)^2\right]^{-1} \left[1 + \alpha^2(wh - 4r^2)^2\right]^{-1} \tag{1}$$

   with w and h being the width and height of the blob respectively, r the radius of the ball and α a scaling factor, all calculated in meters.
5. The found balls are transformed into robot coordinates.

The result is an almost 100% detection rate at 30 Hz when the ball is inside the field of view of the camera, and closer than 9 m. False positives are uncommon, but when present, they are filtered out by the ball model.

3.2.1 RTDB Multi-network Extension

We use the Real-time Database library of CAMBADA (RTDB, [7]) for inter-process as well as inter-robot communication. This database is based on records that can be marked either *local* or *shared*. A communication process (comm) is running on all robots, which broadcasts the *shared* records over WIFI using multicast UDP. The same process is also used to receive data to update the local RTDB instance with shared data from peers. This provides a flexible configurable communication architecture for inter-process and inter-robot communication.

With the introduction of the Jetson TK1 board for image processing of the Kinect v2, the processes on the robot are no longer executed on a single processing unit. As a result, the standard RTDB library can no longer fulfill all inter-process communication on a robot. Therefore RTDB and comm are extended to support multiple networks. The new communication architecture is illustrated in Fig. 3. Each robot PC runs two instances of comm. One broadcasts and listens on the wireless interface for inter-robot communication. A second comm instance is connected to a wired LAN interface which is connected to the Jetson board.

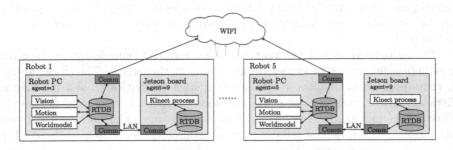

Fig. 3. Inter-process and inter-robot communication architecture using RTDB.

Modifications have been made to RTDB and comm to enable this new configuration. First, a network configuration file has been introduced. This file describes for each network the multicast connection properties, the frequency at which comm should share the agents's shared records, and an option to mark the network *default* to be fully backwards compatible. Two modifications to RTDB have been added to reduce the traffic in the networks. The first one is compression of the data to be sent just before a UDP packet is created. The complete payload of this packet, i.e., data and comm header, is compressed using *zlib* which reduces the payload on average to about 70% of the original size. Using the second modification, the user can specify in the RTDB configuration file which (shared) records have to be broadcasted in a given network. For example, the Robot PC (agent 1–5), illustrated in Fig. 3, is sharing data in two networks. The two networks are configured such that all shared records are broadcasted to all peers through the WIFI network, while only a subset of data is sent to the Jetson board through the LAN network. The Jetson board only needs to know the current robot position and not all team related information. This implementation is also fully backwards compatible; if the network is not specified in the RTDB configuration file, all shared records will be broadcasted.

Tournament Results. One of our weak points in previous years was blocking high balls shot at the goal. Either the goalkeeper did not see them, or they were detected too late to be able to react. During this tournament the goalkeeper was one of our strengths. Especially during games against teams with a strong attacking strategy, many high balls were shot at the goal, detected by the Kinect camera, and stopped by the goalkeeper. During the final match, Team Water shot twelve high balls at our goalie from a distance of more than four meters, eleven were detected by the Kinect, and eight were stopped.

3.3   Obstacle Detection Enhancements

During the past RoboCup tournaments it was observed that the success rate of goal attempts is still too low. For the RoboCup tournament in Hefei 2015 the success rate was approximately 20% averaged over all matches according to the logged game data. By improving the obstacle detection the goalkeepers position can be estimated more accurately, which will increase the success rate of shots at the goal.

The current obstacle detection method is a relatively simple approach, which uses 200 radial rulers to detect dark objects in the image. The disadvantage of this approach is that the resolution decreases dramatically as a function of distance. Hence, at larger distances only wide obstacles are detected accurately. This results in a 0.25 m resolution at an 8 m distance. Considering the image resolution, a resolution of 0.03 m at 8 m distance could be achieved, which is about a factor of 8 better. Hence, the main improvement of the new algorithm focuses on using the available resolution in tangential direction. The new method consists of the following steps:

1. Iterate through radii starting from inside outwards;
2. Apply an intensity threshold for each circle;
3. Apply a circular closing filter to fill small holes;
4. Collect candidate obstacles;
5. Split obstacles that are too wide;
6. Check mandatory features (obstacle is inside field, obstacle large enough in both tangential and radial direction);
7. Collect all valid obstacles;
8. Update the mask with the found obstacles such that no obstacles can be found behind other obstacles.

When comparing the old and new method on the robot, the results as shown in Fig. 4(a) and (b) are obtained. In this experiment, a keeper is positioned at about

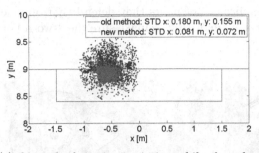 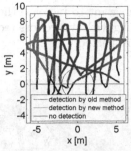

(a) Obstacle detection variation while the robot is moving across the field.

(b) Obstacle detection range comparison while the robot is moving across the field.

Fig. 4. Comparison results of old and new obstacle detection algorithm.

$(-0.5, 9)$ m pointing forward. The dots in Fig. 4(a) illustrate where the obstacle was seen by the robot with the old and new method. It can be seen that the standards deviation is significantly reduced. Figure 4(b) shows that the detection range is also increased. The lines show the trajectory of the moving robot. The color indicates whether the goalkeeper was detected from that position or not. As observed, the new method has an increased detection range.

Tournament Results. After analysis of the Robocup 2015 tournament matches we found that our success rate of shots at goal was around 20%, mainly caused by not detecting the goalkeeper. Analysis of our matches during Robocup 2016 showed that the efficiency of shots at the goal was only slightly higher. This is mainly caused by our changed strategy, more shooting attempts were performed, and probably by more effective defensive actions of our opponents. However, the number of shots directly at an opponent goalkeeper were reduced.

4   Improved Defensive Strategies

Two defensive strategies have been improved during 2016. The first one is described in Sect. 4.1 and describes our improved defense algorithm in standard attack situations. The second defensive strategy elaborates on our goalkeeper stopping penalties. The latter was of great importance during the final match which ended with penalties after a 3-3 draw.

4.1   Defending Attack Actions

Rules with respect to defending within the RoboCup MSL league are strict. When two robots from opponent teams are in a scrum, no other robot is allowed to make direct contact with the scrumming robots. This fault is illustrated by Fig. 5(a). When an opponent comes close to the goal, a defending team might, however, want to increase the number of defenders that defend that opponent. Defending with two robots requires an algorithm to make sure the "two-robots"-rule is respected.

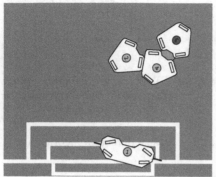 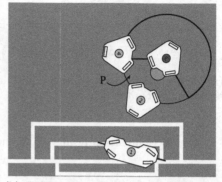

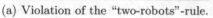

(a) Violation of the "two-robots"-rule.   (b) Robot 2 positions on the line between the ball and the goal, robot 4 will position on the edge of area P.

Fig. 5. Defending one opponent with multiple defenders. Left: violation of the "two-robots"-rule. Right: proposed solution. Cyan: defending team, magenta: attacking team. (Color figure online)

During the RoboCup 2016 a solution was implemented to make sure defending one opponent with two robots is possible, without violating the "two-robots"-rule. Figure 5(b) shows a situation in which the proposed algorithm is controlling the position of the robots. Robot 4 will always try to gain possession of the ball, unless the ball and robot 4 are in the area denoted by P. If the ball and the target of robot 4 are in area denoted by P, robot 4 will actually position on the edge of area P, as shown in Fig. 5(b). Robot 2 will position on the line between the ball and the mid-point of the goal, close to the opponent with the ball. When robot 4 is already in the area denoted by P, robot 2 will not enter area P, and keep some distance to robot 4 to not violate the "two-robots"-rule.

Tournament Results. During the matches at RoboCup 2016 this concept has proven to be very effective, Fig. 6(b) shows a still from the match versus the Chinese team Water where the solution is active. This concept has been proven effective especially versus teams with a relatively slow starting attack. This because, our second defender has an attacking role during the attack, this robot therefore has to make its way from the other side of the field. An improved role-assignment can be a possible solution to overcome this problem and have defense in position even faster.

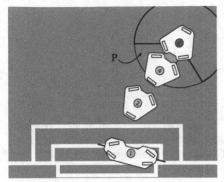

(a) When robot 4 is in the area denoted by P, robot 2 will not enter the area.

(b) Solution active in the final match versus Water (China), the area P is represented by the orange circle-part.

Fig. 6. The implemented solution. Left: preventing violation of the "two-robots"-rule. Right: solution active during match. Cyan: defending team, magenta: attacking team. (Color figure online)

4.2 Defending Penalties

In a penalty situation in the MSL, a robot shoots the ball from a distance of 3 m at a goal that is 2 m wide. The goalkeeper defending the goal has a maximum width of 0.7 m ($\sqrt{2} \times 0.5$ m). It is allowed to equip the goalkeeper with a movable frame that extends the width by 10 cm during one second, once every five seconds. An MSL robot can shoot a ball with a velocity up to 12 m/s, hence the reaction time of the goalkeeper is approximately 0.25 s. Within this time, the goalkeeper should detect the shot direction, and position itself at the right position. If the shot direction estimation is neglected and the complete reaction time of 0.25 s is available for positioning the goalkeeper 0.4 m to one side, an acceleration of approximately 14 m/s^2 is required. Hence, in a real situation, it is impossible for the goalkeeper to stop a penalty when the ball is shot at full speed close to the goal post. Therefore, we implemented a basic algorithm that tries to position the goalkeeper at the right spot in the goal.

During gameplay the goalkeeper solely looks at the current ball-position and predicts where the ball crosses the goal line if the ball has a velocity larger than zero. Based on that, it positions itself at the best position in the goal to stop the ball. During a penalty session, however, the opponent position is taken into account as well. Since all MSL robots rotate around the ball to shoot in a certain direction, the goalkeeper can estimate the shot direction based on the opponent position relative to the ball. This is illustrated in Fig. 7(a) to (c).

The opponent robot (magenta 4) grabs the ball, Fig. 7(a), and starts rotating around the ball to shoot in a goal corner. From the position of the opponent with respect to the ball it can be seen clearly that the shot direction will be the right hand side of the goal (Fig. 7(b)). The goalkeeper starts positioning to that corner and is in time to block the shot.

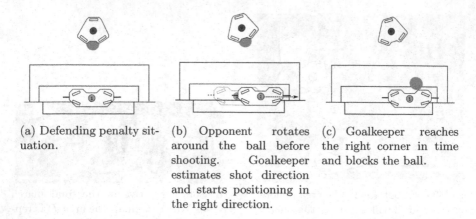

(a) Defending penalty situation.

(b) Opponent rotates around the ball before shooting. Goalkeeper estimates shot direction and starts positioning in the right direction.

(c) Goalkeeper reaches the right corner in time and blocks the ball.

Fig. 7. Defending penalty strategy: goalkeeper estimates shot direction based on opponent position relative to the ball. (Color figure online)

Tournament Results. During Robocup 2016, one penalty was given to our opponent during the round robins which was stopped by the goalkeeper. The final match ended in a draw (3-3) after extension and a penalty shoot-out was performed to find the winner. The goalkeeper was able to stop five out of five penalties by positioning to the right side of the goal based on the opponent position. Hence, the algorithm shows its significant value at the most important moment of the Robocup 2016 competition.

5   Tournament Results

The previous sections of this paper elaborated on improvement of algorithms of the Tech United software during 2016. With these improvements we managed to win the MSL competition of 2016. In total we played eleven matches during the tournament. In the three round robins, nine matches were played, seven matches were won and two times a draw. The semi-final ended in 5-0 and the final game ended in 4-3 after penalties. In total, Tech United scored 85 times and the opponents scored eight times.

During the tournament, the robots in the field drove in total 43.6 km. The goalkeeper, only active inside the goal area, was very active in blocking the goal, the total travelled distance of this robot only was 3.8 km. During 99.5% of the match time, the omnivision or the laser range finder of the goalkeeper found its location. For the other robots a localization percentage of 96.5% was obtained. These numbers, together with a high percentage of having five active robots in the field (over 85%), show the robustness of our robot platform.

6   Conclusions

In this paper we have discussed our improvements during the 2015/2016 season, which enabled us to regain the world championship. The paper elaborated on the improved perception using combined omnivision for a more accurate ball position estimation and integrating the Kinect v2 cameras onto the robots. This resulted in an improved perception of high balls of the goalkeeper. Furthermore, the new obstacle detection algorithm is described. With this algorithm the robots have a more accurate obstacle position estimation and obstacles can be detected from a wider range. This improvement made the attackers more effective in scoring goals. Our updated defensive strategy during game-play and during penalty sessions is described and the numbers show the effect of this. Especially the penalty blocking strategy was very efficient which made the goalkeeper block five out of five penalties during the final match. The tournament statistics in the last section prove the robustness of our improved robots.

Altogether we consider our improvements, made during 2016, successful for the tournament, while at the same time maintaining the attractiveness of our competition for a general audience.

References

1. Ahmad, A., Xavier, J., Santos-Victor, J., Lima, P.: 3D to 2D bijection for spherical objects under equidistant fisheye projection. Comput. Vis. Image Underst. **125**, 172–183 (2014)
2. Martinez, C.L., et al.: Tech United Eindhoven, Winner RoboCup 2014 MSL. In: Bianchi, R.A.C., Akin, H.L., Ramamoorthy, S., Sugiura, K. (eds.) RoboCup 2014. LNCS, vol. 8992, pp. 60–69. Springer, Cham (2015). doi:10.1007/978-3-319-18615-3_5
3. Microsoft. Kinect v2 technical specifications. https://dev.windows.com/en-us/kinect/hardware
4. Tech United Eindhoven MSL. Tech United Eindhoven Team Description 2014 (2014)
5. Neves, A.J.R., Pinho, A.J., Martins, D.A., Cunha, B.: An efficient omnidirectional vision system for soccer robots: from calibration to object detection. Mechatronics **21**(2), 399–410 (2011)
6. NVIDIA: Jetson tk1 technical specifications. http://www.nvidia.com/object/jetson-tk1-embedded-dev-kit.html
7. Almeida, L., Santos, F., Facchinetti, T., Pedreiras, P., Silva, V., Lopes, L.S.: Coordinating distributed autonomous agents with a real-time database: the CAMBADA project. In: Aykanat, C., Dayar, T., Körpeoğlu, İ. (eds.) ISCIS 2004. LNCS, vol. 3280, pp. 876–886. Springer, Heidelberg (2004). doi:10.1007/978-3-540-30182-0_88
8. Kuijpers, W., Neves, A.J.R., van de Molengraft, R.: Cooperative sensing for 3D ball positioning in the RoboCup middle size league. In: Robocup 2016: Robot World Cup XX, Accepted for Publication (2016)

iRAP Robot: World RoboCup Rescue Championship 2016 and Best in Class Mobility Award

Amornphun Phunopas$^{(\boxtimes)}$, Aran Blattler, and Noppadol Pudchuen

King Mongkut's University of Technology North Bangkok, Bangkok, Thailand
amornphun.p@eng.kmutnb.ac.th
https://www.iraprobot.com

Abstract. This paper describes an approach to the rescue robot competition by iRAP Robot in World RoboCup 2016. Rescue Robot League is beneficial as competing robots can be used in real situations when a disaster occurs. The competition demonstrates the performances of the robots and the contribution of each team to robotics in mechanics and algorithms. The rules for this year's competition have greatly changed from the past years'. The rescue robot has been tested and evaluated in performing necessary tasks repetitively to indicate a strong capability to get a high score. This paper presents the history of the iRAP Robot team, the robot design, the results of the competition, and the lessons learned.

Keywords: Rescue robot · iRAP robot · Mobility

1 Introduction

The main purpose of the Rescue Robot League is to develop a rescue robot that can be used in a real disaster situation. The competition measures progress in rescue robotic systems to highlight breakthrough capabilities that responders can understand and appreciate. The rules of the competition are updated every year, especially this year; in 2016 the rules for endurance and repeatability testing changed greatly. Only a single robot is allowed, and it must do the tasks from the preliminary round to the final round with the same configuration. The preliminary round comprised four test suites: Maneuvering, Mobility, Dexterity, and Exploration. Each test suite had five sub-tests. Thus, there was a total of 20 ground robot trials. The RoboCup Rescue Complete Rule Book described the details of the competition (see [1]). The arena layout shows all test suites, which is similar to the real scene, as in Fig. 1. The preliminary test trials had no victims, but to reflect the expected performance in the finals, the robot had to travel in the arena to search for artificial victims.

In any trial, ten checkpoints before doing a ground test consisted of six inspections and four dexterity tasks, as shown in Fig. 2. The score from checkpoints was a multiplier for the number of rounds that the robot performed the repetitions

© Springer International Publishing AG 2017
S. Behnke et al. (Eds.): RoboCup 2016, LNAI 9776, pp. 554–564, 2017.
https://doi.org/10.1007/978-3-319-68792-6_46

Fig. 1. Sample arena layout, showing the locations of all the test lanes set up for concurrent operation and a part of the real arena.

in the ground test. The new rules asked the robot to manipulate objects in the dexterity tasks; therefore, it forced our team to add a gripper to the robot, which formerly had only a robot arm for manipulating a visual system at the end effector. Our robot works in semi-auto mode. It can alert the operator in the six identification modes that are Video Image Resolution, Motion Detection, Thermal Image Resolution, Audio Acuity, Color/Pattern Recognition, and Gas. As well as the dexterity task, the robot had to inspect, touch, rotate and extract the pipes.

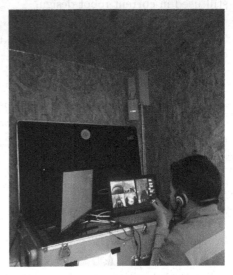

Fig. 2. The operator of the iRAP robot team operated the robot for ten checkpoints from the control station before doing a test suite in preliminaries.

2 Background

A group of students who were fascinated with making robots, formed a Student Robotics Club named iRAP, which stands for the Invigorating Robot Activity Project. Our iRAP robot team has a long history of about ten years and we have participated in the World RoboCup Rescue League since 2006. We have won an award at the competition every time that we have participated, which is seven times in total, and this is summarized in Table 1. From the year 2011, the Rescue Robot League introduced the Best in Class awards, namely: Best in Class Autonomy, Best in Class Manipulation, and Best in Class Mobility. It was a challenge to make the best robot in a class.

The rescue robot evolution, from 2006 to 2015, is shown in Fig. 3. The first era had a tele-operated robot with only a pair of flippers in the front. Many wheel materials were tested, for example, the different kinds of rubber and water tubes. The mechanism and driving system of the robot was improved, making it faster and stronger.

From 2009, besides the teleoperated robot, we had the autonomous robot shown in Fig. 4. The autonomous robot was not required to travel in harsh terrain like the teleoperated robot. Therefore, it had no flippers for climbing but had more sensors for full automation without human control. Knowing its position in the explored map was a big challenge. It had to do path planning and inspect signs and hazardous material labels [2].

From 2010, the teleoperated robot had two pairs of flippers in the front and the rear. As a result, the robot did not need to turn around to go backward and was able to move and climb backward using the rear flippers. This platform is still used in current robot design.

Table 1. The summary of iRAP robot team participating in the RoboCup rescue competition.

Year	Place	Team name	Award
2006	Bremen, Germany	Independent	1st place championship
2007	Atlanta, USA	Independent	1st place championship
2009	Graz, Austria	iRAP_Pro	1st place championship
2010	Singapore	iRAP_Pro	1st place championship
2011	Istanbul, Turkey	iRAP_Judy	- 1st place championship - Best in class mobility
2013	Eindhoven, Netherlands	iRAP_Furious	- 1st place championship - Best in class mobility
2015	Hefei, China	iRAP_Junoir	- 2nd place championship - Best in class mobility
2016	Leipzig, Germany	iRAP robot	- 1st place championship - Best in class mobility

Fig. 3. Teleoperated robot configuration of iRAP robot team from 2006 to 2015

Fig. 4. Autonomous robot configurations of the iRAP robot team from 2009 to 2015

Although last year, 2015, we became the runner-up, we won back the championship in this year. The robot has been developed in many versions to improve its capability in the RoboCup Rescue competition from past failures. For example, we did not get a good score in map plotting last year. It was the main thing that defeated us. The robot could not map out the explored terrain because it lost map data to send them back to the operator station. We solved it by processing and backing up map information in the robot before sending it back to the station. However, the updated rules of the competition allow us to redesign and change one thing every year. For the status of this year, there are two main criteria that we have considered. First, the robot has to be robust enough to compete from the preliminaries to the finals. Second, the robot has to have a gripper for the dexterity task.

3   Robot Design

The four-flippered configuration has a high performance, and it obtained the Best in Class Mobility Award in every competition (see details in Team Description Paper [3]). The robot has four flippers in the front and the rear. It has proved its great capabilities regarding maneuvers and mobility. The configuration looks the same as the previous year. However, inside the robot, the mechanism, materials, and devices are partially different. The new gripper is designed, the new electrical wiring is for more devices, and the new thermal camera is installed onto the robot.

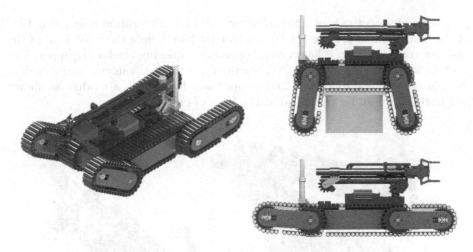

Fig. 5. The current robot design and configuration for participating in RoboCup rescue 2016.

Robot Body and Locomotive Driving Design. Our criteria for the rescue robot design base on the RoboCup Rescue Robot Competition 2016 rules. The competition rules and scoring metric focus both on the basic Urban Search and Rescue (USAR) tasks of identifying live victims and determining the victims' conditions. It provides accurate victim location, and enables victim recovery, all without causing damage to the environment. All teams compete in several missions and test performances with their robots, such as maneuvering, dexterity, and exploration, to define the standard of rescue robot.

The new design of our robot can be seen in Fig. 5. The solid aluminum is machined to be the base frame and the locomotive driving system, with all motors, is placed at the bottom of the base frame. Therefore, the center of gravity is low, which prevents the robot from turning over. The robot can move at an inclined 45° angle. When the robot stretches its front and rear flippers to a horizontal level, the overall length of the base frame must be more than the length of three levels of a standard staircase, so that the robot can climb across the stairway. Moreover, it can climb over an obstacle by using its front or rear flippers to lift itself. Two 24-V DC motors are used to drive the two caterpillar wheels separately. Each side of the caterpillar wheel works together with the flippers, linking the front and rear sprockets, to move forward, turn left, and turn right. The flippers are very useful for climbing over collapsed structures.

Robot Arm and Gripper design. Robot Arm and Gripper design Our robot arm aims to meet the requirements of the competition. First, the robot arm can reach the maximum height of a victim or an object from the ground floor. The second condition requires that the robot arm be able to manipulate an object such as a PVC pipe or door knob in the dexterity test suite. In particular, in the final round, the robot arm must be able to open a door using its gripper to pass through a victim zone. Our robot arm has a configuration resembling that of the PUMA robot arm except for a prismatic joint before the wrist joint of the end effector. Moreover, it has two end effectors: exploring head and gripper. The exploration head consists of a CCTV camera, a thermal camera, and a carbon dioxide sensor. The robot arm and gripper are designed in a module as shown in Fig. 6. They can be assembled at the base of our robot.

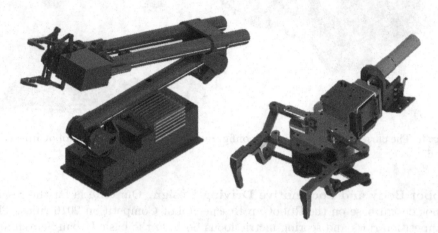

Fig. 6. The robot arm is designed as a module to fit together with the robot. It has a new gripper for dexterity tasks.

The reason that we separate the end effector into two parts is because the Exploring head and the gripper together are too large to pass through a small hole to search for hidden victims.

The Exploring head can inspect the temperature and the motion of the victim. Accordingly, a life signal of the victim can be examined by the carbon dioxide gas sensor because living creatures breathe out carbon dioxide gas. The gripper is designed based on the principle of a four-bar linkage using a worm gear to drive the mechanism because the worm gear is self-locking. The parallel gripper has a wide clamping range with slotted jaw faces that can grip objects tighter.

3.1   Simultaneous Localization and Mapping (SLAM)

In a mobile rescue robot, localization and mapping are very relevant abilities. The ability to sense the surrounding environment could help the operator to get a better grasp of the current situation. By using a 2D grid map representation, we can determine the current position and traveled trajectory of the robot. We can use data from the LIDAR sensor to get the surrounding distances, use odometry data from the robot's track encoder to refer the current position on the map, and use a Mems IMU to correct the robot frame and coordinates. However, in

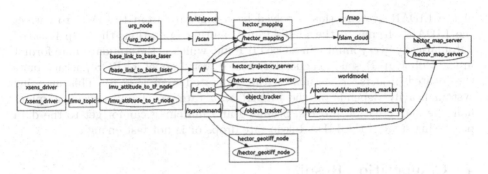

Fig. 7. ROS mapping system diagram of Simultaneous Localization and Mapping (SLAM).

a search and rescue operations scenario such as a collapsed building, there is a possible case that the ground is uneven or rocky. The debris can be scattered in the way, which makes the robot's track slip; the odometry data from the encoders would be useless in such a situation. Our approach is using the mapping system hector_slam [4] ROS packages, which are provided as an open source by Team Hector. Our ROS Mapping System Diagram is shown in Fig. 7. It uses only a LIDAR sensor to estimate the position from the surrounding environment by using a scan matching method. How this was possible is described elsewhere [5]. As the LIDAR platform alone might exhibit 6DOF motion, the scan has to be transformed into a stabilized coordinate frame using the estimated attitude

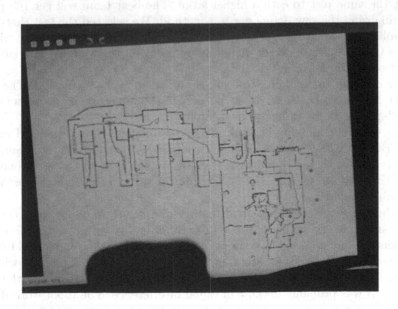

Fig. 8. The generated map and located victims in the finals.

of the LIDAR system; this is solved by using data from the IMU to correct the LIDAR's frame to the map's frame. During operation, the map is saved automatically every minute in a GeoTIFF file, which is the standard map format in the RoboCup Rescue League. The hector_worldmodel [6] ROS package plots the located objects or victims on the generated map (Fig. 8). This mapping system heavily depends on the LIDAR scan rate, so shaky movement might halt the map creation process. Scanning and matching cannot get to the data processing stage if the LIDAR scan rate drops or is not fast enough.

4   Competition Result

The results of the competition are shown in the official website of the World RoboCup 2016 [3]. In the preliminary test, there were 20 ground robot tests as stated in Sect. 1. A score was awarded in each test to qualify for the final round and get the best in class awards. There are four best in class awards in the main competition: Best in Class Dexterity, Best in Class Exploration, Best in Class Mobility, and Best in Class Autonomous Robot Exploration. However, it is expected that every robot can do the maneuvering tests. Each team has a different strategy to pass the different ground tests, focusing on maneuvering, mobility, dexterity, and exploration. It is hard to be the best and focus on every test. The robot can perform at least 12 missions because of the reserved time slots. More time slots may be available in case some teams cancel or cannot finish the mission. Therefore, the robot can probably perform more than 12 missions. There is no need to execute all the ground tests, and it is possible to repeat the same test to earn a higher score. The best team will get 100 points by normalizing the raw points per test method. We selected the test that let us accomplish two goals: first, to qualify in the final round and, second, to win the Best in Class Mobility award; therefore, we focus on the Mobility test suites in Fig. 9 from MOB 1 to MOB 5.

The result of the mobility test suites was what we had expected. The team had the highest score in every test. We earned the full score of 500 points in the five different tests for Best in Class Mobility as shown in Table 2.

The top six teams in the rank of the preliminary round qualified for the finals. Best in Class Awards showed a robot's performance and guaranteed it would pass to the next round as in Table 3, except Best in Class Autonomous Robot Exploration. Overall, the iRAP Robot team had the highest score in the preliminary round.

In the finals, the arena was divided into two areas. Two teams could compete at the same time and switch the areas. The robot had to travel, search for, locate, and identify simulated victims. As in the preliminaries, the robots could repeat to do the mission for the best score. In this round, we had a big problem with the wireless control of the robot. It was not only our team; every team had the same problem. It was probably because of signal interference. The robot worked well, but our score was not good and did not lead. To solve unexpected problems, we tried to fix the problem by changing the wireless router and antenna, but it did

Fig. 9. The five mobility tests from MOB 1 to MOB 5: hurdles, sand/gravel hills, stepfields, elevated ramps, and stair debris.

Table 2. Best in class award in World RoboCup rescue competition 2016.

Award and team	Point
Best in Class Mobility: iRAP Robot King Mongkut's University of Technology North Bangkok	500
Best in Class Dexterity: UPROBOT- ICS University Panamericana Campus Bonaterra	390
Best in Class Exploration: MRL Islamic Azad University of Qazvin	293
Best in Class Autonomous Robot Exploration: TEDUSAR Graz University of Technology	300

not work. Many teams turned to Ethernet cable. In the last minute, we switched to using an Ethernet cable and everything went back to our way. We could get higher scores, and we won the competition as shown in Table 4.

Table 3. The advancing to finals team in World RoboCup rescue 2016.

Team	Country	Point
iRAP robot	Thailand	884.7
MRL	Iran	807.3
GETbot	Germany	577
UPROBOTICS	Mexico	496.1
Nubot	China	479.1
Autonohm	Germany	469.1

Table 4. RoboCup rescue championship 2016.

Award	Team
First place	iRAP robot
Second place	MRL
Third place	GETbot

5   Conclusion

The champion team does not have to have any Best in Class awards. However, our robot had an outstanding performance in mobility and won the first place award. The robot is fairly useful in other tests besides maneuvering and mobility. It is good enough to complete the tasks in the final round. Our team is very adaptive to new competition rules, which are getting more difficult every time. We have developed the new robot and innovated. Furthermore, we have tried to upgrade our robot's capabilities, including the dexterity task and the autonomous robot exploration.

References

1. RoboCup Rescue Complete Rule Book (2016). http://wiki.robocup.org/wiki/Robot_League
2. Hazardous Material Labels. http://wiki.robocup.org/images/2/27/Hazmatlabels.pdf
3. Official Website World RoboCup (2016). http://www.robocup2016.org/
4. Hector slam package. http://wiki.ros.org/hector_slam
5. Kohlbrecher, S., von Stryk, O., Meyer, J., Kingauf, U.: A flexible and scalable SLAM system with full 3D motion estimation. In: IEEE International Symposium of Safety, Security, and Rescue Robot (SSRR), pp. 155–160 (2011). doi:10.1109/SSRR.2011.6106777
6. Hector worldmodel package. http://wiki.ros.org/hector_worldmodel

RoboCup Rescue Simulation System 2016 Champion Team Paper

Pooya Deldar Gohardani(✉), Siavash Mehrabi, and Peyman Ardestani

Mechatronics Research Laboratory, Islamic Azad University, Qazvin Branch,
Qazvin, Iran
pooya.gohardani@gmail.com, siavash.mehrabi@gmail.com,
peyman.ardestani@gmail.com

Abstract. RoboCup Rescue Simulation League competition is a highly competitive league which promotes the research and development of multi-agent and robotic solutions for disaster mitigation. Wining the first place was a goal that we have pursued for years. This success is not the outcome of our recent work, it is the result of years of research and development, so in this paper we will introduce our most considerable developments by team MRL throughout these years. These innovations and developments include developing a visual debugger, partitioning, assignment, sticky movement, blockade avoidance and drainage basin behavior.

Keywords: Champion paper · Rescue simulation · RoboCup

1 Introduction

After occurring disasters such as earthquake, a team of rescue agents consist of police forces, ambulance teams and firefighters will deploy in the city and start search and rescue operations. The search strategy, communication method, estimation of the needed forces in different parts of the city, assignment of the available agents to various tasks and also individual decisions of rescue agents will affect the speed and quality of the aid provided by the agents. Thus computer assistance can be very helpful to maximize the efficiency of agents, this is where RoboCup Rescue Simulation System (RCRSS) [1, 2] comes to work.

The Rescue Simulation is a system for simulating a city after an earthquake happens and is considered an important league in RoboCup. This system, simulates the earthquake and the events that usually occurs after the earthquake, for example shattered buildings, buried civilians in the buildings, blocked roads due to the debris of buildings, fire, explosion of gas stations and even the communication problems that can occur after an earthquake. Utilizing such an elaborate system in real world scenarios demands preparations on different levels.

The intention of the RoboCup Rescue project is to promote research and development in this socially significant domain at various levels involving multi-agent teamwork, coordination, physical robotic agents for search and rescue, information infrastructures, personal digital assistants and decision support systems, evaluation

S. Behnke et al. (Eds.): RoboCup 2016, LNAI 9776, pp. 565–576, 2017.
https://doi.org/10.1007/978-3-319-68792-6_47

benchmarks for rescue strategies and robotic systems that can all be integrated into comprehensive systems in future.

There are three main competitions in the league, and one technical challenge competition. Main competitions are the agent competition, infrastructure competition and virtual robot competition.

The agent competition involves primarily evaluating the performance of agent teams on different maps of the RoboCup Rescue Agent Simulation (RCRSS) platform. Specifically, it involves evaluating the effectiveness of Ambulances, Police Forces, and Fire Brigades agents on rescuing civilians, clearing blocked roads and extinguishing fires in cities where an earthquake has just happened.

The Infrastructure competition involves the presentation of an already existing tool or simulator related to disaster management issues in general. The aim is to evaluate possible enhancements and expansions of the RoboCup Rescue Simulation League environment (both the agent-simulator and the virtual robot platform) based on the new ideas and concepts proposed in these tools and simulators.

The MRL team is one of the most experienced and active teams in Rescue Simulation League since 2004. We took part in the agent competition every year since 2004 and we won the championship twice (in 2006 and 2007)[1]. With the league becoming more popular and competitive the technical committee has released a new version of the Rescue Simulation Platform in 2010 with following features[2] [3]:

- New kernel
- New traffic simulator and GIS
- New communication model
- New perception model
- Modified collapse and blockade simulator
- New ignition simulator
- Adjustment of the map scale to match real-word data
- Introduction of special challenges in addition to normal simulation runs
- Introduction of variable simulation parameters.

These fundamental modifications to the platform demanded a huge change in our agent code as well. We decided on rewriting the whole agent code from the scratch in order to be compatible with the new version of the platform. This was the biggest change in the Rescue Simulation history and all the other teams had to do the same thing as we did.

MRL's activities divided into two stages since 2010. The first stage, from 2010 to the end of 2012's competitions, which was spent on developing base code, utilities and infrastructure suitable for our high-level algorithms and the second stage, after RoboCup 2012 until 2016's competitions, which we spent on developing the actual high-level logic and strategies which differentiate us from the other competitors. Through the first stage we have gained a lot of experience by interacting with the

---

[1] http://wiki.robocup.org/wiki/Rescue_Simulation_League.

[2] http://roborescue.sourceforge.net/2010/rules.pdf.

simulation kernel, that later inspired us for developing the kernel itself and taking part in Rescue Simulation Infrastructure competitions.

By relying on our experience and after years of hard working we achieved the first place for the third time in our team's history in RoboCup 2016[3]. We also won two other first prizes for infrastructure competition and technical challenge in RoboCup 2016 and first prize in IranOpen 2016.

In Sect. 2 we will explain our team organization and preparation then in Sects. 3 to 9 we will introduce some of our most important utilities that are developed and used by our team and finally in Sect. 10 we will discuss about our conclusion and future work.

2 Team Organization and Preparation

After the release of the kernel's new version in 2010, we had to redesign and rewrite almost everything from the scratch to make our code compatible with the new release. All base-code, utilities and algorithms were re-written for the upcoming event.

In order to ensure our success in the future we have decided to change the structure of the team and recruited some energetic and young researchers. Then we divided our workforce to four different activities, which are developing infrastructural algorithms and utilities (e.g. path-planning and messaging), searching for applicable tactics and strategies (e.g. agent strategies, assignment algorithms and optimizations), designing and implementing the results of our research and finally testing and comparing the results of our implementations and picking the most effective solutions. Each task has an assignee who is responsible to make sure that the related task is resolving in time, but the rest of the members are contributing in each part that is needed based on their skills and team decision.

As you can see in Fig. 1, MRL managed to gain better results every year, comparing to past years until finally we achieved the first place.

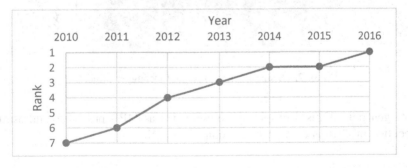

Fig. 1. MRL ranks in agent competition from 2010 to 2016

---

[3] http://www.robocup2016.org/en/schedule-results/results/robocup-rescue/rescue-simulation/.

3 Visual Debugger

Considering the nature of the rescue simulation, monitoring agents' performance and behavior is much easier by visualizing them rather than text-based outputs or logs, therefore it is vital to have a utility that provides a visual representation of output data and is easily extensible for everyone without deep knowledge of the kernel and viewer. MRL has realized this and added many features to the base viewer that made debugging an easy task comparing to debug by logging or by the basic viewer.

The Visual Debugger (Fig. 2) utility has a very similar appearance to the standard rescue simulation viewer and has every feature that is provided by the standard version. The advantage of visual debugger is in extending the viewer and adding new layers of graphic over the standard view in order to provide visual and real time representation of additional data (e.g. output of newly implemented algorithms, specific properties, custom drawings and etc.).

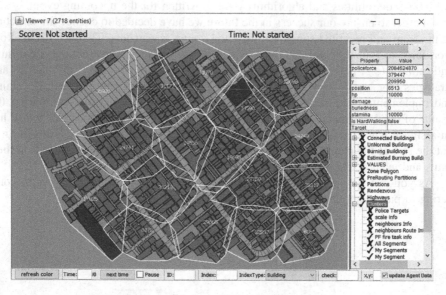

Fig. 2. A simple view of Visual Debugger project

We generalized this debugger and presented it as MRL project for infrastructure competition in 2016 and we won the competition [4].

4 Partitioning

As the world is partially observable to the agents, we needed an approach to let the agents spread over the city in order to fullfill two requierments; first is to find buildings on fire and damaged civilians as fast as possible and second is to prevent congestion in some areas. While the former is a general requirement for all types of agents, the latter is mostly usable for ambulance and police force agents.

To handle this, we decided to use partitioning. We used Voronoi based algorithm [5] for partitioning in 2011. The method was so that, some important points were specified on map as input for Voronoi based algorithm to do the partitioning. But we decided to use K-means [6] clustering for the next year. The problem with previous method was that partitions were not created based on number of buildings in each partition but they were based on geometric clustering, and this could lead to unfair partitioning and inefficient assignment of healthy agents to partitions. So we decided to create variable number of partitions based on count of healthy agents (agents who can walk and are not trapped in buildings) then center of each partition will be determined using K-means algorithm.

The similarity measure for K-means is a function of number of buildings in a partition and distance between each building and center of the partition. This guarantees that there is at least one healthy agent available for each partition. In Fig. 3 the output of the new model is shown. Green circles with cross mark show the center of each partition and smaller circles in one color show center of entities of a specific partition.

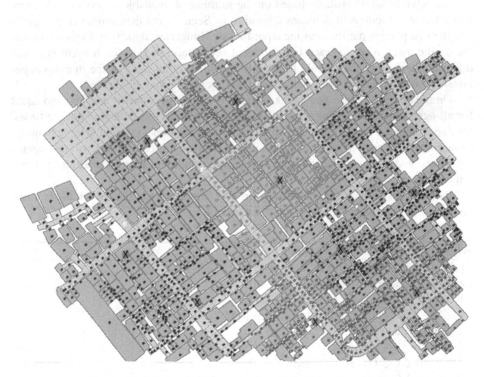

Fig. 3. Partitioning by K-means algorithm (Color figure online)

We have been using this stable and efficient algorithm since 2013 for partitioning.

Algorithm 1 Basic K-means Algorithm

1: Select K points as the initial center.
2: **repeat**
3:     From K partition by assigning all points to the closest center.
4:     Re-compute the center of each partition.
5: **until** no center changes

---

5   Partition Assignment

We didn't have any specific task assignment between the agents at the beginning of the simulation in our previous versions. Our assignment in the middle of scenario was not efficient either, it was mostly based on the distance between agents and available tasks which sometimes causes congestion in some areas and starvation of agent in other areas. The solution we applied was to divide the map into small partitions that may or may not contain any specific task and assign an agent to each starved partition in order to evenly distribute the agents throughout the map, but greedy assignment did not yield any better results. Our other solution was to utilize Hungarian algorithm for efficient assignment.

We have created partitions based on the number of available agents of each type, using the aforementioned K-means algorithm in Sect. 4, and then provided the agents and their respective partitions as the input for our Hungarian algorithm. Please note that we do the assignment for each type of agent separately, because each agent type has different capabilities that should be usually available in all parts of the map homogenously, but the number of available agent for each type may be different.

On the other hand, the data that is needed for some operations is constant and equal for all agent, therefore by applying the same algorithm to this data for multiple times, we expect that the result of this algorithm should be the same. Using this logic helps us to sacrifice CPU time in rare conditions, e.g. in first 3 cycles of the scenario that agents are frozen and cannot move, in order to preserve communication bandwidth for more critical information.

Partition assignment and partitioning process are functioning based on this fact and they are both calculated by each agent separately.

Algorithm 2 Partition Assignment

1: $A \leftarrow$ Find location of all agents
2: $n \leftarrow$ number of agents
3: $M \leftarrow$ perform K-Means clustering on E for n clusters
4: $C \leftarrow$ Find center of all clusters from M
5: **for** $i \leftarrow 1, n$ **do**
6:     **for** $j \leftarrow 1, n$ **do**
7:         $COST(i, j) \leftarrow distance(A_i, C_j)$
8:     **end for**
9: **end for**
10: $\alpha \leftarrow H(COST)$

Here E is the list of all entities in the map which we want to cluster them as a partition; M is the list of produced clusters; distance is a function to calculate euclidean distance between each element of A and C; H is a function which performs Hungarian algorithm on COST matrix and the result (α) is a vector which contains the indices of assigned partition.

6   Sticky Movement Strategy

The main task of an ambulance agent is to maximize the total number of living civilians by the end of the simulation. Our base strategy is to create partitions proportional to number of available agents in the scenario using the k-means algorithm, assign each agent to a partition using Hungarian algorithm and let the agents search and rescue in their assigned partition. But sometimes despite the fact that our assignment is very efficient, the agents have to travel a long way to get to their partition (Fig. 4(a)), which reduces their utilization factor and efficiency. To utilize ambulance as much as possible even in such situations we added a new strategy called "Sticky Movement" which is simply based on potential field motion planning (Fig. 4(b)).

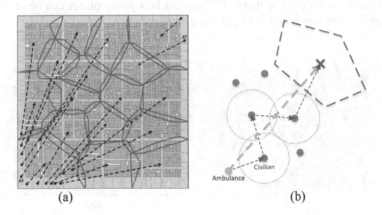

(a)   (b)

Fig. 4. (a) Shows aggregation of agents and (b) shows Sticky Movement (Color figure online)

If an agent detects a civilian closer than a specific threshold to the path (illustrated by green circle) towards the target partition, the agent tries to rescue the civilian before heading towards the target partition. However, doing this sometimes will result in too many ambulances trying to rescue the same civilian; to avoid such conditions we are utilizing an algorithm based on Monte Carlo method [7] to estimate the remaining time until a civilian dies and therefore calculate the optimum number of ambulances needed to rescue that civilian, then we assign only as many as needed ambulances to rescue task and let the rest to go and reach their target partition. This algorithm uses an arbitrary high value as the starting point for the number of agents needed for a civilian to survive and it will be reduced as each civilian get recued faster than our estimated time that it needs to be rescued before death. We are using this method because of the quantized values that kernel exposes as health point and damage of the civilian.

In Fig. 4(a) aggregation of agents in specific zones forces them to travel a long way to get to their partition. And in Fig. 4(b) you can see Sticky Movement of ambulance from the starting point (yellow circle) to the center of target partition (red cross). The green dashed circle shows the threshold of civilians' gravitational pull. The ambulance only rescues the civilians that their gravitational pull crosses its main course.

7   Fire Brigades' Positioning Problem

For situations involving fire it is necessary to act as quick as possible without wasting time on redundant moves. By studying previous results, we have found out that we have lots of redundant moves to find a good place to put the fires off, so we decided to use Maximal Covering [8] to find best positions on the map for fire brigade agents to stand and put the fires off with minimum movement.

To see how it works, you can refer to Fig. 5(a). In this figure you can see three fire points (green, pink and violet buildings) with their corresponding possible positions (colored areas) to put each of them off. Consider how many places can be selected and how many moves can be done to put these fires off.

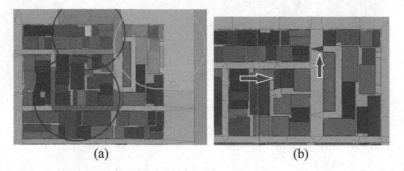

(a)   (b)

Fig. 5. (a) Shows fire points in three different positions and (b) shows found point after solving Maximal Covering (Color figure online)

Solving Maximal Covering problem for these three points helps agents to find a few places that are best to put the fires off, from them with the least movement. Figure 5(b) shows the result of solving Maximal Covering problem for those three mentioned points in Fig. 5(a). At first glance it looks relatively simple to solve this problem but it is actually associated with NP-hard problems [9] and for cases involving many entities it becomes very complex.

8 Blockade Avoidance

Since police agents have distinctive but indirect impact on the other agent's performance, most of MRL's attention was on police agent's coordination and cooperation with other agents. One of the problems we were facing as a result of using new clear method was about serrated blockades that trap agents (Fig. 6). It's clear that this problem reduces the agent's performance drastically.

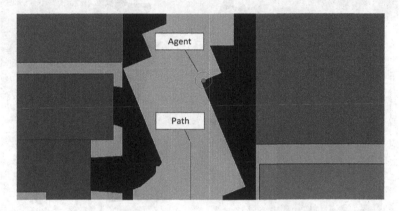

Fig. 6. An agent caught up in fragments of blockage

To overcome this issue and to keep things simple, we tried to clear the blockades so that no jagged blockades be there instead of handling the obstacle avoidance problem. we used Guideline strategy in RoboCup 2014 [10]. In this strategy, a police agent clears the roads along the guidelines to smoothly clear the road without any residues so that the agents can move along faster, without getting stuck. But that was not enough because sometimes we still could find those jagged blockades in some conditions, so in 2015 we introduced another approach alongside the existing one to handle the blockade avoidance.

In this approach, the agent tries to apply following steps to get out of the trap (Fig. 7).

1. Make a convex hull over the blockade
2. Scale it to one and a half (brown polygon)
3. Find bounded rectangle of the scaled shape (green rectangle)
4. Make rays (lines from the trapping point to all directions)
5. Find the nearest intersection point of the bounded rectangle and those rays that does not intersect with the blockade
6. Try to move to the found point
7. You are likely free to go!

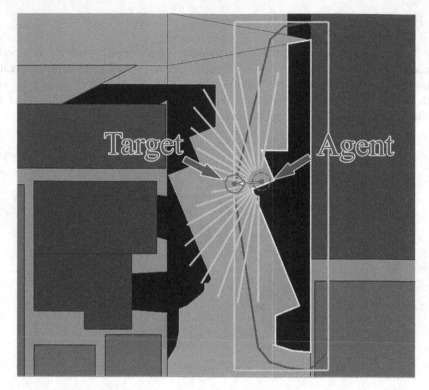

Fig. 7. Ray move of a blocked agent (Color figure online)

9 Drainage Basin Behavior

As we have mentioned before, police actions have indirect impact on other agents' performance. One of the cases that highlights the importance of police decisions is at the beginning of the scenario, which the roads are usually crowded with blockages and moving from one part of the map to another is sometimes impossible. In such situations a small building on fire can turn into an inferno in a matter of a few cycles. It is obvious that the sooner the police agents can manage to open a path from different parts of the map to the fire-site, the higher are the chances for the fire brigades to get to the fire-site and put it off timely.

For RoboCup 2016 we added a new strategy to address the aforementioned issue, based on drainage basin that forms rivers, to deliver a quick access to a newly discovered fire site.

Note that we are assigning each active agent to a specific partition in map. In this strategy each police tries to open a path from the center of its assigned partition to the center of a neighbor partition that has a shortest distance based on A* algorithm to the discovered fire site. As a result, there will be at least one path from each partition to the fire site for fire brigades to access the burning area and put the fire off faster. Figure 8 shows the details.

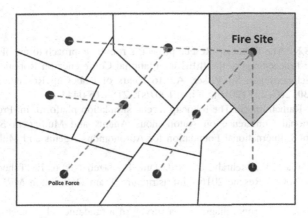

Fig. 8. A tree structure formed from drainage basin behavior of the agents, trying to clear a path from center of their assigned partition to the center of the fire site

10 Concluding Discussion and Future Works

As we have mention in the document, MRL team has tried many different approaches from 2010 to 2016. Our current strategy for coordination of agents is based on clustering using k-means algorithm and assigning the agents to the clusters using Hungarian algorithm. We added "Sticky Movement" for ambulance to optimize the performance of agents and "Drainage Basin Behavior" for police agents to open routes to fire as fast as possible. We also mentioned that we use maximal covering problem for optimizing the fire brigades positioning and minimize the time that is wasted by moving between different targets.

The guideline strategy combined with our blockade avoidance algorithm helps us to escape from traps that are created by serrated blockades.

We have also mentioned the Visual Debugger that accelerates the process of development and debugging of the code.

Our future work will be focused on finding and trying newer and more effective approaches instead of Hungarian, Voronoi and maximal covering. We have planned to implement our code using ADF for next year's competition. We have also planned for implementing a new Move method for the kernel that can solve the problems mentioned in Sect. 8.

As another future work we also want to develop the kernel in order to make it more scalable and bring it closer to its' primary goal which is to be usable in real world situations. We are planning to use Hadoop platform as our infrastructure in order to provide more processing power and high-availability.

Acknowledgment. The 2016 team wish to acknowledge the legacy left by previous members and the considerable financial and administrative support from Mechatronics Research Laboratory, Qazvin Islamic Azad University. We would like to thank Mr. Erfan Jazeb Nikoo and Mr. Sajad Rostami who helped us to prepare this document as well as all Rescue Simulation teams who made the league competitive and exciting.

References

1. Tadokoro, S.K.: The RoboCup-Rescue project: a robotic approach to the disaster mitigation problem. In: Proceedings of the IEEE International Conference on Robotics (2000)
2. Sheh, R., Schwertfeger, S., Visser, A.: 16 Years of RoboCup Rescue. KI - Künstliche Intelligenz 30, 267–277 (2016). doi:10.1007/s13218-016-0444-x
3. Skinner, C., Ramchurn, S.: The robocup rescue simulation platform. In: Proceedings of the 9th International Conference on Autonomous Agents and Multiagent Systems, vol. 1, pp. 1647–1648. International Foundation for Autonomous Agents and Multiagent Systems (2010)
4. Deldar Gohardani, P., Mehrabi, S., Ardestani, P., Jazeb Nikoo, E., Taherian, M.: Visual Debugger RoboCup Rescue 2016 - Infrastructure Team Description MRL (Iran), Leipzig (2016)
5. Aurenhammer, F.: Voronoi diagrams—a survey of a fundamental geometric data structure. ACM Comput. Surv. 23, 345–405 (1991)
6. Hartigan, J.A., Wong, M.A.: Algorithm AS 136: a k-means clustering algorithm. J. R. Stat. Soc. Ser. C 28, 100–108 (1979)
7. Metropolis, N., Ulam, S.: The Monte Carlo method. J. Am. Stat. Assoc. 44, 335–341 (1949)
8. Church, R., Revelle, C.: The maximal covering location problem. Pap. Reg. Sci. 32, 101–118 (1974)
9. Hochbaum, D.S.: Approximating covering and packing problems: set cover, vertex cover, independent set, and related problems. In: Approximation Algorithms for NP-Hard Problems, pp. 94–143. PWS Publishing Company, Boston (1997)
10. Deldar Gohardani, P., Rostami, S., Mehrabi, S., Ardestani, P., Taherian, M.: Robocup Rescue 2015 - Rescue Simulation League Team Description MRL (Iran), Hefei, China (2015)

ToBI – Team of Bielefeld: Enhancing Robot Behaviors and the Role of Multi-robotics in RoboCup@Home

Sebastian Meyer zu Borgsen$^{(\boxtimes)}$, Timo Korthals, Florian Lier, and Sven Wachsmuth

Exzellenzcluster Cognitive Interaction Technology (CITEC), Bielefeld University, Inspiration 1, 33619 Bielefeld, Germany
{semeyerz,tkorthals,flier,swachsmu}@techfak.uni-bielefeld.de
http://www.cit-ec.de/de/ToBI

Abstract. In this paper, we describe the joint effort of the Team of Bielefeld (ToBI) which won the RoboCup@Home competition in Leipzig 2016. RoboCup@Home consists of a defined set of benchmarking tests that cover multiple skills needed by service robots. We present the robotic platforms, technical contributions, and lessons learned from previous events that led to the final success this year. This includes a framework for behavior modeling and communication employed on two human-sized robots Floka and Biron as well as on the small robotic device AMiRo. These were used for a multi-robot collaboration scenario in the Finals. We describe our main contributions in automated testing, error handling, memorization and reporting, robot-robot coordination, and flexible grasping that considers object shape.

1 Introduction

The RoboCup@Home competition [1] aims at bringing robotic platforms to use in realistic domestic environments. In contrast to other leagues like soccer – which predefine and standardize the playing field – here robots need to deal with different apartment layouts, changing decorations, unknown sites, unstructured public spaces, and interfering or cooperating humans who are only very briefly – or not at all – instructed how to interact with the robot. The set of benchmarking tasks is adapted or newly defined each year. These typically require multiple capabilities, like navigation and mapping, person recognition and tracking, speech understanding and simple dialogues, object recognition and manipulation. The integration of these capabilities towards a coherent system behavior that deals with any kind of exception or interference during a task is one of the major challenges of RoboCup@Home. The competition is organized into different stages. Within the first stage, tests focus on a small set of capabilities (e.g. person following and guiding or object recognition and manipulation) scoring the best two tries out of three. The stage is finalized by an integration challenge (GPSR – General Purpose Service Robot) where robots have no predefined task, but need to autonomously sequence a task given by speech. The

© Springer International Publishing AG 2017
S. Behnke et al. (Eds.): RoboCup 2016, LNAI 9776, pp. 577–588, 2017.
https://doi.org/10.1007/978-3-319-68792-6_48

best 50% of the teams proceed to the second stage. Here, robots are tested in an enhanced and longer version of GPSR (EE-GPSR), in a real restaurant as a waiter, and in an individual open performance (Open Challenge). The final is an extended open challenge that is judged by an internal and external jury.

The Team of Bielefeld (ToBI) was founded in 2009 and successfully participated in the RoboCup German Open as well as the RoboCup World Cup from 2009 to 2015. In 2016, the team finally won the global competition and ended first in several of the individual tests (Navigation, Person Recognition, GPSR, EE-GPSR, Restaurant). There are multiple reasons for the performance gain in 2016. Some of these will be discussed in the following sections. Bielefeld University is involved in research on human-robot interaction since more than 20 years especially gaining experience in experimental studies with integrated robotic systems [2,3]. An important lesson learned is that the reproducibility of robotic systems is critical to show the incremental progress – but that this is rarely achieved [4]. This applies to experimentation in robotics as well as to RoboCup. A Technical Description Paper (e.g. [5]) – as typically submitted to RoboCup competitions – is by far not sufficient to describe or even reproduce a robotic system with all its artifacts. The introduction of a systematic approach towards reproducible robotic experiments [6] has been turned out as a key factor to maximally stabilize basic capabilities like, e.g., navigation or person following. Together with appropriate simulation engines [7] it paves the way to an automated testing of complete RoboCup@Home tasks.

In the Open Challenge and the Final, we introduced a multi-robot collaboration scenario that combines small mobile sensor devices with human-sized service robots showing the scalability of the communication [8] and behavior [9] framework. This is an essential contribution to the development of the @Home league because our future homes will be equipped with numerous intelligent devices. A service robot will act in a more human-aware manner if it already knows where people are instead of searching for them. We show how this can be realized in a very flexible manner without completely relying on fragile communication channels.

2 Robot Platforms

In 2016, ToBIparticipated in RoboCup@Home with the two service robots Biron and Floka. Those were assisted by multiple instances of the smaller AMiRo as an extended mobile sensor platform. Figure 1 gives on overview of the three mentioned platforms. While we focus on navigation and HRI with Biron, the body structure of Floka allows advanced bi-manual manipulation.

The robot platform Biron (cf. Fig. 1(a)) is based on the research platform GuiaBot by adept/mobilerobots customized and equipped with sensors that allow analysis of the current situation. The Biron platform has been continuously developed since 2001 and has been used in RoboCup@Home since 2009.

The robot base is a PatrolBot which is maneuverable with $\approx 1.7 \text{ ms}^{-1}$ maximum linear velocity and $>5 \text{ rad s}^{-1}$ rotational velocity. The drive is a two-wheel

(a) Biron   (b) Floka   (c) AMiRo

Fig. 1. Robotic platforms of ToBI. The overall height of Biron is ≈140 cm. The Floka platform has an adjustable height between ≈160 cm and ≈200 cm. The AMiRo has a diameter of 10 cm.

differential drive with two passive rear casters for balance. Inside the base there are two laser range finders with a coverage of 6.28 rad around the robot with a scanning height of ≈30cm above the floor (SICK LMS in the front + Hokuyo UBG-04LX in the back). The upper part of the robot also houses a touch screen (24cm × 18cm) as well as the system speaker. In contrast to most other Patrol-Bots, Biron does not accommodate an internal computer. Instead, two laptops are attached to platform. These are equipped with Intel Core i7-4810MQ processors and 16 GB main memory are running a standard Ubuntu Linux. For person detection/recognition we use a full HD webcam of the type Logitech HD Pro Webcam C920. For object recognition we use a 24 Mpx DSLM camera (Sony Alpha α6000). Two Asus Xtion PRO LIVE Sensors on top of the base provide RGBD data for the robot. As microphones two Sennheiser MKE 400 are installed front- and back-facing, supported by two AKG C 400 BL on the sides. Additionally, the robot is equipped with the Neuronics Katana 450 arm.

Our robot Floka (cf. Fig. 1(b)) is based on the Meka M1 Mobile Manipulator robotic-platform. It has been continuously enhanced within the 'Cognitive Service Robotics Apartment as Ambient Host' project to explore research questions related to human-robot interaction in smart-home environments [10,11].

An omni-directional base with Holomni's caster-wheels and a lift-controlled torso enable navigating in complex environments. In total, the robot has 37 DoF, which break down to joints. It has 7 per arm, 5 per hand, 2 for the head, 2 in the torso, and 9 joints actuate the base including the z-lift. The motors in the arms, torso and hands are Series Elastic Actuators (SEAs), which enable force sensing. The four-fingered underactuated anthropomorphic hands are attached to an ATI Industrial Automation Mini40 force/torque sensor. The sensor-head contains a Primesense Carmine 1.09 short-range RGBD camera and a Ximea MQ042CG-CM 4.2 Mpx Color CMOS Camera. Two AKG C 400 BL are attached to the shoulders. The base is equipped with a Hokuyo UTM-30LX scanning range finder on the front top and a SICK TiM571 integrated in its back. For processing it's back houses a custom processing PC with Intel Core i7-6700 and 16 GB of RAM and Zotac ZBOX SN970 for NVIDIA CUDA. A third PC for real-time control of the actuators with Intel Core i5-3470S and 8 GB of RAM is integrated in the base. All the components controller boards are interfaced over Ethercat with the Meka M3 control framework. This framework is building up on RTAI for Linux to enable a 1 kHz control-loop.

The AMiRo as used in RoboCup@Home is a two wheeled robot with a physical cylindrical shape [12]. It extends and enhances the capabilities of Biron and Floka in many tasks within the Open Challenge and Final. Commonly, multiple AMiRos are applied in conjunction to build a multi-robotic setup which is interconnected via Wi-Fi. AMiRo (cf. Fig. 1(c)) was developed at Bielefeld University with the main objective of research and education. It consists of a set of stackable electronic modules for sensor processing, actuator control, and behavior coordination that fully utilize currently available electronics technology for the construction of mini-robots which are able to show rich autonomous behaviors.

Additionally, practically all common USB or serial device can be attached to extend its sensor and actor capabilities. To name some applied extensions for the RoboCup, the SICK TiM571 is used to perform online SLAM and the captured video is offered via a WebSocket based webserver. An ORBBEC Astra S RGBD camera is used for high precision table top detection and interaction.

3   System Architecture

Our service robots employ distributed systems with multiple clients sharing information over network. On these clients there are numerous software components written in different programming languages. Such heterogeneous systems require abstraction on several levels.

Figure 2 gives an overview of the multiple layers of abstraction in the cooperating robot systems. Each column represents one type of robot. The behavior level (blue) represents the highest level of abstraction for all robots. This can be *skills* or complex *behaviors*. The robot specific software (green) and hardware component interfaces (red) are unified with the BonSAI Sensor Actuator Abstraction Layer (yellow). Even skills from the small AMiRo can be seamlessly integrated into the behavior of the service robots.

Thus, software components can be easily exchanged without changing any behaviors. The system architecture also abstracts from the middleware which is handled on the component layer. The software dependency tree of the system is completely modeled in the description of a *system distribution* which consists of a collection of so called *recipes* [6]. In order to foster reproducibility/traceability

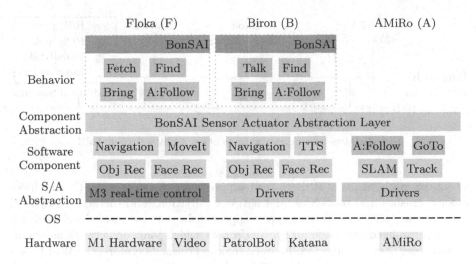

Fig. 2. System architecture of ToBI's service robots (Color figure online)

and potential software (component) re-use of the ToBI system, we provide a full specification in our online catalog platform[1].

The catalog provides detailed information about the soft- and hardware system including all utilized software components, as well as the facility to execute live system tests and experiments remotely. In order to gain access to our remote experiment execution infrastructure please contact the authors.

3.1 Communication Architecture

The communication between software components is mainly based on the Robotic Service Bus (RSB) [8] providing an API which abstracts from different transports (e.g. in-process, socket, Spread) and integrates well with ROS-based nodes. Figure 3 shows the current middleware-oriented communication infrastructure. Numerous essential applications for Floka and Biron have been realized using RSB and ROS. Thus, we decided to run these two systems in conjunction locally on every robot. The message exchange between ROS nodes and RSB participants is handled by ROS4RSB applications, being message bridges living in both habitats. The only exception is the AMiRo due to its hardware constraints in processing power. Therefore, RSB has been chosen as the sole communication bus locally because of its more resource efficient handling of messages [8].

Facing diverse multi-robot setups, ToBIrelies on RSB over Wi-Fi for robot-robot communication. The decision has been made due to the Spread transport mechanism for group communication [13] which is one of the exchangeable

---

[1] https://toolkit.cit-ec.uni-bielefeld.de/systems/versions/robocup-champion-2016-20 16-champion.

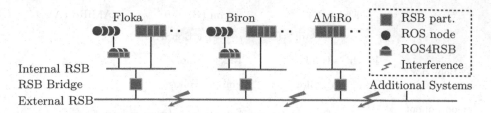

Fig. 3. Intra- and inter-communication architecture of ToBI

transport mechanisms of RSB. Spread supports a rich fault model that includes process crashes and recoveries, and network partitions and merges. Thus, RSB outperforms ROS's multi-master [14] approach in our use case, since ROS still uses a centralized approach for syncing robots which join the network as well as peer-to-peer socket connection between remote nodes. Therefore, the Wi-Fi communication channel is handled by RSB exclusively. Since the small channel bandwidth between the robots does not allow massive data exchange, only selected messages are forwarded via an RSB Bridge from the highly loaded internal communications to the external common bus.

3.2 Reusable Behavior Modeling

For modeling the robot behavior in a flexible manner ToBI uses the Bon-SAI framework. It is a domain-specific library that builds up on the concept of sensors and actuators that allows the linking of perception to action [15]. These are organized into robot *skills* that represent the basic unit of the robot's actions. These basic units are combined into *behaviors* with certain strategies for an informed decision making.

To support the easy construction of more complex robot behavior we have improved the control level abstraction of the framework. BonSAI supports modeling of the control-flow using State Chart XML which can be combined, hierarchically. The coordination engine serves as a sequencer for the overall system by executing BonSAI *skills* to construct the desired robot behavior. Skills can be triggered asynchronously and communicate via events with the coordination engine. This also allows a flexible delegation to other robotic platforms. The BonSAI framework has been released under an open source license.

4   Selected Robot Skills

The performance in the Finals targeted a futuristic apartment scenario where a heterogeneous set of robots is available for diverse tasks (cf. Fig. 4(a)). All robots shared their position and state via a common RSB connection using Wi-Fi so that an additional PC was able to visualize the current common inner world model representation of all robots (cf. Fig. 4(b)).

(a) Final task scenario   (b) Common internal representation

Fig. 4. Final task scenario showing Biron, Floka, and AMiRo

Biron acted as a common domestic worker performing GPSR, Floka as a novel robot with sophisticated grasping skills which were going to be presented, and AMiRos equipped with a LIDAR being the apartment's watchdogs. One human host resided in the apartment's living room with Floka, Biron, and one AMiRo. Additionally, one visiting guest entered the apartment through a long hall way (≈8m) where another two AMiRos were located.

4.1 Multi-robot Interaction

Multi-robot interaction comes into play if parallel but coordinated tasks need to be performed or an event requires an instant reaction at different places. This is shown in the first part of the Final. When a guest appears at the door, the AMiRos and Biron robots collectively solve the task of accompanying the guest on the way to their owner. AMiRos waited in the hall way, acting as a mobile tag while attaching to traversing legs. The first AMiRo followed the guest for a certain distance until it handed over the guest seamlessly to the next one. Positioning information were transferred to Biron, so that it was finally able to take over the guest and introduce him to the owner.

The crucial part of applying multi-robotics is the provision of a fail-safe communication channel and the task allocation. Intercommunication between the robots via Wi-Fi is inherently fragile due to instability in the RoboCup@Home arena caused by noise or coverage, joining and detaching robots, or hardware failures. These link layer interferences cannot be completely eliminated by tweaking the network drivers, e.g. maximizing channel utilization, minimizing connection abortion, or reducing reconnection delays. Thus, we solved the remaining connection abortions on the application layer by our proposed communication (cf. Fig. 3) and behavior architecture (cf. Fig. 2) to keep the multi-robot setup running. Facing the task allocation, we decided to design every robot fully autonomous with state machines loosely linked to each other. Thereby, information exchange is reduced to percepts or symbols representing the current state or requested task allocations.

On every robot runs a stand-alone behavior based on a state-machine representing the robot's capabilities relevant for the task. On the basis of societal agents [16], BonSAI realizes the connection and abstraction layer to allow transparent access to the sensorimotor features, skills, or behaviors of its own or every other remotely accessible feature. This approach makes no difference between the methods used to be triggered by intra- or inter-robot behaviors. If communication breaks, the behaviors define fall-back strategies similar to those which may deal with blocked navigation goals or other unexpected events (Fig. 4).

4.2   Error Handling and Reporting in GPSR

The GPSR task is a challenge to foster the ability of robots to interpret a natural language command and solve the task by combining capabilities. We propose an approach that not only extracts the task from a given sentence but even allows the robot to handle unexpected situations and report by verbal feedback to the operator. Hierarchical grammars are used to cluster the task into eight main-categories based on the sentence's predicate. For each category a set of verbs is defined directly in the grammar. Subcategories of actions are defined by type (person, object or location) and number of the objects in the sentence. Pronouns are replaced by object designators. All gathered information about the task is then stored in a memory as a sequence of action subcategories. Based on this subcategory, BonSAI *behaviors* are executed which directly trigger *skills* or reusable *behaviors* of Stage 1 (Sect. 3.2). These also store information to memory about their success or failure. Thus, the behavior framework allows to trace back a task performance and verbally report about each subtask. ToBI was one of the first teams realizing such a generic approach within the EE-GPSR test.

Fig. 5. The grasping pipeline. On the left output of the CLAFU component is displayed. The RVIZ environment including Floka, the detected planar surface as well as fitted superquadrics are visible in green. (Color figure online)

4.3   Flexible Grasping Considering Object Shapes

Our previous grasping pipeline involved a basic grasp generator producing many potential grasp poses (up to thousands) around a given center pose of the target object. The number of generated grasp poses was implicitly determined by an equidistant sampling around the view-aligned bounding box of the object's point cloud, i.e. neither shape nor orientation of the object were considered. All potential grasps were fed into the MoveIt! [17] planning pipeline to check for feasibility. The first adequate grasp pose was finally selected for grasping. In order to improve the pipeline in speed as well as precision, a new grasp generator was adapted from work by Haschke [18]. The grasp generator is composed of two nodes, an object fitting node and a grasp generation node.

A preprocessed point cloud alongside additional information regarding the recognized type of object(s) is generated by the Classification Fusion (CLAFU) [19] component. The point cloud of objects newly encountered are further fitted by superquadrics. Considered shapes are boxes, spheres and cylinders. The grasp generator analytically generates a reduced set of grasp poses exploiting the shape information and object dimensions. For a box, grasps will be aligned to opposing faces; for cylinders and spheres, the arm will approach from the most comfortable direction and thus resolve the redundancy introduced by the shape's symmetry. The grasps will be filtered for feasibility and collision with the table exploiting the object's and hand's bounding boxes. All remaining grasps are ranked according to several criteria, including preference for side vs. top grasp, comfort, and motion distance of the hand. Thus, only a reduced set of 1 to 10 grasps per object is fed into the MoveIt! [17] planning pipeline for a final feasibility check, determining a collision-free grasp trajectory.

5   Analysis and Lessons Learned

In Fig. 6 the results of the 5 best teams in the predefined tests of RoboCup@Home 2016 are shown. ToBIachieved best performances in the Person Recognition, Navigation, GPSR, Restaurant, and EE-GPSR tests. For most of the required capabilities, available standard libraries were used. Thus, it were not the algorithmic parts in the components that made any difference. The reasons why teams fail in some of the challenges are multifaceted. In many cases,

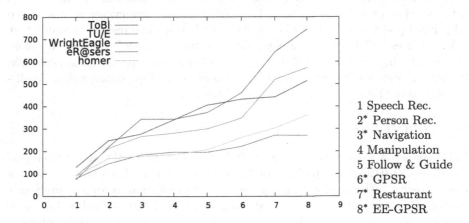

Fig. 6. Accumulated scores from the pre-defined tests in RoboCup@Home. The numbers on the x-axis refer to tests, the X^*-tests have been won by the ToBI-Team.

bugs in the code are a major cause. In other cases, unexpected interferences, external noise, and untested environmental conditions lead to a break-down. At the RoboCup site in Leipzig, our team experienced several of these but learned to deal with it. For example, the floor of the hall was very slippery for the wheels of the Floka robot; thus, we needed to change the drive strategy and odometry model of its omnidirectional base; the multi-robot coordination relied on a very fragile Wi-Fi on-site, so that the middleware was required to deal with partial communication break-downs (cf. Sect. 3.1). This year, we changed to a new people detection and tracking framework [20]. Based on this, a re-usable *following behavior* was implemented that also included strategies for re-initialization, if a person was lost. This BonSAI *behavior* is re-used in the Navigation, Following and Guiding, GPSR, and Restaurant tasks. Introducing new basic skills typically requires a high need for bug-fixing until all possible side effects have been explored. This emphasizes the importance of the development framework used within the competition. We exploited a dedicated toolchain for reproducible experimentation in robotics [21]. In the Cognitive Interaction Toolkit (CITK), there is a versioned description of any – incrementally developed – system distribution including all software and data dependencies which is automatically built on a continuous integration (CI) server. This allows to track down any system change that might have caused an error or repaired it. The CITK also provides an automated testing environment [7]. For RoboCup@Home, we implemented a complete person-following test utilizing a simulation environment based on Morse which is included in the CITK catalog entry referenced in Sect. 3. This test was automatically executed by the CI server as a replicated experiment which helped to stabilize the person detection and tracking *skills* as well as the following *behavior*.

Another important aspect is to design robot behaviors for the complete competition and not only for a single test. For example, furniture or persons sometimes blocked navigation goals in the apartment; thus, the robot needed to deal with these situations all the time – not only when mentioned in the rulebook. A general behavior for memorizing and reporting about these events even achieved additional points for the team in the EE-GPSR test. The reasoning about task performances will be a critical capability for future RoboCup@Home developments. This includes dealing with situations that require the delegation subtasks because a robot is stuck, needs help, or is too far away. Here concepts from multi-robotics come into play as already argued before.

6   Conclusion

In this paper, we have described the main features of the ToBI system which won the RoboCup@Home competition in 2016. This result has been achieved with a team mostly consisting of bachelor and master students that were completely new to RoboCup, with a newly introduced Floka robot, and with a Final performance that heavily relied on a fragile WiFi communication between multiple robots.

Nevertheless, the ToBI robots gave the most stable performance throughout the competition. New elements have been introduced like reporting on success and failure of tasks assigned to the robot in GSPR, re-entering into the arena through a closed door in the Navigation task, the flexible grasping considering object shapes in the Final together with a multi-robot cooperation where a person is handed over from one robot device to the next one. There are a couple of essential elements that made up the success of the team. First of all, we improved the robustness of the ToBI system on all levels, starting with a fail-prove communication framework, an automated testing procedure for new component skills, a re-usable behavior definition that is used and tested across multiple tests, and a development approach that aims at reproducible robotic experiments. Finally, there was an inherent team spirit which highly motivated each individual team member. All these aspects contributed to ToBI's overall success.

Acknowledgments. This research/work was supported by the Cluster of Excellence Cognitive Interaction Technology 'CITEC' (EXC 277) at Bielefeld University, which is funded by the German Research Foundation (DFG).

Thanks to the student team members of 2016 Marvin Barther, Julian Exner, Jonas Gerlach, Johannes Kummert, Luca Michael Lach, Henri Neumann, Nils Neumann, Leroy Rügemer, Tobias Schumacher, Dominik Sixt.

References

1. Wachsmuth, S., Holz, D., Rudinac, M., Ruiz-del Solar, J.: RoboCup@Home - benchmarking domestic service robots. In: Proceedings of the Twenty-Ninth AAAI Conference on Artificial Intelligence, AAAI 2015, pp. 4328–4329. AAAI Press (2015)
2. Wrede, B., Kleinehagenbrock, M., Fritsch, J.: Towards an integrated robotic system for interactive learning in a social context. In: Proceedings IEEE/RSJ International Conference on Intelligent Robots and Systems - IROS 2006, Bejing (2006)
3. Lohse, M., Siepmann, F., Wachsmuth, S.: A modeling framework for user-driven iterative design of autonomous systems. Int. J. Soc. Robot. **6**(1), 121–139 (2014)
4. Amigoni, F., Reggiani, M., Schiaffonati, V.: An insightful comparison between experiments in mobile robotics and in science. Auton. Robots **27**(4), 313–325 (2009)
5. Meyer zu Borgsen, S., Korthals, T., Wachsmuth, S.: ToBI-Team of Bielefeld The Human-Robot Interaction System for RoboCup@Home 2016 (2016)
6. Lier, F., Hanheide, M., Natale, L., Schulz, S., Weisz, J., Wachsmuth, S., Wrede, S.: Towards automated system and experiment reproduction in robotics. In: Burgard, W. (ed.) 2016 IEEE/RSJ International Conference on Intelligent Robots and Systems (IROS). IEEE (2016)
7. Lier, F., Lütkebohle, I., Wachsmuth, S.: Towards automated execution and evaluation of simulated prototype HRI experiments. In: HRI 2014 Proceedings of the 2014 ACM/IEEE International Conference On Human-robot Interaction, pp. 230–231. ACM (2014)
8. Wienke, J., Wrede, S.: A middleware for collaborative research in experimental robotics. In: IEEE/SICE International Symposium on System Integration (SII2011), pp. 1183–1190. IEEE (2011)

9. Siepmann, F., Ziegler, L., Kortkamp, M., Wachsmuth, S.: Deploying a modeling framework for reusable robot behavior to enable informed strategies for domestic service robots. Robot. Auton. Syst. **63**, 619–631 (2012)
10. Holthaus, P., Leichsenring, C., Bernotat, J., Richter, V., Pohling, M., Carlmeyer, B., Köster, N., Meyer zu Borgsen, S., Zorn, R., Schiffhauer, B., Engelmann, K.F., Lier, F., Schulz, S., Cimiano, P., Eyssel, F.A., Hermann, T., Kummert, F., Schlangen, D., Wachsmuth, S., Wagner, P., Wrede, B., Wrede, S.: How to address smart homes with a social robot? A multi-modal corpus of user interactions with an intelligent environment. In: Language Resources and Evaluation Conference, European Language Resources Association (ELRA) (2016)
11. Richter, V., Carlmeyer, B., Lier, F., Meyer zu Borgsen, S., Kummert, F., Wachsmuth, S., Wrede, B.: Are you talking to me? Improving the robustness of dialogue systems in a multi party HRI scenario by incorporating gaze direction and lip movement of attendees. In: Proceedings of the Fourth International Conference on Human-agent Interaction. ACM Digital Library (2016)
12. Herbrechtsmeier, S., Korthals, T., Schöpping, T., Rückert, U.: A modular & customizable open-source mini robot platform. In: 20th International Conference on Systems Theory, Control and Computing (ICSTCC), SINAIA, Romania (2016)
13. Amir, Y., Danilov, C., Miskin-Amir, M., Schultz, J., Stanton, J.: The spread toolkit: architecture and performance. Technical report (2004)
14. Koubaa, A.: Robot Operating System (ROS): The Complete Reference, vol. 1. Springer International Publishing, Heidelberg (2016). doi:10.1007/978-3-319-26054-9
15. Siepmann, F., Wachsmuth, S.: A modeling framework for reusable social behavior. In: De Silva, R., Reidsma, D. (eds.) Work in Progress Workshop Proceedings ICSR 2011, pp. 93–96. Springer, Amsterdam (2011)
16. Arkin, R.C.: Behavior-Based Robotics. Intelligent Robots and Autonomous Agents. The MIT Press, Cambridge (1998)
17. Chitta, S., Sucan, I., Cousins, S.: Moveit!. IEEE Robot. Autom. Mag. **19**(1), 18–19 (2012)
18. Haschke, R.: Grasping and manipulation of unknown objects based on visual and tactile feedback. In: Carbone, G., Gomez-Bravo, F. (eds.) Motion and Operation Planning of Robotic Systems. MMS, vol. 29, pp. 91–109. Springer, Cham (2015). doi:10.1007/978-3-319-14705-5_4
19. Ziegler, L.: The attentive robot companion: learning spatial information from observation and verbal interaction. Ph.D. thesis (2015)
20. Dondrup, C., Bellotto, N., Jovan, F., Hanheide, M.: Real-time multisensor people tracking for human-robot spatial interaction. In: Workshop on Machine Learning for Social Robotics at International Conference on Robotics and Automation (ICRA), ICRA/IEEE (2015)
21. Lier, F., Wienke, J., Nordmann, A., Wachsmuth, S., Wrede, S.: The cognitive interaction toolkit – improving reproducibility of robotic systems experiments. In: Brugali, D., Broenink, J.F., Kroeger, T., MacDonald, B.A. (eds.) SIMPAR 2014. LNCS, vol. 8810, pp. 400–411. Springer, Cham (2014). doi:10.1007/978-3-319-11900-7_34

Improvements for a Robust Production in the RoboCup Logistics League 2016

Tim Niemueller[1]($\boxtimes$), Tobias Neumann[2], Christoph Henke[3],
Sebastian Schönitz[3], Sebastian Reuter[3], Alexander Ferrein[2],
Sabina Jeschke[3], and Gerhard Lakemeyer[1]

[1] Knowledge-Based Systems Group, RWTH Aachen University, Aachen, Germany
niemueller@kbsg.rwth-aachen.de
[2] MASCOR Institute, FH Aachen University of Applied Sciences, Aachen, Germany
[3] Institute Cluster IMA/ZLW & IfU, RWTH Aachen University, Aachen, Germany

Abstract. In 2016, the RoboCup Logistics League (RCLL) scenario has received only minor changes. The Carologistics team used this time to stabilize and improve several of its system's components to make overall production more robust and support a more elaborated domain modeling. This has been made possible especially through our simulation environment. We describe the major aspects of our efforts that led to winning the competition for the third time in a row.

1 Introduction

The RoboCup Logistics League focuses on multi-robot coordination, through application of methods of, e.g., automated reasoning, planning, and scheduling. 2016 was a year of stabilization in terms of the rules of the game. The Carologistics team has made improvements to several software components, especially to the basic behaviors and the domain and behavior modeling for the incremental reasoning agent. In this paper, we report on the specific aspects we consider to be key to our repeated success. In particular the Gazebo-based simulation environment developed over the past few years has helped tremendously to manifest these improvements while also working on enhancements for functional components in parallel. We also describe our outreach efforts beyond the RCLL by establishing a simulation competition at the ICAPS conference with international partners from the planning community.

Our team has participated in RoboCup 2012–2016 and the RoboCup German Open (GO) 2013–2015. We were able to win the GO 2014 and 2015 as well as the RoboCup 2014, 2015, and 2016 (cf. Figure 1) in particular demonstrating flexible task coordination, robust collision avoidance and self-localization. We have publicly released our software stack used in 2016 in particular including our high-level reasoning components[1] [1].

This paper is based on last year's edition [2] highlighting the specific advances and activities towards RoboCup 2016. For a description of the RCLL we refer to [3–5]. In Section 2 we give an overview of our hardware and software platform. We

---

[1] Software stack: https://www.fawkesrobotics.org/projects/rcll2016-release/.

© Springer International Publishing AG 2017
S. Behnke et al. (Eds.): RoboCup 2016, LNAI 9776, pp. 589–600, 2017.
https://doi.org/10.1007/978-3-319-68792-6_49

Fig. 1. Final round of the RoboCup logistics league 2016 in Leipzig, Germany. Teams carologistics (laptop on top) and Solidus (water bottle, background) are competing.

introduce some specific improvements to functional components in Sect. 3 before describing our behavior components in more detail in Sect. 4. We highlight our simulation in Sect. 5 before giving an overview of our continued contributions to the RCLL in Sect. 6 and concluding in Sect. 7.

2   The Carologistics Platform

The standard robot platform of this league is the Robotino by Festo Didactic [6]. The Robotino is developed for research and education and features omnidirectional locomotion, a gyroscope and webcam, infrared distance sensors, and bumpers. The teams may equip the robot with additional sensors and computation devices as well as a gripper device for product handling [2].

2.1   Hardware System

The robot system currently in use is based on the Robotino 3. The modified Robotino used by the Carologistics RoboCup team is shown in Fig. 2 and features two additional webcams, a RealSense depth camera and a Sick laser range finder. The webcam on top of the robot is used to recognize the machine signal lights, the one attached to the pillar of the robot is used to identify machine markers, and the depth camera below the robot's gripper is used to recognize the conveyor belt. We use the Sick TiM571 laser scanner for collision avoidance and self-localization. It has a scanning range of 25 m at a resolution of $1/3°$. An additional laptop increases the computation power and allows for more elaborate methods for self-localization, computer vision, and navigation.

Fig. 2. Carologistics Robotino 2015/2016

Several parts were custom-made for our robot platform. Most notably, a gripper based on Festo fin-ray fingers and 3D-printed parts is used for product handling. It is able to adjust for slight lateral and height offsets using stepper motors for high positioning accuracy. The motor is controlled with an additional Arduino board with a motor shield. The motors smoothly increase and decrease speed to avoid positioning errors. As no encoders are attached, a micro switch for initializing the lateral axis position is used.

2.2 Software Frameworks

The software system of the Carologistics robots combines Fawkes [7] and ROS [8] allowing to use software components from both systems. The overall system, however, is integrated using Fawkes and ROS is used especially for its 3D visualization capabilities. The overall software structure is inspired by the three-layer architecture [9]. It consists of a deliberative layer for high-level reasoning, a reactive execution layer for breaking down high-level commands and monitoring their execution, and a feedback control layer for hardware access and functional components. The communication between single components – implemented as *plugins* – is realized by a hybrid blackboard and messaging approach [7].

The development is split into a core and domain-specific parts. The core framework is developed in public and has just seen its 1.0 stable release after ten years of development.[2] The RCLL domain-specific parts are developed in private and have been made available in the past three years. This has been awarded with the International Harting Open Source Award [10].

3 Advances to Functional Software Components

Here, we discuss some advancements made in 2016 to the plethora of different software components required to run a multi-robot system for the RCLL.

3.1 Basic Components

For this year, we have developed a module for direct communication with the Robotino microcontroller, fully bypassing and eliminating the need for OpenRobotino. A major issue was that OpenRobotino has no concept of time and the age of sensor and odometry data could not be determined once they arrived to our system. Furthermore, a new velocity and acceleration controller has been implemented resulting in smoother driving.

3.2 Driving

For the last years we have been using a stateless path planner with collision avoidance [11] which initially has been developed for the Middle Size League

---

[2] Fawkes website at https://www.fawkesrobotics.org.

by the AllemaniACs team, which we have ported to the Fawkes framework and adapted to use the capability of a holonomic platform like the Robotino. Since the rule change in the RCLL to use the MPS machines in 2015 the playing field lost a great amount of free space which is furthermore often occluded by the MPS stations. This forced us to cope with new situations for our path planner. While we used a forward facing laser for the last years, this season we deployed a second backward facing laser which increased our field of view to 360°. This way obstacles could be seen longer, which resulted in a more stable path planning and realization. Furthermore using this, we could also start to drive backwards which decreased the driving time overall, but especially the time needed to leave an MPS after interfacing with it.

3.3   MPS Detection and Approaching

The MPS stations are detected in two ways, using the tag placed on the machines and a line fitting algorithm on the laser data. To approach the MPS during a game, first the tag detection is used to validate the correct machine and for a first rough alignment. In a second step the laser lines are used for a more precise alignment especially regarding the rotation. During the exploration phase both methods are used concurrently while searching for machines.

3.4   Light Signal Vision

A multi-modal perception component for robust detection of the light signal state on the field has been developed specifically for this domain [12]. It limits the search within the image by means of the laser-detected position of the machine as depicted in Fig. 3. This provides us with a higher robustness towards ambiguous backgrounds, for example colored shirts in the audience. Even if the machine cannot be detected, the vision features graceful degradation by using a geometric search heuristic to identify the signal, loosing some of the robustness towards the mentioned disturbances.

Fig. 3. Vision-based light-signal detection during production (post-processed for legibility) [2].

3.5   Conveyor Belt Detection

The conveyor belts are rather narrow compared to the products and thus require a precise handling. The tolerable error margin is in the range of about ± 3 mm. The marker on a machine allows to determine the lateral offset from the gripper to the conveyor belt. It gives a 3D pose of the marker with respect to the camera and thus the robot. However, this requires a precise calibration of the conveyor belt with respect to the marker. While ideally this would be the same for each

machine, in practice there is an offset which
would need to be calibrated per station [2].
Therefore we are using the approach described
in 3.3 for a pre-alignment which is then
improved with a new depth based conveyor
detection, where a point cloud from an Intel
RealSense F200 camera is used to detect the
conveyor as shown in Fig. 4. This is done by
pruning the point cloud towards our region
of interest by fusing the initial guess of the
belt gathered by the machine position detected

Fig. 4. Depth based conveyor belt
detection. Left RGB picture, right
point cloud with detected conveyor belt and its normal.

with the laser scanner. Afterwards a plane search is done to detect the precise
pose of the front-plane of the conveyor belt and its normal.

4   High-Level Decision Making and Task Coordination

The behavior generating components are separated into three
layers, as depicted in Fig. 5: the
low-level processing for perception and actuation, a mid-level
reactive layer, and a high-level
reasoning layer. The layers are
combined following an adapted
hybrid deliberative-reactive coordination paradigm.

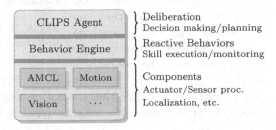

Fig. 5. Behavior layer separation [13]

The robot group needs to cooperate on its tasks, that is, the robots communicate information about their current intentions, acquire exclusive control
over resources like machines, and share their beliefs about the current state of
the environment. Currently, we employ a distributed, local-scope, and incremental reasoning approach [14]. This means that each robot determines only its own
action (local scope) to perform next (incremental) and coordinates with the others through communication (distributed), as opposed to a central instance which
plans globally for all robots at the same time or for multi-step plans.

In the following we describe the reactive and deliberative layers of the behavior components. For computational and energy efficiency, the behavior components need also to coordinate activation of the lower level components.

4.1   Lua-Based Behavior Engine

In previous work we have developed the Lua-based Behavior Engine (BE) [15].
It serves as the reactive layer to interface between the low- and high-level systems. The BE is based on hybrid state machines (HSM). They can be depicted as
directed graphs with nodes representing states for action execution, and/or monitoring of actuation, perception, and internal state. Edges denote jump conditions

implemented as Boolean functions. For the active state of a state machine, all outgoing conditions are evaluated, typically at about 15 Hz. If a condition fires, the active state is changed to the target node of the edge. A table of variables holds information like the world model, for example storing numeric values for object positions. It remedies typical problems of state machines like fast growing number of states or variable data passing from one state to another. Skills are implemented using the light-weight, extensible scripting language Lua.

Separating the different behaviors of the robot into small parts or skills improves maintainability. Each of these small skills can be put together to form greater and more complex behaviors while each parts stays a small maintainable component. This allows for the opportunity to tune the behaviors for specific situations.

In 2016 we analyzed the time needed in each part of our skills to identify the time consuming behaviors. We then focused our efforts on improving these skills. Doing so, we decreased the time needed to align at a machine while at the same time we were able to increase the robustness

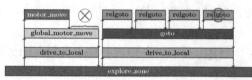

Fig. 6. Used game-time assigned to different skills used during an (simulated) example game.

of the alignment. In the example in Fig. 6, we eliminated the time in `global_motor_move` after the sub-skill `motor_move` returned and also the sub-calls to local movement via `relgoto` (red crossed circles).

4.2 Reasoning and Planning

The problem at hand with its intertwined world model updating and execution naturally lends itself to a representation as a fact base with update rules for triggering behavior for certain beliefs. We have chosen the CLIPS rules engine [16], because using incremental reasoning the robot can take the next best action at any point in time whenever the robot is idle. This avoids costly re-planning (as with approaches using classical planners) and it allows us to cope with incomplete knowledge about the world. Additionally, it is computationally inexpensive. More details about the general agent design and the CLIPS engine are in [17].

The agent for 2016 is based on the continued development effort of our CLIPS-based agent [13]. We have finalized generic world model synchronization capabilities that allow to mark specific facts in the fact base to be shared with other robots. While each robot acts as an own autonomous agent, a central robot dynamically determined through leader election is responsible for generating a consistent view and distributing it to all robots. This way each agent can still work autonomously if the connection to the other robots are interrupted and no information is lost if a single robot (or even the leader) fails. Furthermore, we increased the sophistication of our domain model. The robot group robustly produced lower complexity products during the competition and was able to achieve multiple deliveries per game. There were also partial productions of higher complexity products. Robots were also able to cooperate on MPS usage and we could minimize the MPS handover times.

We have evaluated several different possibilities for the implementation of agent programs in the RCLL including CLIPS, OpenPRS, and YAGI [17] and are making efforts towards a centralized global planning system.

5   Multi-robot Simulation in Gazebo

The character of the RCLL game emphasizes research and application of methods for efficient planning, scheduling, and reasoning on the optimal work order of production processes handled by a group of robots. An aspect that distinctly separates this league from others is that the environment itself acts as an agent by posting orders and controlling the machines' reactions. This is what we call

environment agency. In the RCLL, the large playing field and material costs are prohibitive for teams to set up a complete scenario for testing, let alone to have two teams of robots. Additionally, members of related communities like planning and reasoning might not want to deal with the full software and system complexity. Still they often welcome relevant scenarios to test and present their research. Therefore, we have created an *open simulation environment* [18,19] based on Gazebo³ (see Fig. 7).

Fig. 7. Simulation of the RCLL 2015 with MPS stations [14].

The simulation played a vital role to improve production performance in 2016. Especially the development of a new method of approaching an MPS station meant that experiments on real robots were not possible during several periods. Using the simulation, the domain designers could continuously work on enhancing the production with new capabilities and ensuring an overall robust action selection (through appropriate encoding and prioritization of situations to evaluate) and coordination for multiple robots. Moving from simulation to the real robots is facilitated by exchanging simulation by hardware accessing software components that deal with acquiring sensor data and commanding actuation. The middle and higher levels of the behavior separation are agnostic to this and remain unchanged. The simulation even models network packet loss as is to be expected during RoboCup to avoid overfitting to an environment behaving nicer than in reality. The simulation has also been used for a fully automated tournament of several different task-level executives [17].

5.1   Logistics Robots Planning Competition at ICAPS

As an outcome of the presentation of the RCLL at the workshop on Planning in Robotics at the International Conference on Automated Planning and Scheduling (ICAPS) in 2015 [14], a planning competition in simulation is being prepared.

---

³ More information, media, the software itself, and documentation are available at https://www.fawkesrobotics.org/projects/llsf-sim/.

At ICAPS 2016, a tutorial was held to present the idea, gather feedback, and kickstart interested teams [3]. The particular challenges are to efficiently plan in short time with time-bounded dynamic orders and to provide an effective executive to execute multi-robot plans. Performing the competition in simulation provides a nice alignment with the RCLL. Options have been discussed to perform parts of this competition on real robots in the future. One possibility could be for the winning team of the ICAPS simulation competition to participate in the RCLL, or for the finals to be performed with real robots. The general idea is to foster collaboration and exchange among the planning and robotics communities. The first competition will be held at the ICAPS 2017 at Carnegie Mellon University. For the Carologistics, one benefit is the possibility to compare planning layers in the RCLL scenario which are currently developed. Further information is available at http://www.robocup-logistics.org/sim-comp.

6   League Advancements and Continued Involvement

We have been active members of the Technical, Organizational, and Executive Committees and proposed various ground-breaking changes for the league like merging the two playing fields and using physical processing machines in 2015 [4,5]. Additionally we introduced and currently maintain the autonomous referee box for the competition [20] and develop the open simulation environment described above. We have also been a driving factor in the establishment of the RoboCup Industrial umbrella league [5]. It serves to coordinate and bring closer the efforts of industrially inspired RoboCup leagues. The first steps are the unification to a common referee box system (Sect. 6.1) and the introduction of a cross-over challenge (Sect. 6.4).

6.1   RCLL Referee Box and MPS Stations

The autonomous referee box (refbox) was introduced in 2013 by the Carologistics team [4]. With the goal to automate the playing field and ease the workload of referees the refbox acts as an agent, thereby creating the smart factory aspect of the RCLL scenario. It creates a randomized game layout and schedule and determines appropriate field reactions based on incoming MPS sensor data and robot communication using an extensible and flexible knowledge-based system. It provides a strong industrial grounding [20].

For the 2016 season the changes where moderate, e.g., a first approach for tracking workpieces through barcode scanners was developed, which will be used in 2017. More importantly, the RCLL refbox serves as the foundation for a *common refbox* for the new *RoboCup Industrial* (RC-I) umbrella league.[4] Based on a common framework the individual scenarios can be modeled, starting with the RCLL, RoboCup@Work, and the common cross-over challenge (cf. Section 6.4).

---

[4] Project website: https://github.com/robocup-industrial/rci-refbox.

6.2 Public Release of Full Software Stack

Over the past ten years, we have developed the *Fawkes Robot Software Framework* [7] as a robust foundation to deal with the challenges of robotics applications in general, and in the context of RoboCup in particular. It has been developed and used in several leagues over the past few years [1] as visible in Fig. 8. Recently, the most active example is in the *RoboCup Logistics League* [19].

The Carologistics is the first team in the RCLL to publicly release their software stack. Teams in other leagues have made similar releases before. What makes ours unique is that it provides a complete and *ready-to-run package with the full software* (and some additions and fixes) that we used in the competition in 2015. This in particular *includes* the complete *task-level executive* component, that is the strategic decision making and behavior generating software. This component was typically held back or only released in small parts in previous software releases by other teams (for any league).

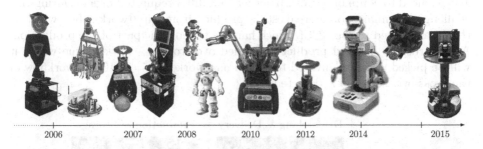

Fig. 8. Robots running (parts of) Fawkes which were or are used for the development of the framework and its components [1].

6.3 RoboCup Logistics League Winter School

In December 2015, the Carologistics Team organized the week-long RoboCup Logistics League Winter School in Aachen (see Fig. 9). Within these days participants from Asia and Europe were introduced to the RoboCup Logistics League

Fig. 9. Participants and the carologistics at the RCLL winter school in 2015.

and the relevant components of the Fawkes software framework. The winter school was structured by theoretical sessions where members of the Carologistics Team presented topics like perception, navigation, simulation, and behavior design. Afterwards hands-on sessions with the Fawkes software framework deepened the theoretical sessions and were applied in simulation and in the real environment. This has been made possible through the generous support of Festo Didactic SE and a RoboCup Federation grant. Videos and further information is available at https://www.carologistics.org/winter-school-2015/.

6.4 RoboCup Industrial Cross-Over Challenge

As a first step for closer cooperation for the industry-inspired leagues under the RoboCup Industrial umbrella, together with stakeholders from the @Work league we have initiated a crossover challenge [21]. It describes several milestones towards closer cooperation. Within the challenge two teams from both leagues need to commonly work together to fulfill a requested order. During this challenge a human worker requests a product from an @work-robot which is then transmitted to the RCLL which handles the logistic part of the production. Afterwards the finished product is handed over to the @work league where it will be picked up and delivered to the human worker. In Fig. 10 the workflow of the cross-over scenario is depicted.

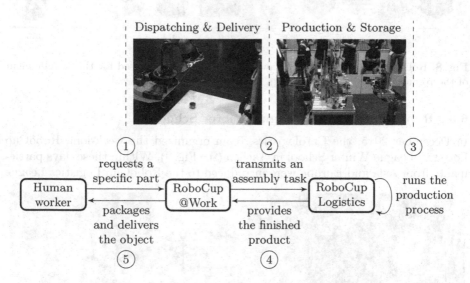

Fig. 10. Workflow of the cross-over scenario between @Work and the RCLL [21].

7 Conclusion

In 2016, we have further adapted to the new game. We upgraded our custom hardware gripper based on the feedback of the 2015 season, and further adapted and extended the behavior and functional components. We have also continued our contributions to the league as a whole through active participation in the league's committees, publishing papers about the RCLL, and initiating a crossover challenge under the RoboCup Industrial umbrella. The development of the simulation we initiated has been transferred to a public project where other teams have joined the effort and it is used in a spin-off simulation competition. Most notably, however, we have released the complete software stack including all components and configurations as a ready-to-run package.

Due to changes in the the the RCLL, we expect products to be identified and tracked by means of a barcode in the future. This allows to award points for intermediate production steps. We plan to integrate a detection component to be run on our robot based, e.g., the ZBar[5] and OpenCV[6] computer vision libraries. This would allow for detecting and overcoming world model inconsistencies.

The website of the Carologistics RoboCup Team with further information and media can be found at https://www.carologistics.org.

Acknowledgement. The team members in 2016 are Alexander Ferrein, Mostafa Gomaa, Christoph Henke, Daniel Künster, Nicolas Limpert, Matthias Löbach, Victor Mataré, Tobias Neumann, Tim Niemueller, Sebastian Reuter, Johannes Rothe, David Schmidt, Sebastian Schönitz, and Frederik Zwilling.

We gratefully acknowledge the financial support of RWTH Aachen University and FH Aachen University of Applied Sciences.

We thank Sick AG, Adolf Hast GmbH & Co. KG and and Xilloc Industrial B.V for sponsoring our efforts by providing hardware and manufacturing support.

F. Zwilling and T. Niemueller were supported by the German National Science Foundation (DFG) research unit *FOR 1513* on Hybrid Reasoning for Intelligent Systems (https://www.hybrid-reasoning.org).

References

1. Niemueller, T., Reuter, S., Ferrein, A.: Fawkes for the RoboCup logistics league. In: RoboCup Symposium 2015 - Development Track (2015)
2. Niemueller, T., Reuter, S., Ewert, D., Ferrein, A., Jeschke, S., Lakemeyer, G.: The carologistics approach to cope with the increased complexity and new challenges of the RoboCup logistics league 2015. In: RoboCup Symposium - Champion Teams Track (2015)
3. Niemueller, T., Karpas, E., Vaquero, T., Timmons, E.: Planning competition for logistics robots in simulation. In: WS on Planning and Robotics (PlanRob) at International Conference on Automated Planning and Scheduling (ICAPS), London, UK (2016)
4. Niemueller, T., Ewert, D., Reuter, S., Ferrein, A., Jeschke, S., Lakemeyer, G.: RoboCup logistics league sponsored by Festo: a competitive factory automation benchmark. In: RoboCup Symposium 2013 (2013)
5. Niemueller, T., Lakemeyer, G., Ferrein, A., Reuter, S., Ewert, D., Jeschke, S., Pensky, D., Karras, U.: Proposal for advancements to the LLSF in 2014 and beyond. In: ICAR - 1st Workshop on Developments in RoboCup Leagues (2013)

---

[5] http://zbar.sourceforge.net/.
[6] http://opencv.org/.

6. Karras, U., Pensky, D., Rojas, O.: Mobile robotics in education and research of logistics. In: IROS 2011 - Workshop on Metrics and Methodologies for Autonomous Robot Teams in Logistics (2011)
7. Niemueller, T., Ferrein, A., Beck, D., Lakemeyer, G.: Design principles of the component-based robot software framework fawkes. In: International Conference on Simulation, Modeling, and Programming for Autonomous Robots (SIMPAR) (2010)
8. Quigley, M., Conley, K., Gerkey, B.P., Faust, J., Foote, T., Leibs, J., Wheeler, R., Ng, A.Y.: ROS: an open-source robot operating system. In: ICRA Workshop on Open Source Software (2009)
9. Gat, E.: Three-layer architectures. In: Kortenkamp, D., Bonasso, R.P., Murphy, R. (eds.) Artificial Intelligence and Mobile Robots, pp. 195–210. MIT Press (1998)
10. Niemueller, T., Neumann, T., Henke, C., Schönitz, S., Reuter, S., Ferrein, A., Jeschke, S., Lakemeyer, G.: International harting open source award 2016: fawkes for the RoboCup logistics league. In: RoboCup Symposium - Harting Award Paper (2016)
11. Jacobs, S., Ferrein, A., Schiffer, S., Beck, D., Lakemeyer, G.: Robust collision avoidance in unknown domestic environments. In: Baltes, J., Lagoudakis, M.G., Naruse, T., Ghidary, S.S. (eds.) RoboCup Symposium 2009 (2009)
12. Mataré, V., Niemueller, T., Lakemeyer, G.: Robust multi-modal detection of industrial signal light towers. In: RoboCup Symposium (2016)
13. Niemueller, T., Lakemeyer, G., Ferrein, A.: Incremental task-level reasoning in a competitive factory automation scenario. In: Proceedings of AAAI Spring Symposium 2013 - Designing Intelligent Robots: Reintegrating AI (2013)
14. Niemueller, T., Lakemeyer, G., Ferrein, A.: The RoboCup logistics league as a benchmark for planning in robotics. In: 25th International Conference on Automated Planning and Scheduling (ICAPS) - WS on Planning in Robotics (2015)
15. Niemueller, T., Ferrein, A., Lakemeyer, G.: A Lua-based behavior engine for controlling the humanoid robot Nao. In: RoboCup Symposium 2009 (2009)
16. Wygant, R.M.: CLIPS: a powerful development and delivery expert system tool. Comput. Ind. Eng. **17**(1–4), 546–549 (1989)
17. Niemueller, T., Zwilling, F., Lakemeyer, G., Löbach, M., Reuter, S., Jeschke, S., Ferrein, A.: Cyber-physical system intelligence. In: Jeschke, S., Brecher, C., Song, H., Rawat, D.B. (eds.) Industrial Internet of Things. SSWT, pp. 447–472. Springer, Cham (2017). doi:10.1007/978-3-319-42559-7_17
18. Zwilling, F., Niemueller, T., Lakemeyer, G.: Simulation for the RoboCup logistics league with real-world environment agency and multi-level abstraction. In: RoboCup Symposium (2014)
19. Niemueller, T., Reuter, S., Ewert, D., Ferrein, A., Jeschke, S., Lakemeyer, G.: Decisive factors for the success of the carologistics RoboCup team in the RoboCup logistics league 2014. In: RoboCup Symposium - Champion Teams Track (2014)
20. Niemueller, T., Zug, S., Schneider, S., Karras, U.: Knowledge-based instrumentation and control for competitive industry-inspired robotic domains. KI - Künstliche Intelligenz **30**, 289–299 (2016)
21. Zug, S., Niemueller, T., Hochgeschwender, N., Seidensticker, K., Seidel, M., Friedrich, T., Neumann, T., Karras, U., Kraetzschmar, G., Ferrein, A.: An integration challenge to bridge the gap among industry-inspired RoboCup leagues. In: RoboCup Symposium (2016)

Staying on Top at RoboCup@Work 2016

Torben Carstensen[1]([✉]), Jan Carstensen[1], Andrej Dick[1], Sven Falkenhain[1],
Jens Hübner[1], Robin Kammel[1], Alexander Wentz[1], Simon Aden[2],
Jan Friederichs[3], and Jens Kotlarski[2]

[1] LUHbots, Leibniz Universität Hannover, Hanover, Germany
info@luhbots.de
[2] Institute of Mechatronic Systems, Leibniz Universität Hannover,
Hanover, Germany
{simon.Aden,jens.Kotlarski}@imes.uni-hannover.de
[3] Hannover Centre for Mechatronics, Leibniz Universität Hannover,
Hanover, Germany
friederichs@mzh.uni-hannover.de

Abstract. The LUHbots won the RoboCup@Work league at RoboCup
2016. This paper gives an overview of major improvements the LUHbots
team implemented since 2015 to stay ahead. We introduce our essential
changes and discuss made mistakes.

1 Introduction

The RoboCup@Work league was established in 2012 [1] to foster the development
and benchmarking of robots in the industrial environment. The main focus of
the league is to improve small but versatile robots capable of doing different
tasks. Those robots are attractive not only to huge firms being able to afford
many robots, but also to small companies. After introducing the league and
tests performed in 2016, we present our major improvements in comparison to
our status as of 2015 [2], which focused on task managing and failure handling.

2 The LUHbots

The LUHbots team was founded in 2012 at the Institute of Mechatronic Systems
at Leibniz Universität Hannover it consists of Bachelor's and Master's students
from mechanical engineering, computer science, and navigation and field robotics (see Fig. 1a). Most of the founding team members have participated in the
research inspired practical lecture RobotChallenge [3]. Today, the team is part
of the Hannover Centre for Mechatronics. In 2012, the LUHbots first competed
in the RoboCup@Work challenge and were able to win the competition [4]. In
2013, the second place was achieved [5]. In 2015, the LUHbots won both the
German Open and the RoboCup in Hefei [2]. This year, in 2016, the LUHbots
won the RoboCup in Leipzig.

© Springer International Publishing AG 2017
S. Behnke et al. (Eds.): RoboCup 2016, LNAI 9776, pp. 601–612, 2017.
https://doi.org/10.1007/978-3-319-68792-6_50

(a) The LUHbots team in Leipzig   (b) The RoboCup@Work league

Fig. 1. RoboCup@Work in 2016

3   The RoboCup@Work

In this section, we introduce the tests and major changes of the 2016 RoboCup @Work world championship. Nine teams participated at the World Cup in Leipzig (see Fig. 1b).

Changed Rules in Comparison to 2015: The arena size has been increased from 25 m² to 60 m². The arena has an entrance and exit area, marked with red-white barrier tape. It is entirely shut either by a wall or by yellow-black barrier tape (see Fig. 2). Different area heights of 0 cm, 5 cm, and 15 cm as well as shelves are available to grasp and place objects. The 0 cm areas are marked by the blue-white barrier tape.

Fig. 2. The RoboCup@Work arena in 2016 (Color figure online)

The teams can no longer choose complexity levels. The new referee box randomly generates all task specifications. The number of manipulation objects has been raised to a total of 14 objects. In some tests, objects need to be placed in a red or blue container (see Fig. 3 left). A new obstacle type, the yellow-black barrier

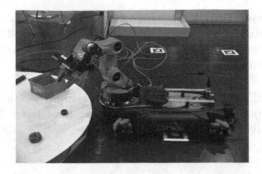 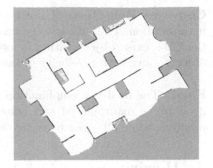

Fig. 3. The picture on the left shows our robot searching for the blue container. The one on the right displays our map used for navigation. (Color figure online)

tape, is used to mark areas where the robot is not allowed to drive through. Additionally, the Conveyer Belt Test (CBT) was added.

Basic Navigation Test: The purpose of the Basic Navigation Test (BNT) is testing navigation in a static environment. The arena is initially known and can be mapped during a set-up phase (see Fig. 3 right). The task consists of reaching and completely covering a series of markers in a specified orientation without any collisions. Two static obstacles and one barrier tape obstacle are positioned in the arena.

Basic Manipulation Test: The Basic Manipulation Test (BMT) focuses on manipulation tasks. The objective is to successfully grasp five objects and place them on a nearby service area. In comparison to 2015, the teams can no longer choose the order, position, or rotation of the objects.

Basic Transportation Test: The Basic Transportation Test (BTT) combines manipulation and navigation. The referee box sends the task description to the robot. It includes information of start and end positions of the objects to be transported. The task order and the particular transport tasks have to be determined autonomously by the robot. After placing all objects, the robot has to leave the arena through the exit. The order, position, and rotation of the objects as well as the pick-up and place down areas are randomly determined.

Three different BTTs are tested. They differ in the following aspects: the area heights, whether obstacles are put in the arena or not, whether five or seven objects need to be transported, whether objects need to be placed into a blue or red container, and whether decoy objects lie on the areas or not.

Precision Placement Test: The Precision Placement Test (PPT) consists of transporting objects and placing them inside small cavities, which are only a few millimetres larger in "diameter" than the object itself. Initially unknown positions of the cavities increase the complexity.

Conveyer Belt Test: The Conveyer Belt Test (CBT) focuses on dynamic manipulation. The task is to successfully grasp three objects. Two variations of the CBT exist: objects either lie on a conveyer belt or on a rotating table. The objects move with a velocity in the range of 2.5 to 5 $\frac{cm}{s}$.

Final: The final is a combination of all the aforementioned tests. Ten objects need to be manipulated and transported. The task time for the final is ten minutes, while all other tests are only five minutes long.

4   Hardware

Our robot is based on the mobile robot KUKA youBot [6], see Fig. 4. Basically, the robot consists of a mobile platform with four Mecanum Wheels [7] and a five degrees-of-freedom (DoF) manipulator which has been remounted to increase the manipulation area [4].

Many improvements have been made this year to rectify the error susceptibility of the robot hardware and to enhance the performance of the robot. In the following chapter, the main changes are described.

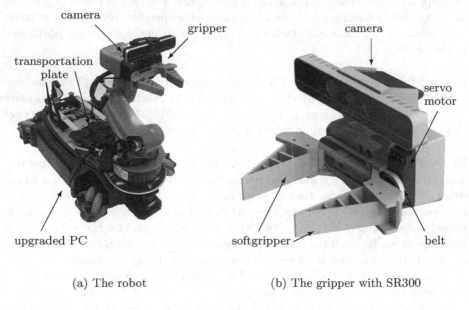

(a) The robot   (b) The gripper with SR300

Fig. 4. Hardware overview

4.1   Computer Upgrade

Unfortunately, the stock built-in Intel Atom computer of the youBot does not provide enough computing power needed to run multiple processes like camera driver, object recognition, and navigation simultaneously. To meet the requirements, the internal PC has been replaced by a Mini-ITX mainboard with an Intel i7-4790T CPU. Moreover, the RAM is increased to 16 GB. For storage, a 256 GB SSD is used. The necessary power of the new PC can not be supplied by the 12 V/5 A output of the youBot power board. The new mainboard's built-in power supply unit allows for an input between 9 V and 24 V. This way, the PC can be supplied from the 24 V output of the youBot power board. Additionally, the upgrade to USB 3.0 is needed to support the new camera (see 4.3).

4.2 Gripper

The gripper of the youBot has been redesigned. Now it is based on a 3D printed component. The usage of a belt drive allows for the reduction of weight and dimension of the gripper. The micro controller and the power regulator are located inside the 3D printed case of the gripper. Furthermore, a camera mount is included. Compared to the previous version [2], the gripper is powered by the youBot manipulator. Like the original youBot gripper it communicates indirectly over the internal EtherCAT bus of the manipulator. This way, there is no need for externally guided cables. The length and weight of the gripper are comparable to the stock gripper, but the gripping width has been improved significantly from 20 mm to 65 mm. Furthermore, the current feedback of the new servo motor allows for a grip check. Fin ray effect fingers are used for safety reasons. They are flexible and do not break in case of a collision.

4.3 Camera

We upgraded the vision system to the "Intel RealSense Camera SR300" (see Fig. 4b). It is a depth camera, just like the previously used "Creative Senz3D", having an improved 3D and 2D image quality and a 1080p RGB resolution. Furthermore, the camera uses USB 3.0 instead of USB 2.0 for a higher data transfer. The quality of the USB extension cable is crucial to ensure that the camera keeps running. Therefore, the camera is connected to the internal PC via a high quality USB-cable to enable the high data transfer rate.

4.4 Transportation Plate on the Robot's Backside

The transportation plate is designed to fit each of the manipulation objects of the RoboCup@Work league. The occurring vibrations while driving are used to slide the objects into their fittings. Even if the objects are not gripped perfectly, grasping errors of one to two centimetres can be resolved. Before taking an object from cargo, it is positioned in the middle of the gripper. Hence, it can be placed with high accuracy. This is crucial, for example during the precision placement test.

5   Approach

Generally satisfied with the results of our approach in 2015 [2], we updated our software to be able to work appropriately with the new changes. Here, we present the changes we have done to stay on top.

5.1   Overview

Our software architecture is based on ROS [8] (see Fig. 5). The yellow nodes (drivers) give access to the sensors. The youBot driver in red can be accessed via the youBot driver API node. The camera data is first processed by the vision node and then filtered and clustered by the observer node, which is triggered by the state machine. The laser scanners and barrier tape detection publish to the navigation stack. The watchdog filters the navigation commands. The task planner and the referee box connection communicate with the state machine. The laser scanner nodes are used unmodified. The standard ROS navigation stack is used, but the global planner has been replaced. As local planner the Dynamic Window Approach (DWA) [9] is used. The youBot driver API is heavily, and the camera driver is slightly modified. All other nodes have been entirely developed by the team.

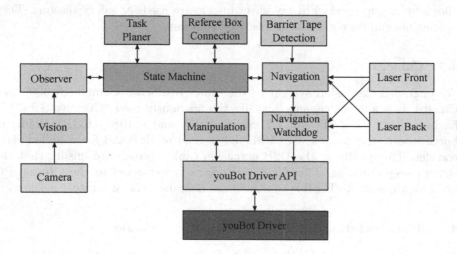

Fig. 5. Overview of the software architecture

5.2   Navigation

Last year, navigation was our primary concern. The ROS DWA local planner of December 2015 was superior to our local planner. Therefore, we changed to the ROS DWA.

Barrier Tape Detection: Three different barrier tapes (yellow-black, red-white and blue-white) have to be tracked. Navigating over a yellow-black barrier tape is counted as a collision. To prevent those collisions, we developed a barrier tape detection algorithm. This node detects the black-yellow tape and displays it on the cost map of the robot (see Fig. 6). To detect the tape, the 2D image of the camera is filtered in the HSV colourspace. The filter is light sensitive. Thus, the colour table needs to be retrained for each new location. Black is difficult to detect on the dark ground. Therefore, it is not tracked. A zero-height point cloud is calculated from the 2D image and the kinematics of the robot.

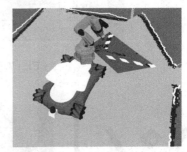

(a) Overlayed point cloud in the RGB image

(b) Barrier detection point cloud in the map

Fig. 6. Barrier detection (Color figure online)

During the competition, we faced the problem of a reflective ground. This results in difficulties in the detection of the tape and the ground. We had to reduce the navigation speed to ensure that the robot can react appropriately.

5.3 Manipulation

The software development kit (SDK) we developed in 2014 still fit the necessary requirements for all tests in 2016. Furthermore, we released the code of the package in April this year. The code and documentation are uploaded to our GitHub:

https://github.com/LUHbots/luh_youbot_os.
https://github.com/LUHbots/luh_youbot_os/wiki.
https://github.com/LUHbots/luh_youbot_os/blob/master/luh_youbot_os_de
scription.pdf.

5.4 Vision

To use the SR300 with ROS, we used the Intel librealsense package from Intel and a custom driver to publish the images in ROS.

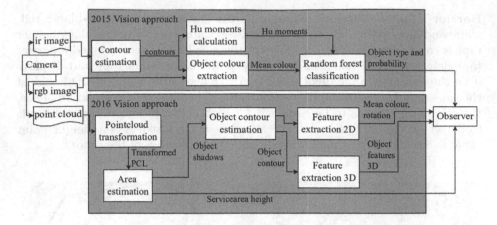

Fig. 7. Current vision system

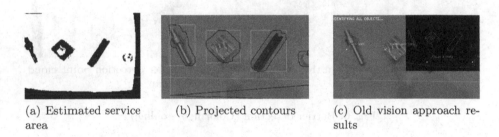

(a) Estimated service area

(b) Projected contours

(c) Old vision approach results

Fig. 8. Subfigure (a) shows the points from the transformed point cloud belonging to a service area. The black areas are potential objects. In (b) the transformed contours are shown and in blue and green the bounding boxes of the objects. Subfigure (c) shows the results of our vision from last year. (Color figure online)

Our vision system consists of three major parts (see Fig. 7). The first part is the vision system from last year, the second is the proposed new approach. All information is collected from a third component - the observer. The first approach mainly relies on the IR image of the camera and estimates a contour around an object in this image. Based on the contour, the node calculates the Hu moments and feeds them in a random forest to classify the objects. The debug output of this approach is shown in Fig. 8c.

The second component is our new approach, running parallel to the old one. Unlike the old approach, we do not classify, we only calculate features from found objects. In the first step, we transform the point cloud into a coordinate system, whose z axis is perpendicular to the floor. With this transformed point cloud, we run a plain segmentation with random sample consensus (RANSAC) and get a consensus set of points belonging to the area. The result of an exemplary

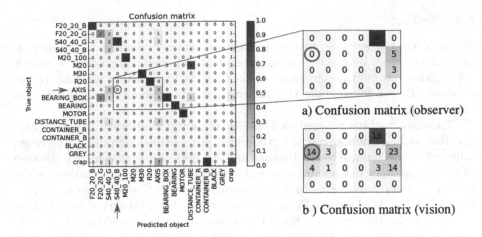

Fig. 9. This figure shows the confusion matrix of our old vision approach (b) compared to our new vision approach (a). It can be seen, that the old vision often mistakes the object *AXIS* with *S40_40_B*, but with our new approach the confusion matrix demonstrates a drastic decreasing of the number of misclassifications. (Color figure online)

calculation is shown in Fig. 8a. The points, which support our estimated service area, are shown in white. Based on the image we are looking for potential objects on the service area. Our potential objects are gaps in the point cloud of the service area. We estimate the contour of these holes and calculate the centre and the occupied area of this contour.

In the next step, the rotation of the object and the mean colour are calculated based on the RGB image. All calculated features and the name and probability of the classified object are sent to the observer.

The vision runs with 10 Hz. To enhance the object detection we removed the frequency limit of the node.

Observer: Since our previous approach suffered from a lot of misclassifications, we implemented an observer, which clusters the objects, their probabilities, and types. The clustering is done with a density-based spatial clustering of applications with noise (DBSCAN) [10] algorithm clustering based on the x-y-z coordinates of the objects and calculates a mean centre, name, and probability.

We extended the observer in order to be able to perform additional plausibility tests. Therefore, it receives additional features from the vision like the colour and the volume of the object. Thanks to this information it can differentiate hard objects, like the *F20_20_G* and *F20_20_B* objects, which can be easily mistaken using our approach we took last year. Furthermore, the observer uses a confusion matrix shown and explained in Fig. 9.

5.5 Testing

We implemented a vision testing framework, which loads our vision and an annotated rosbag. We run the vision and evaluate misclassified objects. With this information, we built a confusion matrix (see Fig. 9), which is fed back to the observer. Hence, it can take this information into account when receiving a classified object.

The state machine is based on SMACH [11], a Python library. It offers introspection and fast development. Python uses just in time compiling. Therefore, a line of code is interpreted at runtime and can crash for syntax errors. Because of various recovery behaviours, a probabilistic task planning and various combinations of tasks, we decided to design automated tests. These tests can be performed on any development PC or on a central server. This server uses Jenkins to schedule the different tests. Since the primary focus is to test the python code and the task planning, the manipulation and navigation is replaced by mocked action servers. The action servers would randomly fail and therefore allow the behaviour to deal with these possible failures. The new version of the referee box allows for random task generation. The Jenkins server schedules several tests per day. After a random task is generated, the behaviour uses the mocked servers to simulate performing the task. All actions are logged and analysed. At the end of the simulation, the points which would have been awarded are calculated. In preparation for the RoboCup event, more than ten thousand simulations were run.

To further increase the testing capabilities, Gazebo is used to simulate navigation. The tests are extended and time keeping is introduced. Using preconfigured values for the manipulation time, it is possible to estimate if the speed is sufficient. The Gazebo youBot model is extended to allow for the detection of collisions and include them into scoring. Since the simulation in Gazebo is computationally expensive, only a few thousand simulations were run.

Simulation: The Gazebo robot simulation is used for an efficient parameter improvement and error localisation of the existing software. The combination of Gazebo and Jenkins is beneficial: the start, end, and data acquisition are automated. Therefore, a big amount of data is collected, that can be used for optimisation. Changes in the current state of the software are refreshed periodically and self-directed. Hence, a problem in new code is found in a short amount of time and without the use of various resources. The optimisation of the navigation is possible if the movement model of the path planning is implemented. A laser scanner extension is available. Standard laser scanner extensions in Gazebo can be adjusted individually. For an automatic evaluation, a collision detector in Gazebo is used.

6   Results

The results of the performed tests are summarised in Table 1.

Table 1. Results of the RoboCup@Work competition in 2016

Place	Team	BNT	BMT	BTT1	BTT2	BTT3	PPT	CBT1	CBT2	Final	Total
1	LUHbots (GER)	250	650	300	0	50	300	0	0	0	1550
2	b-it-bots (GER)	300	200	0	100	200	0	0	600	0	1400
3	Robo-Erectus (SGP)	0	550	300	150	0	0	0	0	0	1000
4	robOTTO (GER)	50	400	0	250	0	0	0	0	200	900
5	AutonOHM (GER)	0	0	0	150	100	0	0	0	100	350
6	SPQR (ITA)	0	0	0	200	100	0	0	0	0	300
6	smARTLabs (ENG)	0	0	0	300	0	0	0	0	0	300
8	WF Wolves (GER)	0	0	0	150	0	0	0	0	0	150
9	AMSTT (SVK)	0	0	0	0	0	0	0	0	0	0

7   Conclusion

This year, rule changes troubled all teams. Besides a referee box and barrier obstacles, new objects resulted in many changes in perception and the manipulation state machine. Although we did not grasp misclassified objects, we had a number of failed grasps. These grasps were mainly due to shadows and reflections but were all handled by grip checks.

Last year, our focus layed on robustness. This year we further increased the robustness. Because of the new tests, which included more actions (e.g. objects to be transported) in less time, speed became more important. During the competition we improved our vision to reduce the number of failed grasps, which resulted in higher CPU load. Even though the frequencies of the nodes were still met and no warnings occurred, the performance was very slow. In two tests, hardware failures lead to a restart. Because of the speed we were unable compensate the penalty.

Our approach aimed to reach all possible points. The majority of the test runs were successful. However, the high number of different possibilities for task specifications did not allow for testing all combinations. In the final run we achieved zero points due to a collision of the manipulator with the wall.

8   Future Work

The vision parameter has to be set individually for every test because of the impact of changing light conditions. We want to improve the stability of the vision. Furthermore, till next year we want to merge the state machine with the manipulation state machine into one C++ state machine.

Acknowledgements. We would like to thank a couple of institutes and persons supporting our work. The team is supported by the Institute of Mechatronic Systems, the Institute of Systems Engineering - Real Time Systems Group, the student affairs office of the faculty of mechanical engineering, the society for the promotion of geodesy and geoinformatics and the Hannover Centre for Mechatronics. The team is being supervised by Jan Friederichs, Simon Aden and Daniel Kaczor.

References

1. Kraetzschmar, G.K., Hochgeschwender, N., Nowak, W., Hegger, F., Schneider, S., Dwiputra, R., Berghofer, J., Bischoff, R.: RoboCup@Work: competing for the factory of the future. In: Bianchi, R.A.C., Akin, H.L., Ramamoorthy, S., Sugiura, K. (eds.) RoboCup 2014. LNCS, vol. 8992, pp. 171–182. Springer, Cham (2015). doi:10.1007/978-3-319-18615-3_14

2. Carstensen, J., Carstensen, T., Aden, S., Dick, A., Hübner, J., Krause, S., Michailik, A., Wigger, J., Friederichs, J., Kotlarski, J.: A failure-tolerant approach for autonomous mobile manipulation in RoboCup@Work. In: Almeida, L., Ji, J., Steinbauer, G., Luke, S. (eds.) RoboCup 2015. LNCS, vol. 9513, pp. 95–105. Springer, Cham (2015). doi:10.1007/978-3-319-29339-4_8

3. Munske, B., Kotlarski, J., Ortmaier, T.: The robotchallenge - a research inspired practical lecture. In: 2012 IEEE/RSJ International Conference on Intelligent Robots and Systems (IROS), pp. 1072–1077, October 2012

4. Leibold, S., et al.: RoboCup@Work league winners 2012. In: Chen, X., Stone, P., Sucar, L.E., van der Zant, T. (eds.) RoboCup 2012. LNCS, vol. 7500, pp. 65–76. Springer, Heidelberg (2013). doi:10.1007/978-3-642-39250-4_7

5. Alers, S., Claes, D., Fossel, J., Hennes, D., Tuyls, K., Weiss, G.: How to win RoboCup@Work? In: Behnke, S., Veloso, M., Visser, A., Xiong, R. (eds.) RoboCup 2013. LNCS, vol. 8371, pp. 147–158. Springer, Heidelberg (2014). doi:10.1007/978-3-662-44468-9_14

6. Bischoff, R., Huggenberger, U., Prassler, E.: Kuka youBot - a mobile manipulator for research and education. In: ICRA (2011)

7. Ilon, B.: Directionally stable self propelled vehicle. July 17 1973. US Patent 3,746,112

8. Quigley, M., Conley, K., Gerkey, B.P., Faust, J., Foote, T., Leibs, J., Wheeler, R., Ng, A.Y.: ROS: an open-source robot operating system. In: ICRA Workshop on Open Source Software (2009)

9. Fox, D., Burgard, W., Thrun, S.: The dynamic window approach to collision avoidance. IEEE Robot. Autom. Mag. **4**, 23–33 (1997)

10. Ester, M., Kriegel, H.-P., Sander, J., Xu, X., et al.: A density-based algorithm for discovering clusters in large spatial databases with noise. KDD **96**, 226–231 (1996)

11. Bohren, J., Cousins, S.: The smach high-level executive [ROS news]. IEEE Robot. Autom. Mag. **4**(17), 18–20 (2010)

Team Delft's Robot Winner of the Amazon Picking Challenge 2016

Carlos Hernandez[1]([✉]), Mukunda Bharatheesha[1], Wilson Ko[2], Hans Gaiser[2], Jethro Tan[1], Kanter van Deurzen[2], Maarten de Vries[2], Bas Van Mil[2], Jeff van Egmond[1], Ruben Burger[1], Mihai Morariu[2], Jihong Ju[1], Xander Gerrmann[1], Ronald Ensing[2], Jan Van Frankenhuyzen[1], and Martijn Wisse[1,2]

[1] Robotics Institute, Delft University of Technology, Mekelweg 2, 2628 Delft, CD, The Netherlands
c.h.corbato@tudelft.nl
[2] Delft Robotics, B.V., Mijnbouwstraat 120, 2628 Delft, RX, The Netherlands

Abstract. This paper describes Team Delft's robot, which won the Amazon Picking Challenge 2016, including both the Picking and the Stowing competitions. The goal of the challenge is to automate pick and place operations in unstructured environments, specifically the shelves in an Amazon warehouse. Team Delft's robot is based on an industrial robot arm, 3D cameras and a customized gripper. The robot's software uses ROS to integrate off-the-shelf components and modules developed specifically for the competition, implementing Deep Learning and other AI techniques for object recognition and pose estimation, grasp planning and motion planning. This paper describes the main components in the system, and discusses its performance and results at the Amazon Picking Challenge 2016 finals.

Keywords: Robotic system · Warehouse automation · Motion planning · Grasping · Deep learning

1 Introduction

The Amazon Picking Challenge (APC) was launched by Amazon Robotics in 2015 [3] to promote research into robotic manipulation for picking and stocking of products. These tasks are representative of the current challenges that warehouse automation faces nowadays. The unstructured environment and the diversity of products require new robotic solutions. Smart mechanical designs and advanced artificial intelligence techniques need to be combined to address the challenges in object recognition, grasping, dexterous manipulation or motion planning.

Amazon chose 16 teams from all over the world to participate in the finals at RoboCup 2016. Team Delft won both the picking and the stowing challenges. Section 2 discusses Team Delft's approach, explaining its design principles and

© Springer International Publishing AG 2017
S. Behnke et al. (Eds.): RoboCup 2016, LNAI 9776, pp. 613–624, 2017.
https://doi.org/10.1007/978-3-319-68792-6_51

the robot hardware. Section 3 details the robot control and all the components integrated for object detection, grasp and motion planning. Finally Sects. 4 and 5 discuss the competition results and the lessons learned. The purpose of this paper is to provide a comprehensive analysis of the complete development of an advanced robotic system that has to perform in real-world circumstances.

2   The Amazon Picking Challenge 2016

The Amazon Picking Challenge 2016 included two competitions: in the Picking Task 12 items from the competition product set had to be picked from an Amazon shelving unit and placed in a tote; in the Stowing Task it was the other way around: 12 items were to be picked from the tote and stowed into the shelf. The maximum allotted time to fulfil each task was 15 min and the system had to operate autonomously. A file containing the task order was given to the system, which included the initial contents of the shelf's bins and the tote, and it had to produce a resulting file indicating the location of all the products.

The set of 39 items used in the challenge (Fig. 1) were representative of those in an Amazon warehouse. Books, cubic boxes, clothing, soft objects, and irregularly shaped objects represented realistic challenges such as reflective packaging, different sizes or deformable shapes. The items could be placed in any orientation inside the bins, sometimes cluttering them, and the target product could be partially occluded by others.

Teams had to place their robots in a 2 m × 2 m workcell, no closer than 10 cm from the shelf. The workspace also posed important challenges to perception and manipulation. The shelf was a metal and cardboard structure divided into a matrix of 3 by 4 bins. The bins were narrow but deep, which limited the manoeuvrability inside and required a long reach. Additionally, the shelf construction resulted in significant deviations in reality from its ideal geometric model.

The performance of the robots during the picking and the stowing tasks was evaluated by giving points for correctly placed items and subtracting penalty points for dropping, damaging or misplacing items. A correct operation could receive 10, 15 or 20 points depending on the cluttering of the bin. Additional bonus points were given for specially difficult objects, for maximum scoring of 185 points in the Picking Task and 246 points in the Stowing Task.

3   Team Delft's Robot

Team Delft was a joint effort of the Robotics Institute of the Delft University of Technology [11] and the robot integrator company Delft Robotics B.V. [4] to participate in the APC 2016. Amongst TUD Robotics Institute research lines is the development of flexible robots capable of automatizing small-scale productions, simplifying their installation and reconfiguration, e.g. through automatic calibration or online self-generated motions. Delft Robotics is a novel systems integrator making these new robotic technologies available to all kind of manufacturing companies. Both parties are closely collaborating within the

Fig. 1. The 39 items in the Amazon Picking Challenge 2016

Factory-in-a-day EU project [5] to reduce installation time and cost of robot automation. Team Delft's goal was to demonstrate and validate this approach in such a challenging industrial benchmark as the APC. The team did not adapt and tune an extant pick-an-place solution to participate in APC, but developed the best solution possible with extant industrial hardware and as many off-the-shelf software components as possible. For that the robot control was based on the ROS framework [7].

The remaining of this section describes the main ideas behind Team Delft's robotic solution.

3.1 Robot Concept

The team analysed the results of the previous edition of the Amazon Picking Challenge in 2015 [3], and decided that making the system *robust* and *fast* was key to win. These characteristics allow the system to perform several attempts to pick each target item, and move occluding objects around if necessary. We also learned that suction was the better performing grasp option, which we confirmed in early tests.

The solution designed is based on an industrial robot arm, a custom made gripper and 3D cameras, as shown in Fig. 2. For the robot arm we chose a 7 degrees of freedom SIA20F Motoman mounted on an horizontal rail perpendicular to the shelf. The resulting 8 degrees of freedom allowed the system to reach all the bins with enough manoeuvrability to pick the target objects.

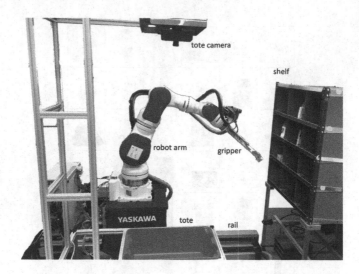

Fig. 2. Team Delft robot setup in the APC workcell.

We customized our own gripper to handle all the products in the competition (see Fig. 3). It has a lean footprint to manoeuvre inside the bins, and a 40 cm length to reach objects at the back. It includes a high flow suction cup at the end, with a 90° rotation allowing two orientations, and a pinch mechanism for the products difficult to suck. Both the suction cup rotation and the pinch mechanism are pneumatically actuated. A vacuum sensor provides boolean feedback whether the suction cup holds anything. For object detection a 3D camera is mounted in the gripper to scan the bins, while another one is fixed on a pole above the tote.

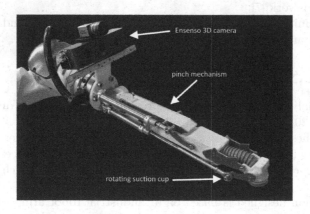

Fig. 3. Team Delft gripper.

The tote is placed on a frame attached to the robot rail. The compressor and the vacuum pump required to actuate the gripper are mounted on another frame that attached to the rail base, so the whole set up could be easily moved in three big blocks. Robust and easy transportation and installation were important requirements.

3.2   Control Pipeline

The system control is based on the sense-plan-act paradigm and path planning for robot motion. This allows for potentially optimal motions, at the cost of more precise sensing information. First, the task is decomposed into a set of pick and place operations on the target items. Then, for each operation in the Picking task the sense-plan-act cycle proceeds as follows[1]. First in the *sense* step the robot moves to take an image of the bin containing the first target item to locate it and get the obstacles information. Then, during the *plan* step a grasping strategy and candidate pose for the gripper to grab it are computed, and a motion plan is generated to approach, grasp and retreat from the bin with the item. Following, in the *act* step the gripper is configured for the selected strategy and the complete motion is executed, including gripper activation to suck or pinch-grasp the item. The vacuum seal in the suction cup is checked to confirm a successful pick. If so, the robot moves to deposit the item in the tote, using simple drop-off motions. This cycle is repeated till all target items are picked. For the Stowing task the loop operates similarly until all items in the tote are stowed in the shelf.

4   Robot Software

Team Delft was fully committed to the ROS-Industrial initiative [9] that aims to create industry-ready, advanced software components to extend the capabilities of factory robots. The robot software is thus based on the ROS framework [7]. We found that the flexibility, modularity and tools provided by ROS allowed us to address the requirements for autonomy and high and reliable performance in the competition, and facilitated development.

The ROS component-based approach allowed for the integration of the different components for task management, object detection, pose estimation, grasping and motion planning into a robust architecture. Following we describe them.

4.1   Task Management

On top of the architecture sits the task manager, responsible for decomposing the Pick and the Stow tasks into a plan of pick and place operations, and manages the state of fulfilment of the whole task. It encodes the competition rules to

---

[1] A video demonstrating the pipeline can be found here: https://www.youtube.com/watch?v=PKgFy6VUC-k.

maximize the scoring, by planning first those operations that scored more points, and keeps track of the location of all the items.

A central coordinator module coordinates the execution of each pick and place operation following the sequential flow presented in Sect. 3.2. It was implemented as a ROS SMACH [2] state machine.

The system can handle some failures applying fallback mechanisms to continue operation. For example, if the robot cannot find the target item, or estimate its pose, it tries different camera viewpoints, then if the problem persists it postpones that target and moves to the next operation. The system can detect if a suction grasp failed by checking the vacuum sealing after execution of the complete grasp and retreat action. If there is no seal the robot assumes the item dropped inside the bin and retries the pick later. If the seal is broken during the placement in the tote, the item is assumed to have dropped in the tote.

4.2 Object Recognition and Pose Estimation

The robot's pipeline involved detecting the target item within the bin or the tote and obtaining a grasp candidate using an estimation of its pose or its centroid, in the case of deformable items. Difficulties included narrow view angles and poor lighting conditions and reflections inside the shelf.

Firstly, the system acquires the $3D^2$ and RGB image with an Ensenso N35 camera. For that, in the Picking task the robot moves the gripper to a pre-defined location in front of the desired bin. In the Stowing task the image is taken by the camera fixed over tote. Then object detection consists of two main steps:

Object Recognition. First, a deep neural network based on Faster R-CNN [8] classifies the objects in the RGB image and extracts their bounding boxes. A pre-trained neural network was further trained to create the two models used for object recognition in both the picking and the stowing tasks. A dataset of about 20 K images of the products in different orientations and with random backgrounds was created to train a "base" model. Then this model was trained with around 500 labelled images of real occurrences of the products in the shelf and in the tote to generate the final recognition models. The result was an almost flawless detection within 150 ms of all the products present in any bin or tote image, as shown in Fig. 4.

Pose Estimation. Pose estimation of non-deformable products was done using Super 4PCS [6] to match the filtered PointCloud of the target item with a CAD model of the object. The 3D information of the bin or the tote is also used later during motion planning for collision detection. Reflections due to packaging and the difficult lighting conditions inside the bin resulted in scarce and noisy 3D data for some products. This proved a big difficulty for the pose estimation method. We included heuristics to correct estimations, e.g. objects cannot be floating on the bin, and also the mentioned fall-back mechanism to take additional images.

---

[2] The 3D data format used was PointCloud.

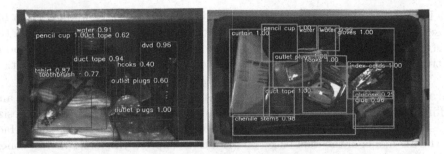

Fig. 4. Example result of the object detection module based on Faster R-CNN for bin and tote images. The estimated bounding boxes are depicted in green and labelled with the identification proposal and the confidence. (Color figure online)

4.3 Grasping and Manipulation

The grasp and manipulation solution is customised to our gripper and our path planning approach. The gripper has three basic modes or configurations (see Fig. 5): *front suction*, *side-top suction*, and *pinch*, each one corresponding to a grasping strategy more suitable different products also depending on the situation.

Fig. 5. The different gripper configurations for the grasping strategies. In the top images, the two configurations for suction rotating the cup. In the image below, the robot is picking the dumbbell using the pinch configuration.

In the *plan* step the best strategy and associated grasp candidate–i.e. a 6D pose to position the gripper–to grasp the target item are chosen, and then the system computes a manipulation plan to move the gripper to the candidate pose, activate it to pick the item, and move out of the bin (or the tote) holding it.

Grasp planning. For non-deformable items pose estimation of the object and offline geometric constraints and user-defined heuristics are used to synthesize grasp candidates. Basically a set of grasp candidates is generated over the surface of the 3D model of the item based on primitive shapes (cylinders, spheres, cones, planes, etc.). These candidates are pruned online using geometry constraints due to the actual item's estimated pose and gripper limitations, e.g. candidates at the back or the bottom[3] of the item are not reachable. Additional heuristics were defined experimentally to prune those grasp candidates specific to each product that proved not suitable. These heuristics were implemented so that new ones could easily be coded for a set of products by including them in the primitive shapes that accounted for different products, while still being able to define ad-hoc constraints that only applied to specific products. Finally, the synthesized candidates are scored based on geometry and dynamic considerations, e.g. poses closer to the centre or mass would tend to provide more stable grasps.

For deformable items the system exploits the power of the suction cup, which is capable of grasping and holding all deformable products in the competition. Instead of computing grasp candidates from the 3D pose estimation of the object, the normals of the segmented object PointCloud are directly used as grasp candidates. The candidates are also scored simply based on the distance to the PointCloud centroid, the closer the better.

Manipulation. Actually grasp planning produces not one but a set of grasp candidates ranked by our scoring criteria. However, the robot might not be able to reach some of these poses with the gripper, due to its kinematic limits or the obstacles, such as the bin or the tote walls, or other items close to the target one. Even if reachable, the robot, with the item attached to the gripper, also needs a retreat trajectory free of obstacles. The first grasp candidate for which a collision-free pick and retreat complete trajectory can be computed is then selected. This will be detailed in Sect. 4.4.

4.4   Motion Planning

For the robot motion strategy we divided the problem considering that the workspace is static (apart from motions due to the robot), and known outside of the shelf. Any online motion planning was required only inside the bins or the tote.

---

[3] These are relative locations assuming we are looking at the object from the tip of the gripper.

Offline Motions. Collision-free trajectories between all relevant locations to approach the bins and the tote and capture the images were computed offline. The trajectories were generated in joint space with the RRT-Connect randomized path planner via MoveIt! [10] and using a URDF[4] model of the workcell including the shelf, the robot on the rail, the gripper, and all the attached frames and equipment.

Online Cartesian Path Planning. To simplify the manipulation problem inside the bins, only collision-free picks were to be attempted. We defined a cartesian approach based on the MoveIt! pick and place pipeline that took the target grasp candidate and computed a combination of linear segments to *approach*, *contact* grasp the target object, *lift* it after grasping and *retreating* with it. The TRAC-IK library [1] is used for inverse kinematics, configured to enforce minimal configuration changes, and then collision checking is done with MoveIt! using the PointCloud information from the camera.

Robot Motion. This way, for the Picking task, offline motions were used in the *sense* phase to acquire the image of the bin containing the target object and to position the gripper ready to enter the bin. Then, during the *plan* phase the approach, contact, lift and retreat segments were generated online, and a drop-off location chosen and an associated offline trajectory retrieved. Finally, a complete motion plan to pick and place the target item is generated by stitching the cartesian segments and the offline drop-off trajectory. This includes time parametrization and the I/O commands required to configure and activate the gripper for grasping, resulting in a complete trajectory that is executed by the robot in the *act* phase. The MotoROS driver was used and enhanced by Team Delft[5] to execute the desired trajectories controlling the complete kinematic chain of the robot and the rail, and also the gripper using the robot controller I/O.

5   Competition Results

Team Delft's robot was the champion of the challenge winning both competitions, with an outstanding performance in the Stowing Task[6]. Table 1 shows the final scores for the Amazon Picking Challenge 2016 Pick and Stow competitions. The overall results of the teams improved considerably over the previous APC edition: average scoring for the top 10 teams increased 38% for the Picking Task, specially considering the increased difficulty in this edition, with more cluttered bins. It is also interesting to mention that all the best robots but Team Delft's placed the tote below the shelf, and initially moved a board to act as a ramp so that any items dropping will fall down to the tote. This trick improved scoring.

---

[4] Unified Robot Description Format http://wiki.ros.org/urdf.

[5] This contribution, as well as other ROS components developed for APC will be open to the community.

[6] Video recordings of Team Delft's competition runs can be found here https://youtu.be/3KlzVWxomqs (picking) and here https://youtu.be/AHUuDVdiMfg (stowing).

We considered this mechanical solution early at the concept brainstorming, but finally discarded it because due to the rail there was no free space for a clean and robust design. We did not want to include any provisional duck-tape solution. However, Team Delft's robust and fast concept outperformed the rest achieving more successful pick and place operations, which was the aim of the competition.

In the Stowing Task Team Delft's robot successfully stowed 11 items of the 12, dropping the remaining one while manipulating one of the other products. The system only had to retry one of the picks from the tote, to finish the task in a total time of 7 min 10 s.

Table 1. Amazon Picking Challenge 2016 scores of the best four robots.

	Stowing scores		Picking scores
214	Team Delft	105	Team Delft (0:30 first pick)
186	NimbRo picking	105	PFN (1:07 first pick)
164	MIT	97	NimbRo picking
161	PFN	67	MIT

The picking task proved much harder than the stowing. The robot picked successfully 9 out of 12 items, the first one in only 30 s. The robot dropped one of the targets and was not able to pick the remaining two. The system dropped a non-target item during manipulation. The system also successfully moved 5 items between the shelf's bins to clear occlusions for required picks. Two of those move operations allowed it two successfully pick two target products. Team Delft called the end of the run after 14 min and 45 s.

5.1   Analysis

Team Delft's robot reliable and performing capabilities were the key to its success. Its gripper could grasp all 39 items in the competition, including the dumbbell and the pencil cup using the pinch grasp, in any orientation and bin location. However, the grasp on heavy and big items was not completely reliable. The dumbbell proved specially difficult, since the grasp approach needed extreme accuracy to succeed.

The object recognition module had an specially outstanding performance robust to varying light conditions. However, pose estimation was strongly affected by reflections, which produced scarce PointCloud data.

Most difficulties for our system were encountered when trying to find a collision-free motion plan to approach the target object. This rejected many targets that were retried later. In the next attempt, removing occluding items was done, but sometimes the cluttering of the bin caused a stall situation in which items were preventing each other from being picked.

Overall, the Picking Task proved far more difficult than the Stowing Task, with many teams scoring half the points. This is because picking from the shelf required more manipulation, with items occluding each other. The Stowing task was basically a standard bin picking problem: all items in the tote were to be picked, and gravity helps having some easily accessible at the top. Also, the stowing in the shelf could be done with pre-computed motions to shove the target item in the bin, blindly pushing back any previous content.

5.2 Lessons Learned

Considering the results described in the previous section and the complete experience developing the robot for the Amazon Picking Challenge, we reached several conclusions about our concept design premises and how to improve it.

The most important idea is that manipulation requires contact with the environment. Team Delft's pure planning approach to grasping and manipulation treated contact as collisions to avoid, and simply by-passed this constraint for the target object. This caused a lot of rejected plans to grasp items from cluttered bins, some of them becoming actually unrealisable. Force-feedback and compliance in the gripper seem unavoidable to achieve a reliable solution. Also, creating a single gripper capable of handling such a variety of products proved difficult. None of the teams managed to pick the dumbbell, for example. Having different grippers and switching between them on the fly seems a more efficient and robust solution.

On the perception side, Deep Learning neural networks proved an excellent solution for object recognition, but they also are a really promising solution to pose estimation and even grasp planning, as the results of other teams suggest.

Notwithstanding the discussed improvements, Team Delft's concept based on speed and reliability proved successful. The ready-for-industry approach we took, with installation and setup procedures, and professional team coordination during the competition, allowed to keep robustly improving the robot's performance till reaching close to its top limit right at the competition.

6 Concluding Remarks

This paper provides a comprehensive overview of Team Delft's robot winner of the Amazon Picking Challenge 2016. The key to Delft's robot success was a concept aimed for robustness and speed, relying on an end-to-end engineering process integrating well establish industry practices and cutting-edge AI and robotics technologies.

There was a new Stowing Task in the 2016 edition of the challenge, to bin-pick products from a tote and stow them in a shelf. The overall high scores by many teams, and the excellent performance of Team Delft's robot, suggest that the bin picking problem for diverse, medium-size products can be addressed by current robotic technology. Speed is still far from human performance ($\sim$100 items an hour, compared to 400 items an hour in the case of a human), but considering that Team Delft's robot could have been speed-up probably 50% with faster motions and faster processing, we are confident to predict that robot technology is getting there. However, the Picking task results, proved that general manipulation, including diverse objects and cluttered spaces, still remains an open problem for robotics.

Acknowledgements. All authors gratefully acknowledge the financial support by the European Union's Seventh Framework Programme project Factory-in-a-day (FP7-609206) We would like to thank RoboValley (http://www.robovalley.com), the ROS-Industrial consortium, our sponsors Yaskawa, IDS, Phaer, Ikbenstil and Induvac, the people at the Delft Center for Systems and Control and TU Delft Logistics for their support, also Lacquey B.V. for helping us handle our heavy rail, and finally special thanks to Gijs vd. Hoorn for his help during the development of the robotic system.

References

1. Beeson, P., Ames, B.: TRAC-IK: an open-source library for improved solving of generic inverse kinematics. In: Proceedings of the IEEE RAS Humanoids Conference, Seoul, Korea, November 2015
2. Bohren, J.: SMACH (2016). http://wiki.ros.org/smach
3. Correll, N., Bekris, K.E., Berenson, D., Brock, O., Causo, A., Hauser, K., Okada, K., Rodriguez, A., Romano, J.M., Wurman, P.R.: Lessons from the amazon picking challenge. CoRR abs/1601.05484 (2016)
4. Delft Robotics, B.V. http://www.delftrobotics.com/
5. Factory-in-a-day. http://www.factory-in-a-day.eu
6. Mellado, N., Aiger, D., Mitra, N.J.: Super 4PCS fast global pointcloud registration via smart indexing. Comput. Graph. Forum **33**(5), 205–215 (2014)
7. Quigley, M., Conley, K., Gerkey, B.P., Faust, J., Foote, T., Leibs, J., Wheeler, R., Ng, A.Y.: ROS: an open-source robot operating system. In: ICRA Workshop on Open Source Software (2009)
8. Ren, S., He, K., Girshick, R., Sun, J.: Faster R-CNN: towards real-time object detection with region proposal networks. In: Advances in Neural Information Processing Systems (NIPS) (2015)
9. ROS-Industrial. http://rosindustrial.org/
10. Sucan, I.A., Chitta, S.: MoveIt!. http://moveit.ros.org
11. TUD Robotics Institute. http://robotics.tudelft.nl

First International HARTING Open Source Prize Winner: The igus Humanoid Open Platform

Philipp Allgeuer[✉], Grzegorz Ficht, Hafez Farazi, Michael Schreiber, and Sven Behnke

Autonomous Intelligent Systems, Computer Science,
University of Bonn, Bonn, Germany
{pallgeuer,ficht,hfarazi}@ais.uni-bonn.de, behnke@cs.uni-bonn.de
http://ais.uni-bonn.de

Abstract. The use of standard platforms in the field of humanoid robotics can lower the entry barrier for new research groups, and accelerate research by the facilitation of code sharing. Numerous humanoid standard platforms exist in the lower size ranges of up to 60 cm, but beyond that humanoid robots scale up quickly in weight and price, becoming less affordable and more difficult to operate, maintain and modify. The igus® Humanoid Open Platform is an affordable, fully open-source platform for humanoid research. At 92 cm, the robot is capable of acting in an environment meant for humans, and is equipped with enough sensors, actuators and computing power to support researchers in many fields. The structure of the robot is entirely 3D printed, leading to a lightweight and visually appealing design. This paper covers the mechanical and electrical aspects of the robot, as well as the main features of the corresponding open-source ROS software. At RoboCup 2016, the platform was awarded the first International HARTING Open Source Prize.

1 Introduction

The field of humanoid robotics is enjoying increasing popularity, with many research groups having developed robotic platforms to investigate topics such as perception, manipulation and bipedal walking. The entry barrier to such research can be significant though, and access to a standard humanoid platform can allow for greater focus on research, and facilitates collaboration and code exchange.

The igus® Humanoid Open Platform, described in this paper, is a collaboration between researchers at the University of Bonn and igus® GmbH, a leading manufacturer of polymer bearings and energy chains. The platform seeks to close the gap between small, albeit affordable, standard humanoid platforms, and larger significantly more expensive ones. We designed the platform to be as open, modular, maintainable and customisable as possible. The use of almost exclusively 3D printed plastic parts for the mechanical components of the robot is a result of this mindset, which also simplifies the manufacture of the robots.

© Springer International Publishing AG 2017
S. Behnke et al. (Eds.): RoboCup 2016, LNAI 9776, pp. 625–633, 2017.
https://doi.org/10.1007/978-3-319-68792-6_52

This allows individual parts to be easily modified, reprinted and replaced to extend the capabilities of the robot, shown in Fig. 1. A demonstration video of the igus® Humanoid Open Platform is available.[1]

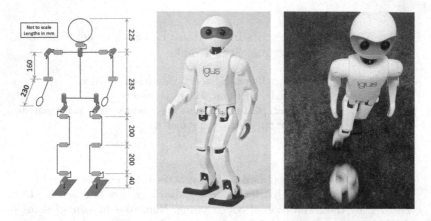

Fig. 1. The igus® Humanoid Open Platform and its kinematic structure

2   Related Work

A number of standard humanoid robot platforms have been developed over the last decade, such as for example the Nao robot by Aldebaran Robotics [1]. The Nao comes with a rich set of features, such as a variety of available gaits, a programming SDK, and human-machine interaction modules. The robot however has a limited scope of use, as it is only 58 cm tall. Also, as a proprietary product, own hardware repairs and enhancements are difficult. Another example is the DARwIn-OP [2], distributed by Robotis. At 45.5 cm, it is half the size of the igus® Humanoid Open Platform. The DARwIn-OP has the benefit of being an open platform, but its size remains a limiting factor for its range of applications.

Other significantly less widely disseminated robots include the Intel Jimmy robot, the Poppy robot from the Inria Flowers Laboratory [3], and the Jinn-Bot from Jinn-Bot Robotics and Design GmbH in Switzerland. All of these robots are at least in part 3D printed, and the first two are open source. The Jimmy robot is intended for social interactions and comes with software based on the DARwIn-OP framework. The Poppy robot is intended for non-autonomous use, and features a multi-articulated bio-inspired morphology. Jinn-Bot is built from over 90 plastic parts and 24 actuators, making for a complicated build, and is controlled by a Java application running on a smartphone mounted in its head. Larger humanoid platforms, such as the Asimo [4], HRP [5] and Atlas robots, are an order of magnitude more expensive and more complicated to operate and

---

[1] Video: https://www.youtube.com/watch?v=RC7ZNXclWWY.

maintain. Such large robots are less robust because of their complex hardware structure, and require a gantry in normal use. These factors limit the use of such robots by most research groups.

3   Hardware Design

The hardware platform was designed in collaboration with igus® GmbH, which engaged a design bureau to create an appealing overall aesthetic appearance. The main criteria for the design were the simplicity of manufacture, assembly, maintenance and customisation. To satisfy these criteria, a modular design approach was used. Due to the 3D printed nature of the robot, parts can be modified and replaced with great freedom. A summary of the main hardware specifications of the igus® Humanoid Open Platform is shown in Table 1.

Table 1. igus® Humanoid Open Platform specifications

Type	Specification	Value
General	Physical	92 cm, 6.6 kg, Polyamide 12 (PA12)
	Battery	4-cell LiPo (14.8 V, 3.8 Ah), 15–30 min
PC	Product	Gigabyte GB-BXi7-5500, Intel i7-5500U, 2.4–3.0 GHz
	Options	4 GB RAM, 120 GB SSD, Ethernet, Wi-Fi, Bluetooth
CM730	Microcontroller	STM32F103RE, 512 KB Flash, 64 KB SRAM
	Interfaces	3 × Buttons, 7 × Status LEDs
Actuators	Total	8 × MX-64, 12 × MX-106
	Per Limb	2 × MX-64 (head), 3 × MX-64 (arm), 6 × MX-106 (leg)
Sensors	Encoders	4096 ticks/rev per joint axis
	IMU	9-axis (L3G4200D, LIS331DLH, HMC5883L)
	Camera	Logitech C905 (720p), with 150° FOV wide-angle lens

3.1   Mechanical Structure

The plastic shell serves not only for outer appearance, but also as the load-bearing frame. This makes the igus® Humanoid Open Platform very light for its size. Despite its low weight, the robot is still very durable and resistant to deformation and bending. This is achieved by means of wall thickness modulation in the areas more susceptible to damage, in addition to strategic distribution of ribs and other strengthening components, printed directly as part of the exoskeleton. Utilising the versatile nature of 3D printing, the strengths of the plastic parts can be maximised exactly where they are needed, and not unnecessarily so in other locations. If a weak spot is identified through practical experience, as indeed happened during testing, the parts can be locally strengthened in the CAD model without significantly impacting the remaining design.

3.2   Robot Electronics

The electronics of the platform are built around an Intel i7-5500U processor, running a full 64-bit Ubuntu OS. DC power is provided via a power board, where external power and a 4-cell Lithium Polymer (LiPo) battery can be connected. The PC communicates with a Robotis CM730 subcontroller board, whose main purpose is to electrically interface the twelve MX-106 and eight MX-64 actuators, all connected on a single star topology Dynamixel bus. Due to a number of reliability and performance factors, we redesigned and rewrote the firmware of the CM730 (and CM740). This improved bus stability and error tolerance, and decreased the time required for the reading out of servo data, while still retaining compatibility with the standard Dynamixel protocol. The CM730 incorporates 3-axis gyroscope and accelerometer sensors, is connected externally to an additional 3-axis magnetometer via an I^2C interface, and also connects to an interface board that has three buttons, five LEDs and two RGB LEDs.

Further available external connections to the robot include USB, HDMI, Mini DisplayPort, Gigabit Ethernet, IEEE 802.11b/g/n Wi-Fi, and Bluetooth 4.0. The igus® Humanoid Open Platform is nominally equipped with a single 720p Logitech C905 camera behind its right eye, fitted with a wide-angle lens. A second camera can be optionally mounted behind the left eye for stereo vision.

4   Software

The ROS middleware was chosen as the basis of the software developed for the igus® Humanoid Open Platform. This fosters modularity, visibility, reusability, and to some degree the platform independence. The software was developed with humanoid robot soccer in mind, but the platform can be used for virtually any other application. This is possible because of the strongly modular way in which the software was written, greatly supported by the natural modularity of ROS, and the use of plugin schemes.

4.1   Vision

The camera driver used in the ROS software nominally retrieves images at 30 Hz in 24bpp BGR format at a resolution of 640 × 480. For further processing, the captured image is converted to the HSV colour space. In our target application of soccer, the vision processing tasks include field, ball, goal, field line, centre circle and obstacle detection, as illustrated in Fig. 2 [6]. The wide-angle camera used introduces significant distortion, which must be compensated when projecting image coordinates into egocentric world coordinates. We undistort the image with a Newton-Raphson based approach (top right in Fig. 2). This method is used to populate a pair of lookup tables that allow constant time distortion and undistortion operations at runtime. Further compensation of projection errors is performed by calibrating offsets to the position and orientation of the camera frame in the head of the robot. This is essential for good projection performance (bottom row in Fig. 2), and is done using the Nelder-Mead method.

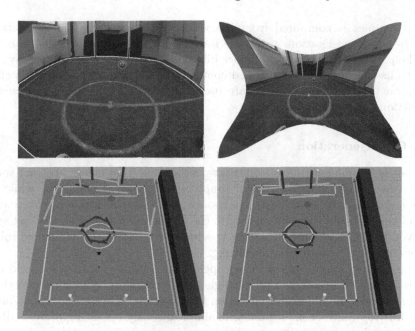

Fig. 2. Top: A captured image (left) with ball (pink circle), field line (red lines), field boundary (yellow lines), and goal post (blue lines) detections annotated, and the corresponding raw captured image with undistortion applied (right). Bottom: Projected ball, field line and goal post detections before (left) and after (right) kinematic calibration (Color figure online).

4.2 State Estimation

State estimation is a vital part of virtually any system that utilises closed-loop control. The 9-axis IMU on the microcontroller board is used to obtain the 3D orientation of the robot relative to its environment through the means of a non-linear passive complementary filter [7]. This filter returns the full 3D estimated orientation of the robot with use of a novel way of representing orientations—the *fused angles* representation [8]. An immediate application of the results of the state estimation is the fall protection module, which disables the torque in order to minimise stress in all of the servos if a fall is imminent.

4.3 Actuator Control

As with most robots, motions performed by the igus® Humanoid Open Platform are dependent on the actuator's ability to track their set position. This is influenced by many factors, including battery voltage, joint friction, inertia and load. To minimise the effects of these factors, we apply feed-forward control to the commanded servo positions. This allows the joints to move in a compliant way, reduces servo overheating and wear, increases battery life, and reduces the problems posed by impacts and disturbances [9]. The vector of desired feed-forward output torques is computed from the vectors of commanded joint positions, velocities and accelerations using the full-body inverse dynamics of the robot, with help of the Rigid Body Dynamics Library. Each servo in the robot is configured to use exclusively proportional control. Time-varying dimensionless effort values on the unit interval $[0, 1]$ are used per joint to interpolate the current proportional gain.

4.4 Gait Generation

The gait is formulated in three different pose spaces: joint space, abstract space, and inverse space. The *joint space* simply specifies all joint angles, while the *inverse space* specifies the Cartesian coordinates and quaternion orientations of each of the limb end effectors relative to the trunk link frame. The *abstract space* however, is a representation that was specifically developed for humanoid robots in the context of walking and balancing.

The walking gait is based on an open loop central pattern generated core that is calculated from a gait phase angle that increments at a rate proportional to the desired gait frequency. This open loop gait extends the gait of our previous work [10]. Since then, a number of simultaneously operating basic feedback mechanisms have been built around the open loop gait core to stabilise the walking [11]. The feedback in each of these mechanisms derives from the fused pitch and fused roll state estimates, and adds corrective action components to the central pattern generated waveforms in both the abstract and inverse spaces [8].

4.5 Motions

Often there is a need for a robot to play a particular pre-designed motion. This is the task of the motion player, which implements a nonlinear keyframe

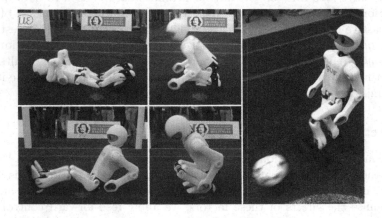

Fig. 3. Dynamic get-up motions, from the prone (top row) and supine (bottom row) lying positions, and a still image of the dynamic kick motion.

interpolator that connects robot poses and smoothly interpolates joint positions and velocities, in addition to modulating the joint efforts and support coefficients. This allows the actuator control scheme to be used meaningfully during motions with changing support conditions. To create and edit the motions, a trajectory editor was developed for the igus® Humanoid Open Platform. All motions can be edited in a user-friendly environment with a 3D preview of the robot poses. We have designed numerous motions including kicking, waving, balancing, get-up, and other motions. A still image of the kicking motion is shown in Fig. 3 along with the get-up motions of the igus® Humanoid Open Platform, from the prone and supine positions.

5   Reception

To date we have built seven igus® Humanoid Open Platforms, and have demonstrated them at the RoboCup and various industrial trade fairs. Amongst others, this includes demonstrations at Hannover Messe in Germany, and at the International Robot Exhibition in Tokyo, where the robots had the opportunity to show their interactive side (see Fig. 4). Demonstrations ranged from expressive and engaging looking, waving and idling motions, to visitor face tracking and hand shaking. The robots have been observed to spark interest and produce emotional responses in the audience.

Fig. 4. Example human interactions with the igus® Humanoid Open Platform, including waving to children (left), and face tracking (middle).

Despite the recent design and creation of the platform, work groups have already taken inspiration from it, or even directly used the open-source hardware or software. A good example of this is the Humanoids Engineering and Intelligent Robotics team at Marquette University with their MU-L8 robot [12]. In their design they combined both an aluminium frame from the NimbRo-OP and 3D printed parts similar to those of the igus® Humanoid Open Platform, as well as using ROS-based control software inspired by our own. A Japanese robotics business owner, Tomio Sugiura, started printing parts of the igus® Humanoid

Open Platform on an FDM-type 3D printer with great success. Naturally, the platform also inspired other humanoid soccer teams, such as the WF Wolves [13], to improve upon their own robots. The NimbRo-OP, which was a prototype for the igus® Humanoid Open Platform, has been successfully used in research for human-robot interaction research at the University of Hamburg [14]. We recently sold a set of printed parts to the University of Newcastle in Australia and await results of their work.

In 2015, the robot was awarded the first RoboCup Design Award, based on criteria such as performance, simplicity and ease of use. At RoboCup 2016, the platform also won the first International HARTING Open Source Prize, and was a fundamental part of the winning TeenSize soccer team. These achievements confirm that the robot is welcomed and appreciated by the community.

6   Conclusions

Together with igus® GmbH, we have worked for three years to create and improve upon an open platform that is affordable, versatile and easy to use. The igus® Humanoid Open Platform provides users with a rich set of features, while still leaving room for modifications and customisation. We have released the hardware in the form of print-ready 3D CAD files[2], and uploaded the software to GitHub[3]. We hope that it will benefit other research groups, and encourage them to publish their results as contributions to the open-source community.

Acknowledgements. We acknowledge the contributions of igus® GmbH to the project, in particular the management of Martin Raak towards the robot design and manufacture. This work was partially funded by grant BE 2556/10 of the German Research Foundation (DFG).

References

1. Gouaillier, D., Hugel, V., Blazevic, P., Kilner, C., Monceaux, J., Lafourcade, P., Marnier, B., Serre, J., Maisonnier, B.: Mechatronic design of NAO humanoid. In: International Conference on Robotics and Automation (2009)
2. Ha, I., Tamura, Y., Asama, H., Han, J., Hong, D.: Development of open humanoid platform DARwIn-OP. In: SICE Annual Conference (2011)
3. Lapeyre, M., Rouanet, P., Grizou, J., Nguyen, S., Depraetre, F., Le Falher, A., Oudeyer, P.-Y.: Poppy project: open-source fabrication of 3D printed humanoid robot for science, education and art. In: Digital Intelligence 2014, September 2014
4. Hirai, K., Hirose, M., Haikawa, Y., Takenaka, T.: The development of Honda humanoid robot. In: International Conference on Robotics and Automation (1998)
5. Kaneko, K., Kanehiro, F., Morisawa, M., Miura, K., Nakaoka, S., Kajita, S.: Cybernetic human HRP-4C. In: Proceedings of 9th IEEE-RAS International Conference on Humanoid Robotics, Humanoids, pp. 7–14 (2009)

---

[2] Hardware: https://github.com/igusGmbH/HumanoidOpenPlatform.
[3] Software: https://github.com/AIS-Bonn/humanoid_op_ros.

6. Farazi, H., Allgeuer, P., Behnke, S.: A monocular vision system for playing soccer in low color information environments. In: Proceedings of 10th Workshop on Humanoid Soccer Robots, International Conference on Humanoid Robots, Seoul, Korea (2015)
7. Allgeuer, P., Behnke, S.: Robust sensor fusion for biped robot attitude estimation. In: Proceedings of 14th International Conference on Humanoid Robotics (2014)
8. Allgeuer, P., Behnke, S.: Fused angles: a representation of body orientation for balance. In: International Conference on Intelligent Robots and Systems, IROS (2015)
9. Schwarz, M., Behnke, S.: Compliant robot behavior using servo actuator models identified by iterative learning control. In: Behnke, S., Veloso, M., Visser, A., Xiong, R. (eds.) RoboCup 2013. LNCS (LNAI), vol. 8371, pp. 207–218. Springer, Heidelberg (2014). doi:10.1007/978-3-662-44468-9_19
10. Missura, M., Behnke, S.: Self-stable omnidirectional walking with compliant joints.: In: 8th Workshop on Humanoid Soccer Robots, Humanoids (2013)
11. Allgeuer, P., Behnke, S.: Omnidirectional bipedal walking with direct fused angle feedback mechanisms. In: Proceedings of 16th IEEE-RAS International Conference on Humanoid Robots, Humanoids, Cancún, Mexico (2016)
12. Stroud, A., Morris, M., Carey, K., Williams, J.C., Randolph, C., Williams, A.B.: MU-L8: the design architecture and 3D printing of a Teen-Sized humanoid soccer robot. In: 8th Workshop on Humanoid Soccer Robots, Humanoids (2013)
13. Tasch, C., Luceiro, D., Maciel, E.H., Berwanger, F., Xia, M., Stiddien, F., Martins, L.T., Wilke, L., Dalla Rosa, O.K., Henriques, R.V.B.: WF Wolves and Taura Bots Teen Size (2015)
14. Barros, P., Parisi, G.I., Jirak, D., Wermter, S.: Real-time gesture recognition using a humanoid robot with a deep neural architecture. In: Proceedings of 14th IEEE-RAS International Conference on Humanoid Robotics, Humanoids (2014)

International Harting Open Source Award 2016: Fawkes for the RoboCup Logistics League

Tim Niemueller[1]([✉]), Tobias Neumann[2], Christoph Henke[3],
Sebastian Schönitz[3], Sebastian Reuter[3], Alexander Ferrein[2],
Sabina Jeschke[3], and Gerhard Lakemeyer[1]

[1] Knowledge-based Systems Group, RWTH Aachen University, Aachen, Germany
niemueller@kbsg.rwth-aachen.de
[2] MASCOR Institute, FH Aachen University of Applied Sciences, Aachen, Germany
[3] Institute Cluster IMA/ZLW & IfU, RWTH Aachen University, Aachen, Germany

Abstract. Since 2014, we have made three releases of our full software stack for the *RoboCup Logistics League* (RCLL) based on the Open Source *Fawkes Robot Software Framework*. They include all software components of the team Carologistics which won RoboCup 2014, 2015, and 2016. The software is based on experience from participating in a number of leagues with the AllemaniACs RoboCup@Home team being another active contributor. We think that these releases have made the RCLL more accessible to new teams and helped established ones to improve their performance. The team is proud to have been selected for the third place of the 1st International Harting Open Source Award in 2016. In this paper, we give an overview of the framework and its development.

1 Introduction

Autonomous mobile robots comprise a great deal of complexity. They require a plethora of software components for perception, actuation, task-level reasoning, and communication. These components have to be integrated into a coherent and robust system in time for the next RoboCup event. Then, during the competition, the system has to perform stable and reliably. Providing a software framework for teams to use tremendously eases that effort. Even more so when providing a fully integrated system specific for a particular domain.

Over the past ten years, we have developed the *Fawkes Robot Software Framework* [2] as a robust foundation to deal with the challenges of robotics applications in general, and in the context of RoboCup in particular. It has been developed and used in the Middle-Size [3] and Standard Platform [4] soccer leagues, the RoboCup@Home [5,6] service robot league, and now in the *RoboCup Logistics League* [7,8]. The frameworks or parts of it have also been used in other contexts [9,10]. In Fig. 1 the timeline of some robots used with Fawkes is depicted. Although Fawkes is designed as a general framework to fit various robotics applications, in this paper we focus on its use in the RCLL.

© Springer International Publishing AG 2017
S. Behnke et al. (Eds.): RoboCup 2016, LNAI 9776, pp. 634–642, 2017.
https://doi.org/10.1007/978-3-319-68792-6_53

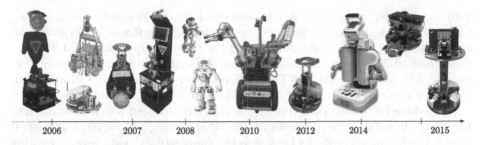

2006   2007   2008   2010   2012   2014   2015

Fig. 1. Robots running (parts of) Fawkes which were or are used for the development of the framework and its components in the past ten years [1].

We have been the first team in the RCLL to publicly release their software stack. Teams in other leagues have made similar releases before [11]. What makes ours unique is that it provides a complete and *ready-to-run package with the full software* (and some additions and fixes) that we used in several competitions – which we won. This in particular *includes* the complete *task-level executive* component, that is the strategic decision making and behavior generating software. The major parts of the domain model are also made publicly available.

In the RCLL all teams use the same hardware platform "Robotino" by Festo Didactic. This means that there is *no hardware barrier* that prevents teams from using the software effectively and quickly. Even more so, with the *3D simulation environment* based on Gazebo which we have developed [12] and provide, teams can immediately start using our software system for their own development. We provide extensive documentation and are expanding it continuously.

In 2016, the RCLL software stack based on Fawkes[1] was selected for the third place of the 1st International Harting Open Source Prize.

In the following we will briefly describe the framework, some major components, and our simulation environment in Sect. 2 with a highlight on the task-level executive in Sect. 3. We conclude in Sect. 4.

2   Fawkes Robot Software Framework

The software stack is based on the *Fawkes Robot Software Framework*[2] which is Open Source software. The development is split into a core and domain-specific parts. The core framework, Fawkes, is developed in public. We have just released the first stable release 1.0. The domain-specific components are developed in private as they are considered to be our competitive edge. We have made several releases in the past few years, one after each RoboCup event since 2014.

Fawkes was initially started in 2006 as an effort to build a capable and faster software platform for a new generation of Mid-Size league robots of the *AllemaniACs*[3] *RoboCup Team* (cf. Fig. 1). It was used for the first time at RoboCup

---

[1] Latest release: https://www.fawkesrobotics.org/p/rcll2016-release.

[2] Fawkes website at https://www.fawkesrobotics.org.

[3] Website of the AllemaniACs at https://robocup.rwth-aachen.de.

2007 in Atlanta. Since then it was also used on our domestic service robot Caesar [6] in the RoboCup@Home league winning the RoboCup in 2006 and 2007, placing second in 2008, and winning the German Open 2007 and 2008 [5]. From 2008 to 2010 we participated as team ZaDeAt [4], a joint team from University of Cape Town (ZA), RWTH Aachen University (DE) and Technical University of Graz (AT), in the Standard Platform League. During this time we developed the Lua-based Behavior Engine [13], a component which was ported to ROS in 2010 and used, for example, on HERB at CMU [9]. Since 2012 we participate in the RoboCup Logistics League as the *Carologistics*[4] *joint team* consisting of the Knowledge-Based Systems Group, the Institute Cluster IMA/ZLW & IfU (both RWTH Aachen University), and the Institute for Mobile Autonomous Systems and Cognitive Robotics (FH Aachen University of Applied Sciences). We won the RoboCup and RoboCup German Open titles 2014–2016. Fawkes is also used in combination with ROS on a PR2 in a project on hybrid reasoning [10].

The overall software structure is designed as a three-layer architecture [14] and follows a component-based paradigm [15–17]. It consists of a deliberative layer for high-level reasoning, a reactive execution layer for breaking down high-level commands and monitoring their execution, and a feedback control layer for hardware access and functional components. The communication between single components – implemented as *plugins* – is realized by a hybrid blackboard and messaging approach [2]. Other teams use monolithic approaches or messaging by standardized interfaces [18].

Fawkes and ROS

The most popular robot software framework is the Robot Operating System (ROS) [19]. It has a rich ecosystem of existing software components. Its development started at about the same time. Fawkes and ROS can be fully integrated, for example with Fawkes running as a ROS node. Some plugins have been extended directly to interact with ROS, e.g., for visualizing component-specific information, the main purpose of ROS on the Carologistics' and AllemaniACs' robots. Generic adapter plugins translate between the middleware differences and message types. For example, Fawkes can either provide its navigation capabilities to ROS, or integrate ROS' move_base component for path planning.

Fawkes uses a monolithic approach, running most components as dynamically loaded plugins multi-threaded in a single process, while ROS focuses on a multi-process approach of federated nodes. Fawkes uses a hybrid blackboard/messaging communication architecture, while ROS uses a publisher/subscriber middleware. While Fawkes uses a development model focused on a few core repositories used to develop the components, for ROS components are developed rather separately.

Software Components

Fawkes already contains a wide variety of more than 125 software components and more than two dozen software libraries, many of which are used in the RCLL.

---

[4] Website of the Carologistics at https://www.carologistics.org.

These cover a wide range of functionalities, from plugins providing infrastructure, over functional components for self-localization and navigation, and perception modules via point clouds, laser range finders, or computer vision, to behavior generating components following reactive or deliberative paradigms. In the following we describe some examples with a particular focus on the RCLL. The behavior components are explained in more detail in Sect. 3.

Navigation. Fawkes comes with an implementation of Adaptive Monte Carlo Localization which is an extended port from ROS. In the RCLL, we use a pre-specified map and a laser range finder to determine and track the position of the robot on the field. For locomotion path planning we use a layered structure. A component called *navgraph* has a topological graph of the playing field, where nodes specify travel points or points of interest like machines, and edges denote passages free from static obstacles. When moving to a specific point the navgraph plugin determines a path on this graph to reach the goal. It then instructs the *colli* [20], a local path planner and collision avoidance module we have developed. Based on the next (intermediate) goal on the path it follows a collision-free path.

Perception. The detection and recognition of the light signal of a machine as shown in Fig. 2. While it might seem like a routine task for computer vision, it is complicated by several factors. Since the lights can be on and off, the brightness of the image varies significantly. Additionally, background clutter colored alike the light signal makes detection difficult. A full search for the light signal in an image therefore results in many false positives and negatives. Thus we use a multi-modal laser-based search space reduction [21].

Fig. 2. Machine signal detection used in the RCLL 2016. The markings denote the detected lights [21].

Simulation. The RCLL emphasizes research and application of methods for efficient planning, scheduling, and reasoning on the optimal work order of production processes handled by a group of robots. An aspect that distinctly separates this league from others is that the environment itself acts as an agent by posting orders and controlling the machines. This is what we call *environment agency*. Therefore, we have created an *open simulation environment* [12] depicted in Fig. 3 to support research and development. There are three core aspects in this context: (1) The simulation should be a turn-key solution with simple interfaces, (2) the world must react as close to the real world as possible, including in particular the machine responses and signals, and (3) various levels of abstraction are desirable depending on the focus of the user, e.g. whether to simulate laser data to run a self-localization component or to simply provide the position.

In recent work [12], we provide such an environment.[5] It is based on the well-known Gazebo simulator addressing these issues: (1) its wide-spread use

---

[5] Simulation is available at https://www.fawkesrobotics.org/p/rcll-sim/.

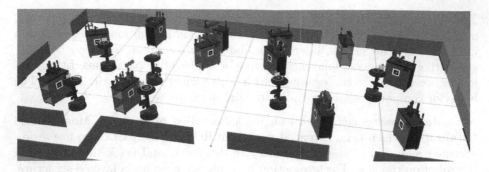

Fig. 3. The simulation of the RCLL in Gazebo based on Fawkes.

and open interfaces already adapted to several software frameworks in combination with our models and adapters provide an easy to use solution; (2) we have connected the simulation directly to the referee box, the semi-autonomous game controller of the RCLL, so that it provides precisely the reactions and *environment agency* of a real-world game; (3) we have implemented *multi-level abstraction* that allows to run full-system tests including self-localization and perception or to focus on high-level control reducing uncertainties by replacing some lower-level components using simulator ground truth data.

The simulation also forms the basis for a new logistics robots competition in simulation [22]. It is intended to build a bridge between the planning and robotics communities and foster closer cooperation for integrating state-of-the-art planning systems into a robotics scenario.

3   Task-Level Coordination and Execution

In the model as depicted in Fig. 4, behavior specification takes place in the upper two layers. The layers are combined following an adapted hybrid deliberative-reactive coordination paradigm. On the lower level, processing for perception and actuation takes place. Task coordination is performed using an incremental rea-

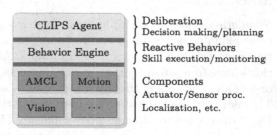

Fig. 4. Behavior layer separation [23].

soning approach [23] on the top level and a reactive middle layers creates a consistent and unified interface to the lower level components. In the RCLL, the top level takes care about selecting the next tasks to accomplish and to coordinate with the other robots. The middle layer provides a reactive framework for modeling, implementing, executing, monitoring, and (locally repairing) basic skills like moving a place, but also multi-step actions like retrieving a workpiece.

For computational and energy efficiency, the behavior components need also to coordinate activation of the lower level components to solve computing resource conflicts.

In the following, we describe these two components as a core contribution of the Fawkes framework in the RCLL in a little more detail.

Lua-based Behavior Engine

In previous work we have developed the Lua-based Behavior Engine (BE) [13]. It integrates as a plugin into Fawkes and has also been ported to and used in ROS [9]. The ROS integration is also available as part of Fawkes allowing for a direct hybrid development of behaviors based on Fawkes and ROS.

The BE implements individual behaviors – called skills – as hybrid state machines (HSM). They can be depicted as a directed graph (cf. Fig. 5 to the right) with nodes representing states for action execution and monitoring. Edges denote jump conditions implemented as Boolean functions. For the active state of a state machine, all outgoing conditions are evaluated, typically at about 15 Hz. If a condition fires, the active state is changed to the target node of the edge. A table of variables holds information like the world model, for example storing numeric values for object positions. It remedies typical problems of state machines like fast growing number of states or variable data passing from one state to another. Skills are implemented using the light-weight, extensible scripting language Lua.

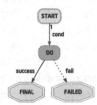

Fig. 5. Hybrid state machine.

For the RCLL, more than thirty skills have been implemented with a hierarchical structure where more complex skills like retrieving a workpiece build on more basic ones like approaching and aligning at an MPS.

Incremental Reasoning Agent

The problem at hand with its intertwined world model updating and execution naturally lends itself to a representation as a fact base with update rules for triggering behavior for certain beliefs. We have chosen the CLIPS rules engine [24]. *Incremental reasoning* means that the robot does not create a full-edged plan at a certain point in time and then executes it. Rather, when idle it commits to the "then-best" action. This avoids costly re-planning (as with approaches using planners), it allows to cope with incomplete knowledge about the world, and it is computationally inexpensive. The decision is based on the current situation as determined through a world model that is weakly synchronized with the other robots and eventually consistent [25]. Adding a new rule is simplified through more specific rules augmenting more general ones.

The robots must communicate to coordinate with the group in order to avoid multiple robots choosing the same task. A mechanism for mutual exclusion denotes one robot as leader through dynamic election. For each task to perform and resource to use, locks must be acquired ensuring that conflicts are resolved early. Robots who fail to obtain re-evaluate their choice with respect to the updated knowledge (that another robot is already performing that task).

Another set of rules controls and monitors the execution of the basic behaviors through the Behavior Engine to accomplish the task. For example, consider a task to retrieve a basic element and delivering it to another machine. This is broken down in several skills. Should the basic element be dropped on the way, the robot can repair the task by retrieving another one, or make a new decision.

4   Conclusion

The integration of a complete robot system even for medium-complex domains such as the RCLL can be tedious and time consuming. We had made the decision early in 2012 when joining the RCLL to go for a more complex, but then also more robust and flexible system. This was finally rewarded by winning the RoboCup 2014, 2015, and 2016 RCLL competitions.

The public release of a fully working and thoroughly tested integrated software stack lowers the barrier of entry for new teams to the league and fosters research and exchange among members of the RoboCup community in general, and in the RoboCup Logistics League in particular. We have organized the first RCLL Winter School in 2015 to disseminate this work and to discuss future directions with other members of the community. These effort were honored with the third place of the 1st International Harting Open Source Award 2016. We continue to develop Fawkes as Open Source software.

Acknowledgments. The Carologistics team members in 2015/2016 are: A. Ferrein, M. Gomaa, C. Henke, S. Jeschke, N. Limpert, D. Kuenster, G. Lakemeyer, M. Löbach, V. Mataré, T. Neumann, T. Niemueller, S. Reuter, J. Rothe, D. Schmidt, S. Schönitz, and F. Zwilling.

The AllemaniACs team members in 2015/2016 are: G. Gierse, T. Hofmann, B. Maleki-Fard, T. Niemueller, S. Schiffer, and F. Zwilling.

We gratefully acknowledge the financial support of RWTH Aachen University and FH Aachen University of Applied Sciences.

F. Zwilling and T. Niemueller were supported by the German National Science Foundation (DFG) research unit *FOR 1513* on Hybrid Reasoning for Intelligent Systems (https://www.hybrid-reasoning.org).

References

1. Niemueller, T., Reuter, S., Ferrein, A.: Fawkes for the RoboCup logistics league. In: Almeida, L., Ji, J., Steinbauer, G., Luke, S. (eds.) RoboCup 2015. LNCS, vol. 9513, pp. 365–373. Springer, Cham (2015). doi:10.1007/978-3-319-29339-4_31
2. Niemueller, T., Ferrein, A., Beck, D., Lakemeyer, G.: Design principles of the component-based robot software framework Fawkes. In: Ando, N., Balakirsky, S., Hemker, T., Reggiani, M., von Stryk, O. (eds.) SIMPAR 2010. LNCS, vol. 6472, pp. 300–311. Springer, Heidelberg (2010). doi:10.1007/978-3-642-17319-6_29
3. Beck, D., Niemueller, T.: AllemaniACs 2009 Team Description. Technical report, KBSG, RWTH Aachen University (2009)

4. Ferrein, A., Steinbauer, G., McPhillips, G., Niemueller, T., Potgieter, A.: Team ZaDeAt 2009 - Team Report. Graz University of Technology, and University of Cape Town, Technical report, RWTH Aachen University (2009)
5. Schiffer, S., Lakemeyer, G.: AllemaniACs Team Description RoboCup@Home. Technical report, KBSG, RWTH Aachen University (2011)
6. Ferrein, A., Niemueller, T., Schiffer, S., Lakemeyer, G.: Lessons learnt from developing the embodied AI platform caesar for domestic service robotics. In: Proceedings of AAAI Spring Symp, 2013 - Designing Intelligent Robots: Reintegrating AI (2013)
7. Niemueller, T., Reuter, S., Ewert, D., Ferrein, A., Jeschke, S., Lakemeyer, G.: Decisive factors for the success of the carologistics RoboCup team in the RoboCup Logistics League 2014. In: Bianchi, R.A.C., Akin, H.L., Ramamoorthy, S., Sugiura, K. (eds.) RoboCup 2014. LNCS, vol. 8992, pp. 155–167. Springer, Cham (2015). doi:10.1007/978-3-319-18615-3_13
8. Niemueller, T., Reuter, S., Ewert, D., Ferrein, A., Jeschke, S., Lakemeyer, G.: The carologistics approach to cope with the increased complexity and new challenges of the RoboCup logistics league 2015. In: Jeschke, S., Isenhardt, I., Hees, F., Henning, K. (eds.) Automation, Communication and Cybernetics in Science and Engineering 2015/2016, pp. 619–635. Springer, Cham (2016). doi:10.1007/978-3-319-42620-4_46
9. Srinivasa, S.S., Berenson, D., Cakmak, M., Collet, A., Dogar, M.R., Dragan, A.D., Knepper, R.A., Niemueller, T., Strabala, K., Vande Weghe, M., Ziegler, J.: HERB 2.0: lessons learned from developing a mobile manipulator for the home. Proc. IEEE **100**(8), 2410–2428 (2012)
10. Niemueller, T., Abdo, N., Hertle, A., Lakemeyer, G., Burgard, W., Nebel, B.: Towards deliberative active perception using persistent memory. In: Proceedings of the Workshop on AI-based Robotics at the International Conference on Intelligent Robots and Systems (IROS) (2013)
11. Röfer, T., Laue, T.: On B-Human's code releases in the standard platform league – software architecture and impact. In: Behnke, S., Veloso, M., Visser, A., Xiong, R. (eds.) RoboCup 2013. LNCS, vol. 8371, pp. 648–655. Springer, Heidelberg (2014). doi:10.1007/978-3-662-44468-9_61
12. Zwilling, F., Niemueller, T., Lakemeyer, G.: Simulation for the RoboCup Logistics League with real-world environment agency and multi-level abstraction. In: Bianchi, R.A.C., Akin, H.L., Ramamoorthy, S., Sugiura, K. (eds.) RoboCup 2014. LNCS, vol. 8992, pp. 220–232. Springer, Cham (2015). doi:10.1007/978-3-319-18615-3_18
13. Niemüller, T., Ferrein, A., Lakemeyer, G.: A Lua-based behavior engine for controlling the humanoid robot Nao. In: Baltes, J., Lagoudakis, M.G., Naruse, T., Ghidary, S.S. (eds.) RoboCup 2009. LNCS, vol. 5949, pp. 240–251. Springer, Heidelberg (2010). doi:10.1007/978-3-642-11876-0_21
14. Gat, E.: Three-layer architectures. In: Artificial Intelligence and Mobile Robots. MIT Press (1998)
15. McIlroy, M.D.: Mass produced software components. In: Software Engineering: Report On a Conference Sponsored by the NATO Science Committee (1968)
16. Brugali, D., Scandurra, P.: Component-based robotic engineering (part I). IEEE Robot. Autom. Mag. **16**(4), 84–96 (2009)
17. Brugali, D., Shakhimardanov, A.: Component-based robotic engineering (part II). IEEE Robot. Autom. Mag. **17**(1), 100–112 (2012)
18. Mamantov, E., Silver, W., Dawson, W., Chown, E.: RoboGrams: a lightweight message passing architecture for RoboCup soccer. In: Bianchi, R.A.C., Akin, H.L., Ramamoorthy, S., Sugiura, K. (eds.) RoboCup 2014. LNCS, vol. 8992, pp. 306–317. Springer, Cham (2015). doi:10.1007/978-3-319-18615-3_25

19. Quigley, M., Conley, K., Gerkey, B.P., Faust, J., Foote, T., Leibs, J., Wheeler, R., Ng, A.Y.: ROS: an open-source robot operating system. In: ICRA Workshop on Open Source Software (2009)
20. Jacobs, S., Ferrein, A., Schiffer, S., Beck, D., Lakemeyer, G.: Robust collision avoidance in unknown domestic environments. In: Baltes, J., Lagoudakis, M.G., Naruse, T., Ghidary, S.S. (eds.) RoboCup 2009. LNCS, vol. 5949, pp. 116–127. Springer, Heidelberg (2010). doi:10.1007/978-3-642-11876-0_11
21. Mataré, V., Niemueller, T., Lakemeyer, G.: Robust multi-modal detection of industrial signal light towers. In: RoboCup Symposium (2016, to appear)
22. Niemueller, T., Karpas, E., Vaquero, T., Timmons, E.: Planning competition for logistics robots in simulation. In: WS on Planning and Robotics (PlanRob) at International Conference on Automated Planning and Scheduling (ICAPS), London, UK (2016)
23. Niemueller, T., Lakemeyer, G., Ferrein, A.: Incremental task-level reasoning in a competitive factory automation scenario. In: Proceedings of AAAI Spring Symposium 2013 - Designing Intelligent Robots: Reintegrating AI (2013)
24. Wygant, R.M.: CLIPS: a powerful development and delivery expert system tool. Comput. Industr. Eng. 17(1–4), 546–549 (1989)
25. Vogels, W.: Eventually Consistent. ACM Queue 6(6), 14–19 (2008)

Author Index